THE WAITE GROUP'S

COM/DCOM
Primer Plus

Chris Corry
Vincent Mayfield
John Cadman
Randy Morin

SAMS

A Division of Macmillan Computer Publishing
201 West 103rd St., Indianapolis, Indiana, 46290 USA

EXECUTIVE EDITOR   Tracy Dunkelberger
ACQUISITIONS EDITOR   Holly Allender
DEVELOPMENT EDITOR   Jeff Durham
MANAGING EDITOR   Jodi Jensen
PROJECT EDITOR   Tonya Simpson
COPY EDITOR   Kate Talbot
INDEXER   Heather Goens
PROOFREADER   Cynthia Fields
TECHNICAL EDITORS   John Cadman, Alexander Kachour, Vincent Mayfield, Randy Morin
SOFTWARE DEVELOPMENT SPECIALIST   Michael Hunter
TEAM COORDINATOR   Michelle Newcomb
INTERIOR DESIGN   Gary Adair
COVER DESIGN   Aren Howell
LAYOUT TECHNICIAN   Brian Borders

International Standard Book Number: 0-672-31492-4

Library of Congress Catalog Card Number: 98-88868

Printed in the United States of America

First Printing: December 1998

00 99   4   3   2

About the Authors

Chris Corry served his time in the IT consulting world, where he spent six years at American Management Systems developing advanced object-oriented technologies for telecommunications clients. He has dabbled in the fast-paced world of the Internet startup and is currently living out his adolescent fantasy of developing Star Wars computer games at LucasArts Entertainment Company.

Vincent (Vinny) W. Mayfield lives in Niceville, Florida with his Labrador Retrievers Gunner and Tank. He is a Senior Software Engineer and a Microsoft Certified Professional with over 10 years of experience developing software and over five years developing windows-based applications with C and C++. He has served in the US Army Reserves and the US Air Force. Presently, Vinny is a Senior Software Engineer and Project Manager for Nichols Research Corporation in Shalimar, Florida. With Nichols Research, Vinny is developing Microsoft Windows-based applications with Visual C++, MFC, and Access. Vincent is a contributing author of *ActiveX Programming Unleashed* and contributing author of *Visual C++ 5.0 Developer's Guide*. He has also done freelance technical consulting with his own company, Bit~Wise Technology Solutions, and done technical editing on numerous books for Macmillian Publishing. Vinny is an FAA Commercial Instrument rated pilot. When not punching holes in the sky or pounding the keyboard, Vinny enjoys spoiling his two nieces Kaitlyn and Mary and his nephew Anthony. In addition, Vinny is a Star Trek fanatic, an aviation enthusiast, a military history buff, and enjoys roughing it in the great outdoors. Vinny holds a BS in mathematics with minors in computer science and aerospace science and an MS in international relations.

John Cadman is founder and president of PowerUp Consulting, Inc., a consulting company focused on delivering quality, cutting-edge solutions and integrations. He has designed and developed many solutions both utilizing and based on COM and DCOM spanning industries such as eCommerce, banking and finance, retail, document management, and imaging. He is also a published author and contributor of technical articles relating to COM/DCOM. John has provided COM/DCOM support and mentoring all over the United States and internationally in France, Spain, and Mexico.

Randy Charles Morin has degrees in both computer science and commerce from the University of Windsor. He is currently employed as a software developer at 724 Solutions Inc. in Toronto, Ontario. Randy is married to Bernadette and they have one daughter, Adelaine. They live together in Brampton, Ontario, Canada. Randy spends most of his free time as Webmaster of the KBCafe Web site and playing with his daughter while watching NHL hockey games. GO! LEAFS! GO!

Table of Contents

Contents

Chapter 7: Breaking the Process Boundary Using Local Servers 209

Chapter 8: Building COM Objects Using the ActiveX
Template Library 279

Tell Us What You Think!

As the reader of this book, *you* are our most important critic and commentator. We value your opinion and want to know what we're doing right, what we could do better, what areas you'd like to see us publish in, and any other words of wisdom you're willing to pass our way.

As the Executive Editor for the Advanced Programming and Distributed Architectures team at Macmillan Computer Publishing, I welcome your comments. You can fax, email, or write me directly to let me know what you did or didn't like about this book—as well as what we can do to make our books stronger.

Please note that I cannot help you with technical problems related to the topic of this book, and that due to the high volume of mail I receive, I might not be able to reply to every message.

When you write, please be sure to include this book's title and author as well as your name and phone or fax number. I will carefully review your comments and share them with the author and editors who worked on the book.

Fax: 317-817-7070
Email: `programming@mcp.com`
Mail: Tracy Dunkelberger
         Executive Editor
         Advanced Programming and Distributed Architectures Team
         Macmillan Computer Publishing
         201 West 103rd Street
         Indianapolis, IN 46290 USA

INTRODUCTION:

SETTING OFF ON THE RIGHT FOOT

Welcome to *The Waite Group's COM/DCOM Primer Plus*. Boy, what a mouthful! Two of the hottest new technologies in the programming world are Microsoft's Component Object Model (COM)and the Distributed Component Object Model (DCOM). Most programmers in the know constantly strive to stay on the tip of the technology spear. Let's face it, in today's cutthroat world of computing, if you stagnate, you will find yourself at the butt of the shaft. There is a lot of commotion over these new technologies. However, as I am sure you will find by reading this book, COM and DCOM are not just computing buzzwords.

This book is a primer with a focus on learning COM and DCOM in the friendly learning format that has become the trademark of *Primer Plus* books. The programming examples in this book use Microsoft's Visual C++ 6 Development Suite; some examples use the Microsoft Foundation Class Library 6 (MFC 6).

Who Should Read This Book

One might ask, "Why the award-winning *Primer Plus* format? Aren't the *Primer Plus* books for beginners?" Traditionally, yes, the *Primer Plus* books are for beginners. COM and DCOM are advanced topics. These topics cannot be taught to a programmer who lacks certain basic knowledge. Far too many basic skills are needed in order to properly learn these new technologies. This is similar to the notion that in order to do Calculus, one must possess a solid foundation of algebra and analytic geometry.

Although COM and DCOM are advanced topics, they are perfect technologies to teach by example. This book is for you if you are an intermediate to advanced programmer and are looking for a beginning to intermediate introduction to COM and DCOM. You must have a firm understanding of C++, event-driven programming, the Microsoft Windows family of operating systems, the Visual C++ Development Suite, and the Microsoft Foundation Classes. Now, having said that, I do not want to scare you off. If you are weak in any of these areas, take a look at a few of the other books available from Macmillan Computer Publishing to polish your skills in the prerequisites for *The Waite Group's COM/DCOM Primer Plus*.

In concert with the *Primer* format, you will learn by doing. In this book, you will start with the fundamentals of COM programming and gradually be guided into the more advanced topic of DCOM programming. In each chapter, you will learn by examining a series of explanations, followed by examples to demonstrate the concepts. Through the code examples and exercises, you will solidify basic concepts.

The Waite Group's COM/DCOM Primer Plus includes a CD-ROM with all the code from the examples. Furthermore, this book is graphical in nature, with screen shots and graphics to give you a visual perspective. This is accomplished with code examples and exercises to present basic concepts and solidify your understanding. All you need to start is a willingness to learn.

Through the use of this book, you will learn skills to aid you in leveraging COM/DCOM technologies in the development and implementation of commercial-grade applications for the Microsoft Windows family of operating systems. You will learn to do this using Visual C++ 6 and MFC. Visual C++ is one of the most popular development tools in the industry today, and MFC is one of the best class libraries for developing applications for Microsoft Windows.

Book Conventions

Throughout this book I use the following icons to draw your attention to certain information that is important or useful.

URLs

The URL sidenote is used to point out an Internet URL that has information pertinent to the topic being discussed or that might have additional useful information. The following is an example of a URL note.

URL

Microsoft Corporation Internet URL: `http://www.microsoft.com/`.

Tips

Tips present useful tidbits of information to aid you in doing something. Here is an example of a tip:

TIP

In Microsoft Developer Studio, if you hold the Alt key while holding down the left mouse button you can highlight and select a column of text in the Developer Studio Editor.

Notes

Notes annotate an item of special significance to the current topic.

NOTE

Anyone with some minimum programming skills and a willingness to learn can master COM/DCOM.

Cautions

Cautions point out instances where you should exercise caution in performing a certain action that could potentially be hazardous.

CAUTION

Great care should be exercised when editing the System Registry because you could potentially render a system unusable.

Chapter Outline

The following is the layout of what lies ahead for you.

Chapter 1: An Overview of Microsoft's Object Technologies

This chapter explains the following topics: COM, OLE, ActiveX, and the evolution of Microsoft's object technologies.

Chapter 2: The Object Revolution

This chapter explores what might be called the *object revolution* and introduces you to basic object-oriented concepts such as encapsulation, inheritance, and polymorphism. You will find out that there are two types of inheritance and which type COM supports. Finally, you learn the basics of the component object model by first looking at what COM is and why its mastery is so important. You delve into the notion of interfaces and mapping the IUnknown.

Chapter 3: Building COM Objects and Interfaces

In this chapter you learn how to start building component-based programs using COM. COM is the precursor to DCOM, and the two technologies are intrinsically linked. Learning about DCOM means learning about COM first.

Chapter 4: Implementing a COM Client and Server

You will implement your first COM client and COM server. You learn issues regarding the layout and architecture of your components, as well as registering them in the Registry. Additionally, you learn Unicode and internationalizing your components.

Chapter 5: COM Programming with MFC

This chapter finds you exploring COM programming with MFC. You will discover the clever way in which the MFC development team used interface maps to enable you to create light and fast COM components quickly.

Chapter 6: Using Aggregation to Simulate Inheritance

In this chapter you examine aggregation and discover that it's the primary mechanism used by COM objects for code reuse. Aggregation will help resolve the problems associated with new versions of your components.

Chapter 7: Breaking the Process Boundary Using Local Servers

Armed with the knowledge you have acquired so far, you will explore developing components that step across boundaries on a single machine. These components are local servers, and Chapter 7 shows how easy it is to create local servers.

Chapter 8: Building COM Objects Using the ActiveX Template Library

You will learn how to build COM objects using the ActiveX Template Library. This chapter shows you how the clever use of C++ templates can simplify and enhance your ability to build COM objects.

Chapter 9: A Distributed Objects Overview

Now you really start to learn how Microsoft has taken its COM technology and extended it to include the network. This first chapter gives you a high-level picture of what programming with DCOM entails.

Chapter 10: Security

This chapter demonstrates DCOM security. You will find that the new security enhancements are not just for DCOM; they affect nondistributed COM as well. You also learn Win32 security, including user profiles and access tokens. You will look at restricting access to running objects and at configuring a class to always run in the security context of a user. Finally, you learn how to assure message integrity, as well as integrating DCOM interfaces with the new Cryptography API.

Chapter 11: Using Different COM Threading Models

In this chapter you learn the principles of how to build an NT service. You will delve into how to wrap a COM interface into a service, and you will address the life-cycle concerns of your COM objects.

Chapter 12: Automation Unveiled

In this chapter, you will learn how to make your distributed objects thread-safe by exploring the two types of threading models: the free threading model and the apartment threading model.

Chapter 13: Using Distributed Objects

This chapter consolidates everything you've learned and puts it to work building a true distributed object application.

Programming Conventions

In this book, I will strive to follow these guidelines: "The Microsoft Foundation Class Library Development Guidelines" and the "Windows Interface Guidelines for Software Design."

URL

"The Microsoft Foundation Class Library Development Guidelines" is available from Microsoft at the following Internet URL:
`http://www.microsoft.com/visualc/sitemap.htm`.

URL

"The Windows Interface Guidelines for Software Design" is available from Microsoft Press at 1-800-MS-PRESS or at the following Internet URL:
`http://www.microsoft.com/mspress/`.

"The Microsoft Foundation Class Library Development Guidelines" is for people who want to write extension libraries to MFC; however, I have found that the basic principles and conventions in this paper are good practices for those who develop applications using MFC. Please take a moment to download this document and to become familiar with the programming conventions expressed in it.

"The Windows Interface Guidelines for Software Design" is a great resource for keeping you in concert with the other applications written for the Windows family of operating systems. This book outlines the guidelines for setting up your applications' user interface to conform to the conventions set by the operating system. It is very important to try to adhere to these standards whenever possible. One of the great things about Microsoft Windows is that every application looks and feels the same. For the user, this means familiarity and ease of use. For corporations, it means less money spent on training. By adhering to these standards, you can ensure your application will be well received by your users.

What You Will Need

To do the programming exercises in this book, you will need the following items:

- Microsoft Windows 95 OSR2, Windows 98, or Windows NT 4.0
- Visual C++ 6 Professional or Enterprise Edition
- Microsoft Foundation Class Library v6.0 (Comes VC++ 6)

Microsoft Windows 95 OSR2, Windows 98, or Windows NT 4.0

Information on where to purchase Microsoft Windows 95 OSR2, Windows 98, or Microsoft Windows NT 4.0 can be obtained by calling Microsoft Technical Support Sales at 1-800-936-3500.

Visual C++ 6 Professional or Enterprise Edition

Information on where to purchase Visual C++ 6 Professional or Enterprise Editions can be obtained by calling Microsoft Technical Support Sales at 1-800-936-3500.

Microsoft Foundation Class Library v6.0 (with VC++ 6)

Microsoft Foundation Class Library v6.0 comes with Visual C++ 6 and cannot be purchased separately.

CHAPTER 1

AN OVERVIEW OF MICROSOFT'S OBJECT TECHNOLOGIES

In this chapter, you will learn about the following:

- The evolution of component technology
- An overall understanding of OLE
- The Component Object Model
- How to develop and implement ActiveX components and services
- The Distributed Component Object Model for COM component interoperation

Sifting Through the Acronyms: COM, DCOM, OLE, and ActiveX

In almost every sphere of software engineering, *software component construction* has crept into our vocabulary and into our practices. Component software, through the ingenious salesmanship of skillful marketers, has fast become the panacea for all our software development ills. We look to it as the end of our pilgrimage to seek object-oriented nirvana. We see it as our silver bullet.

Note

The *silver bullet* comes from an interesting article written by F. P. Brooks, Jr. and titled "No Silver Bullet: Essence and Accidents of Software Engineering," which appeared in *IEEE Computer*, Vol. 20, No. 4, in April 1987.

Acronyms and fast-changing technology have left many of us in the industry trying to navigate through the mumbo jumbo in our quest to sort out the charlatans from the real McCoys. Trying to keep up with the daunting pace of the personal computer (PC) industry and the constant metamorphosis of computer technology can be compared to putting one's mouth over the opening of a fire hydrant and turning it on.

One company that can be described as a technological fire hydrant is Microsoft. The driving force of Bill Gates and Microsoft has many of us gasping for breath as we try to understand such acronyms as COM, OLE, ActiveX, and DCOM. Just when we feel we understand a technology from Redmond, a new acronym or technology emerges or changes its name.

What are we to do? This book will demystify some of the Microsoft technologies for you. The primary focus of this book is on the Component Object Model (COM) and the Distributed Component Object Model (DCOM). However, you cannot understand DCOM without first grasping COM. Likewise, to understand COM, you must step back and look at the bigger picture and understand OLE and ActiveX.

The Evolution of Component Technology

You will begin your journey to understanding COM and DCOM by looking at the evolution of component technology. Although object-oriented technology has had an evolution all its own, a spinoff of object-oriented technology, termed *component technology*, has had its own evolution. The component technology evolution has a majority of its roots in the Microsoft Windows family of operating systems. Although there were other contributors to the component revolution with quasi-component–based development, using libraries of functions in FORTRAN, and Smalltalk classes, Microsoft has defined component-based technology as we see it today. This began with the custom control.

Custom Controls

The term *control*, or *custom control*, has been around since Windows 3.0, when it was first defined. A custom control is nothing more than a dynamic link library (DLL) that exports a defined set of functions. Unlike a DLL, a custom control can manipulate properties and handle the firing of events in response to user or programmatic input.

In the early days of Microsoft Windows, the Visual Basic (VB) development environment caught on in the development community, and component technology took off. VB programmers found that custom controls were necessary because they needed better ways to express the user interface of their applications. Many times, there was simply no way to perform a complex operation in Visual Basic. Unfortunately, or fortunately, depending on your perspective, these C language DLLs had no way of allowing Visual Basic to query the control for information on the properties and methods supported by the control. This made custom controls difficult to use in the Visual Basic development environment.

Visual Basic Extensions

In 1991, Microsoft unveiled the VBX. *VBX* stands for Visual Basic Extension. The idea was that these little reusable software components could be embedded in their container application. To everyone's surprise, VBXs took off like wildfire. Companies cropped up all over the place, developing these little reusable software components. VBXs were able to provide a wide range of functionality, from a simple text label to a complex multimedia or communications control. They were written in C and C++ and provided a wide variety of capabilities that otherwise could not have been possible in a Visual Basic application. VBXs were extremely popular.

Because VBXs became popular, demand for them grew within the developer market. Soon developers wanted them for 32-bit applications and even on non-Intel platforms such as the DEC Alpha, RISC, Power PC, and the MIPS. Developers wanted to extend VBXs by using Visual Basic for Applications to connect VBXs with applications such as Access, PowerPoint, Excel, Project, and Word.

Unfortunately, VBXs are severely restricted. They were built on a 16-bit architecture that is not designed as an open interface. They were primarily designed to accommodate the Visual Basic environment. This made VBXs almost impossible to port to a 32-bit environment. Seeing the value and popularity of VBXs, Microsoft wanted to capitalize on this market. Microsoft was looking for an object-oriented architecture that was extensible and that supported a data-driven approach, as opposed to an application-driven approach. The result was OLE 1.0.

OLE 1.0

In 1991, Microsoft introduced a new specification called OLE 1.0. The acronym stood for *object linking and embedding*. OLE 1.0 was basically a method of handling compound documents. A *compound document* is a way of storing data in multiple formats—such as text, graphics, video, and sound—in a single document. At the time, *object-oriented* was the new programming buzzword, and the OLE 1.0 specification was a move toward a more object-oriented paradigm. Furthermore, OLE 1.0 was an effort to move toward a more document-centric approach, instead of an application-centric approach.

Unfortunately, OLE 1.0 was coldly received by software developers. Very few independent software vendors (ISVs) and corporations raced to embrace OLE 1.0 and to OLE-enable their applications. This reluctance to deploy OLE 1.0 in applications was mainly due to OLE 1.0 being very complex and having a steep learning curve. OLE 1.0 had to be coded using a very complex C application programming interface (API), which embodied programming concepts germane to OLE. These new concepts were foreign to most developers.

OLE 2.0

Undaunted by the limited success of OLE 1.0, Microsoft continued to strive to improve OLE. In 1993, Microsoft released the OLE 2.0 specification, which encompassed more than just compound documents. It sported an entire architecture of object-based services that could be extended, customized, and enhanced. The foundation of this services architecture was the Component Object Model. The services available through this architecture are

- COM
- Clipboard
- Drag and drop

- Embedding

- In-place activation

- Linking

- Monikers (persistent naming)

- OLE Automation

- OLE controls

- OLE documents

- Structured storage

- Uniform data transfer (UDT)

From a programmatic view, OLE 2.0 is a series of services built on top of each other, as shown in Figure 1.1. These services form an architecture of interdependent building blocks built on the COM foundation.

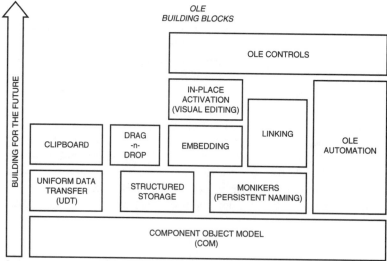

Figure 1.1 The foundation of OLE is COM, with each successive service built on the technologies of the others.

The release of OLE 2.0 had such an effect on standard ways of computing that it received two prestigious industry awards: a Technical Excellence award from *PC Magazine* and the MVP award for software innovation from *PC/Computing*. Adding to the OLE 2.0 success was a new and improved programming interface. Developers could now move to OLE-enabled applications much more easily. The OLE 2.0 services incorporate many principles embodied in object-oriented programming: encapsulation, polymorphism, and an object-based architecture. Further adding to the success of OLE 2.0 was the release in February 1993 of Visual C++ 1.0 with the Microsoft Foundation Class (MFC) Library version 2.0. MFC had wrapped the OLE API in a C++ class library, thus making it much easier for programmers to use the OLE services architecture.

Today, OLE is no longer the acronym for *object linking and embedding*. That term is obsolete. Now Microsoft refers to it as simply OLE, pronounced *o-lay*. Notice that no version number is attached to OLE anymore. Because OLE is an extensible architecture, it can be enhanced and extended without changing its basic foundation. A testimonial to this capability is OLE controls. OLE controls were not part of the original release of OLE. OLE controls were not added to the available OLE services until almost a year after the original release. In fact, objects created with OLE 1.0 still work and interact with modern OLE applications. However, their functionality is limited to the original 1.0 specification, so no need for versions exists. From here on, this chapter refers to OLE unless specifically outlining a feature of OLE 1.0 or 2.0.

Understanding OLE

To understand OLE, you must look at it from two levels: first from the eyes of the end user and then from the programmer's eyes.

OLE Through the Eyes of the End User

Although many software engineers forget this, the end user is the very reason for their existence as software developers. Because the end user is the main reason why software is developed, this section views OLE through the user's eyes. This will help you grasp the benefits and available services of OLE. The end user's view is simple, less technical, and very understandable. I firmly believe that users decide in the first 10 minutes of using an application whether they like it. This sets the stage for all further experiences with that application. Therefore, an application's intuitiveness, appearance, ease of use, capability to accomplish work or entertain, and performance are of paramount importance.

Note

Working with end users can be frustrating. Always keep in mind that the "devil-spawned end user"—as the cartoon character *Dilbert*, by Scott Adams, would say—is the main reason for our existence as software engineers. They depend on us to bridge the technical, and their less technical, view of the world. Most end users could care less about data structures and programming languages or that your tree control algorithm takes only 1/10 of a second. They just want intuitive applications that help make their lives easier. The best software engineers never forget this and always tackle every programming endeavor with the end user in mind.

Microsoft, and Apple before it, knew that a large portion of the software has to have a human-to-machine interface. This is why Windows and the Macintosh each have a standard interface—not only from a user's perspective but also from a programmer's.

Users interact with OLE in three ways:

- OLE documents

- OLE Automation

- OLE controls

Even though these are the ways that the end user sees OLE, all the other OLE services are part of these three in some way. For example, COM is a part of all three; linking and embedding are part of OLE documents.

Through the End User's Eyes—OLE Documents

As a computer professional, I'm sure you have seen or worked with Microsoft Word or Excel. Microsoft Word is the classic example of an OLE document. This chapter doesn't outline the functionality of Word; it merely points out the features of OLE. However, do not be deceived. OLE documents are not always classic word processors. It is easy to think so, because of the word *documents*. Think of an OLE document as a piece of Velcro. You have two pieces: the hook side (the document) and the pile side (the document container).

The first feature of OLE documents is a common user model. This simply means that the user interface (UI) features used to access OLE documents are similar from application to application. The common user model features document-centricity and takes advantage of OLE's integrated data capabilities.

Note

OLE user-interface design guidelines are well documented in *The Windows Interface Guidelines for Software Design*, Microsoft Press, 1995.

One of these integrated data capabilities is called *linking and embedding*. Data objects of different types, created from other applications, can be embedded or linked into an application's OLE document. This enables the user to manipulate the object in the host application without returning to the creating application. The object is simply edited in place (therefore the term *in-place editing*). The user interface is modified in the host application with menus, toolbars, and context menus from the application that created the object.

In Figure 1.2, note the two kinds of data—text and an embedded Visio drawing. Note the layout of the toolbars and the menu in Figure 1.2. In Figure 1.3, they are different. Notice how they change.

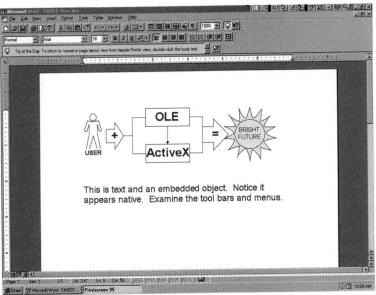

Figure 1.2   A Microsoft Word document with embedded text and graphics.

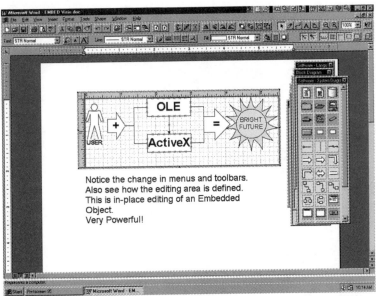

Figure 1.3   A Microsoft Word document with the Visio drawing activated for in-place editing.

If you double-click the Visio drawing, the Word application changes, and new user interface objects are added to Word from Visio (see Figure 1.3). Notice that the Word user interface performs a metamorphosis and now has the Visio toolbars, floating dialog boxes, and menu items, as well as the Visio drawing and rulers. The user can then edit this drawing object without switching applications. This is called *in-place editing*. In addition, you can drag and drop these objects between and within applications.

These features are implemented in the same way from application to application. Therefore, there is a smaller learning curve for users when they get new applications, because the applications function similarly and have a common user model.

Through the End User's Eyes—OLE Automation

The next level of visibility to the user is OLE Automation. OLE Automation enables the user to access and modify objects through properties and methods, using a high-level language such as Visual Basic for Applications (VBA), VBScript, or JavaScript. This enables the user to customize objects and the interactivity between objects to perform operations the way the user defines. Microsoft Excel spreadsheets are the classic OLE Automation objects. The user can create Excel spreadsheets that update a Microsoft Graph object or update information in a Microsoft Access or Borland Paradox database.

The greatest part about OLE Automation is that you do not have to be a programmer to take advantage of it. One example of this is demonstrated through VBA. Microsoft has made VBA easy to learn by the use of a macro recorder (see Figure 1.4), which records your keystrokes in VB code, and an object browser, which you use to paste the proper code where you need it. Anyone can learn to use it.

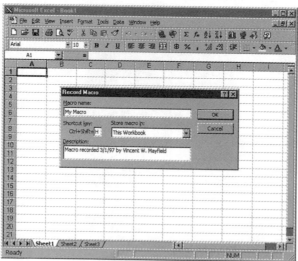

Figure 1.4   Microsoft Excel with the Record macro invoked.

In addition to VBA, VBScript and JavaScript are available. Microsoft has been very kind to us and provided the ActiveX Control Pad for free. The ActiveX Control Pad (see Figure 1.5) is an easy way for nonprogrammers to embed ActiveX controls. These are OLE Automation objects in Web pages, as you will see later, and you can programmatically manipulate them with VBScript or JavaScript. An example of this would be a Calendar ActiveX control changing the month when the user types a new month.

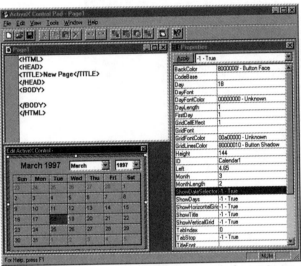

Figure 1.5   The ActiveX Control Pad with the VBScript editor.

Through the End User's Eyes—OLE Controls

This leads us to OLE controls. OLE controls are the last area of OLE visibility to the end user. They are self-contained, reusable components that can be embedded in applications. To the user, they are nothing more than a control that takes the user's input and passes it to the application that contains it. However, some OLE controls are static in nature, such as a picture control. OLE controls are also OLE Automation objects that can have properties set at both compile time and runtime, and OLE controls also have methods that can perform certain operations. The difference between OLE controls and OLE Automation objects is that OLE controls are self-contained objects.

OLE controls provide two-way communication between the control and the container. They have even more special capabilities beyond simple OLE Automation: They can respond to events and initiate events.

An example of a property would be the date value or the background color in the Microsoft Access Calendar Control shown in Figure 1.6. A method might be a function that changes the date value or the background color. To clarify an event, when the user clicks a day, the Calendar control might have an event fired that lets the container know that a day has been clicked. These properties, methods, and events make OLE controls powerful. They give the programmer and the end user a cornucopia of functionality, as shown in Figure 1.6.

In future sections, you will discover that OLE controls have been renamed ActiveX controls and have been enhanced so that they can be used across the Internet. These components have a profound effect in the area of application development (see Figure 1.7) because they are prebuilt. From the end user's perspective, they provide increased functionality and lower software costs.

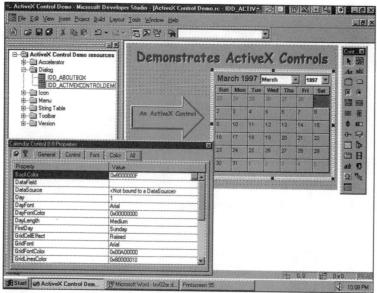

Figure 1.6 The properties, methods, and events of the Microsoft Access Calendar control during development in the Visual C++ Developer Studio.

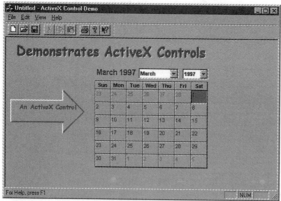

Figure 1.7 Two OLE controls embedded in an application. These controls come with Visual C++.

OLE from the Programmer's Viewpoint

This section presents the OLE services from a programmatic view. For each service, you are given a description of the technology and a programmer's view of the interfaces to these OLE services. In addition, you will also look at the MFC classes that support each OLE service. Pay particular attention to understanding what each service does and where it fits into the architecture. The explanations highlight the interfaces to these objects and some key properties and methods where appropriate. Some of these services are discussed in detail in later chapters because they pertain to and integrate into ActiveX.

Notice that these are the same technologies the end user sees. However, the end user's view is a visual one, and the programmer's view is a menagerie of interfaces that must be mastered to provide the slick visual representation the end user sees. These sections are intended to give you an overview of the OLE architecture.

As discussed earlier, the OLE services form building blocks on which each element in the architecture is based, as shown in Figure 1.8. An example of how these services build on each other is OLE documents. You can see in Figure 1.8 that OLE documents are made up of embedding, linking, and in-place editing. Embedding is built using structured storage, drag and drop, and uniform data transfer. Linking is built on embedding, moniker, and drag and drop. At root, all these technologies are built on COM and use COM.

In the case of the Word document with an embedded Visio drawing, you are using the OLE technology of embedding to embed the Visio drawing. Embedding requires structured storage. As demonstrated earlier, you can double-click the embedded Visio drawing to start in-place editing. From this example, you can see how the OLE technologies are structured as interdependent building blocks. If it's not clear now, it will become apparent as you read on.

This architecture starts with the foundation, the Component Object Model.

The Component Object Model (COM)

When Microsoft designed OLE, it had object-oriented programming in mind. COM objects are much like instantiated C++ classes or an ADA package. In fact, COM was designed with C++ programmers in mind. It supports encapsulation, polymorphism, and reusability. However, COM was also designed to be compatible at the binary level and thus differs from a C++ object.

As a programmer, you are aware that compiled programming languages such as C, C++, Pascal, and ADA are machine-dependent. As a binary object, a COM object concerns itself with how it interfaces with other objects. When not used in the environment of its creator, an interface is exposed that can be seen in the non-native environment. It can be seen because it is a binary object and therefore not machine-dependent. This does not require the host environment or an interacting object to know anything about the COM object. When the object is created in the womb of its mother application, COM does not concern itself with how that object interacts within it. This interaction is between the mother application and the child object.

When the object interacts with the rest of the world, however, COM is concerned about how to interface with that object. It's important to note that COM is not a programming language; it is a binary standard that enables software components to interact with each other as objects. COM is not specific to any particular programming language. COM can work with any language that can support the binary layout of a COM object. It is a programming model to facilitate the programmability of this standard. For the purposes of this book, you will look at COM as implemented with C++.

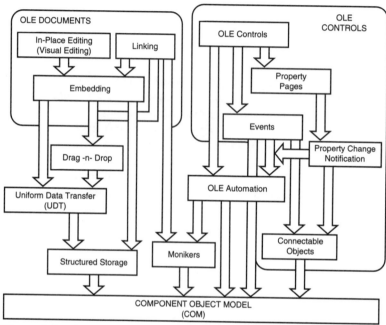

Figure 1.8   A programmatic view of OLE.

Interfaces

COM objects expose their functionality through interfaces. An *interface* is a binding contract between the COM object and the world. Interfaces in C++ are implemented through abstract base classes. All their member functions are *pure virtual*. This means that the derived class must implement the functionality. With an interface, you can strongly type your internal implementation by your interface and isolate the inner workings of your component. Let's examine how an interface is implemented in C++ by looking at Listing 1.1.

Listing 1.1   A Simple Interface

```
1: interface IStrikeEagle : IUnknown
2: {
3: public:
```

```
4:        virtual void __stdcall TakeOff() = 0;
5:        virtual void __stdcall Fly() = 0;
6:        virtual void __stdcall DropSmartBomb() = 0;
7:        virtual void __stdcall Land() = 0;
8: };
```

In line 1, notice first the declaration **interface**, which declares an interface called **IStrikeEagle**. An interface is defined as a C/C++ **struct** so that the members are automatically declared public and you don't have to declare them. For clarity, I have evoked the **public** keyword, but it is not necessary. You want the interface and its members to be public because this is the implementation that you want to expose to the world. It tells everyone what your object does, but hides how it does it.

In lines 4–7 are the methods that the interface exposes to the world. As a whole, the COM object contains the data (properties) and behavior (methods) that are implemented behind the publicly exposed and well-defined interface. This containment demonstrates the object-oriented principle of encapsulation, which is discussed in more detail in Chapter 2, "The Object Revolution." The internal implementation of a COM object is expressed as a class or potentially multiple classes. That class is derived from the interface, which is an abstract base class. The COM class contains the core of the COM object. In a moment, I will present an example of a class.

The IUnknown

Now, let's go back to line 1 of Listing 1.1. Notice that after the scope resolution operator, you have **IUnknown**. COM objects each have a common interface. No matter what they do, COM objects all must implement the **IUnknown** interface. This interface is the main interface for all others. It is the base interface from which all other COM interfaces are derived. The **IUnknown** interface provides you with a way to access the interfaces that your COM object exposes. It has the following member functions (methods):

- ULONG AddRef(void)

- ULONG Release(void)

- HRESULT QueryInterface(REFIID id, void **ipv)

Vtables

Each object implements a vtable. A vtable is nothing more than an array of pointers to member functions implemented in the object (see Figure 1.9). This vtable is shared between all the instances of the object also maintaining the private data of each object. A client application evokes an instance of the interface and gets a pointer to a pointer that points to the vtable. Each time a new interface to the object is instantiated, the reference count of objects is incremented with **AddRef()**. Conversely, each time a reference is destroyed, the reference counter is decremented with **Release()**. After the reference count is zero, the object can be destroyed. To see what interfaces an object supports, you can use **QueryInterface()**.

COM interfaces are never directly accessed. They are always accessed through a pointer. The `QueryInterface(REFIID id, void **ipv)` function takes a reference `id` and a void pointer. Notice the double indirection on the pointer: `**ipv`. The `id` is a 128-bit unique ID that identifies the interface you are retrieving. The `ipv` pointer is where the pointer to the interface you are trying to retrieve is stored. Consider this code fragment:

```
IUnknown *pUnknown = CreateInstance();
IStrikeEagle* pIStrike = NULL;

if (pUnknown->QueryInterface(IID_IStrikeEagle,(void**)&
➥pIStrike) == NOERROR)
{
    pIStrike->TakeOff();
    pIStrike->Fly();
    pIStrike->DropSmartBomb();
    pIStrike->Land();
    pIStrike->Release();
}
```

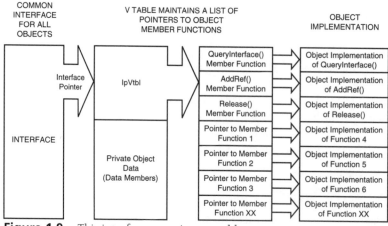

Figure 1.9 This interface maps into a vtable.

Now I am sure you can see the value here, but I'm also sure you are wondering what `pUnknown` is. The `pUnknown` is an interface pointer to the object's `IUnknown`. You got that pointer by using the function `CreateInstance()`. `CreateInstance()` is a function that knows how to create a new object and return a pointer to the `IUnknown` interface. You then use the `IUnknown` interface pointer to call `QueryInterface()` for the interface that you want to use. In this case, it is the `IStrikeEagle` interface. You then do the work that you want to do, using the exposed methods of your interface—`TakeOff()`, `Fly()`, `DropSmartBomb()`, and `Land()`—and then you `Release()` the interface pointer. You access those functions through the pointer to the object's interface `pIStrike`. You don't have to worry about the `IUnknown` pointer because it knows how to delete itself. What you have just seen is the use of an instance of the COM object Strike Eagle. By using the `IStrikeEagle` interface, you were able to `TakeOff()`, `Fly()`, `DropSmartBomb()`, and `Land()` your Strike Eagle.

So far, I have given a general overview of COM. A more in-depth overview is necessary to really grasp COM. Chapter 2 and Chapter 3, "Building COM Objects and Interfaces," delve into COM in more detail. You need some basic COM terminology to understand the rest of the OLE technologies.

Structured Storage

Unfortunately, most platforms today have different file systems, making sharing data a very difficult task. In addition, these file systems arose during the mainframe days, when only a single application was able to update and, in some cases, access that data at any one time. COM is built with interoperability and integration between applications on dissimilar platforms in mind. To accomplish this, COM must have multiple applications write data to the same file on the underlying file system. OLE structured storage addresses this need.

Structured storage is a file system within a file. Think of it as a hierarchical tree of storage and streams. Within this tree, each node has only one parent, but each node can have from zero to many children. Think of it like the Windows 95 Explorer. The folders are the storage nodes, and the files are the streams. Structured storage provides an organization chart of data within a file, as seen in Figure 1.10. In addition, this organization of data is not limited to files but includes memory and databases.

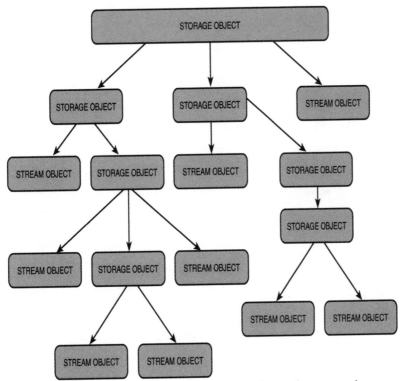

Figure 1.10   Structured storage is a hierarchical tree of storage and streams.

Stream objects contain data. This data can be native data or data from other outside objects. Storage objects are compatible at the binary level; therefore, in theory, they are compatible across OLE-compliant platforms. However, you know that minute differences exist between the various platforms. In Figure 1.10 notice the tree of the structured storage object. The definition of the tree is dependent on how the object's creator defined the storage of the object.

Structured storage objects are manipulated by using the following OLE interfaces:

- `IPersistStorage`

- `IStorage`

- `IStream`

As the name implies, `IStorage` manipulates storage objects and `IStream` manipulates streams. Rarely would you want to manipulate stream or storage objects individually. More than likely, you would want to manipulate the persistent storage object with the `IPersistStorage`. *Persistent storage* is data that will continue to exist even after an object is destroyed. For example, if you want to allow the user to define the color of an object such as a text label, you would persistently store that object's foreground and background colors. The next time the object was created, you could read in from persistent storage the colors previously chosen by the end user. You could then apply those attributes to the object and thus maintain the user's preferences. `IPersistStorage` enables you to do this by performing the following operations:

- `IsDirty`

- `InitNew`

- `Load`

- `Save`

- `SaveCompleted`

- `HandsOffStorage`

A great way to see what structured storage looks like is with a utility that comes with Visual C++ 6.x called DfView (DocFile Viewer). DfView is in the \Visual Studio\Common\Tools\ directory of Visual C++. DfView enables you to look at a compound file, also known as an *OLE document*. OLE documents implement structured storage. Figure 1.11 shows an example of DfView (this is the Word document with an embedded Visio drawing object, seen earlier in Figure 1.2).

If you double-click a stream object, you can see its binary contents (see Figure 1.12).

MFC provides an encapsulation of `IPersistStorage` and `IStorage` through an easy-to-use class called `COleDocument`. In addition, to aid in the manipulation of storage and streams, MFC provides `COleStreamFile`. It is important to note that compound documents in MFC are not only OLE documents and ActiveX documents but also any file type that represents the structured storage of data.

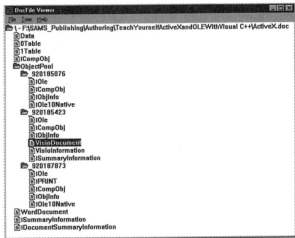

Figure 1.11   DfView (DocFile Viewer) shows the hierarchical tree of a structured storage object.

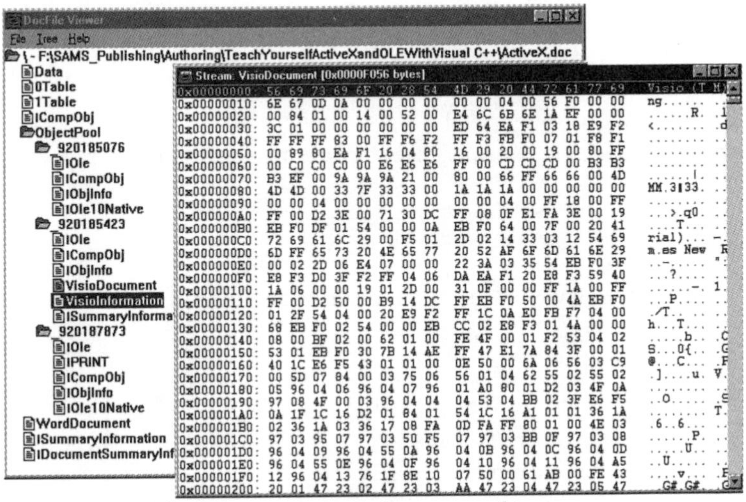

Figure 1.12   The binary contents of a stream object.

Monikers (Persistent Naming)

Monikers are a way to reference a piece of data or object in an object-based system such as OLE. When an object is linked, a moniker is stored that knows how to get to that native data. For example, if you link a sound file into a Word document, the WAV file is not stored natively in that document. A moniker is created that can intelligently locate the WAV file object, as the moniker stores the location of that WAV file. Think of a moniker as a map to where X marks the spot.

To use a moniker to locate and bind to an object, you must use the `IMoniker` interface and call `IMoniker::BindToObject`. By using the intelligent persistent name of that object, the `IMoniker` interface negotiates the location of that object and returns a pointer to the interface of that object's type. The moniker itself then dies. Think of it as similar to dereferencing a pointer in C or C++ to locate a piece of data. Remember that monikers are persistent. `IMoniker` is derived from `IPersistStream`, and thus it can serialize itself into a stream. This gives it persistence. These are the five basic types of monikers:

- File monikers
- Item monikers
- Anti monikers
- Pointer monikers
- Composite monikers

File Monikers

File monikers store a filename persistently. In binding the text filename to the file object, a pointer to the file object interface is returned so that you can manipulate that file object.

Item Monikers

Item monikers point to a specific place inside a file, such as a paragraph or a portion of an embedded video.

Anti Monikers

Anti monikers delete the last moniker in a series or chain of monikers, as in a composite moniker.

Pointer Monikers

Pointer monikers simply point to other monikers, wrapping them in a chain. However, it should be noted that pointer monikers are not persistent.

Composite Monikers

A *composite moniker* is an ordered collection of monikers. At the root of a composite moniker is a file moniker that references the document pathname. It then holds a series of item monikers. You use composite monikers when you need to have a collection of monikers within a single object.

MFC Encapsulation of Monikers

In the previous section "Structured Storage," you learned that MFC has a class called `COleStreamFile`. The purpose of this class is to encapsulate the functionality of `IStream` to provide access to the streams of data in a compound file. Derived from `COleStreamFile` is CMonikerFile. CMonikerFile is a class that encapsulates the functionality of monikers provided in the IMoniker interface. This class gives the ability to gain access to IStreams named by IMoniker. It's important to note that this class does not encapsulate the entire IMoniker interface. It provides the capability to work with the streams of a compound file. So, if you want to bind to storage or an object, you must implement the IMoniker interface directly. This means you will not be able to use MFC directly to implement all the moniker types stated previously.

Uniform Data Transfer (UDT)

Through OLE, you can use structured storage to store your objects and monikers to find your objects, but there has to be a mechanism to move this data from the place it is stored (linked or embedded) to where you can output it to the client for manipulation. Uniform data transfer (UDT) does this and also notifies the data object and the client of changes in the data. UDT provides this service through the IDataObject interface and is used primarily in three areas:

- The Clipboard
- OLE drag and drop
- Linking and embedding

Clipboard

The system Clipboard is a system-level service used for interprocess communications. A *system-level service* is a function that is built into the Windows operating system. Because it's a system-level service, all applications have access to it. OLE can use the Clipboard to do UDT of objects between processes. With an IDataObject pointer, you can use the function OleSetClipboard() to take a cut or copied object and expose this object to all processes through the Clipboard. Likewise, when you want to paste data from the Clipboard, you can use your IDataObject pointer to use the OleGetClipboard() function. This is a very powerful mechanism because it maintains the integrity of the object as a whole, enabling you to move complex object data types between applications.

Visual C++ and MFC provide access to the Clipboard through the use of member functions in the classes CWnd and COleClientItem.

Drag and Drop

Drag and drop is a method by which the user can select and move objects within an application and between applications. UDT is used to perform drag-and-drop actions. On the selection of the object, the source application packages the object and uses an IDataObject pointer to call DoDragDrop(). The source uses the IDropSource interface, which yields a pointer to its implementation. This pointer is passed to DoDragDrop(). The source controls the mouse cursors and handles the object in case of a cancellation.

When the user brings the dragged object to its new client location or target, the client application evokes the IDropTarget interface. With the pointer to the IDropTarget, the client application tracks the object in relation to itself with the functions available in the

`IDropTarget` interface. One function named `IDropTarget::Drop()` is called when the object is dropped on the target. `Drop()` passes the `IDataObject` pointer of the source to the target. Now that the client has the `IDataObject` pointer, it's free to manipulate the object.

Drag-and-drop support is encapsulated in the following MFC classes:

- `COleDropSource`
- `COleDropTarget`
- `COleClientItem`
- `COleServerItem`
- `COleDataSource`

Embedding and Linking

A *linked* object is an object that is not stored within a single OLE document on your hard drive, but rather elsewhere external to the document, such as another file, in another directory on your computer's hard drive. In the document, a moniker is stored that references the linked object. This OLE function uses UDT to move the data from the data object source to the container application so that the data can be rendered, as appropriate. Linked objects are manipulated through the `IOleLink` interface. By linking an object instead of embedding it, you cut down on the size of the compound file. In addition, you expose the linked object so that multiple people can use it.

An *embedded* object is an object that is stored through the OLE structured storage mechanism as native data within an OLE document itself. Although this increases the size of the compound file, it provides a single file object that can contain multiple data types.

OLE Documents

OLE documents are nothing more than compound files that use structured storage to hold the objects that make up the document. These objects can be native data, or through the use of monikers, they can link to data outside the document. In addition, an OLE document can contain objects created by other processes, embedded as if they were natively a part of the document. OLE documents are handled through interfaces, just like any other OLE object. As you can see, OLE documents are a conglomeration of several OLE services. Here are some of the interfaces used to implement OLE document interfaces:

- `IOleItemContainer`
- `IPersistFile`
- `IClassFactory`
- `IOleInPlaceActiveFrame`
- `IOleInPlaceUIObject`
- `IOleInPlaceSite`

`COleDocument` encapsulates the functionality of OLE documents and ActiveX documents in MFC. However, it's important to note that a series of classes in MFC are used together to provide this functionality.

In-Place Activation

OLE documents support *in-place activation*, or what is commonly referred to as *visual editing*. This enables you to edit embedded objects in a container application as if they were native. When you activate visual editing in the container, the user interface of the container morphs to support selected user-interface functions of the server application that created the object. A whole series of interfaces exists to enable you to implement and support in-place activation. These interfaces all begin with `IOleInPlace`. Some of the interfaces you can use to implement and support in-place activation are the following:

- `IOleInPlaceObject`
- `IOleInPlaceActiveObject`
- `IOleInPlaceSite`
- `IOleInPlaceActiveFrame`
- `IOleInPlaceUIObject`
- `IOleInPlaceSite`

OLE Automation

OLE Automation basically enables you to manipulate the properties and methods of an application from within another application through the use of high-level macro languages and scripting languages such as VBScript and JavaScript. This enables you to customize objects and provide interoperability between applications.

In the world of OLE Automation are OLE Automation components and OLE Automation controllers. An *OLE Automation component* is a service that is exposed by an application for use by another. Microsoft Excel is a good example of this because it exposes services that can create and manipulate worksheets, cells, and rows.

Services available through an OLE Automation component are stored in a type library. A type library is stored in a binary file with a .TLB extension. Object Description Language is used to define the services of an OLE Automation component. Object Description Language instructions are stored in a file with the extension .ODL. The ODL file is compiled into a type library. In Visual C++ 6.x, there is a nice utility that reads type libraries and graphically displays the services provided by OLE Automation components.

The utility in Visual C++ is named the OLE\COM Object Viewer application and is in the \Visual Studio\Common\Tools\ directory of Visual C++. Figure 1.13 shows the OLE/COM Object Viewer, which can be used to view OLE and COM objects graphically.

Notice that the Type Library Viewer screen shows the disassembled type library in Object Description Language (see Figure 1.14). It also displays the constants, properties, methods, and interfaces to the Automation component.

OLE Automation clients are applications that use the services provided by OLE Automation controllers. OLE Automation clients work through an interface named `IDispatch`. This dispatch interface exposes the available services to the controller application.

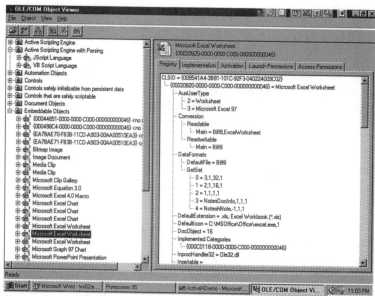

Figure 1.13 The OLE/COM Object Viewer that comes with Visual C++ 6.x.

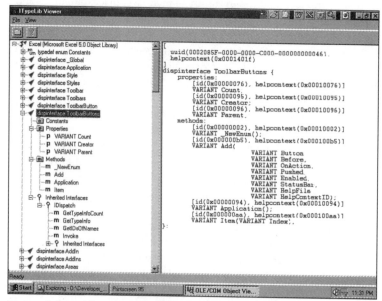

Figure 1.14 The OLE/COM Object Viewer's function Type Library Viewer.

OLE Controls

As discussed previously, *OLE controls* are self-contained reusable components that can be embedded in applications. They are also OLE Automation objects that can have properties set at both compile time and runtime. OLE controls also have methods that can perform certain operations. These components have a very profound effect in the area of application development. Also called *OLE control extensions*, OLE controls are commonly referred to as *OCXs*.

In more technical terms, an OLE control is an embeddable COM object that is implemented as an in-process server dynamic link library. It supports in-place activation as an inside-out object.

As an OLE in-process object, an OLE control is loaded into the address space of its container. As you are probably aware, every WIN32 process has a 4GB address space.

Note

A *WIN32 process* is a running instance of an application loaded into memory.

The lower 2GB is where the application is loaded and the upper 2GB is where the system is loaded. An OLE control is loaded in the lower 2GB with the application. Therefore, they share the same resources with the application; thus the term *in-process*.

An OLE control is also a server. Why is it a server? Well, it provides two-way communication between the container application and the control. It can also respond to user-initiated events such as mouse movements, keyboard input, and programmatic scripting input, and it can pass that input to the container application for action.

OLE controls are also *in-place–activated*. This means that they can be placed in the active state by the user or the container and edited or manipulated. This is a functionality that OLE controls inherit from OLE documents. Like a dynamic link library (DLL), the OLE control is a library of functions. In fact, an OLE control might be considered a super DLL. More than just a super DLL, an OLE control is a detached object that can fire and respond to events and process messages; it has unique properties and possesses multithreaded capabilities. Although OLE controls are also known as *OCXs* because of their file extension, they are actually DLLs. OCXs can contain several controls. Unlike DLLs, OCXs respond to user input and support two-way communication or notification, between themselves and their container.

An OLE control can have its own data set and can act as an OLE Automation component because you can manipulate its properties and methods. OLE controls can be both 16-bit and 32-bit, as well as Unicode. Like OLE Automation objects, OLE controls can have properties set at both compile time and runtime, and OLE controls also have methods that can perform certain operations. The difference between OLE controls and OLE Automation objects is that they are self-contained objects. They provide two-way communication between the control and the container. In addition, OLE controls do not have to have a user interface. As such they can provide hidden services such as a timer, communications, or mail.

OLE controls cannot stand alone; they must be embedded in an OLE container. They provide prepackaged components of functionality that are reusable and customizable. OLE controls are at the top of the OLE architecture; they are built on several OLE technologies.

In addition, OLE controls can be used in a wide variety of development tools, such as Delphi, Visual C++, Borland C++, Gupta, Visual Basic, Oracle Developer 2000, and PowerBuilder. OLE controls can also be used in a variety of nonprogramming environments, such as Microsoft Word, Microsoft Excel, Lotus, HTML, and Internet Explorer. OLE controls are a very powerful reusable component.

An Overview of ActiveX

You have probably heard a lot of media hype about ActiveX. The question is, "Is ActiveX really new?" Well, yes and no. After all the marketing fluff, you are probably left wondering, "What can ActiveX do for me? More importantly, what are the foundations of ActiveX? What technologies does ActiveX include, and how can I incorporate them in my applications by using Visual C++ and MFC?" These are some of the same questions I found myself asking when I returned from the Software Development 96 Conference in March 1996.

During a lecture I attended, someone suggested that ActiveX was nothing more than Internet-aware OLE controls. I started asking questions, and someone else informed me that ActiveX is nothing more than a sly marketing attempt to sell OLE under a different name. I was left perplexed and confused because no one could give me a definitive answer about the internals and framework of ActiveX or even an explicit definition of ActiveX. I decided to find out for myself.

I found that ActiveX is composed of a group of technologies or components to develop and implement applications for the Internet. I soon understood why no one could give me a clear definition. At the core of these technologies is OLE. ActiveX is an extension of OLE technologies across the Internet, but it's more than that—it also comprises a series of Internet and multimedia services that can be used to create rich Internet applications. Because I have covered OLE, I will now give you a look at ActiveX, which is really OLE, renamed and extended.

OLE Technologies Extended Through ActiveX

ActiveX has taken the OLE technologies and extended them beyond the bounds of the local machine to enterprisewide networks and the Internet. Specifically, OLE technologies have aggrandized into the following ActiveX services:

- ActiveX documents
- ActiveX controls
- COM
- Internet monikers

This is not the total effect. Elements of OLE are also present in the new ActiveX technologies, as you will see in the next section, "ActiveX Technologies." For now, let's concentrate on the evolution of OLE technologies into ActiveX.

ActiveX Documents

ActiveX has taken OLE documents and extended them across the Internet. This technology is a way for existing OLE documents, such as Microsoft Word, Microsoft Project, and Microsoft PowerPoint, to be activated by a Web browser and opened through a viewer. Thus, you can have compound files with various data that can contain linked and embedded objects being accessed across the World Wide Web (WWW). Using the ActiveX hyperlinks technology, you can extend OLE documents across the Web. ActiveX hyperlinks are discussed in the next section.

Asynchronous Storage

The capability to bring ActiveX documents across the WWW gives rise to another ActiveX technology, asynchronous storage. Basically, this extends structured storage across the Web, enabling the storage to happen asynchronously. Obviously, with the slow bandwidth of the Internet, if you allowed a storage operation to happen synchronously, nothing else could happen on the client or server until the transfer of data to or from persistent storage took place. Using ActiveX hyperlinks and the technology of asynchronous monikers, you can accomplish asynchronous storage.

ActiveX Controls

An *ActiveX control* is a superset of an OLE control that has been extended for the Internet environment. This does not mean that ActiveX controls can be used only in the Internet environment; quite the contrary, they can be used in any container that can support their interfaces. ActiveX controls must still be embedded in a container application. When an end user encounters a page with an ActiveX control, that control is downloaded to the client machine if it's not already there and used. This is, of course, provided that the user's browser supports ActiveX controls. The two most prevalent browsers that support ActiveX controls are Microsoft Internet Explorer and Netscape, with the help of the Ncompass plug-in.

The major difference between the OLE control and the superset ActiveX control is that the standard is different. In the new standard, an ActiveX control must support at least the `IUnknown` interface and be self-registering. It is a simple COM object. Obviously, the control must have more interfaces than just `IUnknown`, or it would have no functionality. The idea is that the control supports only the interfaces it needs, so it can be as lightweight as possible. In contrast, in the previous standard an OLE control was required to support a whole armada of COM interfaces, whether the control needed them or not. This made some controls bloated with code that was not used or needed. In the world of Internet development, this code bloat is unacceptable.

Internet Monikers

With the advent of ActiveX and the extension of COM across the net, monikers were also extended and incorporated into this architecture. This gave rise to two new types of monikers:

- URL monikers
- Asynchronous monikers

URL Monikers

A *URL* is a universal resource locator, used for Web-based addressing of objects. As you learned earlier, monikers are an intelligent naming system. By using the `IMoniker` interface to a moniker object and the intelligent name, you can locate the object. This capability was simply extended to include URLs, because of the capability of passing objects across the Internet from DCOM.

Asynchronous Monikers

Previously, monikers carried out their binding to the object synchronously. Nothing could happen until the binding was complete. On the high-latency, slow-link communications network of the Internet, holding up operations while binding is accomplished is unacceptable. With asynchronous monikers, the interfaces to the object negotiate the transmission of the binding process to perform it asynchronously. Right now, URL monikers are the only implementation of asynchronous monikers.

New ActiveX Technologies

ActiveX brings to the table some new technologies that are not necessarily related to OLE. However, these technologies facilitate the creation of interactive applications for the World Wide Web. Until now, the Internet has contained relatively static content. Now, with the ActiveX technologies, you can build dynamic HTML pages as a result of a database query, embed sound and video into your Web pages, and link to documents on a remote server—basically enabling you to *activate* the Internet. These new ActiveX Technologies are

- ActiveX hyperlinks
- ActiveX conferencing
- ActiveX server extensions
- Code signing
- HTML extensions
- ActiveMovie

ActiveX Hyperlinks

ActiveX hyperlinks basically allow in-place activation from HTML files of non-HTML–based documents. Using an ActiveX document container, you can access Microsoft Word, Microsoft Excel, Microsoft PowerPoint, Visio, and CorelDraw! documents from a hypertext link in an HTML document.

ActiveX Conferencing

The ActiveX conferencing services are a suite of technologies that enable real-time, multiparty, multimedia communication over the Internet. This is much like video teleconferencing except that you can do it on a PC. Just think what this does for programmers; we could all work at home and telecommute. This is a programmable interface opening up endless possibilities for innovation.

ActiveX Server Extensions

ActiveX server extensions, formerly known as the *ISAPI Internet Server API*, are used to give functionality to Internet servers. Previously this could be done only using common gateway interface (GCI) code. ActiveX server extensions provide an alternative means of achieving this functionality. Usually, server extensions are implemented using a dynamic link library (DLL) and provide some functionality not provided by the HTTP server, such as connecting to a database.

ActiveX Scripts

ActiveX scripts bring OLE Automation to the Internet. Automation controllers can now access Automation component services across the Internet with DCOM and ActiveX support for scripting. You can use a variety of scripting languages, such as VBScript, JavaScript, Perl, Visual Basic for Applications, Lisp, and Scheme.

Code Signing

Code signing is a new technology that enables electronic signatures for code. This provides security from tampering of interactive applications across the Net. Basically, the application vendors will provide a digital signature for their code that compiles with the code signing specification. On the client side, when an application or component is downloaded from the Net, it calls a Win32 API function named `WinVerifyTrust()`. This function checks the digital signature and verifies it.

HTML Extensions

Hypertext Markup language (HTML) is the language for all Web-based document production. To support ActiveX controls and ActiveX Scripts, extensions had to be made to the HTML language. In addition, Web browsers had to be modified to accommodate the new language extensions. Now you can add ActiveX controls to Web pages by using the HTML `<OBJECT>` tag.

ActiveMovie

ActiveMovie is a new technology to replace the old media control interface and video for Windows. ActiveMovie is an audio and video streaming framework. With ActiveMovie, you can play back MPEG, AVI, and Apple Quicktime movies. If you worked for Ford Motor Company building active Web pages, you could embed the ActiveMovie control into your Web pages with ActiveMovie. You could then have the control asynchronously download and play at the same time an mpeg of a Ford truck climbing a steep mountain. ActiveMovie and ActiveX conferencing are related in that they are based on the same video streaming technologies.

Distributed COM (DCOM)

Distributed COM, also known as *DCOM* and formerly known as *Network OLE*, is the basic extension of binary COM objects across LANs, WANs, and the Internet. Now you can instantiate and bind objects across a network. Chapter 9, "A Distributed Objects Overview," gives you more background on DCOM.

For now, I will give you an initial taste of DCOM. Keep it in mind as you read future chapters. DCOM is a high-level network protocol that enables COM-based components to interoperate across a network. DCOM makes it so that the programmer doesn't have to write network code or even know how to write network code. DCOM, like COM, is not a programming language. It is a specification and a service, built with and built on COM, which provides a transparent network protocol enabling COM components to interoperate across a network. Basically, it enables COM objects to talk with each other across a network. DCOM is not an object-oriented method for object-oriented programming, like COM. However, because DCOM was built with COM and is implemented using COM, it utilizes COM's object-oriented technology to provide its services. To understand what DCOM does, you need to see what problem it solves–communication between processes on different computers, also known as the Distributed Computing Environment (DCE). You will explore this more in Chapter 9.

Summary

This chapter discusses OLE, ActiveX, COM, and DCOM. Because OLE is an object-oriented architecture founded on COM, it is an extendible services architecture. Each OLE component is a building block for the rest of the technologies. Microsoft has extended this architecture to ActiveX to facilitate the creation of Internet-enabled applications. ActiveX builds on OLE by using COM and DCOM. You've had a sneak preview of COM and DCOM. I have laid a high-level foundation for them. The next chapters go into the details and solidify your understanding of COM and DCOM.

CHAPTER 2

THE OBJECT REVOLUTION

Everywhere you turn, there's talk of object-oriented design, object-oriented analysis, and object-oriented development tools—there are even companies out there selling object-oriented versions of the classic mainframe language COBOL. Nowadays everyone seems to have his own idea about what it means to be object-oriented. However, scholars agree that since the term *object-oriented* was coined by Alan Kay in 1970, *object-oriented* has become a conglomerate of a handful of principles. These principles are

- Inheritance
- Polymorphism
- Encapsulation

This chapter begins by reviewing the basic tenants of what it means to be object-oriented (OO). Programming with COM and DCOM requires an intimate understanding of object-oriented principles. You will also discover that Microsoft took a unique approach in the way that it supports the object-oriented principle of inheritance.

Objects and Classes

It's probably not going to come as any surprise to you that object-oriented programming revolves around objects. Now the dictionary will tell you that in the most philosophical sense, an object is something "intelligible or perceptible by the mind," but that's pretty abstract. In the context of object-oriented programming, an *object* is a software package containing data elements (called *attributes* or *properties*) and the functions that perform operations (called *methods*) for manipulating and accessing that data. Sure, it's still abstract, but at least now it's framed in programming terms.

Let's take a look at an example. Suppose you were asked to write a program to track the number of hamburgers made at a fast-food restaurant. Intuition would tell you to build a Hamburger object that would wrap together all the code dealing with hamburgers and all the data that might belong to a hamburger (the number of pickles, whether the hamburger has onions or bacon, and so on).

Objects can also represent things that don't physically exist. In the hamburger example, it might make sense to have a HamburgerCounter object.

In object-oriented programming terms, Hamburger and HamburgerCounter are two examples of a class. A *class* is an abstract description of the behaviors and data found in an object. Your program might have only one Hamburger class, but many distinct and separate Hamburger objects. Think of a class as a template for creating an individual object. Each object, being a member of the Hamburger class, would be semantically identical to the other objects. An object is said to be an *instance* of a particular class, and the process of creating one of these instances is referred to as *instantiation*.

If you take a closer look at what an object is, you'll find that an instance is composed of both data and behavior. The object's data is sometimes referred to as the object's *attributes* or *member variables*. The attributes of an object belong only to that particular instance. You might have two instances of the Hamburger class, for example, but the two objects could have different NumberOfPickles attributes. One hamburger could contain a value of True in its HasKetchup attribute, whereas another could have False—same class, two very different hamburgers!

The behaviors of an object are accessed through class-specific functions named *methods*. Depending on the tool or language you are using, methods are also referred to as *operations*, object *functions*, or *messages*. Methods indicate to an object that you want it to perform some specific task. For example, the HamburgerCounter class could specify that all HamburgerCounters know how to reset themselves and prepare for a new batch of burgers. The HamburgerCounters could know how to report on their status and could have a DisplayStatus() method. Figure 2.1 shows the relationship between the Hamburger class and object instances, attributes, and methods.

Note

In OOP, an object's attributes are considered private and should be directly accessible only by the object itself. If an object wants to expose its data to an external source, it does so through assessor functions. These methods are sometimes called Get and Set functions.

An external source never directly manipulates an object's data. In the case of the Hamburger object, you would not directly allow a user of your Hamburger object to modify the NumberOfPickles attribute. Instead, you would provide a SetNumberOfPickles() method. This enables the Hamburger object to control access to its data. If you allow direct manipulation of your data, you violate the OO principle of information hiding and encapsulation.

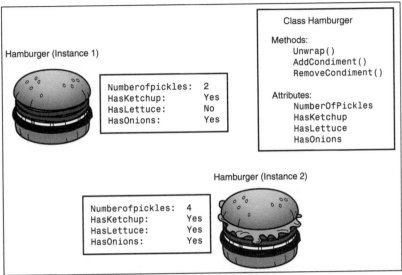

Figure 2.1 A logical view of the `Hamburger` and `HamburgerCounter` classes.

What It Means to Be Object-Oriented

Now that you have an understanding of objects and classes, you need to explore the meaning of *object-oriented*. As I mentioned at the beginning of this chapter, three principles embody what it means to be object-oriented: encapsulation, inheritance, and polymorphism.

Encapsulation

Three critical concepts are important when you are deciding whether to call a programming system object-oriented. Depending on the language or product that you're talking about, these concepts—encapsulation, inheritance, and polymorphism—can take radically different forms. The way one language implements inheritance, for example, can be so different from another product that users of the first product might not even recognize the inheritance features of the other. These differences are what often lead to so much controversy and contention between the various industry players. Although considerable controversy exists among the various vendors, the academic community has definitive criteria for what constitutes the OO principles.

Encapsulation refers to the idea that well-designed classes should hide the details of their implementation from the outside world. Classes present to the world an *interface* that is used to dictate the protocol that objects use when interacting with each other. In much the same way that the steering wheel, accelerator, and brake represent the interface to your car, the collection of methods supported by a class represent the class's interface. Encapsulation means implementing an object in a manner that does not affect the class's interface.

As you learned in Chapter 1, when talking about the details of Microsoft's OLE and COM technologies, the word *interface* has special meaning apart from the traditional object-oriented vernacular. So be careful. Depending on its context, *interface* could mean several different things. Right now I'm using it in a rather generic OOP sense. I'll warn you when you start to get into COM and OLE-specific interfaces.

Let's take a look at an example that shows why encapsulation can be a valuable feature. Suppose you are writing a program that will enable the user to create electronic versions of those ubiquitous yellow sticky notes that most people use at work. Your virtual sticky notes can be pasted to your Windows desktop and are persistent; that is to say, the user can turn off the computer, and when he or she turns it back on again, the notes will reappear in exactly the same place, with exactly the same contents. This implies that the notes can be saved to some form of nonvolatile storage and then read back in when needed. One way to accomplish this is to have a `StickyNote` class with a `Save()` method. When the user finishes entering or updating the text on the note, your `Save()` method can stream the text to a file on the computer's hard drive. Figure 2.2 depicts this program design.

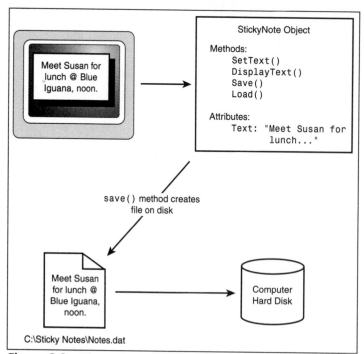

Figure 2.2   The Sticky Note program, using the computer's hard disk for persistent storage.

Of course, your new program sells fabulously well, and before you know it, the orders are coming in faster than you can cash the checks. One day you receive a call from a very large Fortune 500 company, asking for 10,000 copies of your new program. There's just one catch: They want all the sticky notes to be saved into a corporate database so that anyone can access their sticky notes from any computer in the company.

No problem. Your `StickyNote` class encapsulates all the logic for saving to the persistent store. Your program knows that `StickyNote` object instances have a `Save()` method, but it has no idea about how the method is implemented. All you have to do is rewrite the `StickyNote` class's `Save()` method to go to the database. The rest of your program doesn't need to change at all. Figure 2.3 shows how the new and improved version of the Sticky Note program works. Note that the interface to the `StickyNote` class has not changed; only the implementation of the `Save()` method has been modified.

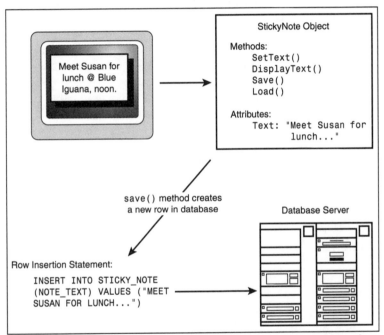

Figure 2.3   The new Sticky Note program, using a SQL database for persistent storage.

Of course, this example is rather contrived, and object-oriented programming offers several other mechanisms for solving this problem more elegantly. All the same, you see why encapsulation can be so useful.

Because this book is about COM and DCOM, it's important to note that COM and, in turn, DCOM support encapsulation. As a whole, a COM object contains the data (properties) and behavior (methods) that are implemented behind a publicly exposed and well-defined interface. This containment demonstrates the object-oriented principle of encapsulation.

Encapsulation makes sense to us because it exists in nature. This is what being object-oriented does for us. It allows us to reduce the complexity of our software system and to see things as we do in nature. A great example of encapsulation is the cell. A cell contains membranes that serve as the interface for passing chemical messages, information (data) encapsulated in protein chains, behavior carried out by structures under cell control. Object-oriented programming requires encapsulation. However, nothing particular to object-oriented programming specifies how encapsulation is carried out. Consequently, nothing should prevent you from using encapsulation in a program written in a non–object-oriented language such as C or FORTRAN.

Inheritance

On the other hand, *inheritance* is an object-oriented principle that can't be artificially created. The reason for this is that it's implemented at the compiler level. Inheritance binds one object tightly to the implementation of another object. This must be accomplished at the machine level.

Inheritance enables your classes to model relationships between objects where one class is a specialized form of another. In its simplest form, inheritance involves two classes. The first class, the more general of the two, is called the *base class* or *superclass*. The second class, the specialization, is called the *derived class* or *subclass*. The inheritance relationship is often called an *is-a* relationship, because the derived class "is a" form of the base class.

Let us examine the inheritance hierarchy in Figure 2.4. This diagram shows a base class named `Animal` and a single derived class named `Dog`. The `Dog` derived class, in turn, is the base class for two derived classes, `Collie` and `Terrier`. Now the *is-a* semantics should make a little more sense. A `Terrier` "is a" `Dog` and so "is a" `Collie`. Both `Terriers` and `Collies` are `Animals`, as are all `Dogs`. As you can see, inheritance is a transitive relationship.

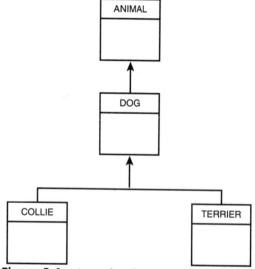

Figure 2.4   A simple inheritance hierarchy with one base class and two derived classes.

A Quick Word About Notation

Numerous types of notation exist to represent object-oriented systems. Some of these types include Booche OOD, Rumbaugh OMT, Microsoft COM Notation, Shlaer-Mellor OOA, and Jacobson Use Cases. In the past year, one object-oriented notation has emerged as the industry standard for representing object-oriented systems: the Unified Modeling Language(UML).

UML is an amalgamation of three of the most popular notations: Booche OOD, Rumbaugh OMT, and Jacobson Use Cases. A company called Rational Corporation, formed by the big three in object-oriented analysis and design—Grady Booche, Ivar Jacobson, and James Rumbaugh, has submitted UML to the Object Management Group, an industry standards committee. OMG has approved UML version 1.0. Because UML draws from the best of the top three object-oriented notations, it has been very well received by everyone in the industry.

A discussion of UML is beyond the scope of this book. To find more information on UML, visit Rational Corporation's Web site at `http://www.rational.com/`. For now, it suffices to say that the boxes in Figure 2.4 represent classes. The lines that connect the classes denote which class is the base class. The class with the arrow pointing at it is the base class, and the class with the arrow pointing away from it is the derived class.

From a practical standpoint, inheritance, as described so far, is simply a notational and organizational feature. With object inheritance, derived classes actually inherit attributes and methods of the base class.

Let's go back to the Dog example. Suppose the `Dog` class had a method called `Bark()` that an application would call whenever it wanted its `Dog` objects to bark. Well, guess what? Then every `Collie` and `Terrier` instance would have a `Bark()` method, too, without any extra coding on your part. That's the beauty of inheritance. If you can think of behaviors and attributes that are general enough to push up into a base class, every derived class will benefit from your efforts.

When Good's Not Good Enough: Method Overriding

You're probably thinking that inheritance sounds pretty good. It should be clear that using inheritance in your programs facilitates code reuse because now programmers can benefit from the hard work you put into building your base classes.

What happens, though, when the behaviors you've inherited from a superclass don't quite make sense in the context of your specialization? A `Dog` class's `Bark()` method might display `Whoof!`, but does that behavior make sense when you create a derived `Chihuahua` class? After all, if there ever was a class that should display `Yip-yip!` in response to `Bark()`, the `Chihuahua` is it.

That's where *overriding* comes in. Overriding refers to the practice of selectively redefining an inherited interface to meet the needs of the derived class. In the example, the author of the `Chihuahua` class can override the `Bark()` method to display `Yip-yip!` without disturbing the rest of the interface inherited from `Dog`. Figure 2.5 depicts the relationship between a base method and its overrides.

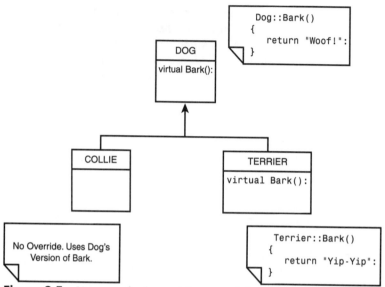

Figure 2.5   Using method overriding to redefine inherited behavior.

Multiple Inheritance

One of the most contentious debates in the object-oriented community is about *multiple inheritance*. Multiple inheritance means allowing a class to inherit from two or more superclasses. However, multiple inheritance introduces some potential problems.

Take the inheritance tree depicted in Figure 2.6. In this diagram, you can see an inheritance tree of vegetables, with `Broccoflower` inheriting from both `Broccoli` and `Cauliflower`.

What you have in Figure 2.6 is not only multiple inheritance, but also the potential problem that I mentioned earlier: a multiple inheritance loop. Because both `Broccoli` and `Cauliflower` are derived from `Vegetable`, the `Broccoflower` class indirectly inherits from `Vegetable` twice. This fact, among others, can lead to a variety of different problems.

Without diving too deep in compiler design theory, the first problem is that some object-oriented languages don't have a way of knowing which branch they should follow to get at methods in the topmost base class (for example, `Vegetable`) that are never overridden. In other languages, this information might be discernible, but at a significant performance expense. After all, not all inheritance trees contain inheritance loops, and a particular method might belong to a base class that can be accessed only through a single path. Searching for that path can be time-consuming.

Another problem relates to overriding. In Figure 2.6, you can see that the `Vegetable` class has declared a method named `GetColor()`, which returns the color of the vegetable in question. Both `Broccoli` and `Cauliflower` have overridden this method, with `Broccoli` returning `Green` and `Cauliflower` returning `White`. Now the problem is—independent of what color the `Broccoflower` class *should* return— what happens if `Broccoflower` *doesn't* override `GetColor()` at all? Whose `GetColor()` should be called, `Broccoli`'s or `Cauliflower`'s?

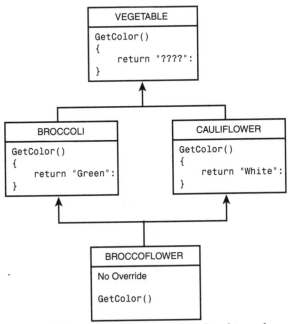

Figure 2.6   A multiple inheritance class hierarchy.

I'm afraid that no definitive answer to this problem exists. Some languages solve the problem in a language-specific manner; others simply punt and don't support multiple inheritance at all. Most industry pundits, including several noted C++ gurus, recommend staying away from multiple inheritance altogether, even if you are working in a programming language that implements the feature. Despite multiple inheritances pitfalls, it has redeeming value. There are situations in which multiple inheritance is useful, as you will see in Chapter 3, "Building COM Objects and Interfaces."

Polymorphism

The last of the primary object concepts, *polymorphism*, enables you to write programs that manipulate very specific objects in a generalized fashion. *Polymorphism* is a Greek word that means "having multiple forms." In OO, it refers to the capability to hide different implementations behind a common interface.

Polymorphism is a feature that enables you to treat derived classes as if they were really instances of a superclass.

Examine Figure 2.7 closely and then ask yourself, "What is this a picture of?"

Figure 2.7   Three insects.

Of course, this is a vague question. Ask one person, and he or she might tell you that it's just a picture of some insects. Someone else might reply that it's a picture of a beetle, a dragonfly, and an ant. If you're fortunate enough to stumble on an entomologist, you might be enthusiastically informed that this is a picture of a *sagra busqueti*, an *anax junius*, and a *monomorium pharaonis*. The interesting thing is that none of these responses are wrong; they're simply from varying perspectives.

However, at the risk of sounding insensitive, the creatures in Figure 2.7 are, fundamentally, bugs. All three exhibit basic characteristics shared by all insects: six legs, one pair of antennae, a ringed or segmented body, and three well-defined body regions. Therefore, even if you didn't know anything about *anax junius* but were told that this creature is an insect, you could still say something about the attributes of this animal.

Polymorphism takes this ability a step further, so let's take a look at an object-aware version of the bug picture. Figure 2.8 shows an inheritance tree that includes two of our creepy little friends.

This is a straightforward inheritance hierarchy, with both the `Dragonfly` and `Ant` subclasses inheriting a few methods and attributes from the `Insect` superclass. Note that the `Dragonfly` class overrides the `CanFly()` method that it inherits from `Insect`. The assumption here is that the method implementation for `CanFly()` found in `Insect` always returns `False`. `Dragonfly` overrides this method so that it can be re-implemented to return `True`. This way, when you ask a `Dragonfly` whether it can fly, it will accurately respond `True`, whereas everything else will continue to respond in the negative.

Now imagine that someone has blindfolded you and then placed three insect objects into your hand. You don't know what kind of insects they are, but you do know that they share the same common `Insect` superclass. How would you pick out the one insect object that could fly? One way would be to call the `CanFly()` method on each object and look for a `True` return value. Getting back a `True` doesn't tell you what insect you're holding—it could be a `Wasp`, a `Dragonfly`, or a `Bumble-Bee`—but it does enable you to answer the question at hand.

This is polymorphism at work. Even though your "vision" is restricted to viewing these objects as `Insects`, they are all really subclasses of `Insect`. When you call the `CanFly()`

method, polymorphism ensures that the correct method is called; if you call `CanFly()` on a `Dragonfly` object, it will always call the overridden version and return `True`, even if you think the object is just an `Insect`.

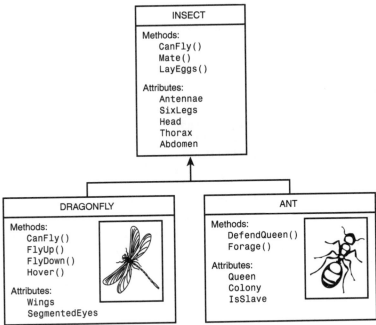

Figure 2.8   An insect inheritance hierarchy.

Polymorphism is a tremendously powerful capability. It enables you to manipulate and control disparate objects in the same fashion, as long as they share a common base class. The capability to construct similar objects that respond in different ways to the same message is one of the most profound tenets of the object-oriented programming movement.

Abstract Base Classes

In some of the preceding examples, you might have noticed that a few of the classes represent some rather ambiguous concepts. Take the `Vegetable` class depicted in Figure 2.6. Certainly, it is fair to say that this class could have many useful and generalized methods common to all vegetables. It's much harder, however, to pin down how these methods would actually be implemented in the `Vegetable` class.

In Figure 2.6, the `Vegetable` class is shown having a single method called `GetColor()`. This is a perfectly reasonable behavior to place into the `Vegetable` class; all vegetables have coloring of some sort, and it's exactly these types of common attributes and behaviors that you want to move as high up in the class hierarchy as possible. The real problem is coming up with a sane and logical implementation that would apply to all vegetables.

You could, of course, code `Vegetable` so that its `GetColor()` always returned `Green`, and effectively force non-green `Vegetable` subclasses to override this method. However, if you have any sense of what is good and right, this possibility should churn your stomach. Such a totally arbitrary implementation is inelegant and semantically inaccurate. The simple fact of the matter is that not all vegetables are green, and it doesn't make sense to imply that they are. (Okay, give me a second to calm down.)

On the other hand, you could code `Vegetable` so that the `GetColor()` method always returns something that isn't a color. In Figure 2.6 the class returns `???`; other possibilities include things like `Undefined`, `Not supported`, or `Override me`. It's probably safe to say that this approach is a little better than simply choosing a default color, but not by much.

Enter the concept of the *abstract base class*. Abstract base classes are built with the intention that a program will never create object instances of this type. Instead, an abstract base class is used as an object interface starting point. Programmers derive a new class from the abstract base class and override its methods as appropriate. The only objects that are ever instantiated belong to derived classes of the abstract base class. Classes derived from abstract base classes are called *concrete classes*; these classes are designed to be instantiated and directly manipulated.

Abstract base classes are quite useful, but explicit support for the concept varies between languages and tools. In C++, for example, abstract base classes are fully supported. The language enforces the rule that abstract base classes cannot be instantiated, in addition to allowing the programmer to designate certain methods as required to be implemented in the derived class. The Smalltalk programming language, on the other hand, does not have this formal level of support. I'll talk more about C++'s support for abstract base classes in future sections.

Class Objects

No, it's not a typo. The title of this section is "Class Objects," which might sound as though I'm mixing up some of my terminology. Au contraire. This section is about special objects that represent classes, as opposed to objects that simply represent instances of classes.

Let's briefly review what classes and object instances are. A *class* is a rather abstract description of object-based functionality. It describes what attributes an object has and what methods the object understands and responds to. In the context that I've been describing, a class is not a tangible entity; you can't *do* anything with a class in the same way that you can with an object instance. Object instances are the concrete manifestations of the class. You can think of a class as the vision of a logical programming entity with encapsulated attributes and behaviors, and the object instance as being the implementation of that vision.

In some programming systems, classes are objects as well. These *class objects* are responsible for managing the creation and, sometimes, the destruction of instances. For this reason, class objects are sometimes referred to as *class factories* or *metaclass objects* (Smalltalk). A *class factory* is an object that knows how to create instances of a particular class. Some class objects can also implement behaviors that are related to the overall class functionality but don't make sense being bound to a single object instance. If this is all a little confusing, don't worry. Class objects are rather abstract ideas, and it takes a little bit of time to become comfortable with them. Figure 2.9 depicts the relationship between the `Hamburger` object instances and their class object.

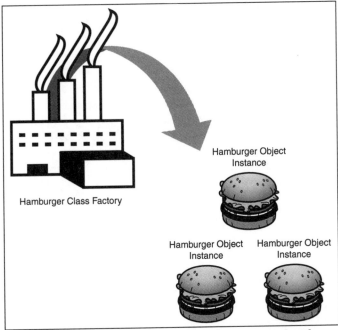

Figure 2.9   Hamburger objects and the Hamburger class factory.

Looking at Objects from a C++ Perspective

So far, this chapter has centered on those abstract concepts that make the object-oriented approach to writing software unique and compelling. You might have noticed that the preceding examples do not include any code samples or talk about language features that are not universal. Object-oriented programming takes many different forms, and it's more often the specific language or development tool that colors the programmer's overall impressions of the development process. To avoid the biases that a language-oriented approach can introduce, the earlier sections emphasize ideas and practices instead of languages and products.

Now it's time to get away from that. The reality is that software is built using languages and tools. You can talk theory all you want, but at the end of the day if you haven't done any programming, you don't have a program.

The next few sections briefly look at how the C++ language approaches the problem of writing object-oriented programs. C++ is widely accepted as the language of COM. Although it's certainly possible to write COM and DCOM programs in other languages, most COM objects are likely to be implemented in C++. You might ask yourself why C++. Well, there really is no definitive answer, but I will try to give you an acceptable explanation. Basically, it's because C++ is a mature OO language that natively supports all three of the OO principles: encapsulation, inheritance, and polymorphism.

Because C++ is the language used throughout most of this book, it's important to understand how the language achieves encapsulation, inheritance, and polymorphism.

Encapsulation in C++

As alluded to in the overview section on encapsulation, nothing in C++ dictates or mandates encapsulation. However, the simple use of a class is, in itself, encapsulation. As you design and program object-oriented systems in C++, or any other language for that matter, you should keep in mind encapsulation. It is very easy in C++ to build classes that do a poor job of encapsulating their behavior.

Take a look at Listing 2.1. This listing shows how you might code a declaration of the StickyNote class presented earlier.

Listing 2.1 STICKY1.H—A Poorly Encapsulated Declaration of the StickyNote Class

```
class StickyNote
{
public:

    // Public methods
    void Save(const string& strDatabaseName,
            const string& strDatabaseUser,
            const string& strDatabasePassword);

    void Load(const string& strDatabaseName,
            const string& strDatabaseUser,
            const string& strDatabasePassword);

    // Public data (Yeeech!)
    string strNoteText;
};
```

For several reasons, this is not a well-encapsulated class design. First, the arguments to Save() and Load() are directly accessing a database for storage of the note text. By directly accessing a database, StickyNote is now tied to a particular implementation. The first time a database object needs new parameters, the interface will have to be changed. Secondly, the class user has direct access to the text. What I am getting at here is that the details of the class have not been hidden behind a well-defined interface. Listing 2.2 is an improved version of the same class declaration.

Listing 2.2 STICKY2.H—A Well-Encapsulated Declaration of the StickyNote Class

```
class NoteStorage
{
    //... Methods implemented by all backing stores ...
};

class StickyNote
{
public:
```

```
    // Public methods
    void SetText(const string& strNewNoteText);
    void Save(NoteStorage& PersistPlace);
    void Load(NoteStorage& PersistPlace);

private:

    // Now this data is private
    string strNoteText;
};
```

C++ is unique in the OOP world because it allows methods and attributes to be associated with *access specifiers*. The access specifiers—`public`, `private`, and `protected`—enable a programmer to indicate who is allowed to call the method or access a particular attribute. A `public` method, for example, may be called by any external entity. Conversely, a `private` method may be called only within the same class. The `protected` keyword serves as an intermediate level of protection between `public` and `private` member variables and methods of a class. `Protected` members of a base class are accessible only to friends of the base class and members and friends of derived classes. A friend is a concept unique to C++. If a class, function, or variable is declared outside the scope of a particular class as a friend of that class, it is granted access to the `private` and `protected` members of that class. A friend serves as a way in certain unique situations to enhance the performance of an application or when it's absolutely necessary to circumvent the C++ access specifiers. You can think of C++ access specifiers as a security guard, carefully screening everyone who wants to use your objects. If you attempt to call a method that you don't have access to, the C++ compiler will generate a compiler error. This is one feature of C++ that enables you to implement encapsulation. By marking variables or methods as private, you can hide the implementation details of your class. As discussed earlier, C++ gives you the ability to implement encapsulation; however, as you saw in Listing 2.1, C++ will allow you to build classes that do not implement encapsulation.

In Listing 2.2, you can see that the public attribute `strNoteText` has been made private and that users of the class now use the `SetText()` method to modify the variable indirectly. This gives the object more control over how that variable is managed. It would now be simple, for example, to modify the class so that the note is saved every time the text changes. This was not possible with the design in Listing 2.1 because the object had no way of knowing when the text change occurred.

Note

You should limit your use of the `friend` and `public` specifiers. The `private` and `protected` access specifiers can be circumvented in a number of ways, most notably by using a `friend` class. As Bjarne Stroustrup, the father of C++, wrote in his book *The Annotated C++ Reference Manual* (Addison-Wesley, 1990), "The C++ access control mechanisms provide protection against accidents—*not* against fraud."

The more serious problem of where notes are saved has also been solved. Now the type and location of note storage has been encapsulated out into its own class, NoteStorage. If you were really going to write this program, you'd probably choose to make NoteStorage an abstract class and then create subclasses for each of the different backing stores (TextFileStorage, DatabaseStorage, and so on). The real trick is coming up with a generic enough interface for NoteStorage that will enable you to save and load your sticky notes from both a text file and a database. Of course, I'll leave this to you to do as an exercise.

Inheritance in C++

C++ has full and robust support for class inheritance. As you would expect, a derived class inherits all the public attributes and methods of its superclass. A superclass is also referred to as a *base class*. C++'s powerful and intuitive implementation of inheritance enables you to model complicated and sophisticated inheritance trees.

In the previous Dog example, I stipulated that each individual breed of dog had to be derived from a common base class. The class, Dog, was in turn derived from a class named Animal. In C++, specifying the base class after the new class's name, as shown in Listing 2.3, creates an inheritance relationship. This header file shows one possible set of declarations you could use to create the classes depicted in Figure 2.4.

Listing 2.3   DOGS1.H—A Dog Inheritance Hierarchy

```
class Animal
{
public:

    // Public methods
    string GetName() const;
    void    SetName(const string& strNewName);

    //... Other methods common to Animals ...

private:

    // We assume that all Animals have a name
    string strName;

    // ... Other attributes common to Animals ...
};


class Dog : public Animal
{
public:

    // Public methods
    void Bark();

    //... Other methods and attributes common to Dogs ...
};
```

```
class Collie : public Dog
{
    //... Methods and attributes specific to Collies ...
};


class Terrier : public Dog
{
    //... Methods and attributes specific to Terriers ...
};
```

In this inheritance tree, instances of Dog, Collie, and Terrier will all have the GetName()/SetName() methods that they inherited, either directly or indirectly, from the base class Animal.

Method Overriding in C++

Overriding a method is also easily accomplished in C++. Derived classes that must override a method inherited from a base class only have to create a new declaration and implementation in the context of the new class. The only catch is that the method must be declared virtual in the base class. The virtual keyword signals to the compiler that this method might be used in a polymorphic manner and might be the target of overrides in derived classes.

Let us look at another example. Remember the Animal example? In that example, the Chihuahua needed to Yip instead of Whoof. The code in Listing 2.4 shows a short program that demonstrates a fully functional inheritance tree demonstrating just this overriding behavior.

Listing 2.4 DOGS2.CPP—Overriding the Dog Class's Bark() Method

```
#include <iostream>
#include <string>


class Dog
{
public:

    // Public methods (notice virtual keyword)
    virtual void Bark();
};

void Dog::Bark()
{
    cout << "Whoof!";
}


class Collie : public Dog
{ };
```

continued on next page

continued from previous page

```
class Chihuahua : public Dog
{
public:

    // Overriden method
    void Bark();
};

void Chihuahua::Bark()
{
    cout << "Yip-yip!";
}


void main()
{
    Collie     Lassie;
    Chihuahua  Pepe;

    cout << "A collie goes \"";
    Lassie.Bark();
    cout << "\"\n";
    cout << "A Chihuahua goes \"";
    Pepe.Bark();
    cout << "\"\n";
}
```

As one would expect, this program prints out

```
A collie goes "Whoof!"
A Chihuahua goes "Yip-yip!"
```

The collie class inherits `Bark()` from its parent class, and because it does not override the method, the implementation used is the one found in the base class.

Polymorphism in C++

The C++ language fully supports polymorphism, but a couple of important prerequisites must be met first. The first was encountered in the previous example; only methods that are marked as `virtual` have the capability to be used in a polymorphic fashion. Additionally, a polymorphic method invocation can occur only through a pointer (or reference) to an object.

Let's revisit the insect example. Recall that Figure 2.8 depicts an inheritance tree in which `Dragonfly` and `Ant` classes were derived from the base class `Insect`. The `Insect` class possessed a polymorphic `CanFly()` method that was supposed to return `True` if the insect in question could fly and `False` otherwise. Given three anonymous insect objects, Listing 2.5 demonstrates how you can use polymorphism and the `CanFly()` method to pick out the one instance of a flying species.

Listing 2.5   INSECTS.CPP—Using Polymorphism to Find Out Which Insects Can Fly

```cpp
#include <iostream>
#include <string>

class Insect
{
public:

   // Public methods
   virtual bool CanFly() const;
};

bool Insect::CanFly() const
{
   return false;
}


class Dragonfly : public Insect
{
public:

   // Overriden method
   bool CanFly() const;
};

bool Dragonfly::CanFly() const
{
   return true;
}


class Beetle : public Insect
{ };


class Ant : public Insect
{ };


void main()
{
   Beetle    ABeetle;
   Ant       AnAnt;
   Dragonfly ADragonFly;

   // Fill up our array of bug pointers
   Insect*   InsectArray[] = { &AnAnt, &ADragonFly, &ABeetle };

   // Ask each insect if it can fly
   for (int loop = 0; loop < 3; loop++) {

      cout << "Insect #" << loop+1;
```

continued on next page

continued from previous page

```
                    // Here's the polymorphic method call
                    if (InsectArray[loop]->CanFly() == true)
                        cout << " can ";
                    else
                        cout << " cannot ";

                    cout << "fly.\n";
                }
            }
```

In this short program, you find three classes: `Dragonfly`, `Beetle`, and `Ant`. Each of these classes inherits from the `Insect` base class. Because the dragonfly is the only insect of the three that can fly, the `Dragonfly` class overrides the virtual `CanFly()` method to return `True`.

The bulk of this example occurs in the `main()` function. In the `main()` function, the program creates one instance each of the insect derived classes and then places the address of each insect into a random location in an array. Note that the array is declared to be of type "pointer to `Insect`"; there is no mention in the array declaration of classes derived from `Insect`. When the program loops through the array and uses each pointer to call the `CanFly()` method, the function call is routed to the method implementation that corresponds to the actual object type, irrespective of the fact that the code is treating all three of the objects as though they were just instances of the `Insect` class.

The following is the output of this example:

```
Insect #1 cannot fly.
Insect #2 can fly.
Insect #3 cannot fly.
```

Abstract Base Classes in C++

As previously described, an abstract base class is an inheritance-tree placeholder, a description of an interface that can never be directly instantiated but exists exclusively so that another class can derive from it and inherit its interface. At first glance, the idea might seem hopelessly esoteric; however, abstract base classes are extremely useful.

In C++, a class is said to be an abstract base class if it has one or more pure virtual methods. Just like a regular virtual method, a *pure* virtual method indicates that the compiler should generate code to perform a polymorphic lookup whenever the method is invoked. However, very much unlike a regular virtual method, a pure virtual method has no implementation at all within the class that it is declared.

I realize this definition of a pure virtual method might not appear to make much sense. How is it that you can indicate that a method is pure virtual but not provide a method implementation? What happens when you try to call the function?

This is the beauty of abstract base classes in C++. A child class that derives itself from an abstract base class is required to override all the derived class's pure virtual methods. Couple this with the fact that the language guarantees you can't create an instance of an abstract base class, and you start to realize that an implementation will always be found somewhere down the inheritance tree.

Take another look at Figure 2.6. I've already mentioned how the `Vegetable` class is a perfect candidate for an abstract base class. I bet you've never gone down to the grocery store and bought a vegetable. Sure, you've bought carrots, potatoes, lettuce, and a whole host of other produce items that happen to be vegetables. But you've never picked up a "vegetable" and carried it to the checkout line; it's always been a concrete type of produce that you can think of as belonging to the vegetable abstract base class.

Listing 2.6 shows how you might code the declaration of the vegetable abstract base class. Just like the class hierarchy depicted in Figure 2.6, there are two `Vegetable` derived classes, `Broccoli` and `Cauliflower`.

Listing 2.6 `VEGGIE.CPP`—An Abstract `Vegetable` Class and Its Concrete Subclasses

```
class Vegetable
{
public:

    // Pure virtual method makes Vegetable abstract
    virtual string GetColor() = 0;
};


class Broccoli
{
public:

    // Override inherited method as required by abstract base class
    string GetColor();
};

string Broccoli::GetColor()
{
    return "Green";
}


class Cauliflower
{
public:

    // Override inherited method as required by abstract base class
    string GetColor();
};

string Cauliflower::GetColor()
{
    return "White";
}
```

Note that if you were to try to get away without providing an override of `GetColor()` in either the `Broccoli` or `Cauliflower` class, the compiler would return an error complaining about how `GetColor()` was missing from the derived class. If you were to try to instantiate an instance of class `Vegetable`, you would get an error indicating that the class had an incomplete implementation.

As you can see, the use of abstract classes has also solved the somewhat thorny philosophical question of what color a vegetable is. You can now respond that vegetables, in the large, have no color and that only specific vegetable types do.

Class Objects in C++

So far, I've been happy to point out that C++ handles the fundamental concepts of object-oriented programming with relative ease. Although it can certainly be debated whether the concept of metaclass objects or class objects (as described earlier) should be considered an immutable tenet of object-oriented theory, one thing cannot be disputed: C++ does not have native support for metaclass objects.

Note

It's important to make a distinction here regarding class objects. The term *class object* has multiple meanings, depending on its context. In this context, I am referring to a class object as an object that creates instances of a particular class. But when I'm referring to C++, the term *class objects* refers to variables of a class, as defined by Bajarne Stroustroup in C++ *Programming Language 2nd Edition*. Later in the chapter, you will see that COM has a concept of a class object that is a creator of instances of an object. I will try to clarify the context of a class object further.

To understand COM, you must be clear on a few terms and their meanings. You will encounter much term mangling from many sources, so you will need to translate the terms you hear and read into understandable concepts.

- Object—In C++, an object is a region of storage. In object-oriented design, an object is an instance of a class.

- Class—In C++, class is a keyword that declares a type. This keyword was specified in support of object-oriented programming concepts.

How do you create an object of a particular class? In C++, there are operators, **new** and **delete**, to create instances directly on the stack or on the heap. Object-oriented programming has a concept of a metaclass, as discussed earlier, which is not natively supported in the C++ language. Some languages directly support this concept, such as Smalltalk. Using C++, you can certainly implement a metaclass object, or a factory object that separates the creation of an object from the actual object. I highly recommend that you learn more about creational design patterns by reading *Design Patterns* by Gamma, Helm, Johnson, and Vlissides.

Earlier in this chapter, I explained the notion of a class factory. To refresh your memory, a *class factory* is an object that knows how to create instances of a particular class. This is a core concept of COM. Sometimes, the term *class object* will be used to refer to a class factory. Do not be confused by this terminology. In C++, the term *class object* refers to an instance of a class, and no native language construct supports class factories. As you read and learn more about COM, understand that all references to *class object* refer to an object that knows how to create an object of a particular class. The terms *class factory* and *class object* are often used interchangeably.

Let's take a look at an example that demonstrates some of these capabilities. Finishing up the chapter where we started, imagine you wanted to build a class factory that would enable you to control the construction of `Hamburger` objects. Listing 2.7 shows just such a class.

Listing 2.7   HAMFACT.CPP—A Hamburger Class Factory

```cpp
#include <iostream>
#include <string>


class Hamburger
{
public:

    // Constructor
    Hamburger(const unsigned short usNewNumPickles) :
            usNumPickles(usNewNumPickles)
    { }

    // Public methods
    unsigned short GetNumPickles() const;

private:

    // Private member data
    unsigned short usNumPickles;
};

unsigned short Hamburger::GetNumPickles() const
{
    return usNumPickles;
}


class HamburgerFactory
{
public:

    // Constructor
    HamburgerFactory() : ulTotalNumHamburgers(0UL) { }

    // Public methods
    Hamburger* CreateInstance();

    // How many hamburgers have been made so far?
    unsigned long GetHamburgerTotal() const;

private:
```

continued on next page

continued from previous page

```cpp
    // Private attributes
    unsigned long ulTotalNumHamburgers;
};

Hamburger* HamburgerFactory::CreateInstance()
{
    ulTotalNumHamburgers++;
    return new Hamburger(4);
}


unsigned long HamburgerFactory::GetHamburgerTotal() const
{
    return ulTotalNumHamburgers;
}

using namespace std;

void main()
{
    // Instantiate the factory
    HamburgerFactory  factHamburgers;

    // Create a new hamburger
    Hamburger* pHamburger = factHamburgers.CreateInstance();

    cout << "New hamburger has "
        << pHamburger->GetNumPickles()
        << " pickles.\n";

    // Destroy the hamburger
    delete(pHamburger);

    // Create and destroy a few more
    for (int loop = 0; loop < 7; loop++) {
        pHamburger = factHamburgers.CreateInstance();
        delete(pHamburger);

    }

    // How many hamburgers were created in all?
    cout << factHamburgers.GetHamburgerTotal()
        << " hamburgers were created.\n";
}
```

In the first part of this example, you can see the declaration and implementation of a pretty minimalist Hamburger class; all you can really do with one of these hamburgers is get and set the number of pickles that it has. Of a little more interest is the HamburgerFactory class. This class object knows how to create new Hamburger objects.

The first question you might have is, "Why?" After all, it seems a lot more straightforward just to create a new object instance with the new operator. Although there certainly are cases where using class objects is overkill and provides little benefit, there are a host of useful features that are best implemented using the class object concept.

For example, notice in Listing 2.7 that the factory object keeps track of how many hamburgers it has created. If you were simply using the C++ `new` and `delete` operators, this is information that you would have to track yourself. Also notice that the `HamburgerFactory` ensures that all instances of its `Hamburger` objects are created with exactly four pickles. The control of this hamburger attribute is removed from the program and is now safely encapsulated inside the factory class. Of course, this hard-coding behavior is not always desirable, but it's difficult and error-prone to try and implement this sort of cross-class control with something other than a factory-like object.

Looking at Objects from a COM Perspective

In this chapter, I have defined what it means to be object-oriented and the three key principles that embody OO. I have also explained how C++ supports the three key object-oriented principles of encapsulation, inheritance, and polymorphism. This brings us to the pinnacle of this chapter: How COM supports the key object-oriented principles. For the remainder of the chapter, you will explore how COM supports each of the major object-oriented programming concepts. Keep in mind that the next few sections are the most important in the chapter because they lay the foundation required to understand and implement COM.

Note

It's important to note that both COM and DCOM are the same object model; fundamentally, DCOM is really just a network protocol for COM. For the remainder of this chapter, you will concentrate on COM. However, everything I discuss about COM applies to DCOM as well, unless explicitly noted.

Encapsulation in COM

Previously, I talked about how the methods supported by a class are collectively referred to as the class's *interface* in the generic object-oriented sense. COM takes this concept one step further by formalizing the definition of an interface and then allowing a component to expose more than one interface.

Interfaces

As touched on in Chapter 1, "Distributed COM," COM objects expose their functionality through interfaces. The interface is a binding contract between the COM object and the world. This interface exposed by the COM object is simply an ordered collection of semantically related methods. These methods are the tasks that an external user of your object expects your object to perform.

Interfaces in C++ are implemented as abstract base classes. All their member functions are pure virtual. As discussed in the earlier section on C++, because your member functions are pure virtual, this means that the derived class must implement the functionality of that function. With an interface, you can strongly type your internal implementation by your interface and isolate the inner workings of your component. This means that the outside world will not have a clue how your COM object accomplishes its work; it will only know what work can be performed.

This is a very important concept, so I am going to reiterate it in another way. The COM specification stipulates that objects that support an interface are accessible through a pointer to an array of function pointers. (Remember the vtable discussed in Chapter 1?) The pointer to the actual object is not revealed to the client or, for that matter, to COM itself, *Ever!* Clients of the object see only the interface pointer, not the object pointer. This is one of the toughest concepts for C++ programmers to wrap their minds around, because they are used to describing an object by using the keyword `class`. When a client gets a pointer to an instance of a class, it can access any data or method directly through that pointer. In COM, clients have a pointer to an array of function pointers—the object is unreachable, completely opaque.

This concept is also referred to as *separation of interface* (functionality) *from implementation* (object data and functionality). This restriction forces the programmer to think differently about objects, whether he is programming the client or the component. This object model breeds a new discipline, a new way of thinking about objects. All implementation details are invisible, completely encapsulated, exposed to the world only through an interface, a set of functions.

Why is it so important to separate the interface (functionality) from implementation (object data and functionality)? Keep in mind that COM was created to solve the following problems in component software development:

- Programming language independence—COM objects can be programmed in any language that can support the binary layout that COM specifies.

- Reusability—Because COM objects are encapsulated and their implementation is isolated from the interface, they are reusable.

- Interoperability—COM objects promote interoperability among applications and objects. More than one application or component can share the same COM object.

- Location transparency—COM objects are location-independent. As you will see with DCOM, you can put COM objects on the same computer or on different computers. To COM, it makes no difference.

- Independent, uncoordinated evolution—Because COM is extensible, COM objects can evolve without breaking their predecessors.

- Deployment—COM objects are self-contained, reusable components, making them relatively easy to deploy and use.

- Efficiency—COM objects are efficient in that they are small, light, fast, and easy to deploy, can evolve, and can be deployed anywhere.

As I continue to discuss COM, these key problems and how COM solves them will become apparent.

URL

I highly recommend that you read the COM specification to enrich and deepen your understanding of COM. The COM specification is available from Microsoft free of charge at the Internet URL
`http://www.microsoft.com/com/`.

As I pointed out in Chapter 1, you can think of an interface as a contract between an object and the programs that use it. An interface represents a guarantee that the interface's methods will always be available to the clients of that object. After an interface is defined, it cannot change because to COM, this interface definition defines a binary layout that permits language-independent access.

Note

The immutability of interfaces is how COM addresses the problem of versioning. If a programmer determines that one of her interfaces must be altered in a subsequent version (either by adding, removing, or modifying methods), the correct procedure is to create a new interface altogether. For example, consider an `ISmellyDog` interface that you want to extend by adding a `Wash()` method. To minimize breakage within the current clients of `ISmellyDog`, you would create an `ISmellyDog2` interface that is identical to `ISmellyDog` but adds the new method. Now your component can support new and old clients by supporting *both* interfaces.

COM's multiple interface concept allows the programmer a significant amount of flexibility and control over the management of encapsulation. In this respect, I would say that COM components exhibit a greater capability to tune encapsulation than many standard C++ classes.

Inheritance in COM

COM has been beaten up and its object-orientedness questioned because of the issue of whether it supports inheritance. From earlier discussions, you know that inheritance means that a class can be derived from a base class and that the derived class inherits the interface and implementation of the base class. You also learned that inheritance binds one object tightly to the implementation of another object. Because these are bound so tightly together, a change in a base class can cause a ripple effect down the line of derived classes, creating the potential of breaking some implementation in a derived class.

Inheritance can be classified into two types: implementation inheritance and interface inheritance. Implementation inheritance is the type of inheritance just discussed. *Interface inheritance* is a type of inheritance in which the derived class inherits only the interface of the base class, not the implementation. Interface inheritance is what COM implements.

Implementation inheritance is controversial because it is considered not to be true inheritance by some OO purists. This is exactly why COM has had its object-orientedness questioned and why some people COM have dubbed COM as object-based, as opposed to object-oriented. The reason is that those who question COM do so because with COM, you cannot derive one COM object from another. Instead, you create a new Interface within the same object.

It's also important to note that, whereas COM in its implementation of interfaces only supports interface inheritance, COM objects *do* support implementation inheritance internally. The COM class supports implementation inheritance in COM. The COM class is the class derived from the public interface. This is where the functionality of the COM object is implemented. Nothing prevents you from using implementation inheritance internally.

Note

From another source: The reason for COM to support only implementation inheritance in its implementation of interfaces, as Dale Rodgerson states in his book *Inside COM*, is the following:

"COM doesn't support implementation inheritance because implementation inheritance binds one object tightly to the implementation of another object. If the implementation of the base object changes, the derived objects break and must be changed."

Let's look at this from a slightly more technical aspect. When you get a pointer to an interface, that interface pointer is a pointer to the vtable pointer. As discussed in Chapter 1 (See Figure 1.9), the vtable pointer is a pointer to an array of pointers to the public functions that the interface exposes.

In examining this statement, you can see that to achieve the specified binary layout, the interface describes behavior only. A class describes an object, which is more than behavior. The class description is made up of the objects of various types (data), the functions the object can perform (behavior), and access restrictions to the object's data and functions. An interface is not an object. An interface pointer is an indirect pointer to an array of functions.

You can use the built-in C++ compiler support for inheritance to create classes with the correct binary layouts.

The IUnknown

All interfaces inherit from the IUnknown, and interface inheritance is key to the C++ compiler generating the correct binary layout of the component. Remember that an interface contains no data members and that all the methods are declared as pure virtual. When the C++ compiler sees a class that derives from an abstract base class (or interface), it creates an array of pointers to functions that resolve the virtual functions declared in the interface.

Thus, this array of pointers resolves to the concrete class object's implementation of these functions. It then places a pointer to this array in a variable called the `vptr`. Conveniently for COM programmers, this is the binary layout that COM requires. Therefore, all you have to do is define a class in C++ that has only pure virtual methods, and the compiler will generate a vtable and a `vptr` for you, which is exactly the binary layout specified by COM. This is exactly what you will do in the hands-on to come.

Two techniques simulate the effects of implementation inheritance in a COM interface. The first, *containment*, is the practice of building components that reuse multiple interfaces by binding several components together and placing them under the control of a single, collective umbrella component. The second technique, *aggregation*, is very similar to containment but relies less on the umbrella component for routing method calls to the contained subcomponents.

Take a look at Figure 2.10. Here you can see a COM component diagram that conceptually shows how a program might use containment to model the Dog inheritance relationship discussed in previous sections.

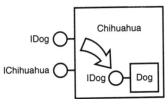

Figure 2.10   Using COM containment to simulate inheritance.

Two different components are depicted in this diagram, **Dog** and **Chihuahua**. The **Dog** component simply exposes a single interface, **IDog**. The **Chihuahua** component exposes two different interfaces, **IDog** and **IChihuahua**. Containment is used by **Chihuahua** to help with the implementation of the **IDog** interface. The **Chihuahua** component maintains an internal instance of the **Dog** component and forwards each of the **Chihuahua::IDog** methods on to the equivalent methods of the **Dog::IDog** interface in the contained **Dog** component.

Aggregation works in a similar fashion, except the **IDog** interface pointer returned by **Chihuahua::QueryInterface()** really is the **IDog** interface pointer that belongs to the contained **Dog** component. In other words, containment relies on the outermost component channeling method calls to inner components, whereas aggregation exposes inner components as though they were actually part of the outer component.

If this all sounds a little convoluted to you, you're not alone. The containment and aggregation strategies simply aren't as elegant as the built-in inheritance features of the native C++ language. Why would Microsoft decide to do such a thing? Remember that COM is a binary standard that is supposed to be language-neutral. Not all C++ compilers generate compatible binaries with other compilers. After you've done a few months of interface-based programming, you'll learn to appreciate the advantages.

Basically, COM makes a trade off. Internally a COM component does support implementation inheritance, but as far as the rest of the world is concerned, it only supports interface inheritance. It also supports implementation inheritance through containment and aggregation. Is COM still object-oriented? You bet! COM sets out to solve the problem of versioning and reusability. The designers of COM chose a solution to solve these problems. Their solution: to remove implementation inheritance in their implementation of interfaces and instead support only inheritance of the interface. Does this make it less object-oriented? In the opinion of this author, the answer is no. COM is still object-oriented. COM is successful in solving the problems it sets out to resolve. As for the debate, I'll only say that COM has been highly successful in the industry and I feel it will be here for some time to come.

Method Overriding in COM

Because COM doesn't directly support inheritance, it obviously doesn't support the concept of method overriding. However, in much the same way that containment can be used to model inheritance, containment can also be used to provide method-overriding capabilities.

Building on the example used in the previous section, imagine now that you want to override the IDog::Bark() method in your Chihuahua component to return Yip-yip!. Assuming that you are using containment to forward the IDog interface onto the internal instance of the Dog component, the current definition of Chihuahua::IDog::Bark() does nothing more than call the internal Dog's IDog::Bark().

To override this method, all you have to do is short-circuit the Bark() request. In other words, instead of forwarding the call onto the Dog component, your Chihuahua should simply provide a method implementation that returns the desired result. Figure 2.11 shows the conceptual modifications that would be made to the Chihuahua component to make this strategy work.

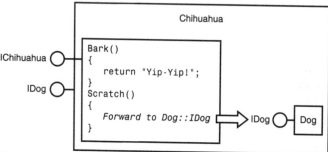

Figure 2.11 Short-circuiting containment to simulate method overriding.

Although this scheme of method overriding is rather inelegant, it certainly provides the same functional capability as the native C++ variant. Clients of the Chihuahua interface don't have to be aware that containment or aggregation is at work.

Polymorphism in COM

COM does a nice job of supporting polymorphism, despite the fact that it doesn't directly support inheritance. The key to polymorphism in COM is `QueryInterface()`. C++ has its runtime type conversion support for inheritance, the *dynamic cast,* and COM has its runtime discovery mechanism, `QueryInterface`.

As mentioned in Chapter 1, every COM object is required to expose at least one interface. This interface, `IUnknown`, hosts the `QueryInterface()` method. `QueryInterface()` is the mechanism by which component clients gain access to other interfaces. Want a pointer to the `IDog` interface? Call `QueryInterface()`. Want a pointer to the `IWashingMachine` interface? Call `QueryInterface()`.

Note

It should be noted that although `QueryInterface()` is the most often-used mechanism for obtaining interface pointers, it's by no means the only one. A component can design any method so that it returns an interface pointer. `QueryInterface()` is just the one method that all components are guaranteed to understand and implement.

So let's talk insects. Recall that in the previous polymorphism examples, the goal was to have a base `Insect` class with derived classes that provide specialized implementations of common protocol (for example, `CanFly()`). As you might imagine, COM's innovative support of inheritance puts a different spin on things. Take a close look at Figure 2.12, which depicts how the example might look in the COM world.

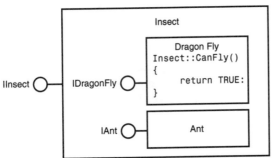

Figure 2.12   Polymorphic insect behaviors in the COM world.

As you can see, the inheritance tree of the previous examples has been replaced with three components: `Insect`, `Dragonfly`, and `Ant`. Both `Dragonfly` and `Ant` use the containment strategy described earlier to expose an `IInsect` interface. In the `Dragonfly` component, the `IInsect::CanFly()` method has been short-circuited to return `True`.

The key to obtaining polymorphic behaviors is passing around component objects by their IUnknown interface pointers. In COM, you can think of an object's IUnknown pointer as the attribute that an application can use to uniquely identify a specific object instance. Two objects, even if they are of the same component type, must always return different IUnknown pointer values. In later chapters, you will see exactly how this is accomplished, but rest assured that the implementation of this behavior is trivial.

Now you are probably beginning to see how polymorphism is going to work. If I gave you three IUnknown pointers, you could call QueryInterface() on each of them, requesting the IInsect interface pointer. Then you could call CanFly() on each of those interfaces. In the case of Ant, the CanFly() method invocation will be passed onto the embedded Insect component, which will return False. Dragonfly's IInsect::CanFly() method, however, has been short-circuited to return True. Voilá! Polymorphism without C++ inheritance.

Class Objects in COM

COM is built on an architecture that relies on class factories, or class objects.

In COM, objects are created by class factories. This is because the simple act of creating a new object is much trickier in COM than it might first appear. Class factories provide a nice clean interface to the creation of new objects. As you will see in later chapters, component creation is nontrivial because of the tremendous power and flexibility afforded by COM, not because of any particular limitations of the object model.

A class factory is just another COM component that exposes the IClassFactory (or IClassFactory2) interface. The IClassFactory interface is very small and is composed of only two methods. IClassFactory2, which adds functionality designed to help with the commercial licensing of components, adds only a few more methods and is functionally similar.

The crux of IClassFactory is the method called CreateInstance().which creates object instances as its central purpose; it creates a new component instance and returns a requested interface pointer.

Applications can directly interact with class factories, and, indeed, the more technically intricate programs probably do so often. However, the COM infrastructure provides a variety of convenience methods for bypassing class factories altogether (which should be used only when appropriate, of course). You'll become much more familiar with class factories in later chapters. You'll even write one.

Summary

In this chapter, you've learned about the fundamental driving principals that differentiate object-oriented programming technologies from predecessors. Using the concepts of encapsulation, inheritance, and polymorphism, you can build object-oriented programs in an extensible and flexible fashion. The C++ language has all the prerequisite infrastructure for the construction of these object-based applications. The Component Object Model, which can be programmed in C++, is generally object-oriented but has some important restrictions and requirements to adhere to.

CHAPTER 3

BUILDING COM OBJECTS AND INTERFACES

In this chapter, you will learn about the following:

- The differences between and roles of clients and servers
- Unique identifiers such as GUIDs, CLSIDs, and REFIIDs
- The structure of an interface class and how interfaces are built.

- The role of the IUnknown Interface
- How to create Registry entries
- A working example of a COM client and in-process server

The computer industry is currently in a frenzy, and there is much fervor over the Internet. New companies have cropped up all over the Net to tap into the revenue that can be generated by leveraging services with Internet technologies for the consumer. Many of these companies have become overnight sensations, making some entrepreneurs millions in the process. Because of the hype, new technologies have emerged, and new acronyms relating to the Internet and Internet technologies have been coined almost daily.

Trying to stay abreast of this fast-changing area of computing can be a daunting task, to say the least. As you learned in Chapter 1, "An Overview of Microsoft's Object Technologies," although Microsoft entered the Internet craze a little late, it has been an active contributor and leader in innovating Internet technologies. If you are feeling intimidated by the vast number of technologies, terms, and acronyms that have emanated from Redmond lately, let me put your mind at ease. You will be pleased to find out that the foundation of nearly all the new technologies coming from Microsoft is COM (and DCOM).

I have spent the past two chapters explaining what COM is and why it plays such an important role in Microsoft's overall technology strategy. Now it's time to apply what you have learned and build your own COM component. Don't worry, you're not alone. I will guide you every step of the way.

Getting Your Hands Dirty with Low-Level COM

The COM/DCOM technologies are complicated, and it takes a while to climb the learning curve. Microsoft recognized this reality when OLE was in its infancy, so Microsoft went to great lengths to integrate COM support into the Microsoft Foundation Classes (MFC). To this day, MFC remains one of the easiest ways to integrate COM support into your C++ programs. For this reason, most of the discussions found in this book center around developing COM applications by using the MFC libraries. This chapter, however, concentrates on basic COM programming.

In many respects, MFC does such a good job of hiding the mechanics of the COM architecture that you can miss or forget the underlying principles of COM. This is analogous to mathematics. In math classes, I learned how to use the quadratic equation. One professor let the class use a programmable calculator. I programmed the quadratic equation, as well as other equations, into my calculator. After a semester of using the calculator, I took another course with an instructor who, as you might have guessed, did not allow calculators. I fumbled around and had to spend a few days relearning the principles of the quadratic equation and the other equations that I had become so dependent on the calculator to perform for me. I had to relearn to do them by hand. The calculator provided me with a layer of abstraction.

Like the calculator, MFC provides a layer of abstraction from COM. By doing much of the work for you, MFC hides the details of implementing a COM component. If you do not learn the fundamentals of COM or you become too dependent on the layer of abstraction that MFC provides, you might one day find yourself scrambling to relearn the basics of COM for a client that wants a component that was not done with MFC. Fortunately, this chapter focuses on learning to do COM by hand, and then in Chapter 5, "COM Programming with MFC," you will learn how to do COM with MFC, letting MFC do a big portion of the work for you. To really understand what's happening inside a COM-based application, you will need to start with the basics.

Note

Learning COM can be frustrating. It's complicated, but considering the problems it solves in component development, this is understandable. The key is not to become discouraged. COM programming is a way of thinking that most of us are unused to. No one gets it on the first try. It takes a solid foundation and practice. You must retrain your mind to think COM. Be patient and keep your eye on the goal: to learn COM. This book will guide you to that goal.

Clients and Servers

If you're not using a computer, it sits unused. Although this might seem intuitively obvious, the point is completely valid. To clarify this a little further, an investment in a computer (or a technology, or a programming tool, and so on) is pointless if you're not going to use the tool.

COM reinforces this rather obvious point by conceptually splitting the object model down the middle. On one side you have the client and on the other side you find the server. Examine Figure 3.1 to visualize this further.

Note

You might already be familiar with the phrase *client/server computing*, which generally refers to applications being spread across multiple machines, with each machine responsible for maintaining a particular functional focus. A typical three-tier client/server application architecture, for example, would be composed of a graphical user interface on one machine, some application logic on a second machine, and a database on yet a third machine. Microsoft has adopted a variation of the common industry vernacular for client/server and subtly changed it. Let us examine how Microsoft has applied client server to COM.

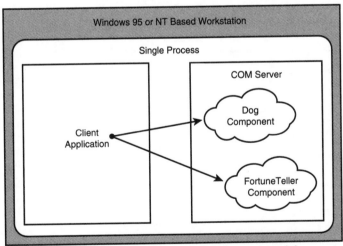

Figure 3.1   A very basic COM client and server model.

Figure 3.1 is very simple. A COM component (or components) resides inside a server; the client is the program or application that is using the component. Both the client and the server exist within the same process, running on the same machine. Now take a look at Figure 3.2 to see another view of how clients and servers might interact with each other.

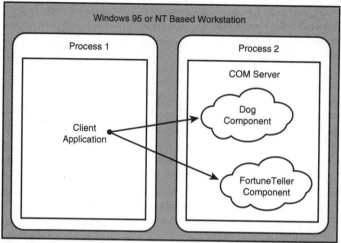

Figure 3.2 A COM client and server in different processes.

This figure looks very similar, except that the client and the server are now located in different processes. Both entities, however, are still found on the same machine. Finally, take a look at Figure 3.3 for yet a third view of client/server partitioning.

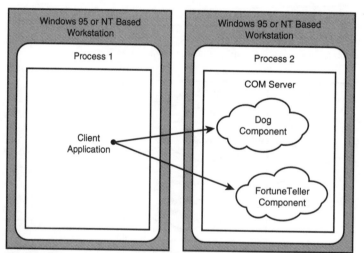

Figure 3.3 A COM client and server running on different machines.

This figure depicts a separation of clients and servers that is probably most in line with what most people associate with client/server computing. In Figure 3.3, you can see that the client program and the COM server are executing on separate machines and are communicating over a network.

Which of these diagrams most accurately depicts the standard COM architecture? The answer is all three. To be more precise, the first two figures are directly supported by regular COM, and the functionality depicted in Figure 3.3 is supplied by DCOM.

The client is a program that needs the services provided by COM components. In other words, a COM client is just an executable. On the other hand, a COM server can take several different forms, and it is these different forms that usually dictate which of the three architectural configurations are possible.

In-Process Servers

In Figure 3.1, you can clearly see that the client and server reside within the same process and address space. In COM, a server that can share the same address space as the client is referred to as an *in-process server*. In-process servers are packaged into standard Windows DLLs. COM takes on the responsibility of loading the DLL when required and unloading the DLL when it can be determined that the client is no longer using the component. A single DLL can host many different objects, or a component designer can choose to place individual components into their own DLLs.

Local Servers

To enable the configuration depicted in Figure 3.2, COM cannot rely on DLLs. Instead, a component that can be used from outside the client process is referred to as living in a *local server*. Local servers are implemented as full-fledged executable programs (EXEs). Like in-process servers, a local server can host multiple objects, or the designer might choose to place each of his components into a server program.

The COM Runtime Library

It's important that I take a moment to change directions to introduce something that needs to be discussed before I go any further. Something that I have not explained before is that COM has a runtime library. This library was built with—you guessed it—COM. The COM runtime libraries provide services, functions, and interfaces to support COM. This is so that each time you write a COM component, you don't have to reinvent the wheel. It also provides some services necessary to have components interact across processes. I will be describing some of these services as I continue the discussion of servers.

Now that I have discussed two of the three types of servers, you might be wondering how COM gets the client and server to talk to each other. Within a process or between processes on the same computer, COM uses LRPCs.

Lightweight Remote Procedure Calls

COM uses a communication mechanism called *Lightweight Remote Procedure Calls* (LRPC) to communicate between processes on a single machine. LRPC is a scaled-down version of Remote Procedure Calls, which I will explain in a moment, and is designed to facilitate interprocess communication. LRPC is proprietary to COM. Using LRPC, COM provides this communication in a completely transparent fashion: It intercepts calls from the client or object. It then uses LRPC to forward the call to the component, or possibly the server, in the other process. This is how an application such as Word can talk to an application such as Visio in order to embed a Visio drawing object in a Word document object. Each of the objects is a COM object. The client (Word) gets an interface pointer to the COM object provided by the server (Visio). The COM runtime libraries use LRPC to forward the messages of one object to the other.

Marshaling

Getting the call from the client to the server is only half the battle. You must have access to the address space of the other application. When using an interface pointer, yours truly must copy the structure referenced by the pointer over to the other process address space so that you can use it. Doing this is called *marshaling*.

To perform this process, COM objects use an interface, from the COM runtime library, called `IMarshal`. `IMarshal` does the work involved in marshaling and unmarshaling parameters before and after a function call. It copies the structure from one process to the other so that the information can be referenced. Referencing data from one COM component in one process to another COM component is a difficult task, one that COM, the COM runtime libraries, and LRPC does behind the scenes. Communication between computers on the same machine is a tricky task, but communication between computers on different machines is a more tedious problem to solve. Let's talk about this problem and about communicating with remote servers.

Remote Servers

The final configuration, as shown in Figure 3.3, relies on the DCOM technology to route client requests to servers running on other machines. Servers located on a different machine than their clients are referred to as *remote servers*. A DCOM remote server can exist as either a DLL or an executable program. Like any in-process or local server, a remote server can be home to many different object instances at once.

One of the truly neat things about COM is that the client is unaware of whether it's interacting with an in-process or local server. COM provides a standard set of objects and APIs that are used to connect clients with the components that they want to use. These APIs hide the differences that can exist between in-process and local server implementations. Although the implementation of the servers can be quite different, the clients can be written once in a consistent fashion. You have seen how COM provides this transparency locally, but how does COM provide it remotely? The first concept to understand is proxies.

Proxies

When you're writing a simple (non-COM) program in C++, interacting with objects that are compiled into your program is a straightforward exercise. Your program can simply call object methods, and the compiler generates an in-process jump to the address of the method in question. If the object resides inside a DLL, the procedure is identical. This is because the operating-system program loader ensures that when your program is started, all necessary DLLs are brought into memory, and the correct addresses of the methods inside the DLLs are wired to the calling points inside your program.

You can probably see how this same strategy would work for an in-process COM server. Because the server is in a DLL, the COM subsystem can load up the server DLL and perform an analogous wiring operation. When you're talking about local or remote COM servers running in a different address space, however, it becomes less clear how the client can seamlessly call in to the COM component. The fact of the matter is, a client can't be directly wired to a local server. It uses a proxy.

One of COM's most important chores is to ensure that when a client asks for a particular component, the client is given an object that supports the requested interface. In the simplest cases, the object that COM gives the client is the component. When the COM server is in-process, this is exactly what happens. However, when the server is local (and therefore located in another address space), COM gives the client a special kind of object called a *proxy*. A proxy is an object that resides in the same address space as the client and responds to all the interfaces supported by the targeted component. From the client's perspective, the proxy *is* the component.

When the client invokes a method on one of the component's interfaces, the proxy bundles up all the method arguments into some portable set of data structures and ships the whole bundle over to the local server program through a Remote Procedure Call (RPC).

Remote Procedure Calls (RPC)

RPC is an interprocess communication mechanism defined in the Open Software Foundations DCE RPC specification. Using RPC, applications on different machines can communicate with each other by using a variety of network transport mechanisms. The RPC mechanism is unique because it uses the other IPC mechanisms to establish communications between the client and the server. RPC can use named pipes, NetBIOS, or Windows Sockets to communicate with remote systems. DCOM uses RPC to enable COM components to communicate between machines in different processes. Because RPC enables programs to communicate with each other across address spaces, the proxy can move method arguments into the address space of the local server with relative ease.

On the server side, the RPC is received by a piece of code referred to as the RPC *stub*. The stub breaks the argument data structures apart and calls the appropriate method on the real component. When the method call is complete, the component returns control to the stub (along with any return arguments). The stub bundles up the return arguments, packs them into a portable format, and then RPCs them back to the proxy. The proxy unpacks any return data and relinquishes control back to the client. Figure 3.4 depicts the relationship between clients, proxies, RPC stubs, and local servers.

The great thing about this scheme is that it provides *location transparency*. That is to say, the location of a COM component and its server are transparent to the client. Now, I'll give you exactly one guess how DCOM gives the client programs the capability to call remote servers running on another machine. I hope you said, "Proxy objects and RPCs!" Isn't location transparency wonderful?

If you compare Figure 3.4 to Figure 3.1, you can see that using a local server adds a considerable amount of complexity to the equation. Of course, using a remote server that resides on another machine only compounds the technical challenges that need to be met. For these reasons, local and remote servers are considerably more difficult to build from scratch. In this chapter, I'll be demonstrating how to build an in-process COM server only. In later chapters, you'll learn how to use MFC to build local servers. Finally, in the second part of the book, you'll learn how to build remote DCOM servers, also with the aid of MFC.

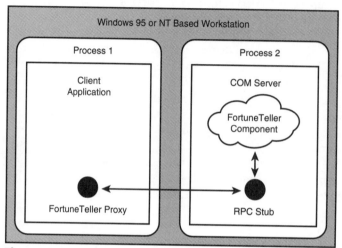

Figure 3.4 Local COM servers rely on proxies and RPC stubs.

Note

For the rest of this chapter, I am going to restrict my discussion to issues that arise when the client and server are located on the same machine (with an emphasis on in-process servers). I won't discuss how to build remote servers until Chapter 9, "A Distributed Objects Overview," where I will really delve into the specifics issues that revolve around DCOM.

A Server's Work Is Never Done

Whether your components are located inside an in-process server or a local server, certain capabilities need to be supported by your server in order to meet the COM specification. Although the implementation of these capabilities is certain to vary based on the server type, the functional requirements are the same.

The next few sections start to outline some of the procedures for which in-process and local COM servers are responsible. I will still stick to general descriptions; in later sections, I will dive into specifics. If something still isn't completely clear to you after reading these sections, there's a good chance that your questions will be answered when you get to the hands-on examples later on in the chapter.

Who Goes There?

When a client indicates to COM that it wants to use a particular component, some way must exist for COM to know where to find the requested server. You can think of COM as one big dating service, hooking up clients with servers and looking for that perfect match. Although the image of COM acting as a computerized Chuck Woolery might be a little unsettling, the process is considerably less haphazard than the "Dating Game" ever was. After all, COM components aren't nearly as fickle as human beings.

The primary mechanism that COM uses to help match clients with servers is the Windows Registry. If you're not familiar with it, the Registry is a giant hierarchical structure of persistent data. The Windows 95 and Windows NT operating systems use it extensively to manage your system configuration and to store much of the information needed to help with the smooth functioning of application programs. Both Windows 95 and NT use the Registry to store initialization and configuration data for the operating system itself, as well as the applications and hardware drivers that reside on that computer.

COM uses the Registry to track which component servers are installed on your system. The Registry contains information on which components are available to clients, exactly where the server DLLs and/or executables are located, and a host of other details required by COM over the course of an application run.

This server information has to get into the Registry somehow, and I hope you're not surprised to learn that the burden is going to fall on your shoulders. When implementing a server, you will have to ensure that your server implements the functions necessary to get this information into the Registry. The process of placing this information into the Registry is referred to as *server registration*. Conversely, the process of removing all this information from the Registry is referred to as *server unregistration*. Unregistration is used when your server is being removed from the system because the server and its constituent components are no longer needed by the user. Unregistration of COM servers typically takes place as part of an application's uninstall process.

You can register your server in two ways. The first method involves manually poking values into the Registry by using a script that can be read by the **REGEDIT** utility. These registration scripts need to be shipped with your server and run by either the user or your installation program. This method is probably best suited for use during the development of your components, because a registration script is easily modified and rerun.

COM servers can also be self-registering. A local server should self-register itself in response to a **/RegServer** command-line argument (or unregister itself in response to an **/UnregServer** command-line argument). If the **/RegServer** argument is set, the server is responsible for poking the required entries into the Registry. This is most commonly accomplished using the Registry Win32 API functions supported by the operating system.

In-process servers can also support self-registration, although the process is not as straightforward. An in-process server that supports self-registration exports two publicly recognized functions, **DllRegisterServer()** and **DllUnregisterServer()**. **DllRegisterServer()**, if it exists, should use the Win32 Registry APIs to place all required entries into the system Registry. **DllUnregisterServer()** is responsible for removing the same entries. An application that wants to register the server needs to load the server into memory by using the **LoadLibrary()** Win32 API call, get the address of the appropriate function by using

GetProcAddress(), and then call the function directly. The biggest disadvantage to this whole scheme is that users cannot directly register the server from the command line, as they can with Registry scripts or self-registering local servers. A self-registering in-process server requires another program to load the server's DLL and call the registration function manually. Now for the good news. Windows NT and Windows 95 both come with a program, regsvr32.exe, that will register your server. Simply run it from the command line like this:

```
"regsvr32 c:\myproject\bin\myserver.dll"
```

Class Factories

You'll recall the discussion about class factories in Chapter 2, "The Object Revolution." Class factories are used by COM to aid in the creation and destruction of components. Therefore, it makes sense that every server must be able to provide a class factory for each of its components. This means that every server needs to support at least two COM components: your component and your component's class factory.

Because class factories represent the beginning of the COM object life cycle, it would make intuitive sense that the process of creating a factory object would be different from the process for creating other COM objects. After all, if all class factories were created by class factories, where would that get us? This chicken-and-egg problem would send us into an endless cycle of looking for class factories.

COM solves this problem by requiring servers to implement bootstrap functionality that will deliver class factory objects into the hands of the COM subsystem. This is one of those areas where the functional implementation is quite different, depending on whether the server in question is an in-process or local server.

If you're building an in-process server from scratch, handing off your class factory to COM is easy because COM is going to ask you for it. When a client wants to start interacting with one of your components, COM will consult the Registry to determine where the correct server can be found. Imagine a program saying to COM, "Give me a new **Dog** object." COM looks in the Registry and sees that the **Dog** server is an in-process server that can be found at c:\COM Servers\Dog.dll. Knowing that the server is in-process, COM loads the DLL and then calls a function that all in-process servers must implement, **DllGetClassObject()**. COM calls this function, passing in the name of the class factory that it's looking for. All the server needs to do at this point is create the class factory object and return it back to the COM subsystem. Simple.

This procedure is a little different when you're talking about local servers. Because COM can't simply load up an executable and call in to it, local servers need to register all their class factories with COM as a startup task. They do this by calling the COM API function **CoRegisterClassObject()**. COM will wait until it senses that the desired class factory has been registered and then use the class factory to create new components. Clearly, this is a little backwards from how in-process servers work. In the in-process example, the server is reactive and responds to the specific class factory query presented by COM. In the local server case, the server needs to be more proactive and register all its class factories without knowing which ones will actually be used.

Shutting Down Your COM Component

The final task that all servers must implement is clean-up logic. If a dozen programs are each using a few local servers, this can add up to a large number of concurrently running programs. It's clearly in the best interest of overall system performance to kill these local servers as soon as it's determined that they're no longer needed. The same issue exists with in-process servers, although the performance penalties imposed by a DLL being loaded into a program's address space are typically less severe than those implied by a local server.

Because of the inherent differences that exist between DLLs and executables, the procedures for unloading a server vary, depending on whether the server is in-process or local. Not surprisingly, the differences closely parallel the approach taken for enabling COM access to your server's class factories.

If your server is in-process, you can get away with being reactive. Periodically, COM will call a function in your DLL, called `DllCanUnloadNow()`. If your server determines that it can be unloaded, it merely has to return an affirmative answer. If, for a variety of possible reasons, your server determines that it cannot be unloaded yet, you can simply decline the unloading offer. Rather civilized, isn't it?

When you get down to it, local servers have it even easier than in-process servers. Because a local server is a full-fledged program, COM enables it to be master of its own domain. Whenever a local server determines that it can be unloaded, it simply ends. It doesn't get much simpler than that.

Local servers (not DLLs) should register their running class objects as "running" to let COM know that it doesn't have to go to the overhead of creating another process; this one can serve up objects of a particular type (`CLSID`).

If your server is local, you also must ensure that your server's class factories are revoked before the server shuts down. If your server shuts down while COM still thought that it had valid pointers to your class factories, the computer system would terminate unexpectedly! This would leave the computer user having to reboot his computer, and it might possibly cause the user to lose some mission-critical data. Luckily, revoking a class factory is even easier than registering it. Every class factory that was handed over to COM, using `CoRegisterClassObject()`, must be reclaimed with a corresponding call to `CoRevokeClassObject()`.

Now you have a high-level understanding of what's involved in unloading a COM server. However, a piece of the picture is missing. What exactly are the conditions under which a server knows that it can be unloaded? The short answer is that a server can be unloaded when its internal object counter and lock counters are all at zero. Remember when I discussed reference counting in Chapters 1 and 2? This is what I'm referring to here. In a little bit, I will explain more about reference counting.

Identify Your Classes with GUIDs

Now that I have described clients and servers, I need to switch gears and return to the discussion on building a COM component.

Fundamentally, the COM programmer is concerned with two things: building components that can be shared across a network and extracting interfaces from those components that will expose object functionality. Classes and interfaces are two of the most important core concepts in COM, and the COM subsystem is intimately concerned about the management and manipulation of both these data types.

Whenever you're responsible for managing something, it helps to assign the managed thing a name. If you were stocking inventory at a supermarket, how would you track the amount of products on the shelves? You certainly wouldn't think to yourself, "I have six boxes of those bright pink circles that people eat with milk in the morning." You would name the product ("Neon-Pops Cereal") and henceforth refer to the product by its given name. Of course, none of this should be very earth-shattering to you. After all, we all use the concept of names every day.

COM refers to both components and interfaces by name, but unlike the names human beings are familiar with, the names assigned to components and interfaces are a little less familiar. A component, for example, might be named `EDFF2BC0-1FAF-11d0-8B7B-9493759B380C`. One of its supported interfaces might be known as `EDFF2BD1-1FAF-11d0-8B7B-9493759B380C`. These specially formatted COM names are referred to as Globally Unique Identifiers, or GUIDs. GUID is pronounced *Goo-ID*.

Of course, a number of really good reasons exist why GUIDs look so unusual. Right now, as you read this, hundreds of other programmers are preparing to build a host of COM-based and DCOM-based components. Every single one of those programmers is going to have to name her component. Now imagine the chaos that would ensue if Microsoft allowed all of us to come up with string-based names for our components. Somewhere, at some point, a name collision would occur.

The whole point of GUIDs is to avoid name collisions and enforce the uniqueness of names across all components and interfaces. With COM being moved out onto the Internet through the use of DCOM technologies, the need for uniqueness becomes even more important. The Microsoft GUID generation utilities use a sophisticated algorithm to help ensure that the GUIDs generated on your computer are unique across every computer on the planet. This algorithm uses a combination of counters, the current date and time, and the address burned into your network card to generate a unique ID for your component or interface. This GUID is a 128-bit (16-byte) constant that is guaranteed to be unique across space and time so that your component can be uniquely identified.

Now that you know why you need to use GUIDs, it might help to learn how you obtain them and what you should do with them after you have them.

Generating GUIDs

Visual C++ 6 ships with a couple of utilities that you can use to generate GUIDs. The UUID-GEN program is a command-line program, whereas **GUIDGEN** is a graphical utility. Both are a cinch to use. Make sure that you always use one of these utilities to generate new GUIDs. Never (never, *never!*) make up GUIDs. Use the tool provided. Remember that GUIDs need to be globally unique and that duplicate GUIDs can wreak havoc within the COM subsystem. Do your part and practice safe GUID generation.

Note

Every rule has an exception, and it's probably going too far to say that you should use only the UUIDGEN or GUIDGEN utilities to get your GUID. It's critical, however, that if you are not using these utilities, you obtain your GUIDs from a source that is ultimately receiving the GUIDs as a result of a call to the COM API function CoCreateGuid(). As you might expect, this method creates and returns a new GUID. This is exactly the mechanism that GUIDGEN uses to obtain its GUIDs. (It's interesting to note that UUIDGEN does not use CoCreateGuid() but relies on the equivalent function, UuidCreate(), which is associated with the operating system's RPC engine. CoCreateGuid() is simply implemented as a wrapped call to UuidCreate().)

Using UUIDGEN to Obtain GUIDs

To obtain a single new GUID, you can run the UUIDGEN program with no command-line arguments. You can also redirect the output of the utility into a text file to capture the GUID in an editable form, or you can use the -o command-line argument to have the utility place the GUID directly into a file.

```
C:\uuidgen -oNewGUID.txt
C:\type NewGUID.txt
23c175b0-1fbf-11d0-8b7b-9493759b380c

C:\
```

You can also use the -n command-line parameter to generate a bunch of GUIDs at the same time. Follow the -n parameter with the number of GUIDs that you want to generate.

```
C:\uuidgen -n10
e4297790-1fbf-11d0-8b7b-9493759b380c
e4297791-1fbf-11d0-8b7b-9493759b380c
e4297792-1fbf-11d0-8b7b-9493759b380c
e4297793-1fbf-11d0-8b7b-9493759b380c
e4297794-1fbf-11d0-8b7b-9493759b380c
e4297795-1fbf-11d0-8b7b-9493759b380c
e4297796-1fbf-11d0-8b7b-9493759b380c
e4297797-1fbf-11d0-8b7b-9493759b380c
e4297798-1fbf-11d0-8b7b-9493759b380c
e4297799-1fbf-11d0-8b7b-9493759b380c

C:\
```

Note that you shouldn't place a space between the -n command-line option and the number of GUIDs that you want generated, nor should you place a space between the -o command-line option and the filename that you want the GUIDs to be written into.

Caution

If you don't have a network card installed on your computer, or the UUIDGEN program cannot read the card's network address, you'll receive the following message: Warning: Unable to determine your network address. The UUID generated is unique on this computer only. It should not be used on another computer. In this case, the GUIDs being generated are considerably less unique. Another programmer, who's also working on a machine that doesn't have a network card, now has a higher chance of generating an identical GUID, especially if you're both generating GUIDs at the same time. As a general rule, always generate your GUIDs on a machine that doesn't cause this warning to be displayed.

UUIDGEN also has a couple of other options for outputting GUIDs in a format prepackaged for direct insertion into your source code.

Using GUIDGEN to Obtain GUIDs

The GUIDGEN utility serves exactly the same purpose as the UUIDGEN program, but provides you with a rudimentary graphical interface. GUIDGEN cannot generate more than a single GUID at once, and it can't dump GUIDs to a text file. It does, however, support the Windows Clipboard, so you can paste GUIDs directly into your source file.

GUIDGEN takes no command-line parameters and displays a single dialog box, depicted in Figure 3.5.

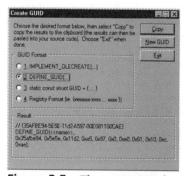

Figure 3.5 The GUIDGEN utility.

As you can see from the figure, the GUIDGEN utility does have a few more generation options than UUIDGEN. For example, it can generate GUIDs in a format that supports the IMPLEMENT_OLECREATE macro that MFC uses to declare GUIDs.

> ### Caution
>
> Unlike the UUIDGEN utility, GUIDGEN will not warn you when it cannot deter-
> mine your computer's network address. It's a good idea to always run
> UUIDGEN first to make sure that GUID generation is functioning correctly and
> then use the GUIDGEN only after you've verified that everything's working.

GUIDGEN isn't a very fancy program, but if there's anything that you don't like about it, you can always change it yourself. The full source code for GUIDGEN is shipped as an MFC sample program. Consult the Visual C++ Books Online for more details.

Placing GUIDs into Source Code

GUIDs are designed to be opaque; you should be able to manipulate GUIDs without ever needing to know what they're actually composed of. That being said, you should know that a GUID maps onto a structure that can be found in the WTYPES.H header file. The WTYPES.H header file is located in your Visual C++ directory at \VC98\include\. Although the vast major-ity of your application can be unaware of what a GUID is composed of, the part of your program that declares and initializes your GUIDs needs to know something of the GUID structure. Microsoft supplies a number of macros to help with this task, but eventually you'll probably want to just look up the structure definition and see what you're dealing with. Here is what you would find in the WTYPES.H header file:

```
typedef struct  _GUID
    {
    DWORD Data1;
    WORD Data2;
    WORD Data3;
    BYTE Data4[ 8 ];
    }GUID;
```

As you can see, the GUID structure is composed of four attributes, totaling 16 bytes of storage space. If you look at one of the GUIDs that I previously generated, you'll see that the fields in the GUID structure roughly correspond to the sections of the generated GUID that are separated by dashes.

```
23c175b0-1fbf-11d0-8b7b-9493759b380c
```

The GUIDs that are generated by the UUIDGEN and GUIDGEN utilities are represented in hexadecimal fashion. Therefore, each byte is represented by a single double-digit hexadecimal number. In this GUID, then, the Data1 field corresponds to 23c175b0, Data2 corresponds to 1fbf, Data3 corresponds to 11d0, and the Data4 field corresponds to the remaining part (8b7b9493759b380c). The only unusual part of this process is that the two bytes that appear in the fourth GUID subgroup (that is, 8b7b) are folded into the Data4 attribute.

I have talked about using GUIDs to name classes and interfaces. Now I need to discuss CLSID and IID types. Both these types are really just typedefs to the standard GUID structure. To put it a little more simply, CSLIDs and IIDs are symbolic constants used to better define what a GUID is used for. A CLSID is a GUID that names a class/component, and an IID is a GUID that names an interface. As a convention, variable identifiers for class IDs typically have a CLSID_ prefix, whereas variable identifiers for interface IDs typically have an IID_ prefix. Therefore, a Chihuahua component might declare the following GUIDs:

```
CLSID CLSID_Chihuahua;
IID IID_IDog;

static const CLSID CLSID_Chihuahua =
{ 0x86ecd437, 0x1fd9, 0x11d0, { 0x8b, 0x7c, 0xe4, 0x45, 0xc9,
0xbd, 0x31, 0xc } };

static const IID IID_IDog =
{ 0x86ecd438, 0x1fd9, 0x11d0, { 0x8b, 0x7c, 0xe4, 0x45, 0xc9,
 0xbd, 0x31, 0xc } };
```

Because all CLSIDs and IIDs are really just GUIDs, it's just as legal to declare these variables in the following fashion:

```
static const GUID CLSID_Chihuahua =
{ 0x86ecd437, 0x1fd9, 0x11d0, { 0x8b, 0x7c, 0xe4, 0x45, 0xc9,
0xbd, 0x31, 0xc } };

static const GUID IID_IDog =
{ 0x86ecd438, 0x1fd9, 0x11d0, { 0x8b, 0x7c, 0xe4, 0x45, 0xc9,
0xbd, 0x31, 0xc } };
```

This is one of the formats in which your GUIDs can appear if you cut and paste by using the GUIDGEN utility. Microsoft also provides a helper macro that makes these sorts of definitions a little cleaner. The macro, DEFINE_GUID, takes as a first parameter the name of the variable that you're declaring and then the components of the GUID, broken up into the first DWORD, the second and third WORDs, and finally followed by the remaining eight hexadecimal byte values. The preceding definitions for CLSID_Chihuahua and IID_IDog, therefore, could have been created using the DEFINE_GUID macro in the following fashion:

```
DEFINE_GUID(CLSID_Chihuahua,
       0x86ecd437, 0x1fd9, 0x11d0, 0x8b, 0x7c,
       0xe4, 0x45, 0xc9, 0xbd, 0x31, 0xc);

DEFINE_GUID(IID_IDog,
       0x86ecd438, 0x1fd9, 0x11d0, 0x8b, 0x7c,
       0xe4, 0x45, 0xc9, 0xbd, 0x31, 0xc);
```

There is one important reason why you should probably use the Microsoft DEFINE_GUID macro. Because declaring class and interface IDs involves establishing global, static constants that are accessible from anywhere within your application, you need to make sure that the actual GUIDs themselves are defined only once, in a single source file.

This is actually more difficult than it might first sound. You can't, for example, simply place a GUID definition in a header file and have everyone who needs the GUID include that header file. If the header file is included more than once, the compiler will throw an error saying that the program now contains duplicate symbols for the GUID variables. What you really want to do is declare the GUIDs in a header file that is used by all your source files, but actually define the GUIDs in only one source file. The `DEFINE_GUID` macro goes a long way toward helping you with this task.

In its default form, the `DEFINE_GUID` macro ignores all the GUID pieces that you feed into it. The following code

```
DEFINE_GUID(IID_IDog,
    0x86ecd438, 0x1fd9, 0x11d0, 0x8b, 0x7c,
    0xe4, 0x45, 0xc9, 0xbd, 0x31, 0xc);
```

expands into nothing more than

```
extern "C" const GUID IID_IDog;
```

In other words, the GUID is declared, but not actually defined. However, if you have declared the preprocessor macro `INITGUID` before including the standard OLE header files, the `DEFINE_GUID` macro will be defined so that this `DEFINE_GUID` call expands into

```
extern "C" const GUID IID_IDog = \
{ 0x86ecd438, 0x1fd9, 0x11d0, { 0x8b, 0x7c,  0xe4,  0x45,  0xc9,
0xbd,  0x31,  0xc } };
```

As you can see, now the GUID is fully declared and defined. The important thing to keep in mind is that a given GUID needs to be included into your source code with the `INITGUID` macro set exactly once. If you don't use `INITGUID` at least once, the linker will fail because it will report that it can't find any definition for the GUIDs that you have declared and used within your program. On the other hand, if more than one source file tries to include GUIDs and has the `INITGUID` flag set, you'll run into the same duplicate symbol problem described previously.

The HRESULT Return Type

Most of your interactions with the COM APIs will require you to deal with COM's ubiquitous return type, the `HRESULT`. Unlike a conventional API that might return a simple error code, the `HRESULT` can be thought of as a ministructure within a single four-byte `unsigned long`. This structure allows an `HRESULT` a considerable amount of flexibility in describing the success or failure of a given operation.

Note

With older versions of Windows, you might encounter applications that return a type called an `SCODE`. In previous versions of Windows and OLE, an `SCODE` was a fundamentally different error type than `HRESULT`. In the current versions of Windows 95 and NT, however, an `SCODE` and an `HRESULT` are identical. The use of the `SCODE` is deprecated, and you will find that all new interfaces coming from Microsoft use `HRESULT`. Because the examples in this book deal exclusively with 32-bit code, and I shamelessly admit that no attempt at Windows 3.1 compatibility is being made, I will be using only `HRESULT`s.

An HRESULT is composed of three distinct parts: a severity code, a facility code, and a description code. The COM subsystem provides macros to help extract each of these "fields" from the HRESULT. You should always rely on these macros rather than dig into the HRESULT and try to discern individual fields manually. Using the HRESULT macros will help preserve compatibility in the unlikely event that Microsoft decides to change the definition of HRESULT.

The severity field within an HRESULT is used to indicate whether the HRESULT signals an error or success condition. Generally speaking, if you try to perform an operation and it fails, the severity of the returned HRESULT will indicate an error occurred. One of the nice things about having the severity represented by its own field—as opposed to being implied by the description field—is that it enables Windows or a component to define more than one success code. A component, for example, could define one success code that would be returned when an operation was an unqualified success, and another that would be returned when the operation succeeded but in a suboptimal fashion.

Caution

Because a successful operation can be indicated by multiple HRESULT codes, it's not enough to simply compare an HRESULT against an often used success constant such as S_OK. Instead, use the FAILED() and SUCCEEDED() macros described later in this section.

The facility code indicates the broad functional group that the HRESULT belongs to. Microsoft has defined several such groups, only one of which, FACILITY_ITF, should be used for your own HRESULT values. Table 3.1 shows the currently defined facilities that can be returned in an HRESULT.

Table 3.1 Valid Facilities Used in HRESULTs

Facility Name	Description
FACILITY_NULL	Used for HRESULTs that are general in nature and can be shared across all facilities. S_OK and S_FALSE are two examples of such HRESULTs.
FACILITY_ITF	Custom interfaces (for example, any interfaces created by someone other than Microsoft) need to ensure that any HRESULTs they return use this facility code. This implies that two interfaces could return exactly the same HRESULT and have it mean two different things, depending on which interface created the HRESULT.
FACILITY_DISPATCH	This facility is reserved for HRESULTs associated with OLE Automation technologies.
FACILITY_RPC	This facility is reserved for HRESULTs associated with remote procedure calls.
FACILITY_STORAGE	This facility is reserved for HRESULTs associated with OLE structured storage interfaces.

Facility Name	Description
FACILITY_WIN32	The Win32 API functions return all manner of error codes, depending on the function in question. FACILITY_WIN32 is used to group standard Win32 error codes in an HRESULT form.
FACILITY_WINDOWS	This is a catch-all facility for any additional error codes used by Microsoft that do not fall into the description of any of the previous facilities.

The last field within an HRESULT, the description code, is what most programmers think of when they hear return value. It's a context-specific code that describes exactly what took place.

The symbolic constants that represent HRESULTs returned from Microsoft code are named using a standard and consistent format that you will probably want to adopt in your own interfaces. The first part of the name represents a more specific context than the facility code, the second part represents the severity, and the third part represents a mnemonic for the description. For example, the E in CLIPBRD_E_BAD_DATA indicates that an error occurred. The functional area responsible for generating this HRESULT was the Microsoft Clipboard code and apparently something happened that involved bad data. In DRAGDROP_S_DROP, you can see that the drag-and-drop component has returned a value that implies that a successful drop operation occurred. Finally, an HRESULT such as S_OK is easy to interpret: The operation was successful, and everything is okay.

I mentioned earlier that you should use only the standard Microsoft macros to extract fields out of an HRESULT. Table 3.2 shows the macros that you should use to manipulate HRESULTs. Be sure to consult the Visual C++ Books Online in the article in the COM specification titled "Error Codes and Error Handling" for more information on the use of these macros.

Table 3.2 Commonly Encountered Macros Used to Manipulate HRESULTs

Macro	Description
FAILED()	Returns TRUE if the passed-in HRESULT represents a failed operation; otherwise, FALSE
IS_ERROR()	Returns TRUE if the HRESULT's severity field indicates an error condition; functionally identical to FAILED()
SUCCEEDED()	Returns TRUE if the passed-in HRESULT represents a successful operation; otherwise, FALSE
HRESULT_SEVERITY()	Extracts and returns the severity field, given an HRESULT
HRESULT_FACILITY()	Extracts and returns the facility field, given an HRESULT
HRESULT_CODE()	Extracts and returns the description field, given an HRESULT
MAKE_HRESULT()	Constructs and returns an HRESULT, given three values representing a severity, a facility, and a description code

Anatomy of an Interface

By this point, you're probably starting to wonder how COM interfaces are represented in C++. C++, after all, has no native support for anything called an *interface*. I discussed interfaces at length in Chapters 1 and 2. To refresh your memory for a moment, I'm going to touch on interfaces again. You will recall that I mentioned in Chapter 2 that one of Microsoft's goals in creating COM and OLE was to establish an object model that was language-independent. That means that Microsoft had to create a binary specification that describes what COM objects look like when they are laid out in memory. This specification had to be general enough that it could be implemented in any language that supports basic concepts such as pointers and functions. Of course, a particular language is free to hide its COM support in any way that it sees fit, but all languages must ultimately interact and manipulate COM objects at the same binary level as all other COM-aware programming languages.

At the core of C++ objects being usable COM objects is the vtable. Remember that an *interface* is simply a grouping of semantically related COM methods? An interface's vtable is an in-memory table of pointers. Each entry in the vtable points to the address of an interface method. Figure 3.6 depicts how a sample vtable might look for the **IDog** interface discussed in Chapter 2.

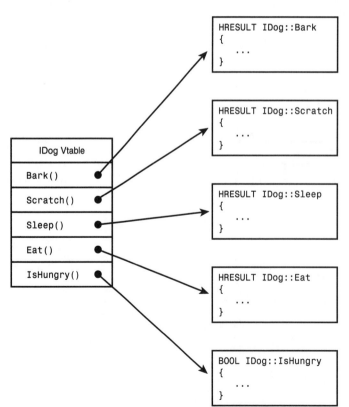

Figure 3.6 A vtable for an **IDog** interface.

A COM interface pointer is simply an indirect pointer to the interface's vtable. An interface can own hidden, private data that is manipulated through calls to the interface's methods. This data, if it exists, is stored in memory immediately following the vtable. Figure 3.7 shows the complete picture.

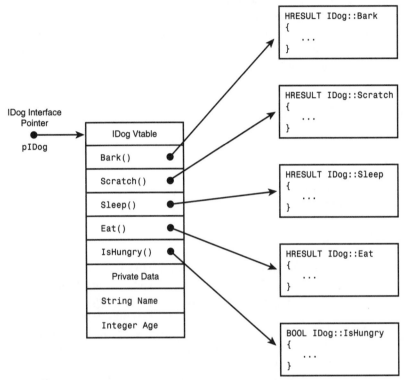

Figure 3.7 The entire **IDog** interface layout in memory.

The nice thing about this memory layout is that C++ uses exactly the same memory layout for C++ objects that have virtual functions. This means that a COM interface can be easily represented by a C++ abstract base class.

Of course, this alignment of COM and C++ objects isn't a coincidence at all. COM's binary layout is directly modeled after C++'s binary layout. The word *vtable*, in fact, comes from C++ and was part of the C++ vocabulary a long time before COM came along; it stands for *virtual function table*.

Unlike C++, however, the COM specification explicitly details the in-memory representation of objects. The C++ standard, on the other hand, is mute on this point.

When you're building COM interfaces, the convention is to describe an interface as a C++ abstract base class with all pure virtual functions. A component that wants to support a given interface need only inherit from the interface class and implement the required methods.

You might be thinking that because a COM object shares a common structure with C++ objects, cross-language compatibility is compromised. However, this really isn't the case. Although the COM binary object specification is directly based on the structure of C++ objects, a C++ object has much additional plumbing that is required to fully support C++ functionality in its entreaty. Although a COM interface can be implemented as a simple C++ object, not all C++ objects are COM interfaces. In other words, the COM binary object specification can be thought of as a subset of the C++ binary object specification.

Listing 3.1 shows how the **IDog** interface might be declared in C++. Note that this isn't exactly the way that one declares COM interfaces in C++, but it's really close. You'll learn exactly how an interface class is declared when you encounter the Fortune2 program later in the chapter.

Listing 3.1   IDOG1.H—A Declaration of the **IDog** Interface in C++

```
class IDog : public IUnknown
{
public:
    virtual HRESULT Bark() = 0;
    virtual HRESULT Scratch() = 0;
    virtual HRESULT Sleep() = 0;
    virtual HRESULT Eat() = 0;
    virtual BOOL    IsHungry() = 0;
};
```

As you can see, the declaration of an interface is straightforward in C++.

In this C++ example, note that the **IDog** interface is derived from the **IUnknown** interface. In COM, every interface is derived from **IUnknown**. If the language you're working in does not support inheritance, you must ensure that every interface supports the **IUnknown** protocol and that the appropriate pointers are loaded into your interface's vtable. The **IUnknown** interface provides a mechanism for gaining access to any of the other interfaces exposed by a component. This means that a client, given a pointer to any of your component's interfaces, can use **IUnknown** to gain access to any other interfaces exposed by your component.

Note

A COM component can expose multiple interfaces. In fact, your components will always expose at least two, including **IUnknown**. Complicated components might expose many more than that. A full-featured ActiveX control, for example, can expose more than 15 different interfaces.

The subject of multiple-interface support is more complicated than you might think. I'll explain multiple-interface support in the next chapter, when you start to learn about COM programming using MFC.

Now look at Listing 3.2. In this short piece of code, you can see the exact same interface as it would appear to the C programmer.

Listing 3.2   IDOG2.H—A Declaration of the `IDog` Interface in C

```
// Forward declaration
typedef struct IDog IDog;

// Vtable structure
typedef struct
{
    // IUnknown methods
    HRESULT (*QueryInterface )(IDog    *This,
                               REFIID riid,
                               void   **ppvObject);
    ULONG   (*AddRef )(IDog *This);
    ULONG   (*Release )(IDog *This);

    // IDog methods
    HRESULT (*Bark)(void);
    HRESULT (*Scratch)(void);
    HRESULT (*Sleep)(void);
    HRESULT (*Eat)(void);
    BOOL    (*IsHungry)(void);

} IDogVtable;

// The actual IDog interface structure
typedef struct
{
    struct IDogVtable *lpVtable;
} IDog;
```

As you can see, the C version of the interface is a little more involved. Programming COM objects from C requires more effort because the vtable must be explicitly declared and set up. You must first declare the vtable structure itself, complete with the pointer entries for each method in the interface. Then you must declare the actual interface structure, which contains nothing but a pointer to the vtable.

Because C doesn't support object inheritance, you need to make provisions for manually placing the `IUnknown` interface method pointers directly into the component's vtable structure. This ensures that a component written in C will still behave in exactly the same manner as the same component written in C++.

Although programming COM objects in C is not as pretty in C, it certainly can be done. The remainder of this book, however, focuses exclusively on 32-bit COM and DCOM examples built in C++. C++ makes the process of building COM clients and servers much easier. I emphatically recommend using C++ for your COM and DCOM programming, because C++ naturally supports the COM binary layout.

Exploring `IUnknown`

Recall from the discussion of polymorphism in Chapter 2 that the `IUnknown` interface must be implemented by all COM components. The `IUnknown` interface holds a position of considerable prominence in COM because a client program never obtains a direct pointer to your component. Instead, the client interacts with your COM objects exclusively through the use of interface pointers, and `IUnknown` is the only interface that all objects are guaranteed to expose. Many COM APIs and interfaces create new objects and return them to clients in the form of an `IUnknown` interface pointer. If you're used to writing programs that pass around pointers to objects, you'll need to readjust your thinking to focus on passing `IUnknown` pointers instead.

The `IUnknown` interface is remarkably simple, but behind its unassuming exterior lies a tremendous amount of power. The entire object model relies extensively on the three methods of `IUnknown`.

```
// Interface IUnknown
class IUnknown
{
public:
    virtual HRESULT QueryInterface(REFIID riid,
                                   void **ppvObject) = 0;
    virtual ULONG AddRef() = 0;
    virtual ULONG Release() = 0;
};
```

It doesn't look like much, does it? As you'll see in the next few sections, there's a whole lot more to `IUnknown` than first meets the eye.

Showing a Different Face, Using `QueryInterface()`

Arguably, the `QueryInterface()` method of the `IUnknown` interface is the most important method in all COM. Because interfaces are at the heart of all object interactions within COM, the obvious question is how does an application or component obtain these interface pointers? The equally obvious (by now) reply is to use `QueryInterface()`.

`QueryInterface()` takes two arguments: a GUID that identifies the requested interface, and the address of the pointer that you want the requested interface pointer returned in. A `REFIID`, by the way, is simply a C++ `const` reference to an interface GUID. Any GUIDs passed into APIs and methods that accept a `REFIID` will pass your GUID structure by reference, instead of the by-value mechanism that would involve copying the GUID structure onto the stack (which is much slower). Listing 3.3 shows how you might use the `QueryInterface()` method to obtain a component's `IChihuahua` interface, given that component's `IUnknown` pointer.

Listing 3.3 QUERYINT.CPP—Using `QueryInterface()` to Obtain an Interface Pointer

```
... IUnknown interface pointer is in variable pIUnknown ...

HRESULT hResult = E_FAIL;
IChihuahua *pIChihuahua = NULL;

// Query the component's IChihuahua interface
hResult = pIUnknown->QueryInterface(IID_IChihuahua,
                                    (void**) &pIChihuahua);
```

```
// Were we successful?
if (FAILED(hResult)) {

    // Determine what went wrong
    switch (hResult) {

        // Does the component even support this interface?
        case E_NOINTERFACE:
            cout << "Component does not expose IChihuahua.\n ";
          cout << "or could be a problem with the proxy/stub. \n";
            break;

        // Has COM been initialized for this thread
        case CO_E_NOTINITIALIZED:
            cout << "COM not initialized.\n";
            break;

        // Has the component run out of memory?
        case E_OUTOFMEMORY:
            cout << "Out of memory!\n";
            break;

        // Some other error
        default:
            cout << "Unrecognized error.\n";
    }

    return hResult;
}
```

As you can see, several things might go wrong when you try to obtain an interface pointer. Perhaps the error you are most likely to encounter is E_NOINTERFACE, which will be returned to you if the component you're working with doesn't support the requested interface. After receiving E_NOINTERFACE, the caller must decide how to proceed. A client program that has determined that an important component doesn't expose IChihuahua, for example, might try to obtain an IDog interface in the hope that partial functionality could be salvaged, or the client might decide that it really requires an IChihuahua in order to proceed. In this case, E_NOINTERFACE is a more serious error condition.

Reference Counting: AddRef() and Release()

The two remaining methods within IUnknown are functionally related. Together, AddRef() and Release() help to coordinate a COM component's reference count. The component's reference count helps a component to determine whether it's a candidate for destruction.

In a typical COM-based application, situations often arise in which multiple components and pieces of client code are simultaneously using and interacting with the same objects. The problem with this state of affairs is that it can be hard for a client to determine when an object is no longer being used.

Imagine a client application that is using a single `Chihuahua` component. Two separate parts of the program, a `Kennel` object and a `Veterinarian` object, have obtained pointers to the component's `IDog` interface pointer by using `QueryInterface()`. The `Kennel` class has no knowledge of the `Veterinarian` class, and vice versa. How does the client (or the server, for that matter) know when the `Chihuahua` object is no longer being used? The `Kennel` object knows when it's finished with the object, and the `Veterinarian` class knows when it's finished with the object, but neither the `Kennel` nor the `Veterinarian` can be sure that it has sole access to the object. Who is in a position to know what objects are still referring to the `Chihuahua`?

The COM solution to this problem is to make the `Chihuahua` itself aware of the external entities using the object. All COM objects keep a running count of how many other objects and programs are using the object. When this count drops to zero, the object knows that it's no longer being used and becomes eligible for destruction.

Of course, it's a little inaccurate to say that the `Chihuahua` object knows about all the objects that are using the component. It's the responsibility of the client to help out with the maintenance of the component's internal reference count, using the `AddRef()` and `Release()` methods.

In several cases, the component client needs to become an active participant in the management of the object's reference count. Whenever the client makes a copy of an interface pointer, the object's reference count needs to be incremented by making a call to the component's `AddRef()` method. Whenever a client's pointer to an interface is destroyed, by going out of scope or being overwritten, the object's reference needs to be decremented by making a call to the component's `Release()` method. Note that neither the `AddRef()` nor the `Release()` method takes arguments. Both methods respond with the reference count as a return value.

The final thing to keep in mind is that when an object's reference count falls to zero, the component can be destroyed at any time thereafter. In reality, most COM components self-destruct immediately. In C++, this is accomplished by deleting the object's `this` pointer from inside the `Release()` method. Because an object's reference count can theoretically fall to zero after any call to `Release()`, it's absolutely forbidden to try to use an interface pointer after calling `Release()` on it. A good practice is to set the interface pointers you've just released to `NULL`.

Caution

You might find the concept of performing `delete this` rather disturbing; some of you might not have even known that this is legal C++ (it certainly looks like it should be illegal!).

It's absolutely critical, after your object's `Release()` method has performed the `delete this` action, that no further code involving the object be executed. In fact, as a safety precaution, I urge you to code your components so that the line of code that immediately follows `delete this` is always the method return statement.

Let's take a look at a few examples. Whenever a component is newly created, an interface is handed back to the client directly or indirectly through the component's class factory (I'll go into the specifics of this process a little bit later in the chapter). At this point, the component has a reference count of one because there is only a single interface copy out in the public domain.

Subsequent successful calls to QueryInterface() will cause the object's reference count to be bumped up by one. It is the component's responsibility to implement this behavior inside the object's QueryInterface() method. This rule of thumb can be further generalized by saying that whenever a component returns an interface pointer from *any* method—not just QueryInterface()—the object's reference count must be incremented.

Table 3.3 shows a series of sample events that could happen over the life span of an object. Follow the descriptions closely as the interface pointers are copied, overwritten, and finally released. The following example assumes that one IUnknown interface pointer initially exists in a variable named pIUnknown (so the reference count begins at one).

Table 3.3 Reference Counter Interface Pointers

Code	Reference Count	Description
IDog *pIDog1 = 0; IDog *pIDog2 = 0; IChihuahua *pIChihuahua1 = 0;	1	These are variable declarations that will be used through out this example.
pIUnknown->QueryInterface (IID_IDog, (void**) &pIDog1);	2	Returning the new IDog interface pointer causes the object's reference count to be automatically increased by one.
pIDog2 = pIDog1; pIDog2->AddRef();	3	Because the object has no way of knowing that the client has made a copy of the pIDog1 interface pointer, the the client needs to manually increment the reference count by calling AddRef().It doesn't matter whether AddRef() is called on pIDog1 or pIDog2; they both point to the same interface pointer.
pIDog1->Release(); pIDog1 = NULL;	2	In anticipation of setting the pIDog1 interface pointer NULL, to the client must call Release() to decrement the reference count.

pIUnknown->QueryInterface
    (IID_IChihuahua,
    (void**) &pIChihuahua1);
	3	Returning the new interface pointer causes the object's reference count to be automatically increased by one.

continued on next page

continued from previous page

Code	Reference Count	Description

```{```
``` (void**) &pIChihuahua1);```
``` IChihuahua *pInner = 0;```
``` pInner = pIChihuahua1;```
``` pInner->AddRef();```
	4	Here you start a new level of scope. The variable `pInner` is local to the new scope. The client needs to manually increment the object's reference count by calling `AddRef()`, because of the pointer copy from `pIChihuahua`.

```pInner->Release();``` ```}```	3	Because the scope is about to come to an end and the `pInner` variable will be destroyed, the client must call `Release()` before `pInner` goes away.

```pIChihuahua1->Release();```
```pIDog2->Release();```
```pIDog2->Release();```
	1	Because the client is done using both these interface pointers, `Release()` is called on each. Now, only a single reference count exists on the object, from the original `pIUnknown` pointer.

```pIUnknown->Release();```	0	The client releases the final outstanding interface pointer. The object's reference count drops to zero, and the component self-destructs.

As you might imagine, the intricacies of reference counting can become involved. However, it's very important that any clients of the component accurately track interface pointer usage. The price that you will pay for being off by even a single call to `AddRef()` or `Release()` can be heavy. Missed calls to `Release()` can lead to memory and resource leaks, and missed calls to `AddRef()` can cause parts of your applications to be left with dangling pointers to invalid memory (which will almost certainly lead to program crashes).

COM gurus such as Kraig Brockschmidt—who wrote *Inside OLE*, which is considered the Bible of OLE programming—and Don Box, who wrote the very popular COM book titled *Essential COM*, often refer to a reference counting pattern called *Acquire-Use-Release*. Generally speaking, a client calls a COM API function or component method that returns a new interface pointer, thus *acquiring* it. The fundamental assumption is that the component incremented its reference count before returning the pointer. The client *uses* the returned interface to perform some set of operations or to accomplish some function. Finally, the client, when finished with the interface pointer, *releases* the interface, which causes a reference count decrement. Keep these three steps in mind at all times, and you can't go too wrong.

Knowing Which IUnknown

A component's `IUnknown` pointer must exhibit a couple of important qualities. First and foremost, a component might have only a single `IUnknown` pointer value that remains constant over the run of the application. This rather simple requirement is easily accomplished in the sample programs in this chapter, but it's important that you keep it in mind. The low-level COM examples that you'll be introduced to are quite simple and revolve around components that expose only a single interface (in addition to `IUnknown`, of course).

However, COM makes no stipulations about the internal structure of your components. For all COM knows, your component might be composed of many subobjects, each responsible for handling a single interface. In fact, this is one of the techniques that can be used by your components to support multiple interfaces. Just remember that a component's IUnknown pointer must always be constant over the lifetime of the component.

The main reason for this requirement is that an object's IUnknown pointer can be used to uniquely identify the object within a given client program. Say, for example, that a client program has obtained two interface pointers. One of these pointers is to an IDog interface, and the other is to an IChihuahua interface. You need to be able to tell whether these pointers are both owned by the same object or are pointers into two completely separate components.

Previously, you learned that every interface inherits from IUnknown and can therefore respond to the same protocol supported by IUnknown. This means that your client program can call QueryInterface() on both the IDog and IChihuahua interfaces, requesting the component's IUnknown interface pointer. To determine whether the interface pointers come from the same object, after you have obtained the pointers from the QueryInterface() method, the pointers can simply be compared to each other to determine whether they are equal. If they are, the IDog and IChihuahua pointers belong to the same object. If the IUnknown pointers differ, the client application knows that it's dealing with two different components. Listing 3.4 shows the code used to make this determination of equality.

Listing 3.4 COMPARE.CPP—Comparing Two Interface Pointers to See Whether They Belong to the Same Component

```
... IDog interface pointer is in variable pIDog...
... IChihuahua interface pointer is in variable pIChihuahua...

HRESULT hResult;
IUnknown* pDogIUnknown = 0;
IUnknown* pChihuhuaIUnknown = 0;

// Get the IUnknown interface pointer for the IDog
hResult = pIDog->QueryInterface(IID_IUnknown,
                                (void**) &pDogIUnknown);
if (FAILED(hResult)) {
   ... Error processing ...
}

// Get the IUnknown interface pointer for the IChihuahua
hResult = pIChihuahua->QueryInterface(IID_IUnknown,
                                (void**) &pChihuahuaIUnknown);
if (FAILED(hResult)) {
       ... Error processing ...
}

// Do both these interface pointers belong to the same object?
If (pDogIUnknown == pChihuahuaIUnknown) {
   cout << "The IDog and IChihuahua interfaces belong to "
        "the same component.\n";
else
   cout << "The IDog and IChihuahua interfaces DO NOT belong to "
        "the same component.\n";
```

Although it's important that an object always return the same `IUnknown` interface pointer, it's probably just as important that the set of interfaces supported by a given component remain constant over the object's lifetime. If a component can call `QueryInterface()` and get back a valid `IDog` pointer, there should never be a time when the same call to `QueryInterface()` would return an `E_NOINTERFACE` error. A component is free to play all the games it wants in obtaining interface pointers that are returned back to clients. Regardless of how the objects gets the pointers, however, the component must always be able to satisfy a request for an interface that the component is known to expose.

Summary

In this chapter, I covered some of the fundamental mechanics of building COM objects. You have seen that COM is divided into COM clients and COM servers and that COM servers are composed of three types: in-process, local, and remote. You also learned how an interface is implemented with C++ as an abstract base class whose functions are pure virtual. Armed with these basic mechanics, you can now construct your first COM client and COM server. Chapter 4, "Implementing a COM Client and Server," demonstrates exactly that. So turn the page and let's get started.

CHAPTER 4

IMPLEMENTING A COM CLIENT AND SERVER

In this chapter, you will learn about the following:

- How to build a functional COM client and in-process server

- The role of the Registry throughout the COM subsystem

A ren't you about to explode with the anticipation of building your own COM component? The wait is finally over. In this chapter, you will build and implement a COM client and server. By the end of this chapter, you should be able to use the techniques that you learned here to create your own COM clients and servers. Perhaps more importantly, because this chapter approaches the task of building COM objects from a low-level perspective that forsakes the use of MFC or other helper class libraries, you will gain a good understanding of what's going on inside the typical COM-based application.

Introducing the World's Most Trivial Sample Program: Fortune1

Throughout this chapter, I am going to refer to an ongoing sample program. The COM example you will do is basic. You are doing an extremely simple example because I want to keep the emphasis on introducing you to the various steps involved in building COM components. In the interest of simplicity, your first COM component will have only one interface. This interface will have, in turn, exactly one method. COM servers don't come much simpler than this, yet I think you'll find that this single method provides plenty of room for instruction. In fact, you're liable to be surprised by how much work goes into supporting this single interface. Most of the source code that you'll be working with is concerned with supporting the mechanics of interacting with the COM subsystem. Extending this example to include more methods should be a simple exercise.

I'm sure that you're eager to jump right in, but take a moment to look at Listing 4.1. This header file contains the declaration for a single C++ class, `CFortuneTeller`.

Listing 4.1 FORTUNE1.H—The Simple C++ Header File for the `CFortuneTeller` Class

```cpp
#ifndef FORTUNE_H
#define FORTUNE_H

// Get needed include files
#include <string>
#include <windows.h>

// New class declaration
class CFortuneTeller
{
public:

    // Constructor
    CFortuneTeller();

    // Lone public method
    string GetFortune();
};

#endif
```

As you can see, there's not a whole lot that you can do with a `CFortuneTeller` object. In fact, the only thing that you can do with a `CFortuneTeller` is ask it for a fortune. The `GetFortune()` method returns a standard ANSI string object that, one would assume, contains a brilliant and witty commentary on pertinent life issues. Thankfully, the `AcceptPayment()` method has not been implemented yet.

Listing 4.2 shows the implementation for this class. Again, there's not a whole lot to the implementation of this class.

Listing 4.2 FORTUNE1.CPP—The Simple C++ Implementation for the `CFortuneTeller` Class

```cpp
#include <stdlib.h>
#include <time.h>
#include <sys/types.h>
#include <sys/timeb.h>
#include "fortune.h"

// Our list of fortunes
static string g_astrFortunes[] =
    {
        "You are strong in body and spirit",
        "You are strong in perspiration and odor.",
        "Good fortune smiles upon the distributed.",
        "You will solve the world hunger problem.",
        "I never met an object I didn't like.",
        "Edit, Compile, Link, Crash, Sigh.",
```

```
        "Never judge a stack dump by its arguments.",
        "Card-carrying member of the Bug Police.",
        "You make Dilbert look charming and sophisticated.",
        "BMW, The Ultimate Driving Machine."
    };

// Constant that tracks the number of fortunes we know about
static const ULONG g_ulNumFortunes =
    sizeof(g_astrFortunes) / sizeof(string);

// Constructor
CFortuneTeller::CFortuneTeller()
{
    // Seed the random number generator
    struct _timeb timebuffer;
    _ftime(&timebuffer);
    srand(timebuffer.millitm);
}

// Lone public method
string CFortuneTeller::GetFortune()
{
    return g_astrFortunes[rand() % g_ulNumFortunes];
}
```

The CFortuneTeller class, as depicted here, knows only ten fortunes (and I'm afraid that none of them are brilliant or witty). Of course, the list of fortunes can be easily extended but...why bother?

The constructor of the CFortuneTeller class seeds and initializes the random number generator that ships with the Visual C++ runtime library. The CFortuneTeller class seeds the random number generator with the milliseconds value of the current time to help provide more random-appearing numbers from run to run. The GetFortune() method simply generates a random index into the fortune array and returns the selected string.

The CFortuneTeller class is especially useless if no one is out there to use it, so direct your attention to Listing 4.3. The CLIENT1.CPP file shown here compiles into the Fortune1 program.

Listing 4.3   CLIENT1.CPP—A Client Program for the Simple C++ CFortuneTeller Class

```
#include <iostream>
#include "Fortune1.h"

int main()
{
    CFortuneTeller  MadameX;

    cout << "Fortune1 - Basic C++ Fortune Program\n";
    cout << "\"" << MadameX.GetFortune() << "\"" << endl;

    return 0;
}
```

Listing 4.3 is a trivial program that uses the `CFortuneTeller` class to help it print out a fortune to standard output. Over time, you'll be extending this simple program to become an actual COM client.

Now that the stage has been set, it's time to start looking at the steps that you'll take to transform the `CFortuneTeller` class into a bona fide COM component.

The Fortune2 Sample Program

As part of the effort to transform `CFortuneTeller` into a COM component, a number of important things have to happen. Perhaps most importantly, a decision needs to be made about what type of server the component will live in. For the sake of simplicity, I'll present the Fortune2 example in only the in-process flavor. The `ComFortuneTeller` source files and its partnered factory class, `ComFortuneTellerFactory`, are placed in the `\Chap4\Fortune2\InProc\` directory. Other server-side files, including Visual C++ 5.0 project files, can be found in the same directory. Source files and project files that are specific to the Fortune2 client application can be found in `\Chap4\Fortune2\Client\`. Finally, files common to both clients and servers can be found in `\Chap4\Fortune2\Common\`.

Building the `IFortuneTeller` Interface

Microsoft has defined a host of COM interfaces that ship with the Windows 98, Windows 95, and Windows NT 4 and NT 5 operating systems. These interfaces are fully established and well described. Programmers are expected to use some of the interfaces through components that Microsoft also provides with the operating system. In other cases, programmers themselves are expected to implement some of these built-in interfaces, with the intent that other COM components will use these interfaces as a commonly defined protocol to communicate with your objects.

Our FortuneTeller program, however, is an example of a *custom interface*. This means that Microsoft didn't write the interface and that the interface doesn't ship with the operating system. Most interfaces provided by Microsoft are used in the implementation of OLE and ActiveX technologies. The following are some of these interfaces:

- `IOleControl`—An interface to implement OLE/ActiveX controls

- `IMonikers`—An interface that encapsulates the functionality needed to implement the various types of monikers

- `IFont`—An interface that encapsulates the Windows font objects

- `IStorage`—An interface that encapsulates the storages in OLE structured storage

- IStream—An interface that encapsulates the streams in OLE structured storage

- IMarshal—An interface that encapsulates the functionality needed to marshal interfaces

Usually, you will write your own components, which provide value to your client applications. If a need exists for your components to support some of the predefined interfaces, they are there to support you. The real value of COM is that it enables you to create components that provide custom-crafted interfaces tailored to the needs of the problems that you want to solve.

Examining the IFortuneTeller Interface

Keeping that in mind, the interface should command the majority of your initial attention. As you learned when we discussed the IDog interface in Chapter 3, "Building COM Objects and Interfaces," all interfaces must be derived from the IUnknown interface. In Fortune2, your interface needs to support only a single method, so the construction of the interface class will be straightforward. Listing 4.4 shows the interface declaration.

Listing 4.4   IFORTUNE.H—The Declaration of the IFortuneTeller Interface

```
#ifndef IFORTUNE_H
#define IFORTUNE_H

// Get needed include files
#include "GUIDs.h"

// New interface declaration
DECLARE_INTERFACE_(IFortuneTeller, IUnknown)
{
  // IFortuneTeller
  STDMETHOD(GetFortune)(/* out */ BSTR*) PURE;
};

typedef IFortuneTeller* PIFortuneTeller;

#endif
```

I am sure you are wondering why this interface doesn't look like the IDog example discussed in Chapter 3, as I'm sure you are wondering about the DECLARE_INTERFACE_ and STDMETHOD macros. You are also probably wondering what a BSTR is.

Don't fret, I am going to explain these new items to you. Yes, the preceding interface declaration—brief as it might be—looks rather strange. Trust me on this one. There's no rocket science going on here.

Start by looking at the top of the file. The first thing that happens is that the GUIDS.H header file is included. This header file, which I won't bother showing here, simply brings in the various GUIDs that a client or server needs in order to use the IFortuneTeller interface. The GUIDS.H header file is also responsible for bringing in necessary operating system include files such as WINDOWS.H and OLE2.H.

The `DECLARE_INTERFACE` Macro

The first real line of the interface declaration looks as though it was written in a different language. `DECLARE_INTERFACE_` appears to be a macro, but what does it do? What does it evaluate to?

Visual C++ provides a host of macros that are used in the declaration and definition of COM methods. These macros exist primarily to help keep your code compatible across languages (C, C++) and platforms (Windows 3.x, Win32). You never know when one of your customers is going to come along and offer you a million dollars to port your spectacularly useful `FortuneTeller` component to another language or operating system. The `DECLARE_INTERFACE` macro is used to declare a new interface. There are actually two variations of this macro. The first, `DECLARE_INTERFACE`, is used when you are creating an interface that does not inherit from another interface. The second form, `DECLARE_INTERFACE_` (note the trailing underscore) is used when your new interface inherits from another interface. Because the vast majority of interfaces inherit from `IUnknown`, use of the second macro variant is much more common. `DECLARE_INTERFACE_` takes two parameters: the name of the new interface and the name of the interface's superclass.

In C++, the `DECLARE_INTERFACE_` macro simply establishes the inheritance relationship between your new interface class and its superclass and declares the actual class itself. The first line of your `IFortuneTeller` interface declaration,

```
DECLARE_INTERFACE_(IFortuneTeller, IUnknown)
```

is evaluated by the preprocessor and replaced with

```
interface IFortuneTeller : public IUnknown
```

The `interface` Keyword

Of course, the next question is, What does that `interface` keyword mean? In truth, the `interface` token is just a symbolic constant. Microsoft has redefined the C++ keyword `struct` as `interface` token. Therefore, the first line of the interface declaration is processed by the compiler as the following code:

```
struct IFortuneTeller : public IUnknown
```

Microsoft has chosen to have `interface` evaluate to `struct` so that you don't have to insert many `public` access specifiers at the beginning of your interface declarations. COM doesn't support the concept of public versus private methods, so all methods that appear in an interface class must be public. A C++ `struct` has exactly the same semantics as `class`, except that the default access specifier is `public` instead of `private`.

The `STDMETHOD` Macro

The real core of the `IFortuneTeller` interface is the declaration of the `GetFortune()` method. The `GetFortune()` method declaration uses the `STDMETHOD` macro which, like `DECLARE_INTERFACE`, also comes in two flavors. The first version of the macro, `STDMETHOD`, assumes that the method you are declaring returns a standard COM HRESULT value. The macro accepts the name of the macro as a single argument. The second version of this macro, **STD-METHOD_** (again, note the trailing underscore), enables you to specify your own return type. **STDMETHOD_**'s two arguments correspond to the method's return type and the name of the method itself. In C++, use of the **STDMETHOD** macros ensures that all your interface methods are declared `virtual`, and the methods use the `__stdcall` calling convention.

Although there are two versions of the **STDMETHOD** macro, you really should use the first form, which declares every method to return an HRESULT. Microsoft has established a set of interface design rules, one of which notes that all interface methods should return an HRESULT. This convention enables the part of the COM subsystem that handles remote processing (that is, local and remote COM servers) to report RPC errors in a logical and consistent manner. By making the **IFortuneTeller** interface return the fortune string in an output parameter, as opposed to through the method's return type, you prepare the **IFortuneTeller** class for distribution outside the client process. The **out** comment that I've embedded into the interface declaration serves as a reminder that the BSTR address being passed into this method will be used as an output argument.

The PURE Macro

The **PURE** macro found at the end of the method declaration evaluates to the `= 0` that's needed to designate a C++ method as being a pure virtual function. When all is said and done, **IFortuneTeller**'s single method,

```
STDMETHOD(GetFortune)(/* out */ BSTR*) PURE;
```

is preprocessed into

```
virtual HRESULT __stdcall GetFortune(BSTR*) = 0;
```

Take a look at Listing 4.5, which shows what the **IFortuneTeller** interface declaration looks like after all the COM macros have been expanded into their full form.

Listing 4.5   NOMACRO.H—The Declaration of the **IFortuneTeller** Interface After Macro Preprocessing

```
#include "GUIDs.h"

struct IFortuneTeller : public IUnknown
{
    virtual HRESULT __stdcall GetFortune(BSTR*) = 0;
};
```

Now that looks much more manageable, doesn't it? In fact, it looks downright trivial.

The last part of the **IFortuneTeller** puzzle is the BSTR type, which is more involved and is one of the topics addressed in the next section.

Unicode and Internationalized Strings

When novice C programmers first start learning about character strings, their eyes generally glaze over as they start to wrestle with the rather abstract concept of a string actually being represented by a pointer to a contiguous sequence of bytes. As you know, each byte in a C string represents a single character. It's not a hard concept to grasp, but it takes a little getting used to.

C++ programmers, on the other hand, have the luxury of ignoring C-style strings altogether. Most C++ programmers use a string class to help hide the management of unwieldy textual data. A good string class can fully insulate a programmer from the hassles of standard library functions such as `strcat()` and `strcpy()`. In fact, string classes are so prevalent that Visual C++ 6 comes with several, the two most commonly used being the ANSI standard–compliant `string` class (that is, the ANSI class named `string`) and the MFC `CString` class.

Unfortunately for the COM programmer, an inherent conflict exists here. C++ string classes are nice, but they are *very* language dependent. If COM is to be language-independent, in no way can string objects be passed in and out of COM objects.

There's another related problem here. Windows 95 and Windows NT have become the most widely used operating systems in the world. When you consider releasing your application into the international market, conversations invariably lead to talk of Unicode. Unicode is a double-byte character set that has been defined to help with the problem of writing applications with a multilingual audience. The 65,000 or so characters supported by Unicode are enough to handle virtually every character found in every language on the planet.

A full-fledged discussion of the issues revolving around Unicode application development are beyond the scope of this book. However, Unicode cannot be ignored, because Unicode is the *lingua franca* of COM. That's right, all the standard COM APIs and method interfaces require Unicode strings. All strings that are shared between clients and local (or remote) servers are passed around in Unicode format.

Note

Technically speaking, you can build an in-process or local server that doesn't have to use Unicode or BSTRs. However, throughout the book you'll find that I use BSTRs exclusively whenever I want to pass strings through COM interfaces. BSTRs become very important when writing Automation-aware clients and servers, and I want to start preparing you early. As you'll see, this is hardly an egregious proposition because using BSTRs imposes little additional performance overhead compared to regular Unicode strings. Even better, using BSTRs becomes easier after you make the move to MFC.

One of the nice things about development under Windows NT is that Unicode support is built right in to the operating system. This doesn't mean that NT programmers can ignore Unicode issues altogether, but it certainly can make life easier. Don't get too excited, though. Windows 95, unfortunately, does not have pervasive Unicode support. In fact, the Unicode support in Windows 95 is only strong enough to enable your application to translate regular ASCII strings back and forth between Unicode, and little more. What this means is that if you want your components to work on both Windows 95 and Windows NT, you're going to have to rely predominately on ASCII strings and translate to and from Unicode as necessary.

Note

If it makes you feel any better, the MFC `CString` class that you will begin using in Chapter 5, "COM Programming with MFC," provides a number of useful behaviors that will help simplify your application's use of Unicode.

Translating ANSI Strings to and from Unicode

The Win32 API provides two functions to help your application translate text from Unicode strings to ANSI character strings (and back again, of course). These two functions, `MultiByteToWideChar()` and `WideCharToMultiByte()`, are rather inconvenient to use, so I've enlisted the help of two utility functions.

Note

Note that in the previous paragraph, I was careful to say *ANSI* strings, not *ASCII* strings. An ASCII string always uses a single-byte character set. That means that every character in an ASCII string is represented by a single byte. The terms *ANSI string* and *ASCII string* are often used interchangeably, but there is an important distinction. An ANSI string *can* use a multiple-byte character set, in which a given character is represented by one or more bytes. The examples in this book use only standard ASCII strings, so you don't have to worry about it too much. It's important to understand that a given ANSI string and a given ASCII string are not always equivalent.

Now before I get myself into trouble, let me confess that I didn't write these utility functions. The two utility functions, `AnsiToUnicode()` and `UnicodeToAnsi()`, were written by Microsoft to help simplify the use of the native Win32 API functions. In addition to providing a very straightforward way to translate strings between the two different string types, `AnsiToUnicode()` and `UnicodeToAnsi()` use the COM memory allocator to create memory buffers.

Note

AnsiToUnicode() and UnicodeToAnsi() are detailed in an OLE Knowledge Base article that is included on the Visual C++ 6 CD-ROM. The same article is also available if you have access to a recent copy of the Microsoft Developer Network CD-ROM. Search for the Knowledgebase Article Q138813 to obtain more information on these useful functions.

Now, I am sure you want to know what the OLE task memory allocator is. You'll recall that an in-process component server shares the same memory space as a client application because it exists in a DLL. Local and remote COM servers, however, execute in a different address space than the component client. Because a client can't be sure that a component exists in the same address space, memory for strings that are passed as method arguments to a component, or memory returned to clients from a component, must be controlled by the COM subsystem.

These memory management services are encapsulated in (what else) a COM object, referred to as the *default COM memory allocator*. Although the memory allocator exposes a memory management interface (IMalloc), it's usually more convenient to simply call the COM APIs that wrap the default memory allocator object.

Both AnsiToUnicode() and UnicodeToAnsi() use the default COM memory allocator. AnsiToUnicode() takes two arguments: a standard ANSI C-style source string and a pointer to the address of a variable that will be used to store the target Unicode string. The target address variable doesn't need to allocate any memory to hold the new Unicode string; this task is handled by AnsiToUnicode(). The AnsiToUnicode() function allocates new memory for the Unicode string by using the COM memory allocator function CoTaskMemAlloc(). Data allocated with the COM memory allocator can be passed between clients and servers, with either party freeing the shared memory by using the function CoTaskMemFree().

The UnicodeToAnsi() function is very similar. It, too, takes two parameters: a Unicode source string and a pointer to the address of a variable that will be used to store the target ANSI string. Unlike AnsiToUnicode(), there's not a compelling reason to use the COM memory allocator to obtain memory for the target ANSI string. Recall that OLE is a Unicode-only subsystem, so you'll never be passing regular ANSI strings between COM clients and servers. Just remember that every call to UnicodeToAnsi(), like every call to AnsiToUnicode(), will result in a piece of memory that needs to be freed using CoTaskMemFree().

Unfortunately, even though you've learned how to translate strings to and from Unicode, you're not finished yet. Although OLE requires you to use Unicode strings, the standard type for passing strings between COM clients and servers is the BASIC string (BSTR). Although BSTRs are very close to being standard Unicode strings, there are some important differences.

BSTR, the COM String Type

The BSTR type is a product of the same Microsoft team responsible for the development of Visual Basic. The developers on this team recognized the need to provide a generic COM interface that a scripting engine (or interpreted language such as Visual Basic) could use to gain access to any of a component's interfaces. Their efforts in this area led to the development of the **IDispatch** interface, which lies at the heart of OLE Automation. Because the developers were most concerned about how they could give applications written in Visual Basic access to COM objects, it was only natural that they devised a way to support Visual Basic strings (and therefore the type name *BSTR, Basic STRing*).

Unlike native strings in C and C++, which are simply runs of contiguous characters terminated by a **NULL** character, a Visual Basic string is conceptually composed of two fields. The first field is a 4-byte unsigned **long** value that represents the total number of bytes in the string (*not* to be confused with the total number of Unicode characters in the string). The second field is the string itself, terminated by a **NULL** (the length field does not include the **NULL** character at the end of the character buffer).

Remember that COM operates in the world of Unicode, where every character takes up two bytes (an **OLECHAR** is just another name for **wchar_t**, the integral 2-byte–wide character type supported by Visual C++). Despite the two fields found in a Basic string, you might be surprised to discover that the actual BSTR type is just a standard Unicode **char** pointer. You'll probably be even more surprised to learn that a non-**NULL** BSTR doesn't point to the whole string structure, but instead points to the beginning of the Basic string character buffer. With BSTR defined in this manner, an application can treat a BSTR as if it were a regular Unicode string. Figure 4.1 shows what a BSTR looks like laid out in memory.

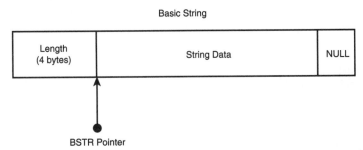

Figure 4.1   The memory layout of a BSTR string.

The BSTR API is composed of functions such as **SysAllocString()**, **SysFreeString()**, **SysReAllocString()**, and yes, **SysStringLen()**.

`CFortuneTeller` Rebuilt as `ComFortuneTeller`

The moment of truth is at hand. We have discussed COM clients and servers, GUIDs, HRESULTs, interfaces, BSTRs, and a host of other concepts needed to build your first COM component. Many other COM concepts and abstractions are so interrelated that programmers new to COM have to accumulate a lot of up-front knowledge before they can get their first programs up and running. Guess what? Now you've learned the basics, and it's time to get on with the good stuff.

You've seen what the `IFortuneTeller` interface looks like, but as I've already discussed, an interface is simply a contract between the COM component and the outside world as to what functionality the COM component provides. The interface describes the methods exposed by a COM component that implements the interface. The next logical step is to actually implement the `IFortuneTeller` interface. Let's examine the `ComFortuneTeller` class.

The `ComFortuneTeller` Class

Take a look at Listing 4.6. This listing contains the header file that declares the `ComFortuneTeller` class.

Listing 4.6   `FORTUNE2.H`—The Declaration of the `ComFortuneTeller` Class

```
#ifndef FORTUNE_H
#define FORTUNE_H

// Get needed include files
#include "IFortune.h"

// New class declaration
class ComFortuneTeller : public IFortuneTeller
{
public:

    // Constructor
    ComFortuneTeller();

    // IUnknown

    STDMETHOD(QueryInterface)(REFIID, LPVOID*);
    STDMETHOD_(ULONG, AddRef)();
    STDMETHOD_(ULONG, Release)();

    // IFortuneTeller
    STDMETHOD(GetFortune)(/*[out,retval]*/BSTR*);

protected:
```

```
    // Reference count
    ULONG m_cRef;
};

typedef ComFortuneTeller* PComFortuneTeller;

#endif
```

There shouldn't be any surprises here. You can see that the `ComFortuneTeller` class inherits from the `IFortuneTeller` interface. Remember that the `IFortuneTeller` interface class in turn is inherited from the `IUnknown` interface class. In practical terms, this means that the `ComFortuneTeller` class has four pure virtual functions for which it has to provide implementations.

Now that you know what the `ComFortuneTeller` class is supposed to look like, turn your attention to the actual implementation of the class in Listing 4.7. Although I'm showing you the full class implementation now, I'm going to organize my discussion of the implementation around the two interfaces that `ComFortuneTeller` supports: `IUnknown` and `IFortuneTeller`.

Listing 4.7   FORTUNE2.CPP—The Implementation of the `ComFortuneTeller` Class

```
// Get needed compiler include files
#include <stdlib.h>
#include <time.h>
#include <sys/types.h>
#include <sys/timeb.h>
#include <string>

// Get needed system and custom include files
#include "Utility.h"
#include "Counts.h"
#include "Fortune2.h"
#include "Factory2.h"


// Our list of fortunes
static string g_astrFortunes[] =
    {
        "You are strong in body and spirit.",
        "You are strong in perspiration and odor.",
        "Good fortune smiles upon the distributed.",
        "You will solve the world hunger problem.",
        "I never met an object I didn't like.",
        "Edit, Compile, Link, Crash, Sigh.",
        "Never judge a stack dump by its arguments.",
        "Card carrying member of the Bug Police.",
        "You make Dilbert look charming and sophisticated.",
        "BMW, The Ultimate Driving Machine."
    };

// Constant that tracks the number of fortunes we know about
static const ULONG g_ulNumFortunes =
```

continued on next page

continued from previous page

```
            sizeof(g_astrFortunes) / sizeof(string);


    // Constructor
    ComFortuneTeller::ComFortuneTeller()
            : m_cRef(0)
    {
        // Be annoying and verbose
        VerboseMsg("Constructing new ComFortuneTeller object.");

        // Seed the random number generator
        struct _timeb timebuffer;
        _ftime(&timebuffer);
        srand(timebuffer.millitm);
    }



    //
    // IUnknown methods
    //

    STDMETHODIMP ComFortuneTeller::QueryInterface(REFIID rIID,
                                                  LPVOID* ppInterface)
    {
        VerboseMsg("In ComFortuneTeller::QueryInterface");

        // Set the interface pointer
        if (rIID == IID_IUnknown) {
            VerboseMsg("   Requesting IUnknown interface.");
            *ppInterface = this;
        }

        else if (rIID == IID_IFortuneTeller) {
            VerboseMsg("   Requesting IFortuneTeller interface.");
            *ppInterface = this;
        }

        // We don't support this interface
        else {
            VerboseMsg("   Requesting unsupported interface.");
            *ppInterface = NULL;
        }

        // Bump up the reference count
        if (*ppInterface) {
            ((LPUNKNOWN) *ppInterface)->AddRef();
            return NOERROR;
        }

        return E_NOINTERFACE;
    }

    STDMETHODIMP_(ULONG) ComFortuneTeller::AddRef()
```

```
{
   // Increment the reference count
   m_cRef++;

   // Convert to string and display
   VerboseMsg("In ComFortuneTeller::AddRef. Reference count = "
              + ULongToANSI(m_cRef));

   return m_cRef;
}

STDMETHODIMP_(ULONG) ComFortuneTeller::Release()
{
   // Decrement the reference count
   m_cRef--;

   // Convert to string and display
   VerboseMsg("In ComFortuneTeller::Release. Reference count = "
              + ULongToANSI(m_cRef));

   // Is this the last reference to the object?
   if (m_cRef)
      return m_cRef;

   // Decrement the server object count
   Counters::DecObjectCount();

   // Self-destruct
   VerboseMsg("   ComFortuneTeller reference count is 0.
              ➥Deleting self.");
   delete this;
   return 0;
}


//
// IFortuneTeller methods
//

STDMETHODIMP ComFortuneTeller::GetFortune(BSTR* pbstrFortune)
{
  VerboseMsg("In ComFortuneTeller::GetFortune");

  // Initialize the output string
  *pbstrFortune = NULL;

  // Convert the ANSI string to Unicode
  LPOLESTR pszFortuneW;
  AnsiToUnicode(g_astrFortunes[rand() % g_ulNumFortunes].c_str(),
                &pszFortuneW);

  // Create a BSTR out of the Unicode string
  *pbstrFortune = SysAllocString(pszFortuneW);
```

continued on next page

continued from previous page

```
    // Release the Unicode string memory
    CoTaskMemFree(pszFortuneW);

    if (*pbstrFortune)
      return NOERROR;
    return E_OUTOFMEMORY;
}
```

The `ComFortuneTeller` constructor implementation is straightforward; the method initializes the component's reference count to zero and seeds the random number generator in exactly the same manner as the original `CFortuneTeller` class.

The `VerboseMsg()` Function

As you start to inspect the larger sample programs, you're bound to encounter calls to the global function `VerboseMsg()`. I've defined this function in the utilities header file used by both the client programs and server programs in this chapter.

The `VerboseMsg()` function takes a reference to a single ANSI string object, but by default does nothing with it. In fact, in the default case, the `VerboseMsg()` is really a no-op. It performs absolutely no function whatsoever. However, when the source code is compiled with the `QUE_VERBOSE` preprocessor macro defined, the `VerboseMsg()` function springs to life and begins to function. Granted, the behavior of the function is hardly earth-shattering; all the function does is display the input string to the console.

What is more interesting is that the `VerboseMsg()` call is sprinkled liberally through the examples I'll be presenting in the rest of this chapter. I've included these calls not so much as debugging aids, but as a way to open a window into the client and server binaries. As I mentioned at the beginning of the chapter, the FortuneTeller example is so trivial that it's hard to imagine that it could be very instructional. It only takes a `QUE_VERBOSE` compile to prove otherwise.

Take, for example, the output of the Fortune2 client program with the `VerboseMsg()` method disabled. The output of this program is virtually identical to the output of Fortune1, the program I showed you earlier that had a simple C++ implementation with no COM involved at all.

```
C:\fortune2
Fortune2 - Simple COM Fortune Client Program
"You make Dilbert look charming and sophisticated."

C:\
```

Now rebuild the Fortune2 server DLL and client program with the `QUE_VERBOSE` flag defined. (An easy way to do this is to go to the Visual C++ Developer Studio's Build menu and select the Settings option. In the Main Settings dialog box, navigate to the C/C++ tab, select the Preprocessor category, and add the string `QUE_VERBOSE` to the Preprocessor Definitions edit field. Now close the dialog box and select Rebuild All from the Build menu.) If you rerun the Fortune2 client program now, you should see the following:

```
C:\fortune2
Fortune2 - Simple COM Fortune Client Program
VERBOSE: Calling COM API CoInitialize.
```

```
VERBOSE: Requesting FortuneTeller class factory.
VERBOSE: In DllGetClassObject
VERBOSE:    Creating new ComFortuneTellerFactory object
VERBOSE: Constructing new ComFortuneTellerFactory object.
VERBOSE: In ComFortuneTellerFactory::QueryInterface
VERBOSE:    Requesting IClassFactory interface.
VERBOSE: In ComFortuneTellerFactory::AddRef. Reference count = 1
VERBOSE: Creating new FortuneTeller object instance.
VERBOSE: In ComFortuneTellerFactory::CreateInstance
VERBOSE:    Creating new ComFortuneTeller object
VERBOSE: Constructing new ComFortuneTeller object.
VERBOSE: In ComFortuneTeller::QueryInterface
VERBOSE:    Requesting IFortuneTeller interface.
VERBOSE: In ComFortuneTeller::AddRef. Reference count = 1
VERBOSE: Releasing FortuneTeller class factory.
VERBOSE: In ComFortuneTellerFactory::Release. Reference count = 0
VERBOSE:    ComFortuneTellerFactory reference count is 0. Deleting self.
VERBOSE: Getting fortune from FortuneTeller object.
VERBOSE: In ComFortuneTeller::GetFortune
VERBOSE: Translating fortune from Unicode to ANSI text.
"You make Dilbert look charming and sophisticated."
VERBOSE: Releasing fortune and BSTR strings.
VERBOSE: Releasing FortuneTeller object.
VERBOSE: In ComFortuneTeller::Release. Reference count = 0
VERBOSE:    ComFortuneTeller reference count is 0. Deleting self.

C:\
```

As you can tell, an awful lot is going on here for such a simple program. I encourage you to trace through the output of a program run with the QUE_VERBOSE flag set at least once. It's certainly easier than walking through the whole thing in the debugger, and I think you'll find yourself getting a better feel for what's going on.

ComFortuneTeller's Implementation of IUnknown

The first few ComFortuneTeller methods belong to the IUnknown interface. The most predominate of the three methods that IUnknown declares is the QueryInterface() method.

ComFortuneTeller's QueryInterface() method serves two central purposes, in addition to returning a pointer to the requested interface back to the method's caller. First, the QueryInterface() method verifies that the caller is not asking for an interface that the component does not support. Because the caller might not be the entity responsible for creating the component in the first place (the object could have, for example, been passed to the caller as a function or method argument), there's a perfectly legitimate chance that the caller has no idea what type of component it is dealing with. Your components should always be sensitive to the fact that they might be dealing with an uninformed audience. For this reason, it's critical that your objects return E_NOINTERFACE whenever the caller is asking for an interface that your component doesn't support.

In addition to returning interface pointers and validating that the caller is requesting a supported interface, the `QueryInterface()` is also responsible for ensuring that the reference count of the object is incremented before the interface pointer is returned back to the caller. Clients expect a successful call to `QueryInterface()` to increment the reference count automatically, and as I've already mentioned, you can pay a heavy price for not paying close attention to your reference counts. The reason is that the memory might never be released or might be released before you are done with it. If it is released before you are done with it, your code might try to access an object that doesn't exist. If the reference count never reaches zero, your object will never unload. You would have a memory leak. Therefore, it is very important to pay close attention to reference counts.

The next two `IUnknown` methods are concerned with reference counting. Take a look first at the `AddRef()` method. This is another simple method, which does nothing more than bump up the component's reference count by one.

`Release()`, on the other hand, has more meat to it. The first thing the method does is decrement the component reference count. If the reference count is still greater than zero, the component knows that no clients are still holding on to interface pointers that belong to this object. At this point, the object knows that it can be destroyed.

```
// Is this the last reference to the object?
if (m_cRef)
    return m_cRef;

// Decrement the server object count
Counters::DecObjectCount();

// Self-destruct
delete this;
```

As you can clearly see, before the object destroys itself by deleting its **this** pointer, the component needs to decrement the server object count. As I mentioned at the beginning of this chapter when discussing server fundamentals, all COM servers need to track the total number of objects (*not* including class factory objects) that exist within the server at any given time. The server will use this information later to determine whether the server is able to be unloaded from memory. (Obviously, it would be a very bad thing if the server were removed from memory and there were still active objects living inside it). Although this server object count is implemented by many programmers as a global variable, I encourage you to think carefully about this decision. (Watch out! I'm about to step up on my soapbox.)

Global Data

Most programmers are taught from the beginning that global data is a bad thing. The main rationale for making this blanket statement is that classes and functions can inadvertently modify global data in ways that other objects within the server might not have anticipated. If you have written your classes to be dependent on global data being constant from one point in your code to another, you're placing your program in jeopardy. The problem, of course, is that everyone has access to global data, which means that you can't always be sure that another object hasn't changed the global data in a way that you don't expect.

The problem only deepens when you're developing programs under Windows 98, 95, or NT, which are operating systems that preemptively multitask at the thread level. In a multithreaded environment, you can never be certain that global data hasn't been modified without your knowledge, unless you use some external means to ensure otherwise. Although you can use many different strategies to help coordinate access to global data, one of the most effective involves *stewarding*.

A *steward* is an object that is responsible for managing the access to global data. The steward object serves as a traffic cop that manages and restricts access to global data. The steward may employ internal mechanisms such as semaphores to help guarantee serialized access to the global data members. Recall that a *semaphore* is a construct used in multithreaded programming; it flags you that some activity is completed. Even if you know that your server is not operating in a multithreaded environment or that the opportunities for corrupted data are rare, it's always a good idea to steward global data anyway. This will enable you to evolve your code if at some future point you recognize the need to strictly enforce serialization.

In the FortuneTeller2 sample program, the `Counters` class acts as a steward for the server's global object count and the server's lock count (more on server locks shortly). Classes never directly access the object count variable, but always go through the static member functions of the `Counters` class to increment, decrement, and read the current counter values.

In its current form, the `Counters` class is very simple. Listing 4.8 shows the declaration for the class as it appears in the class header file.

Listing 4.8   `COUNTS.H`—The Declaration of the `Counters` Data-Stewarding Class

```
#ifndef COUNTS_H
#define COUNTS_H

#include "StdInc.h"

//
// The Counters class is a simple encapsulation of the server lock
// and the server object count global variables.
//

class Counters
{
public:

    // Public query methods
    static ULONG GetLockCount();
    static ULONG GetObjectCount();

    // Counter increment.decrement methods
    static VOID IncLockCount();
    static VOID DecLockCount();
    static VOID IncObjectCount();
    static VOID DecObjectCount();
```

continued on next page

continued from previous page

```
private:

    // Lock and object count variables
    static ULONG m_cLocks;
    static ULONG m_cNumObjects;
};

#endif
```

The various public methods of the **Counters** are declared as static so that the application doesn't have to actually instantiate a **Counters** object. This is usually more convenient for programmers because they don't have to worry about what software entity should be responsible for the steward instance declaration. Listing 4.9 shows the straightforward implementation for this class.

Listing 4.9   COUNTS.CPP—The Implementation of the **Counters** Data-Stewarding Class

```
// Get needed system and custom include files
#include "Counts.h"

// Initialize static data
ULONG Counters::m_cLocks = 0UL;
ULONG Counters::m_cNumObjects = 0UL;


//
// Public methods
//

ULONG Counters::GetLockCount()
{
    return m_cLocks;
}

ULONG Counters::GetObjectCount()
{
    return m_cNumObjects;
}

VOID Counters::IncLockCount()
{
    m_cLocks++;
}

VOID Counters::DecLockCount()
{
    m_cLocks—;
}

VOID Counters::IncObjectCount()
{
    m_cNumObjects++;
}
```

```
VOID Counters::DecObjectCount()
{
   m_cNumObjects—;
}
```

Although there's nothing to the `Counters` class right now, and the class doesn't really do anything to alleviate the dangers of using global data, the `Counters` class (and the stewarding pattern, in general) does suggest a more formalized mechanism for declaring and accessing global information. At the very least, the `Counters` class provides a convenient place to insert debugging routines that you can use to track down elusive global data bugs. Finally, if you use a stewarding class to wrap all your global data, you can dramatically cut down on your server's pollution of the global namespace.

ComFortuneTeller's Implementation of IFortuneTeller

All this `IUnknown` business is merely infrastructure required to help coordinate the component's behaviors with the COM subsystem at large. However, the whole reason that you are ostensibly building the `ComFortuneTeller` class is because you want a fortune-telling component. This functionality is embodied by the implementation of the `IFortuneTeller` interface.

The `IFortuneTeller` interface is composed of a single method, `GetFortune()`, which returns a single BSTR through an output parameter. The method is essentially composed of three core lines of code.

```
AnsiToUnicode(g_astrFortunes[rand() % g_ulNumFortunes].c_str(),
              &pszFortuneW);

// Create a BSTR out of the Unicode string
*pbstrFortune = SysAllocString(pszFortuneW);

// Release the Unicode string memory
CoTaskMemFree(pszFortuneW);
```

The `ComFortuneTeller` class stores the various fortunes in an array of ANSI `string` objects. `ComFortuneTeller` can extract a normal C-style string from a `string` object by calling the class's `c_str()` method, and that's exactly what `ComFortuneTeller` does as it calls the `AnsiToUnicode()` function.

The `AnsiToUnicode()` function returns a Unicode version of the randomly selected fortune in the `pszFortuneW` variable. Although a Unicode string and a BSTR are similar, they are not identical. For this reason, Microsoft has been kind enough to provide you with a whole API for allocating and managing BSTRs. The `SysAllocString()` function that `ComFortuneTeller` uses here creates a new BSTR given a Unicode string. The new BSTR is a completely different string, located at a different memory address, so all calls to `SysAllocString()` need to be paired with a corresponding call to `SysFreeString()`. In this in-process server example, the responsibility for calling `SysFreeString()` falls on the calling client program.

The `AnsiToUnicode()` function allocates new memory for the Unicode string by using the COM memory allocator. Because the `SysAllocString()` API also allocates memory for the new BSTR and copies the Unicode string into the BSTR, there is no need to keep the Unicode string around. (Incidentally, `SysAllocString()` also uses the COM memory allocator.) The `GetFortune()` method finishes up by freeing the Unicode string with a call to `CoTaskMemFree()` and returning the new BSTR back to the caller.

The ComFortuneTellerFactory Class

Now that you've seen what the implementation of the FortuneTeller component looks like, it's time to turn your attention to how instances of `ComFortuneTeller` are created. As discussed previously, every COM object is instantiated by a class factory. This implies that you need to write a class factory component for `ComFortuneTeller`.

The IClassFactory Interface

In COM, the class factory protocol is embodied in a standard interface named `IClassFactory`. This interface is short, being composed of only two methods.

```
// Interface IClassFactory
class IClassFactory : public IUnknown
{
public:
    virtual HRESULT CreateInstance( IUnknown *pUnkOuter,
                                    REFIID riid,
                                    void **ppvObject) = 0;
    virtual HRESULT LockServer(BOOL fLock) = 0;
};
```

The workhorse of `IClassFactory` is the `CreateInstance()` method, which creates a new object and returns a pointer to one of the object's requested interfaces. The latter two of `CreateInstance()`'s three arguments should look familiar to you. They are, after all, exactly the same arguments that you pass in to a call to `IUnknown::QueryInterface()`. The only difference here is that the object doesn't exist yet and needs to be instantiated before the interface pointer can be returned to the caller.

The first argument to `CreateInstance()`, on the other hand, is probably unfamiliar to you. In Chapter 2, "The Object Revolution," I briefly discussed some of the strategies that COM servers can employ to simulate inheritance. In one of the strategies, aggregation, an outer object contains an inner object and exposes the inner object's interfaces as if they were the outer object's own. The first argument to `CreateInstance()` will contain the `IUnknown` interface pointer of the outer controlling component if your component is being aggregated into another component. However, because I haven't yet explained how to build components that expose multiple custom interfaces, the FortuneTeller server does not support aggregation, and this will be reflected in the implementation of `ComFortuneTellerFactory`. For now, you can safely ignore the `pUnkOuter` argument.

The second method in the interface, `LockServer()`, is used primarily as a performance enhancement for clients that tend to create and destroy objects frequently. Imagine a client that regularly creates a single Dog object, uses it for a short period, releases it, creates a new Dog object, uses it for a short period, and so on. (I call this the "create-use-release-repeat" usage pattern.) The first time the client creates a Dog, the server that hosts the Dog class is started up. If the server is an in-process server, this startup overhead isn't particularly excruciating, but a fair amount of additional processing is involved because the DLL is loaded into memory and the Dog component's class factory is created. The situation only grows worse, however, when the Dog class is hosted by a local COM server. Starting up a local server involves spawning off a whole new operating system process, which is considerably more work than loading up a new DLL into memory. Now the client uses the new Dog object for a short time and releases it. The server's object reference count falls to zero, and the server is removed from memory, by unloading the DLL or by the local server process terminating itself. Now the client turns right around and says, "I want a new Dog." Ouch! Time to reload the entire server and go through the whole process again.

The server lock mechanism provides a way to prevent exactly this type of behavior. Without a way to lock the server in memory, a server could end up spending a significant amount of time being continuously created and destroyed, rather than hosting objects and doing its real job. The server lock count is just a second reference count. A server is never unloaded until its object count *and* its lock count are both zero. This enables clients with the create-use-release-repeat usage pattern to lock the server and rest assured that the server will only need to be loaded once. Subsequent calls to create a new object will occur without needing to reload the server, even if the server's object count has fallen to zero. The only thing that a client program has to be careful about is ensuring that every call to `LockServer(TRUE)` is eventually paired with an ensuing call to `LockServer(FALSE)`.

Note

COM also supports creating objects through the `IClassFactory2` interface. The `IClassFactory2` interface provides exactly the same services as `IClassFactory`, but does so for components that are *licensed*. Licensing a component is a form of copy protection. For someone to use a licensed component, the client needs to provide a valid key that is used to unlock the class factory and allow the creation of new component objects. COM does not dictate the specifics of how the component implements a licensing strategy. The contents of a license key and what makes it valid or invalid, for example, is application-defined. `IClassFactory2` simply provides an interface for components to use in a license-based environment.

Implementing `ComFortuneTellerFactory`

Now it's time to take a look at what the FortuneTeller class factory looks like. The `ComFortuneTellerFactory` component needs to implement two interfaces: `IUnknown` and `IClassFactory` (remember, *everyone* has to implement `IUnknown`). Listing 4.10 shows the header file that contains the declaration for the `ComFortuneTellerFactory` class.

Listing 4.10 `FACTORY2.H`—The Declaration of the `ComFortuneTellerFactory` Class Factory Component

```
#ifndef FACTORY2_H
#define FACTORY2_H

// Get needed include files
#include "IFortune.h"

// New class declaration
class ComFortuneTellerFactory : public IClassFactory4
{
public:

    // Constructor
    ComFortuneTellerFactory();

    // IUnknown
STDMETHOD(QueryInterface)(REFIID, LPVOID*);
    STDMETHOD_(ULONG, AddRef)();
    STDMETHOD_(ULONG, Release)();

    //IClassFactory members
    STDMETHOD(CreateInstance)(LPUNKNOWN, REFIID, LPVOID*);
    STDMETHOD(LockServer)(BOOL);

protected:

    // Reference count for class factory
    ULONG m_cRef;
};

typedef ComFortuneTellerFactory* PComFortuneTellerFactory;

#endif
```

Like every good interface, the `IClassFactory` interface is derived from `IUnknown`. Because both `IUnknown` and `IClassFactory` are standard system interfaces provided by Microsoft, you don't have to worry about providing a separate `IClassFactory` interface declaration as you did for `IFortuneTeller`. The declaration of the factory class indicates that the `ComFortuneTellerFactory` will be providing implementations for all the methods specified in the `IUnknown` and `IClassFactory` interfaces. Listing 4.11 shows the actual class factory code for the `ComFortuneTellerFactory`. This is the code that will create and manage the `ComFortuneTellerFactory` objects.

Listing 4.11   FACTORY2.CPP—The Implementation of the ComFortuneTellerFactory
Class Factory Component

```
// Get needed compiler include files
#include <iostream>

// Get needed system and custom include files
#define INITGUID
#include "Utility.h"
#include "Factory2.h"
#include "Fortune2.h"
#include "Counts.h"


// Constructor
ComFortuneTellerFactory::ComFortuneTellerFactory()
        : m_cRef(0)
{
    // Be annoying and verbose
    VerboseMsg("Constructing new ComFortuneTellerFactory object.");
}


//
// IUnknown methods
//

STDMETHODIMP ComFortuneTellerFactory::QueryInterface(REFIID rIID,
➥LPVOID* ppvInterface)
{
    VerboseMsg("In ComFortuneTellerFactory::QueryInterface");

    // Initialize returned interface pointer
    *ppvInterface = NULL;

    // Set the interface pointer
    if (rIID == IID_IUnknown) {
        VerboseMsg("   Requesting IUnknown interface.");
        *ppvInterface = this;
    }

    else if (rIID == IID_IClassFactory) {
        VerboseMsg("   Requesting IClassFactory interface.");
        *ppvInterface = this;
    }

    // We don't support this interface
    else {
        VerboseMsg("   Requesting unsupported interface.");
        *ppvInterface = NULL;
        return E_NOINTERFACE;
    }
```

continued on next page

continued from previous page

```
                // Bump up the reference count
                ((LPUNKNOWN) *ppvInterface)->AddRef();

            return NOERROR;
        }

        STDMETHODIMP_(ULONG) ComFortuneTellerFactory::AddRef()
        {
            // Increment the reference count
            m_cRef++;

            // Convert to string and display
            VerboseMsg("In ComFortuneTellerFactory::AddRef. Reference count = "
                        + ULongToANSI(m_cRef));

            return m_cRef;
        }

        STDMETHODIMP_(ULONG) ComFortuneTellerFactory::Release()
        {
            // Decrement the reference count
            m_cRef—;

            // Convert to string and display
            VerboseMsg("In ComFortuneTellerFactory::Release. Reference count = "
                        + ULongToANSI(m_cRef));

            // Is this the last reference to the object?
            if (m_cRef)
                return m_cRef;

            // Self destruct
            VerboseMsg("   ComFortuneTellerFactory reference count
        ➡is 0. Deleting self.");
            delete this;
            return 0;
        }


        //
        // IFortuneTeller methods
        //

        STDMETHODIMP ComFortuneTellerFactory::CreateInstance
                                    ➡(LPUNKNOWN pUnkOuter,
                                    REFIID rIID,
                                    LPVOID* ppvInterface)
        {
            PComFortuneTeller   pObj;
            HRESULT             hResult;

            VerboseMsg("In ComFortuneTellerFactory::CreateInstance");
```

```
    // Initialize returned interface pointer
    *ppvInterface = NULL;

    // Check for a controlling unknown
    if (pUnkOuter && rIID != IID_IUnknown)
       return CLASS_E_NOAGGREGATION;

    //Create the object-passing function to notify on destruction.
    VerboseMsg("   Creating new ComFortuneTeller object");
    pObj = new ComFortuneTeller;

    // Out of memory?
    if (!pObj) {
       VerboseMsg("   FortuneTeller object creation failed.");
       return E_OUTOFMEMORY;
    }

    // Now obtain the requested interface
    hResult = pObj->QueryInterface(rIID, ppvInterface);

    // Destroy the object if the desired interface couldn't be obtained
    if (FAILED(hResult)) {
       delete pObj;
       return hResult;
    }

    // Everything looks good. Bump up the server object count
    Counters::IncObjectCount();

    return NOERROR;
}

STDMETHODIMP ComFortuneTellerFactory::LockServer(BOOL fLock)
{
    VerboseMsg("In ComFortuneTellerFactory::LockServer");

    // Are we locking or unlocking?
    if (fLock) {

       // Locking
       VerboseMsg("   Incrementing server lock count");
       Counters::IncLockCount();
    }
    else {

       // Unlocking
       VerboseMsg("   Decrementing server lock count");
       Counters::DecLockCount();
    }

    return NOERROR;
}
```

Much is happening in this source file, but most of the methods that belong to the `IUnknown` interface implementation should look very familiar to you. `QueryInterface()`, `AddRef()`, and `Release()` all have implementations that are almost identical to the implementations in `ComFortuneTeller`. In fact, the implementation of `IUnknown` looks very similar across all COM classes. Oh sure, there are variations, especially between components that use containment and aggregation to support interface sharing, but generally speaking, if you've seen one `IUnknown`, you've seen them all.

That's not to say that *no* differences exist between `ComFortuneTeller::IUnknown` and `ComFortuneTellerFactory::IUnknown`. In the `ComFortuneTellerFactory`'s version of `QueryInterface()`, the only valid interface IDs that are accepted and understood are `IID_IUnknown` and `IID_IClassFactory`. `ComFortuneTellerFactory`'s `AddRef()`, however, is identical to `ComFortuneTeller`'s. (Yes, I know that the text outputted in the call to `VerboseMsg()` is different, but give me a break, won't you?) The only remaining differences between the two `IUnknown` implementations lie in `Release()`. The `ComFortuneTeller` version of `Release()` is careful to decrement the server object count before the object destroys itself. However, because class factories are not included in the server object count, the `Counters::DecObjectCount()` call is absent from `ComFortuneTellerFactory::Release()`.

You need to examine the differences between the `ComFortuneTellerFactory` and the `ComFortuneTeller` because you do things a little differently when you use a class factory to create and manage your objects, as opposed to managing them in the class itself. The really interesting part of `ComFortuneTellerFactory` is the implementation of `IClassFactory`'s two methods. Most of the action takes place inside `CreateInstance()`, which I'll reproduce here a little at a time so that you can refer to the code as I explain it.

The first thing that `CreateInstance()` does is to see whether the component is being used by another object as part of an aggregation relationship.

```
// Check for a controlling unknown
   if (pUnkOuter && rIID != IID_IUnknown)
       return CLASS_E_NOAGGREGATION;
```

As I mentioned earlier, I haven't explained how components implement aggregation relationships, so the `ComFortuneTeller` class doesn't support this feature. The `ComFortuneTellerFactory` checks whether aggregation is being used and, if it is, returns the `CLASS_E_NOAGGREGATION` error HRESULT. This, by the way, is the standard error returned when someone tries to use a component as part of an aggregation, but the component doesn't support aggregation. I will cover adding aggregation support later.

Next, `CreateInstance()` creates the new `ComFortuneTeller` object instance and checks to make sure that available memory hasn't been exhausted.

```
//Create the object passing function to notify on destruction.
pObj = new ComFortuneTeller;

// Out of memory?
if (!pObj) {
   return E_OUTOFMEMORY;
}
```

The new object instance has now been created, but remember that client applications are never given direct access to the object pointer. Instead, clients are given pointers to interfaces. Now in many cases, the pointer to the interface and the pointer to the object will be the same, but it is an important distinction all the same. At no point in the client program, for example, should you ever see a declaration of a pointer that will point to a `ComFortuneTeller` object.

```
// Bad -- Should not appear in client code (fine for server code)
ComFortuneTeller  *pFortuneTeller;
```

However, clients will often declare and use pointers to interfaces.

```
// Good -- Useful in both clients and servers
IFortuneTeller  *pIFortuneTeller;
```

Keeping this in mind, the next task for `CreateInstance()` is to obtain an interface pointer to return back to the client. The client has indicated the interface that it wants in the `rIID` variable, so obtaining the interface pointer should be as simple as calling `QueryInterface()` on the newly created object instance.

```
// Now obtain the requested interface
hResult = pObj->QueryInterface(rIID, ppvInterface);
```

```
// Destroy the object if the desired interface couldn't be obtained
if (FAILED(hResult)) {
    delete pObj;
    return hResult;
}
```

Of course, if the new object doesn't support the requested interface, the whole deal is off. The new object instance should be destroyed, and the error code is returned back to the client.

Now that the object has been successfully created and the requested interface obtained, the last remaining chore for `CreateInstance()` is to increase the server object count.

```
// Everything looks good. Bump up the server object count
Counters::IncObjectCount();
```

The only thing that `ComFortuneTellerFactory` needs now is an implementation for the `IClassFactory` method `LockServer()`, which is trivial. If the method is called with a boolean value of `TRUE`, the server lock count maintained by the `Counter` class is incremented; if the method is called with a boolean value of `FALSE`, the server lock count is decremented.

Completing the In-Process Server

The pieces are starting to fall together. You now have a complete implementation of the COM object, in addition to a functional class factory. The only remaining code left to implement are those items specific to an in-process server.

At the beginning of the chapter, I talked about issues related to how COM obtains class factories from servers and how servers communicate to COM that they are ready to be unloaded.

This is one area where in-process and local servers vary dramatically. For an in-process server (the type currently being built here), the solution to both these problems involves two functions that are exported from the server DLL. Listing 4.12 shows the implementation of `DllGetClassObject()` and `DllCanUnloadNow()` for the `IFortuneTeller` in-process server.

Listing 4.12 DLLSERV.CPP—`DllGetClassObject()` and `DllCanUnloadNow()`, the Two Functions That All In-Process Servers Must Implement

```cpp
// Get needed compiler include files
#include <iostream>

// Get needed system and custom include files
#include "Utility.h"
#include "Counts.h"
#include "Factory2.h"


//
// Function exported from in-process server DLL that is called
// by COM to obtain an interface pointer to a particular class factory.
//

STDAPI DllGetClassObject(REFCLSID rClsId,
                         REFIID rIID,
                         LPVOID* ppvInterface)
{
    HRESULT                    hResult;
    PComFortuneTellerFactory pFactory;

    VerboseMsg("In DllGetClassObject");

    // Make sure we're not being asked for
    // a class factory that we don't know about
    if (rClsId != CLSID_FortuneTeller2) {
        VerboseMsg("   COM is requesting a class
        ➥other than CLSID_FortuneTeller2");
        return E_FAIL;
    }

    // Instantiate the new class factory
    VerboseMsg("   Creating new ComFortuneTellerFactory object");
    pFactory = new ComFortuneTellerFactory;

    // Out of memory?
    if (!pFactory) {
        VerboseMsg("   ComFortuneTellerFactory object creation failed.");
        return E_OUTOFMEMORY;
    }

    // Now obtain the requested interface
    hResult = pFactory->QueryInterface(rIID, ppvInterface);

    // Destroy the factory if the desired interface
```

```
    // couldn't be obtained
    if (FAILED(hResult)) {
        delete pFactory;
        return hResult;
    }

    return NOERROR;
}


//
// Function exported from in-process server DLL that is
// called by COM to determine whether the server can be
// unloaded from memory.
//

STDAPI DllCanUnloadNow()
{
    VerboseMsg("In DllGetClassObject");
    VerboseMsg("    Server Lock Count:    " +
            ULongToANSI(Counters::GetLockCount()));
    VerboseMsg("    Server Object Count: " +
            ULongToANSI(Counters::GetObjectCount()));

    // If the server lock count and the object count are both zero,
    // the server can be unloaded
    return ((Counters::GetLockCount() == 0L &&
            Counters::GetObjectCount() == 0L) ? S_OK : S_FALSE);
}
```

DllGetClassObject()

The `DllGetClassObject()` method is called by COM whenever it needs to obtain a class factory for a given component. The function takes a class ID that identifies which class factory COM is looking for and an interface ID that identifies which interface within the factory is being requested (remember, a class factory may expose `IClassFactory` or `IClassFactory2`).The parallels between `DllGetClassObject()` and `ComFortuneTellerFactory::CreateInstance()` are significant. This shouldn't come as any surprise because you can think of `DllGetClassObject()` as the `CreateInstance()` counterpart method responsible for instantiating class factories. In fact, there are only a few substantive differences between the two pieces of code.

`DllGetClassObject()` needs to ensure that the COM subsystem is asking for a component class factory that actually resides within the current server. This check is straightforward because the class ID of the requested factory is passed as an argument into the function.

```
// Make sure we're not being asked for a class factory
// that we don't know about
if (rClsId != CLSID_FortuneTeller2) {
    return E_FAIL;
}
```

The question of whether the class is part of an aggregation is not relevant to the request for the class factory, so this logic does not appear in `DllGetClassObject()`. Apart from these two discrepancies, the rest of the function is identical to `CreateInstance()`. The function creates a new factory instance and checks to make sure that the program hasn't run out of memory. The requested interface is obtained from the factory instance, and assuming everything went smoothly, the interface pointer is returned back to the COM subsystem.

DllCanUnloadNow()

`DllCanUnloadNow()` plays counterpoint to `DllGetClassObject()`, working to communicate to the COM subsystem when it is acceptable to unload the in-process server from memory. The implementation of `DllCanUnloadNow()` (which, by the way, takes no arguments) is extremely simple and requires even less code than `DllGetClassObject()`. In fact, the entire `DllCanUnloadNow()` function can be summed up in a single line of code:

```
return ((Counters::GetLockCount() == 0L &&
        Counters::GetObjectCount() == 0L) ? S_OK : S_FALSE);
```

An in-process server can be safely unloaded if the server's object count has fallen to zero and no outstanding server locks are waiting to be released. Both these counters are tracked from within the `Counters` class and are easily accessible by calling the appropriate static `get` methods.

With `DllGetClassObject()` and `DllCanUnloadNow()` successfully exported from the in-process DLL, the server is now complete and ready for use. A COM server is useless, however, if no one knows how to use it. It's time to build a client program.

Caution

It is critical that the `DllGetClassObject()` and `DllCanUnloadNow()` functions are explicitly exported from the server DLL (you can verify this by using the DUMPBIN utility that comes with Visual C++ 6). The first time I built an in-process server, I tried desperately to export the functions by using the standard `__declspec(dllexport)` mechanism. Unfortunately, I soon realized that this strategy does not work because of collisions with the predefined function prototypes declared in the standard OLE header files. In the end, I had to admit defeat and manually export the two functions, using a standard Win32 `.DEF` file. Save yourself some frustration and don't even try to get `__declspec(dllexport)` working with `DllGetClassObject()` and `DllCanUnloadNow()`.

Building the Client

Now you finally have an in-process COM server. What you really have is a DLL that will just sit there unless someone knows how to access the server, create new objects, and then use them. In short, you need to build a client.

A *client* is any software entity that uses the COM components implemented by a COM server. Remember, the COM server is where you implement your COM class factory and COM class. The client simply uses the interface exposed by the COM objects implemented by the server. By definition, COM servers themselves can be clients of other servers. However, the simple example that I present now will be a binary executable that obtains a fortune and displays it to **cout**, just as the Fortune1 program did. No, I agree that it's not the world's most visually impressive client program, but I tend to believe that simplicity is elegance. If you feel compelled to paste an ornate graphical interface on Fortune2, please be my guest. Just remember, the main thing that you should get out of this program is an understanding of how to build a COM client application.

As far as COM is concerned, your client program is composed of at least four logical sections. In the *initialization* portion of the client, APIs are called that initialize the COM subsystem and prepare it for use. Most client programs will need to execute the initialization phase of their code only once, when the program first starts up.

In the *acquisition* portion of a program, the client obtains class factories and then uses them to create new instances of COM objects. By acquisition, I am referencing the beginning of a COM client, where you will create a class factory and request that it create an object and return you an interface pointer to that COM object so that you can do some work with the COM object. Clients might opt to streamline this process by using various COM APIs that enable you to skip over the process of explicitly obtaining a class factory and instead let you create new COM objects directly. (I'll demonstrate both methods.)

The *usage* portion of a program takes the objects obtained in the acquisition phase and actually uses them. By usage, I am referring to the point at which you actually use the COM object to do some work for you. The client will typically query the objects for particular interfaces and then invoke methods on those interfaces that are required to satisfy the functional requirements of the client. Of course, any client program of appreciable size will probably bounce between the acquisition and usage phases many times during the run of the program.

The final phase of the program, *termination*, occurs as the client is shutting down and prepares to end. During this phase, a socially responsible COM client will call APIs that uninitialize the COM subsystem and indicate that the client program will not need COM again.

Because the Fortune2 client program is so short, I'll show the code to you here. The next few sections guide you through each of the client application sections, explaining the programming in more detail. Without further ado, take a look at Listing 4.13, which shows the client code for the Fortune2 program.

Listing 4.13   CLIENT2.CPP—Client Code for the Fortune2 Program

```cpp
#include <iostream>
#define INITGUID
#include "Utility.h"
#include "IFortune.h"

int main()
{
    HRESULT         hResult;
    IClassFactory   *pIClassFactory;
    IFortuneTeller  *pIFortuneTeller;
    BSTR            bstrFortune;
    LPSTR           pszFortune;

    cout << "Fortune2 - Simple COM Fortune Client Program\n";

    // Prepare COM for use
    VerboseMsg("Calling COM API CoInitialize.");
    hResult = CoInitialize(NULL);
    if (FAILED(hResult)) {
        ReportError("Could not initialize COM.", hResult);
        return 1;
    }

    // Retrieve the FortuneTeller class factory
    VerboseMsg("Requesting FortuneTeller class factory.");
    hResult = CoGetClassObject(CLSID_FortuneTeller2,
                               CLSCTX_INPROC_SERVER,
                               NULL, IID_IClassFactory,
                               (void**) &pIClassFactory);
    if (FAILED(hResult)) {
        ReportError("Could not obtain FortuneTeller
                ➥class factory.", hResult);
        return 1;
    }

    // Create a new FortuneTeller object and return an IFortuneTeller
    // interface pointer
    VerboseMsg("Creating new FortuneTeller object instance.");
    hResult = pIClassFactory->CreateInstance(NULL, IID_IFortuneTeller,
                                        (void**) &pIFortuneTeller);
    if (FAILED(hResult)) {
        ReportError("Could not create a new FortuneTeller
        ➥object.", hResult);
        return 1;
    }

    // We're done with the class factory
    VerboseMsg("Releasing FortuneTeller class factory.");
    pIClassFactory->Release();
    pIClassFactory = NULL;
```

```
// Get our fortune, in BSTR form
VerboseMsg("Getting fortune from FortuneTeller object.");
pIFortuneTeller->GetFortune(&bstrFortune);

// Convert the fortune into a regular string
VerboseMsg("Translating fortune from Unicode to ANSI text.");
UnicodeToAnsi(bstrFortune, &pszFortune);

// Show the user the fortune
cout << "\"" << pszFortune << "\"" << endl;

// Release the memory for both the ANSI string and the BSTR
VerboseMsg("Releasing fortune and BSTR strings.");
CoTaskMemFree(pszFortune);
SysFreeString(bstrFortune);

// We're done with the FortuneTeller object
VerboseMsg("Releasing FortuneTeller object.");
pIFortuneTeller->Release();
pIFortuneTeller = NULL;

// We're all done with COM
CoUninitialize();

return 0;
}
```

Initialization

Every client program (and every local server as well) needs to initialize the COM subsystem before using it. This task is performed by a single call to the COM API `CoInitialize()`. The `CoInitialize()` function prepares the COM subsystem for use by the current process. Internally, the `CoInitialize()` function allocates a variety of data structures that will hold important information specific to your use of COM. `CoInitialize()` determines your program's process number and uses this as a unique ID by which it can track the progress of your program's COM-related activities. `CoInitialize()` takes a single pointer argument, which should always be set NULL.

```
// Prepare COM for use
   VerboseMsg("Calling COM API CoInitialize.");
   hResult = CoInitialize(NULL);
   if (FAILED(hResult)) {
      ReportError("Could not initialize COM.", hResult);
      return 1;
   }
```

`CoInitialize()` needs to be called only once for every process, but you won't hurt anything if you call it multiple times. The first time that the function is called successfully, the API will return S_OK. Subsequent calls to `CoInitialize()` will return S_FALSE, signifying that COM is already initialized and ready to go.

Caution

When an application calls `CoInitialize()`, the unstated assumption is that any objects acquired in the current thread of execution may only be used within that thread. In other words, calling `CoInitialize()` essentially restricts you to using COM in a single-threaded manner. You may be relieved to hear that Windows NT 4.0 does support true, multithreaded COM applications; it just requires some extra work on your part. For now, remember that you will have to call `CoInitialize()` inside every thread that will be using COM.

Retrieving an Interface Pointer to the `Fortuneteller` Object

After a client has initialized COM, it's ready to rock-and-roll. The next step is to actually create an instance of a COM component. This is accomplished using several standard COM APIs.

As I've mentioned many times in this chapter, new COM objects are created using a partnered class factory. Creating a new object, therefore, is as simple as obtaining access to a class factory and then using the factory's `CreateInstance()` method to instantiate a new COM object. The first part of this process, obtaining the factory, is achieved by a call to the COM API `CoGetClassObject()`.

```
// Retrieve the FortuneTeller class factory
hResult = CoGetClassObject(CLSID_FortuneTeller2,
                           CLSCTX_INPROC_SERVER,
                           NULL, IID_IClassFactory,
                           (void**) &pClassFactory);
if (FAILED(hResult)) {
   ReportError("Could not obtain FortuneTeller class
   ➥factory.", hResult);
   return 1;
}
```

The `CoGetClassObject()` function accepts a number of important arguments that dictate how the class factory will be obtained. The first argument is the class ID that specifies exactly which factory you want to get your hands on. This is the same class ID that will eventually end up percolating its way into your in-process server's `DllGetClassObject()` function.

The next argument indicates the type of server with which you want to be connected. Your program passes a value—or several values logically ORed together—that is a member of the CLSCTX enumeration. Each value in the CLSCTX enumeration corresponds to a particular type of COM or OLE server. If you pass multiple CLSCTX values into `CoGetClassObject()`, you are indicating that any of the indicated server types are acceptable to you.

The most commonly used COM server types are **CLSCTX_INPROC_SERVER**, **CLSCTX_LOCAL_SERVER**, and **CLSCTX_REMOTE_SERVER**. Each of these CLSCTX values corresponds to in-process, local, and remote server implementations, respectively (as if you couldn't have figured that one out on your own). Additionally, there is the **CLSCTX_SERVER** value, which is just an ORing of all three COM server types. When your program passes a value of **CLSCTX_SERVER** in to **CoGetClassObject()**, you are indicating that you don't really care what type of server you get hooked up with; you just want a server that can service the class you're interested in. Because you know that the FortuneTeller2 server is an in-process–only server, the Fortune2 client passes in a value of **CLSCTX_INPROC_SERVER** for this parameter. The client works equally as well, however, if you pass in **CLSCTX_SERVER** or any other value that includes **CLSCTX_INPROC_SERVER**.

The third parameter passed into **CoGetClassObject()** is used to indicate what machine the server is running on if you intend to use a remote server implementation. In other words, if you are using DCOM to access a server located on another machine, this is where you would specify which machine the server is running on. Hold that thought. I'll be returning to this very parameter value later in Part II, "Stepping Up to Distributed COM," when I start to detail how to migrate your applications to DCOM. For now, because your server is in-process, the client program should specify a **NULL** value for **CoGetClassObject()**'s third parameter.

The fourth parameter indicates which class factory interface you want to acquire. Although the standard COM interfaces for class factories are **IClassFactory** and **IClassFactory2**, there isn't anything to prevent you from creating a custom class factory interface. When dealing with an in-process server for the first time, COM simply passes the requested interface ID through to the server's **DllGetClassObject()** method. At that point, your class factory is free to return any interface pointer that the client has requested, even if it isn't an **IClassFactory** or an **IClassFactory2**.

The final parameter passed into **CoGetClassObject()** is the address of the interface pointer that you want the class factory interface to be returned in. Assuming that the call to **CoGetClassObject()** succeeds, the pointer address passed in to the function will come back as an interface pointer that you can then use to create new object instances.

This is exactly what the Fortune2 client does. After the client has obtained a pointer to the factory's **IClassFactory** interface, a new object is created with a call to **CreateInstance()**.

```
// Create a new FortuneTeller object and return an IFortuneTeller
   // interface pointer
   VerboseMsg("Creating new FortuneTeller object instance.");
   hResult = pIClassFactory->CreateInstance(NULL, IID_IFortuneTeller,
                                            (void**) &pIFortuneTeller);
   if (FAILED(hResult)) {
      ReportError("Could not create a new FortuneTeller
      ➥object.", hResult);
      return 1;
   }

   // We're done with the class factory
   pIClassFactory->Release();
   pIClassFactory = NULL;
```

This call to `CreateInstance()` should look familiar after the discussion of the `ComFortuneTellerFactory` implementation. This method creates a new `ComFortuneTeller` component and returns the object's `IFortuneTeller` interface pointer. After the new object has been created, there's no need to keep the factory around, so the client releases the factory interface pointer and sets it to `NULL`.

Now that I've explained the component creation process, I want to show you a shortcut. Although it is still the preferred method for creating lots of objects all at once, the `CoGetClassObject/CreateInstance` method is a little complicated if you simply want to create a single new instance of a COM component. The good news is that you can combine the two steps of obtaining a class factory and then calling `CreateInstance()` by using the COM API `CoCreateInstance()`. As you will see, the `CoCreateInstance()` function combines aspects of both `CoGetClassObject()` and `CreateInstance()`.

```
// Create a new FortuneTeller object and return an IFortuneTeller
// interface pointer
hResult = CoCreateInstance(CLSID_FortuneTeller2,
                           NULL, CLSCTX_INPROC_SERVER,
                           IID_IFortuneTeller,
                           (void**) &pIFortuneTeller);
if (FAILED(hResult)) {
   ReportError("Could not create a new FortuneTeller
   ➥object.", hResult);
   return 1;
}
```

Note

For your convenience, I've provided a version of the `CLIENT2.CPP` source file that uses the `CoCreateInstance()` API. The new source file is named `CLIENT2B.CPP` and can be found in the `\Chap4\Fortune2\Client` directory. Note that the Fortune2 client project uses the `CLIENT2.CPP` file by default. If you want to rebuild the client using `CLIENT2B.CPP`, you'll have to remove `CLIENT2.CPP` from the project and then add `CLIENT2B.CPP`.

Let's quickly review the arguments that you pass in to this function.

- The first parameter is the class ID of the factory that should be used to create the new object instance; it corresponds to the first parameter passed in to the `CoGetClassObject()`.

- The second parameter is a pointer to a wrapping object's `IUnknown` interface; this argument corresponds to the first parameter passed in to `IClassFactory::CreateInstance()`.

- The third parameter is a CLSCTX enumerated value that tells COM what type of server you expect to service the object creation request; it corresponds to the second argument passed in to `CoGetClassObject()`.

- The fourth argument is the interface ID being requested from the new object; this parameter corresponds to the second parameter passed in to `CreateInstance()`.

- Finally, the fifth argument is the address of a pointer used as an output parameter for the returned interface pointer; it corresponds to the last argument passed in to `CreateInstance()`.

As you can see, with the `CoCreateInstance()` API, everything old is new again. Clearly, `CoCreateInstance()` isn't doing anything too tricky. In fact, you could almost intuit what the implementation of `CoCreateInstance()` must look like. Listing 4.14 shows my best guess at what the Microsoft code for `CoCreateInstance()` resembles.

Listing 4.14   CREATE.CPP—A Speculative Implementation of the `CoCreateInstance()` API

```
STDAPI MyCreateInstance(REFCLSID rClsId,
                        LPUNKNOWN pUnkOuter,
                        DWORD dwClsContext,
                        REFIID rIID,
                        LPVOID *ppvInterface)
{
    HRESULT         hResult;
    IClassFactory   *pIClassFactory;

    // Initialize returned interface pointer
    *ppvInterface = NULL;

    // Retrieve the class factory
    hResult = CoGetClassObject(rClsId, dwClsContext,
                               NULL, IID_IClassFactory,
                               (void**) &pIClassFactory);
    if (FAILED(hResult))
       return hResult;

    // Create the new object
    hResult = pIClassFactory->CreateInstance(NULL, rIID, ppvInterface);
    if (FAILED(hResult))
       return hResult;

    // We're done with the class factory
    pIClassFactory->Release();

    return hResult;
}
```

Looks familiar, doesn't it? All I did was cut and paste the code from the Fortune2 client program, remove any references to the fortune telling component, and rename a couple of variables.

Usage

After your application has obtained an interface pointer for a new object, the next step is to use it. Of course, how you use a particular object will completely depend on what interfaces the component supports and what your program wants to accomplish. In the case of the Fortune2 client, the program simply calls the **IFortuneTeller**'s single method, GetFortune(), and then jumps through the necessary hoops to translate the returned BSTR into a human-readable string.

```
// Get our fortune, in BSTR form
pIFortuneTeller->GetFortune(&bstrFortune);

// Convert the fortune into a regular string
UnicodeToAnsi(bstrFortune, &pszFortune);

// Show the user the fortune
cout << "\"" << pszFortune << "\"" << endl;

// Release the memory for both the ANSI string and the BSTR
CoTaskMemFree(pszFortune);
SysFreeString(bstrFortune);

// We're done with the FortuneTeller object
pIFortuneTeller->Release();
pIFortuneTeller = NULL;
```

Like all good COM clients, note how the Fortune2 program makes sure to call **Release()** on interface pointers that will no longer be used.

Termination

Finally, COM client applications need to ensure that they terminate in a clean fashion and that the COM subsystem is notified that the client will no longer be requiring COM services. After an application determines that no COM objects are in use any longer and every interface pointer has been appropriately released, the program terminates the COM subsystem by calling **CoUninitialize()**. This API function spins off a modal message loop that ensures that no outstanding COM messages are waiting to be processed—recall that, like client programs, local servers also need to call `CoInitialize()` and `CoUninitialize()`—and makes sure that the data structures that were initially allocated by COM when your program called `CoInitialize()` are correctly released. In fact, every call to `CoInitialize()` should have a matching call to `CoUninitialize()`.

```
// We're all done with COM
CoUninitialize();
```

With the termination phase complete, the program is free to shut down the rest of its operations and end. Although Fortune2 is not an elaborate application, it demonstrates the fundamental steps undertaken by a COM client. Sure, Fortune2 is about as simple a client program as you'll ever see, but you're going to find yourself using the basic techniques employed by Fortune2 over and over again in your own COM programs.

Registering the Server

Finally! Now that the server is built and the client implemented, it's time to sample the fruits of your labor. After building the in-process server DLL and the client program, testing the whole system is as simple as running the Fortune2 client program—or is it?

```
C:\fortune2
Fortune2 - Simple COM Fortune Client Program
VERBOSE: Calling COM API CoInitialize.
VERBOSE: Requesting FortuneTeller class factory.
Error: "Could not obtain FortuneTeller class factory."
HRESULT: 0x80040154

C:\
```

The problem is that although you have built a perfectly valid client and server, the crucial object-matchmaking service that COM provides, and that I spoke about at the beginning of the chapter, doesn't know how to connect the client program up to the requested server. If you look in the `WINERROR.H` header file, you'll find that error 0x80040154 corresponds to `REGDB_E_CLASSNOTREG`. The client program is not working because the server has not been registered.

OLEView: Your New Best Friend

For some time, COM and OLE programmers have been using the indispensable OLEView utility. OLEView, a browser that enables you to examine all the COM servers installed on your system, ships with Visual C++ 6.

COM and OLE maintain all their configuration information inside the system Registry. Although this data is structured in a reasonably sane manner, the sheer volume and scope of the data make managing this information by using `REGEDIT` a real pain. OLEView, on the other hand, puts a pretty face on the task of maintaining COM/OLE–related Registry entries. However, OLEView is much more than just a pretty face. Browsing your system using OLEView often gives you significant and new insights into how COM operates and, in many cases, how other COM programmers have designed and implemented their COM components. You *will* find that OLEView is your new best friend.

Registry Fundamentals

Class registration information is stored inside the system Registry. You can think of the Registry as a giant tree of data, with named branches that are referred to by a key. Each portion of the key refers to a node that is termed a *subkey*. Each subkey can have associated with it a collection of data attributes that are referred to as *values*. A value itself is composed of three pieces: a name, a type, and the value data. Take a close look at the following example, which shows a breakdown of the HKEY_CURRENT_USER\Console\Command Prompt key:

```
HKEY_CURRENT_USER
Value: "Default"      (Value not set)


                    \Console
                    Value: "Default"      (Value not set)
                    Value: "CursorSize"   REG_DWORD   0x00000019


                            \Command Prompt
                            Value: "Default"      (Value not set)
                            Value: "FaceName"     REG_SZ      "Terminal"
                            Value: "FullScreen"   REG_DWORD   0x00000001
```

In this example the HKEY_CURRENT_USER\Console\Command Prompt key is composed of three subkeys: HKEY_CURRENT_USER, Console, and Command Prompt. In the system Registry, all subkeys have at least one value that is called the *default value*. Most Registry subkeys do not have any data stored in the default value; if you open the REGEDIT Registry browsing utility, you'll see that for many subkeys, the default value is noted as not being set. Many of the subkeys used by COM, however, make use of the default value.

Two of these sample subkeys, Console and Command Prompt, have values associated with them, apart from the default value. The Console subkey has a single value named CursorSize. The CursorSize value is of type REG_DWORD, which indicates that the value's data is contained within a single 4-byte chunk of memory. In this case, the value's actual data is the number 0x00000019.

The Command Prompt subkey has two values. The FullScreen value is a DWORD that is currently set to one. The FaceName value is of type REG_SZ, which indicates that the value is stored as a NULL-terminated string. The data for this value is the string, Terminal.

COM Classes and the Registry

COM stores a tremendous amount of information about its servers. Still more information is maintained by other OLE subsystems. When taken as a whole, the OLE Registry tree can be overwhelming, but luckily, you need be concerned about only a few special keys for now.

COM classes are registered beneath the `HKEY_CLASSES_ROOT\CLSID` key. Each class is listed as a subkey off `HKEY_CLASSES_ROOT\CLSID`, where the name of the class subkey corresponds to the class GUID. In the case of the fortune teller example, the `FortuneTeller2` CLSID is the same as the `CLSID_FortuneTeller2` GUID `89A48671-20B3-11d0-8B80-EA9EFFE6330C`. By convention, the class subkey is surrounded by braces; for `FortuneTeller2`, the new subkey would look like the following:

`HKEY_CLASSES_ROOT\CLSID\{89A48671-20B3-11d0-8B80-EA9EFFE6330C}`

Note

By the way, don't try to enter this information into the Registry by using `REGEDIT`. I've provided `REGEDIT` scripts, called REG files, on the book's CD-ROM. You can customize and use them to enter all your Registry information at once.

In COM, the default value for the class subkey contains a string that names your component in a friendly, human-readable form. By convention, the default value of a subkey is depicted using an equal sign, like so:

`\{89A48671-20B3-11d0-8B80-EA9EFFE6330C} = "FortuneTeller2 Object"`

The class subkey has several critical subkeys hanging off it, which will vary depending on the type of server being registered. For `FortuneTeller2`, which is served by an in-process server, you want to add the `InprocServer32` subkey. The `InprocServer32` subkey should have a default value of type REG_SZ, which contains the fully qualified path and DLL name of the `FortuneTeller2` server. It's very important that the pathname be fully qualified and point to the exact location of the DLL. COM will refuse to load the server if this information is not supplied at this level of detail. Therefore, assuming that you have moved the `Fort2Srv.DLL` file into the `C:\COM Servers` directory, the `InprocServer32` subkey should look like this:

```
\
  {89A48671-20B3-11d0-8B80-EA9EFFE6330C}\
                    InprocServer32 = "C:\COM Servers\Fort2Srv.DLL"
```

Although technically speaking, this is the only entry you need to make in the Registry for the client program to function correctly now, another entry should be present. Like `InprocServer32`, the `NotInsertable` subkey also hangs off the main class subkey. `NotInsertable` prevents the name of the component from appearing in OLE dialog boxes that are used when inserting objects into compound documents. Although placing `NotInsertable` into the Registry is not, strictly speaking, required for the `FortuneTeller2` component to work correctly, it helps communicate to anyone browsing the Registry that this class does not support insertion into OLE documents.

Caution

Because I don't know where you are building the code that has shipped on this book's CD-ROM, you will need to modify each Registry script that I have supplied for server registration. The paths specified within the scripts are sample paths only and might not correspond to the locations on your hard drive where you placed your COM servers. If you do not make these Registry script modifications, the sample client programs will not work, even if you have run the scripts through **REGEDIT**.

Now don't get me wrong. There are many other Registry entries that the `FortuneTeller2` component could add to the Registry. None, however, would functionally change how the component operates. As you start to build progressively more sophisticated components, additional Registry entries will be required. For now, and I stress that this is only for now, the `InprocServer32` and `NotInsertable` subkeys are all that matter (and even now, `NotInsertable` could be left out without suffering any ill effects).

Now, with the Registry entries in place, you are finally ready to run your client for the first time. When run on my home machine (just a second ago), the Fortune2 program blurts out the following:

```
C:\fortune2
Fortune2 - Simple COM Fortune Client Program
"You are strong in perspiration and odor."

C:\
```

Ah, the sweet smell of success. I don't know about you, but I don't mind being insulted by a computer when I wrote the program that's giving me lip.

Summary

It has been a long road, but in this chapter you followed the construction of a COM client and server from inception to implementation. The concepts and techniques covered in this chapter have been presented at a low level, but most of the information that you've covered here will end up serving you well as you work through later chapters.

CHAPTER 5

COM PROGRAMMING WITH MFC

In this chapter, you will learn about the following:

- COM objects that expose multiple interfaces
- How to use interface maps to register nested handler classes

Now that you have a good feeling for COM basics, I want to turn your attention to how the Microsoft Foundation Class libraries can help make the sometimes arduous task of COM programming easier.

Many programmers think of MFC as a class library primarily focused on building graphical user interfaces, and I would be hard pressed to argue with them. However, a ton of OLE code is in MFC, and it would be a mistake to characterize MFC as a one-trick pony. Much of MFC's OLE code is concerned with ActiveX controls and documents, which I do not cover in this book, but there is core MFC functionality that exists purely for the sake of building COM clients and servers. It is this core COM functionality that you'll learn about in this chapter.

An Introduction to the MFC

Microsoft started development of MFC in the early nineties when object-oriented programming—and development in C++ specifically—was becoming more and more prevalent. At the time, Microsoft wasn't even selling a C++ compiler, and most Windows and OS/2 programming was done in C. Borland, Microsoft's fiercest rival in the arena of programming tools and languages, was successfully pushing C++ as a mainstream programming language for DOS, and it was clear to many developers that C++ was on the verge of displacing C as the professional's language of choice.

The original MFC development team wasn't even called the *MFC team*; it was the AFX group. *AFX* stands for *Application Frameworks*, which underscores the team's original charter. AFX was to be an elegant set of C++ application infrastructures that would help developers conquer the Windows learning curve and provide a central resource for reusable source code. Unfortunately for the AFX team, when it finally released the first version of AFX for internal use by other Microsoft development, one thing was clear. AFX was too complicated for novice programmers.

To be fair, I've heard several different accounts of what the first version of AFX was really like. Some say that AFX was actually an elegantly abstracted view of what a windowing system should be. AFX contained a lot of technology that was (and in some cases, still is) ahead of its time. Unfortunately, with its own completely new windowing system and garbage collection scheme, AFX had very little to do with Windows programming. Instead, AFX had become a utopian view of what Windows programming should be like—except that writing AFX programs was prohibitively complicated and the resulting programs were invariably large and slow.

It was back to the drawing board for the AFX team. This time the marching orders were clear; the class libraries, now rechristened *MFC*, had to be easily approachable for novice programmers and experienced Windows developers alike. Above all else, the new MFC libraries were to be small and fast.

Ironically, after MFC 1.0 was publicly released in 1992, many object-oriented programmers howled that MFC was too much like the underlying Windows API and didn't go far enough in hiding the messy details that were part and parcel of every Windows application. However, for the majority of C++ers, who either didn't care or were more concerned with building programs than fighting holy wars, MFC hit a chord. MFC was fast and relatively small, and it did help make writing Windows programs easier.

Over the years, Microsoft has evolved MFC in much the same way that it has evolved its operating systems. As new technologies and feature sets have been integrated into the underlying OS, MFC has grown to accommodate the new functionality. With its intimate knowledge of, and close ties to, the other development groups at Microsoft, the MFC team has been able to support new operating-system features in MFC long before its competitors. In fact, MFC has flourished and is now the preeminent class library available for Windows programming.

MFC and OLE/ActiveX

I've talked elsewhere about how Microsoft has clearly and unambiguously fingered DCOM and OLE/ActiveX as the cornerstones of a far-reaching and comprehensive technology vision. With DCOM and ActiveX playing such a prominent role in Microsoft's future, it should come as no surprise that MFC is central to Microsoft's strategy for getting DCOM and ActiveX technologies into the hands of the masses of developers who build applications for Windows operating systems. MFC, now in version 6.0, has supported OLE 2.0 since MFC 2.5 was released in 1993. Perhaps more importantly, each new release of MFC adds a host of new capabilities that leverage MFC's support for OLE to help deploy new ActiveX and Internet-related feature sets. Nowhere is the convergence of the Internet and OLE more apparent than in MFC.

Much of the OLE code found within MFC is concerned with supporting ActiveX controls and documents. Despite what some people would have you believe, even with a host of wizards and generated code, an ActiveX control is a sophisticated piece of software.

The ActiveX Template Library

Microsoft has another story to tell when it comes to building COM objects by using a C++ framework. Microsoft has formally introduced a new C++ framework, called the *ActiveX Template Library* (ATL), that now comes with Visual C++. The ATL is a new framework, independent of MFC, that programmers can use to build fast and efficient COM object classes.

The ATL uses C++ templates to write COM objects. ATL approaches the problem of building COM components from a new and completely original point of view. The fundamental techniques used by the ATL are different from MFC, but the underlying fundamental principles of COM are the same.

If MFC is so great and its future so bright, why has Microsoft added ATL to the component-building equation? For a couple of reasons. MFC makes the construction of COM objects much easier than if you had to code the classes yourself, from scratch. On the other hand, building those classes by using the ATL is even easier than using MFC. Because the ATL approach relies on C++ templates, COM objects built with the ATL appear a little more intuitive to the experienced C++ programmer. ATL has also been carefully designed to be as small as possible and doesn't require that you include a class library DLL with your application. Finally, ATL also provides native support for some of the new COM threading models that made their appearance with Windows NT 4.0.

Much debate continues about which COM approach is better: generic COM (as in Chapter 4, "Implementing a COM Client and Server"), MFC, or now ATL (which is not discussed in this book). Keep in mind, they are all good approaches. Consider them all options in your COM programming arsenal. I've found that a good rule of thumb is to look at the graphical user interface (GUI) requirements of your COM objects. If your objects have any sort of GUI requirements or you plan on using your objects in Visual C++ projects that build ActiveX controls, MFC offers more support. If, on the other hand, you simply need an elegant way to write COM object classes that have no user interface requirements, I encourage you to take a close look at the ATL. Last, if you really need speed and portability, but can sacrifice the time necessary to write COM objects this way, use generic COM.

Schizophrenic Components and Their Multiple Interfaces

Any presentation of MFC's COM support has to begin with a discussion of how components expose multiple interfaces. At first, you're liable to find this a little strange. After all, in the last chapter, you built a fully functional in-process COM server with a small touch on the topic of multiple interfaces. It seems only logical that you do something similar in this chapter, but simply substitute MFC where appropriate.

As it turns out, MFC's COM support is intrinsically bound to how MFC supports multiple interfaces. First, you must become familiar with building components that expose multiple interfaces anyway (and, no, `IUnknown` does not count as a second interface for the purpose of this discussion). Certainly, if you aspire to building applications that integrate with higher-level OLE and ActiveX technologies, exposing multiple interfaces will have to become second nature to you. Finally, MFC makes the task of exposing multiple interfaces a snap. You see, learning about multiple interfaces is your next logical step toward total DCOM enlightenment.

Multiple-Interface Support Is Not Aggregation

I want to underscore that building a component that exposes multiple interfaces is not the same as creating components by using aggregation. In previous chapters, I noted that the technique of aggregation is used in COM to simulate implementation inheritance. Keep in mind that multiple-interface support is just a way for a single component to expose several different interfaces, each of which the component is responsible for implementing and supporting. Although on the surface it might appear that aggregation supports a similar goal, when a component uses aggregation to expose multiple interfaces, it's actually relying on contained subcomponents to provide the implementation for interfaces that it exposes as its own. For now, you are concerned only with exposing multiple interfaces in which only a single COM class is involved.

Multiple Interfaces and Multiple Inheritance

I need to touch first on multiple inheritance. Intuitively, it would seem that using multiple inheritance would be a perfect candidate for implementing multiple interfaces (even the names sound similar). To illustrate my point, imagine a SportsCar component that exposes two custom interfaces, ISteerable and ICar. Listing 5.1 shows what these interfaces might look like.

Listing 5.1   ICARSTUFF.H—Two Interfaces That a COM SportsCar Object Might Want to Expose

```
DECLARE_INTERFACE_(ISteerable, IUnknown)
{
    STDMETHOD(TurnLeft)() PURE;
    STDMETHOD(TurnRight)() PURE;
    STDMETHOD(UTurn)() PURE;
};

DECLARE_INTERFACE_(ICar, IUnknown)
{
    STDMETHOD(StartIgnition)() PURE;
    STDMETHOD(Accelerate)() PURE;
    STDMETHOD(Brake)() PURE;
    STDMETHOD(PopHood)() PURE;
```

```
    STDMETHOD(CheckOil)() PURE;
};
```

This interface partitioning makes a certain amount of sense. Many objects can be steered, but not necessarily automobiles (ships, bicycles, elephants, and so on). Separating out the steering protocol is a logical abstraction.

Now, it would seem that multiple inheritance could be used to easily bind both these interfaces into a single component class. Listing 5.2 shows how you might do this.

Listing 5.2   SPORTCAR.H—The Declaration for a COM SportsCar Class That Exposes Both ISteerable and ICar

```
class ComSportsCar : public ISteerable, public ICar
{
public:

    // IUnknown
    STDMETHOD(QueryInterface)(REFIID, LPVOID*);
    STDMETHOD_(ULONG, AddRef)();
    STDMETHOD_(ULONG, Release)();

    // ISteerable
    STDMETHODIMP TurnLeft();
    STDMETHODIMP TurnRight();
    STDMETHODIMP UTurn();

    // ICar
    STDMETHODIMP StartIgnition();
    STDMETHODIMP Accelerate();
    STDMETHODIMP Brake();
    STDMETHODIMP PopHood();
    STDMETHODIMP CheckOil();

protected:

    // Reference count
    ULONG m_cRef;
};
```

Why doesn't COM support this sort of construct? Well, actually COM does enable you to use multiple inheritance in exactly this fashion. The MFC supports multiple interfaces, and it doesn't use multiple inheritance. There is a good reason why Microsoft forsook the use of a built-in and readily accessible language feature of multiple inheritance in favor of multiple interfaces.

Generally speaking, many of the arguments against using multiple inheritance for COM and DCOM programming are the same as the arguments against using multiple inheritance in general. The problems associated with multiple inheritance are well documented, but I will briefly explain some of the most serious MFC-related and COM-related problems that face the programmer who makes use of multiple inheritance.

The Clash of the Symbols

The first problem that I'll discuss is related to duplicate symbols. Specifically, what happens when you want to inherit from two different interface classes, but both classes contain a method with the same name. Take a look at Listing 5.3. In this file, you will find the declaration of two interfaces, ICircle and IWindow. Presumably, the ICircle interface is for objects that can be rendered to the screen in some circular format. The IWindow interface, on the other hand, looks like a standard interface for any component that wants to display itself in a standard user-interface window.

Listing 5.3 COLLIDE.H—Two Separate Interfaces with Duplicate Method Names

```
DECLARE_INTERFACE_(ICircle, IUnknown)
{
    STDMETHOD(SetRadius)        (ULONG ulRadius) PURE;
    STDMETHOD(CalcArea)         (PFLOAT pfltArea) PURE;
    STDMETHOD(CalcCircumference)(PFLOAT pfltCircum) PURE;
    STDMETHOD(Draw)             () PURE;
};

DECLARE_INTERFACE_(IWindow, IUnknown)
{
    STDMETHOD(Initialize)       (ULONG ulXPos, ULONG ulYPos,
                                 ULONG ulWidth, ULONG ulHeight);
    STDMETHOD(SetTitleBarText)  (BSTR bstrTitleText);
    STDMETHOD(SetVertScrollBar) (BOOL boolVertScrool);
    STDMETHOD(SetHorzScrollBar) (BOOL boolHorzScrool);
    STDMETHOD(Draw)             () PURE;
};
```

Both these interfaces seem reasonable in their own right. However, imagine a component that wants to expose both these interfaces. Using multiple inheritance here causes a problem with the Draw() method. There need to be two functional representations of Draw(): one as it applies to the Circle interface and one as it applies to the Window interface. However, when the two Draw() method prototypes are identical, the compiler will allow the programmer to provide only a single implementation of Draw(). That means that it's impossible for you to provide one Draw() method that operates in one way if the user obtained the object pointer through QueryInterface(IID_ICircle...) and operates in a different way if the object pointer was obtained through QueryInterface(IID_IWindow...).

Can you think of a set of methods that would experience this symbol crash in every single COM object you built? How about QueryInterface(), AddRef(), and Release()? Because every interface inherits from the IUnknown, every use of multiple inheritance will have collisions on IUnknown's methods. Practically speaking, this might not be as much of a problem as might appear at first glance. After all, the IUnknown methods are pretty much boilerplate and follow the same general structure every time. AddRef() and Release() reference count, QueryInterface() checks for valid arguments and returns a pointer to this. Unfortunately, some sophisticated applications might want to reference count at the interface level, as opposed to the object level. A component might need to separately track how many ICircle and IWindow interface pointers have been returned to the client. This becomes impossible in a multiple inheritance situation because only one set of methods would be used to implement the IUnknown interface and your code would never be able to divine whether it was called through an ICircle interface or an IWindow interface.

Exposing Multiple Interfaces by Using Nested Classes

MFC doesn't use multiple inheritance to support multiple interfaces. Fine. That still doesn't explain how MFC *does* support multiple inheritance, although you probably have a good idea, based on the name of this section. Yes, MFC uses the concept of nested classes to support multiple interfaces. The first time I heard this, I was impressed. After all, it's a clever idea. The more I thought about it, though, the more I realized that the nested class approach was going to require a bit of programmatic wizardry to pull it off. Let's take a look.

The Fortune3 Sample Program

To illustrate the construction of an MFC COM class that exposes multiple interfaces, I'm going to resurrect the Fortune sample program. The new sample program, Fortune3, will still allow the user to obtain a life-enriching fortune. However, the new version will also support a new interface that returns quotations. The IQuotation interface is shown in Listing 5.4. The IFortuneTeller interface remains unchanged from the Fortune3 program, so I won't show you it again.

Listing 5.4   IQUOTE.H—The Declaration of the IQuotation Interface

```
#ifndef IQUOTE_H
#define IQUOTE_H

// Get needed include files
#include "GUIDs.h"

// New interface declaration
DECLARE_INTERFACE_(IQuotation, IUnknown)
{
  // IFortuneTeller
  STDMETHOD(GetQuotation)(/* out */ PBSTR, /* out */ PBSTR) PURE;
};

typedef IQuotation* PIQuotation;

#endif
```

As you can plainly see, the IQuotation interface is virtually identical to IFortuneTeller. For the sake of this sample program, I distinguish a quotation from a fortune by the fact that every quotation has a known author. Therefore, the `IQuotation` interface enables the client to obtain a quotation and the quotation's author by calling the `GetQuotation()` method.

The new `ComFortuneTeller` class will be a COM component built by using MFC that supports both the `IFortuneTeller` and `IQuotation` interfaces. The new client program will also be an MFC program (albeit, with a minimalist implementation) that will randomly display a fortune or a quotation.

The MFC Version of `ComFortuneTeller`

From a functional standpoint, the new and improved MFC version of `ComFortuneTeller` will need to fulfill the same implementation responsibilities as the non-MFC version had to. The Fortune3 `ComFortuneTeller` will still need to provide implementations of `IUnknown`, in addition to providing the logic for both the `IFortuneTeller` and `IQuotation` interfaces. Although MFC can lend a little help with the construction of the custom interfaces, you'll find that MFC makes implementing `IUnknown` a no-brainer.

Let's start out by going over the `ComFortuneTeller` header file. Listing 5.5 shows the declaration of the new `ComFortuneTeller` class. Don't be intimidated by all the macros. I realize that this version of `ComFortuneTeller` appears much different than the class I presented to you in the last chapter, but in truth you'll find that the new version has much in common with its Chapter 4 cousin.

Listing 5.5   FORTUNE3.H—The Declaration of the MFC `ComFortuneTeller` Class

```
#ifndef FORTUNE_H
#define FORTUNE_H

// Get needed include files
#include "IFortune.h"
#include "IQuote.h"


class ComFortuneTeller : public CCmdTarget
{
public:

    // Constructor and destructor
    ComFortuneTeller();
    virtual ~ComFortuneTeller();

protected:

    // IFortuneTeller members
    BEGIN_INTERFACE_PART(CInnerFortune, IFortuneTeller)
        STDMETHOD(GetFortune)(PBSTR);
    END_INTERFACE_PART(CInnerFortune)

    // IQuotation members
    BEGIN_INTERFACE_PART(CInnerQuote, IQuotation)
        STDMETHOD(GetQuotation)(PBSTR, PBSTR);
```

```
    END_INTERFACE_PART(CInnerQuote)

    DECLARE_INTERFACE_MAP()
    DECLARE_OLECREATE(ComFortuneTeller)
    DECLARE_DYNCREATE(ComFortuneTeller)
};

typedef ComFortuneTeller* PComFortuneTeller;

#endif
```

Although the ComFortuneTeller class declaration is only 11 lines long, a lot is going on here. I'm going to go through the header file once relatively quickly, and then I'll come back around again with a more detailed analysis.

The header file shown in Listing 5 can be divided into three different parts. The first part of the declaration, which shows ComFortuneTeller being derived from CCmdTarget and contains the prototypes for the class's constructor and destructor, is straightforward. Sure, you probably want to know how CCmdTarget factors into the grand scheme of things, but at least the first section is normal, standard C++.

The second section contains the declarations of two nested classes, but you wouldn't know it from looking at the code. The declarations of the two classes are hidden in a tangled morass of MFC macros (try saying *that* ten times quickly!). Rest assured that the two chunks of code wrapped with BEGIN_INTERFACE_PART and END_INTERFACE_PART are hidden class declarations. Each declared class is responsible for implementing one of the two interfaces that the new ComFortuneTeller class will be supporting.

The last section of this header file contains three macros: DECLARE_INTERFACE_MAP, DECLARE_OLECREATE, and DECLARE_DYNCREATE. As obfuscated as these macros might first appear, they each perform a critical service. You needn't know exactly what code each macro expands into, but it's very important that you understand what each macro is used for.

The IUnknown Implementation in the CCmdTarget Class

Unlike the low-level, from-scratch COM programming you did in Chapter 3, "Building COM Objects and Interfaces," and in Chapter 4, MFC COM components are not derived from IUnknown—at least, not directly. Instead, MFC COM classes inherit from the MFC class CCmdTarget. Although you can think of CCmdTarget as MFC's IUnknown, CCmdTarget is actually one of those linchpin classes that MFC would be lost without. CCmdTarget contains not only some important and fundamental COM functionality, but it also provides critical infrastructure required by every window class in MFC. Throw in support for Automation and some essential message-handling plumbing, and you start to realize that CCmdTarget is a very important class for COM and user-interface classes alike.

As far as COM is concerned, CCmdTarget gives COM objects a base class that provides a ready-made implementation of IUnknown. Take a close look at Listing 5 which shows the declaration for the CCmdTarget class. CCmdTarget is declared in the AFXWIN.H header file in your \vc98\mfc\include directory, but I've cleaned up the version in Listing 5. seq Listing List6 * Mergeformat 6 to include just those parts of the class that you're interested in right now. The class is huge, and most of the class's functionality isn't relevant to building COM objects. There's much more to `CCmdTarget` than I'm showing in Listing 5.6, and I'll show you even more when I discuss COM aggregation. For now, however, you need to take small bites and chew your MFC thoroughly before swallowing.

Listing 5.6 `AFXWIN.H`—An Excerpt from the MFC Header File AFXWIN.H, Containing the Declaration of the `CCmdTarget` Class

```
class CCmdTarget : public CObject
{

    ... A lot of stuff we don't care about right now...

public:

    DWORD InternalQueryInterface(const void*, LPVOID* ppvObj);
    DWORD InternalAddRef();
    DWORD InternalRelease();

    DWORD ExternalQueryInterface(const void*, LPVOID* ppvObj);
    DWORD ExternalAddRef();
    DWORD ExternalRelease();

    ... A lot more stuff we don't care about right now...

};
```

As you look at the declaration of `CCmdTarget`, you should notice that some things are both familiar and new at the same time. By this point, the `QueryInterface()`, `AddRef()`, `Release()` triplet of methods should be instantly recognizable as an implementation of an `IUnknown` interface. In `CCmdTarget`, however, two groups of methods are grouped with either an `Internal` or `External` prefix.

The distinction between the internal and external `IUnknown` methods is important only when your COM objects are taking part in an aggregation relationship. Remember that you use COM aggregation to reuse a COM class that is already complete and fully functional. In other words, aggregation is COM's mechanism for achieving the reuse of code that's typically accomplished in C++ by using inheritance. For now, it's enough for you to understand that `CCmdTarget` implements the tracking of your component's reference count for you. In fact, `CCmdTarget` also implements `QueryInterface()` for you. All these behaviors are at your disposal by calling the `External` set of methods. Therefore, in any situation in which you would normally call `AddRef()`, you should ensure that your component calls `ExternalAddRef()`. Need to call `QueryInterface()`? Call `ExternalQueryInterface()` instead. The great thing about this deal is that you are off the hook for functionally implementing `AddRef()`, `Release()`, and `QueryInterface()`.

Be careful, though. Note that in the preceding sentence I was careful to say that you are off the hook for *functionally* implementing the `IUnknown` methods. As you will see in the next section, you are still responsible for implementing a standard set of IUnknown methods for each interface that your component supports. However, unless you want to do something tricky, all your IUnknown method implementations can just be pass-throughs to the CCmdTarget external versions. I'll walk you through this procedure when it comes time to implement ComFortuneTeller's nested interface classes.

Declaring Nested Classes

When you use MFC to build a COM component, you are actually constructing an outer wrapper class that maintains a nested class for each interface that you want your component to support. To help you with the declaration of these nested classes, MFC provides the BEGIN_INTERFACE_PART and END_INTERFACE_PART macros.

Take a closer look at how I've declared the nested class in ComFortuneTeller that will be responsible for implementing the IFortuneTeller interface.

```
// IFortuneTeller members
BEGIN_INTERFACE_PART(CInnerFortune, IFortuneTeller)
    STDMETHOD(GetFortune)(PBSTR);
END_INTERFACE_PART(CInnerFortune)
```

The first macro that I use here is BEGIN_INTERFACE_PART. This macro takes as its two arguments the name that you want to assign to the nested class and the interface class from which the nested class should be derived. You can find the BEGIN_INTERFACE_PART macro in the MFC header file AFXDISP.H. This macro declares the beginning of a new class and includes the standard methods required to support the IUnknown interface. Here's the definition of BEGIN_INTERFACE_PART:

```
#define BEGIN_INTERFACE_PART(localClass, baseClass) \
class X##localClass : public baseClass \
{ \
public: \
    STDMETHOD_(ULONG, AddRef)(); \
    STDMETHOD_(ULONG, Release)(); \
    STDMETHOD(QueryInterface)(REFIID iid, LPVOID* ppvObj); \
```

For a macro with such an impressive name, BEGIN_INTERFACE_PART is simple. One important thing to note, however, is that the macro prepends an X to the name of the nested class passed in by the caller. To be honest, I'm not quite sure why Microsoft had the macro do this. Some sources claim that the X helps to reduce namespace pollution, but I don't buy it. How in the world does pasting an X to the front of the classname prevent pollution of the class namespace? It's far more likely that the MFC development team saw value in marking a nested interface class in some unique fashion. When you see code that references a class, beginning with the telltale X, you can be sure that the class was constructed with the intent of implementing a COM interface.

The END_INTERFACE_PART macro is even simpler. END_INTERFACE_PART finishes the class declaration and then declares an instance of the class with a variable name of m_xinner-class-name. Finally, the macro makes sure that the nested class is a friend of the outer class, which ensures that any of the inner classes will have unfettered access to the outer class's member data and methods. The definition of END_INTERFACE_PART looks much the way you would expect.

```
#define END_INTERFACE_PART(localClass) \
        } m_x##localClass; \
        friend class X##localClass; \
```

Between the BEGIN_INTERFACE_PART and END_INTERFACE_PART macros is where you need to place the declarations for those methods that are required to implement the nested class's partnered interface. Remember that because the inner class is directly derived from the interface class, you must make sure that all the interface's methods are represented in your inner class. You don't have to worry about the methods that belong to IUnknown; these are taken care of for you by BEGIN_INTERFACE_PART. However, you do have to make sure that everything else is correctly declared.

Now that you know how the macros operate, let's see how the declarations of the nested classes look when the macros are fully expanded and evaluated.

```
// IFortuneTeller members
class XCInnerFortune : public IFortuneTeller
{
public:
    STDMETHOD_(ULONG, AddRef)();
    STDMETHOD_(ULONG, Release)();
    STDMETHOD(QueryInterface)(REFIID iid, LPVOID* ppvObj);
    STDMETHOD(GetFortune)(PBSTR);
} m_xCInnerFortune;
friend class XCInnerFortune;

// IQuotation members
class XCInnerQuote : public IQuotation
{
public:
    STDMETHOD_(ULONG, AddRef)();
    STDMETHOD_(ULONG, Release)();
    STDMETHOD(QueryInterface)(REFIID iid, LPVOID* ppvObj);
    STDMETHOD(GetQuotation)(PBSTR, PBSTR);
} m_xCInnerQuote;
friend class XCInnerQuote;
```

Based on these declarations, it's clear that the implementation of the ComFortuneTeller class will also have to contend with implementing the two nested classes, XCInnerFortune and XCInnerQuote. How about that? You began this section thinking that you had to implement just one class, and now you need to implement three.

The INTERFACE_MAP, OLECREATE, and DYNCREATE Macros

The last section of the ComFortuneTeller header file contains the use of three macros. Like many other macros used throughout MFC, the OLECREATE and DYNCREATE macros follow the DECLARE_/IMPLEMENT_ pattern; you place the DECLARE macro inside a class declaration to signal that you want your class to support a given piece of functionality, and then you use the **IMPLEMENT_** macro to add implementation code for the desired functionality inside your class's **.cpp** file. Using a **DECLARE** macro without the appropriate **IMPLEMENT_** counterpart will lead to compile-time errors or, even worse, code that might compile but doesn't function correctly.

The **INTERFACE_MAP** macro is a little different from **OLECREATE** and **DYNCREATE**. Instead of being partnered with an appropriate **IMPLEMENT** macro in your class's .cpp file, the **DECLARE_INTERFACE_MAP** macro is paired with a corresponding **BEGIN_INTERFACE_MAP/END_MESSAGE_MAP** set of macros. Let's take a closer look at interface maps now.

Note

If you are really interested in the details of how the **INTERFACE_MAP**, **OLE-CREATE**, and **DYNCREATE** macros work their magic, I recommend you check out *MFC Internals* (Addison-Wesley Developers Press, 1996) by Scott Wingo and George Sheppard. Scott and George dissect MFC's COM support (macros and all) in detail.

Declaring MFC Class Factories by Using DECLARE_DYNCREATE and DECLARE_OLECREATE

Throughout MFC, you will encounter situations in which the MFC framework will need to create instances of your class. In many of these cases, the creation of the new object instance needs to occur deep within the bowels of the framework itself. In other words, the object creation will not occur within code that you are responsible for writing. This happens often in applications that use the MFC document/view architecture, but it also occurs in applications that use MFC for little more than providing support for COM. When you are talking about COM, the capability of the framework to create instances of your class is particularly important because—now hold on to your seat because this is pretty cool—MFC will provide a class factory for your COM class automatically (almost). That's right, you don't have to go through the hassle of creating a new factory class for every COM component that you build. Neat, huh?

Instrumenting your class to allow for automatic class-factory support involves using two sets of macros: the **DYNCREATE** macro and the **OLECREATE** macro. The **DECLARE/IMPLE-MENT_DYNCREATE** macro pair establishes within your class the capability to have the MFC framework dynamically create instances of your objects. This macro is not specifically used to support COM and OLE; if you are an experienced MFC GUI programmer, you will probably recognize these macros from other applications you have built that use the document/view architecture. It's important to note that the **DYNCREATE** macros alone do not provide your class with a class factory. It is the **OLECREATE** macros that provide you with a class factory, but the implementation of the MFC class factory relies on the member data and behaviors that the **DYNCREATE** macros add to your class.

Like `DECLARE_INTERFACE_MAP`, the declaration forms of `DYNCREATE` and `OLECREATE` are extremely simple. Both `DECLARE_DYNCREATE` and `DECLARE_OLECREATE` require you to pass in the name of the COM class that you are building, but apart from that, you just need to ensure that the macros appear at the end of your class declaration.

```
// Allow dynamic creation
DECLARE_DYNCREATE(ComFortuneTeller)

// Declare a class factory
DECLARE_OLECREATE(ComFortuneTeller)
```

After you've used the declarative form of these macros in your class's header file, you need to make sure that each is paired up with a matching `INPLMENT_DYNCREATE` or `IMPLEMENT_OLECREATE` macro call inside your class's `.cpp` file. I'll show you an example of this in the next section, when I discuss the implementation of the `ComFortuneTeller` class.

Implementing the MFC `ComFortuneTeller` Class

At this point, the `ComFortuneTeller` class has been declared, and by a variety of MFC macros, the class has been instrumented to include support for two nested interface classes, an interface map, and a class factory. Now let's see what's involved in finishing the construction of `ComFortuneTeller`.

Listing 5.7 shows the entire implementation of the `ComFortuneTeller` class. Take a few minutes to quickly skim through the source code. As I move through the file and explain different facets of the implementation, I'll reproduce code segments as necessary. However, it's a good idea to closely examine the source code before reading on.

Listing 5.7   FORTUNE3.CPP—The Implementation of the MFC-Based `ComFortuneTeller` Class

```
// Get needed include files
#define INITGUID
#include <stdlib.h>
#include <time.h>
#include <sys/types.h>
#include <sys/timeb.h>
#include "Fortune3.h"
#include "Utility.h"


// Support dynamic creation
IMPLEMENT_DYNCREATE(ComFortuneTeller, CCmdTarget)

// Support a class factory
IMPLEMENT_OLECREATE(ComFortuneTeller, "FortuneTeller3",
0x28200682, 0x35b6, 0x11d0, 0x8b, 0xbd, 0xfa, 0x6e, 0xaa, 0x2d, 0x62, 0xd);

// Map the various interfaces onto the nested interface classes
BEGIN_INTERFACE_MAP(ComFortuneTeller, CCmdTarget)
    INTERFACE_PART(ComFortuneTeller, IID_IFortuneTeller, CInnerFortune)
```

```
      INTERFACE_PART(ComFortuneTeller, IID_IQuotation,    CInnerQuote)
END_INTERFACE_MAP()


// Our list of fortunes
static CString g_astrFortunes[] =
    {
        "You are strong in body and spirit.",
        "You are strong in perspiration and odor.",
        "Good fortune smiles upon the distributed.",
        "VB Programmer for Hire — Cheap!!",
        "I never met an object I didn't like.",
        "Edit, Compile, Link, Crash, Sigh.",
        "Never judge a stack dump by its arguments.",
        "Card carrying member of the Bug Police.",
        "You make Dilbert look charming and sophisticated.",
        "BMW, The Ultimate Driving Machine."
    };

// Constant that tracks the number of fortunes we know about
static const ULONG g_ulNumFortunes =
    sizeof(g_astrFortunes) / sizeof(CString);


// Our list of quotations
struct CQuoteTuple
{
    // Ctor
    CQuoteTuple(CString strNewQuote, CString strNewAuthor)
                        : m_strQuotation(strNewQuote),
                          m_strAuthor(strNewAuthor)
    { }

    // Member data
    CString    m_strQuotation;
    CString    m_strAuthor;
};

static CQuoteTuple g_aQuotations[] =
    {
        { CQuoteTuple("Most writers steal a good thing when they can,\n"
                      " And when 'tis safely got 'tis worth the winning.\n"
                      " The worst of 't is we now and then detect 'em,\n"
                      " Before they ever dream that we suspect 'em.",
                      "Bryan Waller Proctor") },
        { CQuoteTuple("Husbands never become good;\n"
                      " they merely become proficient.",
                      "H. L. Mencken") },
        { CQuoteTuple("Americans may have no identity,\n"
                      " but they do have wonderful teeth.",
                      "Jean Baudrillard") },
        { CQuoteTuple("Justice ... limps along,\n"
                      " but it gets there all the same.",
```

continued on next page

continued from previous page

```
                                       "Gabriel García Márquez") },
            { CQuoteTuple("In politics if you want anything said, ask a man.\n"
                          " If you want anything done, ask a woman.",
                          "Margaret Thatcher") }
   };

   // Constant that tracks the number of fortunes we know about
   static const ULONG g_ulNumQuotations =
      sizeof(g_aQuotations) / sizeof(CQuoteTuple);


   //
   // Constructor and destructor
   //

   ComFortuneTeller::ComFortuneTeller()
   {
      VerboseMsg("In FortuneTeller constructor.\n");

      // Seed the random number generator
      struct _timeb timebuffer;
      _ftime(&timebuffer);
      srand(timebuffer.millitm);

      AfxOleLockApp();
   }

   ComFortuneTeller::~ComFortuneTeller()
   {
      VerboseMsg("In ComFortuneTeller destructor.\n");
      AfxOleUnlockApp();
   }


   //
   // Nested FortuneTeller IUnknown members
   //

   STDMETHODIMP_(ULONG)
   ComFortuneTeller::XCInnerFortune::AddRef()
   {
      METHOD_PROLOGUE(ComFortuneTeller, CInnerFortune)
      return pThis->ExternalAddRef();
   }

   STDMETHODIMP_(ULONG)
   ComFortuneTeller::XCInnerFortune::Release()
   {
      METHOD_PROLOGUE(ComFortuneTeller, CInnerFortune)
      return pThis->ExternalRelease();
   }

   STDMETHODIMP
```

```
ComFortuneTeller::XCInnerFortune::QueryInterface(REFIID riid,
    ➥PPVOID ppv)
{
   METHOD_PROLOGUE(ComFortuneTeller, CInnerFortune)
   return pThis->ExternalQueryInterface(&riid, ppv);
}



//
// IFortuneTeller interface members for nested FortuneTeller class
//

STDMETHODIMP
ComFortuneTeller::XCInnerFortune::GetFortune(PBSTR pbstrFortune)
{
   METHOD_PROLOGUE(ComFortuneTeller, CInnerFortune)
   VerboseMsg("In GetFortune.\n");

   // Initialize the output string
   *pbstrFortune = NULL;

   // Create a BSTR out of the fortune
   *pbstrFortune = g_astrFortunes[rand() % g_ulNumFortunes].
     ➥AllocSysString();

   return NOERROR;
}



//
// Nested Quotation IUnknown members
//

STDMETHODIMP_(ULONG)
ComFortuneTeller::XCInnerQuote::AddRef()
{
   METHOD_PROLOGUE(ComFortuneTeller, CInnerQuote)
   return pThis->ExternalAddRef();
}

STDMETHODIMP_(ULONG)
ComFortuneTeller::XCInnerQuote::Release()
{
   METHOD_PROLOGUE(ComFortuneTeller, CInnerQuote)
   return pThis->ExternalRelease();
}

STDMETHODIMP
ComFortuneTeller::XCInnerQuote::QueryInterface(REFIID riid,
                                        ➥PPVOID ppv)
{
   METHOD_PROLOGUE(ComFortuneTeller, CInnerQuote)
   return pThis->ExternalQueryInterface(&riid, ppv);
```

continued on next page

continued from previous page

```
}


//
// IQuotation interface members for nested Quotation class
//

STDMETHODIMP
ComFortuneTeller::XCInnerQuote::GetQuotation(PBSTR pbstrQuotation,
                                            PBSTR pbstrAuthor)
{
    METHOD_PROLOGUE(ComFortuneTeller, CInnerQuote)
    VerboseMsg("In GetQuotation.\n");

    // Initialize the output strings
    *pbstrQuotation = NULL;
    *pbstrAuthor = NULL;

    // Select our quote
    CQuoteTuple *pQuote = &g_aQuotations[rand() % g_ulNumQuotations];

    // Create BSTRs out of the quotation and author strings
    *pbstrQuotation = pQuote->m_strQuotation.AllocSysString();
    *pbstrAuthor = pQuote->m_strAuthor.AllocSysString();

    return NOERROR;
}
```

Implementing MFC Class Factories, Using IMPLEMENT_DYNCREATE and IMPLEMENT_OLECREATE

Now you have seen how your COM classes can use the **DECLARE_DYNCREATE** and **DECLARE_OLECREATE** macros to declare support for MFC-provided class factories. Lo and behold, the first thing that you find in the **.cpp** file is the implementation side of the **DYNCREATE** and **OLECREATE** macros. I hope you're not surprised . . .

Let's take a look at **IMPLEMENT_DYNCREATE** first. The use of this macro is almost as simple as its **DECLARE_DYNCREATE** sister.

```
// Support dynamic creation
IMPLEMENT_DYNCREATE(ComFortuneTeller, CCmdTarget)
```

IMPLEMENT_DYNCREATE takes two parameters: the name of the class assuming the dynamic creation capabilities and the name of the new dynamic class's superclass. In this example, the class you are writing is **ComFortuneTeller**, which is derived from **CCmdTarget**.

The **IMPLEMENT_DYNCREATE** macro expands to provide **ComFortuneTeller** with a native method named **CreateObject()**. **CreateObject()** is used by the MFC-provided class factory to create new instances of **ComFortuneTeller**, typically in response to either a **CoCreateInstance()** or **IClassFactory::CreateInstance()** call. The

IMPLEMENT_DYNCREATE macro also provides ComFortuneTeller with a CRuntimeClass instance, which I described previously.

Now that the class has a standard mechanism for creating new object instances, the final step is to provide an implementation for the MFC-provided class factory. This is accomplished using the IMPLEMENT_OLECREATE macro.

```
// Support a class factory
IMPLEMENT_OLECREATE(ComFortuneTeller, "FortuneTeller3",
0x28200682, 0x35b6, 0x11d0, 0x8b, 0xbd, 0xfa, 0x6e, 0xaa, 0x2d, 0x62, 0xd);
```

Although this macro appears to accept a whopping 13 parameters, looks can be deceiving. You can think of IMPLEMENT_OLECREATE actually taking three arguments, the third parameter being the COM component's CLSID broken down into the same 11 parts that you find in the ubiquitous DEFINE_GUID macro. The first argument of this macro is the name of the class that the new class factory will service, and the second parameter is the publicly known external name of the COM class in string form.

The DECLARE_OLECREATE macro ensures that your COM class maintain a static, class-wide instance of COleObjectFactory. This class encapsulates MFC's support for implementing COM class factories. The IMPLEMENT_OLECREATE macro initializes the COleObjectFactory instance and provides the factory with all the information that it will need to create new ComFortuneTeller instances. One of the arguments passed into the COleObjectFactory constructor is your class's CRuntimeClass object; now you can see why your class needs to use both the DYNCREATE and OLECREATE macros.

Remember

The COleObjectFactory class supports both the IClassFactory and IClassFactory2 interfaces. Recall that the IClassFactory2 interface provides exactly the same functionality as IClassFactory but includes support for licensing COM objects.

Declaring and Implementing Interface Maps

MFC is replete with many different types of maps. There are connection maps, dispatch maps, event sink maps, message maps, and, yes, interface maps. Generally speaking, you can think of a map, regardless of its type, as providing a way for MFC to look up a piece of executable code, based on some sort of unique identifier. In the case of a message map, for example, MFC uses a Windows message ID to help look up a handler method belonging to one of your MFC subclasses.

Interface maps are no exception to this pattern. MFC uses an interface map when it's trying to determine which class should be used to implement a particular COM interface. Can you think of a case in which MFC might need this sort of information? How about QueryInterface()? I've already talked in general terms about how your COM classes inherit the implementation for QueryInterface() from CCmdTarget. CCmdTarget uses interface maps to track down the appropriate nested interface handler class for a given interface ID.

The really nice thing about interface maps is how easy they are to use. There are only two simple steps that you must follow in order to allow `CCmdTarget` to take on all your `QueryInterface()` programming responsibilities. First, you must use the `DECLARE_INTERFACE_MAP` macro in the declaration of your COM class. Second, you must create the map itself in your COM class's implementation file. You create the interface map by using a series of macros that register your nested interface implementation classes and associate each nested class with a specific interface IID.

The first part of this procedure, using the `DECLARE_INTERFACE_MAP` macro, couldn't be easier. Simply place the macro at the bottom of your class declaration. That's it!

```
// Establish support for an interface map
DECLARE_INTERFACE_MAP()
```

This macro instruments your class with the various methods and pieces of member data required to support the interface mapping process. The second part of the interface mapping procedure, creating the interface map itself, is done inside your class's `.cpp` file.

In the `ComFortuneTeller` header file, I made sure to include the declaration of an interface map. Now that we're in the implementation file, it's time to see how the interface map is loaded up and initialized.

The interface map tells MFC—the `CCmdTarget` code, to be specific—which classes are responsible for implementing a given interface. When an application or the COM subsystem needs to obtain a given interface pointer, the `QueryInterface()` call is fielded by `CCmdTarget`. The `CCmdTarget` class uses the interface ID passed into `QueryInterface()` to look up the appropriate interface handler class and then returns the address of the class as the requested interface pointer.

```
// Map the various interfaces onto the nested interface classes
BEGIN_INTERFACE_MAP(ComFortuneTeller, CCmdTarget)
    INTERFACE_PART(ComFortuneTeller, IID_IFortuneTeller, CInnerFortune)
    INTERFACE_PART(ComFortuneTeller, IID_IQuotation,     CInnerQuote)
END_INTERFACE_MAP()
```

You start building the interface map by using, appropriately enough, the `BEGIN_INTERFACE_MAP` macro. This macro defines a couple of helper member functions and then starts the definition of the interface map itself. The `BEGIN_INTERFACE_MAP` macro takes two arguments. These arguments are identical to the parameters that you pass into the `IMPLEMENT_DYNCREATE` macro, namely, the name of the COM component class and the name of the component's superclass.

The interface map is simply an array of interface map entries. An interface map entry is a very small, two-value structure that associates an IID with the location of the interface handler class. Each map entry is placed into the interface map by using the `INTERFACE_PART` macro. The `INTERFACE_PART` macro accepts the name of the component class, the IID for the interface being placed into the map, and the name of the nested class responsible for implementing the given interface. The ID `ComFortuneTeller` now exposes two interfaces; two entries are placed into the interface map (one for `IFortuneTeller` and one for `IQuotation`).

The interface map is completed by invoking the `END_INTERFACE_MAP` macro. The ID `END_INTERFACE_MAP` simply inserts a `NULL` interface entry and closes the array definition; there is no need to pass any arguments into this macro.

With the interface map complete, the `ComFortuneTeller` class now has the capability to enable `CCmdTarget` to accurately respond to `QueryInterface()` calls. This is a very good thing; letting `CCmdTarget` handle `AddRef()` and `Release()` for you is nice, but much more coding is involved in the implementation of a typical `QueryInterface()` method. Now you barely have to deal with `IUnknown` at all. (I'll explain exactly what I mean by *barely* in a few pages.) `CCmdTarget` takes care of all the `IUnknown` housekeeping for you.

Counting Object Instances in MFC Servers

The next piece of code worthy of comment is `ComFortuneTeller`'s constructor and destructor (you didn't expect me to make a wisecrack about the choice of quotations, did you?). Normally, these two methods would not be deserving of comment; in fact, except for two tiny differences, the `ComFortuneTeller` constructor and destructor are exactly the same as the Fortune2 versions.

```
//
// Constructor and destructor
//

ComFortuneTeller::ComFortuneTeller()
{
    VerboseMsg("In FortuneTeller constructor.\n");

    // Seed the random number generator
    struct _timeb timebuffer;
    _ftime(&timebuffer);
    srand(timebuffer.millitm);

    AfxOleLockApp();
}

ComFortuneTeller::~ComFortuneTeller()
{
    VerboseMsg("In ComFortuneTeller destructor.\n");
    AfxOleUnlockApp();
}
```

Notice the two MFC-specific statements in this code: the call to `AfxOleLockApp()` in `ComFortuneTeller`'s constructor and the call to `AfxOleUnlockApp()` in the destructor.

As you might expect from your experience with coding the Fortune server, every MFC COM server maintains a global object count. Rather than wrap this count with a class, as I did in Fortune2, the MFC enables applications to bump this count up and down by making calls to `AfxOleLockApp()` and `AfxOleUnlockApp()`, respectively. When the COM subsystem calls the server's `DllCanUnloadNow()` function, the server simply consults the global object count, now managed by MFC, to determine whether any outstanding objects are still instantiated.

MFC doesn't maintain separate object and server lock count variables. This might cause you to wonder how the `COleObjectFactory` class implements its `LockServer()` method (remember this guy from the `IClassFactory` interface?). It's simple. The `LockServer()` method simply calls `AfxOleLockApp()` if the passed-in boolean indicates a lock increment, and it calls `AfxOleUnlockApp()` if the boolean indicates a lock decrement. In other words, MFC still maintains server locks, but it rolls both the server lock count and the global object count into the same variable.

Implementing `IUnknown` for Nested Classes

Now that I've covered much of the logistical implementation of `ComFortuneTeller`, it's time to take a look at how the nested interface handler classes are implemented. The first thing I'd like to do, before going into the specific implementations of the `IFortuneTeller` and `IQuotation` interfaces (which are trivial anyway), is to investigate how `ComFortuneTeller`'s nested classes implement the `IUnknown` interface.

I know that I've insisted that the `CCmdTarget` class will handle all your `IUnknown` implementation needs. Don't worry, I'm not going back on my word. However, `CCmdTarget` needs a little bit of help with mapping the nested classes' `IUnknown`'s onto the `IUnknown` interface supported by `CCmdTarget`.

You might be surprised that the nested classes need to implement `IUnknown` at all. After all, `XCInnerFortune` and `XCInnerQuote` are hidden from everyone and are exclusively managed by the outer `ComFortuneTeller` class. They don't *need* an `IUnknown` class; they should be able to simply freeload off the `IUnknown` implementation provided by `ComFortuneTeller` (through `CCmdTarget`). The problem is that each of the nested classes is derived from an interface class, which is in turn derived from the `IUnknown` interface class. The rules of C++ dictate that the nested classes are not themselves abstract (for example, they don't declare any pure virtual functions themselves); they must each implement each and every inherited pure virtual function. Yes, this includes the `IUnknown` methods.

In a nutshell, you must come up with a way for the nested classes to redirect their `IUnknown` interfaces to the `IUnknown` interface supported by the `CCmdTarget` base class. Let's take a look at a nested class implementation.

```
//
// Nested FortuneTeller IUnknown members
//

STDMETHODIMP_(ULONG)
ComFortuneTeller::XCInnerFortune::AddRef()
{
    METHOD_PROLOGUE(ComFortuneTeller, CInnerFortune)
    return pThis->ExternalAddRef();
}

STDMETHODIMP_(ULONG)
ComFortuneTeller::XCInnerFortune::Release()
{
    METHOD_PROLOGUE(ComFortuneTeller, CInnerFortune)
    return pThis->ExternalRelease();
}

STDMETHODIMP
ComFortuneTeller::XCInnerFortune::QueryInterface(REFIID riid,
➥PPVOID ppv)
```

```
{
    METHOD_PROLOGUE(ComFortuneTeller, CInnerFortune)
    return pThis->ExternalQueryInterface(&riid, ppv);
}
```

What you have here is the `IUnknown` implementation for the `XCInnerFortune` nested class (the implementation for `XCInnerQuote` is identical, except for the obvious exceptions where classname changes are required).

When you get down to it, each of these methods does exactly the same thing. The first line of each method involves the invocation of a macro named `METHOD_PROLOGUE`. The next line forwards the `IUnknown` method call on to the `pThis` variable. What's `pThis`, and where did it come from?

The `pThis` variable is the `this` pointer for the `ComFortuneTeller` object. I'll give you a second to let this sink in. I remember that the first time I heard this singular fact, it took me a minute to get it. You want the `AddRef()` method—or `Release()` or `QueryInterface()`— to simply turn around and call the `IUnknown` methods that `ComFortuneTeller` inherits from `CCmdTarget`. Inside `XCInnerFortune`, the `this` pointer will refer to the `XCInnerFortune` object instance nested inside the `ComFortuneTeller`, not the `ComFortuneTeller` instance itself. The `pThis` variable points to the outer-wrapping `ComFortuneTeller` object. After the method has the `pThis` pointer, redirecting the methods to `ComFortuneTeller` (and `CCmdTarget`) is a simple matter of calling the appropriate method. The diagram in Figure 5.1 shows the relationship between the `this` pointer and the `pThis` pointer.

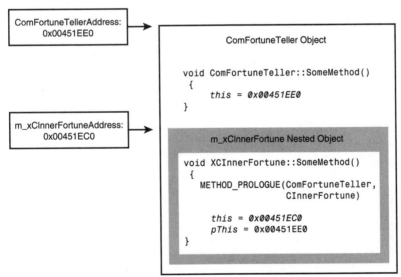

Figure 5.1 The value of the `pThis` pointer in relation to the `this` pointer, when in a nested class.

The last question is, Where did the `pThis` pointer come from? In a two-line method, there really aren't many possibilities. It would be a reasonable guess to assume that the `METHOD_PROLOGUE` macro has something to do with it.

The `METHOD_PROLOGUE` macro declares the `pThis` variable and, subtracting the offset of the nested class from the current `this` pointer, sets the variable so that it points to the outer object instance. Because of the nature of the `pThis` assignment, the `METHOD_PROLOGUE` macro requires the name of the outer class and the name of the nested class as parameters. With the `pThis` variable thus set, the nested class method is free to use `pThis` whenever access to the outer class is required.

Note

The `METHOD_PROLOGUE` macro also switches in the correct module state. Module states are an important concept to be aware of when you're programming MFC using DLLs or multiple threads, but they're a little tricky to grasp (at least, they were for me when I first learned about them). The good thing is that the use of module states is almost completely hidden from the average MFC programmer. However, I mention them here because in a few isolated cases the MFC COM programmer needs to be module state–aware. I'll talk more about module states in the section titled "Implementing `DllGetClassObject()` and `DllCanUnloadNow()`", in which I discuss the implementation of the exported functions `DllGetClassObject()` and `DllCanUnloadNow()`.

It's important to realize that when I say the `pThis` pointer can be used whenever access to the outer class is required, I'm not simply referring to using `pThis` from within the nested class's `IUnknown` methods. When you're implementing non-`IUnknown` interface functionality, it's common to find that the nested class needs access to methods or member data that belongs to the outer class. Try to think of the nested class as an integral part of the entire COM object class. The class is nested only to accommodate the MFC infrastructure. If it weren't for MFC, each of the nested class methods would need to exist in one form or another inside the `ComFortuneTeller` class. The close coupling of the outer class to each of its nested classes is reinforced by the `END_INTERFACE_PART` macro declaring each of the nested classes as a friend of the outer class. This gives nested classes full access to member data and methods that might be private to the outer class.

The `IMPLEMENT_NESTED_IUNKNOWN` Macro

Do you smell another macro?! After looking over the code for implementing `XCInnerFortune` and `XCInnerQuote`'s `IUnknown` interface, you might be wondering whether there's a way to implement this code by using a macro. As I'll show you in a moment, there certainly is. You might be surprised to find that Microsoft does not provide such a macro through the MFC framework. (I mean, these are the folks who seem to feel that a program isn't complete unless it uses 13,000 different MFC macros.) In fact, during the beta testing of MFC 2.5, Microsoft did provide just such a macro. However, the macro was removed before the release because Microsoft felt that the macro made source code harder to debug and understand. My take on this is that an MFC program already uses so many macros that using one more in this case isn't likely to cause you an exceptional amount of additional grief.

Without further ado, I present IMPLEMENT_NESTED_IUNKNOWN:

```
#define IMPLEMENT_NESTED_IUNKNOWN(outerclass, innerclass)      \
                                                               \
    STDMETHODIMP_(ULONG)                                       \
    outerclass::X##innerclass::AddRef()                       \
    {                                                          \
        METHOD_PROLOGUE(outerclass, innerclass)               \
        return pThis->ExternalAddRef();                       \
    }                                                          \
                                                               \
    STDMETHODIMP_(ULONG)                                       \
    outerclass::X##innerclass::Release()                      \
    {                                                          \
        METHOD_PROLOGUE(outerclass, innerclass)               \
        return pThis->ExternalRelease();                      \
    }                                                          \
                                                               \
    STDMETHODIMP                                               \
    outerclass::X##innerclass::QueryInterface(REFIID riid,    \
                                              PPVOID ppv)      \
    {                                                          \
        METHOD_PROLOGUE(outerclass, innerclass)               \
        return pThis->ExternalQueryInterface(&riid, ppv);     \
    }
```

I consider this macro to be so useful that I've included it in the UTILITY.H header file that most of the sample programs rely on. The macro dramatically cuts down the amount of code that you would have to write to support a given interface, at the expense of some clarity. If you don't believe me, take a look at FORTUNE3B.CPP, which is included in the Fortune3 in-process server build directory. This source file is exactly the same as the FORTUNE3.CPP file shown in Listing 5.7, except that it uses the IMPLEMENT_NESTED_IUNKNOWN macro. The FORTUNE3B.CPP source file is more than 20% shorter than FORTUNE3.CPP. (Of course, real-world COM implementation files will be significantly longer, so you shouldn't expect to see anywhere near this amount of savings during normal, everyday usage.)

Implementing the IFortuneTeller and IQuotation Interfaces

With every other part of the ComFortuneTeller implementation covered, all that remains to be done is the actual construction of the nested interface methods that have nothing to do with IUnknown. The IFortuneTeller::GetFortune() method is almost exactly the same as in Fortune2, so I won't rehash that one, but I do want to make some general comments about IQuotation::GetQuotation() that also apply to the implementation of the IFortuneTeller interface. Here's ComFortuneTeller's GetQuotation() method again:

```
//
// IQuotation interface members for nested Quotation class
//

STDMETHODIMP
```

```
ComFortuneTeller::XInnerQuote::GetQuotation(PBSTR pbstrQuotation,
                                            PBSTR pbstrAuthor)
{
    METHOD_PROLOGUE(ComFortuneTeller, CInnerQuote)
    VerboseMsg("In GetQuotation.\n");

    // Initialize the output strings
    *pbstrQuotation = NULL;
    *pbstrAuthor = NULL;

    // Select our quote
    CQuoteTuple *pQuote = &g_aQuotations[rand() % g_ulNumQuotations];

    // Create BSTRs out of the quotation and author strings
    *pbstrQuotation = pQuote->m_strQuotation.AllocSysString();
    *pbstrAuthor = pQuote->m_strAuthor.AllocSysString();

    return NOERROR;
}
```

This method is really just a variation on the original **IFortuneTeller** interface implementation that I showed you in the Fortune2 program. In Chapter 3, I spent a fair amount of time talking about Unicode and how the BSTR type is the standard data type used for passing strings between COM clients and servers. None of this changes when you're working with the MFC framework, but the **CString** class can help ease some of the pain of working with BSTRs.

If you look closely, you will notice that I modified the MFC-based **ComFortuneTeller** class to use **CStrings**, instead of relying on the ANSI string class. I did this mainly because **CString** is BSTR-aware; your application can construct a new **CString** based on an existing BSTR, and a **CString** can construct a new BSTR from the **CString**'s current contents. These two capabilities alone remove the need for you to use the ugly **AnsiToUnicode()** and **UnicodeToAnsi()** utility functions.

One of the nice things about building your COM objects by using MFC is that you gain access to many little features that make your life easier. The **CString** class is a good example. It's almost worth using MFC just so you don't have to worry about ANSI-to-Unicode conversions!

Finishing the MFC-Based Fortune3 Server

With the **ComFortuneTeller** class fully implemented, just a few details need to be attended to before the server is complete. Like every MFC executable or DLL, the server needs to contain an application instance that is derived from the **CWinApp** class. In the case of an in-process server, the application class is remarkably simple, but it's important that you pay close attention to several implementation details. In most cases, the infrastructure code required to build an in-process server is exactly the same for every in-process server. As you'll soon see, the **CInProcServerApp** class that I'll be discussing next will be used throughout the book whenever we need to build an in-process server with MFC.

When the server's application class is complete, the final task is to ensure that the server has implemented and correctly exported the standard in-process server functions, `DllGetClassObject()` and `DllCanUnloadNow()`.

Implementing the `DllGetClassObject()` and `DllCanUnloadNow()` Functions

The `CWinApp`-derived class used by all the in-process servers in this book is named `CInProcServerApp`. I've whittled this class down to the bare minimum required to support a COM component, so `CInProcServerApp` overrides only two methods from its `CWinApp` superclass. In fact, because the class is so small and isn't directly used by any other objects, `CInProcServerApp` is both declared and defined inside the class source file. Listing 5.8 shows the first half of INPROCSRV.CPP, which contains the implementation of the `CInProcServerApp`.

Listing 5.8   INPROCSRV.CPP—The First Half, Containing the Declaration and Implementation of the Server's `CWinApp`-Derived `CInProcServerApp` Class

```
// Get needed include files
#include "StdInc.h"
#include "Resource.h"


//
// Main application/server class
//

class CInProcServerApp : public CWinApp
{
public:

    // Public methods inherited from CWinApp
    virtual BOOL InitInstance();
    virtual int ExitInstance();
};

// Our one-and-only application object
CInProcServerApp TheApp;


BOOL CInProcServerApp::InitInstance()
{
    AfxOleLockApp();
    return COleObjectFactory::RegisterAll();
}

int CInProcServerApp::ExitInstance()
{
    AfxOleUnlockApp();
    return 0;
}
```

As you can see, **CInProcServerApp** overrides only the **InitInstance()** and **ExitInstance()** methods. **InitInstance()** is called by the MFC framework when the in-process server DLL is initially loaded into the client program's address space. It provides the server with the opportunity to initialize data and prepare the server for operation. **ExitInstance()** is called when the DLL is about to be unloaded from memory and provides a good place for a server to deallocate and free resources.

Not a whole lot is going on in this class. The **AfxOleLockApp()** function is called in **InitInstance()**, which causes the server's global lock count to be incremented by one. Conversely, the **ExitInstance()** method decrements the global lock count with a corresponding call to **AfxOleUnlockApp()**. The only thing here that might be out of the ordinary is a call to the static method, **COleObjectFactory::RegisterAll()**.

The static **RegisterAll()** method is one of those MFC methods that acts quite differently depending on what type of COM server you are building. If you are building a local COM server, for example, **RegisterAll()** walks through the list of all the factories in the server and registers them with the COM subsystem by using the **CoRegisterClassObject()** API. (Remember that a local COM server resides inside an executable and runs in a different address space than the client.) However, Fortune3 is an in-process server; in-process servers register their class factories only when asked, by way of a COM subsystem call to the exported function **DllGetClassObject()**.

That's not to say, however, that the call to **RegisterAll()** in the **CInProcServerApp's** **InitInstance()** method serves no purpose. MFC also initializes a number of critical data structures inside **RegisterAll()**, independent of the type of server you're building. Your servers will not function if this initialization has not occurred, so the call to **RegisterAll()** is very important and may not be omitted.

We're approaching the end now. With the **CWinApp**-derived application class complete, let's take a look at Listing 5.9, which shows the second half of the **INPROCSRV.CPP** file. Here are four functions that are exported from the DLL proper. The first two, **DllGetClassObject()** and **DllCanUnloadNow()**, should be familiar to you. The second two, **DllRegisterServer()** and **DllUnregisterServer()**, were not present in the Fortune2 version of the server and are concerned with self-registration and unregistration. I'll cover self-registration in the next section.

Listing 5.9 INPROCSRV.CPP—The Second Half, Containing the Implementation of the Standard Functions Exported from In-Process Servers

```
//
// Standard exported methods for in-process servers
//

//
// Called when COM needs a new class factory
//

STDAPI DllGetClassObject(REFCLSID rclsid, REFIID riid, LPVOID* ppv)
{
    AFX_MANAGE_STATE(AfxGetStaticModuleState());
    return AfxDllGetClassObject(rclsid, riid, ppv);
```

```
}

//
// Called by COM to check whether the server can be unloaded
//

STDAPI DllCanUnloadNow()
{
    AFX_MANAGE_STATE(AfxGetStaticModuleState());
    return AfxDllCanUnloadNow();
}

//
// Method used to support self-registration
//

STDAPI DllRegisterServer()
{
    AFX_MANAGE_STATE(AfxGetStaticModuleState());
    COleObjectFactory::UpdateRegistryAll();
    return S_OK;
}

//
// Method used to support self-unregistration
//

STDAPI DllUnregisterServer()
{
    AFX_MANAGE_STATE(AfxGetStaticModuleState());

    // Load up various strings from the resource stringtable
    CString strClassID, strProgID;
    strClassID.LoadString(ID_STR_CLASSID);
    strProgID.LoadString(ID_STR_PROGID);

    // Transform the string-format CLSID into a real CLSID
    CLSID CLSID_Component;
    BSTR bstrClassID = strClassID.AllocSysString();
    CLSIDFromString(bstrClassID, &CLSID_Component);
    SysFreeString(bstrClassID);

    // Unregister the class
    return AfxOleUnregisterClass(CLSID_Component, strProgID);
}
```

The AFX_MANAGE_STATE Macro

MFC provides an elaborate infrastructure for manipulating and controlling module states. A *module state* can be thought of as a collection of data that resides within a particular context. Module states are what programmers typically regard as global variables and other such readily accessible data. There are module states that belong to DLLs, processes, and threads. Whenever a module boundary is crossed—moving from code in an application into code that resides in a DLL, for example—MFC requires that the module state be appropriately set. Setting the correct module state is critical for building MFC programs that are running on a dynamically multithreaded Win32 operating system. If you do not set the module state, your programs might not function correctly, or at all.

If you're a bit confused by module states, don't worry. Managing module states *is* confusing and takes getting used to. The good news is that the vast majority of the time, MFC takes care of all this module state switching stuff for you. However, on rare occasions you are required to take on some of this responsibility yourself. Functions directly exported from an MFC DLL fall into this category. Because module states don't have anything to do with COM or DCOM per se, I don't want to distract you by launching into a full-fledged tutorial on MFC module states. If you want to learn more, I encourage you to consult the Visual C++ Books Online. In particular, Tech Note TN058: *MFC Module State Implementation* is a good place start. The *MFC Internals* book that I mentioned earlier is also a good source of information.

For the purpose of the Fortune3 server code, understand that

```
AFX_MANAGE_STATE(AfxGetStaticModuleState());
```

will automatically switch in the appropriate module state for the Fortune3 in-process server and the current thread. This macro also ensures that when you exit from the current function, the module state is restored to what it was before the function was called. If you want to ignore this whole module state mess, make sure that your exported DLL functions include this macro and forget that you ever heard about module states. (I'm not saying this is a good idea, mind you. Knowledge is power, and all that stuff. If you have the time, you should make a point of checking out Tech Note 58.)

With the `AFX_MANAGE_STATE` macro out of the way, I'm down to talking about two MFC functions. `DllGetClassObject()` turns around and simply calls the global MFC function `AfxDllGetClassObject()`. In a similar fashion, `DllCanUnloadNow()` turns around and calls `AfxDllCanUnloadNow()`. Unfortunately, neither of these functions is documented in the Visual C++ Books Online.

However, for all intents and purposes, just knowing that these functions exist is enough. The `AfxDllGetClassObject()` method walks the server's list of factories, returning the factory associated with the passed-in CLSID. The implementation of `AfxDllCanUnloadNow()` is just as straightforward. `AfxDllCanUnloadNow()` consults several data structures and lists to ensure that no outstanding objects are instantiated and that no factories have reference counts greater than one. When you get down to it, these two functions, which are really the only two functions we've run across that are totally undocumented, have very reasonable implementations and are used in a completely intuitive manner. Wouldn't it be nice if everything worked this way?

Self Registration and Unregistration

In Chapter 3, I briefly discussed the concept of server self-registration. You'll recall how local servers can support self-registration by sensing the `/RegServer` command-line switch and then manually populating the system registry with the appropriate registration data. Self-unregistration is similar, but responds to the /UnregServer command-line flag. In-process servers can also support self-registration (or unregistration) by exporting a method named DllRegisterServer(), or in the case of self-unregistration, DllUnregisterServer(). Because an in-process server resides in a DLL and doesn't receive command-line arguments, a helper application is required to load the in-process server and call the DllRegisterServer() or DllUnregisterServer() methods as appropriate.

One of the best things about building servers with MFC is that you pretty much get self-registration and unregistration for free. As you can see in Listing 5.9, the DllRegisterServer() method requires a single call to the static COleObjectFactory method UpdateRegistryAll(). This method iterates over each of the factories residing within the server, querying the factory's CLSID and creating the appropriate registry entries. Nothing could be simpler!

Of course, things can always be *harder*. You might be a little surprised to learn that the DllUnregisterServer() method is a little more complicated than DllRegisterServer(), although the additional complications are largely of my own doing. Because the CInProcServerApp class is designed to be reusable, no hard-coded CLSIDs or classnames are compiled into the class. Instead, the class retrieves two standard strings from a string table compiled into the resource portion of the server DLL. The first string, IDS_CLASSID (with an identifier value of 102), is a single CLSID, formatted in standard registry format. The second string, IDS_PROGID (with an identifier value of 103), is a standard ProgID that corresponds to the class in question.

Caution

That only a single CLSID is stored in the string table reveals an important limitation of CInProcServerApp: The class will self-unregister only a single COM class. Although this limitation is acceptable for the relatively simple examples that appear throughout this book, you might want to extend CInProcServerApp's scheme for component unregistration to allow support for multiple classes. Keep in mind that MFC fully supports the hosting of multiple COM classes inside a single server. It's only my simple-minded CInProcServerApp that imposes the single-class limitation. (It should be noted that CInProcServerApp can self-register more than one class. The limitation lies in the number of classes that the class can self-unregister.)

Because the CLSID is in a standard NULL-terminated string, DllUnregisterServer() first translates the string into a GUID by using the CLSIDFromString() API. (Unfortunately, CLSIDFromString() requires a Unicode string, so you have to translate the string into Unicode first.) Finally, the code calls AfxOleUnregisterClass(), which accepts a CLSID and a ProgID. As you might assume, AfxOleUnregisterClass() removes the appropriate component entries from the system registry. The ironic thing about this whole process is that the first thing AfxOleUnregisterClass() does is to take your CLSID and translate it back into a string. I guess Microsoft assumes that programmers are more likely to have their CLSIDs available in GUID form as opposed to string (which is probably true). Obviously, that's not the case in the **CInProcServerApp** class.

Caution

Don't forget that if you plan to reuse **CInProcServerApp** in your own servers, you must compile into your DLL a string table with the **IDS_CLASSID** and **IDS_PROGID** strings. If you forget to create these resources (which I find myself doing constantly), the self-unregistration features of the class will not function.

COM provides a useful feature that enables one component to emulate another, effectively tricking a client application into thinking that it's dealing with an object of one class when it's really interacting with a completely different component type. This can be accomplished because clients interact with COM objects only through interface pointers, and many classes can expose the same interfaces.

All the same, you're probably wondering how COM pulls this off. After all, the client explicitly requests the services of a specific class by passing a CLSID into **CoGetClassObject()** or **CoCreateInstance()**. COM catches and redirects the request at the registry. When COM first consults the registry to determine where the requested server DLL or executable can be found, it can find a **TreatAs** entry. The **TreatAs** key is located at the same key level as the **InprocServer32** entry, and its default value is a CLSID that tells COM what class should really be used to service the client's request.

For example, pretend that a competitor has written a successful Web browser component named SuperWeb. The main registry entry for this component might look something like this:

```
...\
    CLSID\
        {3A771D40-76E7-11D0-8C5C-00400539F36B}\
            InprocServer32 = "C:\COM Servers\SuperWeb.DLL"
```

Assume that you've built your own Web browser component, which blows SuperWeb away, feature for feature. Your Web browser, WebRaider, might have registry entries that look like so:

```
...\
    CLSID\
        {6E5DDE10-76E8-11D0-8C5C-00400539F36B}\
            InprocServer32 = "C:\COM Servers\WebRaider.DLL"
```

In addition to superior HTML-processing capabilities, your browser has backward-compatibility features that enable it to be used by any client designed to use the SuperWeb component. Although you can't magically transform SuperWeb client programs into WebRaider clients, you can place a **TreatAs** key in SuperWeb's registry entry; this key will redirect all the SuperWeb clients to your WebRaider component. As long as your WebRaider component implements all the SuperWeb interfaces in a manner consistent with the original class, clients looking for SuperWeb should be able to use your component while being none the wiser.

Here's what the SuperWeb registry entry might look like after you've injected your **TreatAs** key:

```
...\
   CLSID\
      {3A771D40-76E7-11D0-8C5C-00400539F36B}\
         InprocServer32 = "C:\COM Servers\SuperWeb.DLL"
         TreatAs = "{6E5DDE10-76E8-11D0-8C5C-00400539F36B}"
```

There is a potential *gotcha* that you must keep in mind when using the **TreatAs** entry. The **AfxOleUnregisterClass()** function used in Listing 5.9 has a rather brutish implementation. Although the API does make sure that it doesn't blow away a whole class entry if both 16-bit and 32-bit servers are registered, it makes no such provisions for the **TreatAs** key. Even if a class has a **TreatAs** entry that redirects clients to another component, **AfxOleUnregisterClass()** will delete all the class's registration information. This will break client code, even though a COM class might be registered that is capable of servicing those clients. In the vast scheme of things, this is a rare occurrence, but you should be aware of it all the same.

The **REGSVR32** Utility

Your server should support self-registration, with **DllRegisterServer()**. There is also another way to register your components by hand if you need to before you complete your component. Visual C++ ships with a little utility called **REGSVR32**. REGSVR32's sole purpose in life is to register and unregister in-process servers. To register the Fortune3 server, type the following command line from within the server DLL directory:

```
C:\COM Servers>regsvr32 fort3srv.dll

C:\COM Servers>
```

You will see a message box appear (like the one in Figure 5.2) that indicates the server registration was successful.

Figure 5.2 Registering the Fortune3 server by using the **REGSVR32** utility.

REGSVR32 also understands self-unregistration. If you specify the **/u** command-line switch, **REGSVR32** will invoke the DLL's **DllUnregisterServer()** method.

```
C:\COM Servers>regsvr32 /u fort3srv.dll

C:\COM Servers>
```

Adding the Finishing Touches

With the server registered, you're about ready to take the new MFC-based `ComFortuneTeller` server out for a spin. There's just one problem: Your client program needs to be updated to test out the new functionality provided by the `IQuotation` class. That shouldn't be much of a problem. Let's whip one up.

Note

Because the new Fortune3 server still supports the `IFortuneTeller` inter-face, you can actually use the Fortune2 client program to check whether the `IFortuneTeller` implementation of the new server is functioning correctly. The easiest way to accomplish this is to insert a `TreatAs` key into the Fortune2 component's registration information. Open up `REGEDIT` and search for Fort2Srv.dll, the name of the DLL containing the Fortune2 in-process serv-er. `REGEDIT` will find the DLL name in the component's `InProcServer32` key. Create a new key for the `TreatAs` entry and set its default value to the CLSID of Fortune3 (`{28200682-35B6-11D0-8BBD-FA6EAA2D620D}`). Now try rerun-ning the Fortune2 client program. The program will execute exactly as it did before, except that now it will use the new MFC-based Fortune3 server instead of the Fortune2 server that you built in Chapter 4.

The Fortune3 Client Program

The client program that tests the new Fortune3 server is also an MFC-based application, but it has a minimalist user interface (to put it charitably). In fact, with its single call to `AfxMessageBox()`, the Fortune3 client is probably the most graphically simple-minded pro-gram that you can build in MFC. Listing 5.10 shows the source code for the new client program. Like the Fortune2 client, it all fits into a single file and is quite straightforward.

Listing 5.1   `CLIENT3.CPP`—The Client Code for the Fortune3 Program

```
#define INITGUID
#include "Utility.h"
#include "IFortune.h"
#include "IQuote.h"


// The main MFC application class
class CFortuneTellerApp : public CWinApp
{
public:

    // The single, overridden virtual method
    BOOL InitInstance();
};
```

```
// The one and only CFortuneTellerApp object
CFortuneTellerApp FortuneTeller;


//
// Everything happens inside here
//

BOOL CFortuneTellerApp::InitInstance()
{
    HRESULT        hResult;
    IUnknown       *pIUnknown;

    // Prepare COM for use
    VerboseMsg("Calling COM API CoInitialize.\n");
    hResult = CoInitialize(NULL);
    if (FAILED(hResult)) {
        ReportError("Could not initialize COM.", hResult);
        return FALSE;
    }

    // Create a new FortuneTeller object and return an IUnknown
    // interface pointer
    VerboseMsg("Creating new FortuneTeller3 object instance.\n");
    hResult = CoCreateInstance(CLSID_FortuneTeller3,
                               NULL, CLSCTX_INPROC_SERVER,
                               IID_IUnknown,
                               (PPVOID) &pIUnknown);
    if (FAILED(hResult)) {
        ReportError("Could not create a new FortuneTeller3 object.",
        ➥hResult);
        return FALSE;
    }

    // Fortune or Quotation?
    if (rand() % 2) {

        //
        // It's a Fortune
        //

        IFortuneTeller    *pIFortuneTeller;
        BSTR              bstrFortune;

        // Get an IFortune interface pointer
        VerboseMsg("Getting IFortuneTeller interface pointer.\n");
        hResult = pIUnknown->QueryInterface(IID_IFortuneTeller,
                                            (PPVOID) &pIFortuneTeller);
        if (FAILED(hResult)) {
            ReportError("Could not obtain FortuneTeller interface.",
            ➥hResult);
            pIUnknown->Release();
```

continued on next page

continued from previous page

```
                    return FALSE;
            }

            // Get our fortune, in BSTR form
            VerboseMsg("Getting fortune from FortuneTeller object.\n");
            pIFortuneTeller->GetFortune(&bstrFortune);

            // Show the user the fortune
            CString  strFortune((LPCWSTR) bstrFortune);
            ::AfxMessageBox("\"" + strFortune + "\"",
                            MB_ICONINFORMATION ¦ MB_OK);

            // Release the memory for the BSTR
            VerboseMsg("Releasing fortune BSTR.\n");
            SysFreeString(bstrFortune);

            // We're done with the IFortuneTeller interface
            VerboseMsg("Releasing IFortuneTeller interface.\n");
            pIFortuneTeller->Release();
        }

        else {

            //
            // It's a Quotation
            //

            IQuotation      *pIQuotation;
            BSTR            bstrQuotation;
            BSTR            bstrAuthor;

            // Get an IQuotation interface pointer
            VerboseMsg("Getting IQuotation interface pointer.\n");
            hResult = pIUnknown->QueryInterface(IID_IQuotation,
                                            (PPVOID) &pIQuotation);
            if (FAILED(hResult)) {
                ReportError("Could not obtain Quotation interface.",
                ➥hResult);
                pIUnknown->Release();
                return FALSE;
            }

            // Get our quotation and author, in BSTR form
            VerboseMsg("Getting quotation and author from
            ➥FortuneTeller object.\n");
            pIQuotation->GetQuotation(&bstrQuotation, &bstrAuthor);

            // Show the user the quotation
            CString  strQuotation((LPCWSTR) bstrQuotation);
            CString  strAuthor((LPCWSTR) bstrAuthor);
            ::AfxMessageBox("\"" + strQuotation + "\"\n\n" +
                            "\t— " + strAuthor,
                            MB_ICONINFORMATION ¦ MB_OK);
```

```
        // Release the memory for the BSTRs
        VerboseMsg("Releasing quotation and author BSTRs.\n");
        SysFreeString(bstrQuotation);
        SysFreeString(bstrAuthor);

        // We're done with the IQuotation interface
        VerboseMsg("Releasing IQuotation interface.\n");
        pIQuotation->Release();
    }

    // We're done with the FortuneTeller object
    VerboseMsg("Releasing FortuneTeller object.\n");
    pIUnknown->Release();
    pIUnknown = NULL;

    // We're all done with COM
    CoUninitialize();

    return CWinApp::InitInstance();
}
```

The client program is almost like two copies of the Fortune2 client, bundled into a single program. Based on a random number, the program decides whether it wants to use the **IFortuneTeller** or **IQuotation** interface. The client uses the **CoCreateInstance()** API to create an object instance outright, instead of going through all the factory rigmarole. Because you know that you're going to need only one instance of the class, it doesn't make a whole lot of sense to obtain a factory that you're just going to release right away.

It's worth noting that the client program also uses the **CString** class to help simplify some of the BSTR handling that the Fortune2 program had to go through.

As far as MFC is concerned, the client application is really just an example of a carefully planned program abort. In a normal MFC program, the developer typically creates a main program window in the **InitInstance()** method and registers the window with the framework. The Fortune3 client does none of this. Instead, it's content to go about its business culling all the information necessary to display its single message box. When the program exits from **InitInstance()** and MFC realizes that a main application window was never created, the framework aborts the program, and execution ends. I'd hesitate to call it elegant, but it certainly is functional.

There's not a whole lot more to say about the client. Although it's longer than the Fortune2 client program, the code that deals with the **IQuotation** interface is virtually identical to the code that services the **IFortuneTeller** interface. The only difference is that **GetQuotation()** returns two strings and **GetFortune()** returns just one. Figure 5.3 shows the final product, a message box with a minimally formatted fortune or quotation.

Figure 5.3 The Fortune3 client program in action.

Summary

You've covered a lot of ground in this chapter. From multiple interfaces, to interface maps, to external `IUnknowns`, I hope you've gained an appreciation for how the Microsoft Foundation Classes can help make the process of building sophisticated COM components easier and more efficient. MFC doesn't shield you from all the complexities of COM programming, but classes that would normally be very tricky or tedious to build from scratch are much easier to construct, using MFC-based techniques.

CHAPTER 6

USING AGGREGATION TO SIMULATE INHERITANCE

In this chapter, you will learn about the following:

- The ins and outs of aggregation
- Working with two in-process COM components

Now that you've seen how to build COM classes by using the MFC, I want to spend some time talking about aggregation. Aggregation is Microsoft's solution to the fact that COM interfaces do not support implementation inheritance. Keep in mind that COM enables you to build extensible software that can evolve over time and does not require intrusive maintenance. Aggregation helps you do this.

I'm sure you are aware that Microsoft Word has a spelling checker. That spelling checker is a COM component. Have you recently upgraded to Word 97? Did you realize that you just upgraded your COM-based spelling checker? As long as the new spelling checker supports your old spelling checker's interface, applications can take advantage of the new spelling checker's features without requiring the replacement or installation of older applications. This is the goal of COM. The way that Microsoft is able to update your spelling checker without breaking the older versions of programs that use that spelling checker component is *aggregation*. COM supports aggregation, which is just like inheritance.

The concept of aggregation, and its subsequent use in the development of COM components, approximates the results that you would achieve if you were building the same sort of functionality in a straight, non-COM C++ program.

What Does Aggregation Do for Us?

Aggregation revolves around a simple principal. If you want to build a COM class that exposes several interfaces, and some of those interfaces are already supported by components that have already been built, why not save yourself some work and reuse the preexisting components in your new class? Take a look at an example.

Suppose that one day you're approached by a friend who asks you to build a COM class for him. He needs you to build a `Robot` component that can be controlled through COM interfaces and that knows how to display itself in a program window. The `Robot` also has to make weird noises on demand.

You're in luck. It just so happens that some time ago you decided to purchase a COM `Robot` component from another programmer. This COM class supports a couple of useful interfaces. The first interface, `IRobot`, provides methods for moving the robot around a virtual area. Coincidentally, the second interface, `ISimpleDrawable`, can be used to draw the robot into an application's window. After close examination of the component's interface headers, you realize that the only requirement that your current robot can't fulfill is the capability to make strange noises. Unfortunately, your friend has expressed to you how important the weird sound feature is to him, and considering that he is paying for a custom COM component, you must find a way to meet your customer's requirements.

This presents a dilemma. Because you purchased your current `Robot` component from a third party, you don't have source code for the class. You know what interfaces the robot supports, but that's about it. Now if you didn't know better, you might be inclined to shrug your shoulders, toss out the old `Robot` component, and develop a new `Robot` class from scratch that meets your friend's requirements. But not you. You're going to use aggregation.

Aggregation will enable you to create a new component (let's call it `NoisyRobot`) that supports three interfaces: `IRobot`, `ISimpleDrawable`, and `INoise`. However, your new component is going to implement only the `INoise` interface. The other two interfaces will be implemented by a nested instance of your original `Robot` component. Using this strategy, you should be able to create the `NoisyRobot` component in no time.

The Mechanics of Aggregation

When aggregation is being used, an outer COM component wraps one or more instances of another COM class. For the rest of this chapter, I will call the exterior component instance the *outer object* and will refer to the internal component instance as the *inner object*.

When a client calls an outer object's `QueryInterface()` method to obtain an interface pointer, the component looks at the requested interface ID and checks whether the interface is one that is natively supported by the outer object. If the outer object does support the requested interface, the `QueryInterface()` call is handled in the same manner as any normal COM class. On the other hand, if the outer object does not natively support the requested interface, the outer object forwards the `QueryInterface()` call on to its inner object instance. Assuming that the inner object does support the interface, the call to the inner `QueryInterface()` will set the client's interface pointer, and the client will be unaware that the requested interface will henceforth be supported by an object instance of a completely different COM class.

Unfortunately, there's a subtle problem with this strategy. Remember that every interface is inherited from `IUnknown`. This means that the client, given an interface pointer from either the outer object or an inner object, should be able to call `QueryInterface()` and obtain any interface supported by either object. After all, the whole point of aggregation is to provide the appearance of a single object, even though multiple objects are collaborating to provide the class implementation.

The `IRobot` Interface Pointer

Keeping all that in mind, imagine what would happen under the following circumstances. The client application calls `CoCreateInstance()` to instantiate a new `NoisyRobot` object. During initialization, the `NoisyRobot` creates a new instance of the `Robot` class. At this point, the client has a pointer to the `NoisyRobot`'s `IUnknown`, and the `NoisyRobot` has a pointer to the `Robot`'s `IUnknown`. Now the client calls `QueryInterface()` on the `NoisyRobot`, asking for an `IRobot` interface pointer. `NoisyRobot` knows that he doesn't support `IRobot` (remember, he only implements `INoise`), so he calls `QueryInterface()` on the `Robot`'s `IUnknown` pointer, passing in the target pointer that he obtained from the client. The `Robot`, inside its `QueryInterface()`, recognizes `IRobot` as an interface that he supports and sets the client pointer accordingly. The state of affairs at this point is depicted in Figure 6.1.

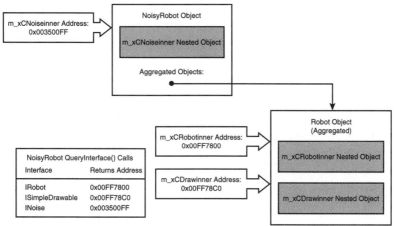

Figure 6.1   The client, `Robot`, and `NoisyRobot` after a `QueryInterface()` serviced by `Robot`.

The `INoise` Interface Pointer

So far so good. The client now has a fully functional `IRobot` pointer, and for all the client knows, the interface pointer belongs to `NoisyRobot`. But you are about to run into a problem. The client now needs an `INoise` interface, so it makes a call to `QueryInterface()`. The problem is that the client calls `QueryInterface()` on the `IRobot` pointer, not on the `IUnknown` pointer that belongs to the `NoisyRobot`. Because the `IRobot` interface pointer actually belongs to the `Robot`, the `QueryInterface()` call never passes through the `NoisyRobot`. The `Robot` doesn't know anything about `NoisyRobot` or `INoise`, so when it examines the requested interface ID and realizes that the interface is not supported, the method returns an error back to the client. The poor client program doesn't know what has gone wrong.

The central problem here is that the `Robot` object has no idea that it's part of an aggregation, and it doesn't realize that `QueryInterface()` calls always need to go through the outer object first. If there were some way to ensure that the `IUnknown` interface for the `Robot` always deferred to the `NoisyRobot IUnknown`, everything would work correctly. `QueryInterface()` always has to go through the outer object because even if a requested interface is supported by the inner object, the outer object might want to catch such requests and implement its own version of the interface.

Making the Inner Object Aware of Aggregation

The solution to this problem is to tell the inner object that it is being aggregated during the creation process. At the time of instantiation, the outer object can hand one of its `IUnknown` interface pointers to the inner object. The inner object can then hold on to this pointer and forward any `IUnknown` method calls on to the outer object. Note that reference counting calls also need to be passed on to the outer object; because the inner and outer object act together as a single entity, only one reference count should be maintained, and as the controlling entity, this responsibility falls on the outer object. This cautious dance of the `IUnknowns` can become intricate; check out Figure 6.2 for an illustration of the outer `IUnknown` pointer handoff.

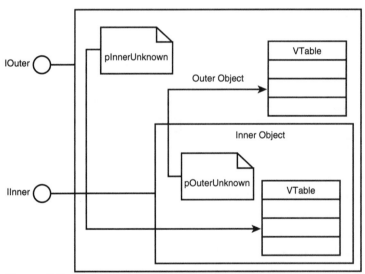

Figure 6.2 Passing off the controlling `IUnknown` pointer in an aggregation.

Aggregation, MFC-Style

MFC provides several methods that you can use to help with the construction of *aggregatable objects* (that is, COM classes that can become inner objects). More impressively, however, MFC provides `CCmdTarget` for managing `IUnknown` pointers in an aggregation and for routing `QueryInterface()` calls to the correct place.

Enabling a component to be aggregated involves a single, almost trivial change to your COM class. In the object's constructor, all you have to do is make a call to the **CCmdTarget** method **EnableAggregation()**. When you call this method, MFC performs some vtable trickery that will enable aggregation to operate smoothly. Calling this method has a negligible effect on your class if it's never used in an aggregation, but a call to this method is required for aggregation to work correctly. Therefore, because you can never anticipate who might want to use your class as part of an aggregation, it's a good idea to always call this method from inside your class's constructor, unless you have an explicit reason for not allowing aggregation.

Creating an object that is an aggregator requires more effort, but it's still pretty straightforward. However, before you start looking at some examples, I want to briefly discuss the difference between internal and external **IUnknown** implementations. Recall that earlier in this chapter I talked about how **CCmdTarget** provides two varieties of **IUnknown** methods. When you aggregate an object, these two **IUnknown** methods are how you distinguish between the inner and outer **IUnknown**s.

First, the internal **CCmdTarget IUnknown** methods—that is, **InternalAddRef()**, **InternalRelease()**, and **InternalQueryInterface()**—are the full-blown implementations of a traditional **IUnknown** interface. **InternalAddRef()** and **InternalRelease()** manage a standard reference count variable and operate in the same manner as any other versions of **AddRef()** and **Release()**.

InternalQueryInterface() also operates much as you would expect. The method uses the object's interface map to search for a supported interface pointer. If the interface isn't found, the **InternalQueryInterface()** method asks any aggregated inner objects whether they support the interface (assuming any inner objects exist). In short, the internal **IUnknown** methods are a standard **IUnknown** implementation.

Therefore, if the internal **IUnknown** methods are real, what does that imply for the external **IUnknown** methods that I've been telling you to call? The external **IUnknown** methods are actually just wrappers around calls to the internal versions of the same methods, with an important twist. If the class has had an outer, controlling **IUnknown** passed to the object during construction, the external methods instead forward the method call on to the controlling **IUnknown**, rather than to the internal version of the method. As an example, here's the **ExternalAddRef()** method code, pulled directly from the MFC source.

```
DWORD CCmdTarget::ExternalAddRef()
{
    // delegate to controling unknown if aggregated
    if (m_pOuterUnknown != NULL)
        return m_pOuterUnknown->AddRef();

    return InternalAddRef();
}
```

The **CCmdTarget** class maintains a member variable, **m_pOuterUnknown**, that is non-**NULL** if the class is the inner object in an aggregation. As you can see, **ExternalAddRef()** checks for the outer **IUnknown** and calls **AddRef()** on it if it exists. Otherwise, the method is just a pass-though to the internal version of the **AddRef()** method.

Now you can see why I urged you to always call external versions of the **IUnknown** methods. Assuming that your object calls **EnableAggregation()** in the constructor, you can never be sure whether your object is being used as a normal COM component or whether your class is being used as part of an aggregation. Calling the external **IUnknown** methods ensures that your object will operate correctly in both cases.

Building the Robot Component

Before you start digging into the implementation code for an outer class, I need to present the class that you will be aggregating.

The **IRobot** Interface

As discussed in the introduction to the aggregation section, in this example the standard **Robot** component supports two interfaces. The first interface, **IRobot**, supports methods that enable you to move a robot around a virtual world. Listing 6.1 shows the **IRobot** interface declaration.

Listing 6.1   IROBOT.H—The Declaration of the **IRobot** Interface

```
#ifndef IROBOT_H
#define IROBOT_H

// Get needed include files
#include "GUIDs.h"

// New interface declaration
DECLARE_INTERFACE_(IRobot, IUnknown)
{
  // IRobot
  STDMETHOD(Initialize)          (ULONG ulXPos, ULONG ulYPos) PURE;
  STDMETHOD(TurnTo)              (USHORT usDegrees) PURE;
  STDMETHOD(GetCurrentHeading)   (PUSHORT pusDegrees) PURE;
  STDMETHOD(GetCurrentPosition)  (PULONG pulXPos, PULONG pulYPos) PURE;
  STDMETHOD(MoveForward)         (ULONG ulNumUnits) PURE;
  STDMETHOD(MoveBackward)        (ULONG ulNumUnits) PURE;
};

typedef IRobot* PIRobot;

#endif
```

The interface is simple and to the point. An application uses the **Initialize()** method to place the robot at an (x,y) coordinate. **TurnTo()** spins the robot so that it's pointed toward the appropriate heading (specified in degrees). **MoveForward()** and **MoveBackward()** advance the robot forward and in reverse, and the **GetCurrentHeading()** and **GetCurrentPosition()** methods enable the client to query information about the robot's current orientation.

The `ISimpleDrawable` Interface

The second interface exposed by the `Robot` component, `ISimpleDrawable`, is even easier to understand. `ISimpleDrawable`, whose declaration is show in Listing 6.2, supports a single method, `Draw()`.

Listing 6.2   `IDRAWBL.H`—The Declaration of the `ISimpleDrawable` Interface

```
#ifndef IDRAWBL_H
#define IDRAWBL_H

// Get needed include files
#include "GUIDs.h"

// New interface declaration
DECLARE_INTERFACE_(ISimpleDrawable, IUnknown)
{
  // ISimpleDrawable
  STDMETHOD(Draw) (HDC hDC) PURE;
};

typedef ISimpleDrawable* PISimpleDrawable;

#endif
```

The `ISimpleDrawable` interface is used to interact with objects that have some sort of visual representation. If a class exposes `ISimpleDrawable`, the implication is that the object can be displayed and that the object knows how to display itself. The interface's `Draw()` method accepts a handle to standard Windows device context. This device context must be a valid device context; the object is to use the context as a canvas onto which the object will paint itself.

Note

It's probably worth mentioning that OLE provides two interfaces that serve similar, albeit more elaborate, purposes. The standard interfaces `IViewObject` and `IViewObject2` are used by OLE and ActiveX whenever a subsystem must interact with components that are displayable. For example, an ActiveX control typically must draw itself onto a Web browser's current document page, so most ActiveX controls expose `IViewObject2`. The `IViewObject` family of interfaces is considerably more capable (and complicated) than my puny `ISimpleDrawable` interface. Exposing `IViewObject2` requires the implementation of seven methods; the `IViewObject2` version of `Draw()` alone accepts a total of 10 parameters. With my user interface requirements being as modest as they are, you can see why I decided to write `ISimpleDrawable` rather than try to implement—and call—a full-blown `IViewObject2` interface.

The `ComRobot` COM Class

The declaration of the `ComRobot` class should be familiar to you because it's similar to the Fortune3 example in Chapter 5, "COM Programming with MFC." The class, shown in Listing 6.3, declares the nested interface handlers for `IRobot` and `ISimpleDrawable`, in addition to providing the prerequisite class factory plumbing.

Listing 6.3   ROBOT1.H—The Declaration of the `ComRobot` Class

```
#ifndef ROBOT1_H
#define ROBOT1_H

// Get needed include files
#include "IRobot.h"
#include "IDrawbl.h"


class ComRobot : public CCmdTarget
{
public:

    // Constructor and destructor
    ComRobot();
    virtual ~ComRobot();

protected:

    // IRobot members
    BEGIN_INTERFACE_PART(CRobotInner, IRobot)
        STDMETHOD(Initialize)          (ULONG ulXPos, ULONG ulYPos);
        STDMETHOD(TurnTo)              (USHORT usDegrees);
        STDMETHOD(GetCurrentHeading)   (PUSHORT pusDegrees);
        STDMETHOD(GetCurrentPosition)  (PULONG pulXPos, PULONG pulYPos);
        STDMETHOD(MoveForward)         (ULONG ulNumUnits);
        STDMETHOD(MoveBackward)        (ULONG ulNumUnits);
    END_INTERFACE_PART(CRobotInner)

    // ISimpleDrawable
    BEGIN_INTERFACE_PART(CDrawInner, ISimpleDrawable)
        STDMETHOD(Draw)(HDC hDC);
    END_INTERFACE_PART(CDrawInner)

    DECLARE_INTERFACE_MAP()
    DECLARE_OLECREATE(ComRobot)
    DECLARE_DYNCREATE(ComRobot)

private:

    // Member data
    USHORT m_usCurrHeading;
    ULONG  m_ulCurrXPos, m_ulCurrYPos;
```

```
   // Private methods
   VOID DrawHeading(CDC& DC);
};

typedef ComRobot* PComRobot;

#endif
```

You can also see that the class declares some private data. These data members will maintain the robot's current location and heading. The private `DrawHeading()` method is a helper method that is called whenever the robot is asked to draw itself through the `ISimpleDrawable` interface. Finally, you have the implementation of the `ComRobot` class itself in Listing 6.4.

Listing 6.4   `ROBOT1.CPP`—The Implementation of the `ComRobot` Class

```
#define INITGUID
#include <math.h>
#include "Robot1.h"
#include "Utility.h"


IMPLEMENT_DYNCREATE(ComRobot, CCmdTarget)

IMPLEMENT_OLECREATE(ComRobot, "Robot",
0xc8bd7017, 0x34fd, 0x11d0, 0x8b, 0xb9, 0xed, 0xea, 0x36,
➥0xf8, 0xb3, 0xc);

BEGIN_INTERFACE_MAP(ComRobot, CCmdTarget)
   INTERFACE_PART(ComRobot, IID_IRobot, RobotInner)
   INTERFACE_PART(ComRobot, IID_ISimpleDrawable, DrawInner)
END_INTERFACE_MAP()


// Useful constants
const ULONG  BufferZoneRadius  = 40;
const ULONG  TriangleHeight    = 7;
const ULONG  TriangleHalfWidth = 7;
const ULONG  RobotHeight       = 65;
const ULONG  RobotWidth        = 55;


//
// Constructor and destructor
//

ComRobot::ComRobot()
          : m_usCurrHeading(0UL),
            m_ulCurrXPos(0UL),
            m_ulCurrYPos(0UL)
{
   VerboseMsg("In ComRobot constructor.\n");
```

continued on next page

continued from previous page

```
        // Allow other components to aggregate us if they need to
        EnableAggregation();

        AfxOleLockApp();
    }

    ComRobot::~ComRobot()
    {
        VerboseMsg("In ComRobot destructor.\n");
        AfxOleUnlockApp();
    }


    //
    // Nested Robot IUnknown members
    //

    STDMETHODIMP_(ULONG)
    ComRobot::XRobotInner::AddRef()
    {
        METHOD_PROLOGUE(ComRobot, RobotInner)
        return pThis->ExternalAddRef();
    }

    STDMETHODIMP_(ULONG)
    ComRobot::XRobotInner::Release()
    {
        METHOD_PROLOGUE(ComRobot, RobotInner)
        return pThis->ExternalRelease();
    }

    STDMETHODIMP
    ComRobot::XRobotInner::QueryInterface(REFIID riid, PPVOID ppv)
    {
        METHOD_PROLOGUE(ComRobot, RobotInner)
        return pThis->ExternalQueryInterface(&riid, ppv);
    }


    //
    // IRobot interface members for nested Robot class
    //

    STDMETHODIMP
    ComRobot::XRobotInner::Initialize(ULONG ulXPos,
                                      ULONG ulYPos)
    {
        METHOD_PROLOGUE(ComRobot, RobotInner)
        VerboseMsg("In XRobotInner::Initialize.\n");

        // Set our starting position
        pThis->m_ulCurrXPos = ulXPos;
        pThis->m_ulCurrYPos = ulYPos;
```

```
   return NOERROR;
}

STDMETHODIMP
ComRobot::XRobotInner::TurnTo(USHORT usDegrees)
{
   METHOD_PROLOGUE(ComRobot, RobotInner)
   VerboseMsg("In TurnTo.\n");

   // Set the new heading, taking care to ensure that the value
   // lies between 0 and 360 (higher values will wrap around)
   pThis->m_usCurrHeading = usDegrees % 360;

   return NOERROR;
}

STDMETHODIMP
ComRobot::XRobotInner::GetCurrentHeading(PUSHORT pusDegrees)
{
   METHOD_PROLOGUE(ComRobot, RobotInner)
   VerboseMsg("In GetCurrentHeading.\n");

   *pusDegrees = pThis->m_usCurrHeading;

   return NOERROR;
}

STDMETHODIMP
ComRobot::XRobotInner::GetCurrentPosition(PULONG pulXPos,
➥PULONG pulYPos)
{
   METHOD_PROLOGUE(ComRobot, RobotInner)
   VerboseMsg("In GetCurrentPosition.\n");

   *pulXPos = pThis->m_ulCurrXPos;
   *pulYPos = pThis->m_ulCurrYPos;

   return NOERROR;
}

STDMETHODIMP
ComRobot::XRobotInner::MoveForward(ULONG ulNumUnits)
{
   METHOD_PROLOGUE(ComRobot, RobotInner)
   VerboseMsg("In MoveForward.\n");

   pThis->m_ulCurrXPos += (LONG)(ulNumUnits *
                            cos(Radians(pThis->m_usCurrHeading)));
   pThis->m_ulCurrYPos -= (LONG)(ulNumUnits *
                            sin(Radians(pThis->m_usCurrHeading)));

   return NOERROR;
}
```

continued on next page

continued from previous page

```
STDMETHODIMP
ComRobot::XRobotInner::MoveBackward(ULONG ulNumUnits)
{
    METHOD_PROLOGUE(ComRobot, RobotInner)
    VerboseMsg("In MoveBackward.\n");

    pThis->m_ulCurrXPos += (LONG)(ulNumUnits *
                        cos(Radians(pThis->m_usCurrHeading
                        ↪+ 180)));
    pThis->m_ulCurrYPos -= (LONG)(ulNumUnits *
                        sin(Radians(pThis->m_usCurrHeading
                        ↪+ 180)));

    return NOERROR;
}


//
// Nested Draw IUnknown members
//

STDMETHODIMP_(ULONG)
ComRobot::XDrawInner::AddRef()
{
    METHOD_PROLOGUE(ComRobot, DrawInner)
    return pThis->ExternalAddRef();
}

STDMETHODIMP_(ULONG)
ComRobot::XDrawInner::Release()
{
    METHOD_PROLOGUE(ComRobot, DrawInner)
    return pThis->ExternalRelease();
}

STDMETHODIMP
ComRobot::XDrawInner::QueryInterface(REFIID riid, PPVOID ppv)
{
    METHOD_PROLOGUE(ComRobot, DrawInner)
    return pThis->ExternalQueryInterface(&riid, ppv);
}


//
// ISimpleDrawable interface members for nested Draw class
//

STDMETHODIMP
ComRobot::XDrawInner::Draw(HDC hDC)
{
    HRESULT hResult;
    CDC     DC;
```

```
    METHOD_PROLOGUE(ComRobot, DrawInner)
    VerboseMsg("In XDrawInner::Draw.\n");

    hResult = DC.Attach(hDC);
    if (FAILED(hResult)) {
        VerboseMsg("Failed to attach hDC to CDC object
        ➥in XDrawInner::Draw.\n");
        return hResult;
    }

    // Draw the heading tick
    pThis->DrawHeading(DC);

    CDC memorydc;

    CBitmap m_bmRobotBitmap;
    m_bmRobotBitmap.LoadBitmap("Robot");

    memorydc.CreateCompatibleDC(&DC);
    CBitmap* pOldBitmap = memorydc.SelectObject (&m_bmRobotBitmap);

    hResult = DC.BitBlt(pThis->m_ulCurrXPos - (RobotWidth / 2),
                        pThis->m_ulCurrYPos - (RobotHeight / 2),
                        RobotWidth,
                        RobotHeight,
                        &memorydc,
                        0,
                        0,
                        SRCCOPY);

    memorydc.SelectObject (pOldBitmap);

    if (FAILED(hResult)) {
        VerboseMsg("Failed to draw Robot rectangle.\n");
        return hResult;
    }

    return NOERROR;
}

VOID ComRobot::DrawHeading(CDC& DC)
{
    // Our heading indicator should be filled in blue
    CBrush  TriangleFillBrush(Blue);
    CBrush  *pOldBrush = DC.SelectObject(&TriangleFillBrush);

    // Calculate some trig stuff and hold on to it for later
    DOUBLE dCosHeading = cos(Radians(m_usCurrHeading));
    DOUBLE dSinHeading = sin(Radians(m_usCurrHeading));

    // Top of triangle
    ULONG ulTopX = m_ulCurrXPos + (BufferZoneRadius * dCosHeading) +
                   (TriangleHeight * dCosHeading);
```

continued on next page

continued from previous page

```
        ULONG ulTopY = m_ulCurrYPos - (BufferZoneRadius * dSinHeading) -
                       (TriangleHeight * dSinHeading);

        // Right vertice
        ULONG ulRightVerticeX = m_ulCurrXPos + (BufferZoneRadius
        ➥* dCosHeading) +
                                (TriangleHalfWidth * dSinHeading);
        ULONG ulRightVerticeY = m_ulCurrYPos - (BufferZoneRadius
        ➥* dSinHeading) +
                                (TriangleHalfWidth * dCosHeading);

        // Left vertice
        ULONG ulLeftVerticeX = m_ulCurrXPos + (BufferZoneRadius
        ➥* dCosHeading) -
                               (TriangleHalfWidth * dSinHeading);
        ULONG ulLeftVerticeY = m_ulCurrYPos - (BufferZoneRadius
        ➥* dSinHeading) -
                               (TriangleHalfWidth * dCosHeading);

        // Create the polygon array
        POINT   aPoints[] = { { ulTopX,         ulTopY,         },
                              { ulLeftVerticeX,  ulLeftVerticeY, },
                              { ulRightVerticeX, ulRightVerticeY } };
        DC.Polygon(aPoints, 3);

        // Restore the brush
        DC.SelectObject(pOldBrush);
}
```

The implementation of the `Robot` class is straightforward and looks very much like the implementation of the `ComFortuneTeller` class for the server in the Fortune3 example. Notice the call to `EnableAggregation()` in the class constructor. The `NoisyRobot` component that I'll be going over shortly will not work unless the `EnableAggregation()` call is made from within the aggregated inner class object.

With the `DrawHeading()` method, I wanted the robot's heading indicator to revolve around the robot so that it was always pointing in the direction that the robot was facing. As far as the mechanics of the `DrawHeading()` method, it's a simple Windows GDI and a little trigonometry. I am not going to cover the GDI code here because the focus of this book is COM and DCOM.

The Client and the Server

The server implementation is almost a direct copy of the server code presented for the Fortune3 example in Chapter 5, so I'm not going to duplicate the code here. The client program, however, is another story.

The robot client is composed of two main classes. The central application class—derived from `CWinApp`, like every good MFC application citizen—is responsible for initializing the COM subsystem and creating the main window. Listing 6.5 shows the short declaration and implementation of `CRobotApp`.

Listing 6.5 ROBOT1.CPP—The Implementation of the Client's CRobotApp Class

```
#define INITGUID
#include "MainWin.h"
#include "Utility.h"


class CRobotApp : public CWinApp
{
public:

   // Overrides
   virtual BOOL InitInstance();
   virtual int ExitInstance();
};

// The one and only CRobotApp object
CRobotApp RobotApp;


BOOL CRobotApp::InitInstance()
{
   // Prepare COM for use
   VerboseMsg("Calling COM API CoInitialize.\n");
   HRESULT hResult = CoInitialize(NULL);
   if (FAILED(hResult)) {
      ReportError("Could not initialize COM.", hResult);
      return FALSE;
   }

   // Create the main frame window
   m_pMainWnd = new CMainWindow;
   m_pMainWnd->ShowWindow(m_nCmdShow);
   m_pMainWnd->UpdateWindow();

   return TRUE;
}

int CRobotApp::ExitInstance()
{
   // We're all done with COM
   CoUninitialize();

   return CWinApp::ExitInstance();
}
```

The Client Main Window

The main window, encapsulated into a class named, appropriately enough, CMainWindow, is responsible for interacting with the Robot component and trapping user-interface events. The CMainWindow class is declared in the MAINWIN.H header file, which is shown in Listing 6.6.

Listing 6.6   MAINWIN.H—The Declaration of the Client's CMainWindow Class

```
#ifndef MAINWIN_H
#define MAINWIN_H

#include "StdInc.h"
#include "IRobot.h"
#include "IDrawbl.h"


class CMainWindow : public CFrameWnd
{
public:

    CMainWindow();
    virtual ~CMainWindow();

protected:

    afx_msg int  OnCreate(LPCREATESTRUCT);
    afx_msg void OnPaint();
    afx_msg void OnKeyUp(UINT nChar, UINT nRepCnt, UINT nFlags);

    DECLARE_MESSAGE_MAP()

private:
    ISimpleDrawable   *m_pISimpleDrawable;
    IRobot            *m_pIRobot;
};

#endif
```

The CMainWindow class is derived from the MFC class window class, CFrameWnd. CFrameWnd provides the implementation for a standard frame window, including niceties such as a title bar and system menu. The CMainWindow class declares private data to manage two interface pointers (one for an IRobot and one for an ISimpleDrawable). The class overrides the OnCreate() method so that it can provide some startup code. CMainWindow also captures paint and key press events, which MFC will route to the OnPaint() and OnKeyUp() methods.

Now take a look at Listing 6.7, which shows the implementation of the CMainWindow class, as well as the main source code for the Robot client program.

Listing 6.7   MAINWIN.CPP—The Implementation of the Client's CMainWindow Class

```
#include "MainWin.h"
#include "Utility.h"


BEGIN_MESSAGE_MAP(CMainWindow, CFrameWnd)
    ON_WM_CREATE()
    ON_WM_PAINT()
    ON_WM_KEYUP()
END_MESSAGE_MAP()
```

```
CMainWindow::CMainWindow()
        : m_pISimpleDrawable(NULL),
          m_pIRobot(NULL)

{
   Create(NULL, "Robot Client Program");
}

CMainWindow::~CMainWindow()
{
   // Release COM interfaces
   if (m_pISimpleDrawable) {
      m_pISimpleDrawable->Release();
      m_pISimpleDrawable = NULL;
   }
   if (m_pIRobot) {
      m_pIRobot->Release();
      m_pIRobot = NULL;
   }
}

int CMainWindow::OnCreate(LPCREATESTRUCT lpcs)
{
   HRESULT  hResult;

   if (CFrameWnd::OnCreate(lpcs) == -1)
      return -1;

   // Create a new Robot object and return an IRobot
   // interface pointer
   VerboseMsg("Creating new Robot object instance.\n");
   hResult = CoCreateInstance(CLSID_Robot,
                              NULL, CLSCTX_INPROC_SERVER,
                              IID_IRobot,
                              (PPVOID) &m_pIRobot);
   if (FAILED(hResult)) {
      ReportError("Could not create a new Robot object.", hResult);
   }

   else {

      try
      {

         // Initialize the robot
         VerboseMsg("Initializing Robot object.\n");
         hResult = m_pIRobot->Initialize(150, 150);
         if (FAILED(hResult)) {
            ReportError("Could not initialize the
            ➥new Robot object.", hResult);
            throw FALSE;
         }
```

continued on next page

continued from previous page

```
                    // Obtain a drawable interface pointer (we'll hold on to this
                    // interface pointer for the duration of the view lifetime)
                    VerboseMsg("Obtaining ISimpleDrawable interface.\n");
                    hResult = m_pIRobot->QueryInterface(IID_ISimpleDrawable,
                                          (PPVOID)
                                            ➥&m_pISimpleDrawable);
                    if (FAILED(hResult)) {
                        ReportError("Could not obtain ISimpleDrawable
                        ➥interface.", hResult);
                        throw FALSE;
                    }

                    VerboseMsg("Object initialized fine.\n");
                }
                catch(HRESULT)
                {
                    VerboseMsg("Robot construction failed.\n");

                    // Clean up
                    m_pIRobot->Release();
                    m_pIRobot = NULL;
                }
            }

            return 0;
        }

        void CMainWindow::OnPaint()
        {
            CPaintDC dc(this);

            if (m_pISimpleDrawable)
                m_pISimpleDrawable->Draw(dc);
        }

        void CMainWindow::OnKeyUp(UINT nChar, UINT nRepCnt, UINT nFlags)
        {
            USHORT usHeading;

            switch(nChar) {

            case VK_LEFT:
                if (m_pIRobot) {
                    m_pIRobot->GetCurrentHeading(&usHeading);
                    m_pIRobot->TurnTo(usHeading + 15);
                    Invalidate(TRUE);
                }
                break;

            case VK_RIGHT:
                if (m_pIRobot) {
                    m_pIRobot->GetCurrentHeading(&usHeading);
                    if (usHeading < 15)
```

```
                usHeading = 360 + usHeading;
            m_pIRobot->TurnTo(usHeading - 15);
            Invalidate(TRUE);
        }
        break;

    case VK_UP:
        if (m_pIRobot) {
            m_pIRobot->MoveForward(30);
            Invalidate(TRUE);
        }
        break;

    case VK_DOWN:
        if (m_pIRobot) {
            m_pIRobot->MoveBackward(30);
            Invalidate(TRUE);
        }
        break;
    }
}
```

The CMainWindow creates an instance of the Robot component when the window is first created. This code, found in the OnCreate() method, instantiates the robot and initializes the robot's position to coordinates (150,150). OnCreate() also sets the m_pISimpleDrawable member variable by calling QueryInterface() and asking for an ISimpleDrawable interface pointer.

The OnPaint() method provided by CMainWindow is trivial. The class instantiates a device context that can be used to paint in the window's client area and then calls the Draw() method, found in the ISimpleDrawable interface. Because the object is responsible for its own appearance, all the tricky painting code is relegated to the COM component. The client has the luxury of remaining completely unaware of what the robot looks like and how much screen real estate the object will take up.

Finally, the OnKeyUp() method catches keyboard presses made by the user. Navigating the robot is simple; the left arrow rotates the robot 15 degrees to the left, the right arrow rotates the robot 15 degrees to the right, the up arrow moves the robot forward, and the down arrow moves the robot backward. The OnKeyUp() method captures each of these key presses, manipulates the robot object accordingly, and invalidates the window (which causes the windows to be repainted).

I'll be the first to admit that the final result doesn't exactly take your breath away, but it's still kind of fun to run the client and take your robot out for a spin. Figure 6.3 shows the Robot client program in action.

Caution

Don't forget to register your Robot server with the COM subsystem by using the REGSVR32 utility program. The Robot client program will not function correctly until the server is correctly registered.

Figure 6.3 The Robot client program.

Aggregation in Action: The `NoisyRobot` Component

Although the ComRobot is moderately interesting, the whole discussion of ComRobot is just a prelude to the main event. What you really want to see is a COM component that uses aggregation: Enter ComNoisyRobot. The NoisyRobot component aggregates the Robot class in order to add the INoise interface. INoise, whose declaration is depicted in Listing 6.8, exposes a single method, MakeNoise().

Listing 6.8   INOISE.H—The Declaration of the INoise Interface

```
#ifndef INOISE_H
#define INOISE_H

// Get needed include files
#include "GUIDs.h"

// New interface declaration
DECLARE_INTERFACE_(INoise, IUnknown)
{
  // INoise
  STDMETHOD(MakeNoise)() PURE;
};

typedef INoise* PINoise;

#endif
```

How a component decides to implement INoise is, of course, up to the component, but the ComNoisyRobot will respond to a MakeNoise() call by playing a random wave resource that is compiled into the server DLL.

Listing 6.9 shows the declaration of the `ComNoisyRobot` class. On the surface, the class looks like an ordinary MFC-based COM component, but a couple of crucial elements here should not be overlooked.

Listing 6.9   `ROBOT2.H`—The Declaration of the `ComNoisyRobot` Class

```
#ifndef ROBOT2_H
#define ROBOT2_H

// Get needed include files
#include "INoise.h"


class ComNoisyRobot : public CCmdTarget
{
public:

    // Constructor and destructor
    ComNoisyRobot();
    virtual ~ComNoisyRobot();

protected:

    // Overridden method required for aggregation
    virtual BOOL OnCreateAggregates();

    // INoise members
    BEGIN_INTERFACE_PART(CNoiseInner, INoise)
        STDMETHOD(MakeNoise)();
    END_INTERFACE_PART(CNoiseInner)

    DECLARE_INTERFACE_MAP()
    DECLARE_OLECREATE(ComNoisyRobot)
    DECLARE_DYNCREATE(ComNoisyRobot)

private:

    // Aggregation pointer
    IUnknown   *m_pAggrIUnknown;
};

typedef ComNoisyRobot* PComNoisyRobot;

#endif
```

Two important things should be noted about the `ComNoisyRobot` class declaration. The first is the declaration of the `m_pAggrIUnknown` member data pointer. This pointer is where the `ComNoisyRobot` class will hold on to the `IUnknown` interface belonging to the inner `Robot` component.

The second part of the `ComNoisyRobot` declaration worthy of note is the overriding of the virtual method `OnCreateAggregates()`. This is a method that is called by the class factory as part of the component construction process. It is inside `OnCreateAggregates()`

that the `ComNoisyRobot` class will create the inner `Robot` object instance. It's important to note that the creation of your aggregation's inner object (or objects) needs to occur inside `OnCreateAggregates()`, as opposed to your class's constructor. As you will see, you need to pass your component's `IUnknown` pointer in to the `CoCreateInstance()` call that will construct your aggregate object.

Caution

If you're not using an MFC-based class factory to instantiate your component, you will need to ensure that the `OnCreateAggregates()` method is called at some point in the object creation process. The vast majority of programmers will not have to worry about this step because the class factory provided by the **DYNCREATE** and **OLECREATE** macros will call this method automatically.

Now that you've seen what the `ComNoisyRobot` class will look like, take a quick browse through Listing 6.10. This listing shows **ROBOT2.CPP**, the implementation of the `ComNoisyRobot` class.

Listing 6.1   `ROBOT2.CPP`—The Implementation of the `ComNoisyRobot` Class

```
#define INITGUID
#include <stdlib.h>
#include <time.h>
#include <sys/types.h>
#include <sys/timeb.h>
#include "Robot2.h"
#include "Utility.h"
#include "resource.h"
#include <mmsystem.h>


// Sound identifiers
int g_aiSoundIds[] =
   {
       WAV_BLADDLE,
       WAV_COW,
       WAV_GAMESHOW,
       WAV_GARGLE,
       WAV_LAUGH,
       WAV_OHNO,
       WAV_OOOO,
       WAV_OUCH,
       WAV_TAXI
   };

// Constant that tracks the number of longer sounds
static const ULONG g_ulNumOtherSounds =
   sizeof(g_aiSoundIds) / sizeof(int);
```

```
IMPLEMENT_DYNCREATE(ComNoisyRobot, CCmdTarget)

IMPLEMENT_OLECREATE(ComNoisyRobot, "NoisyRobot",
0xf8d4bfd6, 0x4277, 0x11d0, 0x8b, 0xe2, 0xad, 0x32, 0xe5,
➡0x41, 0xaf, 0xc);

BEGIN_INTERFACE_MAP(ComNoisyRobot, CCmdTarget)
    INTERFACE_PART(ComNoisyRobot, IID_INoise, CNoiseInner)
    INTERFACE_AGGREGATE(ComNoisyRobot, m_pAggrIUnknown)
END_INTERFACE_MAP()


//
// Constructor and destructor
//

ComNoisyRobot::ComNoisyRobot()
        : m_pAggrIUnknown(NULL)
{
    VerboseMsg("In ComNoisyRobot constructor.\n");

    // Seed the random number generator
    struct _timeb timebuffer;
    _ftime(&timebuffer);
    srand(timebuffer.millitm);

    // Allow other components to aggregate us if they need to
    EnableAggregation();

    AfxOleLockApp();
}

ComNoisyRobot::~ComNoisyRobot()
{
    VerboseMsg("In ComNoisyRobot destructor.\n");

    // Release our aggregate
    if (m_pAggrIUnknown) {
        m_pAggrIUnknown->Release();
        m_pAggrIUnknown = NULL;
    }

    AfxOleUnlockApp();
}


//
// Virtual functions overriden from CCmdTarget
//

BOOL ComNoisyRobot::OnCreateAggregates()
{
    HRESULT    hResult;
```

continued on next page

continued from previous page

```
                // Create a new Robot object to aggregate with
                VerboseMsg("Creating new Robot aggregate.\n");
                hResult = CoCreateInstance(CLSID_Robot,
                                           GetControllingUnknown(),
                                           CLSCTX_INPROC_SERVER,
                                           IID_IUnknown,
                                           (PPVOID) &m_pAggrIUnknown);
            if (FAILED(hResult)) {
                ReportError("Could not create a new Robot aggregate.", hResult);
                return FALSE;
            }

            return TRUE;
        }


        //
        // Nested Robot IUnknown members
        //

        STDMETHODIMP_(ULONG)
        ComNoisyRobot::XCNoiseInner::AddRef()
        {
            METHOD_PROLOGUE(ComNoisyRobot, CNoiseInner)
            return pThis->ExternalAddRef();
        }

        STDMETHODIMP_(ULONG)
        ComNoisyRobot::XCNoiseInner::Release()
        {
            METHOD_PROLOGUE(ComNoisyRobot, CNoiseInner)
            return pThis->ExternalRelease();
        }

        STDMETHODIMP
        ComNoisyRobot::XCNoiseInner::QueryInterface(REFIID riid, PPVOID ppv)
        {
            METHOD_PROLOGUE(ComNoisyRobot, CNoiseInner)
            return pThis->ExternalQueryInterface(&riid, ppv);
        }


        //
        // INoise interface members for nested Noise class
        //

        STDMETHODIMP
        ComNoisyRobot::XCNoiseInner::MakeNoise()
        {
            METHOD_PROLOGUE(ComNoisyRobot, CNoiseInner)
            VerboseMsg("In XCNoiseInner::MakeNoise\n");

            PlaySound(MAKEINTRESOURCE(g_aiSoundIds[rand()
            ➥% g_ulNumOtherSounds]),
```

```
                     AfxGetResourceHandle(),
                     SND_RESOURCE ¦ SND_ASYNC);

     return NOERROR;
}
```

Allow me to start the discussion of the `ComNoisyRobot` class by pointing out those aspects of the class that are relatively standardized and worthy of little note. The `IUnknown` implementation of the nested `XCNoiseInner` class is exactly what you would expect and is virtually identical to the implementations that you'll find in the `Robot` and `Fortune3` components. The implementation of the `MakeNoise()` method is also rather pedestrian; the method randomly selects a wave file identifier from the `g_aiSoundIds` array and plays the appropriate resource, using the Win32 multimedia API `PlaySound()`.

Now look at the new stuff. One of the first things that probably leaps out at you is the implementation of the interface map. Although the general structure looks the same as previous examples, there's a new macro in town: `INTERFACE_AGGREGATE`.

```
BEGIN_INTERFACE_MAP(ComNoisyRobot, CCmdTarget)
   INTERFACE_PART(ComNoisyRobot, IID_INoise, CNoiseInner)
   INTERFACE_AGGREGATE(ComNoisyRobot, m_pAggrIUnknown)
END_INTERFACE_MAP()
```

The `INTERFACE_PART` macro is required to notify MFC that the outer `ComNoisyRobot` class will be implementing the `INoise` interface. The `INTERFACE_AGGREGATE` macro, on the other hand, tells COM that the `ComNoisyRobot` class will be relying on an aggregated class to help with interface implementation. The `INTERFACE_AGGREGATE` macro accepts two arguments, the name of the outer class and the name of a member variable that will contain an `IUnknown` (or `IUnknown`-derived) pointer to the aggregate.

You might be surprised to find that the `ComNoisyRobot` class does not have to specifically indicate to MFC *which* interfaces will be serviced by the inner, aggregated class. This is because of the algorithm that MFC uses when trying to track down an interface pointer during a call to `QueryInterface()`. MFC can determine from the interface map those interfaces that `ComNoisyRobot` directly supports; that part is easy. If, however, MFC still hasn't found an interface pointer after checking all the outer object's native interface entries, the framework (specifically, `CCmdTarget`) proceeds to check aggregates. Each aggregate entry in the interface map has a pointer to an `IUnknown` pointer, provided by the outer object through the `INTERFACE_AGGREGATE` macro. MFC can determine whether the aggregate supports the requested interface simply by calling `QueryInterface()` on each of the aggregate entries that it finds in the interface map. If the `QueryInterface()` method returns `E_NOTIMPL`, MFC knows that the aggregate doesn't support the requested interface, and it moves on to the next aggregate (if there is one, of course).

The last thing that differentiates `ComNoisyRobot` is the inclusion of the virtual method `OnCreateAggregates()`. This method, which I've duplicated, is called by the component's class factory after the outer object instance has been fully instantiated:

```
BOOL ComNoisyRobot::OnCreateAggregates()
{
   HRESULT    hResult;
```

```
    // Create a new Robot object to aggregate with
    VerboseMsg("Creating new Robot aggregate.\n");
    hResult = CoCreateInstance(CLSID_Robot,
                               GetControllingUnknown(),
                               CLSCTX_INPROC_SERVER,
                               IID_IUnknown,
                               (PPVOID) &m_pAggrIUnknown);
    if (FAILED(hResult)) {
        ReportError("Could not create a new Robot
        ➥aggregate.", hResult);
        return FALSE;
    }

    return TRUE;
}
```

The `OnCreateAggregates()` method is where your aggregation class should instanti-ate all its constituent inner objects. In the `ComNoisyRobot` server, this means creating a new `Robot` instance by using the standard `CoCreateInstance()` API. A pointer to the `Robot`'s `IUnknown` interface is stored in the class's `m_pAggrIUnknown` member variable; remember that this was the variable that was registered with MFC as being the aggregate pointer in the `INTERFACE_AGGREGATE` macro.

Note

As you can see from Listing 6.10, the `ComNoisyRobot` class calls `EnableAggregation()` in the constructor. Just because the `ComNoisyRobot` class itself is implemented by using aggregation doesn't mean that the `NoisyRobot` component couldn't be used as part of another component's aggregation. You can nest aggregations arbitrarily deep, so don't forget to call `EnableAggregation()` in your constructors.

That's about it for the `ComNoisyRobot` component class. Like the `Robot` example, the main application class is identical to the class presented for the Fortune3 example, so I'm not going to duplicate that code here (don't worry, all the code is supplied on the includ-ed CD-ROM).

The `NoisyRobot` client program is almost exactly the same as the client program that I showed you for the `Robot` server. However, a few trivial modifications need to be made that enable you to exercise the new `INoise` interface that the `NoisyRobot` component pro-vides. Because all the changes are in the `CMainWindow` class, Listing 6.11 shows the new implementation file.

Listing 6.11 `MAINWIN.CPP`—The Implementation of the `NoisyRobot` Client's `CMainWindow` Class

```
#include "MainWin.h"
#include "Utility.h"
```

```
BEGIN_MESSAGE_MAP(CMainWindow, CFrameWnd)
   ON_WM_CREATE()
   ON_WM_PAINT()
   ON_WM_KEYUP()
END_MESSAGE_MAP()


CMainWindow::CMainWindow()
         : m_pISimpleDrawable(NULL),
           m_pIRobot(NULL),
           m_pINoise(NULL)
{
   Create(NULL, "NoisyRobot Client Program");
}

CMainWindow::~CMainWindow()
{
   // Release COM interfaces
   if (m_pISimpleDrawable) {
      m_pISimpleDrawable->Release();
      m_pISimpleDrawable = NULL;
   }
   if (m_pIRobot) {
      m_pIRobot->Release();
      m_pIRobot = NULL;
   }
   if (m_pINoise) {
      m_pINoise->Release();
      m_pINoise = NULL;
   }
}

void CMainWindow::OnPaint()
{
   CPaintDC dc(this);

   if (m_pISimpleDrawable)
      m_pISimpleDrawable->Draw(dc);
}

int CMainWindow::OnCreate(LPCREATESTRUCT lpcs)
{
   HRESULT   hResult;

   if (CFrameWnd::OnCreate(lpcs) == -1)
      return -1;

   // Create a new NoisyRobot object and return an IRobot
   // interface pointer
   VerboseMsg("Creating new NoisyRobot object instance.\n");
   hResult = CoCreateInstance(CLSID_NoisyRobot,
                              NULL, CLSCTX_INPROC_SERVER,
                              IID_IRobot,
```

continued on next page

continued from previous page

```
                                    (PPVOID) &m_pIRobot);
            if (FAILED(hResult)) {
                ReportError("Could not create a new
                ➥NoisyRobot object.", hResult);
            }

            else {

                try
                {

                    // Initialize the robot
                    VerboseMsg("Initializing Robot object.\n");
                    hResult = m_pIRobot->Initialize(150, 150);
                    if (FAILED(hResult)) {
                        ReportError("Could not initialize the new
                        ➥Robot object.", hResult);
                        throw FALSE;
                    }

                    // Obtain a drawable interface pointer (we'll hold on to this
                    // interface pointer for the duration of the view lifetime)
                    VerboseMsg("Obtaining ISimpleDrawable interface.\n");
                    hResult = m_pIRobot->QueryInterface(IID_ISimpleDrawable,
                                        (PPVOID)
                                        ➥&m_pISimpleDrawable);
                    if (FAILED(hResult)) {
                        ReportError("Could not obtain
                        ➥ISimpleDrawable interface.", hResult);
                        throw FALSE;
                    }

                    // Obtain a noise interface pointer (we'll hold on to this
                    // interface pointer for the duration of the view lifetime)
                    VerboseMsg("Obtaining INoise interface.\n");
                    hResult = m_pIRobot->QueryInterface(IID_INoise,
                                                (PPVOID) &m_pINoise);
                    if (FAILED(hResult)) {
                        ReportError("Could not obtain
                        ➥INoise interface.", hResult);
                        throw FALSE;
                    }

                    VerboseMsg("Object initialized fine.\n");
                }
                catch(HRESULT)
                {
                    VerboseMsg("Robot construction failed.\n");

                    // Clean up
                    m_pIRobot->Release();
                    m_pIRobot = NULL;
```

```
          if (m_pISimpleDrawable) {
             m_pISimpleDrawable->Release();
             m_pISimpleDrawable = NULL;
          }
       }
    }

    return 0;
}


void CMainWindow::OnKeyUp(UINT nChar, UINT nRepCnt, UINT nFlags)
{
    USHORT usHeading;

       switch(nChar) {

       case VK_LEFT:
          if (m_pIRobot) {
             m_pIRobot->GetCurrentHeading(&usHeading);
             m_pIRobot->TurnTo(usHeading + 15);
             Invalidate(TRUE);
          }
          break;

       case VK_RIGHT:
          if (m_pIRobot) {
             m_pIRobot->GetCurrentHeading(&usHeading);
             if (usHeading < 15)
                usHeading = 360 + usHeading;
             m_pIRobot->TurnTo(usHeading - 15);
             Invalidate(TRUE);
          }
          break;

       case VK_UP:
          if (m_pIRobot) {
             m_pIRobot->MoveForward(30);
             Invalidate(TRUE);
          }
          break;

       case VK_DOWN:
          if (m_pIRobot) {
             m_pIRobot->MoveBackward(30);
             Invalidate(TRUE);
          }
          break;

       case 'N':
          if (m_pINoise)
             m_pINoise->MakeNoise();
          break;
    }
}
```

The `NoisyRobot`-aware `CMainWindow` class adds a new member variable, `m_pINoise`. This member variable is set inside the `OnCreate()` method at the same time that the class creates the new `NoisyRobot` object instance and sets the `ISimpleDrawable` interface pointer member variable. This interface pointer is subsequently used in the `OnKeyUp()` method whenever the user presses the *n* key (or *N* key). The `CMainWindow` class verifies that the `m_pINoise` variable has been set and then calls the `INoise` method `MakeNoise()`. Although the new client program looks exactly the same as the `Robot` client program, you'll now be treated to an interesting sound whenever the user presses the correct key.

When all is said and done, you'll find yourself with a new component, `NoisyRobot`, that can be manipulated and controlled by clients in exactly the same fashion as any other COM object. The difference, of course, is that `NoisyRobot` uses COM aggregation to dramatically cut down on the amount of additional code required to add functionality to the `Robot` component.

Summary

You've covered a lot of ground in this chapter. From multiple interfaces to aggregation, interface maps to external `IUnknowns`, I hope you've gained an appreciation for how the Microsoft Foundation Classes can help make the process of building sophisticated COM components easier and more efficient. MFC doesn't shield you from all the complexities of COM programming, but classes that would normally be very tricky or tedious to build from scratch are much easier to construct using MFC-based techniques. In Chapter 7, "Breaking the Process Boundary Using Local Servers," I am going to discuss taking our in-process servers and breaking that process boundary by using local servers.

CHAPTER 7

BREAKING THE PROCESS BOUNDARY USING LOCAL SERVERS

In this chapter, you will learn about the following:

- The role of local servers
- The necessities of marshaling
- Describing components by using Interface Definition Language (IDL)
- How to build a proxy/stub DLL

The Component Object Model is, when you get down to it, a programmatic exercise in deception. Now I'm not talking about cloak-and-dagger deception (although I bet a few CIA programmers are writing COM servers as we speak). I'm talking about the deception involved in making an object appear as though it's something that it's not. Using COM, all objects are accessed through interface pointers and are created through factories, so objects behave as if the client program is directly manipulating the individual COM components. But the reality is (here's where the deception part comes in), absolutely nothing says that a COM component has to reside in the same address space as its client.

COM programmers often talk at great length about *location transparency*, which is the rather nebulous term we use to describe the decoupling of client programs from knowledge of where their components are physically located. From the client's point of view, the location of COM objects is ultimately unknown. As my mother used to say whenever she was trying out a new recipe on us, "If it looks like chicken and tastes like chicken, it's chicken. Even when it's not." This holds equally true for COM objects. If a component looks like your object and acts like your object, does it really matter if the entity you're directly interacting with actually isn't your object? This chapter is about how COM works its magic and creates the illusion of location transparency.

Location transparency is another implementation of proper encapsulation. That is, Microsoft hides the details of determining whether a COM server is in-process, out-of-process, or remote. This enables the programmer to call COM servers in the same way for all three types of servers, reducing the learning curve.

Why Build a Local Server?

So far, this book has presented examples of four fully functional COM servers. I don't know if you've noticed this yet (I've tried to be subtle), but every single one of these components has been hosted inside an in-process server. There's a good reason for this, of course. Quite simply, building a local server is harder than building an in-process server and requires some additional effort. Whenever COM calls span process boundaries (it would be more accurate to say *apartment boundaries*, but that's another discussion), parameters must be marshaled between the processes. Local servers require additional effort to generate this required marshaling code.

Rest assured that building a local server requires only a little more work on your part, and everything that you've learned so far still holds. In fact, you can use exactly the same code to implement both in-process and local servers; the only difference between the two lies in how the actual servers are constructed and registered.

Still, you might be wondering why you should be interested in building local servers when you just about have in-process servers down pat. There are, after all, plenty of good reasons to stick with in-process servers. For example, in-process servers can be significantly faster when compared to local servers.

I can think of a couple of reasons why someone might elect to use a local server over an in-process server. If it is critical that your client applications remain active and running over extended periods of time, local servers might be a better solution. Client programs that use an in-process COM server are vulnerable to objects that haven't been adequately debugged or tested. Because in-process servers are loaded directly into the address space of the client, a fatal error in the COM object is going to crash the entire client application. A fatal error in a local server, on the other hand, will bring down the process in which the local server is running, but will return an error to the client application (which is considerably more graceful and considerate than the slap in the face provided by a program crash). Local servers have more control over their threading models and thus can build in their own scalability features.

To the client, whether the server is in-process, local, or remote is usually not important. This is called *location transparency*. COM relies on location and activation information in the registry. You'll learn about all this later in this book.

The Man in the Middle: Marshaling

The life of an in-process server is uncomplicated. When a client needs the services of a class residing inside the server, the server is directly loaded into the client program's address space. Interface pointers are passed directly between the server and the client, as are method arguments. In short, using an in-process server is no different than using a DLL (which shouldn't be too surprising, considering that in-process servers *are* DLLs).

But what happens when the server being used is a local server? A local server, because it runs inside its own process, does not share a common address space with the client. If the client has an interface pointer and wants to make a method call, on that interface, that involves passing in a BSTR, there has to be some way to get that BSTR into the address space of the server process. Likewise for arguments and return values coming back from the server. These pieces of data all need to be transported from the server address space back into the client address space.

COM solves this problem by providing a set of services and interfaces that are collectively referred to as the *marshaling* architecture. The charter of marshaling is easily understood: to provide COM clients and servers with a mechanism to share data across different processes. The implementation of a marshaling layer can be rather involved. Luckily for you, COM hides all the details of marshaling from both clients and servers. Your code remains blissfully unaware of the existence of any marshaling code.

The marshaling architecture is a generic specification for describing how COM entities in separate processes should interact and communicate with each other (you'll sometimes see this set of generic marshaling interfaces referred to as *custom marshaling*). Like many of the COM interfaces used by OLE, marshaling is an empty framework for achieving some goal. Microsoft supplies an implementation called the Standard Marshaller, which you get by default if you don't implement and advertise your implementation inside `QueryInterface`.

Standard marshaling communicates between processes by using light-weight remote procedure calls (LRPCs) and has been extended, with the release of Windows NT 4.0 and DCOM, to work across machines separated by a network, using full-blown remote procedure calls (RPCs). This point is worth underscoring, because the same operating system running on different hardware (for example, Windows NT running on a DEC Alpha, compared to NT running on an Intel box) may have different representations of common integral types such as integers, floating point numbers, and strings. It goes without saying that communicating between completely different operating systems (for example, Windows NT talking to a UNIX box) faces similar hurdles. Thankfully, standard marshaling takes care of any required conversions and insulates you from having to write messy conversion routines. In short, standard marshaling provides a comprehensive strategy for solving the problem of moving data between clients and servers.

Proxies and Stubs

One of COM's most important chores is to ensure that when a client asks for a particular component, the client is given an object that can respond to the interface supported by that component. Now, I realize that this sounds like a rather weird way of describing the process. Of course COM gives clients objects that act like the requested component. After all, the object that COM gives the client *is* the component!

Sometimes. When the COM server is in-process, this is exactly what happens. However, when the server is local (and therefore located in another address space), COM gives the client a special kind of object called a *proxy*. A proxy is an object that resides in the same address space as the client and responds to all the interfaces that are supported by the targeted component. From the client's perspective, the proxy *is* the component.

When the client invokes a method inside one of the component's interfaces, the proxy bundles up all the method arguments into some portable set of data structures and ships the whole bundle over to the local server program through a remote procedure call. Because Microsoft's RPC technology enables programs to communicate with each other across address spaces, the proxy can move method arguments into the address space of the local server with relative ease.

On the server side, the RPC is received by a piece of code referred to as the. When the method call is complete, the component returns control back to the stub (along with any return arguments). The stub bundles up the return arguments, packs them into a portable format, and then RPCs them back to the proxy. The proxy unpacks any return data and relinquishes control back to the client. Figure 7.1 depicts the relationship between clients, proxies, RPC stubs, and local servers.

Now, I'll give you exactly one guess how DCOM provides client programs with the capability to call remote servers running on another machine. That's right, RPC proxies and stubs.

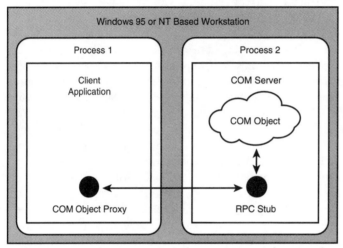

Figure 7.1   Local COM servers rely on proxies and RPC stubs.

I'm sure you're wondering—and if you're not, you should be—where these proxy and stub objects come from. It turns out that there are actually two answers to that question.

For all the standard COM and OLE interfaces such as `IClassFactory`, `IMoniker`, and `IDispatch`, Microsoft provides proxy/stub implementations that COM uses automatically without any further assistance from either your client or server code. One of the reasons for the word *standard* in standard marshaling is that Microsoft has done its job and provided seamless marshaling for all the interfaces that it provides.

That leaves custom interfaces, those interfaces that you and I have developed on our own without any intervention or support from Microsoft. The bad news is that you yourself are responsible for building those proxies and stubs. The good news is that building these objects is a cinch. The only catch is that you will need to fundamentally change the way you approach the development of your interfaces.

Interface Definition Language

Actually, you can take more than one approach to writing a set of proxy/stub objects. You can always, for example, sit down and code each proxy and stub class manually. To do so, however, would require a significant amount of effort. You would have to learn the lowest level details of how standard marshaling works, immersing yourself in arcane details such as NDR (network data representation), RPC invocation, and low-level COM interfaces such as `IRpcProxyBuffer` and `IRpcStubBuffer`.

The biggest problem with manually writing your own proxies and stubs is interpreting how various method arguments and return values should packaged. If one of your interface methods accepts a pointer to a structure that has several data members and pointers to other structures, which in turn have pointers to other structures, which in turn . . . well, you get the point. The mesh of data structures passed between process could potentially become complicated. Proxy/stub code needs to be savvy enough to recognize those data elements that can be directly packed up (for example, integral data types) and those data elements that are passed using pointers and need to be dereferenced to get at the "real" data.

If you don't get my point, allow me to clarify: Writing your own proxy/stub code can be hard. It's not an impossible undertaking—but you don't have to do it. You have help from a secret weapon. You have IDL.

IDL stands for *Interface Description Language*, which is a pretty good three-word description for what IDL really is. An IDL file describes your COM classes and interfaces in a declarative language that vaguely resembles C++, but is most certainly not C++. You don't, however, write any of your object's implementation code in IDL. Instead, you feed your IDL file into MIDL (the Microsoft IDL compiler), and the compiler spits out the code for your proxy/stub objects.

You Say ODL, I Say IDL

In your travels, you might run into discussions of ODL files and the `MKTYPLIB` utility. This can be pretty confusing because much of the older OLE literature makes numerous references to ODL (Object Definition Language) files. Don't worry. You won't have to learn yet another interface language.

ODL files and the `MKTYPLIB` utility were previously used by programmers to help build type-libraries, an important element in the construction of automation clients and servers (I cover automation in Chapter 12, "Creating ActiveX Objects Using MFC Automation"). With Visual C++ 4.0 (and obviously 5.0), Microsoft added support for ODL syntax and type-library generation directly into its IDL compiler. By adding support for ODL files directly into MIDL, Microsoft has effectively removed the need for the older `MKTYPLIB` utility. Indeed, `MKTYPLIB` still ships with Visual C++ to maintain backwards compatibility with older makefiles, but all your new files, both IDL and ODL, should be compiled using the MIDL compiler. MIDL will accept an ODL file as readily as it will accept an IDL file.

The cut-over from ODL to IDL still isn't quite complete. For example, the Visual C++ AppWizard generates an ODL file when building automation server projects. Because Visual C++ doesn't directly support MIDL and the generation of proxy/stub code, I'll be showing you how to add more comprehensive IDE support for the MIDL compiler later in the chapter. (Note that although AppWizard still generates ODL files, Visual C++ does use MIDL to build type libraries. However, Visual C++'s use of MIDL is restricted to using the compiler as a drop-in substitute for `MKTYPLIB`.)

IDL is a large language with a tremendous amount of declarative expression and potential complexity. For most applications, however, you'll probably be using only a subset of IDL keywords to describe your COM classes and interfaces. As you write your IDL, keep in mind that IDL was not initially designed as a way to describe COM classes and interfaces. Microsoft originally envisioned its IDL as a way to describe RPC interfaces that could be used to communicate between Windows NT machines. The IDL variant that Microsoft used as a starting point for its own interface language was the RPC IDL originally specified by the Open Software Foundation (now named *X/Open*) for the Distributed Computing Environment (DCE). Because DCE was developed as a C-based application environment, the IDL language feels much more like C than C++. Because it was Microsoft's original goal, IDL can also be used to generate non-COM, C-based RPC proxies and stubs. Of course, Microsoft has extended the IDL to incorporate keywords that are specific to COM components, but much of the additional syntax that can make IDL seem so complicated is directly transplanted from DCE.

Writing the Custom Component IDL File

I think an example is in order. Listing 7.1 shows an IDL file that defines a class, `PizzaOrderTaker1`, and its single interface, `IPizzaOrderTaker`. Take a close look at this IDL file; it's going to form the foundation of the `PizzaOrderTaker` examples that I'll be presenting later in the chapter. In particular, pay special attention to those parts of the file that appear to be identical to C/C++, and to those unrecognizable parts that are obviously IDL-specific extensions.

Listing 7.1 PIZZA1.IDL—The IDL File for the COM `PizzaOrderTaker` Class

```
// Bring in needed system IDL files
import "wtypes.idl";
import "unknwn.idl";

//
// Misc. enums and typedefs
//
typedef enum
    {
        Pepperoni = 1,
        Sausage,
        GroundBeef,
        GreenOlives,
        ProsciuttiniHam,
        Pastrami,
        GreenPeppers,
        Mushrooms,
        Onions,
        Tomatoes,
```

```
        Pesto,
        JalapenoPeppers,
        CheddarCheese,
        FontinaCheese,
        RicottaCheese,
        FetaCheese,
        Pineapple,
        ExtraCheese,
        Bacon,
        Broccoli,
        GenoaSalami,
        Zucchini,
        BlackOlives,
        Anchovies,
        ChickenBreast,     // Double topping
        Shrimp,            // Double topping
        ArtichokeHearts    // Double topping

    } Topping;

typedef enum
    {
        FullPizza,
        HalfPizza,
        QuarterPizza

    } ToppingSize;

typedef enum
    {
        Individual,
        Small,
        Large

    } PizzaSize;

typedef enum
    {
        Visa,
        MasterCard,
        AmericanExpress

    } CreditCard;

typedef struct
    {

        BSTR bstrCustName;
        BSTR bstrAddress;
        BSTR bstrPhone;

    } DeliveryInfo;
```

continued on next page

continued from previous page

```
//
//   Interface information for IPizzaMaker
//
[ object, uuid(F4C06194-6420-11d0-8C23-00400539F36B) ]
interface IPizzaOrderTaker : IUnknown
{
   HRESULT ResetPizza      ();
   HRESULT SetPizzaSize    ([in]  PizzaSize      eNewSize);
   HRESULT GetPizzaSize    ([out] PizzaSize*     peCurrSize);
   HRESULT AddTopping      ([in]  Topping        eNewTopping,
                            [in]  ToppingSize    eNewToppingSize);
   HRESULT RemoveTopping   ([in]  Topping        eRemTopping);
   HRESULT GetNumToppings  ([out] ULONG*         pulNumToppings);
   HRESULT GetTopping      ([in]  ULONG          ulListPos,
                            [out] Topping*       peTopping,
                            [out] ToppingSize*   peToppingSize);
   HRESULT GetPizzaPrice   ([out] ULONG*         pulPrice);
   HRESULT OrderPizza      ([in]  DeliveryInfo*  pDeliveryInfo,
                            [in]  CreditCard     eCreditCardType,
                            [in]  BSTR           bstrCreditCardNum,
                            [out] ULONG*         pulPrice);
}

//
//   Class information for PizzaOrderTaker1
//
[ uuid(47DD0D53-641F-11d0-8C23-00400539F36B), hidden]
coclass PizzaOrderTaker1
{
        interface IPizzaOrderTaker;
};
```

The `PizzaOrderTaker` component provides the means by which a client can describe the desired attributes of a pizza, get a price quote, and then order the meal. What does it mean to call `IPizzaOrderTaker`'s `OrderPizza()` method? Nothing. Remember that the declaration of the interface says nothing about possible *implementations* of that interface. It is only within the context of a COM object that implements the interface that a method takes on real meaning. One object might respond to `OrderPizza()` by contacting an Internet Web server and placing the order through an HTML interface. Better yet, the COM object could be located in the pizza kitchen itself, and clients could send the `OrderPizza()` request directly to the restaurant over the Internet by using DCOM. The important thing to keep in mind is that `IPizzaOrderTaker` is simply a description of protocol.

I'm going to spend the next few sections walking through this IDL file, explaining the primary keywords that aren't immediately obvious and that are different from standard C.

The COM Lifestyle

Don Box, one of the industry's foremost authorities on COM/DCOM and all-around OLE guru, is fond of talking about the "COM lifestyle." When he and other hard-core COM programmers talk about COM programming as a lifestyle, they're talking about interacting with components through interface pointers, they're talking about creating objects through class factories, and they're talking about all the other little details that distinguish programming in COM from traditional C++ development. But they're also talking about a fundamental change in the way that a programmer approaches the development cycle.

In the past, the intelligent object-oriented programmer has devoted up-front time to constructing a comprehensive and well thought-out design for his project. On larger projects, this often involves using an object-oriented design methodology (take your pick), whereas smaller projects will typically use less formalized approaches. In the end, however, it has been the standard practice for a programmer (or a team of programmers) to tuck his design under his arms, retreat into his office or cubicle, and start churning out C++ code.

I would argue that the COM lifestyle adds a new wrinkle to this state of affairs. Now, I'm not referring to the design phase, mind you. Especially on those large projects that can encompass thousands of classes and result in applications that instantiate millions of object instances, an intelligently managed and iterative design cycle is absolutely critical. No, I'm referring to that part about programmers running off and starting to immediately code in the implementation language. Rather than move from design directly to code, programmers living the COM lifestyle move from design to IDL, and it's only after fully describing their objects in IDL that they focus their attention on the code.

Initially describing classes and interfaces in IDL helps to solidify the separation between an object's interface and its implementation. Thinking in IDL enables you to move the development process one step closer to implementation without actually getting to the point of having to write code. Problems in high-level or low-level designs often surface during the writing of your IDL files, rather than later after programmers have started to write and share source code. Additionally, as you will see later in the chapter, MIDL can also generate useful header files that are not exclusively concerned with proxies and stubs.

I urge you to start all your COM programming tasks with IDL and not relegate IDL to something you "have" to work in just to generate the proxies and stubs of local servers. As Don Box once wrote, "Real COM programmers start work in IDL."

Import

The first two lines of this IDL file use the IDL command `import`, which is analogous to the C/C++ `#include` preprocessor directive.

```
import "wtypes.idl";
import "unknwn.idl";
```

Like `#include`, the `import` reserved word logically extends the current IDL file by copying in the contents of the specified file. But watch out. A number of important differences exist between the two commands. When a file is imported, MIDL ignores any function prototypes that it encounters. This is important because MIDL will generate proxy and stub code for any function prototypes that it runs across. That being said, it is valuable to know that MIDL always runs your IDL files through the C preprocessor before entering its compilation phase. That means that any and all of the preprocessor directives that you use from within your C++ code can also be used from inside IDL (including `#include`). Take the following IDL code snippet, for example:

```
#ifdef USE_ENUMS

    typedef enum { Red, Green, Blue } Colors;

#else

    const ULONG Red   = 0;
    const ULONG Green = 1;
    const ULONG Blue  = 2;

    typedef ULONG Colors;

#endif
```

You can't tell the difference between this and standard C/C++, can you? Here you can see how you might use an `#ifdef` to conditionally declare a logical enumerated type as a series of constant `ULONG`s. In addition to the use of preprocessor directives, notice the IDL support for standard C/C++ constructs such as `const`, `typedef`, and `enum`.

By the way, the two files being imported by `PIZZA1.IDL`—`wtypes.idl` and `unknwn.idl` are two standard IDL files provided by Microsoft and are shipped with Visual C++. `Wtypes.idl` provides the declaration of many common Windows and OLE types. For example, the definitions of both `HRESULT` and `ULONG` come from this IDL file. The `unknwn.idl` file contains the declarations for the `IUnknown` and `IClassFactory` interfaces. Because every custom interface is derived from `IUnknown` in one way or another, and because `wtypes.idl` contains the most common definitions used by virtually every program, you will probably find yourself including these files often. Alternatively, you might include another system IDL file such as `objidl.idl` (which includes declarations of other common COM and OLE interfaces), which in turn imports `wtypes.idl` and `unknwn.idl`.

Typedef

Many things in this IDL file should seem immediately familiar. It does, after all, look a lot like C/C++. Nowhere is this more apparent than in the first half of the IDL file, where you find a series of `typedef`s that are declaring four new enumerated types and a structure. These `typedef`s are declared and defined using exactly the same syntax as you would use in C and C++.

```
typedef enum
    {
        Individual,
```

```
    Small,
    Large

} PizzaSize;
```

Unlike C and C++, the **typedef** keyword has an optional syntax that enables the programmer to associate special attributes with the new type being declared. The precise syntax looks like this:

```
typedef [ [attribute-list] ] type-specifier declarator-list;
```

where an attribute list is a comma-separated list of attributes. No fewer than nine different attributes can be legally used in a **typedef** attribute list, but most of them are used only under special circumstances. One of these attributes, **switch_type**, plays an important role in a special kind of IDL union called an *encapsulated union*. I'll talk more about the special IDL unions later in this chapter.

As you can see, IDL relies on a typing system that is very similar to that used by the C programming language. This makes sense because ultimately the IDL will be used to generate C code. By mimicking and adopting the same types used by C, MIDL can literally blast much of the IDL file contents into the generated code proxies and stubs (after verifying correct syntax, of course).

Interface

Immediately following the declaration of the enumerated types and the **DeliveryInfo** structure, you find the interface declaration for **IPizzaOrderTaker**.

```
[ object, uuid(F4C06194-6420-11d0-8C23-00400539F36B) ]
interface IPizzaOrderTaker : IUnknown
{
   HRESULT ResetPizza      ();
   HRESULT SetPizzaSize    ([in]  PizzaSize      eNewSize);
   HRESULT GetPizzaSize    ([out] PizzaSize*     peCurrSize);
   HRESULT AddTopping      ([in]  Topping        eNewTopping,
                            [in]  ToppingSize    eNewToppingSize);
   HRESULT RemoveTopping   ([in]  Topping        eRemTopping);
   HRESULT GetNumToppings  ([out] ULONG*         pulNumToppings);
   HRESULT GetTopping      ([in]  ULONG          ulListPos,
                            [out] Topping*       peTopping,
                            [out] ToppingSize*   peToppingSize);
   HRESULT GetPizzaPrice   ([out] ULONG*         pulPrice);
   HRESULT OrderPizza      ([in]  DeliveryInfo*  pDeliveryInfo,
                            [in]  CreditCard     eCreditCardType,
                            [in]  BSTR           bstrCreditCardNum,
                            [out] ULONG*         pulPrice);
}
```

The **interface** keyword is followed by the name of the interface being declared. The name of the base interface from which the current interface is being inherited follows after the current interface name, separated by a colon. Like **typedef**, the **interface** keyword can be preceded by a list of optional attributes. Unlike **typedef**, which has no required attributes, the **interface** keyword requires that you at least specify the **object** and uuid attribute when declaring a custom COM interface. The **object** attribute signals to MIDL that this interface is a custom interface; the **uuid** attribute contains the IID that belongs to the custom interface.

Method Prototypes

The IDL syntax affords a tremendous amount of flexibility in describing how isolated software components can communicate with each other. Although much of a typical interface declaration resembles the prototypes for C++-style methods, you will find that these prototypes incorporate new attributes and syntax that you won't find in either C or C++. This is because the problem of crossing address spaces introduces a few wrinkles that simply don't exist in the world of a C/C++ program, where all the functions and objects reside in the same address space.

Take, for example, the simple case of a program that wants to send an array of characters from one machine to another. In straight C/C++, the prototype for such a method might look like this.

```
void ExchangeBuffer(CHAR *pBuffer, ULONG ulBufferLen);
```

As an RPC, this function generates a few questions. Does the buffer pointed to by **pBuffer** initially contain data that should be marshaled to the target process? Or is this buffer going to be filled in on the other side and returned, in which case the current contents of the buffer should be ignored and don't need to be marshaled. Or does this buffer initially contain data that needs to be marshaled on both the call and the return?

One of the techniques used to help answer these questions is the use of **in/out** specifiers. As you can see by looking at the declaration of **IPizzaOrderTaker**, even individual method arguments in IDL can have an attribute list associated with them. The most important of these attributes are the directional specifiers, which tell the MIDL compiler whether an argument is an input parameter, an output parameter, or both.

Note

On those method arguments that are not marked as being either in, out, or in and out, the default is to assume that an argument is an in parameter.

Input Parameters

A parameter is marked as being an input parameter by using the [in] attribute. As an example, take a look at IPizzaOrderTaker's OrderPizza() method.

```
HRESULT OrderPizza ([in]  DeliveryInfo*  pDeliveryInfo,
                    [in]  CreditCard     eCreditCardType,
                    [in]  BSTR           bstrCreditCardNum,
                    [out] ULONG*         pulPrice);
```

The [in] attribute implies that the parameter is filled in with a value at the time of method invocation. In the OrderPizza() IDL, pDeliveryInfo, eCreditCardType, and bstrCredCardNum are all [in] arguments. Input parameters are marshaled by the generated proxy and are passed over to the server. Input parameters have pass-by-value semantics; the server cannot change the value of the parameter, and the argument is not marshaled from the server back to the client after server-side execution of the method.

What's really happening when you pass argument with an [in] parameter? Because an input parameter already has memory associated with it (you have to fill the parameter in before making the call), no memory is allocated on the client by the proxy. This is irrespective of whether the argument is passed into the method by reference (for example, the DeliveryInfo structure pointed to by pDeliveryInfo) or by value on the stack (the CreditCard enum passed into eCreditCardType).

On the server side, the stub receives the message packet from the proxy and allocates enough memory to hold the incoming parameter as part of the marshaling process. The method call is then invoked by the stub; because the parameter is marked as an input parameter, your method implementation might not modify the contents of the argument. (Actually, you can modify the contents of the argument all you want, but the marshaling architecture won't return your changes back to the client.) After you return from the method, the stub frees up the memory used by the parameter. The server does not return any [in] parameters back to the client.

Output Parameters

Using an output parameter, specified by using the [out] parameter attribute, is similar to using an input parameter, except some of the steps followed by the proxy and stub are reversed. In the case of the OrderPizza() example, the pulPrice() variable is an output parameter.

One of the central goals of an RPC—and by association, a local or remote server method call—is to make the caller unaware that the method or function implementation resides inside another address space. Therefore, the implication is that a COM client calls a distributed interface in exactly the same manner that it would call an in-process interface. In other words, developers write their C/C++ code the same way that they always have, and the COM RPC layer hides all the ugly details.

In the case of an output parameter, the programmer invokes the call by passing in a pointer to a type that will hold the returned result. Did you catch that? A very important point is made here: Output parameters are always passed by reference (that is, using a pointer). After all, this is exactly the same way that output parameters are programmed in everyday non-COM C++. In the case of the pulPrice parameter in OrderPizza(), the caller passes in the address of an unsigned long that will be filled in with the value of the output parameter returned from the server.

Here's how COM manages the memory of an output parameter. The caller passes in the address of a variable that is capable of holding the return data. The proxy holds on to the address, knowing that it will be used later, but does not marshal the variable's current contents. This is an output parameter, and an output parameter's data is never marshaled from client to server, only a pointer to data.

On the server side, the stub unmarshals the pointer and passes it into the server method. Note that at invocation, the output parameter's contents are undefined. It's the responsibility of the "callee" to allocate the data requested, fill it, and fill the method parameter with a pointer to the data. After the method has filled in the output parameter and the method returns, the stub marshals the data and ships it off to the client, leaving it to the client to free up the memory from the parameter when the client is finished using it.

Input/Output Parameters

A method argument can be both an input and an output parameter. Such parameters are called input/output parameters and are specified using the [in, out] attribute in the IDL file. Input/output parameters are used just the way that you would in any standard C++ program. In essence, they are parameters that combine the qualities of both input and output parameters (no surprises *there*!).

You mark a parameter as being [in, out] whenever you want to pass data over to the server that the server might want to modify. For example, take an interface method that would enable two pizza parlors to exchange inventory information. The caller (assumed to be a representative from restaurant #1) would indicate the item in question and the number of units currently in stock. The server would respond to this method by noting the stock available at restaurant #1 and returning the stock available at restaurant #2 in the same input/output parameter.

```
HRESULT ExchangeInventoryInfo([in] BSTR    bstrInventoryItem,
                              [in, out] ULONG* pulUnitsInStock);
```

The pulUnitsInStock variable is used to both send and retrieve information. This means that the value must be marshaled from the client to the server and from the server back to the client.

Memory management is a natural extension of the need to marshal the parameters in both directions. The proxy sets aside the address of the [in, out] parameter (input/output parameters must always be passed by reference, just like [out] parameters) and saves it for when the RPC call returns. However, unlike an [out] parameter, the [in, out] argument is marshaled up and sent over to the server.

Over on the server, the stub allocates memory for the parameter and fills it in with the data that was marshaled over from the client. Then the stub calls the object's method, where the function can change the value of the parameter to its heart's content, secure in the knowledge that the modified data will be transmitted back to the client. After executing the method, the stub marshals up the parameter value (which might have been changed at this point) and sends the return information back to the client.

Finally, when the client receives the return message packet from the server, the [in, out] parameter is extracted from the marshaled data structures, and the pointer to the data is copied back into the variable that was passed into the initial call.

Coclass

The last section in this sample IDL file uses the coclass keyword. Coclass is used to indicate the declaration of a new COM class type.

```
[ uuid(47DD0D53-641F-11d0-8C23-00400539F36B) ]
coclass PizzaOrderTaker1
{
    interface IPizzaOrderTaker;
};
```

Immediately following the `coclass` keyword is the name of the new component. The `coclass` keyword, which has an attribute list associated with it, requires that you at least specify the `uuid` attribute. As you might expect, the **GUID** found within the `uuid` attribute is the class ID for the component class. This is exactly the same **GUID** that you will use to register the class in the system registry and that you pass into the **IMPLEMENT_OLECREATE** macro when building your COM object using MFC.

The class name is followed by a section listing the previously declared interfaces that the class supports. Here you should list each interface exported by your component. Although including it will not cause any harm, the **IUnknown** interface is implied in the definition of each interface and doesn't need to be specified explicitly.

Note

Most IDL keywords support attribute lists, and many attributes can be used with more than one keyword. For example, the `hidden` attribute can appear in the attribute list of any property or method and in the attribute list of the `coclass, dispinterface, interface,` and `library` statements. You can ignore the terms `property, dispinterface,` and `library` for now. These concepts are related to automation, which is discussed in Chapter 12, "Automation Unveiled."

Integrating MIDL with the Developer Studio

As important as IDL is to the COM programmer, the version of Developer Studio shipped with Visual C++ 5.0 (or earlier) does not automatically recognize IDL files. Although this certainly qualifies as a nuisance, integrating MIDL support into Developer Studio is a simple enough task.

Note

Although Developer Studio does not recognize IDL files, it does recognize files with the `.ODL` extension. Even though Visual C++ ultimately compiles both file types with **MIDL.EXE**, you will still need to add explicit support for IDL files manually.

Start the process by adding your IDL file to the project. Right-click on the IDL file project entry and select Settings from the pop-up menu. When the Build Settings dialog opens, make sure that you're looking at the Custom Build tab.

Click on the first line of the Build Command list box. The list box will become available for editing; this is where you need to place the main MIDL compiler invocation line.

The examples in this book use the following MIDL compile command:

```
midl.exe /nologo /app_config /out ..\Common /h COMTypes.h $(InputPath)
```

You'll probably want to make sure that the /**app_config** switch is specified, but the use of /**out** and /**h** are optional. The /**out** flag tells the MIDL compiler that all generated files should be placed into the directory specified by the next command-line argument. In the case of the sample programs, I'm generating files into the example's Common directory. The /**h** flag tells MIDL that you want to change the name of the generated declarations header file. I like to have all my projects generate into a commonly named header file named **COM-TYPES.H**, but that's a personal preference. If you omit the /h flag, MIDL will generate declarations into a header file that has the same name as the IDL file, but with an .**H** extension.

Regardless of what MIDL-specific command-line options you use, you must make sure that you finish the invocation line with the $(**InputPath**) Developer Studio macro. At compile time, the Developer Studio will replace this macro with the name of your IDL file.

After you've entered the MIDL build command, you'll need to fill in the Output File list box with the names of the files that MIDL will generate. I explain these files in more detail later in the chapter, but for now, make sure you have four entries in this list box. Table 7.1 details these four entries.

Table 7.1   Files Generated by MIDL

Filename	Description
<IDL filename>.H	Declarations header file (or **COMTYPES.H** in the case of the book's sample projects)
*<IDL filename>*_I.C	Interface **GUID** structures
*<IDL filename>*_P.C	Proxy/stub code
DLLDATA.C	Standard proxy/stub DLL definitions and functions

Filling in the Output Files list box (and getting it right) is important because the files that you place in this list box are the files that Developer Studio will use to determine whether the IDL file has been updated and needs to be recompiled.

The COM Pizza Order– Taking Wizard

In case you haven't noticed yet, there's a distinct and consistent theme to the examples in this chapter. Pizza. Now I don't know how you feel about pizza but it's certainly one of my favorite foods. In fact, I like pizza so much that I'm going to feature it prominently in the next few sample programs. (If you're not a big fan of pizza, I suppose you could modify the examples to be salad-centric, or dessert-centric, or whatever you please. Me, though, I'm a pizza man.)

The COM client and server that I introduce in this chapter is going to be a little more elaborate than the programs I've presented in previous chapters. There are a couple of reasons for this. First off, it's all fine and good to see COM at work in a simple program that uses only a single method, but I want to present you with something more polished and ambitious. Because the programs that you'll be developing on your own are likely to be larger than the examples that you've been working with so far, I want to give you exposure to a COM client/server combination with a wider ranging code base. Finally, as my discussions start to evolve into talk of building distributed object servers with DCOM, I want to have a working example that will have legs and will enable us to build on it to create more elaborate and interesting applications. I figure that if all I've given you by the end of the book is a distributed version of `FortuneTeller`, you might feel a little cheated. Have no fear.

For now, though, the emphasis is on building your first local server. In this case, the server will take orders for pizza; you should already be familiar with the capabilities of the program after having seen the server's IDL file. Clients will be able to construct a "virtual" pizza and then place an order for the real thing.

The client program will be an MFC Wizard application. Under Windows 95 and NT, a *wizard* is a program that takes the user's hand and walks him or her through a specific multistep process. Wizards share a common user interface metaphor, so if you've seen one wizard, you've seen them all. As a point of reference, take a look at Figure 7.2. This figure shows the Windows NT 4.0 printer setup wizard, but you can find wizards almost anywhere. (Virtually every setup program these days is implemented as a wizard.)

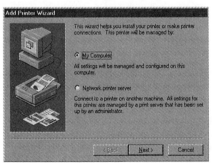

Figure 7.2   The Windows NT 4.0 printer setup wizard.

The wizard that you'll build in this chapter is a pizza order–taking wizard. The application will walk the user through the steps of building a pizza and will then give the user the option of purchasing the pizza through your local server program.

Note

So that I can't be accused of inaccurately portraying the operations of a pizza parlor, the menu in this example is directly based on my favorite pizza restaurant (watch out, shameless plug ahead). If you're ever in the Washington, D.C., area, you owe it to yourself to stop by the Lost Dog Café (5876 Washington Boulevard, Arlington, Virginia). Trust me, they make some great pizzas (try the spinach feta pie).

Although I'll show you how to build the server in both local and in-process forms, you'll spend most of your time focusing on the local version. The nice thing about COM is that you can build a component that is functional in either an in-process or local format, and the class itself is exactly the same, regardless of the server type. In practical terms, you will find that the big difference between an in-process server and a local server lies in the details of how the component is wrapped, as well as in the implementation of the proxy/stub DLL.

The `ComPizzaOrderTaker` Class

The class supported by your in-process and local servers is a standard MFC-implement-ed COM class. Just like the `FortuneTeller` and `Robot` examples presented in the past two chapters, the `PizzaOrderTaker` class relies on standard MFC COM constructs such as `CCmdTarget`, interface maps, and nested interface classes. Let's kick things off by taking a look at Listing 7.2, the header file for the `PizzaOrderTaker` class.

Listing 7.2   `PIZZA1.H`—The Declaration of the `ComPizzaOrderTaker` Class

```
#ifndef PIZZA1_H#define PIZZA1_H// Get needed include files
#include "StdInc.h"
#include "COMTypes.h"


//
// The PizzaOrderTaker COM class
//

class ComPizzaOrderTaker : public CCmdTarget
{
public:

    // Constructor and destructor
    ComPizzaOrderTaker();
    virtual ~ComPizzaOrderTaker();

protected:

    // IPizzaOrderTaker members
    BEGIN_INTERFACE_PART(CInnerPizza, IPizzaOrderTaker)
        STDMETHOD(ResetPizza)     ();
        STDMETHOD(SetPizzaSize)   (PizzaSize      eNewSize);
        STDMETHOD(GetPizzaSize)   (PizzaSize*     peCurrSize);
        STDMETHOD(AddTopping)     (Topping        eNewTopping,
                                   ToppingSize    eNewToppingSize);
        STDMETHOD(RemoveTopping)  (Topping        eRemTopping);
        STDMETHOD(GetNumToppings) (ULONG*         pulNumToppings);
        STDMETHOD(GetTopping)     (ULONG          ulListPos,
                                   Topping*       peTopping,
                                   ToppingSize*   peToppingSize);
        STDMETHOD(GetPizzaPrice)  (PULONG         pulPrice);
```

```
        STDMETHOD(OrderPizza)      (DeliveryInfo* pDeliveryInfo,
                                    CreditCard    eCreditCardType,
                                    BSTR          bstrCreditCardNum,
                                    ULONG*        pulPrice);
    END_INTERFACE_PART(CInnerPizza)

    DECLARE_INTERFACE_MAP()
    DECLARE_OLECREATE(ComPizzaOrderTaker)
    DECLARE_DYNCREATE(ComPizzaOrderTaker)

private:

    // Private, nested tuple class
    struct CToppingTuple
    {
        Topping     eTopping;
        ToppingSize eToppingSize;
    };

    // Private member data
    PizzaSize                              m_eSize;
    CTypedPtrList<CPtrList, CToppingTuple*> m_ToppingList;

    // Private methods
    POSITION FindTopping(Topping eSearchTopping);
};

typedef ComPizzaOrderTaker* PComPizzaOrderTaker;


#endif
```

Being the grizzled COM veteran that you now are, most of the things in this header file should look familiar. As you can see by the use of the **BEGIN_INTERFACE_PART** macro, **ComPizzaOrderTaker** implements only one interface: **IPizzaOrderTaker**. Notice that, unlike previous sample programs, the **PIZZA1.H** header file includes **COMTypes.h**. Remember that **COMTypes.h** is the name of the header file that you instructed MIDL to generate whenever it processed an IDL file. When MIDL compiles **PIZZA1.IDL**, one of the files it creates is **COMTypes.h**. This header file contains the C and C++ interface declaration for the **IPizzaOrderTaker** interface. That's why this example doesn't have an explicit **IPizza.H** header file. In previous examples, you had to manually write an interface header file that contained your interface's class declaration. From here on, MIDL will do all that busy work for you.

In the private section of the class, you'll find the declaration of a nested **CToppingTuple** structure and some member data. The **m_ToppingList** variable is an MFC collection template that you will be using to hold a list of toppings that the user wants on her pizza.

If you're ready to see the implementation of the **ComPizzaOrderTaker** class, take a look at Listing 7.3.

Listing 7.3 PIZZA1.CPP—The Implementation of the ComPizzaOrderTaker Class

```cpp
// Get needed include files
#define INITGUID
#include "Pizza1.h"
#include "Utility.h"


// Support dynamic creation
IMPLEMENT_DYNCREATE(ComPizzaOrderTaker, CCmdTarget)

// Support a class factory
// {47DD0D53-641F-11d0-8C23-00400539F36B}
IMPLEMENT_OLECREATE(ComPizzaOrderTaker, "PizzaOrderTaker1",
0x47DD0D53, 0x641F, 0x11d0, 0x8C, 0x23, 0x0, 0x40, 0x5, 0x39,
➥0xF3, 0x6B);

// Map the various interfaces onto the nested interface classes
BEGIN_INTERFACE_MAP(ComPizzaOrderTaker, CCmdTarget)
    INTERFACE_PART(ComPizzaOrderTaker, IID_IPizzaOrderTaker,
                    ➥CInnerPizza)
END_INTERFACE_MAP()


// List of base pizza prices
ULONG g_aulPizzaPrices[] =
    {
        395, // Individual
        595, // Small
        795  // Large
    };

// List of base topping prices
ULONG g_aulToppingPrices[] =
    {
        50,  // Individual
        100, // Small
        150  // Large
    };

// List of topping modifiers (topping prices are influenced by
// the size of the pizza, but some toppings, like artichokes
// (YECH!), are twice as expensive)
// expensive)
ULONG g_aulToppingMods[] =
    {
        0,   // Not a topping (here to catch errors)
        1,   // Pepperoni
        1,   // Sausage
        1,   // GroundBeef
        1,   // GreenOlives
        1,   // ProsciuttiniHam
        1,   // Pastrami
        1,   // GreenPeppers
```

```
    1,    // Mushrooms
    1,    // Onions
    1,    // Tomatoes
    1,    // Pesto
    1,    // JalapenoPeppers
    1,    // CheddarCheese
    1,    // FontinaCheese
    1,    // RicottaCheese
    1,    // FetaCheese
    1,    // Pineapple
    1,    // ExtraCheese
    1,    // Bacon
    1,    // Broccoli
    1,    // GenoaSalami
    1,    // Zucchini
    1,    // BlackOlives
    1,    // Anchovies
    2,    // ChickenBreast
    2,    // Shrimp
    2     // ArtichokeHearts
};


//
// Constructor and destructor
//

ComPizzaOrderTaker::ComPizzaOrderTaker()
    : m_eSize(Individual)
{
    VerboseMsg("In PizzaOrderTaker constructor.\n");

    // Allow other components to aggregate us if they need to
    EnableAggregation();

    AfxOleLockApp();
}

ComPizzaOrderTaker::~ComPizzaOrderTaker()
{
    VerboseMsg("In PizzaOrderTaker destructor.\n");

    // Call reset to free up memory in the topping list
    m_xCInnerPizza.ResetPizza();

    AfxOleUnlockApp();
}


//
// Nested PizzaOrderTaker IUnknown members
//
```

continued on next page

continued from previous page

```
STDMETHODIMP_(ULONG)
ComPizzaOrderTaker::XCInnerPizza::AddRef()
{
    METHOD_PROLOGUE(ComPizzaOrderTaker, CInnerPizza)
    return pThis->ExternalAddRef();
}

STDMETHODIMP_(ULONG)
ComPizzaOrderTaker::XCInnerPizza::Release()
{
    METHOD_PROLOGUE(ComPizzaOrderTaker, CInnerPizza)
    return pThis->ExternalRelease();
}

STDMETHODIMP
ComPizzaOrderTaker::XCInnerPizza::QueryInterface(REFIID riid,
➥PPVOID ppv)
{
    METHOD_PROLOGUE(ComPizzaOrderTaker, CInnerPizza)
    return pThis->ExternalQueryInterface(&riid, ppv);
}


//
// IPizzaOrderTaker interface members for nested PizzaOrderTaker class
//

STDMETHODIMP
ComPizzaOrderTaker::XCInnerPizza::ResetPizza()
{
    METHOD_PROLOGUE(ComPizzaOrderTaker, CInnerPizza)
    VerboseMsg("In ResetPizza.\n");

    // Clean out the topping list
    POSITION posCurrent = pThis->m_ToppingList.GetHeadPosition();
    while (posCurrent) {
        delete pThis->m_ToppingList.GetNext(posCurrent);
    }
    pThis->m_ToppingList.RemoveAll();

    // Reset the size to Individual
    pThis->m_eSize = Individual;

    return NOERROR;
}

STDMETHODIMP
ComPizzaOrderTaker::XCInnerPizza::SetPizzaSize(PizzaSize eNewSize)
{
    METHOD_PROLOGUE(ComPizzaOrderTaker, CInnerPizza)
    VerboseMsg("In SetPizzaSize.\n");

    // Set the new size
```

```
   pThis->m_eSize = eNewSize;

   return NOERROR;
}

STDMETHODIMP
ComPizzaOrderTaker::XCInnerPizza::GetPizzaSize(PizzaSize* peCurrSize)
{
   METHOD_PROLOGUE(ComPizzaOrderTaker, CInnerPizza)
   VerboseMsg("In GetPizzaSize.\n");

   // Get the current size
   if (peCurrSize)
      *peCurrSize = pThis->m_eSize;

   return NOERROR;
}

STDMETHODIMP
ComPizzaOrderTaker::XCInnerPizza::AddTopping(Topping eNewTopping,
➥ToppingSize eNewToppingSize)
{
   METHOD_PROLOGUE(ComPizzaOrderTaker, CInnerPizza)
   VerboseMsg("In AddTopping.\n");

   // Is this topping already in the list?
   if (pThis->FindTopping(eNewTopping))
      return E_FAIL;

   // Create a new Topping tuple
   CToppingTuple* pTuple = new CToppingTuple;
   pTuple->eTopping = eNewTopping;
   pTuple->eToppingSize = eNewToppingSize;

   // Add the topping to the list
   pThis->m_ToppingList.AddTail(pTuple);

   return NOERROR;
}

STDMETHODIMP
ComPizzaOrderTaker::XCInnerPizza::RemoveTopping(Topping eRemTopping)
{
   METHOD_PROLOGUE(ComPizzaOrderTaker, CInnerPizza)
   VerboseMsg("In RemoveTopping.\n");

   // Find the topping tuple
   POSITION posTopping = pThis->FindTopping(eRemTopping);
   if (!posTopping)
      return NOERROR;

   // We need to free the memory for the tuple
   delete pThis->m_ToppingList.GetAt(posTopping);
```

continued on next page

continued from previous page

```
        // And now remove the list element
        pThis->m_ToppingList.RemoveAt(posTopping);

        return NOERROR;
}

STDMETHODIMP
ComPizzaOrderTaker::XCInnerPizza::GetNumToppings(ULONG* pulNumToppings)
{
        METHOD_PROLOGUE(ComPizzaOrderTaker, CInnerPizza)
        VerboseMsg("In GetNumToppings.\n");

        // Get the current number of toppings
        if (pulNumToppings)
            *pulNumToppings = pThis->m_ToppingList.GetCount();

        return NOERROR;
}

STDMETHODIMP
ComPizzaOrderTaker::XCInnerPizza::GetTopping(ULONG           ulListPos,
                                             Topping*        peTopping,
                                             ToppingSize*    peToppingSize)
{
        METHOD_PROLOGUE(ComPizzaOrderTaker, CInnerPizza)
        VerboseMsg("In GetTopping.\n");

        //
        // Retrieve the position's tuple
        //
        // GetTopping() provides position-oriented retrieval because
        // it's easy to manipulate and understand. However, because the
        // toppings are actually stored in a list, positioned access
        // is slow. Definitely room for improvement here.
        //

        // Validate the list position
        if (ulListPos >= pThis->m_ToppingList.GetCount())
            return E_FAIL;

        // Go to the head of the list
        POSITION posCurrent = pThis->m_ToppingList.GetHeadPosition();
        if (!posCurrent)
            return E_FAIL;

        // Iterate through the list, counting
        ULONG ulCurrentElem = 0UL;
        CToppingTuple* pTuple = NULL;
        while (posCurrent) {

            // Is this a match?
            CToppingTuple* pTuple = pThis->m_ToppingList.GetNext(posCurrent);
            if (ulCurrentElem == ulListPos) {
```

```
         *peTopping = pTuple->eTopping;
         *peToppingSize = pTuple->eToppingSize;
         return NOERROR;
      }
      ulCurrentElem++;
   }

   return E_FAIL;
}

STDMETHODIMP
ComPizzaOrderTaker::XCInnerPizza::GetPizzaPrice(ULONG* pulPrice)
{
   METHOD_PROLOGUE(ComPizzaOrderTaker, CInnerPizza)
   VerboseMsg("In GetPizzaPrice.\n");

   // Start by setting the base price.
   ULONG ulPizzaPrice = g_aulPizzaPrices[pThis->m_eSize];

   // Now walk through the topping list, adding to the current price
   POSITION posCurrent = pThis->m_ToppingList.GetHeadPosition();
   CToppingTuple* pTuple = NULL;
   while (posCurrent) {

      // Get the current topping
      pTuple = pThis->m_ToppingList.GetNext(posCurrent);

      // Calculate the topping price
      ULONG ulToppingPrice = g_aulToppingPrices[pThis->m_eSize] *
                             g_aulToppingMods[pTuple->eTopping];

      // Based on how much of the pizza is covered with this topping,
      // the topping price needs to be scaled
      switch (pTuple->eToppingSize)
      {
         case FullPizza:                        break; // Do nothing
         case HalfPizza:     ulToppingPrice /= 2; break;
         case QuarterPizza:  ulToppingPrice /= 4; break;
      }

      // Add the topping priuce to the total
      ulPizzaPrice += ulToppingPrice;
   }

   // And now return the result
   *pulPrice = ulPizzaPrice;

   return NOERROR;
}

STDMETHODIMP
ComPizzaOrderTaker::XCInnerPizza::OrderPizza(DeliveryInfo* ,
➥// pDeliveryInfo,
```

continued on next page

continued from previous page

```
                                        CreditCard    , // eCreditCardType,
                                        BSTR          , // bstrCreditCardNum,
                                        ULONG*        pulPrice)
    {
        METHOD_PROLOGUE(ComPizzaOrderTaker, CInnerPizza)
        VerboseMsg("In OrderPizza.\n");

        // Set the price
        GetPizzaPrice(pulPrice);

        // Do whatever needs to be done to send the order out
        // (We'll do some things here in Part II of the book)

        return NOERROR;
    }


    POSITION ComPizzaOrderTaker::FindTopping(Topping eSearchTopping)
    {
        // This is about as slow and inefficient a design as you
        // could imagine. I use a linear search here merely to keep
        // the code simple

        // Go to the head of the list
        POSITION posCurrent = m_ToppingList.GetHeadPosition();
        if (!posCurrent)
            return NULL;

        // Iterate through the list, looking for the requested topping
        POSITION posPrev;
        CToppingTuple* pTuple = NULL;
        while (posCurrent) {

            // Is this a match?
            posPrev = posCurrent;
            pTuple = m_ToppingList.GetNext(posCurrent);
            if (pTuple->eTopping == eSearchTopping)
                return posPrev;
        }

        return NULL;
    }
```

Like the header file, much of the ComPizzaOrderTaker implementation should look familiar. The class constructor, destructor, and IUnknown implementation are virtual cut and pastes from previous sample programs. Okay, so the class destructor calls the ResetPizza() method to free up some memory. Apart from the classnames, that is about the only difference that you'll find.

The static arrays of data found at the top of Listing 7.3 are used in several places throughout the class. I've chosen to use array lookups to help simplify some of the code that wouldn't have provided much COM insight anyway. The g_aulPizzaPrices array stores the base prices for the various available sizes of pizza. The g_aulToppingPrices array contains the price of a topping based on the pizza size (the same topping on pizzas of various sizes will cost more or less, depending on the amount of topping needed to cover the entire pizza area). Finally, the `g_aulToppingMods` array contains a list of topping price multipliers. Some toppings (the *premium* toppings) are more expensive than others. The `g_aulToppingMods` array tracks which toppings are more expensive and associates a multiplier value with them. Pepperoni is a normally priced topping, so it has a standard multiplier of one. Shrimp, on the other hand, is twice as expensive, so it has a multiplier of two.

The real meat of the class (pun intended) can be found in the actual implementation methods for the `XCInnerPizza` nested class. `GetPizzaSize()` and `SetPizzaSize()` are certainly the simplest of these methods. The `SetPizzaSize()` method accepts a `PizzaSize` enumerated type and stores the value in the `m_eSize` member variable. `XCInnerPizza`'s other methods are worthy of a quick look.

`ComPizzaOrderTaker` stores the client's currently selected pizza toppings in a collection. In the world of object-oriented programming, *collection* is a frequently encountered word that refers to objects responsible for holding on to other objects. MFC contains several collection classes, some of which rely on C++ templates. For more information on MFC's collection classes, search the Visual C++ Books Online, using the search term *collections topics*.

Note

Visual C++ ships with a set of C++ classes and templates called the *Standard Template Library* (or more commonly referred to as the STL). The STL is a family of template-based collection classes that have been incorporated into the evolving ANSI C++ standardization effort. Although the MFC collection classes are serviceable, the STL is a more robust and technically superior way of dealing with collections. The only disadvantage to using the STL is its steep learning curve. The MFC classes are simple and don't take long to become comfortable with. Because of its breadth and depth, spinning up on STL can take significantly longer.

The `AddTopping()` and `RemoveTopping()` methods enable clients to indicate that they want to add a topping to their pizza or want to change their mind and remove a previously selected topping. The component returns an error if the client tries to add a topping that has already been added or to remove a topping that hasn't been added.

The topping list is really a collection of `CToppingTuples`. `CToppingTuple` is a simple structure used to bind a particular topping value to a topping size. It's not enough to simply track the toppings that the client has requested; you also have to remember how much of the pizza the topping is supposed to cover. The private `FindTopping()` method is used by `AddTopping()` and `RemoveTopping()` to locate the position in the list that corresponds to the appropriate topping.

The `GetNumToppings()` method is another trivial method, simply returning the number of elements in the topping collection. It's important to note, however, that with just two methods—(`GetNumToppings()` and `GetTopping()`—the `IPizzaOrderTaker` interface provides the client with the capability to browse or retrieve the current list of toppings. Although your wizard will not take advantage of this capability, later sample programs will.

The `GetTopping()` method is worth further investigation for a couple of reasons. The functional purpose of this method is clear; using this method the client can determine what topping is at a given position in the topping list. `GetTopping()` accepts a position index and fills in the appropriate topping and topping-size variables. Sounds simple, doesn't it? Well, take a closer look at the code for this method.

```
STDMETHODIMP
ComPizzaOrderTaker::XCInnerPizza::GetTopping(ULONG         ulListPos,
                                             Topping*      peTopping,
                                             ToppingSize*  peToppingSize)
{
    METHOD_PROLOGUE(ComPizzaOrderTaker, CInnerPizza)
    VerboseMsg("In GetTopping.\n");

    // Validate the list position
    if (ulListPos >= pThis->m_ToppingList.GetCount())
        return E_FAIL;

    // Go to the head of the list
    POSITION posCurrent = pThis->m_ToppingList.GetHeadPosition();
    if (!posCurrent)
        return E_FAIL;

    // Iterate through the list, counting
    ULONG ulCurrentElem = 0UL;
    CToppingTuple* pTuple = NULL;
    while (posCurrent) {

        // Is this a match?
        CToppingTuple* pTuple = pThis->m_ToppingList.GetNext(posCurrent);
        if (ulCurrentElem == ulListPos) {
            *peTopping = pTuple->eTopping;
            *peToppingSize = pTuple->eToppingSize;
            return NOERROR;
        }
        ulCurrentElem++;
    }

    return E_FAIL;
}
```

The code for this method seems much longer than one might expect. After all, getting at the desired topping information should just be a matter of calling the appropriate `CTypedPtrList` method that returns the item found at a given index. Unfortunately, this isn't an option, because the MFC list collects do not provide random access methods such as `GetAt()` and `operator[]`. Of course, I could have chosen to use an array, but then the simple addition and removal operations become more complicated. `GetTopping()`, therefore, iterates through the list in a sequential fashion until it reaches the desired position.

You're probably wondering why I'm making such a big deal about a rather esoteric issue, but I want to point out that an important object-oriented principal is at work here. The typical programmer, given only the `IPizzaOrderTaker` interface to look at, would probably assume that `ComPizzaOrderTaker` implemented its topping collection using an array. After all, by accepting an index, the `GetTopping()` method implies that an array-like collection is being used. This is an excellent example of how the separation between interface and implementation provides encapsulation. The interface dictates how clients interact with server objects, but it doesn't mandate how the server objects might choose to implement the object's functionality. In `ComPizzaOrderTaker`, *I* decided to implement the interface by using a list; *you* might have decided to use an array. All that really matters is that the object provides some sort of semantically consistent functionality.

The `GetPizzaPrice()` method is where you can find `ComPizzaOrderTaker`'s core pricing algorithm. I'm not going to go into any of the details here (the code is self-explanatory and is probably of little interest to you unless you're running a pizza parlor), but suffice it to say that the algorithm depends largely on lookups into the reference data arrays. A more ambitious implementation would probably load the array values up from a database, but I didn't want to go overboard. (The commercially viable version of `ComPizzaOrderTaker`, like the rest of the sample programs in this book, is left as an exercise for the reader, royalty free!)

Finally, the `OrderPizza()` method takes in all the information needed to bill a customer's credit card and deliver the product. This implementation clearly does nothing right now, but hopefully, I'm piquing your interest when I say that later versions of `ComPizzaOrderTaker` will rectify this deficiency.

The `PizzaOrderTaker1` Local Server

Now that you have an implementation of the `IPizzaOrderTaker` interface in hand, it's time to turn your attention to the implementation of the local server itself. Remember, the same `ComPizzaOrderTaker` class that you read about in the preceding section can be used without modification in both an MFC in-process server and a local server. The in-process version of the `ComPizzaOrderTaker` server is provided with the rest of the source code, but it relies on the generic in-process server code that I introduced you to back in Chapter 5, "COM Programming with MFC," so I won't repeat that version here. Instead, I want you to concentrate on the local server code that I'm going to present now.

The local server code covered in this section, like the `CInProcServerApp` class of Chapter 5, is a generic piece of code that you can use to implement any COM server. Unlike `CInProcServerApp`, which is used to build in-process servers, the `CLocalServerApp` class that you'll be reading about in this section is specifically designed to support local servers. In fact, `CLocalServerApp` is very similar to `CInProcServerApp`, but with a slightly different structure. I'll be using the exact same code for all the MFC-based local servers that I present in this book; that way, I won't have to waste precious time and space repeating server infrastructure code for each sample server.

Local server code is a little more involved than in-process server code in several respects. A local server is a program executable that relies on command-line arguments to determine whether it should self-register (or self-unregister) itself, so you'll see some additional code that concerns itself with interpreting the contents of the command line.

Local servers are also unique in that, because they are executables, many such servers are also full-blown applications. The word processor that I'm using to write this chapter, Microsoft Word 97, is an example of just such a local COM server. A cursory OLE/COM

Object Viewer (OLEView) check reveals that the main Word executable is home to at least three classes, and I'm sure that I've missed others; the main Word document class exposes at least 29 separate interfaces! Your local servers can also be full-blown applications, but because I'm exclusively concerned with building a local server that does nothing but host COM objects, the code that I'll be discussing does nothing but present the user with a dialog box that asks whether the server should be registered or unregistered.

The local server code is embodied inside the MFC `CWinApp`-derived `CLocalServerApp` class shown in Listing 7.4.

Listing 7.4 `LOCALSRV.CPP`—The `CLocalServerApp` Class

```
// Get needed includes
#include "RegDlg.h"
#include "Resource.h"
#include "CommLine.h"


//
// Main application/server class
//

class CLocalServerApp : public CWinApp
{
public:

    // Public methods inherited from CWinApp
    virtual BOOL InitInstance();

    // New public methods
    VOID RegisterComponent   (const CString& strProgID,
                              BOOL   boolShowConfirmation = TRUE);
    VOID UnregisterComponent(const CString& strClassID,
                              const CString& strProgID,
                              BOOL   boolShowConfirmation = TRUE);
};

// Our one-and-only application object
CLocalServerApp TheApp;


//
// The entire program is run out of this method
//

BOOL CLocalServerApp::InitInstance()
{
    // Initialize OLE libraries
    if (!AfxOleInit()) {
        AfxMessageBox("Could not initialize OLE subsystem.");
        return FALSE;
    }
```

```
// Parse command line for standard OLE commands
CSrvCommandLineInfo CmdInfo;
ParseCommandLine(CmdInfo);

// Check whether launched as OLE server
if (CmdInfo.m_bRunEmbedded || CmdInfo.m_bRunAutomated)
{
    // Application was run with /Embedding or /Automation.

    // Register all OLE servers (factories) as running.
    // This enables the OLE libraries to create objects
    // from other applications.
    COleObjectFactory::RegisterAll();
    return TRUE;
}

// Load up various strings
CString strClassID, strProgID;
strClassID.LoadString(IDS_CLASSID);
strProgID.LoadString(IDS_PROGID);

// Did the user request registration on the command line?
if (CmdInfo.m_bRegister) {
    RegisterComponent(strProgID, FALSE);
    return FALSE;
}

// Did the user request unregistration on the command line?
if (CmdInfo.m_bUnregister) {
    UnregisterComponent(strClassID, strProgID, FALSE);
    return FALSE;
}

// Ask the user whether he wants to register or
// unregister the server
CRegisterDialog    dlgRegister(strProgID);

switch(dlgRegister.DoModal())
{
    case ID_REGISTER:
        RegisterComponent(strProgID);
        break;

    case ID_UNREGISTER:
        UnregisterComponent(strClassID, strProgID);
        break;
}

return FALSE;
}


VOID CLocalServerApp::RegisterComponent(const CString& strProgID,
```

continued on next page

continued from previous page

```
                                         BOOL  boolShowConfirmation)
{
    // Place the server into the system registry
    COleObjectFactory::UpdateRegistryAll();

    // Are we operating silently?
    if (!boolShowConfirmation)
       return;

    // Let the user know that registration is complete
    CString strMsg = "The ";
    strMsg += strProgID;
    strMsg += " server has been registered.";
    AfxMessageBox(strMsg, MB_ICONINFORMATION);
}


VOID CLocalServerApp::UnregisterComponent(const CString& strClassID,
                                          const CString& strProgID,
                                          BOOL  boolShowConfirmation)
{
    // Transform the string-format CLASSID into a real CLSID
    CLSID CLSID_Component;
    BSTR bstrClassID = strClassID.AllocSysString();
    CLSIDFromString(bstrClassID, &CLSID_Component);
    SysFreeString(bstrClassID);

    // Unregister the class
    AfxOleUnregisterClass(CLSID_Component, strProgID);

    // Are we operating silently?
    if (!boolShowConfirmation)
       return;

    // Let the user know that unregistration is complete
    CString strMsg = "The ";
    strMsg += strProgID;
    strMsg += " server has been unregistered.";
    AfxMessageBox(strMsg, MB_ICONINFORMATION);
}
```

The **CLocalServerApp** class is composed of only three methods, but a lot is happening in these three methods (and in the **CRegisterDialog** and **CSrvCommandLineInfo** helper classes that **CLocalServerApp** uses). Like any dialog-based MFC application, most of the action takes place inside **InitInstance()**. **InitInstance()** begins by initializing OLE, using the **AfxOleInit()** method, and then takes a look at what was passed in on the command line.

Processing the Server Command line

One of the keys to understanding how a local server operates is to realize the significance of how various command-line arguments affect server execution. Way back in Chapter 3, "Building COM Objects and Interfaces," I talked about how local servers could be automatically registered or unregistered by passing them special command-line arguments. The server also needs some way to differentiate between being started up by COM in response to a client request and being directly started up by a user from the command line or desktop. To make things easier for you, I've summarized the various options in Table 7.2. Note that the various command-line options found in this table are case-insensitive and may be preceded with either a dash (-) or a forward slash (/).

Table 7.2   Local Server Command-Line Options

Option	Description
RegServer	Indicates that the server should self-register itself in the system registry. The server should not display any user-interface elements and should silently return on completion of registration.
UnregServer	Indicates that the server should unregister itself from the system registry. The server should not display any user-interface elements and should silently return on completion of unregistration.
Embedding	Indicates that the server is being started by the COM subsystem in response to the request of an object client. The word *embedding* is a bit of a misnomer and is a carry-over from the early days of OLE 1.0.
Automation	Indicates that your server is being started by the COM subsystem at the request of an Automation controller. See Chapter 12 for coverage of Automation.

A typical MFC application delegates the processing of command-line arguments to a class named **CCommandLineInfo**. **CCommandLineInfo** is hardly a shining example of how to write an elegant C++ class (among other things, in true MFC fashion, the class has plenty of public member data). The biggest problem that I have with **CCommandLineInfo** is that it doesn't automatically recognize the **RegServer** and **UnregServer** flags, although it can handle **Embedding** and **Automation**. For this reason, I've created my own subclass of **CCommandLineInfo**, named **CSrvCommandLineInfo**. As you can see from the class header file in Listing 7.5, I haven't added a whole lot of new behavior or data to **CSrvCommandLineInfo**.

Listing 7.5   COMMLINE.H—The Declarations for the Command-Line Processing Class, CSrvCommandLineInfo

```
#ifndef COMMLINE_H
#define COMMLINE_H

// Get needed include file
#include "StdInc.h"


class CSrvCommandLineInfo : public CCommandLineInfo
{
public:

    // Ctor
```

continued on next page

continued from previous page

```
                CSrvCommandLineInfo();

                // Overridden public methods
                virtual void ParseParam(LPCTSTR lpszParam, BOOL bFlag,
                                        ⇒BOOL bLast);

                // Public variables (YECH!!)
                BOOL m_bRegister;
                BOOL m_bUnregister;
        };


        #endif
```

Yes, I know I'm being a bit hypocritical here. For the sake of consistency, I've created two public member variables that contain booleans indicating whether the **RegServer** or **UnregServer** parameters were passed in on the command line. I'm trying to strike a subtle balance here, and you should, too. Whenever you're using a framework that you cannot directly modify, you need to weigh the benefits of providing functionality in a "correct" manner versus using the mechanisms advocated by the framework (ideally, the framework has already set the stage for you to do things the correct way). If you deviate from the standards employed by the framework, simply for the sake of being a perfectionist, other programmers familiar with the framework might become confused when they try to use your code. Because the **CCommandLineInfo** class relies on public member data to indicate when standard command-line flags are set, I made sure that I did the same when writing **CSrvCommandLineInfo**.

The implementation of **CSrvCommandLineInfo** is almost trivial, as you can see by the source code in Listing 7.6. In fact, the whole class really comes down to the **ParseParam()** method.

Listing 7.6   COMMLINE.CPP—The Implementation of the **CSrvCommandLineInfo** Class

```
        // Get needed include files
        #include "CommLine.h"


        // Constructor
        CSrvCommandLineInfo::CSrvCommandLineInfo()
            : m_bRegister(FALSE),
              m_bUnregister(FALSE)
        { }


        // Overridden public methods
        void CSrvCommandLineInfo::ParseParam(LPCTSTR lpszParam,
        ⇒BOOL bFlag, BOOL bLast)
        {
            CCommandLineInfo::ParseParam(lpszParam, bFlag, bLast);

            // Is this a flag?
            if (!bFlag)
                return;
```

```
// Is this a register or unregister request?
CString strFlag(lpszParam);
strFlag.MakeUpper();

if (strFlag == "REGSERVER")
    m_bRegister = TRUE;
if (strFlag == "UNREGSERVER")
    m_bUnregister = TRUE;
}
```

The ParseParam() method is called for every argument passed in on the application command line. CSrvCommandLineInfo enables its superclass to do its thing and then does a simple check to see whether the flag was equal to RegServer or UnregServer, setting boolean member flags as appropriate.

Registering the Running Class Factories

The CLocalServerApp class creates an instance of CSrvCommandLineInfo and instructs the object to process the command line. Based on the arguments passed into the server, CLocalServerApp can now determine whether it is being run directly by the user or by the COM subsystem.

If the Embedding or Automation flags are set, the server knows that it has been launched by the COM subsystem. Because the server is running in a different process than the client, COM cannot simply call a known DLL entry point such as the DllGetClassObject() found inside in-process servers. Instead, a local server needs to be more proactive and create all its class factory objects when the server is first started.

```
if (CmdInfo.m_bRunEmbedded || CmdInfo.m_bRunAutomated)
{
    COleObjectFactory::RegisterAll();
    return TRUE;
}
```

The static member function ColeObjectFactory::RegisterAll(), provided by MFC, takes care of all your class factory registration for you. When run by COM, the CLocalServerApp class simply calls the RegisterAll() function and returns TRUE, which indicates to MFC that everything is fine and that the application should continue by creating a Windows message queue and entering a standard message-processing loop.

Registering and Unregistering the Server in the Registry

Of course, a user or some other program could have started the server and passed the RegServer or UnregServer flag in on the command line. The CLocalServerApp class recognizes these flags and takes the steps necessary to perform self-registration or self-unregistration.

CLocalServerApp uses the same techniques as CInProcServerApp to support self-registration and self-unregistration. If the user has indicated that the server should self-register itself, CLocalServerApp calls the RegisterComponent() method. RegisterComponent() simply calls COleObjectFactory::UpdateRegistryAll(), which is the same method that the CInProcServerApp class used to self-register itself. UpdateRegistryAll(), you recall, updates the system registry for all the class factories residing inside the server.

In the case of self-unregistration, appropriately enough, **CLocalServerApp** calls, **UnregisterComponent()**. **UnregisterComponent()**, I am not ashamed to admit, is almost a direct cut and paste of the **DllUnregisterServer()** function exported from a **CInProcServerApp** DLL. A stringified **CLSID** and **ProgID** are passed into this method, both extracted by **CLocalServerApp** from the **IDS_CLASSID** and **IDS_PROGID** entries of a string-table resource. After massaging the **CLSID** string into a **GUID**, using **CLSIDFromString()**, the class calls **AfxOleUnregsiterClass()**.

Caution

Just like **CInProcServerApp**, **CLocalServerApp** can self-unregister only a single COM class.

Presenting the Registration Dialog Box

Finally, if the **CLocalServerApp** class determines that no relevant arguments were passed in on the command line, the class presents the user with a registration dialog box. The registration dialog box is the only user interface that the local server will ever show, because the program has been exclusively designed as a server executable and is not an application intended for direct use by the user. Figure 7.3 shows what this dialog box looks like when invoked from the **PizzaOrderTaker1** local server.

Figure 7.3   The registration dialog box presented by the **PizzaOrderTaker1** local server when run directly.

Like most dialog boxes created by MFC applications, the registration dialog box is controlled by a **CDialog**-derived class, whose declaration you will find in Listing 7.7.

Listing 7.7   REGDLG.CPP—The Declaration of the Local Server's **CRegisterDialog** Class

```
#ifndef REGDLG_H
#define REGDLH_H

// Get needed include files
#include "StdInc.h"
```

```
class CRegisterDialog : public CDialog
{
public:

    // Ctor
    CRegisterDialog(const CString strServerName);

    // Overridden methods
    virtual BOOL OnInitDialog();

    // Public methods
    void OnRegister();
    void OnUnregister();

protected:

    DECLARE_MESSAGE_MAP()

private:

    // Member data
    CString m_strServerName;
};


#endif
```

CRegisterDialog is a simple class, even by dialog-box class standards. This is not surprising, considering the class's limited mission: Ask the client whether it wants to register or unregister the server, and then get out. Listing 7.8 shows the class implementation.

Listing 7.8   REGDLG.CPP—The Implementation of the CRegisterDialog Class

```
// Get needed include files
#include "RegDlg.h"
#include "Resource.h"


BEGIN_MESSAGE_MAP(CRegisterDialog, CDialog)
    ON_BN_CLICKED(ID_REGISTER, OnRegister)
    ON_BN_CLICKED(ID_UNREGISTER, OnUnregister)
END_MESSAGE_MAP()


// Ctor
CRegisterDialog::CRegisterDialog(const CString strServerName)
    : CDialog(IDD_REGISTER, NULL),
      m_strServerName(strServerName)
{ }


// Overridden methods
```

continued on next page

continued from previous page

```
BOOL CRegisterDialog::OnInitDialog()
{
    // Do we know the server name?
    if (m_strServerName != "") {

        // Set the dialog box title bar text
        CString strTitleText = "Local COM Server - ";
        strTitleText += m_strServerName;
        SetWindowText(strTitleText);
    }

    return CDialog::OnInitDialog();
}


// Public methods
VOID CRegisterDialog::OnRegister()
{
    EndDialog(ID_REGISTER);
}

VOID CRegisterDialog::OnUnregister()
{
    EndDialog(ID_UNREGISTER);
}
```

The **CRegisterDialog** class constructor accepts the name of the server as an argument. The server name is used in the **OnInitDialog()** method to set the dialog's title bar text. (**CLocalServerApp** passes **CRegisterDialog** the **ProgID** of the component to use as a server name).

CRegisterDialog's message map routes clicks of the Register and Unregister buttons to **OnRegister()** and **OnUnregister()**, respectively. Each of these message handlers simply closes the dialog box, passing the command ID of the respective button to the standard **EndDialog()** dialog method.

As you can see from Figure 7.3, the registration dialog box also displays an icon alongside the text of the dialog box. This icon is extracted from the executable's resource segment and has a resource ID of **ID_APP_ICON (101)**.

CLocalServerApp handles the return value from the dialog invocation in a very predictable manner. If the user clicked the Register button, **CLocalServerApp** calls **RegisterComponent()**; if the user clicked the Unregister button, **CLocalServerApp** calls **UnregisterComponent()**.

The Proxy/Stub DLL

Up to this point, there haven't been many surprises. In fact, with only a few subtle differences, building the **PizzaOrderTaker1** local server is virtually identical to building an MFC-based in-process server. With the introduction of the proxy/stub DLL, that all changes.

At this point, you can register the server and use OLEView to verify that everything appears to be working fine. (Figure 7.4 shows OLEView browsing **PizzaOrderTaker1**, without a proxy/stub DLL registered.) When you try to expand the class information to look at the component's supported interfaces, OLEView shows you `IUnknown`. No surprises here. This is exactly what all our in-process servers have looked like when browsed with OLEView.

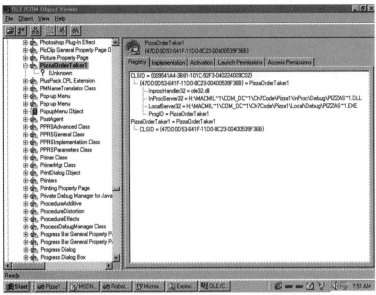

Figure 7.4   Using OLEView to browse the `PizzaOrderTaker1` server, with no proxy/stub DLL registered.

However, if you had a client program that exercised the `IPizzaOrderTaker` interface, you would find that any call to `CoCreateInstance()` requesting an `IPizzaOrderTaker` interface pointer would return an `E_NOINTERFACE` error. Although you could create a new `PizzaOrderTaker` object and even obtain its `IUnknown` interface pointer, any attempt to manipulate the object through a custom interface would be thwarted. The reason for this behavior is obvious. You need proxies and stubs registered to handle the `IPizzaOrderTaker` interface. Proxies and stubs are provided by the operating system for standard interfaces (such as `IUnknown`), but any custom interface that you've dreamed will require its own.

Proxies and stubs are embodied in a proxy/stub DLL. As the name implies, the DLL contains the code for both the client-side proxy and the server-side stub. The implication here is that both the client and the server will need to load the same DLL. This is easy to ensure when dealing with a client and local server running on the same machine. However, when dealing with a client and remote server running on separate machines, you need to make sure that the proxy/stub DLL is registered and installed on both computers.

The proxy/stub is actually two components: the proxy and the stub. The proxy exists in the process space of the caller. The stub exists in the process space of the COM server. In order for the proxy/stub to work, it must be registered on the computer where the calling process exists and on the computer where the COM server exists.

Note

It's worth noting that if you have both an in-process and a local server registered for the same class, COM will always favor the in-process server, given the choice. You leave the decision in COM's hands whenever you call `CoCreateInstance()` and pass in a server context value that presents COM with multiple options. For example, if you call `CoCreateInstance()` with a server context value of `CLSCTX_LOCAL_SERVER`, COM will try to create the new object in a local server, and local server only (even if you have an in-process server registered). However, if you call `CoCreateInstance()` with a server context value such as `CLSCTX_INPROC_SERVER ¦ CLSCTX_LOCAL_SERVER` or `CLSCTX_SERVER`, you leave the decision up to COM (which is not a bad thing, mind you). If both types of server are registered, COM will always use the in-process version in an attempt to maximize performance.

Using IDL, creating a proxy/stub DLL is almost trivial. Guess how many lines of code you need to write? Zero. All the marshaling code is generated by the MIDL compiler, so all you have to do is spackle the different pieces together into a DLL. MIDL will generate four files from your IDL: three C source files and one header file. The three source files need to be compiled and linked together, along with a DEF file that you'll provide. "Viola(!)" Instant proxy/stub DLL. The whole process is depicted in Figure 7.5.

Note

To use the full IDL syntax supported by MIDL, you will need to either define the preprocessor symbol `_WIN32_DCOM` or ensure that the `_WIN32_WINNT` preprocessor symbol is set to a value greater than or equal to 0x0400. Keep in mind, however, that code compiled in this manner might not run correctly (or at all) on versions of NT earlier than 4.0. Similarly, Windows 95 code compiled using the `_WIN32_DCOM` symbol require that the Windows 95 DCOM operating system extensions be installed.

By default, the generated header file assumes the name of your IDL file (but with an `.H` extension, of course). This file contains declarations for all the types and data structures found within the IDL file. The header file also contains the declarations of the IDL's interfaces, in both C and C++ variants. Finally, the header file details the function prototypes used by the proxy and stub to implement the RPCs. This header file is particularly important because it is included by both the COM client and server, who use these declarations in lieu of the hand-coded interface header files that you've included in previous examples.

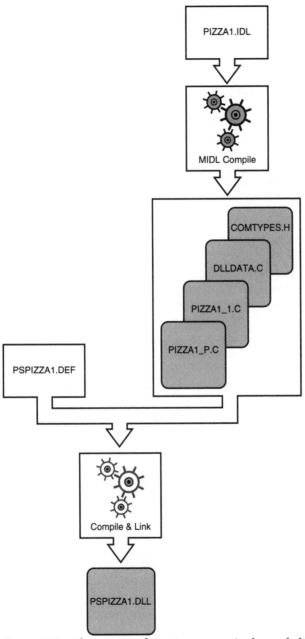

Figure 7.5   The process of creating a proxy/stub marshaling DLL.

> ### Note
>
> Although MIDL defaults the generated header filename to be the same as the IDL file, the examples in this book use command-line arguments to direct MIDL to name the header file COMTYPES.H. This is because the examples use an IDL filename that is typically the same as the CPP and H source files containing the implementing COM class. For example, the local PizzaOrderTaker1 server includes an IDL file PIZZA1.IDL. The ComPizzaOrderTaker implementing class is declared and defined in PIZZA1.H and PIZZA1.CPP, respectively. MIDL defaults would overwrite the PIZZA1.H header file, so the examples would change the generated header filename to COMTYPES.H.

The generated GUID definition source file (I'm going through these in no particular order) is named the same as the IDL file, but with an _I tacked on. In the case of the PizzaOrderTaker1 example, the PIZZA1.IDL file generates PIZZA1_I.C. This file is typically short because it contains nothing but the definitions of the various IIDs and CLSIDs. Because clients and servers also use these GUIDs, this source file is typically compiled and linked into both clients and servers, in addition to the proxy/stub DLL itself.

The actual proxy and stub code is generated into a C source file that has the same name as the IDL file, but with an _P added to the end. Again, using PizzaOrderTaker1 as an example, PIZZA1.IDL generates a proxy/stub source file named PIZZA1_P.C. This source code, because it's specifically concerned with marshaling and implementing proxies and stubs, should only be compiled and linked into the proxy/stub DLL.

The final source file, which is always generated with the name DLLDATA.C, contains methods and data that will be used by the proxy and stub class factories. Although it's not necessary for you to understand the inner workings of the DLLDATA.C code—or the actual proxy/stub source code, for that matter—it's important that you compile the DLLDATA.C file with the preprocessor symbol REGISTER_PROXY_DLL defined. (This symbol can be specified on the General C++ tab of the Build Settings dialog box.) This will automatically provide your proxy/stub DLL with self-registration capabilities.

The final part of the proxy/stub DLL equation is the DEF file that you need to provide. A DEF file for a proxy/stub DLL is exactly like the DEF file for any other in-process server, with one minor addition. Take a look at Listing 7.9, which shows the DEF file for the PizzaOrderTaker1 server proxy/stub DLL.

Listing 7.9 PSPIZZA1.DEF—The DEF File for the PizzaOrderTaker1 Proxy/Stub DLL

```
LIBRARY    PSPizza1

EXPORTS
           DllGetClassObject      PRIVATE
           DllCanUnloadNow        PRIVATE
           DllRegisterServer      PRIVATE
           DllUnregisterServer    PRIVATE

           GetProxyDllInfo        PRIVATE
```

The only change here is the addition of the `GetProxyDllInfo()` entry point, which is a function created by a macro expanded in `DLLDATA.C`. `GetProxyDllInfo()` provides a mechanism for COM to query information about the classes and interfaces supported by the proxy/stub DLL.

Whew! Now that all the constituent parts are in place, it's time to take out that spackle and build the DLL. After all the appropriate files are compiled and the final DLL is linked, you should register the proxy/stub server by using the `REGSVR32` utility.

With the proxy/stub DLL registered, an interesting thing happens to your view of the `PizzaOrderTaker1` component in OLEView. Figure 7.6 tells the story.

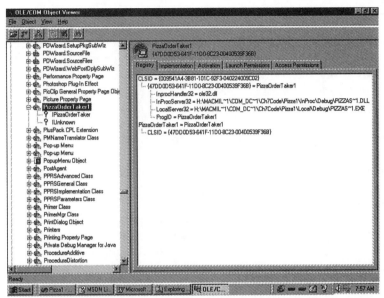

Figure 7.6   Using OLEView to browse the `PizzaOrderTaker1` server after the proxy/stub DLL has been registered.

When the `PizzaOrderTaker1` component is expanded, the `IPizzaOrderTaker` interface magically appears above the `IUnknown` interface entry. Apparently, something is going on here that enables OLEView to logically associate the `PSPizza1` proxy/stub DLL with the local `PizzaOrderTaker1` server and then use the proxy/stub DLL to determine which interfaces the `PizzaOrderTaker1` class exposes.

The technique behind this magic can be found in the registry. When the proxy/stub DLL registers itself, a new class entry is created in the `HKEY_CLASSES_ROOT\CLSID` portion of the registry. The `CLSID` of the registered component is, in the case of a MIDL-generated proxy/stub DLL, the same as the `IID` of the interface that comes first alphabetically in the compiled IDL file. In the case of the `PIZZA1.IDL` file, there is only one interface, `IPizzaOrderTaker`.

```
[ object, uuid(F4C06194-6420-11d0-8C23-00400539F36B) ]
interface IPizzaOrderTaker : IUnknown
{
    ...
```

```
}
```

As expected, you find a new COM class entry based on the interface **IID**.

```
HKEY_CLASSES_ROOT\
            CLSID\
               {F4C06194-6420-11D0-8C23-00400539F36B}\
                  InProcServer32 =
                  ➥"C:\COM Servers\PSPizza1.dll"
```

However, keep in mind that this simple example can be deceiving. If your IDL file had generated proxy/stubs for multiple interfaces, one of which was named **IApple**, the proxy/stub DLL would have been registered under a **CLSID** equal to **IApple** interface's **IID**.

This is all fine and good, but there still needs to be a way for COM to track down the appropriate proxy/stub DLL during a call to **CoCreateInstance()**. The only thing that COM has to go on is the passed-in **IID**. For the sake of tracking down proxy/stub DLLs, the **CLSID** is somewhat of a red herring and doesn't factor into the search algorithm. Why does COM ignore that passed-in **CLSID**? A proxy/stub DLL contains generic marshaling code for a particular set of interfaces, *not for a class*. This means that a single proxy/stub DLL can be used by many classes that all expose the same interfaces (but potentially with very different implementations). In other words, absolutely nothing binds a given proxy/stub DLL to a specific COM class.

I'm sure that you're finding this all very fascinating, but the question still remains. If COM has only an **IID** to go on, how does it find the proxy/stub DLL? When the proxy/stub DLL self-registers, it places information in two places in the registry. The first of these entries, the server data found under **HKEY_CLASSES_ROOT\CLSID**, I have just discussed. The second entry is under the **HKEY_CLASSES_ROOT\Interface** registry key.

HKEY_CLASSES_ROOT\Interface is a key under which you can find a list of all the **IID**s for which COM has registered proxy/stubs. This doesn't mean that **HKEY_CLASSES_ROOT\Interface** holds information on all the interfaces supported by all the registered COM servers in the system, but if you are a local server that has an associated proxy/stub DLL, every custom interface supported by the proxy/stub DLL will appear in this part of the registry.

Every interface found within a given proxy/stub DLL will have an entry directly off **HKEY_CLASSES_ROOT\Interface**, with a key that corresponds to the interface's **IID**. Below the main interface key, you will find an entry detailing the number of methods in the given interface, as well as the **CLSID** of the server that implements the marshaling code. In the case of **IPizzaOrderTaker**, you will find an entry like this:

```
HKEY_CLASSES_ROOT\
            Interface\
               {F4C06194-6420-11D0-8C23-00400539F36B}\
                  NumMethods = "12"
                  ProxyStubClsid32 =
                  ➥"{F4C06194-6420-11D0-8C23-00400539F36B}"
```

In this example, the **ProxyStubClsid32** entry refers to a **CLSID** that is identical to the **IID** of the **IPizzaOrderTaker** interface. However, keep in mind that this is a convention that is arbitrarily set by MIDL and that it applies in this case only because your IDL file contained just a single interface. Remember the example of **IApple**; had your IDL file contained one or more other interfaces with names that alphabetically preceded `IPizzaOrderTaker`, the `CLSID` found in the preceding `ProxyStubClsid32` key would be different.

Now the algorithm that COM follows should be relatively clear. When a client calls `CoCreateInstance()`, it passes COM a requested `CLSID` and `IID`. COM looks up the class in the registry and determines the type of server that will be used to create the new object. If COM determines that the server is of the local variety, the subsystem consults the `HKEY_CLASS-ES_ROOT\Interface` portion of the registry in an effort to find the requested `IID`. After the interface entry has been found, COM consults the `ProxyStubClsid32` entry. Then COM goes to the `HKEY_CLASSES_ROOT\CLSID` portion of the registry to retrieve the name and location of the marshaling DLL. Nothing to it!

The Wizard Client

Now that you have your local server in place, complete with cross-process marshaling support enabled, we're ready to start talking about the client. As I mentioned earlier, the `PizzaOrderTaker1` client is a wizard application that will walk the user through the process of ordering a pizza. The wizard is comprised of four graphical "pages," but before I start to talk about the pages, you need to take a look at the program's central application object. Listing 7.10 shows the source code for the `CWinApp`-derived `CPizzaWizard` class.

Listing 7.10   CLIENT.CPP—The Main Application Class for the `PizzaOrderTaker1` Client, `CPizzaWizard`

```
// Get needed include files
#define INITGUID
#include "InitDlg.h"
#include "SizeDlg.h"
#include "TopDlg.h"
#include "FinalDlg.h"
#include "Resource.h"
#include "GUIDs.h"
#include "Utility.h"


//
// Main application/client class
//

class CPizzaWizard : public CWinApp
{
public:

    // Public method inherited from CWinApp
    virtual BOOL InitInstance();
};

// Our one-and-only application object
CPizzaWizard TheApp;
```

continued on next page

continued from previous page

```
//
// The entire program is run out of this method
//

BOOL CPizzaWizard::InitInstance()
{
   HRESULT  hResult;

   // Standard initialization
   Enable3dControls();

   // Initialize OLE libraries
   if (!AfxOleInit()) {
       AfxMessageBox("Could not initialize OLE subsystem.");
       return FALSE;
   }

   // Create the PizzaOrderTaker object instance
   IPizzaOrderTaker* pIPizzaOrderTaker = NULL;
   hResult = CoCreateInstance(CLSID_PizzaOrderTaker1,
                              NULL, CLSCTX_SERVER,
                              IID_IPizzaOrderTaker,
                              (PPVOID) &pIPizzaOrderTaker);
   if (FAILED(hResult)) {
      ReportError("Could not create a new
      ➥COM PizzaOrderTaker object.", hResult);
      return FALSE;
   }

   // Create our property sheet object...
   CPropertySheet  PropSheets("COM Pizza Order-Taking Wizard");

   // And create the four pages
   // Important Note: Ctors/dtors of each page class
   // AddRef() and Release()
   CInitialDialog  InitialPage;
   CSizeDialog     SizePage(pIPizzaOrderTaker);
   CToppingDialog  ToppingsPage(pIPizzaOrderTaker);
   CFinalDialog    FinalPage(pIPizzaOrderTaker);

   // Add the pages to the property sheet
   PropSheets.AddPage(&InitialPage);
   PropSheets.AddPage(&SizePage);
   PropSheets.AddPage(&ToppingsPage);
   PropSheets.AddPage(&FinalPage);

   // Put ourselves into Wizard mode and fire up the dialog box
   PropSheets.SetWizardMode();
   PropSheets.DoModal();

   // Release the PizzaOrderTaker COM object
   pIPizzaOrderTaker->Release();

   return FALSE;
}
```

If you've never built a wizard before, don't worry. MFC turns the process of writing a wizard into a walk in the park. In many respects, you'll probably find building a wizard easier than creating a full-blown, windowed application.

Although it might not be immediately apparent, a wizard (at least, a wizard written with the help of MFC) is just a tabbed dialog box with some fancy window dressing. MFC provides the `CTabCtrl` class for those enterprising programmers who want to code up tabbed dialogs with lots of custom functionality. For the lazy multitudes (that's the rest of us), Microsoft has (we are thankful) provided the `CPropertySheet` and `CPropertyPage` classes. Whereas `CTabCtrl` is really just a thin layer over the native Windows tab-set common control, the `CPropertySheet` and `CPropertyPage` classes are relatively high-level abstractions that make creating tabbed dialogs a breeze. The best thing about the `CPropertySheet` class is that you can code up a nice little tabbed dialog, call the `SetWizardMode()` method, and presto! Instant wizard! (Okay, maybe there's a little bit more to do, but not much.)

Structurally, the `CPizzaWizard` class of Listing 7.10 is standard fare. Because your wizard is a dialog-based MFC program, all the action takes place in `InitInstance()`. After you take care of the standard housekeeping stuff (enabling 3D controls, initializing COM, and so on), the wizard kicks things into high gear by immediately creating an instance of the `PizzaOrderTaking1` class.

```
// Create the PizzaOrderTaker object instance
IPizzaOrderTaker* pIPizzaOrderTaker = NULL;
hResult = CoCreateInstance(CLSID_PizzaOrderTaker1,
                    NULL, CLSCTX_SERVER,
                    IID_IPizzaOrderTaker,
                    (PPVOID) &pIPizzaOrderTaker);
```

This single instance is passed around to several different objects over the course of the wizard's execution, so it's important that you pay special attention to the reference count on this object instance.

Conceptually, you can think of a property sheet—remember that MFC calls tabbed dialogs *property sheets*—simply as a collection of *property pages*. In the MFC vernacular, a property page represents one tab of a tabbed dialog. As you might have guessed, the `CPropertySheet` class manages the set of pages, and each `CPropertyPage` object manages the contents of a single page.

Surprisingly enough, the `CPropertySheet` class is derived from `CWnd` and not `CDialog`. However, Microsoft has added protocol to `CPropertySheet` so that it looks and acts just like a dialog box. Keep in mind that even though a property sheet object answers much of the `CDialog` protocol, a property sheet does not have a dialog resource (which is the primary reason behind the MFC developers' decision to not derive the class from `CDialog`).

On the other hand, the property page class *is* derived from `CDialog`, and each instance of `CPropertyPage` does have a dialog resource associated with it. For every tab/page that you want to insert into a property sheet, you need to create a dialog box resource and a partnered `CPropertyPage`-derived dialog class. The pizza order–taking wizard has four pages, so there are four `CPropertyPage`-based classes in this program: `CInitialDialog`, `CSizeDialog`, `CToppingDialog`, and `CFinalDialog`. The `CPizzaWizard` class creates a property sheet object and then instantiates each of the page objects separately.

```
// Create our property sheet object...
CPropertySheet  PropSheets("COM Pizza Order-Taking Wizard");
```

```
// And create the four pages
// Important Note: Ctors/dtors of each page class
// AddRef() and Release()
CInitialDialog  InitialPage;
CSizeDialog     SizePage(pIPizzaOrderTaker);
CToppingDialog  ToppingsPage(pIPizzaOrderTaker);
CFinalDialog    FinalPage(pIPizzaOrderTaker);
```

The comment in the preceding code snippet is an important one. By passing off the **IPizzaOrderTaker** interface pointer to each of the property page classes, you are effectively creating a new copy of the pointer (assuming that the object is going to hold on to the pointer for a duration longer than the constructor call). The COM reference-counting rules discussed in Chapter 3 require you to **AddRef()** and **Release()** the interface pointer as appropriate. In the case of the wizard program, I've chosen to make the reference-counting behavior the responsibility of each individual property page class. This way, the property page object is empowered to manipulate and manage the interface pointer without fear or requirement of interference by an external object such as the **CPizzaWizard** application instance.

With the property sheet all loaded up and ready to go, the wizard tabbed dialog is nearly prepared for launch. One critical detail remains, however.

```
// Put ourselves into Wizard mode and fire up the dialog box
PropSheets.SetWizardMode();
PropSheets.DoModal();
```

The **SetWizardMode()** method indicates to MFC that the tabbed dialog is really a wizard and should assume the various user-interface conventions that wizards all share. A wizard, for example, does not have visible tabs. Instead, the user navigates from page to page by using the Back and Next buttons provided by MFC.

With the property sheet object operating in wizard mode, all that remains is a call to the dialog box method **DoModal()**, and up comes the introductory page.

The Introduction Page

The first page displayed by the COM pizza order–taking wizard is fairly brain-dead. I'm including it here because I want to be thorough and because the implementation of the **CInitialDialog** is a simple example of a basic property page implementation. The page itself, as you can see by looking at Figure 7.7, contains few controls. Instead, the right side of the wizard area contains some explanatory text detailing what the wizard does.

The **CInitialDialog** class—which is the **CPropertyPage**-derived class responsible for the display of the first page—is as simple as its appearance might suggest, but it shares many common architectural features with the wizard's more interesting pages. Listing 7.11 shows the header file that contains the **CInitialDialog** declarations.

Listing 7.11   INITDLG.H—The Header File for the Introductory Property Page Class, **CInitialDialog**

```
#ifndef INITDLG_H
#define INITDLG_H
```

```
#include "StdInc.h"
#include "GUIDs.h"


class CInitialDialog : public CPropertyPage
{
public:

    // Ctor & dtor
    CInitialDialog();

    // Overridden methods
    virtual void DoDataExchange(CDataExchange* pDX);
    virtual BOOL OnInitDialog();
    virtual BOOL OnSetActive();

private:

    // Member data
    CStatic  m_Title;
    CFont    m_LargeArialFont;
};


#endif
```

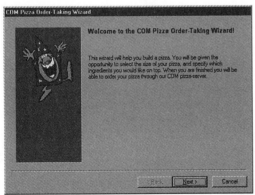

Figure 7.7   The introductory page of the pizza order–taking wizard.

Because **CInitialDialog** class doesn't really do much, you might be surprised to see that the class provides a **DoDataExchange()** method. MFC uses the **DoDataExchange()** method to validate dialog data and to move data between dialog controls and the framework. Typically, however, a dialog box class only overrides **DoDataExchange()** if it wants to perform validation on data values (which **CInitialDialog** clearly does not do) or if the dialog wants to exchange data between dialog controls and an MFC control class. **CInitialDialog** does use **DoDataExchange()** for the latter reason, because the class uses a custom font to display the page's welcoming title.

You're probably not familiar with the **OnSetActive()** method. This method is called by MFC whenever the page is "being entered" and is about to be displayed. As you'll see in the class implementation, wizard classes typically override **OnSetActive()** so that they can manage which control buttons are active or disabled. Listing 7.12 shows the implementation of **CInitialDialog**.

Listing 7.12   INITDLG.CPP—The Implementation of **CInitialDialog**

```
// Get needed include files
#include "InitDlg.h"
#include "Resource.h"
#include "Utility.h"


// Constructor
CInitialDialog::CInitialDialog()
     : CPropertyPage(IDD_INITIAL)
{ }


void CInitialDialog::DoDataExchange(CDataExchange* pDX)
{
   CPropertyPage::DoDataExchange(pDX);
   DDX_Control(pDX, IDS_TITLE, m_Title);
}


BOOL CInitialDialog::OnSetActive()
{
   CPropertyPage::OnSetActive();

   CPropertySheet* pSheet = DYNAMIC_DOWNCAST(CPropertySheet,
   ➥GetParent());
   if (pSheet != NULL)
      pSheet->SetWizardButtons(PSWIZB_NEXT);

   return TRUE;
}


BOOL CInitialDialog::OnInitDialog()
{
   CPropertyPage::OnInitDialog();

   if (m_LargeArialFont.CreatePointFont(100, "Arial Bold")) {
      m_Title.SetFont(&m_LargeArialFont);
   }

   return TRUE;
}
```

The call to the DDX_Control() function in DoDataExchange() ensures that the static text dialog control used to display the page title is kept in sync with the CStatic object referred to by the m_Title member variable. The whole point of these gesticulations is to set the font of the control, which takes place in OnInitDialog().

The OnSetActive() method retrieves the property page's parent window (which should be the property sheet object created inside CPizzaWizard's InitInstance() method) and calls SetWizardButtons(). This method accepts a bit-mask that tells MFC which control buttons should appear along the bottom of the window and which of these buttons should be enabled or disabled. In the case of the first page, there's nowhere to go but forward, so CInitialDialog passes SetWizardButtons() a value of PSWIZB_NEXT, which tells MFC to enable only the Next button.

Predictably, CInitialDialog won't go down in history as the world's busiest class, but you will find very similar code in each of the following three property page classes.

The Size Selection Page

The size selection page, shown in Figure 7.8, is concerned with determining what size of pizza the user wants. As you can see from Figure 7.8, the page presents the user with a single radio button group with one selection for each of the three available sizes (individual, small, or large). Each radio button also offers some explanatory text describing the size.

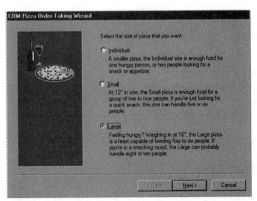

Figure 7.8   The size selection page of the pizza order–taking wizard.

A bit more is going on in this page class, CSizeDialog, although you wouldn't know it from the declaration of the class shown in Listing 7.13. In fact, CSizeDialog looks even simpler than CInitialDialog.

Listing 7.13   SIZEDLG.H—The Header File for the Pizza Size-Selection Property Page Class, CSizeDialog

```
#ifndef SIZEDLG_H
#define SIZEDLG_H
```

continued on next page

continued from previous page

```
#include "StdInc.h"
#include "GUIDs.h"


class CSizeDialog : public CPropertyPage
{
public:

    // Ctor & dtor
    CSizeDialog(IPizzaOrderTaker* pIPizzaOrderTaker);
    virtual ~CSizeDialog();

    // Overridden methods
    virtual BOOL OnInitDialog();
    virtual BOOL OnSetActive();
    virtual BOOL OnKillActive();

private:

    // Member data
    IPizzaOrderTaker* m_pIPizzaOrderTaker;
};


#endif
```

On closer scrutiny, it looks like the only difference between the two page classes lies in CSizeDialog's use of an interface pointer and the OnKillActive() method. Listing 7.14 shows the implementation of CSizeDialog. Although the class clearly shares the same lineage as CInitialDialog, something interesting is happening inside OnKillActive().

Listing 7.14   SIZEDLG.CPP—The Implementation of CSizeDialog

```
// Get needed include files
#include "SizeDlg.h"
#include "Resource.h"
#include "Utility.h"


// Constructor
CSizeDialog::CSizeDialog(IPizzaOrderTaker* pIPizzaOrderTaker)
    : CPropertyPage(IDD_SIZE)
{
    // Set the pointer to the COM PizzaOrderTaker
    m_pIPizzaOrderTaker = pIPizzaOrderTaker;
    m_pIPizzaOrderTaker->AddRef();
}

// Destructor
CSizeDialog::~CSizeDialog()
{
    // Release the COM PizzaOrderTaker
    m_pIPizzaOrderTaker->Release();
```

```
}


BOOL CSizeDialog::OnInitDialog()
{
   CPropertyPage::OnInitDialog();

   // Select the "Individual" radio button
   CheckRadioButton(IDC_RAD_INDIVIDUAL, IDC_RAD_LARGE,
   ➥IDC_RAD_INDIVIDUAL);

   return TRUE;
}


BOOL CSizeDialog::OnSetActive()
{
   CPropertyPage::OnSetActive();

   CPropertySheet* pSheet = DYNAMIC_DOWNCAST(CPropertySheet,
   ➥GetParent());
   if (pSheet != NULL)
      pSheet->SetWizardButtons(PSWIZB_NEXT);

   return TRUE;
}


BOOL CSizeDialog::OnKillActive()
{
   HRESULT hResult;

   CPropertyPage::OnKillActive();

   // Retrieve the pizza size requested
   PizzaSize ePizzaSize;
   int iCheckRadioButton = GetCheckedRadioButton(IDC_RAD_INDIVIDUAL,
                                                  IDC_RAD_LARGE);
   switch(iCheckRadioButton)
   {
      case IDC_RAD_INDIVIDUAL: ePizzaSize = Individual; break;
      case IDC_RAD_SMALL:      ePizzaSize = Small;      break;
      case IDC_RAD_LARGE:      ePizzaSize = Large;      break;

      // There should always be a selected radio button
      default:
         ASSERT(FALSE);
   }

   // Set the COM PizzaOrderTaker's pizza size
   hResult = m_pIPizzaOrderTaker->SetPizzaSize(ePizzaSize);
   if (FAILED(hResult)) {
```

continued on next page

continued from previous page

```
            ReportError("Error setting new pizza size.", hResult);
            return FALSE;
    }

    return TRUE;
}
```

You will find no surprises in the class constructor or destructor; `CSizeDialog` accepts an `IPizzaOrderTaker` interface pointer and holds on to it for the lifetime of the object, releasing the pointer in the class's destructor. `OnInitDialog()` simply ensures that the first radio button is initially selected, and `OnSetActive()` enables the Next wizard button (and yes, this means that the user cannot navigate back to the welcome page—why would he or she want to?). So far, `CSizeDialog` looks like a rather pedestrian class.

Things perk up a bit, however, in `OnKillActive()`. This dramatically named method plays counterpoint to `OnSetActive()`. Rather than call `OnKillActive()` when the page is about to be entered, MFC calls `OnKillActive()` when the page is about to be exited. `CSizeDialog` seizes this opportunity to determine what radio button is currently selected, translate the radio button information into a valid value from the `PizzaSize` enumeration, and make a call to the pizza order–taker's `SetPizzaSize()` method.

The Topping Selection Page

Unlike the `CInitialDialog` and `CSizeDialog` property page classes, the `CToppingDialog` class is a hopping place. This is because, as you can see in Figure 7.9, `CToppingDialog` manages the pizza's toppings. After all, what's the most important part of the pizza? The toppings, of course!

Figure 7.9   The topping selection page of the pizza order–taking wizard.

The user interface conventions employed by `CToppingDialog` are simple. The user selects toppings from the drop-down combo box at the top of the page. The user selects the appropriate radio button, based on whether the user wants the topping to cover the whole pizza, a half, or a quarter. When the topping is correctly indicated, the user presses the Add button. Added toppings are removed from the selection combo box and are moved into the selected-toppings list box. Toppings can be moved back into the selection combo box by selecting the topping in the select-toppings list box and clicking the Remove button.

CToppingDialog's importance becomes obvious by looking at the class's header file (shown in Listing 7.15). With four additional methods and eight member variables, clearly, CToppingDialog is upper crust through and through.

Listing 7.15 TOPDLG.H—The Header File for the Pizza Topping Property Page Class, CToppingDialog

```
#ifndef TOPDLG_H
#define TOPDLG_H

#include "StdInc.h"
#include "GUIDs.h"


class CToppingDialog : public CPropertyPage
{
public:

    // Ctor & dtor
    CToppingDialog(IPizzaOrderTaker* pIPizzaOrderTaker);
    virtual ~CToppingDialog();

    // Overridden methods
    virtual void DoDataExchange(CDataExchange* pDX);
    virtual BOOL OnInitDialog();
    virtual BOOL OnSetActive();

    // Public methods
    void OnAddTopping();
    void OnRemoveTopping();

protected:

    DECLARE_MESSAGE_MAP()

private:

    // Member data
    IPizzaOrderTaker* m_pIPizzaOrderTaker;
    CComboBox         m_ToppingList;
    CButton           m_AddTopping;
    CButton           m_RemTopping;
    CButton           m_WholePizzaRB;
    CButton           m_HalfPizzaRB;
    CButton           m_QuartPizzaRB;
    CListBox          m_SelToppingList;

    // Private methods
    void EnableToppingControls(BOOL boolEnableState);
    void EnableSelToppingControls(BOOL boolEnableState);
};


#endif
```

Okay, so maybe `CToppingDialog` isn't the world's largest class, but there's a lot of activity in this class. Listing 7.16 shows the implementation code.

Listing 7.16   `TOPDLG.CPP`—The Implementation of `CToppingDialog`

```cpp
// Get needed include files
#include "TopDlg.h"
#include "Resource.h"
#include "Utility.h"


BEGIN_MESSAGE_MAP(CToppingDialog, CPropertyPage)
   ON_BN_CLICKED(ID_ADD_TOPPING, OnAddTopping)
   ON_BN_CLICKED(ID_REM_TOPPING, OnRemoveTopping)
END_MESSAGE_MAP()


// Helper class, binding a Topping enum to its string name
struct CStringToEnumAssoc
{
   // We have to have this constructor
   CStringToEnumAssoc(const CString& strTopping,
                      Topping eTopping)
      : m_strTopping(strTopping),
        m_eTopping(eTopping)
   {}

   CString  m_strTopping;
   Topping  m_eTopping;
};

// Array to map string topping name to enum value supported by
// COM PizzaOrderTaker
CStringToEnumAssoc  g_aToppingAssocs[] =
   {
      CStringToEnumAssoc("Not a topping",     (Topping) 0        ),
      CStringToEnumAssoc("Pepperoni",         Pepperoni          ),
      CStringToEnumAssoc("Sausage",           Sausage            ),
      CStringToEnumAssoc("Ground Beef",       GroundBeef         ),
      CStringToEnumAssoc("Green Olives",      GreenOlives        ),
      CStringToEnumAssoc("Prosciuttini Ham",  ProsciuttiniHam    ),
      CStringToEnumAssoc("Pastrami",          Pastrami           ),
      CStringToEnumAssoc("Green Peppers",     GreenPeppers       ),
      CStringToEnumAssoc("Mushrooms",         Mushrooms          ),
      CStringToEnumAssoc("Onions",            Onions             ),
      CStringToEnumAssoc("Tomatoes",          Tomatoes           ),
      CStringToEnumAssoc("Pesto",             Pesto              ),
      CStringToEnumAssoc("Jalapeno Peppers",  JalapenoPeppers    ),
      CStringToEnumAssoc("Cheddar Cheese",    CheddarCheese      ),
      CStringToEnumAssoc("Fontina Cheese",    FontinaCheese      ),
      CStringToEnumAssoc("Ricotta Cheese",    RicottaCheese      ),
      CStringToEnumAssoc("Feta Cheese",       FetaCheese         ),
      CStringToEnumAssoc("Pineapple",         Pineapple          ),
```

```
        CStringToEnumAssoc("Extra Cheese",      ExtraCheese     ),
        CStringToEnumAssoc("Bacon",             Bacon           ),
        CStringToEnumAssoc("Broccoli",          Broccoli        ),
        CStringToEnumAssoc("Genoa Salami",      GenoaSalami     ),
        CStringToEnumAssoc("Zucchini",          Zucchini        ),
        CStringToEnumAssoc("Black Olives",      BlackOlives     ),
        CStringToEnumAssoc("Anchovies",         Anchovies       ),
        CStringToEnumAssoc("Chicken Breast",    ChickenBreast   ),
        CStringToEnumAssoc("Shrimp",            Shrimp          ),
        CStringToEnumAssoc("Artichoke Hearts",  ArtichokeHearts )
    };

// Constant that tracks the number of toppings
static const ULONG g_ulNumToppings =
    sizeof(g_aToppingAssocs) / sizeof(CStringToEnumAssoc);

// Global convenience functions
CString ToppingEnumToStr(Topping  eSearchTopping)
{
    // Map an enum to a string
    for (USHORT usLoop = 1; usLoop < g_ulNumToppings; usLoop++)
        if (g_aToppingAssocs[usLoop].m_eTopping == eSearchTopping)
            return g_aToppingAssocs[usLoop].m_strTopping;

    // We should never get to here
    ASSERT(FALSE);
    return "";
}


Topping ToppingStrToEnum(const CString strSearchTopping)
{
    // Map a string to an enum
    CString strRealSearchTopping =
    ➥strSearchTopping.SpanExcluding("(");
    strRealSearchTopping.TrimRight();
    for (USHORT usLoop = 1; usLoop < g_ulNumToppings; usLoop++)
        if (g_aToppingAssocs[usLoop].m_strTopping ==
        ➥strRealSearchTopping)
            return g_aToppingAssocs[usLoop].m_eTopping;

    // We should never get to here
    ASSERT(FALSE);
    return (Topping) 0;
}




// Constructor
CToppingDialog::CToppingDialog(IPizzaOrderTaker* pIPizzaOrderTaker)
    : CPropertyPage(IDD_TOPPINGS)
{
    // Set the pointer to the COM PizzaOrderTaker
    m_pIPizzaOrderTaker = pIPizzaOrderTaker;
```

continued on next page

continued from previous page

```
            m_pIPizzaOrderTaker->AddRef();
        }

        // Destructor
        CToppingDialog::~CToppingDialog()
        {
            // Release the COM PizzaOrderTaker
            m_pIPizzaOrderTaker->Release();
        }


        void CToppingDialog::DoDataExchange(CDataExchange* pDX)
        {
            CPropertyPage::DoDataExchange(pDX);
            DDX_Control(pDX, IDC_TOPPING_LIST,     m_ToppingList);
            DDX_Control(pDX, IDC_SEL_TOPPING_LIST, m_SelToppingList);
            DDX_Control(pDX, IDC_RAD_WHOLEPIZZA,   m_WholePizzaRB);
            DDX_Control(pDX, IDC_RAD_HALFPIZZA,    m_HalfPizzaRB);
            DDX_Control(pDX, IDC_RAD_QUARTPIZZA,   m_QuartPizzaRB);
            DDX_Control(pDX, ID_ADD_TOPPING,       m_AddTopping);
            DDX_Control(pDX, ID_REM_TOPPING,       m_RemTopping);
        }


        BOOL CToppingDialog::OnInitDialog()
        {
            CDialog::OnInitDialog();

            // Select the first topping in the list
            m_ToppingList.SetCurSel(0);

            // Select the "Whole Pizza" radio button
            CheckRadioButton(IDC_RAD_WHOLEPIZZA, IDC_RAD_QUARTPIZZA,
                        ➥IDC_RAD_WHOLEPIZZA);

            // Because there can be no toppings selected yet, disable
            // the selected toppings list box and the Remove button
            EnableSelToppingControls(FALSE);

            return TRUE;
        }

        BOOL CToppingDialog::OnSetActive()
        {
            CPropertyPage::OnSetActive();

            CPropertySheet* pSheet = DYNAMIC_DOWNCAST(CPropertySheet,
            ➥GetParent());
            if (pSheet != NULL)
                pSheet->SetWizardButtons(PSWIZB_BACK | PSWIZB_NEXT);

            return TRUE;
        }
```

```
void CToppingDialog::OnAddTopping()
{
    HRESULT hResult;

    // Retrieve the topping selected
    Topping eSelTopping;
    CString strSelTopping;
    INT     iCurrSelection = m_ToppingList.GetCurSel();
    m_ToppingList.GetLBText(iCurrSelection, strSelTopping);
    eSelTopping = ToppingStrToEnum(strSelTopping);

    // Retrieve the topping size requested
    ToppingSize eSelToppingSize;
    CString strSelToppingSize;
    int iCheckRadioButton = GetCheckedRadioButton(IDC_RAD_WHOLEPIZZA,
                                                  IDC_RAD_QUARTPIZZA);

    switch(iCheckRadioButton)
    {
        case IDC_RAD_WHOLEPIZZA:
            eSelToppingSize = FullPizza;
            break;
        case IDC_RAD_HALFPIZZA:
            eSelToppingSize = HalfPizza;
            strSelToppingSize = "    (On Half)";
            break;
        case IDC_RAD_QUARTPIZZA:
            eSelToppingSize = QuarterPizza;
            strSelToppingSize = "    (On Quarter)";
            break;

        // There should always be a selected radio button
        default:
            ASSERT(FALSE);
    }

    // Add it to the COM PizzaOrderTaker list first
    hResult = m_pIPizzaOrderTaker->AddTopping(eSelTopping,
    ►eSelToppingSize);
    if (FAILED(hResult)) {
        ReportError("Error adding new pizza topping.", hResult);
        return;
    }

    // Now add the topping to the selected list box...
    CString strNewToppingText(strSelTopping);
    strNewToppingText += strSelToppingSize;
    m_SelToppingList.AddString(strNewToppingText);
    m_SelToppingList.SetCurSel(0);
    EnableSelToppingControls(TRUE);

    // And remove the topping from the topping list
    m_ToppingList.DeleteString(iCurrSelection);
```

continued on next page

continued from previous page

```
        // Select the first topping and the "Whole Pizza" option
        // (if any toppings are left)
        CheckRadioButton(IDC_RAD_WHOLEPIZZA, IDC_RAD_QUARTPIZZA,
        ➡IDC_RAD_WHOLEPIZZA);
        if (!m_ToppingList.GetCount())
            EnableToppingControls(FALSE);
        else
            m_ToppingList.SetCurSel(0);
    }


    void CToppingDialog::OnRemoveTopping()
    {
        HRESULT hResult;

        // Retrieve the topping selected
        Topping eSelTopping;
        CString strSelTopping;
        INT      iCurrSelection = m_SelToppingList.GetCurSel();
        m_SelToppingList.GetText(iCurrSelection, strSelTopping);
        eSelTopping = ToppingStrToEnum(strSelTopping);

        // Remove the topping from the COM PizzaOrderTaker list first
        hResult = m_pIPizzaOrderTaker->RemoveTopping(eSelTopping);
        if (FAILED(hResult)) {
            ReportError("Error removing pizza topping.", hResult);
            return;
        }

        // Now add the topping to the topping combo box...
        CString strTopping = ToppingEnumToStr(eSelTopping);
        m_ToppingList.AddString(strTopping);
        m_ToppingList.SetCurSel(0);
        CheckRadioButton(IDC_RAD_WHOLEPIZZA, IDC_RAD_QUARTPIZZA,
        ➡IDC_RAD_WHOLEPIZZA);
        EnableToppingControls(TRUE);

        // And remove the topping from the selected toppings list
        m_SelToppingList.DeleteString(iCurrSelection);

        // Select the first topping and the "Whole Pizza" option
        // (if any toppings are left)
        if (!m_SelToppingList.GetCount())
            EnableSelToppingControls(FALSE);
        else
            m_SelToppingList.SetCurSel(0);
    }


    //
    // Methods for enabling/disabling control groups
    //
```

```
void CToppingDialog::EnableToppingControls(BOOL boolEnableState)
{
    m_ToppingList.EnableWindow(boolEnableState);
    m_AddTopping.EnableWindow(boolEnableState);
    m_WholePizzaRB.EnableWindow(boolEnableState);
    m_HalfPizzaRB.EnableWindow(boolEnableState);
    m_QuartPizzaRB.EnableWindow(boolEnableState);
}

void CToppingDialog::EnableSelToppingControls(BOOL boolEnableState)
{
    m_SelToppingList.EnableWindow(boolEnableState);
    m_RemTopping.EnableWindow(boolEnableState);
}
```

The first part of Listing 7.16 is concerned with solving a problem that seems to crop up often in Windows programming. It seems as though developers often populate list boxes with items that have a corresponding enum value. Programmers constantly find themselves having to translate back and forth between the string and enum forms of a given element because list boxes can store only strings. I've seen many different ways to deal with this problem, but CToppingDialog uses one of the easiest and time-honored methods.

In this case, a static list of structures is maintained that associates a given enum value with a particular string. More specifically, the g_aToppingAssocs array holds on to a collection of CStringToEnumAssoc objects. The global functions ToppingStrToEnum() and ToppingEnumToStr() enable the CToppingDialog class to easily obtain an enum value, given the associated string, and vice versa.

The constructor, destructor, DoDataExchange(), OnInitDialog(), and OnSetActive() methods are all relatively straightforward, so let's jump ahead to OnAddTopping(). You'll find that OnAddTopping() and OnRemoveTopping() are the heart of the CToppingDialog class.

The message map found at the top of Listing 7.16 indicates that button clicks from the Add and Remove buttons are routed to the OnAddTopping() and OnRemoveTopping() methods, respectively. The first part of OnAddTopping() is concerned with determining exactly what topping has been selected. This involves querying the combo box for the currently selected string and then mapping that string onto a Topping enum by using the ToppingStrToEnum() function. Subsequent code makes a similar determination for the pizza-size radio button group, mapping the radio button selected onto a ToppingSize enum.

Before the class can move the topping into the selected toppings list box, the dialog class ensures that the COM pizza order–taker knows about the addition of the topping. This is accomplished by making a call to IPizzaOrderTaker::AddTopping().

```
hResult = m_pIPizzaOrderTaker->AddTopping(eSelTopping,
↪eSelToppingSize);
if (FAILED(hResult)) {
    ReportError("Error adding new pizza topping.", hResult);
    return;
}
```

After the COM object has been notified, the topping is added to the selected toppings list box and removed from the candidate topping combo box.

The OnRemoveTopping() method follows a similar strategy but comes at it from the other direction. The class queries which topping is being removed from the selected toppings list box and then maps that string onto an **enum** by using the **ToppingStrToEnum()** helper function. The **enum** is passed on to the COM object during a call to the **RemoveTopping()** method.

```
hResult = m_pIPizzaOrderTaker->RemoveTopping(eSelTopping);
if (FAILED(hResult)) {
    ReportError("Error removing pizza topping.", hResult);
    return;
}
```

The operation is finished by removing the topping from the lower list box and adding the topping back into the candidate topping combo box.

The last two methods in the source file, **EnableToppingControls()** and **EnableSelToppingControls()**, are convenience methods used to enable (or disable) a set of dialog controls in a single call. **EnableToppingControls()** manages those controls related to candidate toppings (the controls at the top of the page). **EnableSelToppingControls()** manages the controls related to currently selected toppings (the selected toppings list box and the Remove button). These two methods are used just like the standard MFC windows method **EnableWindow()**; passing in **TRUE** to the method enables the window set, and passing in **FALSE** disables the window set.

The Place-Order Page

The last page in the wizard program is where the user orders his pizza. As you would expect, there are fields where the user can enter the address, phone number, and the all-important credit card number. Some day we'll probably all be ordering pizzas over the Net using smartcards or e-cash, but for now plastic will do just fine. Figure 7.10 shows the final page.

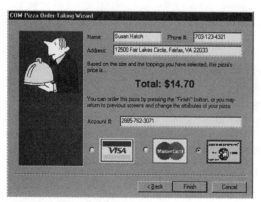

Figure 7.10   The final page of the pizza order–taking wizard.

The ordering page is controlled by a class named **CFinalDialog**. Many controls are on this last page, so you can expect to see **CFinalDialog** contain more code devoted to pure interface programming. Listing 7.17 shows the class header file.

Listing 7.17   FINALDLG.H—The Header File for the Order-Placing Property Page Class, CFinalDialog

```
#ifndef FINALDLG_H
#define FINALDLG_H

#include "StdInc.h"
#include "GUIDs.h"


class CFinalDialog : public CPropertyPage
{
public:

    // Ctor & dtor
    CFinalDialog(IPizzaOrderTaker* pIPizzaOrderTaker);
    virtual ~CFinalDialog();

    // Overridden methods
    virtual void DoDataExchange(CDataExchange* pDX);
    virtual BOOL OnInitDialog();
    virtual BOOL OnSetActive();
    virtual BOOL OnWizardFinish();

private:

    // Member data
    IPizzaOrderTaker* m_pIPizzaOrderTaker;
    CStatic           m_Total;
    CEdit             m_Name;
    CEdit             m_Phone;
    CEdit             m_Address;
    CEdit             m_Account;
    CFont             m_LargeArialFont;

    // Private methods
    CString BuildPriceStr(const ULONG   ulPrice);
    void ExtractFieldData(const CEdit&  EditField,
                          const CString strFieldName,
                          CString&      strNewString,
                          BSTR*         pbstrNewString);
};


#endif
```

Amid the methods and member data, which by now you are probably used to seeing, are some new faces. OnWizardFinish() is a method that MFC calls when the wizard is complete. In the pizza order–taking example, OnWizardFinish() provides the perfect place to send out the completed pizza order.

I'll discuss the other two new methods, BuildPriceStr() and ExtractFieldData(), after you've had a chance to look over the implementation code. As you skim through Listing 7.18, pay special attention to the OnWizardFinish() method because this is where most of the action takes place.

Listing 7.18   `FINALDLG.CPP`—The Implementation of `CFinalDialog`

```cpp
// Get needed include files
#include "FinalDlg.h"
#include "Resource.h"
#include "Utility.h"


// Constructor
CFinalDialog::CFinalDialog(IPizzaOrderTaker* pIPizzaOrderTaker)
    : CPropertyPage(IDD_FINAL)
{
    // Set the pointer to the COM PizzaOrderTaker
    m_pIPizzaOrderTaker = pIPizzaOrderTaker;
    m_pIPizzaOrderTaker->AddRef();
}

// Destructor
CFinalDialog::~CFinalDialog()
{
    // Release the COM PizzaOrderTaker
    m_pIPizzaOrderTaker->Release();
}


void CFinalDialog::DoDataExchange(CDataExchange* pDX)
{
    CPropertyPage::DoDataExchange(pDX);
    DDX_Control(pDX, IDS_TOTAL,   m_Total);
    DDX_Control(pDX, IDC_NAME,    m_Name);
    DDX_Control(pDX, IDC_PHONE,   m_Phone);
    DDX_Control(pDX, IDC_ADDRESS, m_Address);
    DDX_Control(pDX, IDC_ACCOUNT, m_Account);
}


BOOL CFinalDialog::OnInitDialog()
{
    CPropertyPage::OnInitDialog();

    // Make the total in a larger font
    if (m_LargeArialFont.CreatePointFont(160, "Arial Bold")) {
        m_Total.SetFont(&m_LargeArialFont);
    }

    // Select the "Visa" radio button
    CheckRadioButton(IDC_RAD_VISA, IDC_RAD_AMEX, IDC_RAD_VISA);

    return TRUE;
}


BOOL CFinalDialog::OnSetActive()
{
```

```
    HRESULT hResult;

    CPropertyPage::OnSetActive();

    CPropertySheet* pSheet = DYNAMIC_DOWNCAST(CPropertySheet,
    ➥GetParent());
    if (pSheet != NULL)
        pSheet->SetWizardButtons(PSWIZB_BACK | PSWIZB_FINISH);

    // Get the final price for the pizza
    ULONG ulFinalPrice = 0UL;
    hResult = m_pIPizzaOrderTaker->GetPizzaPrice(&ulFinalPrice);
    if (FAILED(hResult)) {
        ReportError("Error getting final pizza price.", hResult);
        return FALSE;
    }

    // Set the price string
    CString strPriceString = "Total: " + BuildPriceStr(ulFinalPrice);
    m_Total.SetWindowText(strPriceString);

    return TRUE;
}


BOOL CFinalDialog::OnWizardFinish()
{
    HRESULT hResult;
    CString strValidate;

    CPropertyPage::OnWizardFinish();

    // Here's the structure where we'll compile together all
    // our delivery info
    DeliveryInfo  CustomerInfo = { NULL, NULL, NULL };

    // And here's our credit card account number BSTR
    BSTR bstrAccountNum = NULL;

    // We need to keep our edit field data around in non-BSTR form
    // so that we can display our final message
    CString strName, strPhone, strAddress, strAccount;

    // Validate our input data (VERY primitively) and fill in
    // data structures and values that will be passed into
    // OrderPizza()
    try {

        ExtractFieldData(m_Name,     "name",
                         strName,    &CustomerInfo.bstrCustName);
        ExtractFieldData(m_Phone,    "phone number",
                         strPhone,   &CustomerInfo.bstrPhone);
        ExtractFieldData(m_Address,  "address",
```

continued on next page

continued from previous page

```
                                  strAddress, &CustomerInfo.bstrAddress);
        ExtractFieldData(m_Account,  "credit card account number",
                            strAccount, &bstrAccountNum);

    }
    catch (BOOL boolReturn)
    {
        SysFreeString(CustomerInfo.bstrCustName);
        SysFreeString(CustomerInfo.bstrPhone);
        SysFreeString(CustomerInfo.bstrAddress);
        SysFreeString(bstrAccountNum);
        return boolReturn;
    }

    // Retrieve the credit card type being used
    CreditCard eCreditCardType;
    CString    strCreditCardType;
    int iCheckRadioButton = GetCheckedRadioButton(IDC_RAD_VISA,
                                                  IDC_RAD_AMEX);
    switch(iCheckRadioButton)
    {
        case IDC_RAD_VISA:
            eCreditCardType = Visa;
            strCreditCardType = "Visa";
            break;
        case IDC_RAD_MASTERCARD:
            eCreditCardType = MasterCard;
            strCreditCardType = "Master Card";
            break;
        case IDC_RAD_AMEX:
            eCreditCardType = AmericanExpress;
            strCreditCardType = "American Express";
            break;

        // There should always be a selected radio button
        default:
            ASSERT(FALSE);
    }

    // Send off the order
    ULONG ulFinalPrice = 0UL;
    hResult = m_pIPizzaOrderTaker->OrderPizza(&CustomerInfo,
                                              eCreditCardType,
                                              bstrAccountNum,
                                              &ulFinalPrice);
    if (FAILED(hResult)) {
        ReportError("Error ordering pizza.", hResult);
        return FALSE;
    }

    // Build the final message to the user and display it
    CString strFinalMsg = "Thank you, ";
    strFinalMsg += strName;
```

```
   strFinalMsg += ", your order has been processed using the "
                  "following information:\n\n";
   strFinalMsg += "\tName: ";
   strFinalMsg += strName;
   strFinalMsg += "\n\tPhone: ";
   strFinalMsg += strPhone;
   strFinalMsg += "\n\tAddress: ";
   strFinalMsg += strAddress;
   strFinalMsg += "\n\nA total of ";
   strFinalMsg += BuildPriceStr(ulFinalPrice);
   strFinalMsg += " has been billed to your ";
   strFinalMsg += strCreditCardType;
   strFinalMsg += " credit card, account number \"";
   strFinalMsg += strAccount;
   strFinalMsg += ".\"\n\nThank you for your patronage!";
   AfxMessageBox(strFinalMsg, MB_ICONINFORMATION);

   // Free all our BSTRs
   SysFreeString(CustomerInfo.bstrCustName);
   SysFreeString(CustomerInfo.bstrPhone);
   SysFreeString(CustomerInfo.bstrAddress);
   SysFreeString(bstrAccountNum);

   return TRUE;
}


CString CFinalDialog::BuildPriceStr(const ULONG ulPrice)
{
   // Format the final price string
   CString strPrice = "$";
   strPrice += ULongToStr(ulPrice / 100);
   strPrice += ".";
   if ((ulPrice % 100) < 10)
      strPrice += "0";
   strPrice += ULongToStr(ulPrice % 100);

   return strPrice;
}


void CFinalDialog::ExtractFieldData(const CEdit&  EditField,
                                    const CString strFieldName,
                                    CString&      strNewString,
                                    BSTR*         pbstrNewString)
{
   // Retrieve edit field text
   EditField.GetWindowText(strNewString);
   if (strNewString == "") {

      // Show message
      CString strMsg = "We need your ";
      strMsg += strFieldName;
```

continued on next page

continued from previous page

```
        strMsg += " before we can deliver your order.";
        AfxMessageBox(strMsg);
        throw FALSE;
    }
    *pbstrNewString = strNewString.AllocSysString();
}
```

Everything looks normal until you hit the **OnSetActive()** method. Like the previous versions of **OnSetActive()** that you've seen in the other page classes, **CFinalDialog** uses **OnSetActive()** to set the various wizard buttons (although this time it is enabling the Finish button). However, **CFinalDialog** also uses **OnSetActive()** to calculate (or recalculate, if the user is returning to the page) and display the total price for the pizza. This enables the user to revisit previous pages and return to the last page for an up-to-date total. More importantly, this technique enables the wizard to provide an accurate total without requiring the various pages to know about each other. Although requiring each page to notify **CFinalDialog** when information changes would hardly be the end of the world, it makes more sense (and seems more elegant) to keep each class distinct and decoupled from each other.

If you look at the code for updating the pizza price, you'll see that the process is quite simple.

```
// Get the final price for the pizza
ULONG ulFinalPrice = 0UL;
hResult = m_pIPizzaOrderTaker->GetPizzaPrice(&ulFinalPrice);
if (FAILED(hResult)) {
    ReportError("Error getting final pizza price.", hResult);
    return FALSE;
}

// Set the price string
CString strPriceString = "Total: " + BuildPriceStr(ulFinalPrice);
m_Total.SetWindowText(strPriceString);
```

Recall that the actual pricing algorithm is in the COM object, so the price quote is generated by a call to the **IPizzaOrderTaker** method **GetPizzaPrice()**. **GetPizzaPrice()** returns the price in cents (for example, for a pizza that costs $13.26, **GetPizzaPrice()** would return 1,326) so the returned value needs to be massaged a little in the **BuildPriceStr()** method before it's ready for public consumption.

OnWizardFinish() is certainly the longest method in the class, but this is largely a consequence of having to deal with several data fields. The primary purpose of **OnWizardFinish()** is to gather all the data required to make the obligatory call to **IPizzaOrderTaker**'s **OrderPizza()** method. Like any good Windows application, **OnWizardFinish()** provides some validation of the collected data to ensure that required information is provided. Unlike good Windows applications, however, **CFinalDialog**'s validation logic is simple; as long as the collected strings are nonempty, the wizard will trundle happily along, assuming that the strings contain valid information.

After all the data fields are extracted and validated, `OnWizardFinish()` fills in a `DeliveryInfo` structure and kicks off a call to the COM object's `OrderPizza()` method.

```
hResult = m_pIPizzaOrderTaker->OrderPizza(&CustomerInfo,
                                          eCreditCardType,
                                          bstrAccountNum,
                                          &ulFinalPrice);
if (FAILED(hResult)) {
    ReportError("Error ordering pizza.", hResult);
    return FALSE;
}
```

With the pizza ordered and the final pizza price in hand, the `CFinalDialog` class cobbles together a final message box (Figure 7.11) that summarizes the details of the transaction. After `OnWizardFinish()` returns with a value of `TRUE`, MFC dismisses the property sheet window, and the wizard exits.

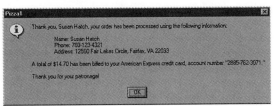

Figure 7.11   The summary message box displayed by the pizza order–taking wizard after the order has been completed.

Summary

With the completion of your first local server also comes the completion of the first part of this book. By now, you should have a pretty good feel for how to build in-process and local servers using MFC. Coupled with your knowledge of COM aggregation, you already have the skills required to start building sophisticated COM clients and servers.

You should now understand the basics of how a local server (out-of-process) differs from an in-process server, how you must marshal data between the caller and the local server, and how this can be accomplished using IDL and a proxy/stub DLL.

CHAPTER 8

BUILDING COM OBJECTS USING THE ACTIVEX TEMPLATE LIBRARY

In this chapter, you will learn about the following:

- The differences between ATL and the MFC

- ATL-based local and in-process server construction

- How to use the ATL Registrar to execute your scripts

The Microsoft Foundation Class (MFC) Library is now more than seven years old, and it has become a fundamental example of what you can accomplish with a large C++ class library. The MFC class library has an undeniable appeal when you evaluate the product's broad and far-reaching scope.

With the release of Visual C++ 6, however, Microsoft is answering the requests of COM programmers who feel that the MFC runtime is too large to facilitate the building of light, fast COM components. With many developers wanting to develop ActiveX controls that need to be downloaded across potentially slow Internet links (an ActiveX control is a COM component), Microsoft recognized the need to develop a lightweight COM class library optimized for speed. Microsoft hopes that this new class library, named the *ActiveX Template Library* (ATL), will help stimulate developer interest in the COM and ActiveX technologies.

Welcome, ATL!

The ActiveX Template Library is big news for COM programmers and should, in fact, change the way in which most developers approach the construction of COM objects. However, it doesn't change the underlying COM principles discussed in this book. The ATL is one of several tools for building COM components. ATL provides a rich class library specifically focused on the needs of the COM developer. In its current incarnation, ATL has a single-minded focus: the construction of the fastest possible custom components, automation objects, and ActiveX controls—all COM components.

The Future of ATL

With the appearance of ATL, the COM/DCOM programmer is now faced with the vexing dilemma of having to decide whether to use MFC or ATL for his or her server development. Each approach has its advantages and disadvantages.

The decision is not, strictly speaking, an either/or issue. It's possible to use ATL in an MFC project, and vice-versa. I recommend that you make the decision to go with one class library or the other, if you can. Using MFC with ATL mitigates many of the advantages of using ATL (namely, speed and size).

If you plan to build large local servers that are also full-blown graphical applications, you're better off going with MFC. MFC helps with the complexity of building graphically sophisticated programs, and ATL provides very little support in this area, although it's improving with each release. MFC also provides high-level interfaces for important application features such as ActiveX documents, Data Access Objects (DAO), and Open Database Connectivity (ODBC) databases.

If your primary concern is building COM/DCOM servers that have little or no user interface requirements, you should probably give ATL the nod. This book is about creating and using COM and DCOM components as application building blocks, so I will be discussing ATL.

ATL and C++ Templates

Because you're a COM programmer, ATL should be music to your ears. Given the chance to "start over," the ATL development team has done an impressive job of providing a class library that's easy to use and doesn't require the overhead of the MFC runtime DLLs. In fact, ATL doesn't require any sort of runtime services at all. This is because, as its name implies, ATL is based on C++ templates, and as a consequence, it has no link dependencies on external libraries at all.

Note

Although components built with ATL do not have to have any dependencies on external libraries, ATL does provide registry access facilities that you will probably want to use. These facilities, provided through a COM component called the *Registrar*, might require the existence of the Registrar server, contained in **ATL.DLL**. However, this tiny DLL is only about 20KB in size, which is a far cry from the more than one megabyte required by the MFC runtime. In fact, the Registrar doesn't even have to be used as an external COM component. If you so choose, you can statically link the Registrar directly into your components. The cost? A startlingly small 5K in production-mode builds.

Because ATL is template-based, the library is contained exclusively in the header files that your components include in their source code. Although using ATL does require the use of inheritance, the inherited class hierarchy is relatively flat because of the extensive use of templates.

Multiple Inheritance

The ATL relies on two fundamental design techniques that utilize the unique syntax and expressive capabilities of C++ to maximum effect. The first, ATL's namesake, is the pervasive use of templates. The second is multiple inheritance.

ATL is an excellent example of how to use multiple inheritance correctly. This is mainly because the use of multiple inheritance in ATL is restricted to the use of *mixin* classes. A C++ mixin is a class that has been designed to be multiply inherited by a host class. Mixins are virtually useless in their own right and must be coupled to a host class in order to provide substantive benefit.

Using mixin classes is one way to effectively share class functionality and reinforce "is-a" relationships, but using mixins alone does not protect a class library from that scourge of multiple inheritance, the inheritance diamond. You recall from Chapter 2, "The Object Revolution," that a multiple inheritance occurs when a class inherits from two classes that are inherited from a common base class. The ATL is designed so that COM component class hierarchies are quite flat. A COM component will typically be part of a hierarchy that is only two or three levels deep. By keeping the inheritance tree short and by using template classes as mixins, the ATL team has sidestepped most of the traditional arguments against multiple inheritance by ensuring that multiple inheritance will be virtually nonexistent.

Automation and Dual Interfaces

ATL fully supports the creation of automation servers and dual interfaces. Most of the examples in this book center on custom interfaces that use standard COM calling semantics, which are based on a binary vtable specification. The various Automation technologies add a level of indirection that enables clients to dynamically query and execute server interfaces at runtime, rather than have to hard-code (and subsequently hard-compile) the interfaces of the objects with which they are interacting.

Automation is a tremendously flexible and powerful set of technologies. Until recently, it was the only way that COM objects could be manipulated from within other development environments such as VBScript, PowerBuilder, and Java. Although ATL certainly provides comprehensive Automation support, the framework can also help with the construction of COM components that expose dual interfaces. A *dual interface object* is one that can be accessed through either Automation *or* COM vtable bindings. Starting with version Visual Basic 5, Microsoft has stated that dual interface support is not required for compatibility with Visual Basic object support features. However, the real benefit of dual interfaces is that those development environments that can access custom interfaces can realize significant performance gains while using the same component implementations as Automation-only clients.

Tear-Off Interfaces

The 3.0 version of ATL supports an intriguing performance enhancement called *tear-off interfaces*.

The idea behind tear-off interfaces is simple. Rather than instantiate a component in its entirety, an object might want to instantiate only its `IUnknown` interface section and other interfaces that it knows are going to be used often. Interface code that is called infrequently can wait until a client actually asks for the interface pointer before instantiating that part of the component. In other words, a component that uses tear-off interfaces is composed of several implementation objects, and creation of the objects that implement rarely used interfaces is deferred until someone wants to use the interfaces in question.

Performance gains are possible with tear-offs, but you must watch for some pitfalls. The use of tear-off interfaces is a fairly advanced ATL topic, and I won't be covering them in this book. Now that you have been properly introduced to ATL, it's time to dig in to some of the underlying architecture of ATL.

The ATL Architecture

Building COM objects using ATL is not a whole lot different than building COM objects using MFC. In fact, it has been said that building components with ATL is easier than using MFC, especially if you've read all the previous chapters and have a good understanding of COM basics.

ATL version 3 (the version included with Visual C++ 6) adds support for ActiveX controls, registry scripting, Microsoft Transaction server components, compiler-specific optimizations, and a host of additional enhancements.

To learn how to build basic custom components by using ATL, all you have to do is understand four classes and a handful of macros. In later sections, I'll show you how to put it all together by porting the `PizzaOrderTaker` server from MFC to ATL.

The `CComModule`

At the heart of every MFC program is an application class derived from `CWinApp`. This application class serves as a focal point for activities that affect the entire executable or DLL. If you choose to build an ATL DLL-based COM server with MFC support (which is one of the options), you will get a `CWinApp` object that so much of MFC depends on. This book's examination of ATL focuses on the use of ATL for building the smallest, fastest possible COM servers—without support for MFC.

Although ATL doesn't use an application class per se, it does have a central *module* class. The module object, which is either an instance of `CComModule` or one of its subclasses, serves the same purpose as `CWinApp`. However, `CComModule` is not as large and complicated as `CWinApp`.

For example, your servers will declare a module object irrespective of whether your class is an in-process or local server. Unlike `CWinApp`, though, `CComModule` does not encapsulate a windows message loop if the server is a local server. Local ATL servers must provide their own message loops; in other words, you have to hand-code your own message loop if you are going to use a local server. Cutting the message loop out of **CComModule** means that an in-process server doesn't have to lug around any more code than it needs.

The module object handles server lock counts, registration of class factories from inside local servers, and coordination with the Registrar for self-registration and unregistration. Compared to the MFC servers that you've looked at in previous chapters, the module object performs some of the functions performed by **CWinApp** and some functions performed by **CCmdTarget**.

If you're building an in-process server, you can get away with simply using the **CComModule** class as is. However, if you are planning on building a local server, you will have to create a subclass of **CComModule**. This is because the standard **CComModule** class doesn't make the distinction between local and in-process servers, and a local server needs to bring itself down when its internal object count reaches zero. Although you can easily accomplish this by overriding the **Unlock()** method and posting a quit message to the server's message queue when the lock count reaches zero, it still requires the creation of a **CComModule** subclass.

As a final quirky touch, ATL requires that you name the global module object **_Module**. This is because several of the ATL macros and templated base classes rely on the existence of a global object named **_Module** that responds to **CComModule** protocol.

CComObjectRoot

When you are using ATL, a COM component is constructed by writing an implementation object that multiply derives from several ATL classes, templates, and, optionally, one or more custom interface classes. **CComObjectRoot** is one of those classes that every COM component must be derived from.

Note

Throughout ATL documentation, you will find references to a class named **CComObjectRootEx**, which is a template parameterized on a thread-model object. The **CComObjectRoot** "class" is really just a **typedef** for the **CComObjectRootEx** template that has been parameterized on the default server threading model.

You can think of **CComObjectRoot** as the main ATL counterpart to MFC's **CCmdTarget**. The fundamental purpose of **CComObjectRoot** is to manage the components' reference count. In the case of an object that is being aggregated, **CComObjectRoot** holds on to the outer component's **IUnknown** pointer and makes sure that **AddRef()** and **Release()** calls are routed to the outer object.

Because reference counting is one of the most important maintenance tasks performed by a COM object, the use of **CComObjectRoot** is not optional. All ATL COM components must be derived from **CComObjectRoot** (or **CComObjectRootEx**).

CComObject

Although `CComObjectRoot` is responsible for managing your objects' reference counts, a quick perusal of the `CComObjectRoot` class declaration or documentation fails to turn up the implementation of the actual `IUnknown` interface. That's because the actual `IUnknown` interface is embodied in the `CComObject` class.

Note

The `CComObject` class comes in several different flavors. `CComObject` is designed for those components that will not (and cannot) ever be aggregated. Conversely, the `CComAggObject` performs the same function as `CComObject` for those components that can be aggregated. Finally, the `CComPolyObject` is used as an optimization when you know that your component will be used as both a standalone object and as part of an aggregation. The important thing to keep in mind is that, generally speaking, all three of these classes serve the same purpose. As I continue to discuss `CComObject`, keep in mind that I am also talking about `CComAggObject` and `CComPolyObject` unless otherwise noted.

`CComObject` is quite different from the other main ATL classes because you don't derive your component implementation classes from `CComObject`. Instead, *CComObject is derived from your component class*. It shouldn't come as a surprise to find that `CComObject` is actually a template; the weird part is that `CComObject` is derived from your class and is also parameterized on your COM class type.

Because you don't have to custom code the `CComObject` class, some sort of trickery must be going on here. After all, the programmers at Microsoft couldn't have possibly anticipated the names of your component classes and then embedded those names in their template code. What is the `CComObject` trick?

The work that `CComObject` class does is accomplished with macros. The macros in question are `DECLARE_AGGREGATABLE`, `DECLARE_NOT_AGGREGATABLE`, `DECLARE_ONLY_AGGREGATABLE`, and `DECLARE_POLY_AGGREGATABLE`. These macros can be placed in the declaration of your class to control the aggregation characteristics of your component and to define the implementation of the `CComObject` (or like) class. Each of these macros expands into a `typedef`, nested within your implementation class, for a creator class. This creator class is used to create instances of your component when clients call `CoCreateInstance()` or `IClassFactory::CreateInstance()`. The creator class `typedef` also provides the name of your component implementation class to the `CComObject` template.

The `DECLARE_AGGREGATABLE` macro ensures that the creator class will use a `CComObject` class (derived from your component class, of course) in those cases in which your component is not being aggregated. If you have used `DECLARE_AGGREGATABLE` and your object is part of an aggregation, the creator class relies on a `CComAggObject` variant. `DECLARE_NOT_AGGREGATABLE`, on the other hand, constructs a creator class `typedef` that uses `CComObject` when there is no aggregation underway and returns a `CLASS_E_NOAGGREGATION` error when an outer class tries to aggregate your objects. `DECLARE_ONLY_AGGREGATABLE` uses `CComAggObject` in the case of an aggregation and `E_FAIL` in all other cases. Finally, `DECLARE_POLY_AGGREGATABLE` uses a `CComPolyObject` instance in both cases.

Note

The default aggregation model used by ATL relies on the `DECLARE_AGGREGATABLE` semantics, so if you don't use any of these macros in your code, your objects will act as if you had called `DECLARE_AGGREGATABLE`. If you want different functionality, you have to use a different macro.

In each case, the `CComObject` family of templates forwards its reference-counting and interface-querying interfaces to corresponding methods in `CComObjectRoot`. However, each `CComObject` class deals with other miscellaneous housekeeping tasks in different ways. Luckily for you, all this ugliness is hidden deep within ATL and is taken care of for you without any intervention required on the part of your code.

CComCoClass

The last major ATL class that you need to be aware of is `CComCoClass`. You might have noticed a very important COM component that I haven't addressed yet: your object's class factory. The class factory is automatically provided for you by ATL, similar to the manner in which MFC provides a class factory for COM objects. Using `CComCoClass` doesn't require a whole lot of effort. As long as your component is derived from `CComCoClass`, ATL ensures that your class is automatically bound to a default class factory object.

Exactly how `CComCoClass` provides your component with a class factory is a little more involved. Inside the declaration of `CComCoClass`, you'll find the use of the `DECLARE_CLASSFACTORY` macro. The `DECLARE_CLASSFACTORY` macro works in much the same way as the various aggregation macros; fundamentally, the macro declares a nested `typedef` for a creator class (in this case, a factory creator, as opposed to an object creator).

In the case of `DECLARE_CLASSFACTORY`, the creator `typedef` employs the services of a class named `CComClassFactory`. The `CComClassFactory` class implements the `IClassFactory` interface used by clients (and the `CoCreateInstance()` API function) to construct new COM object instances. However, your code should never have cause to interact with an actual instance of `CComClassFactory`, because the use of the class is encapsulated by the inherited `CComCoClass` part of your component.

Note

Just like aggregation models, ATL supports a default factory implementation. If you don't place a class factory macro in your own code, ATL will use the `DECLARE_CLASSFACTORY` macro found in `CComCoClass`, which ultimately uses an instance of the `CComClassFactory` class.

You can have your class use a different type of class factory by using a different, overriding class factory macro in the declaration of your component implementation class. The `DECLARE_CLASSFACTORY2` macro, for example, causes `CComCoClass` to collaborate with an instance of `CComClassFactory2` instead of a `CComClassFactory` object. `CComClassFactory2` implements the standard `IClassFactory2` COM interface, which is really just `IClassFactory` with some licensing extensions. Other class factory macros include `DECLARE_CLASSFACTORY_AUTO_THREAD` and `DECLARE_CLASSFACTORY_SINGLETON`. Use of these variants is rare, but you should be aware of their existence.

Mixing In the Custom Interfaces

The final class (or classes) involved in your component's inheritance tree is the actual custom interface class generated by the MIDL compiler. For example, if your component implements three custom interfaces, your implementation will be multiply derived from the three MIDL-generated interface classes (in addition to `CComObjectRoot` and `CComCoClass`).

Implementing your custom interfaces is simply a matter of providing method bodies for each of the functions declared in each of the interface classes. All the interfaces are inherited at the same logical level of scope; the beauty of ATL is that you don't have to mess around with nested classes or call ugly macros to obtain the `pThis` pointer, as you do in MFC. Subclass your component from your interface, provide implementations for your functional methods, and BOOM! You're done.

You might be wondering about `IUnknown`. After all, each of the MIDL-generated interface classes will be derived from `IUnknown`, and I haven't said anything about where in your class definition you need to place your `IUnknown` code. This is because you don't have to worry about `IUnknown` at all! The `IUnknown` interface is handled at the `CComObject` level, which is derived from your class. In fact, `IUnknown` is exactly why `CComObject` (or one of the `CComObject` variants) needs to be derived from your class, rather than have your class derived from `CComObject`. `CComObject` is added to the inheritance tree after you've mixed in the interface classes so that it can provide implementations of the `IUnknown` methods. Remember that `CComObject` ends up forwarding the `IUnknown` protocol to `CComObjectRoot` anyway, so the whole class exists only to capture incoming `IUnknown` methods calls and redirect them to the correct place.

The New ATL Version of PizzaOrderTaker

So far, I've kept the discussion of ATL pretty abstract; a couple of important concepts still need to be explained. All the same, it's time for you to look at some code before I fill in the last few gaps.

As I mentioned earlier, I'm going to show you how to take the `PizzaOrderTaker` example from Chapter 7, "Breaking the Process Boundary Using Local Servers," and implement the server by using ATL instead of MFC. It's not accurate to say that I'm going to port the server to ATL, because I'm going to start over from scratch, but you will find that the functional implementation of the various `IPizzaOrderTaker` methods is very similar.

Declaring the `ComPizzaOrderTaker` Class with ATL

The `ComPizzaOrderTaker` class is identical in ATL, regardless of whether it's being hosted inside an in-process or local server. This is no different from the MFC version, in which you created an IDL file and then an implementation class with its own header and implementation file.

The IDL file that I'm using is almost exactly the same IDL file that I showed you in Chapter 7. However, I did make a single change to the file that has caused me to change the filename to `PIZZA2.IDL`. Although the `IPizzaOrderTaker` interface GUID is the same in both versions, I've given the coclass a new GUID. This will enable your system to host both an ATL and MFC `PizzaOrderTaker` server simultaneously, even though the servers provide identical functionality.

I'm not going to reproduce the entire IDL file here, but Listing 8.1 does show the new declaration for the modified coclass (I'm calling the coclass `PizzaOrderTaker2` here, to distinguish it from the first version presented in Chapter 7).

Listing 8.1   `PIZZA2.IDL`—The IDL File for the COM `PizzaOrderTaker` Class, the ATL Version

```
... Rest of the IDL file omitted ...

//
//  Class information for PizzaOrderTaker2
//
[ uuid(43903313-8857-11D0-8C80-00400539F36B) ]
coclass PizzaOrderTaker2
{
        interface IPizzaOrderTaker;
};
```

As you can see, this is not a profound change. Keep in mind that the `IPizzaOrderTaker` interface has not changed at all. This means that the proxy/stub DLL that you created and registered for the MFC version of the local server will work just as well with ATL local server (and yes, a local ATL server requires marshalling code just like any other local server that hosts objects with custom interfaces).

Okay, all that IDL stuff is merely housekeeping. Take a look at the new implementation class header file in Listing 8.2. It contains a lot of new stuff, so be sure to give it a good once-over before reading on.

Listing 8.2   `PIZZA2.H`—The Declaration of the `PizzaOrderTaker` Class, the ATL Version

```
#ifndef PIZZA2_H
#define PIZZA2_H


// Get needed include files
#include <list>
```

continued on next page

continued from previous page

```cpp
#include "Resource.h"
#include "GUIDs.h"


class ATL_NO_VTABLE ComPizzaOrderTaker :
        public CComObjectRoot,
        public CComCoClass<ComPizzaOrderTaker,
       ➥&CLSID_PizzaOrderTaker2>,
        public IPizzaOrderTaker
{
public:

    // Ctor and dtors
    ComPizzaOrderTaker();
    virtual ~ComPizzaOrderTaker();

    // IPizzaOrderTaker
    STDMETHOD(ResetPizza)     ();
    STDMETHOD(SetPizzaSize)   (PizzaSize      eNewSize);
    STDMETHOD(GetPizzaSize)   (PizzaSize*     peCurrSize);
    STDMETHOD(AddTopping)     (Topping        eNewTopping,
                               ToppingSize    eNewToppingSize);
    STDMETHOD(RemoveTopping)  (Topping        eRemTopping);
    STDMETHOD(GetNumToppings) (ULONG*         pulNumToppings);
    STDMETHOD(GetTopping)     (ULONG          ulListPos,
                               Topping*       peTopping,
                               ToppingSize*   peToppingSize);
    STDMETHOD(GetPizzaPrice)  (PULONG         pulPrice);
    STDMETHOD(OrderPizza)     (DeliveryInfo*  pDeliveryInfo,
                               CreditCard     eCreditCardType,
                               BSTR           bstrCreditCardNum,
                               ULONG*         pulPrice);

    BEGIN_COM_MAP(ComPizzaOrderTaker)
      COM_INTERFACE_ENTRY(IPizzaOrderTaker)
    END_COM_MAP()

    DECLARE_REGISTRY_RESOURCEID(IDR_REGSCRIPT)
    DECLARE_NOT_AGGREGATABLE(ComPizzaOrderTaker)

private:

    // Private, nested tuple class
    struct CToppingTuple
    {
        Topping     eTopping;
        ToppingSize eToppingSize;
    };

    // Convenience typedefs
    typedef std::list<CToppingTuple*>  TupleList;
    typedef TupleList::iterator        TupleListIter;
```

```
    // Private member data
    PizzaSize     m_eSize;
    TupleList     m_ToppingList;

    // Private methods
    TupleListIter FindTopping(Topping eSearchTopping);
};

typedef ComPizzaOrderTaker* PComPizzaOrderTaker;


#endif
```

A lot is going on in this header file, and most of it is new, so I'm going to proceed slowly. Let's start by looking at the basic class declaration.

```
class ATL_NO_VTABLE ComPizzaOrderTaker :

        public CComObjectRoot,
        public CComCoClass<ComPizzaOrderTaker,
        ➥&CLSID_PizzaOrderTaker2>,
        public IPizzaOrderTaker
```

The name of the component implementation class is `ComPizzaOrderTaker`, as in the MFC version that I showed you in Chapter 7. This time around, `ComPizzaOrderTaker` is multiply derived from `CComObjectRoot`, `CComCoClass`, and the `IPizzaOrderTaker` interface class. The `CComObjectRoot` and `IPizzaOrderTaker` inheritance is straightforward, but the `CComCoClass` template requires parameters that are worth discussing.

The `CComCoClass` template accepts two parameters. The first is the name of the class for which a class factory will be provided. The indicated class must be derived from `CComCoClass`. The second template parameter is the address of a GUID that contains the target class's CLSID. As you can see from the preceding code snippet, the `ComPizzaOrderTaker` class provides itself as the first template parameter and the address of `CLSID_PizzaOrderTaker2` for the second.

Is a Vtable Needed?

You might be a little confused by the use of the `ATL_NO_VTABLE` macro that appears in the declaration of the `ComPizzaOrderTaker` class. If you are using Visual C++ 6, this macro expands to `__declspec(novtable)`. This new Microsoft-specific compiler extension indicates to the compiler that it should not initialize the object's vtable in the class constructor. Of course, this makes direct use of the class impossible, so why would you want to do this?

Because the `ComPizzaOrderTaker` class implements an ATL object, the ATL class factory will never actually create instances of your class. Instead, the class factory creates instances of a `CComObject` class that is derived from (in this example) `ComPizzaOrderTaker`. The `CComObject` class is never declared with `ATL_NO_VTABLE` and will always be the most derived subclass, so the vtable will be correctly built and initialized in the `CComObject` constructor. To put it bluntly, a `ComPizzaOrderTaker` object cannot be directly instantiated. Anyway, you are interested only in the `CComObject` subclass.

The typical programmer usually doesn't regard the vtable initialization phase of object construction as significant overhead, but Microsoft isn't taking any chances. The ATL developers wanted to ensure that ATL objects be absolutely as fast as possible.

You must be aware that some problems are associated with the no-vtable technique. The main one is that the constructor of a class that uses `ATL_NO_VTABLE` cannot call virtual methods. If, as part of your object initialization, you need to perform some sort of up-front processing that requires virtual function calls, override the `FinalConstruct()` method and move the code there. `FinalConstruct()` is called by the ATL framework after the object has been fully constructed, so the vtable should be in place and fully functional by the time `FinalConstruct()` is executed.

The nice thing about `ATL_NO_VTABLE` optimization is that if you're unsure about whether your code can safely use it, you can simply omit the macro altogether. Sure, your code will run a little more slowly, but it's important to understand that you can always omit `ATL_NO_VTABLE` without suffering any functional ill effects.

COM Maps

After the class declaration, you encounter prototypes for the constructor, destructor, and all the `IPizzaOrderTaker` interface methods. All the interface methods are declared as normal virtual (that is, `STDMETHOD`) functions. No messy macros, no messy nested classes.

Immediately following the declarations for the interface functions, you find the COM map. COM maps are very similar to the interface maps that you encountered in your MFC servers. It is the COM map that associates a particular interface ID with the implementation class. A `QueryInterface()` call on your object will only return interface pointers for those interfaces registered in the COM map.

The COM map is delineated using the `BEGIN_COM_MAP` and `END_COM_MAP` macros. Interface registration entries are placed between the `BEGIN` and `END` macros.

```
BEGIN_COM_MAP(ComPizzaOrderTaker)
   COM_INTERFACE_ENTRY(IPizzaOrderTaker)
END_COM_MAP()
```

In the case of `ComPizzaOrderTaker`, the server object supports only a single interface (`IPizzaOrderTaker`, of course). A normal custom interface is placed into the COM map, using the `COM_INTERFACE_ENTRY` macro. Many different types of COM map interface entry macros (more than a dozen) exist because they have the most common utility. The `COM_INTERFACE_ENTRY_AGGREGATE` macro is one of the exceptions; it's used when your object is aggregating another class (it is the ATL equivalent of the MFC `INTERFACE_AGGREGATE` macro that you learned about in Chapter 6, "Using Aggregation to Simulate Inheritance").

Most other interface macros are more esoteric. For example, you use a `COM_INTERFACE_ENTRY_FUNC` macro when you want to install a callback function that is called whenever a `QueryInterface()` is performed on your object for a particular interface. I am not going to cover these in detail, but if you're interested in more information on the various interface macros, look in the online help index under "`COM_INTERFACE_ENTRY` Macros."

Of Registries and Aggregates

Immediately following the COM map are two more macros. I've already discussed the `DECLARE_NOT_AGGREGATABLE` macro; its use here indicates that this class cannot be used as part of an aggregation. I didn't choose to use the `DECLARE_NOT_AGGREGATABLE` macro for any special reason. If you wanted to enable `ComPizzaOrderTaker` to be used as an aggregate, all you would have to do is remove the `DECLARE_NOT_AGGREGATABLE` macro call (remember that the default behavior is `DECLARE_AGGREGATABLE`) or replace the macro with `DECLARE_POLY_AGGREGATABLE`.

The next macro, `DECLARE_REGISTRY_RESOURCEID`, indicates that the class's registration information is contained in a registry script stored in the server's resource segment. This script can be given to the Registrar, who uses the script to register or unregister the COM object. I'm going to leave it at that until later on in the chapter when I cover registry scripting and the Registrar in more detail.

ATL Tradeoffs

If you are coming from the world of MFC, you're liable to suffer some culture shock as you start to immerse yourself in the ways of ATL. Without the array of MFC services at your disposal, you might find yourself having to find other outlets for functional help. This is probably best demonstrated by those parts of `ComPizzaOrderTaker` that had previously relied on MFC collection classes to store the list of client-selected pizza toppings. ATL does not have the simple collection classes that MFC does.

To work correctly without dependencies on MFC, I had to modify `ComPizzaOrderTaker` so that it uses an STL list. If you're not familiar with the Standard Template Library (STL), I urge you to start learning as much about the STL as possible. STL code is only going to become more prevalent as compilers mature and the ANSI standard moves closer to ratification. That being said, I've tried to keep my use of STL to a functional minimum, and the STL code in `ComPizzaOrderTaker` (and the rest of the book, for that matter) is straightforward.

The lack of MFC services is most obvious when it comes to graphical interfaces. Although ATL provides some bare-bones windowing and GUI infrastructure, functionality is minimal, and building an application interface with ATL classes is only incrementally easier than writing directly to the Win32 APIs. As you will see later in the chapter, I have sacrificed the MFC server's graphical registration dialog box in favor of a more streamlined user interface (a euphemism for saying that duplicating the MFC server's interface is more trouble than it's worth).

A Short STL Tutorial

One of the largest and most dramatic additions to the ANSI standard occurred in the summer of 1994 with the acceptance of the Standard Template Library, usually referred to as *STL*. The STL is a container class library—implemented with templates—designed using generic programming techniques devised by Alexander Stepanov, Meng Lee, David Musser, and others. It tackles the problem of creating collection classes from an algorithmic vantage point. As a result, the STL classes perform efficiently but are very flexible and extensible. Visual C++ 6 ships with a fully functional version of STL. Before you can start using STL, you must have a firm grasp of three simple concepts: algorithms, iterators, and containers. A program uses *containers* to hold type instances, *iterators* to access and refer to items held by a container, and *algorithms* to process and manipulate container contents. As an example, this code fragment depicts how you might code a search through an array of integers:

```
// Declare the array
vector<int>  MyVector(100, 0);

... Do some things ...

// Now see if the number 7 is in the array
int found = binary_search(MyVector.begin(),
➥MyVector.end(), 7);
```

In this code, `MyVector` is the container. It holds integers, as indicated by its template argument. The algorithm is encapsulated in the `binary_search()` function. Algorithms know nothing about the containers on which they work. Instead, they interact only with iterators, which know how to move about in containers and provide a consistent interface for item insertion and extraction. In the preceding example, `MyVector.begin()` and `MyVector.end()` are two container methods that return iterators.

The STL is a very large class library made up of many different container and algorithm types. It's efficient and sophisticated, enabling programmers to accomplish a great deal in a very few lines of code.

Implementing the ATL ComPizzaOrderTaker Class

After that intricate header file, you're liable to be a little disappointed by the actual class implementation. That's because the only thing that you need to place in an ATL object's source file is the implementation of your various interfaces. Compare that to what you need to do for an MFC-based COM object: Add dynamic creation support with the `IMPLE-MENT_DYNCREATE` macro, define class factory support with the `IMPLEMENT_OLECREATE` macro, provide the interface map, provide trivial method implementations for the nested `IUnknown` methods, and finally, provide implementations for the component interfaces.

Take a look at Listing 8.3. The code in `PIZZA2.CPP` will look very familiar to you if you've read Chapter 7. The only real changes to the source have been made to support the new STL container, which actually requires less code. You're starting to like this STL stuff, aren't you?

Listing 8.3 `PIZZA2.CPP`—The Implementation of the `PizzaOrderTaker` Class, the ATL Version

```
// Get needed include files
#define INITGUID
#include "Pizza2.h"
#include "Utility.h"
```

```
// List of base pizza prices
ULONG g_aulPizzaPrices[] =
    {
        395,  // Individual
        595,  // Small
        795   // Large
    };

// List of base topping prices
ULONG g_aulToppingPrices[] =
    {
        50,   // Individual
        100,  // Small
        150   // Large
    };

// List of topping modifiers (topping prices are influenced
// by the size of the pizza, but some toppings
// (like artichokes—YECH!) are twice as expensive
ULONG g_aulToppingMods[] =
    {
        0,    // Not a topping (here to catch errors)
        1,    // Pepperoni
        1,    // Sausage
        1,    // GroundBeef
        1,    // GreenOlives
        1,    // ProsciuttiniHam
        1,    // Pastrami
        1,    // GreenPeppers
        1,    // Mushrooms
        1,    // Onions
        1,    // Tomatoes
        1,    // Pesto
        1,    // JalapenoPeppers
        1,    // CheddarCheese
        1,    // FontinaCheese
        1,    // RicottaCheese
        1,    // FetaCheese
        1,    // Pineapple
        1,    // ExtraCheese
        1,    // Bacon
        1,    // Broccoli
        1,    // GenoaSalami
        1,    // Zucchini
        1,    // BlackOlives
        1,    // Anchovies
        2,    // ChickenBreast
        2,    // Shrimp
        2     // ArtichokeHearts
    };


//
```

continued on next page

continued from previous page

```
// Constructor and destructor
//

ComPizzaOrderTaker::ComPizzaOrderTaker()
    : m_eSize(Individual)
{
    VerboseMsg("In PizzaOrderTaker constructor.\n");
}

ComPizzaOrderTaker::~ComPizzaOrderTaker()
{
    VerboseMsg("In PizzaOrderTaker destructor.\n");
}


//
// IPizzaOrderTaker interface members
//

STDMETHODIMP
ComPizzaOrderTaker::ResetPizza()
{
    VerboseMsg("In ResetPizza.\n");

    // Clean out the topping list
    m_ToppingList.clear();

    // Reset the size to Individual
    m_eSize = Individual;

    return NOERROR;
}

STDMETHODIMP
ComPizzaOrderTaker::SetPizzaSize(PizzaSize eNewSize)
{
    VerboseMsg("In SetPizzaSize.\n");

    // Set the new size
    m_eSize = eNewSize;

    return NOERROR;
}

STDMETHODIMP
ComPizzaOrderTaker::GetPizzaSize(PizzaSize* peCurrSize)
{
    VerboseMsg("In GetPizzaSize.\n");

    // Get the current size
    if (peCurrSize)
        *peCurrSize = m_eSize;
```

```
      return NOERROR;
}

STDMETHODIMP
ComPizzaOrderTaker::AddTopping(Topping eNewTopping,
                              ToppingSize eNewToppingSize)
{
   VerboseMsg("In AddTopping.\n");

   // Is this topping already in the list?
   if (FindTopping(eNewTopping) != m_ToppingList.end())
      return E_FAIL;

   // Create a new Topping tuple
   CToppingTuple* pTuple = new CToppingTuple;
   pTuple->eTopping = eNewTopping;
   pTuple->eToppingSize = eNewToppingSize;

   // Add the topping to the list
   m_ToppingList.push_back(pTuple);

   return NOERROR;
}

STDMETHODIMP
ComPizzaOrderTaker::RemoveTopping(Topping eRemTopping)
{
   VerboseMsg("In RemoveTopping.\n");

   // Find the topping tuple
   TupleListIter iter = FindTopping(eRemTopping);
   if (iter == m_ToppingList.end())
      return NOERROR;

   // Free the memory for the tuple and remove the list element
   m_ToppingList.erase(iter);

   return NOERROR;
}

STDMETHODIMP
ComPizzaOrderTaker::GetNumToppings(ULONG* pulNumToppings)
{
   VerboseMsg("In GetNumToppings.\n");

   // Get the current number of toppings
   if (pulNumToppings)
      *pulNumToppings = m_ToppingList.size();

   return NOERROR;
}

STDMETHODIMP
```

continued on next page

continued from previous page

```
ComPizzaOrderTaker::GetTopping(ULONG        ulListPos,
                               Topping*     peTopping,
                               ToppingSize* peToppingSize)
{
    VerboseMsg("In GetTopping.\n");

    //
    // Retrieve the position's tuple
    //
    // GetTopping() provides position-oriented retrieval
    // because it's easy to manipulate and understand.
    //
    // Note that list positions use first element-based access
    // and not zero-based access (that is., the first element is
    // at position 1, not 0)

    // Validate the list position
    if (!ulListPos || ulListPos > m_ToppingList.size())
        return E_FAIL;

    // Iterate through the list, counting
    TupleListIter iter = m_ToppingList.begin();
    ULONG ulCurrentElem = 1UL;

    do {

        // Is this a match?
        if (ulCurrentElem == ulListPos) {
            *peTopping = (*iter)->eTopping;
            *peToppingSize = (*iter)->eToppingSize;
            return NOERROR;
        }
        ulCurrentElem++;
        iter++;

    } while (iter != m_ToppingList.end());

    return E_FAIL;
}

STDMETHODIMP
ComPizzaOrderTaker::GetPizzaPrice(ULONG* pulPrice)
{
    VerboseMsg("In GetPizzaPrice.\n");

    // Start by setting the base price.
    ULONG ulPizzaPrice = g_aulPizzaPrices[m_eSize];

    // Now walk through the topping list, adding to the current price
    TupleListIter iter = m_ToppingList.begin();
    while (iter != m_ToppingList.end()) {

        // Calculate the topping price
        ULONG ulToppingPrice = g_aulToppingPrices[m_eSize] *
                               g_aulToppingMods[(*iter)->eTopping];
```

```
      // Based on how much of the pizza is covered with
      // this topping, the topping price needs to be scaled
      switch ((*iter)->eToppingSize)
      {
         case FullPizza:                          break; // Do nothing
         case HalfPizza:     ulToppingPrice /= 2; break;
         case QuarterPizza: ulToppingPrice /= 4; break;
      }

      // Add the topping price to the total
      ulPizzaPrice += ulToppingPrice;

      // On to the next topping
      iter++;
   }

   // And now return the result
   *pulPrice = ulPizzaPrice;

   return NOERROR;
}


STDMETHODIMP
ComPizzaOrderTaker::OrderPizza(DeliveryInfo* , // pDeliveryInfo,
                               CreditCard    , // eCreditCardType,
                               BSTR          , // bstrCreditCardNum,
                               ULONG*        pulPrice)
{
   VerboseMsg("In OrderPizza.\n");

   // Set the price
   GetPizzaPrice(pulPrice);

   // Do whatever needs to be done to send the order out
   // (We'll do some things here in Part II of the book)

   return NOERROR;
}



ComPizzaOrderTaker::TupleListIter
ComPizzaOrderTaker::FindTopping(Topping eSearchTopping)
{
   for (TupleListIter iter = m_ToppingList.begin();
        iter != m_ToppingList.end();
        iter++)
        if ((*iter)->eTopping == eSearchTopping)
           return iter;

   return iter;
}
```

Because I'm not trying to do anything fancy with STL in this example, the code becomes easier to read and is significantly shorter (by nearly 275 lines of code, down from approximately 350 lines in the MFC version).

Building the Local Server

With the `ComPizzaOrderTaker` class out of the way, you can turn your attention to the module class. The module class, you'll recall, is the ATL equivalent of `CWinApp` in MFC, except dumber.

You've now reached the point at which things need to be done a little differently depending on whether you are building a local or in-process server. I'll start by showing you the steps required to build the local server and then move on to the in-process server example, which is even easier.

Module Identification

In addition to ATL classes that are used to help implement a COM component, a local server requires two other things. First, the server must declare a global object named `_Module` that is derived from `CComModule`. Second, the server must provide a `WinMain()` function, which is the starting point for any Windows-based program.

It's important that your local servers use a `_Module` object that is an instance of a class derived from `CComModule`, not an actual instance of `CComModule`. This is because the `CComModule` class doesn't know about the distinction between in-process and local servers, but does maintain the server lock count that determines whether the server can be unloaded. You'll recall that a local server, on sensing that it's no longer hosting objects that have external references, needs to unload and send a quit message to itself. If your server is MFC-based, the framework provides this little piece of logic, and the server is brought down without any required intervention on your part. In ATL, you are responsible for providing this last step. Fortunately, the implementation of this behavior is simple.

In the local-server ATL examples shown throughout this book, you can see that the `_Module` object is always declared as an instance of `QueATLModule`. `QueATLModule` is actually a `typedef` that is conditionally defined, based on whether you specify the `USE_ATL_LOCAL` or `USE_ATL_INPROC` symbol in your project settings. If either of these symbols is defined, the `STDINC.H` header file, used by virtually all the sample program source files, will include the `ATLMOD.H` header file. This include file, shown in Listing 8.4, contains the definition of the server module class.

Listing 8.4   `ATLMOD.H`—The Header File Containing the Definition of the ATL Module Class

```
#ifndef ATLMOD_H
#define ATLMOD_H

//
// Set the module class correctly, depending on
// whether we are an in-process or local server
//

#ifdef USE_ATL_INPROC

    // Set our module class type
    typedef CComModule QueATLModule;
```

```
#endif

#ifdef USE_ATL_LOCAL

    // Check for double inclusion
    #ifdef USE_ATL_INPROC
        #error Specify USE_ATL_INPROC or USE_ATL_LOCAL, but not both.
    #endif

    //
    // This is a local server. Unlock needs to be overridden
    // so that the server can shut itself down when the server
    // lock count reaches zero
    //

    class CExeModule : public CComModule
    {
    public:

        // Ctor and dtor
        CExeModule()
        {
          // Set our thread id
         ulThreadID = GetCurrentThreadId();
        }

        // Overridden methods
        LONG Unlock()
        {
            // Unlock ourselves
            LONG lLockCount = CComModule::Unlock();

            // Was that the last one?
            if (!lLockCount)
            {
                // Yep! Send our suicide message
                PostThreadMessage(ulThreadID, WM_QUIT, 0, 0);
            }

            return lLockCount;
        }

    private:

        ULONG ulThreadID;
    };

    // Set our module class type
    typedef CExeModule QueATLModule;

#endif
```

continued on next page

continued from previous page

```
// Declare the external module instance
extern QueATLModule _Module;
```

```
#endif
```

This header file is divided into two sections, with the second part being by far the larger of the two. Based on what preprocessor symbol has been set for the project, the compiler will compile one of the two sections (but never both).

If you're building an in-process server, the `CComModule` class doesn't need to be subclassed, because the ATL-provided definition of `CComModule` has all the functionality that your server will require. In this case, a `typedef` sets `QueATLModule` as the equivalent of the `CComModule` class.

```
typedef CComModule QueATLModule;
```

However, if you are building a local server, the `CComModule` class needs to be subclassed, and the `Unlock()` method needs to be overridden to post a `WM_QUIT` message to the server in the event that the server lock count has fallen to zero. This subclass, named `CExeModule`, uses the same techniques as the `CExeModule` class generated by the ATL server wizard; in the constructor, the class retrieves the current thread ID, and when the lock count falls to zero, the class uses the Win32 API `PostThreadMessage()` to send a `WM_QUIT` event to the thread's message queue. Because all my server code relies on the `QueATLModule` typedef, `QueATLModule` is set to alias the `CExeModule` class.

Although you are free to use this same technique in your own code, absolutely nothing dictates that you have to do things this way. Regardless of the approach you decide to take, however, you must make sure that your local servers post a `WM_QUIT` message to themselves when their lock count falls to zero.

The Server Object Map

With the module class in place, you can turn your attention to the definition of `WinMain()`. In Listing 8.5, you'll find `ATLLOCALSRV.CPP`, which contains the remaining C++ code specific to ATL local servers. The `WinMain()` function depicted in Listing 8.5 is very similar to the code that the ATL AppWizard pumps out, but I've cleaned it up a bit and slapped on a few coats of fresh paint. You might want to generate a test ATL project and compare Microsoft's generated version of `WinMain()` with mine; functionally, the two versions are identical, but I think you'll find the code in Listing 8.5 to be significantly easier to understand, because it's simplified and takes less code to do the same work.

Listing 8.5 `ATLLOCALSRV.CPP`—The Implementation of an ATL Local Server's `WinMain()` Function

```
// Get needed include files
#include "Pizza2.h"
#include "ATLLine.h"


//
// Object map, indicates which classes are serviced by this server
//
```

```
BEGIN_OBJECT_MAP(ObjectMap)
   OBJECT_ENTRY(CLSID_PizzaOrderTaker2, ComPizzaOrderTaker)
END_OBJECT_MAP()


//
// The global module object
//
QueATLModule _Module;


//
// Standard start function for a Windows executable
//
extern "C"
int WINAPI WinMain (HINSTANCE    hInstance,
                    HINSTANCE    /*hPrevInstance*/,
                    LPSTR        pszCommLine,
                    int          /*nShowCmd*/)
{
    // Process our command line
    CATLCommandLine CommLine(pszCommLine);

    // Crank up COM
    HRESULT hResult = CoInitialize(NULL);
    if (FAILED(hResult)) {
        ReportError("Could not initialize OLE subsystem.", hResult);
        return FALSE;
    }

    // Set up the module object
    _Module.Init(ObjectMap, hInstance);

    // Do we need to self-register?
    if (CommLine.Register())
        hResult = _Module.RegisterServer();

    // Do we need to self-unregister?
    if (CommLine.Unregister())
        hResult = _Module.UnregisterServer();

    // Everything's looking good — start up the server?
    if (CommLine.ShouldRun())
    {
        // Register the class factories with COM
        hResult = _Module.RegisterClassObjects(CLSCTX_LOCAL_SERVER,
                                               REGCLS_MULTIPLEUSE);
        if (FAILED(hResult)) {
            ReportError("Could not register class factories.", hResult);
            return FALSE;
        }
```

continued on next page

continued from previous page

```
        // Main server message loop
        MSG msg;
        while (GetMessage(&msg, 0, 0, 0))
           DispatchMessage(&msg);

        // Unregister class factories
        _Module.RevokeClassObjects();
    }

    // Bring down COM
    CoUninitialize();

    return hResult;
}
```

I'll get to `WinMain()` in just a moment, but I want to start by looking at the object map definition that can be found at the top of Listing 8.5.

```
BEGIN_OBJECT_MAP(ObjectMap)
   OBJECT_ENTRY(CLSID_PizzaOrderTaker2, ComPizzaOrderTaker)
END_OBJECT_MAP()
```

The object map is used to tell COM what classes reside within the server. The map is found at global scope and starts with the **BEGIN_OBJECT_MAP** macro (the name passed into this macro provides the name for the global map variable, which you referred to in `WinMain()`). The object map is completed using the (surprise!) **END_OBJECT_MAP** macro. Ultimately, it's the **OBJECT_ENTRY** macro that you're really interested in. The **OBJECT_ENTRY** macro takes two parameters: the CLSID of your component and the name of your component's implementation class. This macro entry informs ATL that any clients who want to create instances of the class indicated by the provided CLSID should be routed to the bound implementation class. Of course, you may have as many **OBJECT_ENTRY** macro invocations in your object maps as you need. For example, if your server hosted three different COM components, the object map would contain three **OBJECT_ENTRY** macros.

Immediately following the object map, you can find the declarations of the global `_Module` instance, and then immediately following that, you can find the `WinMain()` function. All nonconsole Windows programs use `WinMain()` as their starting point, in much the same way that a standard ANSI C++ program uses `main()` as its starting point. When you're building programs with MFC, the framework provides its own implementation of `WinMain()`, so many MFC programmers have never had to deal with `WinMain()` at all.

In an ATL local server implementation, several things need to happen in `WinMain()`. Specifically, you are responsible for ensuring that the COM libraries are initialized, that command-line arguments are checked for /**RegServer** and /**UnregServer** flags, and that the server has a central message loop.

Command-Line Processing

For the first task, firing up the COM libraries is a simple case of calling the standard `CoInitialize()` and `CoUninitialize()` COM APIs discussed earlier in the book.

Without the benefit of MFC, however, even trivial tasks such as checking the command line become hassles. Scanning a command line for various flags is hardly difficult, but it's not a whole lot of fun. That's why I built the CATLCommandLine class that is used by the ATL local server. Like the CSrvCommandLineInfo class that I derived from MFC's CCommandLineInfo, the CATLCommandLine is designed to provide a simple way for programs to determine which of the various COM command-line arguments have been passed into the server. (Obviously, without MFC you can't reuse the CSrvCommandLineInfo class because it's derived from the framework.) Listing 8.6 shows the header file that contains the CCommandLineInfo class declaration.

Listing 8.6   ATLLINE.H—The Declaration for the CATLCommandLine Class

```
#ifndef ATLLINE_H
#define ATLLINE_H


// Get needed include files
#include "StdInc.h"
#include "Utility.h"


class CATLCommandLine
{
public:

    // Ctor
    CATLCommandLine(PCHAR pszCommandLine);

    // Query methods
    BOOL Register() const
    {
        return m_bRegister;
    }
    BOOL Unregister() const
    {
        return m_bUnregister;
    }
    BOOL ShouldRun() const
    {
        return !m_bRegister && !m_bUnregister;
    }

private:

    // Member data
    BOOL m_bRegister;
    BOOL m_bUnregister;

    // Helper member function
    BOOL FindArg(PCHAR pszBaseString, PCHAR pszSearchArg);
};


#endif
```

CATLCommandLine is very simple; you pass a command line into the object's constructor, and the class checks for the /RegServer or /UnregServer flags. The class is not infallible, but it's very easy to use and gets the job done with a minimal amount of fuss. Listing 8.7 shows the remaining implementation details of CATLCommandLine.

Listing 8.7 ATLLINE.CPP—The Implementation of the CATLCommandLine Class

```
#include "ATLLine.h"
#include "Utility.h"


// Ctor
CATLCommandLine::CATLCommandLine(PCHAR pszCommandLine)
{
    // Initialize our temporary and blast into uppercase
    CHAR  achCommLine[256];
    _ASSERTE(strlen(pszCommandLine) < 256);
    strcpy(achCommLine, pszCommandLine);
    _strupr(achCommLine);

    // Now look for a RegServer or UnregServer argument
    m_bRegister   = FindArg(achCommLine, "REGSERVER")   ? TRUE : FALSE;
    m_bUnregister = FindArg(achCommLine, "UNREGSERVER") ? TRUE : FALSE;
}


BOOL CATLCommandLine::FindArg(PCHAR pszBaseString,
                             PCHAR pszSearchArg)
{
    // Now look for the search string
    PCHAR pszArg = strstr(pszBaseString, pszSearchArg);
    if (pszArg && pszArg != pszBaseString)
    {
        // Is this a command-line argument?
        if (*(—pszArg) == '-' ¦¦ *pszArg == '/')
            return TRUE;
    }
    return FALSE;
}
```

The Size and Efficiency of COM Components with ATL

ATL does several things well, but two of the framework's primary goals are size and efficiency. Microsoft has gone to great extremes to ensure that components built with ATL can be as small and as fast as possible. I've already discussed the ATL_NO_VTABLE macro, but I'll give you another example.

The ATL AppWizard generates several different configurations for a new ATL server project. One of these configurations, MinSize, strives to create final binaries that are as small as realistically possible. In this configuration, the symbol `_ATL_MIN_CRT` is declared, which causes ATL to provide its own definition for every single runtime library function used by ATL itself. This enables the `MinSize` configuration to link without requiring the runtime libraries (and their associated size and overhead) at all.

Whether you intend to be this maniacal about performance, understand that the source code examples depicted in this book have not been optimized and carry around a bit of additional luggage with them. For example, like all the previous sample programs and servers that I've shown you, these ATL servers compile and link in the `UTILITY.CPP` file. This source file uses functionality found in the standard runtime libraries, so relying on `UTILITY.CPP` defeats many of the optimizations that a `MinSize` (or similar) configuration is striving for. Similarly, the `STDINC.H` header file and the `CATLCommandLine` class each rely on various standard runtime library headers. Although convenient, you ultimately pay a price in binary size and to a lesser extent, performance. Of course, the whole reason that I rely on `UTILITY.CPP`, `STDINC.H`, and other calls to the runtime is to simplify the code and provide examples that are effective and instructional. Just keep in mind that if you're concerned about performance—and size, in particular—you'll want to cleanse your code of any "conveniences" and keep your source as close to the metal as possible.

The first thing that the `WinMain()` function does is process the server's command-line arguments, using a `CATLCommandLine` object. In many respects, this command-line object will single-handedly dictate the logic flow through the `WinMain()` function.

After initializing the COM libraries, `WinMain()` initializes the `_Module` object. The `Init()` method requires you to provide the name of the object map global variable (remember, you provided that name in the `BEGIN_OBJECT_MAP` macro call) and an application instance handle. The instance handle is an opaque token that Windows uses to help differentiate applications and DLLs from each other. As you can tell from Listing 8.5, the instance handle is passed by Windows into `WinMain()`, so it is a simple matter to pass this value into the `_Module` object's `Init()` method.

Server Registration and Unregistration

After the `_Module` object has been initialized, the server can turn its attention to the issue of self-registration. With the help of the `CATLCommandLine` class, determining whether the server should self-register is a simple matter of calling the `Register()` method. This method returns `TRUE` if the server was invoked with the `/RegServer` command-line flag.

```
// Do we need to self-register?
if (CommLine.Register())
    hResult = _Module.RegisterServer();
```

The Registrar and the introduction of registry scripting are two of the best new features introduced with ATL 2.0, and they lie at the heart of ATL server registration and unregistration. I cover both these topics in a later section titled "Registering the Class Factories," but because `WinMain()` serves as the kick-off point for the Registrar, you need to be aware of what the preceding code snippet is doing.

How your class handles self-registration depends entirely on what registry macro you used in the declaration of your component implementation class. In the case of the ComPizzaOrderTaker class, the DECLARE_REGISTRY_RESOURCEID macro was used, which indicates that the server is registered using an external registration script that needs to be run through the Registrar. In this case, the RegisterServer() method call will eventually end up using the Registrar. However, other possibilities exist.

The DECLARE_REGISTRY_RESOURCE macro is virtually identical to the DECLARE_REGISTRY_RESOURCEID macro (they both end up using the same internal registration mechanism). For the ComPizzaOrderTaker class, you use the DECLARE_REGISTRY_RESOURCEID macro, passing in the name of a symbolic constant that contains the resource identifier of the registry script resource. DECLARE_REGISTRY_RESOURCE works in much the same fashion, except you pass it a constant string that indicates the correct registry resource script identifier.

Another option is the DECLARE_REGISTRY macro. This is the macro that you should use if you don't want to take advantage of the Registrar and don't plan on writing a registration script; the macro provides a bare-bones implementation that will place only those items in the registration that are minimally required to register your component. The DECLARE_REGISTRY macro requires five parameters, which are detailed in Table 8.1.

Table 8.1   The Five Parameters of the DECLARE_REGISTRY Macro

Argument	Description
class	For the first parameter, you should pass in your component's CLSID, but it really doesn't matter what you pass in here, because the parameter is used for backwards compatibility with previous versions of ATL and is completely ignored.
pid	A string containing the component's ProgID (including any version-specific extensions).
vpid	A string containing the component's version independent ProgID.
descid	For the fourth macro argument, you should pass in a string table ID that will be used to retrieve a component description string. Make sure that you pass a valid identifier here; ATL uses this identifier as a parameter into the Win32 LoadString() API, but the code doesn't check the return code and uses an initialized character array to hold the result. In other words, if you pass an invalid number in this argument, you'll probably end up with garbage in your component description, or you might even experience program crashes.
threadtype	The final macro describes the server's threading model. In this example, you need to pass in THREAD-FLAGS_APARTMENT. (The other options are THREADFLAGS_BOTH or AUTPRXFLAG).

Of course, you can always opt to use the DECLARE_NO_REGISTRY macro. In this case, the RegisterServer() method will do nothing to help register your class, and you will have to provide some other means to register your server. Note that using the DECLARE_NO_REGISTRY macro inside one component does not affect other components' self-registration behaviors; the RegisterServer() method registers those components that provide an appropriate mechanism and only ignores those servers that use the DECLARE_NO_REGISTRY macro.

As far as `RegisterServer()` is concerned, the method takes two arguments. The first—a boolean argument that is defaulted to **FALSE** if the caller doesn't provide it—indicates whether ATL should also register the type libraries that may be associated with a given class. A *type library* is an Automation-specific structure that describes the interfaces and methods supported by a component. Because the `PizzaOrderTaker` server is not an Automation server, there's no type library to register. `RegisterServer()`'s second argument is a pointer to a CLSID. If the CLSID is provided (is non-**NULL**), only the specified component will be registered; a **NULL** argument, which is the default, indicates that all the components in the server should be registered.

```
// Do we need to self-unregister?
if (CommLine.Unregister())
    hResult = _Module.UnregisterServer();
```

The next code segment is virtually identical to the previous three lines of code, except that the methods called handle a server self-unregistration. The call to `RegisterServer()` has been replaced with `CComModule`'s unregistration counterpart, `UnregisterServer()`. Unlike `RegisterServer()`, `UnregisterServer()` accepts only a single argument (a pointer to the targeted CLSID, or **NULL** to unregister every component in the server).

Registering the Class Factories

If the server isn't being run in registration or unregistration mode, the `CATLCommandLine` method `ShouldRun()` will return **TRUE**, and the executable will enter into its main event-processing loop. Before the main event loop can be started up, however, the server needs to register its class factories with the COM subsystem (remember that this is a local server that you're building here). The server needs to be registered before it's run, because initialization information needed to load it is contained in the registry. Registering the server's class factories is as simple as making a call to the `CComModule` method `RegisterClassObjects()`.

```
// Everything's looking good — start up the server?
if (CommLine.ShouldRun())
{
    // Register the class factories with COM
    hResult = _Module.RegisterClassObjects(CLSCTX_LOCAL_SERVER,
                                           REGCLS_MULTIPLEUSE);

    if (FAILED(hResult)) {
        ReportError("Could not register class factories.", hResult);
        return FALSE;
    }

    // Main server message loop
    MSG msg;
    while (GetMessage(&msg, 0, 0, 0))
        DispatchMessage(&msg);

    // Unregister class factories
    _Module.RevokeClassObjects();
}
```

`RegisterClassObjects()` takes two parameters. The first is a class context value, which tells COM what type of server you're running. You've seen the class context value before in calls such as `CoCreateInstance()` and `CoGetClassObject()`, but this time around you're specifying it on the server side (as opposed to the client side). The second parameter to `RegisterClassObjects()` indicates to COM whether a new local server process should be started to each new client requesting a server connection or whether a single local server can be used to service multiple clients. The use of these two arguments can be a little confusing, so let's take a closer look.

Let me start by explaining `RegisterClassObjects()`'s second argument. This parameter can assume one of three different values: `REGCLS_SINGLEUSE`, `REGCLS_MULTIPLEUSE`, or `REGCLS_MULTI_SEPARATE`. If you pass `REGCLS_SINGLEUSE` into `RegisterClassObjects()`, you're telling COM that the class factories for this particular server instance should be made available only to a single client. This means that if another client wants to create instances of your components, COM will physically launch another server process. I can think of only a few occasions when you would want this behavior, because creating a new process is slow and expensive from a performance standpoint. However, if your server needs to serialize access to a single, globally shared resource (a printer, for example), there might be a good reason for this. On the other hand, if you use `REGCLS_MULTIPLEUSE`, you're telling COM that multiple clients can simultaneously access multiple components that are all running within a single instance of your server. This is the case that you will probably encounter the most often. `REGCLS_MULTI_SEPARATE` is a rather special case flag which, when specified, registers the class object only as a multiple-use local server.

Now turn your attention to `RegisterClassObjects()`'s first parameter. The server context parameter can have a value of `CLSCTX_INPROC_SERVER`, `CLSCTX_LOCAL_SERVER`, or both (that is, `CLSCTX_INPROC_SERVER | CLSCTX_LOCAL_SERVER`). This might appear strange. After all, you're talking about a local server here, so why would you ever want to expose your class factories as if they belonged to in-process servers? There are really two answers to this question.

The `RegisterClassObjects()` method ultimately calls the standard COM API `CoRegisterClassObject()`. Although I've never seen it done, it's supposedly valid for an in-process server that's already been loaded into a client address space to proactively register class factories, rather than rely on COM making calls to the exported function `DllGetClassObject()`. Now this seems like a really bad idea to me (how does the server guarantee that it can stay in memory long enough to handle multiple clients?), and I never want to catch you trying this sort of foolishness. However, it is technically allowed, which implies that the `CoRegisterClassObject()` method should be able to accept a server context value of `CLSCTX_INPROC_SERVER`. It goes without saying that you will probably not run into this use case very often.

The second reason for `RegisterClassObjects()`'s support of `CLSCTX_INPROC_SERVER` is that on certain occasions a local server might want to register itself as an in-process server. Say what!?! I realize that this doesn't make much sense on the surface, but imagine a local server that creates instances of a class named `Peanut`. Now imagine that this very same server contains multiple classes, and one of the other hosted classes is a class named `Elephant`. What happens when an `Elephant` object wants to interact with a `Peanut` object? Because the same server hosts both objects, it would be a huge waste of resources to kick off a whole new process just so that the `Elephant`s could have their `Peanut`s. In this example, the `Peanut` objects are really in-process with respect to the `Elephant` objects, and COM enables you to formalize this relationship by registering a server as being both local and in-process. When you do this, COM knows to treat local objects used within the server as if they were being hosted by an in-process server.

If you think this is confusing, Microsoft has unfortunately muddied the waters even further by providing the `REGCLS_MULTI_SEPARATE` option for `RegisterClassObjects()`'s second argument. When you specify `REGCLS_MULTI_SEPARATE` in the second parameter, as a "convenience" feature, COM adds `CLSCTX_INPROC_SERVER` to the server context argument. Are you completely confused yet?

Back to the `Elephants` and `Peanuts` example, you've already established that you want to use `CLSCTX_INPROC_SERVER` and `CLSCTX_LOCAL_SERVER` as the server context because COM will interpret this as meaning that co-located objects will be served in-process. The call to `RegisterClassObjects()` would look something like this:

```
// Register the class factories with COM
hResult = Module.RegisterClassObjects(CLSCTXINPROC_SERVER |
➥CLSCTX_LOCAL_SERVER,
➥REGCLS_MULTIPLEUSE);
```

However, you can accomplish the same result by writing this code like so:

```
// Register the class factories with COM
hResult = Module.RegisterClassObjects(CLSCTX_LOCAL_SERVER,
                               REGCLS_MULTI_SEPARATE);
```

These two method invocations are equivalent, and both are equally accurate. The ironic thing about this whole mess is that the vast majority of local servers can get away with `CLSCTX_LOCAL_SERVER` and `REGCLS_MULTIPLEUSE`, but it's important that you understand these parameters all the same.

After the class factories have been registered with COM, the server enters into its main message loop. This is the part that you never saw in your MFC servers because the framework took care of this step for you. Compared to the messiness you had to wade through for `RegisterClassObjects()`, this simple message loop isn't much to look at, is it?

The message loop will continue to spin until the `_Module` object posts its `WM_QUIT` message, at which point the loop will break and the server will call the module's `RevokeClassObjects()` method. The `RevokeClassObjects()` method is refreshingly straightforward; call it before your local server terminates to ensure that COM knows that those class objects are going away.

With `WinMain()` safely navigated, your excursion through the ATL local server is largely complete. The next section explains what needs to be done as part of the in-process ATL server implementation, and then you can focus your attention on the Registrar and ATL's new registry scripting capabilities.

Note

The `PizzaOrderTaker2` local server, like any local server, will need a proxy/stub DLL for any custom interfaces. Because the `IPizzaOrderTaker` interface is exactly the same as in the Chapter 7 examples, the proxy/stub DLL that you built in that chapter will be perfectly adequate for use with this new local server implementation.

Building the In-Process Server

By comparison to the local server, implementing the code for an in-process server is a breeze. Although the in-process server has more required functions than the local server, the code required to implement these functions is quite simple. (A local server only needs a `WinMain()`; the in-process server needs to implement five different public functions.) Listing 8.8 shows the implementation code for the in-process `PizzaOrderTaker2` server.

Listing 8.8   `ATLINPROCSRV.CPP`—The In-Process `PizzaOrderTaker2` ATL Server Code

```
// Get needed include files
#include "Pizza2.h"


//
// Object map, indicates which classes are serviced by this server
//
BEGIN_OBJECT_MAP(ObjectMap)
    OBJECT_ENTRY(CLSID_PizzaOrderTaker2, ComPizzaOrderTaker)
END_OBJECT_MAP()


//
// The global module object
//
QueATLModule _Module;


//
// Standard exported method called by Windows when important
// system events occur
//

extern "C"
BOOL WINAPI DllMain(HINSTANCE hInstance,
➥DWORD dwReason, LPVOID /*lpReserved*/)
{
    // Is a process starting to use us?
    if (dwReason == DLL_PROCESS_ATTACH) {

        // Fire up the main server module
        _Module.Init(ObjectMap, hInstance);

        // We're not interested in thread attach/detach notifications
        DisableThreadLibraryCalls(hInstance);
    }

    // We're all done with this server, so we need to power down
    // the main module object
    else if (dwReason == DLL_PROCESS_DETACH)
```

```
        _Module.Term();

    return TRUE;
}


//
// Standard exported methods for in-process servers
//

//
// Called when COM needs a new class factory
//

STDAPI DllGetClassObject(REFCLSID rclsid, REFIID riid, LPVOID* ppv)
{
    return _Module.GetClassObject(rclsid, riid, ppv);
}

//
// Called by COM to check if the server can be unloaded
//

STDAPI DllCanUnloadNow()
{
    return _Module.GetLockCount() ? S_FALSE : S_OK;
}

//
// Method used to support self-registration
//

STDAPI DllRegisterServer()
{
    return _Module.RegisterServer();
}

//
// Method used to support self-unregistration
//

STDAPI DllUnregisterServer()
{
    return _Module.UnregisterServer();
}
```

The code presented here approximates the sources generated by ATL AppWizard. There shouldn't be any surprises here as far as what functions are exported from the server DLL. You've seen the same functions exported from each of the other in-process servers built in previous chapters. The only exception is the `DllMain()` function.

Note

Don't forget that an in-process server requires an object map and a `_Module` declaration, just like a local ATL server.

You can think of `DllMain()` as a `WinMain()` for DLLs. Unlike `WinMain()`, which serves as the starting point for a program's execution, the `DllMain()` function serves as a callback function for when important events occur that might affect your DLL. For example, `DllMain()` is called every time a new process or thread starts to use the DLL and every time a current process or thread stops using the DLL.

The reason that you need to provide a `DllMain()` is that the global `_Module` object needs to be initialized for each new process that attaches to the server. As you can see from Listing 8.8, not a whole lot of code is involved. When Windows calls `DllMain()`, it provides a reason code that describes the event taking place. When `DllMain()` receives a `DLL_PROCESS_ATTACH` message, you know that your `_Module`'s `Init()` method should be called. (As an additional performance enhancement, you also tell Windows at this point that you're not interested in thread attach/detach events.) In the case of a `DLL_PROCESS_DETACH`, you need to call `_Module::Term()`.

The remaining in-process functions are trivial because the `CComModule` class has methods that handle each of the required cases without any additional work required by your code. The exported `DllGetClassObject()` function, for example, simply redirects the query to the `CComModule` method `GetClassObject()`. `GetClassObject()` looks up the appropriate class factory and returns it to COM.

It's the same story for most of the other functions. `DllCanUnloadNow()` is only slightly different in that the function needs to manually check the current lock count and ensure that it only returns `TRUE` when the count is zero. All the same, it's still only a single line of code. The `DllRegisterServer()` and `DllUnregisterServer()` functions are simple pass-throughs to the `CComModule` methods `RegisterServer()` and `UnregisterServer()` that I talked about when I covered local server registration.

Note

Both the in-process and local server implementations presented in this chapter contain in their projects a file named `STDATL.CPP`. This source file (which is identical in both cases) incorporates various ATL files that have been designed to be included into a given program only once. The most important ATL file used by `STDATL.CPP` is `ATLIMPL.CPP`. `ATLIMPL.CPP` must be compiled into your servers somewhere; an ATL AppWizard project will always contain a file that actually includes `ATLIMPL.CPP` like a header file into one (and only one) source file.

With the in-process server implementation behind you, you can now move on to Registry scripting, one of the major enhancements to ATL 2.x framework.

Registry Scripting and the Registrar

In Chapter 7, I discuss the inner workings of the COM Pizza Order-Taking Wizard. The wizard, you'll recall, uses the system registry for some of its own configuration information, namely, its list of known components that expose **IPizzaOrderTaker**. To read in this registry-based list of information requires knowledge of the Win32 registry API, and the code's not pretty. Unfortunately, as useful as the registry is, it's not particularly easy or pleasant to manage using the standard APIs. Enter the ATL Registrar.

The Registrar is a script-driven mechanism for maintaining registry-based information. Rather than hassle over whether to call **RegEnumKeyEx()** or **RegOpenKeyEx()**, clients of the Registrar represent their registry commands in a scripting language that is simple to understand and easy to use. After a script has been perfected, it can be compiled into the resource portion of an executable or DLL and run by the Registrar in response to a self-registration or unregistration request. The process is so simple that the only real challenge lies in learning the Registrar's scripting language.

Testing Your Registry Scripts

Because the Registrar itself is a COM component, there's no easy way for you to experiment with registry scripting unless you build a COM component that knows how to call Registrar protocol. It would have been nice if Microsoft had provided a command-line utility that enabled you to run a script, but such a utility is simple enough to write. The **RUNREG.EXE** utility is just such a program (some day I'll get around to making a graphical version); you can use it to experiment with the sample registry scripts that I present throughout the rest of the chapter. The program can be found on the CD-ROM, with the other examples for this chapter. I've provided full source code for this utility, but I do not detail the program's design in the text.

Using **RUNREG.EXE** couldn't be easier. The program is run in either registration or unregistration mode. Depending on the mode, the Registrar will add or remove registry keys/values from your system registry. You specify the mode by passing in either **Register** or **Unregister** on the program command line. Apart from the mode indicator, the only other command-line argument required is the filename of a registry script.

As always, be careful when you mess around with the registry. Deleting a critical key or value can render the operating system unstable, or even worse, unbootable. Make sure that the values you are poking in to the registry (or removing) are yours to fiddle with. My rule of thumb is, Don't mess with any keys or values that you didn't put into the registry in the first place. It's bad enough that a single typo can render your machine useless without having to worry about registry scripts that try to be fancy and muck around with critical internal operating-system registry entries.

Writing a Registry Script

A *registry script* is a logical representation of a tree of registry keys and values. There are no script verbs for adding and deleting keys, for example. Instead, your script shows the Registrar what the registry should look like. These logical trees of keys and values are referred to in the Microsoft literature as *parse trees*.

For every parse tree, you are describing a logical structure that is grounded by one of the central registry keys: HKEY_CLASSES_ROOT, HKEY_CURRENT_USER, HKEY_LOCAL_MACHINE, HKEY_USERS, HKEY_PERFORMANCE_DATA, HKEY_DYN_DATA, or HKEY_CURRENT_CONFIG. Because writing out these keynames can become tiresome, and they are referenced often, the Registrar recognizes root key acronyms. Therefore, the Registrar treats HKEY_PERFORMANCE_DATA and HKPD identically.

Subkeys are denoted by creating a nested level of "scope," using braces in much the same way that you would create a new layer of scope in a C++ program. The subkey name appears in single quotes at the top of the new scope. I realize that this can be difficult to visualize, so take a look at an example. Listing 8.9 shows a very simple registry script.

Listing 8.9 SIMPLE.RGS—A Trivial Registry Script That Creates a Few Subkeys

```
HKCU
{
    'ASubkey'
    {
        'AnotherSubkey'
        {
            'AndYetAnotherSubkey'
        }
        'SiblingOfAnotherSubkey'
    }
}
```

You can use the RUNREG.EXE utility to execute this script in both registration and unregistration mode. Registration mode causes the indicated registry keys to be created, whereas unregistration mode causes the keys to be removed.

In this example, the Registrar will create a single key named ASubKey coming off HKEY_CURRENT_USER (assuming registration, of course). ASubkey has two subkeys of its own, AnotherSubkey and SiblingOfAnotherSubkey. Finally, AnotherSubkey has its own subkey, named AndYetAnotherSubkey. The best way to test that everything is working correctly is to crank up REGEDIT.EXE and browse your keys. Keep in mind that from one run of RUNREG.EXE to the next, you might have to press REGEDIT's refresh key (F5) to ensure that you're looking at the latest and greatest registry entries.

Registry keys can have default values. A default value is assigned to a key by using an equals sign (=) and then providing a value. A string value is denoted using an s followed by a literal string enclosed in single quotes, whereas a numerical (double-word integer) is denoted using a d, followed by a literal string representation of the number enclosed in single quotes. Listing 8.10 shows a registry script that creates some keys with default string and numerical values.

Listing 8.10   DEFVAL.RGS—A Registry Script Illustrating How to Add Default Values to Subkeys

```
HKCU
{
    'Susan'
    {
        'Age' = d '27'
        'MiddleName' = s "Campbell"
        'Address'
        {
            'Apartment' = d '301'
            'City' = s 'Arlington'
            'State' = s 'VA'
        }
    }
}
```

In this example, several subkeys are represented, almost all of which contain default values (the Susan and Address keys being the two exceptions). The Age and Apartment default values are numbers, and the rest of the default values are strings. Pretty simple, huh?

Of course, default values aren't the only kind of values that can be associated with a subkey. A subkey can also contain named values. In a parse tree, a named value looks just like a subkey entry, except that it's preceded by the token val. Listing 8.11 shows a registry script that defines a single Book subkey, with both default and named subkeys.

Listing 8.11   NAMEDVAL.RGS—A Registry Script Illustrating How to Add Named Values to Subkeys

```
HKCU
{
    'Book' = s 'CORBA Design Patterns'
    {
        val 'ISBN' = s '0-471-15882-8'
        val 'Author' = s 'Thomas M., Raphael M.'
        val 'NumPages' = d '334'
    }
}
```

In this example, the Book subkey's default value contains the title of the book. Named values represent the book's ISBN number, the names of the book's authors, and a numerical value showing the book's page count.

Subkeys in a registry script can also be affected by the use of modifiers. Three modifiers are understood by the ATL 2.x Registrar: NoRemove, ForceRemove, and Delete.

The NoRemove modifier indicates that the specified key should never be removed, even during unregistration. This modifier is particularly important for scripts that are responsible for setting class registration data, because COM components are placed beneath the CLSID subkey of HKEY_CLASSES_ROOT. You most definitely do not want to delete the entire CLSID subkey during a server unregistration!

Listing 8.12 shows the LOCALSRV.RGS script. This script, which can be found with the rest of the PizzaOrderTaker2 local server source code, is the script that is used to register the local ATL version of the PizzaOrderTaker server. As you can see, this script makes extensive use of NoRemove.

Listing 8.12   LOCALSRV.RGS—The `PizzaOrderTaker2` Server Registration Script

```
HKCR
{
    'PizzaOrderTaker2' = s 'PizzaOrderTaker2'
    {
        'CLSID' = s '{43903313-8857-11D0-8C80-00400539F36B}'
    }
    NoRemove 'CLSID'
    {
        '{43903313-8857-11D0-8C80-00400539F36B}' = s 'PizzaOrderTaker2'
        {
            'ProgID' = s 'PizzaOrderTaker2'
            'LocalServer32' = s '%MODULE%'
        }
    }
    NoRemove 'AppID'
    {
        '{43903313-8857-11D0-8C80-00400539F36B}' = s 'PizzaOrderTaker2'
        'PizzaSrv2.EXE'
        {
            val 'AppID' = s '{43903313-8857-11D0-8C80-00400539F36B}'
        }
    }
}
HKLM
{
    NoRemove 'SOFTWARE'
    {
        NoRemove 'Que'
        {
            NoRemove 'PizzaOrderTaker Client'
            {
                NoRemove '1.0'
                {
                    NoRemove 'Known Components'
                    {
                        '{43903313-8857-11D0-8C80-00400539F36B}' =
                                    s 'Chapter 8, ATL implementation
                                    ➥(PizzaOrderTaker2)'
                    }
                }
            }
        }
    }
}
```

Before I start to discuss Listing 8.12, I need to warn you that the script shown here cannot be executed by RUNREG as shown. This is because the script uses an embedded replacement macro (the '%MODULE%' syntax found under the LocalServer32 key) which RUNREG doesn't support. If you want to test LOCALSRV.RGS with RUNREG, you need to remove the offending line first. By the way, I'll be covering replacement macros in the upcoming section titled, weirdly enough, "Replacement Macros."

This script is made up of two parse trees. The first tree manages the changes to HKEY_CLASSES_ROOT; these entries are the keys and values required to register your server's COM components (in this case, it's just the PizzaOrderTaker2 component). The second parse tree manages changes to HKEY_LOCAL_MACHINE. This tree contains the keys and values needed to register the PizzaOrderTaker2 component with the wizard client application that you built in Chapter 7.

Caution

In Listing 8.12, the HKEY_CLASSES_ROOT\CLSID and HKEY_CLASSES_ROOT\AppID keys are protected with the NoRemove modifier. I cannot stress this enough: Always protect HKEY_CLASSES_ROOT\CLSID and HKEY_CLASSES_ROOT\AppID with NoRemove! Always! (I think you get the point.) Always!! (I just wanted to make sure.)

NoRemove is also used extensively in the wizard client configuration parse tree. Remember that the wizard will probably know about several different PizzaOrderTaker components. It would be terribly rude for you to blow away the entire set of wizard configurations keys just because you were removing the PizzaOrderTaker2 class from the system. Not only would the wizard no longer know about other PizzaOrderTaker components, but the wizard would also cease to function, because *all* configuration information would have been removed.

Let's move on to the other subkey modifiers. The ForceRemove modifier indicates that during registration the subkey (and any of its descendents) should be completely removed before it's added as part of the registration procedure. This can be useful when you want to guarantee that no external parties have come along and added keys or values to your registry structures. For example, if you wanted to make sure that no one had slipped a TreatAs key into your component registration, you could reregister your component and use ForceRemove on your registration keys. This would ensure that any preexisting keys (including a TreatAs) are completely cleaned out. (*Never* use ForceRemove on the HKEY_CLASSES_ROOT\CLSID and HKEY_CLASSES_ROOT\AppID keys.)

Finally, the Delete modifier serves as the working counterpart of NoRemove. A subkey with a Delete modifier will always be removed, even in the case of script registration. In the TreatAs example, you could use a Delete TreatAs entry to surgically remove the TreatAs key, but allow other keys to remain (assuming, of course, that the parent key was not specified as ForceRemove).

Invoking the Registrar

Assuming that your component did not use the DECLARE_REGISTRY or DECLARE_NO_REGISTRY macros inside its declaration, your registry script will be run automatically when you call the _Module object's RegisterServer() or UnregisterServer() method. For most servers, this is the only extent to which they need to be aware of "invoking the registrar." However, at certain times you might want to explicitly fire off a registry script,

independent   of
server registration or unregistration, such as during development or when you are cleaning out unused registry entries.

Here's an example. Suppose that you need a scheme to determine whether your server experienced a crash the last time it was run. One way you could accomplish this would be to have your server create a known registry "crash key" at server start up. As part of the standard server shutdown sequence, the program would remove the key. If the server were ever started and it immediately found the crash key, the program would know that a previous server run had crashed. Although checking for the existence of the crash key would have to be done manually by using the Win32 registry APIs, the actual setting and removal of the key could be accomplished using registry scripts.

The actual firing of a registry script takes place in the calls to the `CComModule` methods `UpdateRegistryFromResourceD()` and `UpdateRegistryFromResourceS()`. These methods take the same arguments and perform their tasks with identical results. The distinction between the two is found in *how* the script execution is performed. `UpdateRegistryFromResourceD()` is called when you want to use an external COM Registrar component that has been installed on the local machine. If you're uncomfortable with requiring users to first install the Registrar server, or you can't be guaranteed that a Registrar will be installed on your target machine, you can call `UpdateRegistryFromResourceS()`, which will use a Registrar object that is local to your server process (or address space, in the case of an in-process server).

Note

If you plan on using `UpdateRegistryFromResourceS()`, you will have to make sure that the static Registrar code is compiled into your server by including ATL files `STATREG.H` and `STATREG.CPP` into the same source code module that includes `ATLIMPL.CPP`. In the examples that come on the book CD-ROM, `STATREG.H` and `STATREG.CPP` are included in `STDATL.CPP` if you have set the preprocessor symbol `_ATL_STATIC_REGISTRY`. Because other ATL files conditionally compile code based on this symbol (`UpdateRegistryFromResourceS()` isn't even a part of `CComModule` unless you declare `ATL_STATIC_REGISTRY`), it's best that you place it in your project settings, rather than define it in your source code.

The `UpdateRegistryFromResource` methods are identical with respect to their accepted arguments. Each method is overloaded to have two forms. In the first form, the method's first argument is an unsigned integer resource ID that indicates which registry script to process. In the second form, the method's first argument is a string containing the registration script's resource name. In either case, the second argument is a boolean that indicates whether the script should be run as part of a registration or unregistration. Pass in `TRUE`, and the script will be registered; pass in `FALSE`, and it will be unregistered. The third argument, which is defaulted to `NULL`, is an array of macro replacement structures.

Note

The ATL declares a macro that enables you to call a **CComModule** pseudomethod named **UpdateRegistryFromResource()**. I call it a *pseudomethod* because the method never really exists; instead, ATL defines a macro that replaces the string **UpdateRegistryFromResource** with **UpdateRegistryFromResourceD** or **UpdateRegistryFromResourceS**, depending on whether the **_ATL_STATIC_REGISTRY** symbol is declared. This is a simple way to decouple your code from knowledge of what Registrar implementation it's using.

The Undocumented CRegObject Class

Writing a full-fledged ATL program requires that you bite off the responsibility of instantiating a **_Module** object and making sure that it's correctly initialized with your server's instance handle and object map. If all you want to do is run a registry script and you don't have any intention of using other ATL functionality, this whole process seems excessive. It's even worse for console applications that don't have their instance handle handed to them on a silver platter and have to figure it out for themselves (granted, it's a single call to the Win32 API **GetModuleHandle()**, but it's yet one more hoop to jump through). It sure would be nice if you could directly hook into the Registrar class without going through the rest of the ATL rigmarole.

Well, you can, sort of. The **CRegObject** is the class that can provide for all your registry scripting needs. There's just one catch—it's an undocumented class. This means that Microsoft has license to modify this class (or even remove it) without a moment's notice. All the same, there are places where using **CRegObject** makes some sense. The **RUNREG** utility, for example, uses a **CRegObject** instance directly, and the source code is shorter and simpler because of it. The interface of **CRegObject** closely approximates the **IRegistrar** interface, with minor differences. If you want something that's quick and easy to integrate into your code, **CRegObject** certainly qualifies.

Make no mistake, however; using **CRegObject** is a hack, and it should only be used for quick-and-dirty programs, if at all. Future versions of ATL will almost certainly introduce changes to **CRegObject**, and even though it's unlikely that the core protocol that mimics **IRegistrar** will change, it's Microsoft's prerogative to do what ever it wants with undocumented classes.

What are the alternatives to using this hack? Don't be lazy. Instantiate a **_Module** object (calling **GetModuleHandle()** first if you have to) and then call **UpdateRegistryFromResourceS()**. Even better yet, use the COM APIs to go out and use the Registrar component. The nice thing about this last option is that you don't have to include any ATL code in your program (except the **IRegistrar** interface header file). The downside is that you have to be sure that the Registrar component is installed on the machine that your program will be running on.

Replacement Macros

One of the really neat features of the Registrar is that it allows the use of macros. A script macro is surrounded by percent signs (%) and is expanded in place by the Registrar before the execution of your script. Listing 8.13 shows a script fragment that uses a macro named %CarType%.

Listing 8.13   MACRO.RGS—A Registry Script That Uses a Macro

```
HKCU
{
    'Favorite Car' = s 'My favorite car is a %CarType%'
}
```

Assuming that the %CarType% macro was set to the string BMW 325i, this script would create a subkey off HKEY_CURRENT_USER named Favorite Car. This subkey would have a default value of My favorite car is a BMW 325i.

The ATL even supplies a predefined macro named %Module%. This macro will evaluate to the fully qualified path and filename of the program or DLL executing the script. This macro is particularly important for scripts that register components, because the LocalServer32 and InProcServer32 keys require fully qualified executable and DLL names.

	Caution

If you are going to directly use the CRegObject described in the previous section, the %Module% macro will not be available. The %Module% macro is added to the Registrar's internally maintained replacement list by the UpdateRegistryFromResource methods and is not an inherent feature of the Registrar object.

Macro replacement values are passed into calls to UpdateRegistryFromResourceD() and UpdateRegistryFromResourceS() in the form of an array of _ATL_REGMAP_ENTRY structures. The declaration of the _ATL_REGMAP_ENTRY structure can be found in ATLBASE.H and is a coupling of a Unicode string key with a Unicode string value. The key represents the name of the macro, and the value is replacement text. Listing 8.14 shows a code snippet that executes a registry script, setting up the %CarType% macro as just described.

Listing 8.14   MACROSUB.CPP—Executing a Registry Script with Replacement Macros

```
...

USES_CONVERSION;

// Declare our replacement macro list
_ATL_REGMAP_ENTRY  aMacros[] = { { A2OLE("CarType"),
                                 ➥A2OLE("BMW 325i") },
                               { NULL,
                                 ➥NULL             } };
```

```
// Execute the script
hResult = _Module.UpdateRegistryFromResource(IDR_REGSCRIPT,
➥TRUE, aMacros);
```

...

> **Caution**
>
> To date, Microsoft has not documented this anywhere, but the array of
> `_ATL_REGMAP_ENTRY` structures passed into
> `UpdateRegistryFromResource()` must be terminated with an empty entry
> that has a `NULL` key and value. If you do not provide this final array element,
> ATL won't know when it has reached the end of the array, and it will run off
> into random memory. If this happens, your server will crash!

This code snippet is straightforward. The only thing that probably needs explaining is that `USES_CONVERSION/A2OLE` business. It turns out that ATL has been endowed with a robust set of macros that greatly aid in the transformation of strings between their various formats.

Every function or method that plans on using these macros must first invoke the `USES_CON-VERSION` macro (the top of the method is as good a place as any). After that you are free to use the conversion macros with reckless abandon. There are many such macros, but they all follow this form:

source_type2target_type()

where *source_type* and *target_type* are either `A`, `T`, `W`, or `OLE`. Type `A` strings are standard ASCII strings. A type `T` string varies, depending on whether you are building your program with native Unicode support. A type `W` string is a Unicode wide-character string, and a type `OLE` string can vary between standard ASCII strings, depending on the value of various compilation macros. A useful chart depicting the relationship between each of these conversion macros can be found in the online documentation under the topic "String Conversion Macros."

The conversion macros allocate memory for the new strings off memory reserved for the program stack, so when the method returns, the memory is released (and the string becomes invalid).

Adding the New Wizard Configuration Entry

With ATL servers now complete and registered, the final step is to run some clients and make sure everything is operating correctly. Because the registration scripts for each of the servers add the appropriate configuration entries for the Pizza Order-Taking Wizard introduced in Chapter 7, you should be able to test the new ATL servers with the same client program you used to put the MFC servers through their paces. When the wizard is run, you should find that a new Chapter 8 ATL-implemented entry has been added to the wizard's component selection list. All you have to do is select the entry and move on to the next wizard page.

Note

As a convenience I've also provided you with a registry script that adds the wizard configuration information to the system registry. You can run this script using **RUNREG**. Alternatively, I've also provided a **REGEDIT** script you can use to add the required configuration entries. Both these scripts can be found in the client directory of the Pizza2 project area.

With a `PizzaOrderTaker` client that can use either server, you can now experiment with the different implementations to compare performance and memory footprint. Several third-party products on the market provide programmers with plenty of interesting performance metrics, but even the lowly Windows NT task manager can help in this respect. For example, on my primary machine here at home, the NT task manager indicates that the debug version of ATL server has a memory footprint that is about 800K smaller than the MFC version. That's a substantial difference, and in some cases, differences like these can affect your choice of framework.

Summary

The completion of the local server with ATL leaves us ready to examine remote servers and DCOM. By now, you should have a good feel for how to build in-process and local servers using either MFC or ATL. Coupled with your knowledge of COM aggregation, you already have the skills required to start building sophisticated COM clients and servers.

Don't stop reading yet! In the next three chapters, you will learn how DCOM erases the barriers that have typically made it impossible for COM clients to communicate with servers running on another computer. DCOM is the key technology that will enable you to take all your COM-based programs and evolve them into advanced distributed object applications.

CHAPTER 9

A DISTRIBUTED OBJECTS OVERVIEW

In this chapter, you will learn about the following:

- Distributed systems and client server architecture
- The basics of DCOM implementation

I n the last quarter of this book, we are going to concentrate on DCOM. Delivered first with Windows NT 4.0 and then with Windows 98 and Windows NT 5.0, DCOM is the technology that allows programmers to deploy COM components across a network. DCOM can also be added to Windows 95 OSR2 with a special DCOM service pack installed with Visual C++ 6. From an evolutionary perspective, DCOM is the most important thing to happen to COM since COM's initial appearance in OLE 2.0. Why? Because DCOM is Microsoft's foothold in the industry market of distributed object computing. What distributed object computing is—and why it's something to be excited about—is one of the primary topics of this chapter. Microsoft created DCOM as a powerful and compelling technology for building distributed applications. You are going to examine how DCOM is a natural extension of COM and how you can leverage this technology to create rich distributed components and applications.

The Evolution of Distributed Systems

Before I start to discuss the mechanics of DCOM, I think it's beneficial to briefly look back and see how we arrived here. By understanding the problems that Microsoft is trying to solve, you can gain additional insight into what DCOM is.

Fundamentally, DCOM is a technology designed to aid in the construction of distributed systems. I hesitate to use the term *distributed system*, because the concept means many things to different people, but I'll tell you what *I* mean by distributed system and then use this definition throughout the rest of the book.

A distributed system is a collection of software entities physically spread out across two or more computers, working together in concert to achieve a common goal. As you will see, this is a broad definition. In fact, this definition embraces software configurations that traditional systems designers would probably balk at calling *distributed*. For example, by my definition, a client computer that relies on a network operating system such as NT Server or Netware to provide file-sharing services is part of a distributed system. An older DOS program that has no knowledge of networks can use the services of the network operating system without even knowing that the files it is accessing are located on a different computer. Is this really a distributed system? Absolutely. Nothing in my definition precludes using software in ways never anticipated by the original designers. Certainly, nothing in my definition requires every part of a distributed system to have been custom-built with a computer network or intercomputer communication in mind.

Of much more interest are those distributed systems built with explicit knowledge of a computer network or communications link. From the very beginning, these systems are designed so that the system's constituent software components are executed on separate machines.

It's important to realize that the evolution of these types of systems has been just that, an evolution. No one sat down one day and invented two-tier client/server computing. Instead, the ideas and concepts behind the various types of distributed computing have emerged only after an iterative process of writing software, seeing what worked and what didn't, and then rebuilding or starting over. This creative iteration, a fundamental component of the invention process, continues to this day. DCOM is the outgrowth of the evolving technology called *distributed objects*.

Legacy Systems

Of course, in the beginning, there was nothing—or to be more precise, there were only mainframes. As recently as 20 years ago, the mainframe reigned supreme across corporate America. The PC, at least as we think of it today, was just a dream. The mainframe computer is the embodiment of centralized computing; in fact, the mainframe model is the classic.

A mainframe computer is the embodiment of centralized computing; in fact, the mainframe model is the archetypal example of a nondistributed system. Although I am sure that you do not need a lesson in what mainframe computing is, it's important to note it in respect to the evolution of the distributed system.

The mainframe architecture is shown in Figure 9.1.

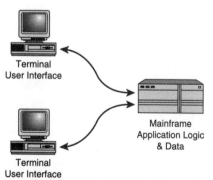

Terminal
User Interface

Terminal
User Interface

Mainframe
Application Logic
& Data

Figure 9.1   A nondistributed mainframe computing architecture.

Mainframes are still very much with us. In fact, here we are in the late 1990s, and the demand for mainframe programmers is actually increasing in some sectors. Telephone companies, credit card companies, insurance firms—most of these businesses process such massive volumes of information that only mainframes are truly up to the task of reckoning with all that data. The mainframe might be down, but it is not out. Until the distributed systems of tomorrow prove that they can handle the same tasks as mainframes while providing significant additional benefit, the mainframe will continue to be a corporate staple.

Client/Server

In the mid-1980s, a new idea began to sweep over the computer industry. A subtle migration toward the PC standard was at a steady trickle and then a torrent. By the end of the 1980s, the PC was the preeminent platform for running *productivity applications*, or those programs (such as word-processing and spreadsheets) that could be leveraged by individuals to improve the quality of their work and increase their productivity. The widespread corporate infiltration of PCs has had several interesting effects, not the least of which has been its catalytic effect in the area of distributed systems.

Probably the most profound distributed systems innovation of the past decade has come about with the emergence of client/server architectures. In a client/server environment, PCs host full-blown applications that rely on services provided by programs running on other machines. The big advantage to the client/server approach is that it exploits the power of the local PC. The graphical user interface (GUI) was made extremely popular with the invention of the Macintosh and Windows operating systems. Users could point and click rather than remember extremely cryptic text-based commands. This improved their efficiency and productivity.

In some respects, the emergence of GUI furthered the idea of client/server computing and the exploitation of the power of the client side. Imagine that you have a GUI running on a server. Sure, it's really fast, but at 1024 768 in 256 colors, you're talking about dumping 1.25MB for every screen refresh across the network. This increase in network traffic is unacceptable in an environment where you have a bandwidth of only 10Mb a second. In addition, heavy-duty transaction processing can take place on larger, more expensive, and more powerful machines over the network, but core application functions such as user interfaces and simple validation can all take place locally on the client workstation.

In fact, one of the more interesting consequences of client/server is that the mainframe can be turned into a sort of superserver, providing database and business logic services for PC-based clients. The bottom line is that in client/server computing, the computing work is shared between the client and the server. Core business processes, transaction-heavy processes, and data all reside on the server. The client takes care of the data validation, user interface features, and operations that can reduce bandwidth.

Client/server has undergone several evolutionary changes over its relatively short lifetime. In the next few sections I'll walk you through the different types of client/server architectures.

Two-Tier

We typically talk about client/server technologies using the abstraction of *tiers*. In the client/server sense, a tier represents a platform that hosts a particular piece of well-defined functionality. A platform, in turn, refers to the combination of hardware and software used by a computer.

The first client/server systems were designed using two tiers. In a two-tier system, the first tier contains a client workstation running the main application. This client-hosted program (or programs) is composed of all the user interface functionality, in addition to all the business logic required by the system. Programmatic considerations, such as how a particular algorithm or heuristic is implemented, are all found inside the client program. Because the client application is responsible for hosting so much core functionality, applications in a two-tier environment are typically referred to as *fat clients*. A fat client is a client computer in a two-tier client server environment that is considered loaded with much of the core functionality of an application.

The second tier of a two-tier architecture is where you find application data. Application data is usually stored in some sort of database and is often stewarded by a database server program. An inventory management system, for example, might use a Microsoft SQL Server relational database to store information about available products. Client applications—of which there can be many, each running on its own client workstation—would send requests to the database whenever the application needed information or data stored in the inventory database. Figure 9.2 shows the two-tier client/server architecture.

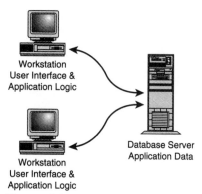

Workstation
User Interface &
Application Logic

Workstation
User Interface &
Application Logic

Database Server
Application Data

Figure 9.2   A two-tier client/server computing architecture.

I don't want to make it sound like two-tier client/server applications have fallen out of favor. They haven't. In fact, a two-tier architecture is a good fit for a smaller, departmental type of application. However, the two-tier architecture does suffer from several deficiencies.

Probably the biggest problem associated with a two-tier architecture is administrative. When a two-tier system grows beyond a particular point, it can be very difficult to maintain over time. For example, say that you've developed a system that supports 50 users (that is, clients) and utilizes five database servers. One day, a user reports a particularly nasty bug that needs to be fixed immediately. Even assuming that fixing the bug is easy, now you have a real problem on your hands. You will need to redeploy the entire application on to all fifty of those client workstations. Doing this by hand can be tremendously tedious and time-consuming. Automating the process can be expensive, even if you go with a shrink-wrapped third-party solution.

Two-tier architectures also suffer from a strong dependency on the structure of their data. Suppose that you were developing a new client-side application that required you to mod-ify the structure of your database. Because all your current applications talk directly to the database server itself, each and every client application would have to be modified to take into consideration the new database structure and formats. Of course, after you changed the client application, you'd need to redeploy the whole system again.

Three-Tier

The three-tier architecture is designed to alleviate some of the problems that you can encounter with a two-tier architecture. Like two-tier, a three-tier system has a data tier that typical-ly hosts a database that stewards application data. However, in a three-tier model, the application is literally split in two. The client still maintains responsibility for the user interfaces and perhaps a limited amount of validation. (Because clients in a three-tier architecture con-tain a minimal amount of functionality, these programs are sometimes referred to as *thin clients*.) The bulk of the business logic and application rules is now separated out from the client tier and placed on a server running in a middle tier. For obvious reasons, these busi-ness logic tiers are often called *midservers* or *application servers*. This architecture is depicted in Figure 9.3.

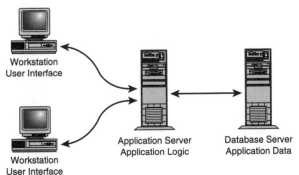

Figure 9.3   A three-tier client/server computing architecture.

In a three-tier architecture, client applications interact exclusively with midservers. The assumption is that the midservers run on larger, more powerful machines and can each han-dle requests from many client machines.

Then how does the addition of this middle tier solve the problems introduced by the two-tier architecture? Although a three-tier architecture doesn't completely resolve the problems of two-tier, it can dramatically reduce them. Take, for example, the maintenance problem posed by having to redeploy applications across all your client workstations. In a three-tier system, any modifications to business logic will only require redeployment of your midservers, of which you supposedly have far fewer. Of course, if you have modifications that affect the user interface aspects of your application, you're out of luck.

Three-tier architectures also insulate client applications from changes in the structure of a system's data. In a three-tier system, clients do not interact directly with the data tier. Instead, clients obtain and manipulate their data exclusively by making requests of midservers. This means that as you encounter situations that require you to modify your data formats, the implications of these changes can be encapsulated by your midservers. Although this requires redeployment of midserver binaries, it should not require a complete redeployment of your client-side applications.

N-Tier

The *en vogue* name for this next approach to client/server development is *n-tier*, which I guess sounds better than *a-whole-lotta-tier*. There seems to be a logical progression in the names of the various client/server architectures, but if you guessed that this next section would be called "Four-Tier," you're out of luck.

N-tier client/server refers to an architecture in which clients interact with midservers, which can in turn interact with other midservers, which can in turn interact with other midservers, and so on, and so on. In other words, rather than limit an architecture to three well-defined tiers, an n-tier system is free to mix and match services as they are needed. The reason for this is that you might want to isolate different business process rules to different midservers. For example, the business rules that apply to your research system, your inventory system, and your personnel system might all reside on different midservers. In effect, this is a form of encapsulation. That way, if the midserver that handles your research department goes down, it doesn't bring down your other mission-critical systems.

The n-tier architecture is really a generalization of the three-tier model. Although some tiers can be used for data management, the majority of tiers become specialized pockets of fine-grained business logic. This works to further compartmentalize functionality and aids in the management of complexity.

This is all fine and good, but the reality is that the technology for effectively implementing n-tier architectures has been slow in coming. Coupled with the relatively minor benefits of n-tier over three-tier, n-tier client/server was starting to look like a ship that was never going to leave the dock. Then along came distributed objects.

Even though absolutely nothing about an n-tier system mandates the use of distributed objects, nine times out of ten when you hear the buzzword *n-tier*, the speaker is talking about a distributed object technology. Distributed objects are notable because the technology solves the implementation problems associated with n-tier architectures. This in itself is probably enough to justify our interest, but distributed object technology is significant for other reasons. Distributed objects represent the marriage of the two most influential software development advances of the past decade: object-oriented programming and client/server.

At its core, distributed object technology is all about location transparency. Does that sound familiar? In Chapter 7, "Breaking the Process Boundary Using Local Servers," you learned how Microsoft was thinking about location transparency when it was developing COM's marshaling architecture, and this foresight is one of the reasons why COM's transition to DCOM has been relatively painless. (In fact, Microsoft has been planning the distribution of COM since the beginning of COM development.)

The idea behind distributed objects is elegantly simple. In a distributed object system, the application manipulates its components as though the objects that it's using were located within the same address space. Indeed, the objects *could* be located within the same address space. They could also, however, be located in a different address space—yes, this includes an address space on a different machine. The diagram in Figure 9.4 shows a representation of a distributed object architecture.

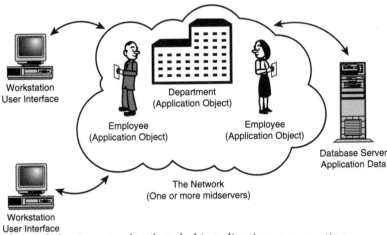

Figure 9.4   An n-tier distributed-object client/server computing architecture.

The real value of distributed objects is in the careful merging of distributed computing with object-oriented design, analysis, and programming. This means that all the benefits of OOP—management of complexity, rigorous service encapsulation, interoperability, flexibility, and code reusability—can be provided in a system that also offers all the benefits of client/server: ease-of-use, resource sharing, rigorous service encapsulation, flexibility, and so on. Certainly, overlap exists in the benefits that these two development methodologies provide, but the overlap is often additive. A client/server system can be flexible, but an object-oriented client/server system is liable to be even more flexible. Of course, doing a poor job of designing the system can lead to disaster regardless of the sophisticated technologies being used, but that's a topic for a different book.

The Web as Client/Server

Whether you are talking about two-tier, three-tier, or n-tier architectures, user interface modifications will always require redeployment of the client—unless your client application is a Web browser. As of late, such tremendous emphasis is placed on the Web as an application development platform that it's become easy to forget that the Web is just another example of a client/server architecture.

Think about it: Browsers are the seminal example of the thin client. A browser is so thin, in fact, that it contains absolutely zero application user interface or business logic. All the system's user interface and business logic can be downloaded from the Web server when requested, in the form of dynamic HTML content, Java applets, ActiveX controls, VBScript, JavaScript, Shockwave, and so on. In fact, the use of the Web as the underlying architecture of a client/server application solves outright the issue of software distribution. Bug fixes in Java applets, for example, can be automatically downloaded as soon as they are made available, without a significant investment in complicated software-distribution techniques.

The Web can be used as part of either a two-tier or three-tier architecture. We are starting to see development tools emerge that couple server-side databases with the expressive power of active Web content. Using standard, off-the-shelf databases, a simple Web site can become host to a sophisticated three-tier application. Because of the ActiveX platform's fundamental reliance on COM, you will find that DCOM can play an important role in Web-based client/server applications.

Distributed COM

The Distributed Component Object Model, also known as DCOM and formerly known as Network OLE, is the basic extension of binary COM objects across LANs, WANs, and the Internet. Now you can instantiate and bind objects across a network.

To put it a little more simply, DCOM is a high-level network protocol that enables COM-based components to interoperate between two process on different computers. DCOM makes it so that the programmer doesn't have to write network code to handle the communication required for distributed components to interact across a network. DCOM is not a programming language. It is a specification and a service, built with and on COM, which provides a transparent network protocol enabling COM components to interoperate across a network. DCOM is not an object-oriented method for object-oriented programming, like COM. However, because DCOM was built with COM and is implemented using COM, it utilizes COM's object-oriented technology to provide its services. To understand what DCOM does, you will look at what problems it solves: communication between processes on different computers, also known as the Distributed Computing Environment (DCE).

In Chapter 6, "Using Aggregation to Simulate Inheritance," I discuss how COM provides identical accessibility to components, irrespective of whether a client is interacting with an in-process server (same address space) or a local server (different address space). Likewise, DCOM crosses process boundaries and, in fact, crosses the physical boundaries between different computers. This enables remote servers and components on one computer to interact with clients on another computer.

Note

Because DCOM is a natural extension of COM, some members of the DCOM development team bristle when COM and DCOM are mentioned as if they were separate subsystems. DCOM is really the connection or network protocol of COM, and as such, COM and DCOM are now one. However, this does not change the fact that COM has now become a distributed object technology with significant new capabilities and implementation challenges.

In the next few sections, I will be dipping beneath the surface to briefly discuss how DCOM works. However, a detailed knowledge of the DCOM implementation is most certainly not required to effectively *use* DCOM. The seamless integration of the DCOM remote technologies with the standard COM subsystem means that from a programmer's perspective, DCOM can look and feel almost exactly like plain old COM. Although it's true that DCOM adds new tools to the developer's toolbox—and using these new features does require DCOM-specific interfaces—most of these capabilities are delivered in a logical and sane fashion. In other words, most developers will never have to worry about how DCOM is implemented at its lowest levels.

Object RPCs

With the release of DCOM on Windows NT 4.0, Microsoft introduced the world to a new, low-level set of call interfaces called the Object Remote Procedure Call (ORPC). The ORPC is really just an improved version of RPC. Remember from Chapter 4, "Implementing a COM Client and Server," that RPC is an interprocess communication mechanism defined in the Open Software Foundation's DCE RPC specification. Using RPC, applications on different machines can communicate with each other by using a variety of network transport mechanisms. The RPC mechanism is unique because it uses the other IPC mechanisms to establish communications between the client and the server. RPC can use named pipes, NetBIOS, or Windows Sockets to communicate with remote systems.

DCOM uses a version of RPC, called ORPC, to enable COM components to communicate between machines in different processes. In fact, the ORPC rests on top of the standard Distributed Computing Environment RPC engine that has been included with NT since the operating system's first release. With ORPC, Microsoft has extended the procedural programming model that underlies standard RPC implementations to accommodate a world bustling with distributed objects.

Note

Although Windows 95 also ships with support for the DCE RPCs, this in itself isn't enough to support DCOM applications. To run DCOM programs from Windows 95, you must install the DCOM for Windows 95 operating-system extensions (colloquially referred to as *DCOM95*) available from Microsoft. When you install Visual C++ 6, DCOM is installed. Windows 98 and Windows NT 5.0 both have DCOM as part of the operating system.

One of the goals of the Distributed Computing Environment was to provide an RPC architecture that was transport-independent. This means that RPC calls can be invoked in a consistent manner across applications, but can be executed using a wide range of wire-based protocols. The current NT RPC implementation includes support for TCP/IP, IP datagrams, Novell IPX/SPX, NetBIOS, and more. Microsoft is even working on adding an HTTP-based RPC transport. By building on top of a proven and functionality-rich RPC implementation, Microsoft has avoided having to reinvent the wheel.

URL

DCOM relies on ORPCs for all its network communications. The ORPC conventions and protocols are described in the Distributed Component Object Model working draft specification available from Microsoft's Web site at the following URL:
`http://premium.microsoft.com/msdn/library/techart/msdn_`
`dcomprot.htm`. If you're hungry for even more low-level details than you find in this chapter, this paper is a good place to start. Although it's rather dense, it will give you a complete picture of what differentiates an ORPC from a regular old RPC, in addition to giving you a comprehensive picture of DCOM from the implementer's perspective.

Even though DCOM ultimately rests on a DCE RPC implementation, a large amount of important behavior has to be implemented as part of the DCOM subsystem. The RPC engine has no knowledge of COM and therefore cannot know how to manage or bind to objects running on other machines. All these mechanisms have had to be built in to the DCOM, and in some cases the ORPC, implementation.

Imagine a local COM server running on a computer that is located in Chicago (if you happen to be reading this in Chicago, cross out all the references to *Chicago* that you find in the next few sections and replace them with *Venus*). Obviously, any client that wants to connect to that server process needs a way of finding out what servers are running on that machine and what object instances reside inside that server. If the server were running on your local machine, there wouldn't be a problem; the COM subsystem knows about all the servers running on your local machine.

What you're really talking about here is binding information. In the world of DCE RPCs, the information needed to connect to a remote server is embodied in a special type of string called a *string binding*. A string binding is a Unicode string that contains information—such as the machine network address, tokens representing the network protocol used to reach the remote machine, communication ports, and endpoint information—that can be used to further narrow and identify the target of an RPC.

The OXID

On a given machine, every running COM server has an associated Object Exporter Identifier (OXID). (Multithreaded servers may have more than one OXID.) The OXID is used as a key into a table of string bindings. Given an OXID, one can look up the string binding required to access the specified server. Note that one implication of this scheme is that several objects could share the same OXID, assuming that the objects were all running within the same server.

Of course, if you're going to have a table of OXIDs, that table is going to have to *belong* to someone. That someone is the OXID resolver, a special object that runs on every machine and is responsible for managing the OXID table (among other things).

This talk of OXIDs and resolvers is all fine and good, but the OXID table is in Chicago, which does us no good. How do clients get at those OXIDs in the first place? And how do clients use these OXIDs to get at string bindings? And as long as I'm asking so many difficult questions, because a single OXID can refer to a server containing multiple objects, how can I make sure that my ORPCs are sent to the right object instance?

Like any good investigative COM programmer, all you have to do is follow the interface pointer.

Passing Interface Pointers

As you're starting to see, distributing COM starts to complicate everything, and that includes the lowly interface pointer. When you were using objects located in an in-process server, life was simple. An interface pointer was usually an indirect pointer to the vtable of the object that you wanted to use. Things became a little hairier when we moved to local servers, because now we found ourselves dealing with proxies that looked and acted like our objects, but were really stand-ins that marshaled calls off to the local server. With remote servers, you're still relying on proxies, but when a remote machine wants to return an interface pointer, it's really sending back something called an OBJREF.

Conceptually, an OBJREF (which stands for Object Reference) is a data structure that provides all the information that you would need to access a specific interface on a specific object in a specific server on a specific machine. In addition to containing the OXID for a given object, the OBJREF contains the string binding for the OXID resolver running on the remote object's machine. This means that your local OXID resolver can ask the resolver on the Chicago machine for the string binding corresponding to the OXID in the remote object's OBJREF. This binding string, along with a unique object identifier and a specialized interface ID also found inside the OBJREF, provide enough information for an ORPC to make its way to the correct object instance. These OBJREFs are useful things to have around.

Optimizing DCOM

Inexperienced programmers and system designers make a common mistake when building their first systems using a distributed object architecture. The technology is so alluring that the temptation exists to build your applications as if all your objects were running in the same, global address space. After all, the whole idea behind distributed objects is to make things appear as if this is the case, even though some objects might be located on remote computers.

To make things even worse, the marketing machines for the various distributed object technology providers—Microsoft or any of the CORBA ORB venders—encourage this sort of naïve approach to distributed systems design. Using a distributed object is just like using a local object, the marketing literature proclaims. Just take your existing programs, and in one fell swoop you have a distributed version. Bah humbug!

What's wrong with this mindset? The reality of distributed objects is that you will *always* have to be aware of where your distribution boundaries lie. This is for the simple reason that a computer network, even a very fast one, is excruciatingly slow compared to the speed of moving data around in the memory of a computer. Things are made worse by the fact that a network is, by nature, a shared resource. Other computers on the network could be generating traffic that will directly affect the performance of your applications. For example, if you build COM interfaces that provide `get/set` method pairs for all your attributes, a remote version of that interface will be touching the wire every time you modify or read the value of that attribute.

You can use a host of strategies to help combat the performance problems inherent in distributed methods calls, and I will be discussing them in the next few sections. The technical arm of Microsoft has done its part by carefully reviewing the design of DCOM and doing everything in its power to minimize the number of times that the subsystem has to hit the wire. As you'll see in the next couple of sections, some of these optimizations are clever, whereas others rely on common sense. Let us start with caching OXIDS.

Caching OXIDs

In the previous section on passing interface pointers, I explained how an OBJREF contains information that a local OXID resolver can use to contact a resolver running on a remote machine. The local resolver usually contacts the remote resolver with the intent of retrieving the string binding for a particular OXID. It could potentially be a huge waste, however, if the local resolver simply discarded the string binding when it was finished making method calls on the interface pointer represented by the original OBJREF. This is because multiple remote objects can share the same OXID, and if the local client decided that it wanted to subsequently use another object in the same server, the local resolver would have to go through the whole process of querying the string binding all over again. Yuck!

The solution to this problem is simple. When a resolver looks up a string binding through a remote resolver, the OXID and its associated string binding are cached. This enables the local client to immediately use interface pointers that originated from inside the same server, without requiring another round trip to the remote machine.

A Faster, Better `IUnknown`

You can take many things for granted when you know that all your objects are running inside the same address space or even on the same machine. Take for example, the familiar `IUnknown` interface that is exposed by every COM object. One of the first things a COM programmer learns is how important it is to `AddRef()` and `Release()` interface pointers correctly. Now, imagine hundreds of thousands (maybe even *millions*) of remote objects, all talking among themselves as a consequence of their normal operation. What do you think the effect would be if every single `AddRef()` and `Release()` actually hit the wire and traveled to the remote object, just to increment or decrement a reference count?

Microsoft realized that this additional network traffic would gobble up bandwidth faster than you can say, "That's too slow." DCOM solves this problem, using several strategies. Unbeknownst to the client, all `IUnknown` method calls on remote objects are routed to a special interface named `IRemUnknown`. The `IRemUnknown` versions of `AddRef()` and `Release()` are capable of simultaneously reference-counting more than one interface pointer and of incrementing or decrementing a reference count by an arbitrary amount. In fact,

DCOM can `AddRef()` more reference counts than your client might need, with the hope that subsequent `AddRef()`s can be serviced without hitting the wire. Finally, `IRemUnknown` typically does not communicate calls to `Release()` back to the remote object until the sum total of all interface pointers on that object reaches zero. Because the remote object doesn't care what its reference count is—as long as it's non-zero, of course—this approach can result in substantially fewer trips to the wire.

Of course, using these strategies does mean that the actual reference count number maintained by the object is no longer an accurate count of exactly how many outstanding live interface pointers there are on an object, but you shouldn't rely on the accuracy of the `AddRef()` and `Release()` return values for anything important anyway.

`IRemUnknown` also optimizes calls to `QueryInterface()` by allowing a single QI method call to return multiple interface pointers. Unlike the `IRemUnknown` versions of `AddRef()` and `Release()`, this functionality is publicly exposed as part of the new COM API, `ComCreateInstanceEx()`.

Pinging and Delta Pinging

When a client program develops problems, it might crash or lock-up. Although this can be annoying and frustratingly difficult to debug, the COM subsystem is capable of sensing that the client has died or is unreachable. COM can determine the inaccessibility of a client by sensing that the client process has outright disappeared (in the case of a crash) or by noting timeouts (in the case of a locked-up client). In either case, COM can signal the server that outstanding reference counts from the dead client should be released.

Note

If you're skeptical about COM being able to trap these sorts of client crashes, try it out. Start up the pizza order-taking wizard, making sure that the registry has only the local version of the server registered. Move through the dialogs, selecting a pizza size and adding a few ingredients. However, when you come to the final page, don't click the Finish button! Instead, open the Windows NT task manager (or press Ctrl+Alt+Delete in Windows 95) and kill the `Pizza1.EXE` application. Now, wait (and then wait some more). After a few minutes, you should see the `PizzaSrv.EXE` local server process suddenly disappear from the task list.

Things are different in the case of a remote server (or a remote client, depending on your perspective). If a client program dies, in no immediately apparent way can the DCOM subsystem on the server machine sense that the client no longer exists.

Microsoft has solved this problem by using a technique called *pinging*. The theory is very simple; periodically the DCOM subsystem on the server machine walks through its list of remote connections and sends a message to the client machine, asking whether the client is still alive. If the client is still operating normally, the client machine returns an acknowledgement. On the other hand, if the server machine doesn't hear back from the client machine after a specified number of pings, the server can assume that the client has died and that any outstanding reference counts owned by that client can be reclaimed. Socket programmers will recognize this strategy as an elaboration of the keep-alive messages sent to sockets in order to maintain open connections.

The designers of DCOM were concerned, however, that all this pinging could get out of hand and that a network could become saturated with nothing more than DCOM ping traffic. To combat this possibility Microsoft provides several ping-related optimizations. First, the developers made sure that pings occurred relatively infrequently (once every two minutes). Although this does imply that it can take a while for a server to realize that a client has died, it will eventually happen. (DCOM waits for three unanswered pings before assuming that the client is dead, for a total potential downtime of six minutes.)

The DCOM development team also recognized that not every interface pointer in use needs to be pinged. By pinging clients at a per-object level of granularity, instead of a per–interface-pointer level of granularity, DCOM still guarantees that every client process will be pinged. That a client can have multiple interface pointers belonging to the same object is irrelevant from the standpoint of ping coverage; a client with multiple interface pointers into a single object will be pinged only once.

The DCOM programmers also came up with the concept of *ping sets*. Rather than send out a separate ping message for every object in use by every client program, DCOM identifies objects to be pinged and places them into a set. The first time a server machine sends out a ping, it sends the entire set list with the message. However, subsequent ping messages simply send out the ping set ID, along with a list of additions and subtractions (that is, the deltas) to the original ping set.

Summary

I hope that this brief overview has given you an insight into what DCOM brings to the table. In this chapter, you learned that DCOM is a high-level network protocol that enables COM components to distribute objects between processes on different computers. DCOM makes it so that you do not have to write network code to handle the communication required for distributed components. DCOM is not a programming language. DCOM is a specification and a service, built with and on COM, which provides a transparent network protocol enabling COM components to interoperate across a network. DCOM is not an object-oriented method for object-oriented programming, like COM. However, because DCOM was built with COM, and because it's implemented using COM, it utilizes COM's object-oriented technology to provide its services.

In the next few chapters, you will see how to implement DCOM components. Starting with Chapter 10, "Security," you will look at a major issue with distributed components—security. Because components contain both the data and the methods that operate on that data, security is important, lest you allow some unauthorized party access to some of your mission-critical business rules or data.

CHAPTER 10

SECURITY

In this chapter, you will learn about the following:

- The Security Support Provider Interface, which enables COM to interact with many security providers

- The basics of NT security

- Changing permissions to launch and access COM objects

- Changing the access rights of a COM object by changing its identity

- Modifying the security context on a processswide basis

- Modifying the security context on a per-call basis

- Integrating DCOM interfaces with the new cryptography API

This chapter describes the building blocks of COM security. Before the release of DCOM, no security was inherent in Microsoft's COM strategy. The introduction of DCOM with Windows NT 4.0 not only added the capability to launch and call COM objects remotely but also provided COM with security. Note that I did not state that it provided DCOM with security, because COM security applies to both remote and local objects. It has become popular to say that "DCOM is COM" when describing why DCOM security applies to local objects. I think it's clearer to view remote objects and COM security as two technologies that make up DCOM but can be implemented exclusively of each other.

The Security Support Provider Interface

For distributed objects to work effectively, COM must be implemented on more that just the Windows NT platform. It has to work on Windows 95, and it does. It also has to work on various other non-Windows platforms, that is, Macintosh, UNIX, and others. How do you implement COM security on these platforms when they lack the fundamental NT security features?

COM security uses Microsoft's Security Support Provider Interface (SSPI) to interface with whatever security infrastructure is available. SSPI provides one interface that is used by COM to query and manipulate the underlying security service. The underlying security service is implemented in a DLL. SSPI executes security calls on the DLL for security service selected by the application. This means that you need not have NT security to use COM security. That said, I will be describing COM security as it relates to NT security, also known as the NTLMSSP (NT Lan Manager Security Service Provider).

An Overview of NT Security

To understand how COM security works, it's best that I begin by describing the NT security model.

Windows NT security is based on the discretionary access control model. This model allows assignment of security attributes to each object of the system. The security attributes specify ownership of the object, a list of users (or groups) with their access permissions and audit attributes.

Security Descriptors

NT security is based on security descriptors. *Security descriptors* describe the security attributes of NT objects. NT objects include directories, files, ports, threads, processes, semaphores, events, drivers, and much more. A security descriptor has an owner SID (security ID), a group SID, a DACL (discretionary access control list), and a SACL (system access control list).

There are two types of security descriptors: self-relative and absolute. *Self-relative* security descriptors are self-contained structures with no indirect pointers. *Absolute* security descriptors may contain indirect pointers. It's important to note the difference, because absolute security descriptors cannot be saved to disk or transmitted, because of the indirect pointers.

Two Win32 API functions exist specifically for converting security descriptors between the two types: `MakeSelfRelativeSD()` and `MakeAbsoluteSD()`.

Security IDs

SIDs uniquely identify users or groups of users. When you create a new user account with the User Manager applet, you are also creating a SID that uniquely identifies that user.

You can find the current user's SID in the Registry under the key `HKEY_USERS`, as in Figure 10.1. I have two accounts set up on my machine: the Administrator account and one user account (rmorin). By logging off and on with the other user account, the SID under the `HKEY_USERS` key changes.

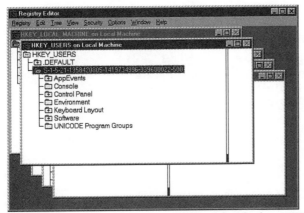

Figure 10.1 The current user's SID under the key HKEY_USERS.

Look at the SID viewer source code in Listing 10.1. This code acquires the access token for the current process. Don't worry about understanding access tokens, because I describe them later in this chapter. Using the access token, I am able to list a group of SIDs. These SIDs will vary, depending on how you execute this code.

Listing 10.1 The SID Viewer

```
#include <windows.h>
#include <strstrea.h>

strstream SidToString(PSID psid)
{
    strstream str;

    // is the sid valid?
    if(!::IsValidSid(psid))
    {
        return str;
    }
    // retrieve identifier authority
    PSID_IDENTIFIER_AUTHORITY pia =
        ::GetSidIdentifierAuthority(psid);
    // append prefix and revision number
    str << "S-" << SID_REVISION << "-";
    // append identifier authority
    if ( (pia->Value[0] != 0) || (pia->Value[1] != 0) )
    {
        str << (USHORT)pia->Value[0]
                    << (USHORT)pia->Value[1]
                    << (USHORT)pia->Value[2]
                    << (USHORT)pia->Value[3]
                    << (USHORT)pia->Value[4]
```

continued on next page

continued from previous page

```
                                << (USHORT)pia->Value[5];
        }
        else
        {
            str << ((ULONG)(pia->Value[5]        )    +
                        (ULONG)(pia->Value[4] <<  8)   +
                        (ULONG)(pia->Value[3] << 16)   +
                        (ULONG)(pia->Value[2] << 24)   );
        }
        // retrieve count of sub authorities
        DWORD dw = *::GetSidSubAuthorityCount(psid);
        // append subauthorities
        for (int i=0 ; i < (int)dw ; i++)
        {
            str << "-" << *::GetSidSubAuthority(psid, i);
        }
        return str;
    }

    int main(int, char **)
    {
        DWORD dwSize = 0;
        HANDLE hToken;

        // retrieve the current process's access token handle
        if (!::OpenProcessToken( ::GetCurrentProcess(),
                                TOKEN_QUERY, &hToken ))
        {
            std::cout << "Error ::OpenProcessToken "
                    << ::GetLastError() << endl;
            return 0;
        }
        // retrieve the size of the token group structure
        if(!::GetTokenInformation(hToken, TokenGroups, NULL,
                                dwSize, &dwSize))
        {
            DWORD dw = ::GetLastError();
            if( dw != ERROR_INSUFFICIENT_BUFFER )
            {
                std::cout << "Error ::GetTokenInformation "
                        << dw << endl;
                return 0;
            }
        }
        // allocate the token group structure
        PTOKEN_GROUPS pTokenGroups = (PTOKEN_GROUPS)
                        ::GlobalAlloc( GPTR, dwSize );
        // retrieve the token group structure
        if(!::GetTokenInformation(hToken, TokenGroups,
                                pTokenGroups, dwSize,
                                &dwSize ))
        {
            std::cout << "Error ::GetTokenInformation "
```

```
                        << ::GetLastError() << endl;
    }
    else
    {
        // dump all the group sids
        for(int i=0; i<(int)pTokenGroups->GroupCount; i++)
        {
            std::cout
            << SidToString(pTokenGroups->Groups[i].Sid).str()
            << endl;
        }
    }

    // clean up
    if ( pTokenGroups )
    {
        ::GlobalFree( pTokenGroups );
    }
    return 0;
}
```

I use the process handle to acquire the access tokens. The process inherits its access tokens from the launching user. I then call `GetTokenInformation()` twice, once to acquire the length of the **PTOKEN_GROUPS** structure and a second time to fill the structure. Last, I cycle through the list of SIDs, convert the SIDs to readable characters, and send the characters to the standard output.

The following is the output for the executable when run from the command line:

```
S-1-5-21-1958420805-1419734996-339680022-513

S-1-1-0

S-1-5-32-544

S-1-5-5-0-5466

S-1-2-0

S-1-5-4
```

The first SID is my user account SID. All user account SIDs begin with **S-1-5-21**. The rest, in order, are the SIDs for the world, my administrator domain, my logon session, the local user, and the interactive user. These SIDs determine my access permissions while the process is running.

Following is a list of well-known SIDs you might encounter:

S-1-0-0	NULL SID
S-1-1-0	World
S-1-2-0	Local

continued on next page

continued from previous page

S-1-3-0	Creator owner ID
S-1-3-1	Creator group ID
S-1-5	NT authority
S-1-5-1	Dialup
S-1-5-2	Network
S-1-5-3	Batch
S-1-5-4	Interactive
S-1-5-6	Service
S-1-5-5-X-Y	Logon session
S-1-5-21-?	User account
S-1-5-32-?	Built-in domain

The dialup SID is assigned to users that connect using RAS. The network SID is assigned to users that connect over a network. The interactive SID is assigned to users that connect locally. The service SID is assigned to processes run as services.

Access Control Lists

The two ACLs (access control lists) in the security descriptor are simply lists of ACEs (access control entries). The DACL is a list of access permissions (ACEs), both allowing and denying access.

Note that an empty DACL and no DACL have special meaning. An *empty DACL* means that no permissions are granted. *No DACL* means that all permissions are granted.

Listing 10.2 shows an example of manipulating the DACL to allow and disallow access to various users. This example creates a Registry key that allows access to the user named "**Administrator**". While I'm logged in as the "**Administrator**", I can delete the Registry key after running the program. However, if I'm logged in with another account (rmorin), the Registry key is not accessible.

Listing 10.2   Creating a Security Descriptor

```
#include <windows.h>
#include <iostream>

int main(int, char **)
{
    PSECURITY_DESCRIPTOR pSD = (PSECURITY_DESCRIPTOR)
        ::LocalAlloc(LPTR, SECURITY_DESCRIPTOR_MIN_LENGTH);

    if (pSD == NULL)
    {
```

```
        std::cout << "LocalAlloc failed." << endl;
        return 0;
}

if (!::InitializeSecurityDescriptor(pSD,
                        SECURITY_DESCRIPTOR_REVISION))
{
    std::cout << "InitializeSecurityDescriptor failed."
            << endl;
    return 0;
}

DWORD cbACL = 1024;
PACL pACLNew = (PACL) ::LocalAlloc(LPTR, cbACL);
if (pACLNew == NULL)
{
    std::cout << "LocalAlloc failed." << endl;
    return 0;
}

if (!::InitializeAcl(pACLNew, cbACL, ACL_REVISION2))
{
    std::cout << "InitializeAcl failed." << endl;
    return 0;
}

DWORD cbSID = 1024;
PSID pSID = (PSID) ::LocalAlloc(LPTR, cbSID);
PSID_NAME_USE psnuType = (PSID_NAME_USE)
                            ::LocalAlloc(LPTR, 1024);
LPSTR lpszDomain;
DWORD cchDomainName = 80;
lpszDomain = (LPSTR) ::LocalAlloc(LPTR, cchDomainName);
if (pSID==NULL || psnuType==NULL || lpszDomain==NULL)
{
    std::cout << "LocalAlloc failed." << endl;
    return 0;
}

if (!::LookupAccountName((LPSTR) NULL,
        "Administrator",
        pSID,
        &cbSID,
        lpszDomain,
        &cchDomainName,
        psnuType))
{
    std::cout << "LookupAccountName failed." << endl;
    return 0;
}

if (!::IsValidSid(pSID))
{
```

continued on next page

continued from previous page

```
                std::cout << "SID is not valid." << endl;
        }
        else
        {
            std::cout << "SID is valid." << endl;
        }

        if (!::AddAccessAllowedAce(pACLNew,
                ACL_REVISION2,
                GENERIC_ALL,
                pSID))
        {
            std::cout << "AddAccessAllowedAce failed." << endl;
            return 0;
        }

        if (!::SetSecurityDescriptorDacl(pSD,
                TRUE,
                pACLNew,
                FALSE))
        {
            std::cout << "SetSecurityDescriptorDacl failed."
<< endl;
            return 0;
        }

        SECURITY_ATTRIBUTES sa;
        sa.nLength = sizeof(SECURITY_ATTRIBUTES);
        sa.lpSecurityDescriptor = pSD;
        sa.bInheritHandle = TRUE;

        DWORD dw = 0;
        HKEY hk = NULL;
        LONG l = ::RegCreateKeyEx(HKEY_LOCAL_MACHINE,
                        "SOFTWARE\\MyKey", 0, "", 0,
                        KEY_READ | KEY_WRITE, &sa, &hk, &dw);

            ::FreeSid(pSID);
            if(pSD != NULL)
            {
                ::LocalFree((HLOCAL) pSD);
            }
            if(pACLNew != NULL)
            {
                ::LocalFree((HLOCAL) pACLNew);
            }
            if(psnuType != NULL)
            {
                ::LocalFree((HLOCAL) psnuType);
            }
            if(lpszDomain != NULL)
            {
                ::LocalFree((HLOCAL) lpszDomain);
```

```
    }

  return 0;
}
```

The ACE defines the access mask for a SID, either user or group. An *access mask* is a set of access rights. Access rights are grouped in three categories: general, standard, and specific.

You might recognize the general access rights; they are, `GENERIC_ALL`, `GENERIC_EXE-CUTE`, `GENERIC_READ`, and `GENERIC_WRITE`. These access rights are generic and therefore might have different meanings for different Windows NT securable objects. The standard access rights (`DELETE`, `READ_CONTROL`, `WRITE_DAC`, `WRITE_OWNER`, and `SYNCHRONIZE`) affect, among other things, access to the security descriptor of the object. The specific access rights are specific to the object type; that is, each object type has its own set of specific access rights.

The second ACL in the SD is the SACL. It has the same structure as the DACL, but contains the auditing settings for the object. I will not discuss this issue in detail because it has little to do with COM security.

User Profiles

Each user account has a profile that describes the user, his password settings, and his permissions. The permissions are set up by granting the user the rights of a user group. You might be more familiar with granting network access rights. Network access rights are one type of access rights.

You can add a new user and modify access permissions with the User Manager. Start the User Manager from the Start menu, as shown in Figures 10.2 and 10.3.

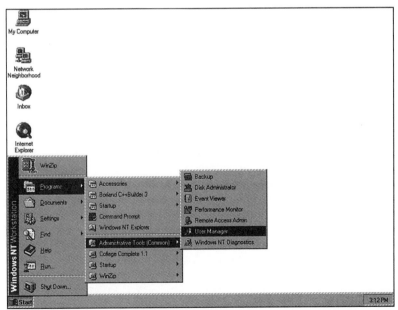

Figure 10.2   The startup User Manager from the Start menu.

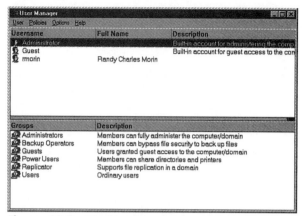

Figure 10.3   The User Manager.

From the User Properties screen, you select the Group button to view and modify the user groups in which the selected user is a member. From the Group Memberships screen, in Figure 10.4, you can add and remove user groups.

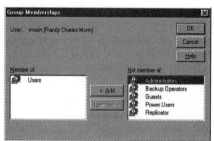

Figure 10.4   Add and remove user groups.

Access Tokens

As a user logs on, he is given an access token that contains a set of SIDs for that user and session. The set of SIDs includes one SID that uniquely identifies the user and a SID for each user group he is a member of.

The list of group SIDs typically includes the world, one or more user groups assigned in the user profile, the logon session, the local user, and the interactive user.

This is a good time to return to the SID viewer. Run the SID viewer once and note the SIDs. Open the User Manager and add a few user groups to your user account. Run the SID viewer again, and you'll note that the SIDs do not change, because the access token is assigned when you log on. Log out and back in and run the SID viewer again. This time, the list of SIDs reflects the new user groups you added.

You should now be more familiar with the NT security model. In the next section, I'll explain how the NT security model relates to COM.

COM Security

Four important topics relate to COM security: authentication, impersonation, launching, and access.

Authentication Security

DCOMCNFG can be used to modify the default authentication level. This utility ships with NT 4, Windows 98, and DCOM for Windows 95 and can be found in the System32 directory on NT installations. Open DCOMCNFG and select the Default Properties tab. This screen should look like Figure 10.5. You can change the authentication level from a list that includes {none}, call, connect, default, packet, packet integrity, and packet privacy.

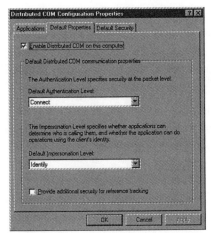

Figure 10.5 DCOMCNFG: Default authentication and impersonation settings.

You can also programmatically change the authentication level by directly modifying the Registry.

```
[ HKEY_LOCAL_MACHINE \ Software \ Microsoft \ OLE ]
➡"LegacyAuthenticationLevel" REG_DWORD =
➡{default_authentication_level}
```

The authentication level tells COM at what level you want the client to be authenticated. The following levels of authentication are available in COM:

RPC_C_AUTHN_LEVEL_DEFAULT	Uses the authentication service's default authentication level
RPC_C_AUTHN_LEVEL_NONE	No authentication
RPC_C_AUTHN_LEVEL_CONNECT	Authenticates only at connection
RPC_C_AUTHN_LEVEL_CALL	Authenticates every call
RPC_C_AUTHN_LEVEL_PKT	Authenticates every packet
RPC_C_AUTHN_LEVEL_PKT_INTEGRITY	Same as RPC_C_AUTHN_LEVEL_PKT and verifies that the data was not modified during transit
RPC_C_AUTHN_LEVEL_PKT_PRIVACY	Same as RPC_C_AUTHN_LEVEL_PKT_INTEGRITY and encrypts the packet

Impersonation Security

Impersonation is the process in which a user, process, or thread, attempts to impersonate another user in order to acquire a different security context.

You can also use **DCOMCNFG** to change the default impersonation levels; refer to Figure 10.5. Also, you can programmatically change the default impersonation level in the Registry.

```
[ HKEY_LOCAL_MACHINE \ Software \ Microsoft \ OLE ]
➥"LegacyImpersonationLevel" REG_DWORD =
➥{default_impersonation_level}
```

The impersonation level tells COM at what level the server can impersonate the client. The following levels of impersonation are available in COM:

- Anonymous—No impersonation is allowed.

- Identify—No impersonation is allowed, except for checking client permissions.

- Impersonate—Impersonation is allowed, except when calling other objects.

- Delegate—Impersonation is allowed, even when calling other objects.

Impersonation is important because the server is doing work for the client. To do the work, the server must acquire a defined set of security privileges. This is done either to limit the server or extend the server. It's sometimes important to acquire rights of the client in order to perform a task that can be performed only under the client's account. It's also important to limit rights normally available to the client in order to limit damage that can be caused by malicious servers.

Activation Security

Activation security grants user permissions to launch objects. COM object launch permissions are stored in the Registry under its **AppID** key, shown in Figure 10.6. **AppID** was introduced with DCOM to uniquely identify a module. Each module (executable or dynamic link library) may contain more than one COM object, and each COM object will have a unique CLSID. Therefore, if you wanted to specify the launch permissions by using the CLSID, you would have to create Registry entries for each COM object. By specifying the launch permissions, using the **AppID**, you reduce the amount of Registry maintenance. Each COM object will have one entry under its CLSID, denoting the object's **AppID**.

```
[HKEY_CLASSES_ROOT \ CLSID \ {class-id}] "AppID" = "{app-id}"
```

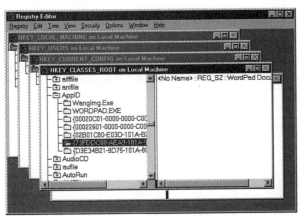

Figure 10.6 Launch permissions in the Registry.

The nondefault launch permissions are found in the Registry under the **AppID**. The value is a self-relative security descriptor. Now you know why you use self-relative security descriptors. Only self-relative security descriptors can be saved in the Registry.

Remember, you can use **MakeSelfRelativeSD()** to convert from an absolute security descriptor. The length of the security descriptor is determined using the **GetSecurityDescriptorLength()** API.

You can set the launch permissions in the Registry, using the following format in the same manner as you save the default launch permissions. Later in this chapter, I describe how to save the default launch permissions by using a self-relative security descriptor.

```
[HKEY_CLASSES_ROOT \ AppID \ {app-id}] "LaunchPermission" =
➡hex: [self-relative security descriptor]
```

You can also set launch permissions for an **AppID** by using **DCOMCNFG**. You might also set these permissions, and others that follow, using a tool called OLEView. I have found OLEView to be unstable and will limit my discussion to **DCOMCNFG** for simplicity.

To set the launch permissions by using **DCOMCNFG**, simply double-click the application in the initial tab and select the Security tab; see Figure 10.7.

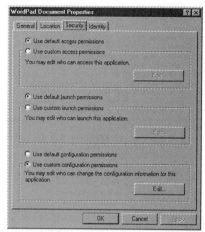

Figure 10.7   DCOMCNFG: Launch permissions.

If an object's launch permissions are not specified, DCOM will use the machine's default launch permissions.

The default launch permissions can also be set using **DCOMCNFG**, as in Figures 10.8 and 10.9. Simply select the Default Security tab and left-click the Edit button in the Default Launch Permissions group box.

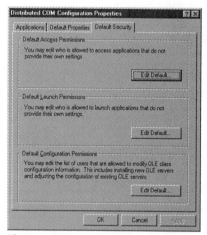

Figure 10.8   DCOMCNFG: Default launch and access permissions.

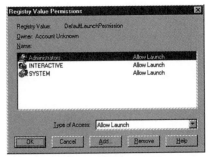

Figure 10.9   DCOMCNFG: NT security permissions.

Listing 10.3 shows how to modify the default launch permissions by modifying the Registry programmatically. This same technique can be applied to the default access permissions and the AppID-specific access and launch permissions.

Listing 10.3   Modify DefaultLaunchPermission in the Registry

```
#include <windows.h>
#include <iostream>
// if this next include file is not found,
// change the line to the next comment
// #include <strstrea>
#include <strstream>

strstream GetFormattedError()
{
    strstream str;
    DWORD dwLastError=::GetLastError();
    if(!dwLastError)
    {
        return str;
    }
    BYTE width=0;
    DWORD flags;
    flags  = FORMAT_MESSAGE_MAX_WIDTH_MASK &width;
    flags != FORMAT_MESSAGE_FROM_SYSTEM
            !FORMAT_MESSAGE_IGNORE_INSERTS;
    char s[1024];
    ::FormatMessage(flags, NULL, dwLastError,
            MAKELANGID(LANG_NEUTRAL, SUBLANG_DEFAULT),
            s, 1024, NULL);
    str << s;
    return str;
}

int main(int argc, char **argv)
{
```

continued on next page

continued from previous page

```cpp
            PSECURITY_DESCRIPTOR pSD = (PSECURITY_DESCRIPTOR)
                ::LocalAlloc(LPTR, SECURITY_DESCRIPTOR_MIN_LENGTH);

            if (pSD == NULL)
            {
                std::cout << "LocalAlloc failed." << endl;
                return 0;
            }

            if (!::InitializeSecurityDescriptor(pSD,
                                    SECURITY_DESCRIPTOR_REVISION))
            {
                std::cout << "InitializeSecurityDescriptor failed."
                            << endl;
                return 0;
            }

            DWORD cbACL = 1024;
            PACL pACLNew = (PACL) ::LocalAlloc(LPTR, cbACL);
            if (pACLNew == NULL)
            {
                std::cout << "LocalAlloc failed." << endl;
                return 0;
            }

            if (!::InitializeAcl(pACLNew, cbACL, ACL_REVISION2))
            {
                std::cout << "InitializeAcl failed." << endl;
                return 0;
            }

            DWORD cbSID = 1024;
            PSID pSID = (PSID) ::LocalAlloc(LPTR, cbSID);
            PSID_NAME_USE psnuType = (PSID_NAME_USE)
                                ::LocalAlloc(LPTR, 1024);
            LPSTR lpszDomain;
            DWORD cchDomainName = 80;
            lpszDomain = (LPSTR) ::LocalAlloc(LPTR, cchDomainName);
            if (pSID==NULL || psnuType==NULL || lpszDomain==NULL)
            {
                std::cout << "LocalAlloc failed." << endl;
                return 0;
            }

            if (!::LookupAccountName((LPSTR) NULL,
                    "Administrator",
                    pSID,
                    &cbSID,
                    lpszDomain,
                    &cchDomainName,
                    psnuType))
            {
                std::cout << "LookupAccountName failed." << endl;
```

```
        return 0;
    }

    if (!::IsValidSid(pSID))
    {
        std::cout << "SID is not valid." << endl;
    }
    else
    {
        std::cout << "SID is valid." << endl;
    }

    if (!::AddAccessAllowedAce(pACLNew,
            ACL_REVISION2,
            1,
            pSID))
    {
        std::cout << "AddAccessAllowedAce failed." << endl;
        return 0;
    }

    if (!::SetSecurityDescriptorDacl(pSD,
            TRUE,
            pACLNew,
            FALSE))
    {
        std::cout << "SetSecurityDescriptorDacl failed."
                    << endl;
        return 0;
    }

    PSECURITY_DESCRIPTOR pSRSD = NULL;
    DWORD cbSD = 0;
    if (!::MakeSelfRelativeSD(pSD, pSRSD, &cbSD))
    {
        DWORD dw = ::GetLastError();
        if( dw != ERROR_INSUFFICIENT_BUFFER )
        {
            std::cout << "Error ::MakeSelfRelativeSD "
                        << dw << endl;
            return 0;
        }
    }
    pSRSD = (PSECURITY_DESCRIPTOR) ::LocalAlloc(LPTR, cbSD);
    if (!::MakeSelfRelativeSD(pSD, pSRSD, &cbSD))
    {
        std::cout << "Error ::MakeSelfRelativeSD "
                    << ::GetFormattedError().str() << endl;
        return 0;
    }

    DWORD dw;
    HKEY hkey;
```

continued on next page

continued from previous page

```
        if (::RegOpenKeyEx(HKEY_LOCAL_MACHINE,
                           "SOFTWARE\\Microsoft\\Ole", 0,
                           KEY_SET_VALUE, &hkey)!=ERROR_SUCCESS)
        {
            std::cout << "Error ::RegOpenKeyEx "
                      << ::GetFormattedError().str() << endl;
            return 0;
        }

        if (::RegSetValueEx(hkey, "DefaultAccessPermission",
                            0, REG_BINARY,
                            (BYTE *)pSRSD, cbSD)!=ERROR_SUCCESS)
        {
            std::cout << "Error ::RegSetValueEx "
                      << ::GetFormattedError().str() << endl;
            return 0;
        }

        ::FreeSid(pSID);
        if(pSD != NULL)
        {
            ::LocalFree((HLOCAL) pSD);
        }
        if(pSRSD != NULL)
        {
            ::LocalFree((HLOCAL) pSRSD);
        }
        if(pACLNew != NULL)
        {
            ::LocalFree((HLOCAL) pACLNew);
        }
        if(psnuType != NULL)
        {
            ::LocalFree((HLOCAL) psnuType);
        }
        if(lpszDomain != NULL)
        {
            ::LocalFree((HLOCAL) lpszDomain);
        }

    return 0;
}
```

The first thing to do is to make a security descriptor. Note that COM uses the specific right that is the first bit of the access mask. Therefore, in place of specifying the access mask constants, you simply take the numeric value of the access mask (1). This is the third parameter of the AddAccessAllowedAce() function call.

After you have completed your security descriptor, you convert the absolute security descriptor to a self-relative security descriptor, using MakeSelfRelativeSD(). The self-relative can easily be saved in the Registry as a REG_BINARY item in the following format. Remember that you are required to use self-relative security descriptors because absolute security descriptors cannot be persisted. By *persisted*, I mean saved as a stream and retrieved later.

```
[HKEY_LOCAL_MACHINE \ SOFTWARE \ MICROSOFT \ OLE]
➥"DefaultLaunchPermission" = hex: [self-relative
➥security descriptor]
```

After running the program, you can view the default launch permissions with **DCOMCNFG**. You can also view them using the Registry Editor, shown in Figure 10.10. The hexadecimal represents the binary view of the self-relative security descriptor.

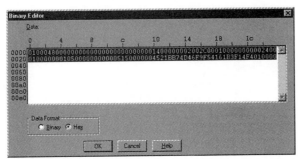

Figure 10.10   Default launch permissions in the Registry.

Call Security

Call security grants users permissions to invoke calls on established objects. You can set the access permissions by using the following format in the same manner you saved the launch permissions:

```
[HKEY_CLASSES_ROOT \ AppId \ {app-id}] "AccessPermission" =
➥hex: [self-relative security descriptor]
```

If an object's access permissions are not specified, DCOM will use the machine's default access permissions. You can set the default access permissions by using the following format in the same manner you saved the launch permissions:

```
[HKEY_LOCAL_MACHINE \ SOFTWARE \ MICROSOFT \ OLE]
➥"DefaultAccessPermission registry" =
➥hex: [self-relative security descriptor]
```

You can also set the default launch permissions by using **DCOMCNFG**; refer to Figures 10.8 and 10.9. Simply select the Default Security tab and left-click the Edit button in the Default Access Permissions group box.

Examples

This is all nice theory, but it's difficult to understand without pursuing a practical example. Listing 10.4 uses a simple automation class that shows how the security works.

Listing 10.4   Automation Permissions

```
#include <windows.h>

//////////////////////////////////////////////////////////////////
// Class Declaraction for Automation.
// This class is entirely defined inline.
// This class is used to call automation objects using the
//   more familiar CreateObject notation available to Visual
//   Basic and Delphi.
//////////////////////////////////////////////////////////////////

class CComVariant : public VARIANT
{
public:
    CComVariant(){};
    CComVariant(VARIANT v)
        :VARIANT(v)
    {
    };
    CComVariant(BSTR bstr)
    {
        vt = VT_BSTR;
        bstrVal = bstr;
    };
};

class Automation
{
public:
    // HRESULT returned from last automation call
    HRESULT hresult;
    // IDISPATCH interface pointer for the existing object
    LPDISPATCH pdisp;
    // hold exception info here
    EXCEPINFO excepinfo;
    // hold argument error here
    UINT uArgErr;

    // Constructor, intializes the data members
    Automation();
    // Copy constructor, intialize data members and call AddRef
    Automation(const Automation & rhs);
    // Destructor, if dispatch is not NULL then release it
    virtual ~Automation();

    // assignment operator
    Automation & operator=(const Automation & rhs);

    // Create the dispatch interface object
    HRESULT CreateObject(WCHAR * str);
    // Retrieve the active dispatch object
    HRESULT GetObject(WCHAR * str);
```

```
    // Invoke a method
    CComVariant Invoke(WCHAR * str, VARIANT * var = NULL,
                       unsigned int cArgs = 0);
    // retrieve a data members value
    CComVariant Get(WCHAR * str);
    // post a data members value
    HRESULT Put(WCHAR * str, CComVariant & var);
};

//////////////////////////////////////////////////////////////
// Construction/Destruction
//////////////////////////////////////////////////////////////

inline Automation::Automation()
: pdisp(NULL),
hresult(S_OK)
{
}

inline Automation::Automation(const Automation & rhs)
: pdisp(rhs.pdisp),
hresult(rhs.hresult)
{
    // return an exception if the dispatch pointer is NULL
    if (pdisp==NULL)
    {
        hresult = DISP_E_EXCEPTION;
    }
    pdisp->AddRef();
}

inline Automation::~Automation()
{
    // Release the object
    if (pdisp != NULL)
    {
        pdisp->Release();
        pdisp = NULL;
    }
}

//////////////////////////////////////////////////////////////
// Assignment operator
//////////////////////////////////////////////////////////////
inline Automation& Automation::operator=(const Automation& rhs)
{
    // If the previous object was not released, do it now.
    if (pdisp != NULL)
    {
        pdisp->Release();
        pdisp = NULL;
    }
```

continued on next page

continued from previous page

```
            pdisp = rhs.pdisp;
            hresult = rhs.hresult;
            pdisp->AddRef();

            return *this;
};


///////////////////////////////////////////////////////////////
// Method GetObject
// Retrieves the active object, does not create a new instance
///////////////////////////////////////////////////////////////

inline HRESULT Automation::GetObject(WCHAR * str)
{
    // If the previous object was not released, do it now.
    if (pdisp != NULL)
    {
        pdisp->Release();
        pdisp = NULL;
    }

    // Convert the progid to a clsid
    CLSID clsid;
    hresult = ::CLSIDFromProgID(str, &clsid);
    if (hresult)
    {
        // CLSIDFromProgID failed
        return hresult;
    };

    // Retrieve the instance of the object
    LPUNKNOWN punk;
    hresult = ::GetActiveObject(clsid, NULL, &punk);
    if (hresult)
    {
        // GetActiveObject failed
        return hresult;
    };

    // Retrieve the interface pointer
    hresult = punk->QueryInterface(IID_IDispatch,
                                    (LPVOID FAR *)&pdisp);
    if (hresult)
    {
        // QueryInterface failed
        return hresult;
    };

    // Release the IUnknown reference.
    hresult = punk->Release();

    return hresult;
}
```

```
/////////////////////////////////////////////////////////////
// Method CreateObject
// Retrieves the a new instance of the object
/////////////////////////////////////////////////////////////

inline HRESULT Automation::CreateObject(WCHAR * str)
{
    // If the previous object was not released, do it now.
    if (pdisp != NULL)
    {
        pdisp->Release();
        pdisp = NULL;
    }

    // Convert the progid to a clsid
    CLSID clsid;
    hresult = ::CLSIDFromProgID(str, &clsid);
    if (hresult)
    {
        // CLSIDFromProgID failed
        return hresult;
    };

    // Create the instance of the object
    LPUNKNOWN punk;
    hresult = ::CoCreateInstance(clsid, NULL, CLSCTX_SERVER,
IID_IUnknown, (LPVOID FAR *) &punk);
    if (hresult)
    {
        // CoCreateInstance failed
        return hresult;
    };

    // Retrieve the interface pointer
    hresult = punk->QueryInterface(IID_IDispatch,
                                   (LPVOID FAR *)&pdisp);

    if (hresult)
    {
        // QueryInterface failed
        return hresult;
    };

    // Release the IUnknown reference.
    hresult = punk->Release();

    return hresult;
}

/////////////////////////////////////////////////////////////
// Method Get
// Retrieves the property's value
/////////////////////////////////////////////////////////////
```

continued on next page

continued from previous page

```
inline CComVariant Automation::Get(WCHAR * str)
{
    // return an exception if the dispatch pointer is NULL
    if (pdisp==NULL)
    {
        hresult = DISP_E_EXCEPTION;
        return CComVariant();
    }

    // Retrieve the dispatch id for the function name
    DISPID dispid;
    hresult = pdisp->GetIDsOfNames(IID_NULL, &str, 1,
                                LOCALE_USER_DEFAULT, &dispid);
    if (hresult)
    {
        // GetIDsOfNames failed
        return CComVariant();
    };

    // Invoke the property GET
    DISPPARAMS dispparams = {0};
    VARIANTARG variantarg;
    VariantInit(&variantarg);
    ::memset(&excepinfo, 0, sizeof(EXCEPINFO));
    uArgErr = 0;
    hresult = pdisp->Invoke(dispid, IID_NULL,
                            LOCALE_USER_DEFAULT,
                            DISPATCH_PROPERTYGET,
                            &dispparams, &variantarg,
                            &excepinfo, &uArgErr);
    if (hresult)
    {
        // Invoke failed
        return CComVariant();
    };

    // return to lhs
    return CComVariant(variantarg);
}

//////////////////////////////////////////////////////////////
// Method Put
// Posts the property's value
//////////////////////////////////////////////////////////////

inline HRESULT Automation::Put(WCHAR * str, CComVariant & var)
{
    // return an exception if the dispatch pointer is NULL
    if (pdisp==NULL)
    {
        hresult = DISP_E_EXCEPTION;
        return hresult;
```

```
    }

    // Retrieve the dispatch id for the function name
    DISPID dispid;
    hresult = pdisp->GetIDsOfNames(IID_NULL, &str, 1,
                                LOCALE_USER_DEFAULT, &dispid);

    if (hresult)
    {
        // GetIDsOfNames failed
        return hresult;
    };

    // Invoke the property PUT
    DISPPARAMS dispparams = {0};
    dispparams.rgvarg = &var;
    DISPID x = DISPID_PROPERTYPUT;
    dispparams.rgdispidNamedArgs = &x;
    dispparams.cArgs = 1;
    dispparams.cNamedArgs = 1;
    VARIANTARG variantarg;
    VariantInit(&variantarg);
    ::memset(&excepinfo, 0, sizeof(EXCEPINFO));
    uArgErr = 0;

    // I'm not sure why you have to call PUTREF with these type
    // but I encountered similar code in "ATLCTL.CPP"
    if (var.vt == VT_UNKNOWN || var.vt == VT_DISPATCH ||
        (var.vt & VT_ARRAY) || (var.vt & VT_BYREF))
    {
        hresult = pdisp->Invoke(dispid, IID_NULL,
                                LOCALE_USER_DEFAULT,
                                DISPATCH_PROPERTYPUTREF,
                                &dispparams, &variantarg,
                                &excepinfo, &uArgErr);

        if (SUCCEEDED(hresult))
            return hresult;
    }

    // If the previous failed or the type did not match then
    // make the standard call.
    hresult = pdisp->Invoke(dispid, IID_NULL,
                            LOCALE_USER_DEFAULT,
                            DISPATCH_PROPERTYPUT,
                            &dispparams, &variantarg,
                            &excepinfo, &uArgErr);

    return hresult;
}

///////////////////////////////////////////////////////////
// Method Invoke
// Executes the method
///////////////////////////////////////////////////////////
```

continued on next page

continued from previous page

```
inline CComVariant Automation::Invoke(WCHAR * str,
                            VARIANT * var, unsigned int cArgs)
{
    // return an exception if the dispatch pointer is NULL
    if (pdisp==NULL)
    {
        hresult = DISP_E_EXCEPTION;
        return CComVariant();
    }

    // Retrieve the dispatch id for the function name
    DISPID dispid;
    hresult = pdisp->GetIDsOfNames(IID_NULL, &str, 1,
                            LOCALE_USER_DEFAULT, &dispid);
    if (hresult)
    {
        // GetIDsOfNames failed
        return CComVariant();
    };

    // Invoke the method
    DISPPARAMS dispparams = {0};
    dispparams.rgvarg = var;
    dispparams.cArgs = cArgs;
    VARIANTARG variantarg;
    VariantInit(&variantarg);
    ::memset(&excepinfo, 0, sizeof(EXCEPINFO));
    uArgErr = 0;
    hresult = pdisp->Invoke(dispid, IID_NULL,
                            LOCALE_USER_DEFAULT,
                            DISPATCH_METHOD,
                            &dispparams, &variantarg,
                            &excepinfo, &uArgErr);
    if (hresult)
    {
        return CComVariant();
    };

    return CComVariant(variantarg);
}

int main(int, char **)
{
    CoInitialize(NULL);
    {
    Automation ob;
    ob.CreateObject(L"MyAutomationServer.MyAutomationObject");
    long l = ob.Get(L"Hello").lVal;
    }
    CoUninitialize();
    return 0;
}
```

The first thing you must do is find or create a simple automation server. I chose to create an automation server named MyAutomationServer with one exposed automation object named MyAutomationObject and one property named Hello. You can do this with just about any tool: Visual C++, Visual Basic, Delphi, C++ Builder, and many more.

After you create the automation server, you have to register it. This is usually done automatically by the executable the first time it is launched. Typically, your automation server will not register its AppID. You can add the AppID with the Registry Editor. Simply add the following values to the Registry:

```
[HKEY_CLASSES_ROOT \ CLSID \ {class-id}] "AppID" = "{class-id}"
```

```
[HKEY_CLASSES_ROOT \ AppId \ {class-id}] "" = "MyAutomationServer"
```

Example1

When you open DCOMCNFG, you'll note an entry in the applications list: MyAutomationServer. Double-click this entry and move to the Security tab; refer to Figure 10.7. Select Use Custom Launch Permissions. Left-click the Edit button. Remove all the current permissions; this will disable launching of the application using COM. Save the setting and close DCOMCNFG.

After these modifications, you will not be able to launch the automation server. Run the sample code in Listing 10.4 and step through the lines of code. You'll note that CoCreateInstance() will return an HRESULT of 0x80070005, which translates to *access denied*.

Example2

The second example uses the same DCOMCNFG settings, so don't change anything. But this time run the automation server executable before you run Listing 10.4. You'll note that CoCreateInstance() doesn't fail this time, and the code executes without error. The automation server was already launched; therefore, the automation client did not need launch permissions.

Run this same sample code again after setting access rights that deny and then allow access for your user account. Step through the code and find out how the low-level COM APIs are executing.

COM Object Identity

When a DCOM object is launched, it assumes the identity of a user in order to acquire security permissions. The identity is retrieved from the Registry setting for the AppID. The object can run as three different users: the interactive user, the activator, or a fixed user account.

To run as the interactive user, add the following Registry value:

```
[HKEY_CLASSES_ROOT \ AppId \ {app-id}] "RunAs" = "Interactive User"
```

To run as a fixed user account, add the following Registry value:

```
[HKEY_CLASSES_ROOT \ AppId \ {app-id}] "RunAs" = "mydomain\myaccount"
```

To run as the activator, omit or delete the Registry value. Objects that are launched as a fixed user or activator on a remote machine will run in a security context of that user. The object might not be able to interact with the desktop and may have other limitations.

You can also select the impersonation user by using **DCOMCNFG**. Simply double-click the application in the initial tab and select the Identity tab, shown in Figure 10.11.

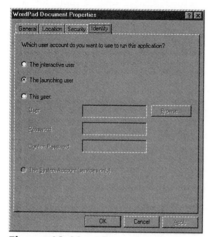

Figure 10.11   The impersonation user in the Registry.

It's easy to modify the Registry to launch an application with whichever identity you require. Listing 10.5 modifies the Registry to launch an application by using the interactive user.

Listing 10.5   Impersonation in the Registry

```
#include <windows.h>
#include <iostream>

int main(int , char **)
{
    HKEY hkey;
    if (::RegOpenKeyEx(HKEY_CLASSES_ROOT,
        "AppID\\{73FDDC80-AEA9-101A-98A7-00AA00374959}",
        0, KEY_SET_VALUE, &hkey)!=ERROR_SUCCESS)
    {
        std::cout << "Error ::RegOpenKeyEx "
                  << ::GetLastError() << endl;
        return 0;
    }

    char * sz = "Interactive User";
```

```
    if (::RegSetValueEx(hkey, "RunAs", 0, REG_SZ,
                  (BYTE *)sz, ::lstrlen(sz))!=ERROR_SUCCESS)
    {
        std::cout << "Error ::RegSetValueEx "
                  << ::GetLastError() << endl;
        return 0;
    }

    return 0;
}
```

Processwide Security

Processwide security is the security permissions that exist for the lifetime of a process. This security may be temporarily modified in the process.

To set processwide security, Microsoft has provided a variety of API functions. `CoGetClassObject()`, `CoCreateInstanceEx()`, and `CoInitializeSecurity()` have parameters that enable the programmer to specify processwide security.

`CoGetClassObject()` and `CoCreateInstanceEx()` have a `COSERVERINFO` structure as a parameter that in turn has a `COAUTHINFO` member. This `COAUTHINFO` member enables the programmer to specify the authentication service, the authorization service, the authentication level, a username, a domain name, and a password.

`CoInitializeSecurity()` takes parameters that include a security descriptor, an array of authentication services, an authentication level, and a default impersonation level.

These functions make it possible to programmatically set processwide security settings without having to configure each client or server workstation.

Security Blankets and Impersonation

COM provides two interfaces to manipulate security on a per-call basis: `IClientSecurity` and `IServerSecurity`.

IClientSecurity

The `IClientSecurity` interface provides COM clients with the capability to control the security used to make calls on the proxy.

To use the `IClientSecurity` interface, it's easier to use the helper functions `CoQueryProxyBlanket()`, `CoSetProxyBlanket()`, and `CoCopyProxy()`. The helper functions hide the process of retrieving and releasing the interface pointers. These three functions have the pseudo implementations shown in Listing 10.6.

Listing 10.6 Client Security Helper Functions

```
HRESULT CoQueryProxyBlanket( IUnknown * pProxy,
    DWORD * pAuthnSvc,
    DWORD * pAuthzSvc,
    OLECHAR ** pServerPrincName,
    DWORD * pAuthnLevel,
    DWORD * pImpLevel,
    RPC_AUTH_IDENTITY_HANDLE * ppAuthInfo,
    DWORD * pCapabilities )
{
    pProxy->QueryInterface(IID_IClientSecurity, (void**)&pcs);
    pcs->QueryBlanket(pProxy, pAuthnSvc, pAuthzSvc,
        pServerPrincName, pAuthnLevel, pImpLevel, ppAuthInfo,
        pCapabilities);
    pcs->Release();
}
HRESULT CoSetProxyBlanket( IUnknown * pProxy,
    DWORD dwAuthnSvc,
    DWORD dwAuthzSvc,
    WCHAR * pServerPrincName,
    DWORD dwAuthnLevel,
    DWORD dwImpLevel,
    RPC_AUTH_IDENTITY_HANDLE   pAuthInfo,
    DWORD dwCapabilities )
{
    pProxy->QueryInterface(IID_IClientSecurity, (void**)&pcs);
    pcs->SetBlanket(pProxy, dwAuthnSvc, dwAuthzSvc,
        pServerPrincName, dwAuthnLevel, dwImpLevel, pAuthInfo,
        dwCapabilities);
    pcs->Release();
}
HRESULT CoCopyProxy( IUnknown * pProxy,
    IUnknown ** ppCopy )
{
    pProxy->QueryInterface(IID_IClientSecurity, (void**)&pcs);
    pcs->CopyProxy(punkProxy, ppunkCopy);
    pcs->Release();
}
```

When do you use `IClientSecurity`? If you want to use a higher security level for some calls that might transmit sensitive information, `IClientSecurity` can provide this higher security level on a temporary basis. Before calling the `SetBlanket()` method, call the `CopyProxy()` method to avoid contention between two calls using the same proxy.

You can also use `QueryBlanket()` to retrieve the current client security settings.

IServerSecurity

The `IServerSecurity` interface provides COM servers with the capability to impersonate the client and query the client's security context.

Again, it's easier to use the helper functions and then use the `IServerSecurity` interface. The helper functions are `CoQueryClientBlanket()`, `CoImpersonateClient()`, and `CoRevertToSelf()`. These three functions have the pseudo implementations shown in Listing 10.7.

Listing 10.7   Server Security Helper Functions

```
HRESULT CoQueryClientBlanket( IUnknown * pProxy,
    DWORD * pAuthnSvc,
    DWORD * pAuthzSvc,
    OLECHAR ** pServerPrincName,
    DWORD * pAuthnLevel,
    DWORD * pImpLevel,
    RPC_AUTHZ_HANDLE * pPrivs,
    DWORD ** pCapabilities )
{
    CoGetCallContext(IID_IServerSecurity, (void**)&pss);
    pss->QueryBlanket(pAuthnSvc, pAuthzSvc, pServerPrincName,
        pAuthnLevel, pImpLevel, pPrivs, pCapabilities);
    pss->Release();
 }
CoImpersonateClient()
{
    CoGetCallContext(IID_IServerSecurity, (void **)&pss);
    pss->ImpersonateClient();
    pss->Release();
}
CoRevertToSelf()
{
    CoGetCallContext(IID_IServerSecurity, (void **)&pss);
    pss->RevertToSelf();
    pss->Release();
}
```

`ImpersonateClient()` and `RevertToSelf()` enable the server objects to impersonate the client object. That is, the server objects acquire the rights and privileges of the client. The server can also use `QueryBlanket()` to retrieve the current client security settings.

`IServerSecurity` has one additional method that does not have a helper function. This method, `IsImpersonating()`, simply indicates whether the server is currently impersonating the client.

DCOM and CAPI

Windows NT 5.0 includes a new authentication service called SChannel security support provider. This authentication service supports SSL (secure sockets layer) and PCT (private communications technology). SSL and PCT are security protocols that have already been implemented in many Internet clients and servers.

The advantage of this authentication service is that it provides support for packet encryption and public-key certificates for authentication. In addition, it's possible to specify the CAPI implementation that will perform the encryption. This means that the security providers and applications will be able to specify different cryptographic implementations by simply providing a CAPI service handle to the SChannel security support provider.

In NT 5.0, the `SOLE_AUTHENTICATION_LIST` parameter of `CoIntializeSecurity()` will enable the application to specify SChannel security as the authentication service and a private certificate for authentication using a CAPI handle.

Summary

In this chapter, you have learned the basics necessary to understanding and manipulating the security settings for a COM server. You should also understand how COM uses SSPI to access the NT security provider and how it can use an alternative security provider through the same SSPI interface. The basic structures that make up the NT security model are now more familiar to you.

COM provides many mechanisms for manipulating the security of a COM server. These include setting permissions for a COM server and acquiring rights by assuming the identity of users. The permissions can be modified using Registry settings and processwide functions. Identities can be assumed by specifying that a COM server launch with a particular user identity or by temporarily assuming identities.

CHAPTER 11

USING DIFFERENT COM THREADING MODELS

In this chapter, you will learn about the following:

- The basics of creating, destroying, and managing your Win32 thread
- Each of the basic thread types
- Thread synchronization functions
- Each of the COM threading models

*T*his chapter describes how to manage threads for best performance while eliminating concurrency problems between your objects and object calls.

COM provides an entire set of threading models that can be used to create COM objects and servers. Unfortunately, because of Windows NT's ancestry (MS-DOS), threading in Windows NT has produced a multitude of complex choices instead of a simple model. Table 11.1 shows the evolution of the thread model in DOS-Windows.

Table 11.1 Evolution of the Thread Model

Operating System	Thread Model
DOS	The operating system is single-processed, and threading is implemented by the application programmer.
16-bit Windows	The operating system uses nonpreemptive multitasking. Threading is still implemented by the application programmer.
32-bit Windows	The operating system uses preemptive multitasking and manages threads for the application programmer.
32-bit COM	The operating system introduces apartments to help programmers serialize COM requests between processes. COM objects are single-threaded.
DCOM	The operating system introduces multithreaded apartments. COM objects are multithreaded, and the application programmer has to worry about thread concurrency.

In the beginning there was an ancient operating system called MS-DOS that didn't provide any facility for multiprocessing or multithreading. MS-DOS applications that required multiple threads of execution had to write their own thread-swapping subroutines.

When multitasking became available on alternative platforms, users demanded a multitasking operating system for Intel machines. Microsoft provided a nonpreemptive multitasking operating system called Windows (the 16-bit variety). Applications ran in one thread with one window message pump.

After a few years of dealing with sluggish nonpreemptive, multitasking operating systems, Microsoft released its 32-bit Windows operating systems (Windows NT and Windows 95). These were true preemptive multitasking systems. Applications started using worker threads to perform background processing.

In the preemptive OS model, the OS is responsible for preempting tasks in order to perform task switching. In the nonpreemptive OS model, the task was responsible for yielding to the OS in order that task switching occur.

At the same time, a young version of COM was using a single-threaded model. When one or more COM methods were invoked, the invocation request was placed on a hidden window's message queue. The COM object serviced one message at a time, and thus concurrency was not an issue. This was acceptable at the time because objects typically serviced one client at a time and those clients were usually single-threaded.

Also, this was convenient because the programmer did not have to write thread-safe code. It resulted, however, in a problem because many early COM objects were not thread-safe. This problem persists today because we have so many legacy objects that require this legacy-threading model. Even today, most COM objects are not thread-safe.

When 32-bit COM was introduced, Microsoft created the apartment model. COM objects existed in apartments, and each apartment ran in a separate thread. COM objects still ran in one thread and serviced one call at a time, but you could have multiple apartments in one process (see Figure 11.1). These apartments were later called *single-threaded apartments* (STA), that is, one thread per apartment. When a COM object in one apartment called a COM object in another apartment, the method invocation had to marshal through a proxy between the apartments. The proxy synchronized the calls to ensure that only one call would be serviced in an apartment at any time.

Two models were available to programmers. Programmers could create one STA for their process and run all objects in that STA or could create more than one STA for their process and run one or more objects in an STA.

Eventually, the single-threaded object was improved on by the introduction of the free-threaded model. This model allowed multiple threads to interact within the same apartment. These apartments are called *multithreaded apartments* (MTA). The multithreaded apartment was created by having incoming COM requests bypass the message queues and call the method directly.

With MTA, any number of COM objects and threads can reside in one MTA apartment (see Figure 11.2). In fact, a process can have only one MTA.

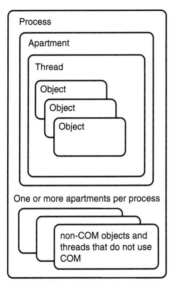

Figure 11.1 The STA apartment model.

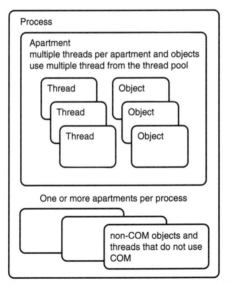

Figure 11.2 The MTA apartment model.

If the client is out-of-process, the stub receives the request from the proxy and calls the COM method directly—again, without the intermediary message queue. However, the responsibility of creating thread-safe objects became the responsibility of the programmer.

Because COM calls need to be marshaled only between apartments, calls between objects within the same free-threaded apartment need not be marshaled.

Legacy COM objects still use the STA model, and therefore, COM has to keep the legacy-threading model to prevent concurrency problems with thread-unsafe COM objects.

Thread Functions

Now, back to thread basics. A process (a running application) can have one or more threads. The processes and threads are managed by Windows to simulate multiple threads running concurrently in one process. The apparent concurrency of threads is accomplished by swapping between threads at small intervals. To create and manage these threads, a programmer can use the following Win32 API functions:

- `CreateThread()`
- `SuspendThread()`
- `ResumeThread()`
- `TerminateThread()`
- `GetExitCodeThread()`
- `ExitThread()`
- `_beginthreadex()`
- Thread local storage functions

CreateThread()

The `CreateThread()` function enables you to create a new thread. Listing 11.1 shows how you can create a thread to periodically dump data to the standard output.

Listing 11.1   Using `CreateThread()`

```
#include <windows.h>
#include <iostream>

DWORD WINAPI ThreadProc(void * p)
{
  std::cout << ":Secondary thread ID = "
            << ::GetCurrentThreadId() << std::endl;
  return 0;
}

int main()
{
  std::cout << ":Primary thread ID = "
            << ::GetCurrentThreadId() << std::endl;
  DWORD dw;
```

```
      HANDLE handle = ::CreateThread(NULL, 0, ThreadProc, NULL, 0,
                                        &dw);
      ::Sleep(1000);
      ::CloseHandle(handle);
      return 0;
}
```

In this section, I will refer to the function `ThreadProc()` as the initiating function. That is, the thread begins when initiating this function and terminates when exiting this function.

SuspendThread() and ResumeThread()

The `SuspendThread()` and `ResumeThread()` functions can be used to pause and restart a thread, as demonstrated in Listing 11.2.

Listing 11.2   Using `SuspendThread()` and `ResumeThread()`

```cpp
#include <windows.h>
#include <iostream>

DWORD WINAPI ThreadProc(void * p)
{
  for (int i=0;i<60;i++)
  {
    std::cout << ":Secondary thread ID = "
              << ::GetCurrentThreadId() << std::endl;
    ::Sleep(100);
  }
  return 0;
}

int main()
{
  std::cout << ":Primary thread ID = "
            << ::GetCurrentThreadId() << std::endl;
  DWORD dw;
  HANDLE handle = ::CreateThread(NULL, 0, ThreadProc, NULL, 0,
                                    &dw);
  ::Sleep(1000);
  std::cout << ":Suspend()" << endl;
  ::SuspendThread(handle);
  for (int i=0;i<10;i++)
  {
    std::cout << ":Primary thread ID = "
              << ::GetCurrentThreadId() << std::endl;
    ::Sleep(100);
  }
  std::cout << ":Resume()" << endl;
  ::ResumeThread(handle);
  ::Sleep(1000);
  ::CloseHandle(handle);
  return 0;
```

TerminateThread()

The `TerminateThread()` function can be used to kill a thread, which is shown in Listing 11.3.

Listing 11.3   Using `TerminateThread()`

```
#include <windows.h>
#include <iostream>

DWORD WINAPI ThreadProc(void * p)
{
  for (int i=0;i<60;i++)
  {
    std::cout << ":Secondary thread ID = "
              << ::GetCurrentThreadId() << std::endl;
    ::Sleep(100);
  }
  return 0;
}

int main()
{
  std::cout << ":Primary thread ID = "
            << ::GetCurrentThreadId() << std::endl;
  DWORD dw;
  HANDLE handle = ::CreateThread(NULL, 0, ThreadProc, NULL, 0,
                                 &dw);
  ::Sleep(1000);
  std::cout << ":TerminateThread()";
  ::TerminateThread(handle, 1);
  ::CloseHandle(handle);
  ::Sleep(1000);
  return 0;
}
```

GetExitCodeThread()

The `GetExitCodeThread()` function can be used to query the exit code from a thread. Because threads run concurrently, an additional function was needed to allow other threads to query the thread's exit code. Listing 11.4 shows how to use the `GetExitCodeThread()` function.

Listing 11.4   Using `GetExitCodeThread()`

```
#include <windows.h>
#include <iostream>

DWORD WINAPI ThreadProc(void * p)
{
  std::cout << ":Secondary thread ID = "
```

```
                    << ::GetCurrentThreadId() << std::endl;
    return 10;
}

int main()
{
  std::cout << ":Primary thread ID = "
            << ::GetCurrentThreadId() << std::endl;
  DWORD dw;
  HANDLE handle = ::CreateThread(NULL, 0, ThreadProc, NULL, 0,
                                 &dw);
  ::Sleep(1000);
  ::GetExitCodeThread(handle, &dw);
  std::cout << ":Thread exit code = " << dw << std::endl;
  ::CloseHandle(handle);
  return 0;
}
```

ExitThread()

The ExitThread() function can be used to exit a thread without completing the thread function. Normally, the thread exits when the thread's initiating function completes. Listing 11.5 shows how you can exit a thread prematurely.

Listing 11.5   Using ExitThread()

```
#include <windows.h>
#include <iostream>

DWORD WINAPI ThreadProc(void * p)
{
  std::cout << ":Secondary thread ID = "
            << ::GetCurrentThreadId() << std::endl;
  ::ExitThread(20);
  std::cout << ":Unreachable";
  return 10;
}

int main()
{
  std::cout << ":Primary thread ID = "
            << ::GetCurrentThreadId() << std::endl;
  DWORD dw;
  HANDLE handle = ::CreateThread(NULL, 0, ThreadProc, NULL, 0,
                                 &dw);
  ::Sleep(1000);
  ::GetExitCodeThread(handle, &dw);
  std::cout << ":Thread exit code = " << dw << std::endl;
  ::CloseHandle(handle);
  return 0;
```

beginthreadex()

The _beginthreadex() function is similar to the **CreateThread()** function except that _beginthreadex() provides the additional benefit of properly initializing and destroying the C runtime library environment. Listing 11.6 shows an example of using the _beginthreadex() function.

Listing 11.6   Using _beginthreadex()

```
#include <afx.h>
#include <process.h>
#include <iostream>
#include <stdlib.h>

#define USES_CREATETHREAD
#define USES_BEGINTHREADEX

/* Structure for each thread's data */

struct _tiddata {
        unsigned long   _tid;
        unsigned long   _thandle;
        int      _terrno;
        unsigned long   _tdoserrno;
        unsigned int    _fpds;
        unsigned long   _holdrand;
        char *          _token;
#ifdef _WIN32
        wchar_t *       _wtoken;
#endif  /* _WIN32 */
        unsigned char * _mtoken;
        char *          _errmsg;
        char *          _namebuf0;
#ifdef _WIN32
        wchar_t *       _wnamebuf0;
#endif  /* _WIN32 */
        char *          _namebuf1;
#ifdef _WIN32
        wchar_t *       _wnamebuf1;
#endif  /* _WIN32 */
        char *          _asctimebuf;
#ifdef _WIN32
        wchar_t *       _wasctimebuf;
#endif  /* _WIN32 */
        void *          _gmtimebuf;
        char *          _cvtbuf;
        void *          _initaddr;
        void *          _initarg;
        void *          _pxcptacttab;
        void *          _tpxcptinfoptrs;
        int             _tfpecode;
        unsigned long   _NLG_dwCode;
        void *          _terminate;
```

```
          void *      _unexpected;
          void *      _translator;
          void *      _curexception;
          void *      _curcontext;
#if defined (_M_MRX000)
          void *      _pFrameInfoChain;
          void *      _pUnwindContext;
          void *      _pExitContext;
          int         _MipsPtdDelta;
          int         _MipsPtdEpsilon;
#elif defined (_M_PPC)
          void *      _pExitContext;
          void *      _pUnwindContext;
          void *      _pFrameInfoChain;
          int         _FrameInfo[6];
#endif  /* defined (_M_PPC) */
          };

typedef struct _tiddata * _ptiddata;

CRITICAL_SECTION cs;

unsigned int __stdcall ThreadProc1(void * p)
{
  DWORD dw = ::GetCurrentThreadId();
  ::srand(dw);
  ::EnterCriticalSection(&cs);
  std::cout << ":Secondary thread ID = " << dw << std::endl;
  dw = ::rand();
  std::cout << ":Random Number = " << dw << std::endl;
  ::LeaveCriticalSection(&cs);
  return 0;
}

DWORD WINAPI ThreadProc2(void * p)
{
  DWORD dw = ::GetCurrentThreadId();
  ::srand(dw);
  ::EnterCriticalSection(&cs);
  std::cout << ":Secondary thread ID = " << dw << std::endl;
  dw = ::rand();
  std::cout << ":Random Number = " << dw << std::endl;
  ::LeaveCriticalSection(&cs);
  return 0;
}

int main()
{
  CMemoryState m1,m2,m3;

  m1.Checkpoint();

  ::InitializeCriticalSection(&cs);
```

continued on next page

continued from previous page

```
        std::cout << ":Primary thread ID = "
                    << ::GetCurrentThreadId() << std::endl;
        std::cout << ":Sizeof _tiddata = "
                    << sizeof(_tiddata) << std::endl;
        HANDLE handle;
        unsigned int ui;
        DWORD dw;
        int i=0;
        for (i=0;i<4;i++)
        {
#ifdef USES_BEGINTHREADEX
            handle = (HANDLE) ::_beginthreadex(NULL, 0, ThreadProc1,
                                               NULL, 0, &ui);
            ::CloseHandle(handle);
#endif
#ifdef USES_CREATETHREAD
            handle = ::CreateThread(NULL, 0, ThreadProc2,
                                    NULL, 0, &dw);
            ::CloseHandle(handle);
#endif
        }
        ::Sleep(6000);
        ::DeleteCriticalSection(&cs);

        m2.Checkpoint();

        if (m3.Difference(m1, m2))
        {
            m3.DumpStatistics();
        }
        return 0;
}
```

The code in Listing 11.6 is very revealing. The structure is the code block allocated by the `beginthreadex()` function to instantiate thread local storage for the C runtime library. If you remove the line `#define USES_CREATETHREAD`, you'll note that the amount of memory leaked decreases by the size of the structure times the amount of threads. To produce this result, you must link with a multithreaded C runtime library.

It's not that the `CreateThread()` function leaks 116 bytes every time it creates a new thread. It is well documented that the `CreateThread()` function should not be used if the thread is going to use the thread local storage structure of the C runtime library.

Thread Local Storage

There are two types of memory: stack frame and heap frame. *Stack frame memory* is local to one thread. *Heap frame memory* is local to one process and shared by all threads in that same process. One type of heap variable is the static variable. Occasionally, it would be nice if static variables had separate local storage for each thread. Listing 11.7 shows a typical example of threads requiring local storage of static variables.

Listing 11.7 Demonstrating the Need for Thread Local Heap Frame Storage

```
int HowManyTimesHasThreadCalledThisFunction()
{
  static int i = 0;
  return i;
}
```

To use thread local storage, you use the **_declspec(thread)** storage class. Listing 11.8 is an example of thread local heap frame storage.

Listing 11.8 Using Thread Local Storage

```
int HowManyTimesHasThreadCalledThisFunction()
{
  _declspec(thread) static int i = 0;
  return i;
}
```

Unfortunately, the **_declspec(thread)** storage class does not work in DLLs. Another method of using thread local heap storage is to use the thread local storage Windows API. Four thread local storage API functions are provided: **TlsAlloc()**, **TlsFree()**, **TlsSetvalue()**, and **TlsGetValue()**.

Listing 11.9 shows a simple example of using the thread local storage Windows API.

Listing 11.9 Using the Thread Local Storage API

```
#include <windows.h>
#include <iostream>

CRITICAL_SECTION cs;
DWORD tls = 0;

void GetThreadId()
{
 DWORD * pdw = new DWORD;
  *pdw = ::GetCurrentThreadId();
  ::TlsSetValue(tls, pdw);
}

void ReleaseTls()
{
  DWORD * pdw = (DWORD *)::TlsGetValue(tls);
  delete pdw;
}

DWORD WINAPI ThreadProc(void * p)
{
  ::GetThreadId();
  ::EnterCriticalSection(&cs);
  std::cout << ":Secondary thread ID = "
            << *(DWORD *)::TlsGetValue(tls) << std::endl;
```

continued on next page

continued from previous page

```
      ::LeaveCriticalSection(&cs);
      ::ReleaseTls();
      return 0;
   }

   int main()
   {
     tls = ::TlsAlloc();
     ::InitializeCriticalSection(&cs);
     std::cout << ":Primary thread ID = "
               << ::GetCurrentThreadId() << std::endl;

     for (int i=0;i<2;i++)
     {
       DWORD dw;
       HANDLE handle = ::CreateThread(NULL, 0, ThreadProc,
                                      NULL, 0, &dw);
       ::CloseHandle(handle);
     }
     ::Sleep(1000);
     ::DeleteCriticalSection(&cs);
     ::TlsFree(tls);
     return 0;
   }
```

Thread Types

The evolution of multitasking, multiprocessing, and multithreading on the DOS Windows systems has resulted in a wide variety of thread types. The next sections describe the different types.

The internals of Win32 know of only two kinds of threads: threads and fibers. All the following thread types are handled by the operating system in the same way and differ only in their implementation.

Worker Thread

The worker thread is the simplest type of thread. This thread usually has a short life span. Typically, long-running functions are spawned to a worker thread to enable the user to continue working on the main thread while the function is completed in the background. All the sample code listings earlier in this chapter use worker threads.

A typical document-style application will provide the ability to create new documents, open existing documents, close open documents, print documents, and save documents. Saving and printing of documents tend to be very long operations. If your application were single-threaded, the user would normally have to wait while the application saved or printed the document. This is when worker threads are useful. You could spawn a worker thread every time the user saved or printed, to free the main thread for further use by the user. Listing 11.10 is pseudocode for how you might code the WndProc() function to use worker threads.

Listing 11.10   Spawning a Worker Thread

```cpp
#include <windows.h>
#include <fstream>

struct DOCUMENTDATA
{
  char szFilename[256];
  long cLength;
  BYTE * pbyte;
};

DWORD SaveDocument(void * p)
{
  DOCUMENTDATA * data = (DOCUMENTDATA *)p;
  std::ofstream os;
  os.open(data->szFilename);
  os.write((char *)data->pbyte, data->cLength);
  os.close();
  return 0;
}

DWORD PrintDocument(void * p)
{
  DOCUMENTDATA * data = (DOCUMENTDATA *)p;
  printstream ps;
  ps.newpage();
  ps.write((char *)data->pbyte, data->cLength);
  ps.endpage();
  return 0;
}

LRESULT CALLBACK WndProc(HWND hWnd, UINT nMsg,
                         WPARAM wParam, LPARAM lParam)
{
  HANDLE handle;
  DWORD dw;
  DOCUMENTDATA * data = GetDOCUMENTDATA();
  switch (nMsg)
  {
    case WM_COMMAND:
    switch (wParam)
    {
      case IDM_NEW:
        NewDocument();
      break;
      case IDM_OPEN:
        OpenDocument();
      break;
      case IDM_CLOSE:
        CloseDocument();
      break;
      case IDM_SAVE:
        handle = ::CreateThread(NULL, 0, SaveDocument,
```

continued on next page

continued from previous page

```
                                          data, 0, &dw);
            CloseHandle(handle);
          break;
          case IDM_PRINT:
            handle = ::CreateThread(NULL, 0, PrintDocument,
                                          data, 0, &dw);
            CloseHandle(handle);
          break;
            ...
      }
      ...
    }
}
```

When designing an application that takes advantage of worker threads (also known as *background processing*), it's important to consider concurrency issues. If your worker thread is accessing the same data as any other thread, you might run into race conditions. Later in this chapter, you'll review some of the available methods for preventing such concurrency problems (see "Thread Synchronization").

Message Queue Thread

A message queue thread is similar to a worker thread, except that it has a message queue where the thread can retrieve and dispatch messages. This thread has the advantage of being able to receive Windows messages from other threads.

GetMessage() and PostThreadMessage()

You can send a message to a thread with the `PostThreadMessage()` function. The thread retrieves messages from its message queue by calling the `GetMessage()` function. Listing 11.11 shows how to create a message queue thread.

Listing 11.11   Non-MFC Thread Messaging

```
#include <windows.h>
#include <iostream>

#define MYMESSAGE (WM_USER+1000)

DWORD WINAPI ThreadProc(void * p)
{
  std::cout << ":Secondary thread ID = "
            << ::GetCurrentThreadId() << std::endl;
  MSG msg;
  while (::GetMessage(&msg, NULL, 0, 0))
  {
    switch(msg.message)
    {
    case MYMESSAGE:
      std::cout << ":Message Received";
      break;
```

```
    default:
      break;
    }
  }
  return 0;
}

int main()
{
  std::cout << ":Primary thread ID = "
            << ::GetCurrentThreadId() << std::endl;
  DWORD dw;
  HANDLE handle = ::CreateThread(NULL, 0, ThreadProc,
                                 NULL, 0, &dw);
  ::Sleep(1000);
  BOOL b = ::PostThreadMessage(dw, MYMESSAGE, 0, 0);
  ::Sleep(1000);
  b = ::PostThreadMessage(dw, WM_QUIT, 0, 0);
  ::Sleep(1000);
  ::CloseHandle(handle);
  return 0;
}
```

A very nice feature in the message queue thread is that WM_QUIT messages are automatically processed by the message queue. The thread exits shortly after the WM_QUIT message is sent.

CWinThread() and AfxBeginThread()

MFC provides two methods of using CWinThread objects. You can derive a class from CWinThread, or you can call AfxBeginThread() to create a CWinThread object. The advantage is that CWinThread implements a lot of functionality that threads normally require. The disadvantage is that creating a CWinThread object requires more CPU time than message queue threads created with the Win32 API.

The CWinThread example shows how to use a CWinThread derived object. I've derived my own class, WorkerThread, from the CWinThread class. Listings 11.12 and 11.13 show the declaration and definition of my WorkerThread class.

Listing 11.12   The WorkerThread Declaration

```
#if !defined(AFX_WORKERTHREAD_H)
#define AFX_WORKERTHREAD_H

#if _MSC_VER >= 1000
#pragma once
#endif // _MSC_VER >= 1000
// WorkerThread.h : header file
//

#define MYMESSAGE (WM_USER+1000)

/////////////////////////////////////////////////////////////////
```

continued on next page

continued from previous page

```
// WorkerThread thread

class WorkerThread : public CWinThread
{
  DECLARE_DYNCREATE(WorkerThread)
  WorkerThread();
protected:

// Attributes
public:

// Operations
public:
  virtual int Run();

// Overrides
  // ClassWizard generated virtual function overrides
  //{{AFX_VIRTUAL(WorkerThread)
  public:
  virtual BOOL InitInstance();
  virtual int ExitInstance();
  //}}AFX_VIRTUAL

// Implementation
protected:
  virtual ~WorkerThread();

  // Generated message map functions
  //{{AFX_MSG(WorkerThread)
  //}}AFX_MSG

  DECLARE_MESSAGE_MAP()
};


/////////////////////////////////////////////////////////////

//{{AFX_INSERT_LOCATION}}

#endif // !defined(AFX_WORKERTHREAD_H)
```

Note that I've overridden the `CWinThread::Run()` method. I did this because I wanted to cut to the chase. `CWinThread` provides too much functionality in its own implementation.

Listing 11.13 The WorkerThread Definition

```
// WorkerThread.cpp : implementation file
//

#include "stdafx.h"
#include "cwinthread.h"
#include "WorkerThread.h"

#ifdef _DEBUG
#define new DEBUG_NEW
```

```
#undef THIS_FILE
static char THIS_FILE[] = __FILE__;
#endif

/////////////////////////////////////////////////////////////
// WorkerThread

IMPLEMENT_DYNCREATE(WorkerThread, CWinThread)

WorkerThread::WorkerThread()
{
}

WorkerThread::~WorkerThread()
{
}

BOOL WorkerThread::InitInstance()
{
  // TODO:  perform a per-thread initialization here
return TRUE;
}

int WorkerThread::ExitInstance()
{
  // TODO:  perform any per-thread cleanup here
  return CWinThread::ExitInstance();
}

BEGIN_MESSAGE_MAP(WorkerThread, CWinThread)
  //{{AFX_MSG_MAP(WorkerThread)
  //}}AFX_MSG_MAP
END_MESSAGE_MAP()

/////////////////////////////////////////////////////////////
// WorkerThread message handlers

int WorkerThread::Run()
{
  MSG msg;
  while (::GetMessage(&msg, NULL, 0, 0))
  {
    switch(msg.message)
    {
    case MYMESSAGE:
      TRACE(":Message Received\n");
      break;
    default:
      break;
    }
  }
  return 0;
}
```

Listing 11.14 contains the dialog client code that creates a new `CWinThread` object, sends messages to the thread, and kills the thread.

Listing 11.14   Calling Objects Inherited from `CWinThread`

```
BOOL CCwinthreadDlg::OnInitDialog()
{
  CDialog::OnInitDialog();

  SetIcon(m_hIcon, TRUE);
  SetIcon(m_hIcon, FALSE);

  CWinThread * p = new WorkerThread;
  p->CreateThread();
  m_idthread = p->m_nThreadID;

  return TRUE;
}

void CCwinthreadDlg::OnOK()
{
  BOOL b = ::PostThreadMessage(m_idthread, MYMESSAGE, 0, 0);
  ::Sleep(1000);
  ::PostThreadMessage(m_idthread, WM_QUIT, 0, 0);
  CDialog::OnOK();
}
```

The `CCwinthreadDlg::OnInitDialog()` function creates a new `WorkerThread` object and saves the thread ID for later use. The `CCwinthreadDlg::OnOK()` function sends a proprietary message to the thread, sleeps while the message is being processed, and then kills the thread and the application. Additional code for the `CWinThread` example is available on the CD-ROM as cwinthread.zip.

Listing 11.15 uses the `AfxBeginThread()` function to create a generic `CWinThread` object.

Listing 11.15   Creating Objects with `AfxBeginThread`

```
static DWORD g_idthread;

HCURSOR CAfxbeginthreadDlg::OnQueryDragIcon()
{
  return (HCURSOR) m_hIcon;
}

UINT ThreadProc( LPVOID pParam )
{
  TRACE("Hello\n");
  MSG msg;
  while (::GetMessage(&msg, NULL, 0, 0))
  {}
  return 0;
}

BOOL CAfxbeginthreadDlg::OnInitDialog()
{
```

```
    CDialog::OnInitDialog();

    SetIcon(m_hIcon, TRUE);
    SetIcon(m_hIcon, FALSE);

    CWinThread * pthread = ::AfxBeginThread(ThreadProc, NULL);
    g_idthread = pthread->m_nThreadID;

    return TRUE;
}

void CAfxbeginthreadDlg::OnOK()
{
    ::PostThreadMessage(g_idthread, WM_QUIT, 0, 0);
    CDialog::OnOK();
}
```

In Listing 11.15, I've implemented the same methods in the dialog client, but rather than use a full **CWinThread** derived object, I simply create the standard **CWinThread** object and provide a thread procedure. Additional code for the **CWinThread** example is available on the CD-ROM as afxbeginthread.zip.

Thread Pools

Three-tier applications are applications divided into three layers: the user interface, the application layer, and the database. Classical two-tier applications had two layers: the user interface and the database. The application was embedded in the user interface.

With today's move toward three-tier applications, the middle tier, or application layer, has become very important. This tier receives requests from the user interface and dispatches requests to the database system. If the application layer resides on a separate processor from the database system, a single-threaded application layer will incur a lot of idle time while it waits for the database system to complete the database requests. To maximize the processing of the application layer, programmers have created multithreaded application layers. These application layers distribute transactions to multiple similar threads. These similar threads are called a *thread pool*. Listing 11.16 shows a simple implementation of thread pooling.

Listing 11.16   Thread Pooling

```
#include <windows.h>
#include <iostream>

#define MYMESSAGE (WM_USER+1000)

HANDLE handle[8];
DWORD dw[8];
bool busy[8]

DWORD ThreadProc(void * p)
{
```

continued on next page

continued from previous page

```
        std::cout << ":Secondary thread ID = " << ::GetCurrentThreadId();
        MSG msg;
        while (GetMessage(&msg, NULL, 0, 0))
        {
          switch(msg.message)
          {
          case MYMESSAGE:
            std::cout << ":Message Received";
            busy[*((int *)p)] = false;
            break;
          case WM_QUIT:
            std::cout << ":Exit Thread";
            return 0;
          default:
            break;
          }
        }
        return 0;
      }

      LRESULT MessageProc(MSG & msg)
      {
        for (int i=0;i<8;i++)
        {
          if (!busy[i])
          {
            busy[i] = true;
            ::PostThreadMessage(dw[i], msg.message, msg.wParam, msg.lParam);
            break;
          }
        }
      };

      int main()
      {
        for (int i=0;i<8;i++)
        {
          std::cout << ":Primary thread ID = " << ::GetCurrentThreadId();
          busy[i] = false;
          HANDLE handle[i] = ::CreateThread(NULL, 0, ThreadProc,
        ➥(void *)&i, 0, &dw[i]);
        }

        MessageLoop();

        for (int i=0;i<8;i++_
        {
          ::CloseHandle(handle[i]);
        }
        return 0;
      }
```

Window Thread

A window thread is a step up from the message queue thread. In addition to having a message queue, the window thread has a window handle. Messages are sent to the message queue by using the window handle instead of the thread ID.

SendMessage(), PostMessage(), and DispatchMessage()

The windows thread uses the save `GetMessage()` function as the message queue thread to retrieve messages. In addition, it has a `DispatchMessage()` function that dispatches messages to the window's procedure (`WndProc`). It also has a `PostMessage()` function to send messages to the window. Another function, `SendMessage()`, also sends messages to the window, but this function blocks until the message has completed. Listing 11.17 is the all-familiar Hello World example found in almost every beginner Windows programming book.

Listing 11.17   The Hello Thread Example

```
#include "windows.h"

LRESULT CALLBACK WndProc (HWND, UINT, WPARAM, LPARAM);
DWORD WINAPI ThreadProc(void * p);
struct TREADSTRUCT
{
  char * szAppName;
  HINSTANCE hInstance;
  int iCmdShow;
};

int WINAPI WinMain (HINSTANCE hInstance,
  HINSTANCE hPrevInstance, LPSTR lpszCmdLine, int iCmdShow)
{
  WNDCLASSEX wndclass;
  static char  szAppName[] = "Hello My Thread";

  wndclass.cbSize = sizeof (wndclass);
  wndclass.style=CS_HREDRAW | CS_VREDRAW;
  wndclass.lpfnWndProc = WndProc;
  wndclass.cbClsExtra = 0;
  wndclass.cbWndExtra = 0;
  wndclass.hInstance = hInstance;
  wndclass.hIcon = LoadIcon (hInstance,IDI_APPLICATION);
  wndclass.hCursor = LoadCursor (NULL, IDC_ARROW);
  wndclass.hbrBackground = (HBRUSH) GetStockObject (WHITE_BRUSH);
  wndclass.lpszMenuName =NULL;
  wndclass.lpszClassName =szAppName;
  wndclass.hIconSm = LoadIcon (NULL,IDI_APPLICATION);
```

continued on next page

continued from previous page

```
        RegisterClassEx (&wndclass);

        DWORD dw;
        TREADSTRUCT ts;
        ts.szAppName = szAppName;
        ts.hInstance = hInstance;
        ts.iCmdShow = iCmdShow;
        HANDLE handle = ::CreateThread(NULL, 0, ThreadProc,
        ➥(void *)&ts, 0, &dw);
        ::CloseHandle(handle);
        ::ThreadProc(&ts);
        return 0;
    }

    DWORD WINAPI ThreadProc(void * p)
    {
      HWND hWnd;
      MSG msg;
      TREADSTRUCT * pts = (TREADSTRUCT *)p;

      hWnd = CreateWindow (
        pts->szAppName,
        "The Hello Program",
        WS_OVERLAPPEDWINDOW,
        CW_USEDEFAULT,
        CW_USEDEFAULT,
        CW_USEDEFAULT,
        CW_USEDEFAULT,
        NULL,
        NULL,
        pts->hInstance,
        NULL);

      ShowWindow (hWnd, pts->iCmdShow);
      UpdateWindow (hWnd);

      while (GetMessage(&msg,NULL,0,0))
      {
        TranslateMessage(&msg);
        DispatchMessage(&msg);
      }
      return msg.wParam;
    }

    LRESULT CALLBACK WndProc(HWND hWnd, UINT iMessage,
                WPARAM wParam, LPARAM lParam)
    {
      HDC hDC;
      PAINTSTRUCT ps;
      RECT rect;
      switch (iMessage)
      {
        case WM_PAINT:
            hDC = BeginPaint (hWnd, &ps);
```

```
      GetClientRect (hWnd, &rect);
      DrawText (hDC, "Hello Thread", -1, &rect,
          DT_SINGLELINE | DT_CENTER | DT_VCENTER);
      EndPaint (hWnd, &ps);
      return 0;
    case WM_DESTROY:
      PostQuitMessage(0);
      break;
    default:
      return DefWindowProc (hWnd, iMessage, wParam, lParam);
  }
  return (0L);
}
```

I've extended the Hello World example to spawn a second thread with a window message pump. Both the primary and secondary threads in Listing 11.17 are classic window threads.

Apartment Thread

An apartment thread builds on the window thread. The apartment is a COM ideology. COM enables a thread to reside inside an apartment. The single-threaded apartment (STA) has a hidden window that is used to synchronize COM calls on the window's message queue. A thread initiates a COM apartment by calling `CoInitialize()` and destroys the apartment by calling `CoUninitialize()`. Listing 11.18 shows how to initiate and destroy a minimal single-threaded apartment.

Listing 11.18 An STA Apartment

```
#include <windows.h>
#include <iostream>

int main()
{
  ::CoInitialize(NULL);
  std::cout << "Hello from my apartment" << std::endl;
  ::CoUninitialize();
  return 0;
}
```

The multithreaded apartment (MTA) does not synchronize COM calls on the window's message queue. This apartment is initialized by calling `CoInitializeEx(NULL, COINIT_MULTITHREADED)` and destroyed by using `CoUninitialize()`. Listing 11.19 shows how to initiate and destroy a multithreaded apartment.

Listing 11.19 An MTA Apartment

```
#include <windows.h>
#include <iostream>

int main()
```

continued on next page

continued from previous page

```
{
    ::CoInitializeEx(NULL, COINIT_MULTITHREADED);
    std::cout << "Hello from my multi-threaded apartment"
            << std::endl;
    ::CoUninitialize();
    return 0;
}
```

Because multiple threads can reside in one MTA apartment, you do not have to initialize a new apartment to use COM in the new thread. In the STA model, you have to create a new apartment in any thread that uses COM. Listing 11.20 shows how to use COM in two separate threads, using the STA model. Listing 11.21 shows how to use COM in two separate threads, using the MTA model.

Listing 11.20   The STA Apartment with Two Threads

```
#include <windows.h>
#include <iostream>

DWORD WINAPI ThreadProc(void * p)
{
    ::CoInitialize(NULL);
    std::cout << "Hello from my second apartment" << std::endl;
    ::CoUninitialize();
    return 0;
}

int main()
{
    ::CoInitialize(NULL);
    std::cout << "Hello from my first apartment" << std::endl;
    DWORD dw;
    HANDLE handle = ::CreateThread(NULL, 0, ThreadProc, NULL, 0,
                                    &dw);
    ::CloseHandle(handle);
    ::Sleep(1000);
    ::CoUninitialize();
    return 0;
}
```

Note again that with STA apartments you must initialize another apartment at the start of every thread if you want to be in an apartment. You must be in an apartment in order to use COM as a client or server.

Listing 11.21   An MTA Apartment with Two Threads

```
#include <windows.h>
#include <iostream>

DWORD WINAPI ThreadProc(void * p)
{
    std::cout << "Hello from my second apartment" << std::endl;
```

```
    return 0;
}

int main()
{
    ::CoInitializeEx(NULL, COINIT_MULTITHREADED);
    std::cout << "Hello from my first apartment" << std::endl;
    DWORD dw;
    HANDLE handle = ::CreateThread(NULL, 0, ThreadProc, NULL, 0,
                                    &dw);
    ::CloseHandle(handle);
    ::Sleep(1000);
    ::CoUninitialize();
    return 0;
}
```

In an MTA apartment, new threads are automatically in the apartment of their parent thread.

Fiber

Fibers are to threads what threads are to processes. As a process may have one or more threads, a thread may have zero or more fibers. Fibers are considered lightweight threads; that is, switching between fibers requires less processing than swapping threads. Threads are managed by the operating system (Windows NT), and the operating system decides when to swap out one thread and swap in another thread. Switching between fibers is controlled directly by the programmer. Listing 11.22 shows how two fibers can be used to manage a sequence of semiconcurrent events.

Listing 11.22   Using Fibers

```
#define _WIN32_WINNT 0x0400

#include <windows.h>
#include <iostream>

struct MYFIBERSTRUCTURE
{
    void * pfiber1;
    void * pfiber2;
};

void __stdcall FiberProc(void *)
{
    MYFIBERSTRUCTURE * pfb =
        (MYFIBERSTRUCTURE *)::GetFiberData();
    std::cout << "Hello from my second second" << std::endl;
    ::SwitchToFiber(pfb->pfiber1);
    std::cout << "Goodbye from my second second" << std::endl;
    ::SwitchToFiber(pfb->pfiber1);
}
```

continued on next page

continued from previous page

```
int main()
{
  MYFIBERSTRUCTURE fb;
  fb.pfiber1 = ::ConvertThreadToFiber(&fb);
  std::cout << "Hello from my first fiber" << std::endl;
  fb.pfiber2 = ::CreateFiber(0, FiberProc, &fb);
  ::SwitchToFiber(fb.pfiber2);
  std::cout << "Goodbye from my first fiber" << std::endl;
  ::SwitchToFiber(fb.pfiber2);
  return 0;
}
```

Thread Synchronization

When you have decided to operate with more than one thread, you must take care to make your applications thread-safe. That is, you have to synchronize your threads when synchronization is important. Four types of synchronization objects exist in Windows NT: events, mutexes, semaphores, and critical sections.

Multithreaded objects that are not thread-safe will eventually run into situations in which two threads accessing the same resource simultaneously will cause undesired results.

Events

An event synchronization object enables one thread to signal one other thread or many other threads that it's time to perform certain tasks. The Win32 API has seven functions that help you manage events.

CreateEvent()	Creates a new event
OpenEvent()	Opens an existing event
WaitForSingleObject()	Waits on one event
WaitForMultipleObjects()	Waits on two events
SetEvent()	Triggers an event
ResetEvent()	Resets an event
PulseEvent()	Triggers and resets an event

Listing 11.23 shows an example of using events to inform a thread when it's time to shut down.

Listing 11.23   Using Events

```
#include <windows.h>
#include <iostream>
```

```
void KillThread()
{
  HANDLE hevent = ::OpenEvent(EVENT_MODIFY_STATE, FALSE,
  ➥"KILL_THREAD");
  ::SetEvent(hevent);
  ::CloseHandle(hevent);
  return;
}

DWORD WINAPI ThreadProc(LPVOID pParam )
{
  std::cout << ":Secondary thread ID = "
            << ::GetCurrentThreadId() << std::endl;

  SECURITY_ATTRIBUTES sa;
  SECURITY_DESCRIPTOR sd;
  sa.nLength = sizeof(SECURITY_ATTRIBUTES);
  sa.bInheritHandle = TRUE;
  sa.lpSecurityDescriptor = &sd;
  if(!::InitializeSecurityDescriptor(&sd,
  ➥SECURITY_DESCRIPTOR_REVISION))
  {
    ::exit (1);
  }
  if(!::SetSecurityDescriptorDacl(&sd, TRUE, (PACL)NULL, FALSE))
  {
    ::exit (1);
  }

  HANDLE hevent = ::CreateEvent(&sa, FALSE, FALSE, "KILL_THREAD");
  if (!hevent)
  {
    ::exit(1);
  }

  ::WaitForSingleObject(hevent, INFINITE);

  std::cout << "Goodbye" << std::endl;

  return 0;
}

int main()
{
  std::cout << ":Primary thread ID = "
            << ::GetCurrentThreadId() << std::endl;
  DWORD dw;
  HANDLE handle = ::CreateThread(NULL, 0, ThreadProc, NULL, 0,
                                 &dw);
  ::Sleep(1000);
  ::CloseHandle(handle);
  ::KillThread();
  return 0;
}
```

Mutex

Mutexes are used to control access to a resource. Like events, mutexes use the `WaitForSingleObject()` and `WaitForMultipleObjects()` functions to wait for ownership of the mutex. Other Win32 API functions that help you manage mutexes are the following:

CreateMutex()	Creates a new mutex
OpenMutex()	Opens an existing mutex
ReleaseMutex()	Releases ownership of the mutex

Listing 11.24 shows how to use a mutex to control access to a global variable.

Listing 11.24 Using Mutexes

```
#include <windows.h>
#include <iostream>

DWORD WINAPI ThreadProc(LPVOID pParam )
{
  std::cout << ":Secondary thread ID = "
            << ::GetCurrentThreadId() << std::endl;
  HANDLE hevent = ::OpenMutex(EVENT_MODIFY_STATE, FALSE, "MYMUTEX");

  for (int i=0;i<4;i++)
  {
     ::WaitForSingleObject(hevent, INFINITE);
     static int count = 0;
     count++;
     std::cout << "I've got the mutex.  Thread = "
           << ::GetCurrentThreadId() << std::endl;
     std::cout << "Threads with mutex = "
           << count << std::endl;
     ::Sleep(100);
     std::cout << "I'll release the mutex.  Thread = "
           << ::GetCurrentThreadId() << std::endl;
     count--;
     ::ReleaseMutex(hevent);
  }

  ::CloseHandle(hevent);
  return 0;
}

int main()
{
  SECURITY_ATTRIBUTES sa;
  SECURITY_DESCRIPTOR sd;
  sa.nLength = sizeof(SECURITY_ATTRIBUTES);
  sa.bInheritHandle = TRUE;
  sa.lpSecurityDescriptor = &sd;
  if (!::InitializeSecurityDescriptor(&sd,
  ➥SECURITY_DESCRIPTOR_REVISION))
```

```
{
  ::exit (1);
}
if(!::SetSecurityDescriptorDacl(&sd, TRUE, (PACL)NULL, FALSE))
{
  ::exit (1);
}

HANDLE hevent = ::CreateMutex(&sa, FALSE, "MYMUTEX");
if (!hevent)
{
  ::exit(1);
}

std::cout << ":Primary thread ID = "
          << ::GetCurrentThreadId() << std::endl;
DWORD dw;
HANDLE handle = ::CreateThread(NULL, 0, ThreadProc, NULL, 0,
                                &dw);
::CloseHandle(handle);
handle = ::CreateThread(NULL, 0, ThreadProc, NULL, 0,
                         &dw);
::CloseHandle(handle);

::Sleep(2000);
::CloseHandle(hevent);
return 0;
}
```

Critical Section

Critical sections are lightweight mutexes. They control access to resources, just like mutexes. The difference between critical sections and mutexes is that mutexes are kernel objects and critical sections are local to one process. If you require control to resources that span across more than one process, you should use a mutex. Otherwise, the lightweight critical section is the better choice. Four Win32 API functions are available to help you manage critical sections:

InitializeCriticialSection()	Creates a critical section
DeleteCriticalSection()	Destroys a critical section
EnterCriticalSection()	Takes ownership of a token for exclusive access to the resource
LeaveCriticalSection()	Releases ownership of a token for exclusive access to the resource

Listing 11.25 shows how, without a control object, access to a resource can cause concurrency problems.

Listing 11.25   An Example of Concurrency Problems

```cpp
#include <windows.h>
#include <iostream>

DWORD WINAPI ThreadProc(void * p)
{
  for (int i=0;i<4;i++)
  {
    std::cout << ":Secondary thread ID = " << ::GetCurrentThreadId();
  }
  return 0;
}

int main()
{
  std::cout << ":Primary thread ID = " << ::GetCurrentThreadId();
  for (int i=0;i<4;i++)
  {
    DWORD dw;
    HANDLE handle = ::CreateThread(NULL, 0, ThreadProc, NULL, 0, &dw);
    ::CloseHandle(handle);
  }
  ::Sleep(6000);
  return 0;
}
```

In Listing 11.25, all 10 threads are trying to write to the same output device. Without synchronization, the threads are likely to write to the output device at the same time. The output of this program might look like Listing 11.26.

Listing 11.26   Output without Synchronization

```
:Primary thread ID = 4294693683
:Secondary thread ID = 4294786279
:Secondary thread ID = 4294786279
:Secondary thread ID = 4294786279
:Secondary thread ID = 4294786279
:Secondary thread ID = 4294761431
:Secondary thre:ad ID = 4294761431
:Secondary thread ID = 4294761:Secondary thread ID = 4294756291
:Secondary thrSecondary thread ID = 4294761983
:Secondary thre431
:Secondary thread ID = 429ead ID = 429475629ad ID = 4294761983
:Secondary thread ID = 4294764761431
1
:Secondary thread ID = 4294756291
1983
:Secondary thread ID = 4294761983
:Secondary thread ID = 4294756291
```

Listing 11.27 shows how to use a critical section to eliminate concurrency problems.

Listing 11.27   Using Critical Sections

```cpp
#include <windows.h>
#include <iostream>

CRITICAL_SECTION g_cs;

DWORD WINAPI ThreadProc(void * p)
{
  for (int i=0;i<4;i++)
  {
    ::EnterCriticalSection(&g_cs);
    std::cout << ":Secondary thread ID = " << ::GetCurrentThreadId();
    ::LeaveCriticalSection(&g_cs);
  }
  return 0;
}

int main()
{
  ::InitializeCriticalSection(&g_cs);

  std::cout << ":Primary thread ID = " << ::GetCurrentThreadId();
  for (int i=0;i<4;i++)
  {
    DWORD dw;
    HANDLE handle = ::CreateThread(NULL, 0, ThreadProc, NULL, 0, &dw);
    ::CloseHandle(handle);
  }
  ::Sleep(6000);

  ::DeleteCriticalSection(&g_cs);
  return 0;
}
```

Semaphore

Semaphores are used to control access to a resource. Like events, semaphores use the
`WaitForSingleObject()` and `WaitForMultipleObjects()` functions to wait for ownership of the semaphore. As mutexes allow one client access to the controlled resource, semaphores
allow one or more (up to a specified limit) clients access to the controlled resource. Other
Win32 API functions that help you manage semaphores are the following:

`CreateSemaphore()`	Creates a new semaphore
`OpenSemaphore()`	Opens an existing semaphore
`ReleaseSemaphore()`	Releases ownership of the semaphore

Listing 11.28 shows how to use a semaphore to control access to a global variable.

Listing 11.28   Using Semaphores

```cpp
#include <windows.h>
#include <iostream>

CRITICAL_SECTION cs;

DWORD WINAPI ThreadProc(LPVOID pParam )
{
  ::EnterCriticalSection(&cs);
  std::cout << ":Secondary thread ID = "
            << ::GetCurrentThreadId() << std::endl;
  ::LeaveCriticalSection(&cs);
  HANDLE hevent = ::OpenSemaphore(SEMAPHORE_ALL_ACCESS,
  ➥FALSE, "MYSEMAPHORE");

  for (int i=0;i<2;i++)
  {
      ::WaitForSingleObject(hevent, INFINITE);
      static int count = 0;
::EnterCriticalSection(&cs);
      count++;
      std::cout << "I've got the mutex.  Thread = "
            << ::GetCurrentThreadId() << std::endl;
      std::cout << "Threads with mutex = "
            << count << std::endl;
      ::LeaveCriticalSection(&cs);
      ::Sleep(100);
      count—;
      ::ReleaseSemaphore(hevent, 1, NULL);
  }

  ::CloseHandle(hevent);
  return 0;
}

int main()
{
  SECURITY_ATTRIBUTES sa;
  SECURITY_DESCRIPTOR sd;
  sa.nLength = sizeof(SECURITY_ATTRIBUTES);
  sa.bInheritHandle = TRUE;
  sa.lpSecurityDescriptor = &sd;
  if(!::InitializeSecurityDescriptor(&sd,
  ➥SECURITY_DESCRIPTOR_REVISION))
  {
    ::exit (1);
  }
  if(!::SetSecurityDescriptorDacl(&sd, TRUE, (PACL)NULL, FALSE))
```

```
{
  ::exit (1);
}

::InitializeCriticalSection(&cs);

HANDLE hevent = ::CreateSemaphore(&sa, 3, 3, "MYSEMAPHORE");
if (!hevent)
{
    ::exit(1);
}

std::cout << ":Primary thread ID = "
          << ::GetCurrentThreadId() << std::endl;
DWORD dw;
for (int i=0;i<5;i++)
{
    HANDLE handle = ::CreateThread(NULL, 0, ThreadProc, NULL, 0,
                                   &dw);
    ::CloseHandle(handle);
};

::Sleep(4000);
::CloseHandle(hevent);
::DeleteCriticalSection(&cs);

return 0;
}
```

The COM Threading Model

Now that you have a good understanding of the threading models available in Windows NT, I'll explain how these models relate to COM and the standard COM programming tools—Visual Basic and Visual C++.

There is an infinite amount of threading models. What I mean is that you can manipulate the threading until you've invented a new, absolutely useless threading model. I've identified three models that are well defined and very practical. They are the single-threaded, apartment-threaded, and free-threaded models.

Single-Threaded

The *single-threaded model* means that all COM objects are handled by one single-threaded apartment (STA). That means, even if you created dozens of objects from different classes and from different clients, the COM objects from the same process would always execute in the same thread. Listing 11.29 shows sample code for a client that calls a random amount of COM objects and methods.

Listing 11.29   A Sample Client Application to Demonstrate Threading

```
#define _WIN32_WINNT 0x0400

#include <windows.h>
#include <iostream>
#include "comhelpers.h"

#include "server\server.h"
#include "server\server_i.c"

CRITICAL_SECTION cs;

DWORD WINAPI thread(void *)
{
  IUnknown * punknown = 0;
  IMyClass * pmyclass = 0;
  IMyClass * pmyclass2 = 0;
  HRESULT hresult = GetUnknown(L"Server.MyClass.1", &punknown);
  hresult = GetInterface(punknown, IID_IMyClass,
  ➥(IUnknown **)&pmyclass);
  punknown->Release();

  hresult = GetUnknown(L"Server.MyClass.1", &punknown);
  hresult = GetInterface(punknown, IID_IMyClass,
  ➥(IUnknown **)&pmyclass2);
  punknown->Release();

  DWORD dw = GetCurrentThreadId();
  unsigned long ot, op;
  for (int i=0;i<GetTickCount()%3+1;i++)
  {
  hresult = pmyclass->GetProcessAndThreadIDs(&ot, &op);
    ::EnterCriticalSection(&cs);
    std::cout << "#1 " << ot << " " << dw << std::endl;
    ::LeaveCriticalSection(&cs);
  }

  for (i=0;i<GetTickCount()%3+1;i++)
  {
  hresult = pmyclass2->GetProcessAndThreadIDs(&ot, &op);
    ::EnterCriticalSection(&cs);
    std::cout << "#2 " << ot << " " << dw << std::endl;
    ::LeaveCriticalSection(&cs);
  }

  pmyclass->Release();
  pmyclass2->Release();

  return 0;
}

int main()
{
```

```
      ::CoInitializeEx(NULL, COINIT_MULTITHREADED);
      ::InitializeCriticalSection(&cs);

      DWORD dw = 0;
      for (int i=0;i<GetTickCount()%3+2;i++)
      {
      HANDLE handle = CreateThread(NULL, 0, thread, NULL, 0, &dw);
      CloseHandle(handle);
      }

      Sleep(10000);
      ::DeleteCriticalSection(&cs);
      ::CoUninitialize();
      return 0;
}
```

If you ran the code in Listing 11.29 on a single-threaded COM server, every call to the `GetProcessAndThreadIDs()` method would return the same thread ID.

If you are using ATL, AppWizard will always generate your projects to use this threading model by default. To change from this model, you have to change the threading model in the call to the `CoInitialize()` function or change the module class that your server inherits from.

Visual Basic also uses the single-threaded model as its default. If you have any visual components in your Visual Basic project, you can use only the single-threaded model. All Visual Basic projects, except for unattended ActiveX EXE and DLLs, use the single-threaded model.

Apartment-Threaded

The apartment model is a step up from the single-threaded model. In this model, each object is created with a separate single apartment thread (STA).

If you ran the code in Listing 11.29 on an apartment-threaded COM server, every call to the same object would return the same thread ID, but calls to different objects would not necessarily return the same thread ID.

To create an apartment-threaded COM server using ATL, you must inherit from the `CComAutoThreadModule`, in place of the `CComModule` (see Listings 11.30 and 11.31). Also, you must specify in each class whether the object is to use the apartment-threaded model (see Listing 11.32).

Listing 11.30   Changes Required to the Module Declaration

```
// stdafx.h : include file for standard system include files,
//      or project-specific include files that are used
//      frequently, but are changed infrequently

#if !defined(AFX_STDAFX_H)
#define AFX_STDAFX_H

#if _MSC_VER >= 1000
```

continued on next page

continued from previous page

```
        #pragma once
        #endif // _MSC_VER >= 1000

        #define STRICT


        #define _WIN32_WINNT 0x0400
        //#define _ATL_SINGLE_THREADED
        //#define _ATL_APARTMENT_THREADED
        #define _ATL_FREE_THREADED


        #include <atlbase.h>
        //You may derive a class from CComModule and use it if you
        //want to override something, but do not change the name of
        //_Module

        class CExeModule : public
          CComAutoThreadModule<CComSimpleThreadAllocator>
        //class CExeModule : public CComModule
        {
        public:
          LONG Unlock();
          DWORD dwThreadID;
        };
        extern CExeModule _Module;
        #include <atlcom.h>

        //{{AFX_INSERT_LOCATION}}
        // Microsoft Developer Studio will insert additional
        // declarations immediately before the previous line.

        #endif // !defined(AFX_STDAFX_H)
```

The changes in the stdafx.h file that are required in order to take advantage of the apartment-threaded model are the following:

- You must define either **_ATL_APARTMENT_THREADED** or **_ATL_FREE_ THREADED** to ensure proper concurrency of global objects.

- You must inherit your **CExeModule** (module) class from the **CComAutoThreadModule** class.

The **CComAutoThreadModule** class maintains a thread pool (actually, it's an apartment pool) that can be used by class factory objects to create COM objects in more than one thread (apartment).

Listing 11.31   Changes Required to the Module Definition

```
        // server.cpp : Implementation of WinMain


        // Note: Proxy/Stub Information
```

```
//    To build a separate proxy/stub DLL,
//    run nmake -f serverps.mk in the project directory.

#include "stdafx.h"
#include "resource.h"
#include "initguid.h"
#include "server.h"

#include "server_i.c"
#include "MyClass.h"


LONG CExeModule::Unlock()
{
   LONG l = CComAutoThreadModule<CComSimpleThreadAllocator>
              ::Unlock( );
//   LONG l = CComModule::Unlock();
  if (l == 0)
  {
#if _WIN32_WINNT >= 0x0400
    if (CoSuspendClassObjects() == S_OK)
      PostThreadMessage(dwThreadID, WM_QUIT, 0, 0);
#else
    PostThreadMessage(dwThreadID, WM_QUIT, 0, 0);
#endif
  }
  return l;
}

CExeModule _Module;

BEGIN_OBJECT_MAP(ObjectMap)
  OBJECT_ENTRY(CLSID_MyClass, MyClass)
END_OBJECT_MAP()


LPCTSTR FindOneOf(LPCTSTR p1, LPCTSTR p2)
{
  while (*p1 != NULL)
  {
    LPCTSTR p = p2;
    while (*p != NULL)
    {
      if (*p1 == *p++)
        return p1+1;
    }
    p1++;
  }
  return NULL;
}

//////////////////////////////////////////////////////////////
//
```

continued on next page

continued from previous page

```
extern "C" int WINAPI _tWinMain(HINSTANCE hInstance,
  HINSTANCE /*hPrevInstance*/, LPTSTR lpCmdLine,
  int /*nShowCmd*/)
{
//this line necessary for _ATL_MIN_CRT
  lpCmdLine = GetCommandLine();
  HRESULT hRes = CoInitialize(NULL);
//  If you are running on NT 4.0 or higher, you can use the
//  following call, instead, to make the EXE free-threaded.
//  This means that calls come in on a random RPC thread
//   HRESULT hRes = CoInitializeEx(NULL, COINIT_MULTITHREADED);
  _ASSERTE(SUCCEEDED(hRes));
  _Module.Init(ObjectMap, hInstance);
  _Module.dwThreadID = GetCurrentThreadId();
  TCHAR szTokens[] = _T("-/");

  int nRet = 0;
  BOOL bRun = TRUE;
  LPCTSTR lpszToken = FindOneOf(lpCmdLine, szTokens);
  while (lpszToken != NULL)
  {
    if (lstrcmpi(lpszToken, _T("UnregServer"))==0)
    {
      _Module.UpdateRegistryFromResource(IDR_Server, FALSE);
      nRet = _Module.UnregisterServer();
      bRun = FALSE;
      break;
    }
    if (lstrcmpi(lpszToken, _T("RegServer"))==0)
    {
      _Module.UpdateRegistryFromResource(IDR_Server, TRUE);
      nRet = _Module.RegisterServer(TRUE);
      bRun = FALSE;
      break;
    }
    lpszToken = FindOneOf(lpszToken, szTokens);
  }

  if (bRun)
  {
    hRes = _Module.RegisterClassObjects(CLSCTX_LOCAL_SERVER,
      REGCLS_MULTIPLEUSE);
    _ASSERTE(SUCCEEDED(hRes));

    MSG msg;
    while (GetMessage(&msg, 0, 0, 0))
      DispatchMessage(&msg);

    _Module.RevokeClassObjects();
  }

  CoUninitialize();
  return nRet;
}
```

One change is required to your class definition; you must call the `CComAutoThreadModule::Unlock()` method in place of the `CComModule::Unlock()` method, as in Listing 11.32.

Listing 11.32   *Changes Required to the Class Declaration*

```
// MyClass.h: Definition of the MyClass class
//
/////////////////////////////////////////////////////////////////

#if
!defined(AFX_MYCLASS_H)
#define AFX_MYCLASS_H

#if _MSC_VER >= 1000
#pragma once
#endif // _MSC_VER >= 1000

#include "resource.h"        // main symbols

/////////////////////////////////////////////////////////////////
// MyClass

class MyClass :
  public CComDualImpl<IMyClass, &IID_IMyClass,
                      &LIBID_SERVERLib>,
  public ISupportErrorInfo,
  public CComObjectRoot,
  public CComCoClass<MyClass,&CLSID_MyClass>
{
public:
  MyClass();
BEGIN_COM_MAP(MyClass)
  COM_INTERFACE_ENTRY(IDispatch)
  COM_INTERFACE_ENTRY(IMyClass)
  COM_INTERFACE_ENTRY(ISupportErrorInfo)
END_COM_MAP()
//DECLARE_NOT_AGGREGATABLE(MyClass)
// Remove the comment from the line above if you don't want
// your object to support aggregation.

DECLARE_CLASSFACTORY_AUTO_THREAD()
DECLARE_REGISTRY_RESOURCEID(IDR_MyClass)
// ISupportsErrorInfo
  STDMETHOD(InterfaceSupportsErrorInfo)(REFIID riid);

// IMyClass
public:
  STDMETHOD(WaitForAMinute)();
  STDMETHOD(GetProcessAndThreadIDs)(unsigned long * pct,
                                    unsigned long * pcp);
```

continued on next page

continued from previous page

```
};

#endif //
!defined(AFX_MYCLASS_H)
```

One more change is required to each COM class definition that you want to participate in the apartment model. You must add the `DECLARE_CLASSFACTORY_AUTO_THREAD()` macro to your class definition; otherwise, the class will be single-threaded. This macro tells the class factory to take advantage of the module's thread pool (apartment pool) to create objects in separate threads (apartments).

Visual Basic enables you to use the apartment model for unattended EXE and DLL projects, which have no visual components. If your project has no visual components, you would be able to check Unattended Execution.

Free-Threaded

Free-threaded is the top-of-the-line threading model of COM objects. This model allows incoming COM calls to use any random thread. This has the advantage that objects can have multiple threads accessing their logic at the same time; that is, they are running in a multithreaded apartment (MTA). The disadvantage is that concurrency problems might arise that require programmers to take special precautions to make their COM classes thread-safe.

If you ran the code in Listing 11.29 on a free-threaded COM server, each call would not necessarily return the same thread ID. Each call would use a random thread, no matter the object instance. From this example, you should see at least one instance in which two threads are accessing the same object.

To create a free-threaded COM object by using ATL, you have to make a couple of changes to the generated code. You must define the `_ATL_FREE_THREADED` to ensure proper concurrency of COM classes, and you must use `CoInitializeEx(NULL, COINIT_MULTITHREADED)` in place of `CoInitialize()` to initialize your server's first apartment.

By defining `_ATL_FREE_THREADED`, your ATL classes inherit code from the `CComObjectRootEx<>` class that is thread-safe. ATL also defines a critical section member variable for your ATL class to help you remove those concurrency problems.

Calling the `CoInitializeEx(NULL, COINIT_MULTITHREADED)` function tells COM to initialize a new multithreaded apartment (an MTA apartment). Normally, you would call the `CoInitialize()` function, which would initialize a new single-threaded apartment (an STA apartment).

Unfortunately, Visual Basic doesn't support free threading. This is somewhat of an advantage because Visual Basic programmers do not have to concern themselves with concurrency problems. This is a real disadvantage because performance in the application suffers when using global single-use objects.

Summary

In this chapter, you have learned the history of threading models in Microsoft's line of operating system, the different threading models available to the programmer, how to use synchronization objects to make your objects thread-safe, and the different COM threading models and how they relate to ATL and Visual Basic.

CHAPTER 12

AUTOMATION UNVEILED

In this chapter, you will learn about the following:

- Automation and events support
- Automation support in MFC

- Automation support in ATL
- Special-meaning DispIDs

A utomation is defined in the glossary of Visual C++ as follows: "A way to manipulate an application's objects from outside the application. Automation is typically used to create applications that expose objects to programming tools and macro languages, create and manipulate one application's objects from another application's, or to create tools for accessing and manipulating objects."

In the early days of OLE (*object linking and embedding*), Automation was the technology to expose an application's object model for client programs to use. In other words, Automation provided other applications with capability to interact with an object as a user might interact with it through UI. The main reason for automation was to make it easy for scripting tool builders and macro language implementations to drive any object. Even pre–version 5 Visual Basic programs that needed to talk to objects required that the objects have automation support.

Put yourself in the shoes of the tool builder for a moment and imagine that you have to build a tool that can access any component. How can you write the under-the-covers object access to any existing and future interfaces? What if these custom interfaces define new data types? How will you access data and methods on an object without pointers that are not supported in Visual Basic? It would be much easier if you could write all object access to one standard interface that used only known data types. Enter `IDispatch`—the Automation interface.

Automation Clients (Controllers) and Servers

In Automation, the client program is called the *Automation controller* or *Automation client*, and the application exposing the object model is called the s*erver component* or *Automation server*. The controller creates the server and talks to it through one generic interface, using that interface to provide *all* the server's services. It can do this without needing to know what other interfaces the server supports. However, to use any component, you need to know what interfaces are supported by a component and the declaration for the interface to write the client code to talk to the component to provide the service, don't you?

Perhaps an example would illustrate how this works. Imagine building a system that empowers people with pizza. Imagine that your system has a component that is a Pizza Order Taker. Hungry customers create a `PizzaOrderTaker` component and are concerned only with ordering pizzas.

```
[
  uuid(…),
  interface IPizzaOrderTaker : IUnknown
{
  HRESULT OrderPizza      ();
  HRESULT GetPizzaSize    ([out,retval]PizzaSize *peCurrSize);
  HRESULT SetPizzaSize    ([in]PizzaSize eNewSize);
  HRESULT AddTopping      ([in]Topping eNewTopping,
                          ➥[in]ToppingSize eNewToppingSize);

  .
  .
  .

};
```

You build customer components that bind to the `IPizzaOrderTaker` interface, and they order pizzas 'til they pop or run out of money. The owner is more interested in the Pizza Order Takers as Employees, so you have your Pizza Order Taker components support an `IEmployee` interface.

```
[
  uuid(…),
  helpstring("IEmployee Interface"),
  pointer_default(unique)
]
interface IEmployee : IUnknown
{
  [propget, helpstring("property LastName")]
  ➥ HRESULT Name([out, retval] BSTR *pVal);
  [propput, helpstring("property LastName")]
  ➥HRESULT Name([in] BSTR newVal);
  . more properties
  . and methods
  .
};
```

Everybody is happy. Thanks to your efficient Pizza Order Takers, customers are popping up all over the place, and the boss is happy to treat everyone the way in which bosses always treat employees.

One day, though, one hungry customer happens to think the `PizzaOrderTaker` is cute and wants to ask for his or her name. The sad part of this scenario is that the customer is just a preprogrammed client that has no knowledge of how to ask the ice-breaking question, "What is your name?" You didn't teach the customer component about `IEmployee` interface, and that's where the `Name` property, along with many other interesting attributes about this Pizza Order Taker, is accessed. Your customer doesn't even know that the cute

PizzaOrderTaker has a name, even though the PizzaOrderTaker would be very willing to answer the question, if asked, because he/she implements IEmployee.

The customer component would need to be programmed to QueryInterface for the IEmployee interface. When the customer got the PizzaOrderTaker's IEmployee interface, the customer would have to know at what position in the binary interface the get_Name method was. This special interface knowledge of how to bind to the IEmployee interface and how to access the methods and properties would have to be programmed in very early in the lifecycle of the customer component development. This is called *early binding*.

The PizzaOrderTaker requires the clients to use the vtable interface or use early binding to the custom interfaces, IPizzaOrderTaker and IEmployee. For performance, this is optimal, but you have seen that this is sad for potential customers that don't know about the other interfaces the PizzaOrderTaker supports. If an IEmployee interface existed, your preexisting customer components would never be able to ask for names or any other friendly information.

This story has a happy ending. Automation controller customer components that talk through one generic interface, IDispatch, can access all of an Automation server's functionality through that one interface. You will examine IDispatch in detail, but at the meat of the interface are two very important methods: Invoke and GetIDsOfNames. Invoke is for accessing the functionality of an object. Somewhat analogous to a windows message being handled by a message procedure, Invoke (in the server's implementation) takes a numeric identifier and maps it to a function. GetIDsOfNames is for resolving human-readable and understandable function names to these identifiers, also called dispIDs.

When using IDispatch, the Automation controller is not early bound to the object, as it would be if it used a custom interface, but waits until runtime to ask GetIDsOfNames for a dispID that resolves a named method or property. Armed with the right dispID, the Automation controller invokes the function. Now, even a client written in Visual Basic or another simple language that supports Automation, is able to access the server's functionality.

Internally, the Automation server's Invoke implementation validates the dispID and unpacks the parameters coming in on the client's call to Invoke. Then Invoke calls the correct function that maps to that dispID. That function would validate the input parameters, do its work, and return to Invoke. Invoke will pack up the return values and the result and then return back to the calling Automation controller.

The simplest of implementations of an Automation controller could take a script like this:

```
Dim MyFriend As Object
Set MyFriend = CreateObject("FriendlyOrderTaker.FriendlyOrderTaker")

Text1.Text = MyFriend.Name
```

and resolve it at runtime to two IDispatch calls on the object, GetIDsOfNames, which returns the dispID of the Name function and a call to Invoke with the dispID. The returned value would be stored in the edit box Text property.

Optimized controllers would cache the dispIDs, thus optimizing the calls to Invoke at runtime.

Automation Features

Besides the previously mentioned way of accessing the functionality of an object, Automation provides a way for clients to discover information about the functionality that the object provides through *type info* (`ITypeInfo`) and *type libraries* (`ITypeLib`).

Errors happen, and any good system provides a mechanism for error reporting. Automation specifies an interface called `IErrorInfo`, and objects can advertise that they support `IErrorInfo` by implementing an interface called `ISupportErrorInfo`.

Many programming projects require data structures and objects that are collections, and Automation has a specification named `IEnumVARIANT`. Automation objects that are collection objects would support this interface. Controllers could get this `IEnumVARIANT` interface from a known, reserved dispID, `DISPID_NEWENUM` (also named `_NewEnum`). A client using this interface is not required to know the type of elements in this collection, because it's a collection of `VARIANT`s.

ITypeInfo and ITypeLib

Type libraries are very useful to Automation clients and servers. Clients need information about a server's methods and properties if the server is to be used at all. Clients can access this information through `IDispatch` at runtime, but a type library provides this information without having to instantiate the server. Scripting language authoring tools can use the type library to cache dispIDs during authoring and provide help on the server's methods and parameters while the user is writing her script. Also, languages that support early binding to components can use the type library to resolve method calls on servers to the `vtbl` custom interface in order to further optimize the use of servers that support a dual interface.

Servers can use the type library to provide an implementation of `IDispatch`. That's right! You don't have to write your own implementation of `IDispatch`; delegate it to the type library methods.

It's easy to create a type library. Use either the MIDL tool or the `MkTypeLib` tool, depending on whether you have described your object in IDL or ODL.

Here are a few of the most helpful methods Automation clients and servers would use on the `ITypeInfo` and `ITypeLib` interfaces:

- `ITypeInfo::GetNames`—Method and property names and parameters. Retrieves the variable with the specified member ID (or the name of the property or method and its parameters) that corresponds to the specified function ID.

- `ITypeInfo::GetIDsOfNames`—Finds the dispIDs and parameter IDs for a method name and a set of parameter names.

- `ITypeInfo::GetContainingTypeLib`—Accesses the containing type library and retrieves the index of the type description within that type library.

- `ITypeInfo::GetDocumentation`—Retrieves `helpstring` for a method or the object itself, or the name of the help file and the Help Context for the method within the `helpfile`.

- `ITypeInfo::Invoke`—Invokes a method on an instance of an object of the type referred to by this type description.

- `ITypeLib::FindName`—Finds out whether a particular `Name` exists in a type library. This could be a name of a method, property, or variable. If it does exist, `ITypeLib::FindName` will return an `ITypeInfo` pointer to the type description(s) that contain the `Name` found in the type library.

- `ITypeLib::GetDocumentation`—Retrieves `helpstring` for a type description or the type library itself, or the name of the help file and the Help Context for the type description within the `helpfile`.

- `ITypeLib::GetTypeInfoCount`—Retrieves a count of the type descriptions in a type library.

- `ITypeLib::GetTypeInfo`—Retrieves a type description from a type library.

- `ITypeLib::GetTypeInfoOfGuid`—Retrieves a type description from a type library for a particular GUID.

- `ITypeLib::IsName`—Finds out quickly whether a name exists and if so, whether as a type description or a member of a type in the type library.

- `ITypeLib::GetTypeInfoType`—Retrieves the type of the type description. Here are the different kinds of types a type description could be:

```
typedef enum tagTYPEKIND {
TKIND_ENUM = 0 ,
TKIND_RECORD ,
TKIND_MODULE ,
TKIND_INTERFACE ,
TKIND_DISPATCH ,
TKIND_COCLASS ,
TKIND_ALIAS ,
TKIND_UNION ,
TKIND_MAX
    } TYPEKIND;

interface ITypeInfo : IUnknown
{
    typedef [unique] ITypeInfo * LPTYPEINFO;

    [local]HRESULT GetTypeAttr([out] TYPEATTR ** ppTypeAttr);

    [call_as(GetTypeAttr)]HRESULT RemoteGetTypeAttr([out]
➥LPTYPEATTR * ppTypeAttr,
                                [out] CLEANLOCALSTORAGE * pDummy);

    HRESULT GetTypeComp([out] ITypeComp ** ppTComp);

    [local]HRESULT GetFuncDesc([in] UINT index, [out]
➥FUNCDESC ** ppFuncDesc);
```

```
[call_as(GetFuncDesc)]HRESULT RemoteGetFuncDesc([in]
➥UINT index, [out] LPFUNCDESC * ppFuncDesc,
                        [out] CLEANLOCALSTORAGE * pDummy);

[local]HRESULT GetVarDesc([in] UINT index,[out]
➥VARDESC ** ppVarDesc);

[call_as(GetVarDesc)]HRESULT RemoteGetVarDesc([in]
➥UINT index, [out] LPVARDESC * ppVarDesc,
                        [out] CLEANLOCALSTORAGE * pDummy);

[local]HRESULT GetNames([in] MEMBERID memid,
➥[out,size_is(cMaxNames),length_is(*pcNames)]
➥BSTR * rgBstrNames,
                [in] UINT cMaxNames, [out] UINT * pcNames);

[call_as(GetNames)]HRESULT RemoteGetNames([in]
➥MEMBERID memid,
                        [out,size_is(cMaxNames),
                        ➥length_is(*pcNames)]
                        ➥BSTR * rgBstrNames,
                            [in] UINT cMaxNames,
                            ➥[out] UINT * pcNames);

HRESULT GetRefTypeOfImplType([in] UINT index,
➥[out] HREFTYPE * pRefType);

HRESULT GetImplTypeFlags([in] UINT index, [out]
➥INT * pImplTypeFlags);

HRESULT GetIDsOfNames([in, size_is(cNames)]
➥LPOLESTR * rgszNames, [in] UINT cNames,
                        [out, size_is(cNames)]
                        ➥MEMBERID * pMemId);

[local]HRESULT Invoke([in] PVOID pvInstance, [in]
➥MEMBERID memid, [in] WORD wFlags,
                        [in, out] DISPPARAMS *
                        ➥pDispParams, [out]
                        ➥VARIANT * pVarResult,
                        [out] EXCEPINFO * pExcepInfo,
                        ➥[out] UINT * puArgErr);

[call_as(Invoke)]HRESULT RemoteInvoke ([in]
➥IUnknown * pIUnk, [in] MEMBERID memid,
➥ [in] DWORD dwFlags,
                        [in] DISPPARAMS * pDispParams,
                        ➥[out] VARIANT * pVarResult,
                        [out] EXCEPINFO * pExcepInfo,
                        ➥[out] UINT * pArgErr,
                        ➥[in] UINT cVarRef,
                        [in, size_is(cVarRef)]
                        ➥UINT * rgVarRefIdx,
                        [in, out, size_is(cVarRef)]
                        ➥VARIANTARG * rgVarRef);
```

```
[local]HRESULT GetDocumentation([in] MEMBERID memid,
➡[out] BSTR * pBstrName,
➡[out] BSTR * pBstrDocString,
                    [out] DWORD * pdwHelpContext,
                    ➡[out] BSTR * pBstrHelpFile);

[call_as(GetDocumentation)]HRESULT RemoteGetDocumentation
➡([in] MEMBERID memid, [in] DWORD refPtrFlags,
                    [out] BSTR * pBstrName,
                    ➡[out] BSTR * pBstrDocString,
                    [out] DWORD * pdwHelpContext,
                    ➡[out] BSTR * pBstrHelpFile);

[local]HRESULT GetDllEntry([in] MEMBERID memid,
➡[in] INVOKEKIND invKind, [out] BSTR * pBstrDllName,
                    [out] BSTR * pBstrName,
                    ➡[out] WORD * pwOrdinal);

[call_as(GetDllEntry)]HRESULT RemoteGetDllEntry(
➡[in] MEMBERID memid, [in] INVOKEKIND invKind,
                    [in] DWORD refPtrFlags,
                    ➡[out] BSTR * pBstrDllName,
                    ➡[out] BSTR * pBstrName,
                    [out] WORD * pwOrdinal);

HRESULT GetRefTypeInfo([in] HREFTYPE hRefType,
➡[out] ITypeInfo ** ppTInfo);

[local]HRESULT AddressOfMember([in] MEMBERID memid,
➡[in] INVOKEKIND invKind, [out] PVOID * ppv);

[call_as(AddressOfMember)]HRESULT
➡LocalAddressOfMember(void);

[local]HRESULT CreateInstance([in] IUnknown * pUnkOuter,
➡[in] REFIID riid,
➡[out, iid_is(riid)] PVOID * ppvObj);

[call_as(CreateInstance)]HRESULT RemoteCreateInstance(
➡[in] REFIID riid,
                    [out, iid_is(riid)]
                    ➡IUnknown ** ppvObj);

HRESULT GetMops([in] MEMBERID memid,
➡[out] BSTR * pBstrMops);

[local]HRESULT GetContainingTypeLib([out] ITypeLib **
➡ppTLib, [out] UINT * pIndex);

[call_as(GetContainingTypeLib)]HRESULT
➡RemoteGetContainingTypeLib(
➡[out] ITypeLib ** ppTLib,
                    [out] UINT * pIndex);
```

```
            [local]void ReleaseTypeAttr([in] TYPEATTR * pTypeAttr);

            [call_as(ReleaseTypeAttr)]
            ➥HRESULT LocalReleaseTypeAttr(void);

            [local]void ReleaseFuncDesc([in] FUNCDESC * pFuncDesc);

            [call_as(ReleaseFuncDesc)]
            ➥HRESULT LocalReleaseFuncDesc(void);

            [local]void ReleaseVarDesc([in] VARDESC * pVarDesc);

            [call_as(ReleaseVarDesc)]
            ➥HRESULT LocalReleaseVarDesc(void);
        }
```

IErrorInfo, ICreateErrorInfo, and ISupportErrorInfo

Automation specifies a rich error-reporting infrastructure. It's up to each Automation server to implement the error reporting and advertise that it supports the error reporting. Languages and controllers that use `IDispatch` interfaces are aware of this error-reporting specification and are built to use it. Therefore, it's highly recommended that you add this support to your Automation servers.

To implement error reporting in the Automation server, the `ISupportErrorInfo` interface must be implemented by the server. `ICreateErrorInfo` and `IErrorInfo` are implemented by an error object supplied to you from the operating system. Here are the steps you need to perform in order to report an error to a controller.

To get your very own error object from the operating system, you would call the API function `CreateErrorInfo`. When you get an error object from the operating system, it is empty and uninteresting. It's up to you to fill it full of useful and interesting information about the error that occurred. To do this, talk to the error object through its `ICreateErrorInfo` interface. Through `ICreateErrorInfo`, you can set a text description of the error, set a path to the help file and a help context (if you have implemented those), set the GUID for the interface that defines the error, and set the ProgID of the interface that returns the error.

After filling the error object full of helpful and interesting information, politely ask it (`QueryInterface`) for its `IErrorInfo` interface and call `SetErrorInfo`, passing the `IErrorInfo` pointer you retrieved.

The call to `SetErrorInfo` sets the error object as the current error object for the current thread of execution. You can now return the `HRESULT` to the caller.

Caution

SetErrorInfo will release the previous error object for this thread of execution, if there was one. Sorry, there is no chaining of error objects through IErrorInfo. Component systems typically have many interactions between components, and an error could happen at any layer. IErrorInfo is very limited when trying to implement an intelligent, accurate report of the errors that could occur as a thread of execution moves through these layers. It's a generic way to report "a single" error, the last one, to a caller. As a generic mechanism, it can be used by generic controllers. If you must chain error objects, you will have to design your own and realize that generic controllers will not be prepared to utilize the extended error reporting you implement.

When the Automation controller receives the bad `HRESULT`, it will ask the server for its `ISupportErrorInfo` interface. It will ask the `ISupportErrorInfo` interface whether it supports errors for a particular IID (*Interface Identifier*—a GUID). Then call `GetErrorInfo` to retrieve the current error object, which returns the `IErrorInfo` interface to the error object. The controller can use this `IErrorInfo` interface to retrieve all the useful and interesting information you filled in when the error occurred.

IEnumVARIANT

Quite often in programming, you must present a list of data to a user or an array of values, as in a spreadsheet. The structures used to organize these collections of data are either native to the programming language or defined by the programmer. You define your structure in code and access it in code from the various parts of the program that must present the data to the user.

COM is not a programming language, but the need for collections of data, both simple and complex, doesn't go away. In recognition of this real-life need, a very generic interface was defined for iterating over collections. When this interface was published and used by a very popular programming tool, Visual Basic, many commercial software products were built to ask *server objects*—which represent collections of data or collections of other objects—for the `IEnumVARIANT` interface.

The Visual Basic `For...Each...Next` syntax uses the `IEnumVARIANT` interface on collection objects. The Visual Basic syntax enormously simplifies the access to collection objects, hiding all the COM semantics from the programmer.

```
For Each vbl In CollectionObject
    List1.AddItem (vbl)
Next
```

To see what is happening under the covers of the preceding three lines of Visual Basic code, try to access the same collection object from C++. In the C++ controller, you would have to do at least the following:

```
IEnumVARIANT * pi = reinterpret_cast<IEnumVARIANT * >
➥(m_CollectionObject->get__NewEnum ( ));
if (pi)
{
    VARIANT val;
    VariantInit(&val);
    HRESULT hr = 0;
    unsigned long cFetch = 1;
    CString sz;
    do
    {
```

```
     hr =pi->Next((unsigned long)1, &val, &cFetch);
     if (FAILED(hr))
         break;
     if (cFetch)
     {
         switch(V_VT(&val))
         {
         case VT_BSTR:
             sz = V_BSTR(&val);
             m_lbCtrl.AddString(sz);
             break;
         case VT_UNKNOWN:
             m_lbCtrl.AddString("Unknown Object");
             break;
         case VT_DISPATCH:
             m_lbCtrl.AddString("Unknown Object");
             break;
         default:
             m_lbCtrl.AddString("??????");
         }
         VariantClear(&val);
     }
 }while (cFetch);
}
pi->Release();
```

Nearly 30 lines of code in a C++ controller are needed to approach the functionality provided in Visual Basic. As an exercise to pursue on your own, I'll leave it to you to add **case** statements to handle other possible variant data types before the **default** statement.

Note that the first line of code in the second example is bound to the object's custom interface and uses the **get__NewEnum(...)** method. If the controller were using the late-bound **IDispatch** interface on the server object, it would have invoked the dispID **DISPID_NEWENUM**, which is a reserved dispID. This reserved dispID makes it possible to build generic controllers that can get the **IEnumVARIANT** interface on any collection object. **DISPID_NEWENUM** is defined as follows:

```
#define   DISPID_NEWENUM    ( -4 )
```

To implement the collection on the server side, you have your choices. If there are not too many and the number of elements is known, the simplest way to implement the **get__NewEnum** method would be to use the ATL-supplied template class **CComEnum**—for example,

```
typedef CComEnum<IEnumVARIANT, &IID_IEnumVARIANT, VARIANT,
    _Copy<VARIANT> > CComEnumVariant;
```

If you are using MFC, no built-in class exists to implement **IEnumVARIANT**. However, there is a good example in an MFC sample—**INPROC**. It has a class named **CEnumVARIANT** that supports **IEnumVARIANT**. A copy of **CEnumVARIANT** is in this chapter's code directory on the accompanying CD-ROM.

If the collection is very large or expensive to build, you might want to be lazy about retrieving the elements until the controller asks for the next element. After all, if you have 10,000 elements in a collection and the client is interested only in the first 25, it would be rude to make the client wait while you build a data structure with 10,000 elements.

The IEnumVARIANT interface is set in stone. There are no methods to traverse to previous elements in the collection, go to the last element, add or remove elements, or go to an element by index or name. In cases like these, you must design your own classes that support IEnumVARIANT and a custom interface with this additional functionality.

Automation Data Types

Automation has restrictions on the types of data that can be passed between controllers and servers. The problem is that the Automation server and the client that interacts between them via IDispatch have only one pair of proxy/stubs. The server knows well how to marshal data passed by methods of IDispatch, but it doesn't know anything about data passed by the methods of other interfaces called through Invoke. Therefore, a set of types that are always supported were chosen. This restriction solves two problems:

- Data in parameters that needs to be marshaled between client and server.

- Automation clients that must program to a set of known data types. Automation clients are most often a scripting language, and when distributed, their implementation cannot change. They must program to a set of known data types. Table 12.1 shows the supported types.

Table 12.1   Supported Data Types

Type	Description
Boolean	An unsigned char indicating TRUE or FALSE.
char	A data item of 8 bits. By default, char is unsigned char.
double	A 64-bit floating point number.
int	The size of an int varies between platforms. On a 32-bit platform, an int is a 32-bit integer, and on 16-bit platforms, an int is 16 bits. On 16-bit platforms, use a type specifier, short, long, or small, to explicitly state the size of the data item. By default, an int is signed.
float	A 32-bit floating point number.
long	A 32-bit integer. By default, long is signed.
short	A 16-bit integer. By default, short is signed.
void	Indicates a procedure with no arguments.
wchar_t	A wide-character type (unsigned short). If you use wchar_t to indicate a string, use the string attribute.
BSTR	A length-prefixed string.

continued on next page

continued from previous page

Type	Description
CURRENCY	An 8-byte, two's complement integer useful for representing money values.
DATE	A `double` value (an 8-byte floating point number).
HRESULT	A `long` value returned from a function call to an interface to describe a result. It's composed of a severity code, context information, a facility code, and a status code.
LPWSTR	A pointer to a null-terminated wide-character (`wchar_t`) string.
LPSTR	A pointer to a null-terminated character (`char`) string.
SCODE	A `DWORD` (`long`) value used on 16-bit systems to indicate a result of a call to an interface or API call.
VARIANT	A 16-byte discriminated union that can be used to pass any of the legal Automation data types.
IDispatch*	A pointer to an object that supports the `IDispatch` interface.
IUnknown*	A pointer to an object that supports the `IUnknown` interface.

As you can see, building an object that supports Automation is very restrictive, and the decision of whether to support Automation controllers must be made before designing the interfaces for your object. For example, how would you define and pass your own structures, as you can with custom interfaces? There is only one provision: The **VARIANT** data type enables you to pass a structure, again, within limits.

A **VARIANT** has two important members: a union that can contain any Automation-compatible type of data and a member that indicates what type of data is contained in the union. As mentioned previously, you can also enclose a custom-defined structure in a **VARIANT** by packaging the structure in a **SAFEARRAY** and placing it at the **parray** member.

```
/* VARIANT STRUCTURE
 *
 *   VARTYPE vt;
 *   WORD wReserved1;
 *   WORD wReserved2;
 *   WORD wReserved3;
 *   union {
 *      LONG            VT_I4
 *      BYTE            VT_UI1
 *      SHORT           VT_I2
 *      FLOAT           VT_R4
 *      DOUBLE          VT_R8
 *      VARIANT_BOOL    VT_BOOL
 *      SCODE           VT_ERROR
 *      CY              VT_CY
 *      DATE            VT_DATE
 *      BSTR            VT_BSTR
 *      IUnknown *      VT_UNKNOWN
 *      IDispatch *     VT_DISPATCH
 *      SAFEARRAY *     VT_ARRAY
 *      BYTE *          VT_BYREF¦VT_UI1
 *      SHORT *         VT_BYREF¦VT_I2
```

```
 *     LONG *          VT_BYREF|VT_I4
 *     FLOAT *         VT_BYREF|VT_R4
 *     DOUBLE *        VT_BYREF|VT_R8
 *     VARIANT_BOOL *  VT_BYREF|VT_BOOL
 *     SCODE *         VT_BYREF|VT_ERROR
 *     CY *            VT_BYREF|VT_CY
 *     DATE *          VT_BYREF|VT_DATE
 *     BSTR *          VT_BYREF|VT_BSTR
 *     IUnknown **     VT_BYREF|VT_UNKNOWN
 *     IDispatch **    VT_BYREF|VT_DISPATCH
 *     SAFEARRAY **    VT_BYREF|VT_ARRAY
 *     VARIANT *       VT_BYREF|VT_VARIANT
 *     PVOID           VT_BYREF (Generic ByRef)
 *     CHAR            VT_I1
 *     USHORT          VT_UI2
 *     ULONG           VT_UI4
 *     INT             VT_INT
 *     UINT            VT_UINT
 *     DECIMAL *       VT_BYREF|VT_DECIMAL
 *     CHAR *          VT_BYREF|VT_I1
 *     USHORT *        VT_BYREF|VT_UI2
 *     ULONG *         VT_BYREF|VT_UI4
 *     INT *           VT_BYREF|VT_INT
 *     UINT *          VT_BYREF|VT_UINT
 *  }
 */
struct  tagVARIANT
    {
    union
        {
        struct  __tagVARIANT
            {
            VARTYPE vt;
            WORD wReserved1;
            WORD wReserved2;
            WORD wReserved3;
            union
                {
                LONG lVal;
                BYTE bVal;
                SHORT iVal;
                FLOAT fltVal;
                DOUBLE dblVal;
                VARIANT_BOOL boolVal;
                _VARIANT_BOOL bool;
                 SCODE scode;
                CY cyVal;
                DATE date;
                BSTR bstrVal;
                IUnknown __RPC_FAR *punkVal;
                IDispatch __RPC_FAR *pdispVal;
                SAFEARRAY __RPC_FAR *parray;
                BYTE __RPC_FAR *pbVal;
```

```
              SHORT __RPC_FAR *piVal;
              LONG __RPC_FAR *plVal;
              FLOAT __RPC_FAR *pfltVal;
              DOUBLE __RPC_FAR *pdblVal;
              VARIANT_BOOL __RPC_FAR *pboolVal;
             _VARIANT_BOOL __RPC_FAR *pbool;
              SCODE __RPC_FAR *pscode;
              CY __RPC_FAR *pcyVal;
              DATE __RPC_FAR *pdate;
              BSTR __RPC_FAR *pbstrVal;
              IUnknown __RPC_FAR *__RPC_FAR *ppunkVal;
              IDispatch __RPC_FAR *__RPC_FAR *ppdispVal;
              SAFEARRAY __RPC_FAR *__RPC_FAR *pparray;
              VARIANT __RPC_FAR *pvarVal;
              PVOID byref;
              CHAR cVal;
              USHORT uiVal;
              ULONG ulVal;
              INT intVal;
              UINT uintVal;
              DECIMAL __RPC_FAR *pdecVal;
              CHAR __RPC_FAR *pcVal;
              USHORT __RPC_FAR *puiVal;
              ULONG __RPC_FAR *pulVal;
              INT __RPC_FAR *pintVal;
              UINT __RPC_FAR *puintVal;
              } __VARIANT_NAME_3;
          } __VARIANT_NAME_2;
      DECIMAL decVal;
      } __VARIANT_NAME_1;
};
```

The COM API defines many functions and macros for dealing with **VARIANT**s, and even better, the VC++ compiler has much friendlier support with the **_variant_t** class. It's strongly recommended to use these functions and macros for forward compatibility.

There is an interface that can describe what functionality exists and how to access each of the methods, and it can provide a mechanism to access the methods of any server that supports this one interface.

How can one interface possibly describe all the future properties and methods for every Automation server that anyone in the world could dream up? That would have to be one extensible interface! Take a look at the **IDispatch** interface:

```
interface IDispatch : IUnknown{

HRESULT GetTypeInfoCount( unsigned int FAR* pctinfo );
HRESULT GetTypeInfo      ( unsigned int iTInfo,
                           LCID lcid,
                           ITypeInfo FAR* FAR* ppTInfo
HRESULT GetIDsOfNames     ( REFIID riid,
                           OLECHAR FAR* FAR* rgszNames,
                           unsigned int cNames,
                           LCID lcid,
```

```
                                DISPID FAR* rgDispId);
HRESULT Invoke                ( DISPID dispIdMember,
                                REFIID riid,
                                LCID lcid,
                                WORD wFlags,
                                DISPPARAMS FAR* pDispParams,
                                VARIANT FAR* pVarResult,
                                EXCEPINFO FAR* pExcepInfo,
                                unsigned int FAR* puArgErr );
```

How would an Automation controller use this interface to access an object model? Also, how could an Automation server expose all its functionality through a predefined interface? To discover the answers, let's examine two of `IDispatch`'s methods in more detail. First, look at the declaration of `GetIDsOfNames`. When controllers have an object, or more accurately, the object's `IUnknown` pointer, they `QueryInterface` for `IDispatch` and call `GetIDsOfNames`, passing a method or property name they are interested in discovering. On the server, the `GetIDsOfNames` implementation fills the caller-allocated parameter `rgDispId` with a dispID that maps to the requested method/property name.

What's a dispID? A *dispID* is a number that identifies a particular method or property on the server object that can be `Invoke`d. The server's methods all have names that can be `Invoke`d only by an ID, a dispatch ID, or a dispID.

The controller asks the server to do some work or return information, calling `Invoke` with the dispID of the method or property it wants to access.

If your controller were actually a scripting tool that hid all this complexity from the programmer, all you would have to do to build the simplest of scripting tools would be to resolve every method call on an object or setting/getting of an object's property to two `IDispatch` methods, `GetIDsOfNames` and `Invoke`. This would be the simplest approach, not the most efficient. As you learn more about Automation, you'll see where efficiencies can be applied.

A little more is involved in calling `Invoke` than just mapping a name to the right dispID. Don't forget all the input and output parameters that the method or property requires. Imagine an object that had a property called `Size`. Is `Size` a numeric value or a string value? The controller needs to know what type of information it will be required to pass in and prepare to receive. That information wasn't available in `GetIDsOfNames`. Well, take a look at the parameters to `Invoke` for a clue to what to do.

`dispIDMember` tells `Invoke` which method the caller is accessing. The next parameter, `riid`, is reserved, and `lcid` is a locale context for multilanguage support, so skip on to the next one. Parameter four, `wFlags`, specifies whether the caller is trying to access a method or a property, and if it is a property, whether it's trying to `get` the value or `put` a new value to the property. Now, for the biggest clue to how to pass the parameters, `pDispParams` points to a structure containing arrays of arguments. Here's the declaration for the structure:

```
typedef struct FARSTRUCT tagDISPPARAMS{
  VARIANTARG FAR* rgvarg;
  DISPID FAR* rgdispidNamedArgs;
  unsigned int cArgs;
  unsigned int cNamedArgs;
} DISPPARAMS;
```

Notice the type of the first member of the `DISPPARAMS` struct—`VARIANTARG`. A `VARIANTARG` is typedef'd as a `VARIANT` in the header files, but semantically, `VARIANTARG` is used for method arguments, and `VARIANT` is used for return values. How do you know what data types to pass? Are there named arguments? Which of the parameters are input and output parameters? If the scripting tool or controller is very simple, it can just try by packing all the parameters into variants in an array. Watch out for this one: A major *gotcha* is the order of parameters in the array. The parameters must be placed in the array in `REVERSE` order, with the last parameter at `rgvarg[0]` and the first parameter at `rgvarg[cArgs-1]`. You still haven't covered named arguments and how a controller could find out about them. Also, your simple controller just guessed about data types, so how do you find out about data types for each of the arguments? For more information about this object, you need to call the other methods on `IDispatch`, `GetTypeInfo`, and `GetTypeInfoCount`.

Building a tool or macro language that only has to know how to use one interface and through that one interface can control any object is powerful. Many companies seized the opportunity and built their own languages and tools that abstract the complexity of interface-based programming. They built the tools to use the `IDispatch` interface of any server and provided a friendly programming syntax. Now that you know what `IDispatch` is, think of all that is going on under the covers inside Visual Basic when you write the following line of VBScript:

```
myOrderNumber = PizzaShop.Order "Pepperoni", "Large"
```

Many CPU cycles are burned up in the client to pack up the arguments, make the call, and unpack the return values. Then the server side has to receive the `Invoke` request, unpack the arguments, route the request to a function inside the server, and repack the return values before returning to the client.

`IDispatch`, the friendly and flexible interface, comes with unavoidable performance costs on every call. For many components, this penalty is too costly. When speed is required, a custom interface is obviously much better than all the `IDispatch` overhead. Wouldn't it be great to have an interface that exposed its functionality through friendly `IDispatch` to scripting tools and interpreted languages and offered the speed of a custom interface to compiled client controllers? Enter dual interfaces.

Dual Interfaces

With dual interfaces, a component can be friendly, flexible, powerful, and fast, offering its functionality through `IDispatch` and a custom interface, which supports VTBL binding, at the same time. This offers the client the choice of using your `IDispatch` interface or binding to the vtable for performance. A component with dual interfaces can be accessed through `IDispatch` from VBScript, but the powerful client written in C++ will not suffer the limitations and lower performance of `IDispatch` accessing it through the virtual table via the custom interface. `dual` is also a keyword in IDL to describe interfaces as supporting both `IDispatch` and VTBL binding. When you mark an interface as `dual`, all the methods and properties in the interface should be accessible through dispIDs, and all parameters should be Automation-compatible types.

When you construct your IDL for a dual interface, you specify it in the interface header.

Now add Automation support to the interfaces defined previously.

```
[
  object,
  uuid(90E43858-4A3A-11D2-AE5E-00E02916DB2F),
  dual,
  helpstring("IFriendlyOrderTaker Interface"),
  pointer_default(unique)
]
interface IFriendlyOrderTaker : IDispatch
{
  [id(1), helpstring("method OrderPizza")]
HRESULT OrderPizza([in]Topping topping, [in]ToppingSize tsize,
➡[in]PizzaSize size);
  [id(2), helpstring("method AddTopping")]
HRESULT AddTopping([in]Topping eNewTopping,
➡[in]ToppingSize eNewToppingSize);
  [propget, id(3), helpstring("property Size")]
HRESULT Size([out, retval] PizzaSize *pVal);
  [propput, id(3), helpstring("property Size")]
HRESULT Size([in] PizzaSize newVal);
  [propget, id(4), helpstring("property Name")]
HRESULT Name([out, retval] BSTR *pVal);
  [propput, id(4), helpstring("property Name")]
HRESULT Name([in] BSTR newVal);
};

  coclass FriendlyOrderTaker
  {
    [default] interface IFriendlyOrderTaker;
    interface IPizzaOrderTaker;
    interface IEmployee;
  };
```

This snippet of IDL shows a new interface that derives from **IDispatch** and supports all the functionality of the **IPizzaOrderTaker** and the **IEmployee** interfaces. The component is described in the last snippet (**coclass**) to support three interfaces:

- **IFriendlyOrderTaker**—Both custom and **IDispatch** interface

- **IPizzaOrderTaker**—Custom interface

- **IEmployee**—Custom interface

By accessing the Friendly Pizza Order Taker through the **IDispatch** interface, friendly Automation controllers can ask for all the services that could ever be envisioned for new and improved Pizza Order Takers as the functionality evolves.

Early bound controllers could take advantage of the performance gains available through using the custom interface **IFriendlyOrderTaker** to access the known functionality published in the custom interface.

Automation and Events Support

If your object is a source of events, be sure that the event source interface is derived from `IDispatch`. If you don't, some controllers will not be able to build sinks for receiving the event notifications your object can send.

Automation Support in MFC

MFC has a great deal of support for building both Automation controllers and servers. For building servers, the `CCmdTarget` class can support `IDispatch`. For building controllers, the `COleDispatchDriver` class is very handy.

To support `IDispatch`, the `CCmdTarget` class relies on a dispatch map. The *dispatch map* contains the external names of your server's methods and properties and the internal member name of the function to map client requests to. Each entry in the map also contains the parameters and return values. The dispatch map must be declared in your header file and defined in your implementation file.

To declare the dispatch map in your class, add the macro `DECLARE_DISPATCH_MAP` at the end of your class declaration. That takes care of the first part. Now add the matching macros, `BEGIN_DISPATCH_MAP` and `END_DISPATCH_MAP` to your class's implementation file. The `BEGIN_DISPATCH_MAP` macro takes two parameters, the name of your class and the name of its base class. Between the `BEGIN_DISPATCH_MAP` and `END_DISPATCH_MAP` macros, describe your class's methods and properties by using the macros `DISP_FUNCTION`, `DISP_PROPERTY`, `DISP_PROPERTY_EX`, and `DISP_PROPERTY_NOTIFY`. That's all there is to it. `CCmdTarget` now knows enough about your class to implement `IDispatch` for you.

To map client requests to your class's internal methods, you supply `DISP_FUNCTION` an external name and internal method name within your class. It also needs to know about the parameters and return values of your method, which are supplied also as parameters to the `DISP_FUNCTION` macro.

`DISP_PROPERTY` maps the methods to get and set properties to a member variable. At times, this default behavior is inadequate.

To give you more control, take a look at `DISP_PROPERTY_EX`. This is handy when a member variable is not desired or when you might want to expose a property as read-only. `DISP_PROPERTY_EX` doesn't rely on a member variable, but on member methods, to get and set the property. You still need to specify the type of the property you are exposing. If you want to make the property read-only, place `SetNotSupported` in the place of the method name normally used to set the property.

If you don't need the control provided by `DISP_PROPERTY_EX`, but need to trigger some other code when a property is reset, use `DISP_PROPERTY_NOTIFY`. `DISP_PROPERTY_NOTIFY` maps `get` and `set` methods to a member variable and notifies you when it has changed value. This is handy when you don't want to implement the `get` and `set` methods, but need to do extra processing based on a property's value.

From the client side, COleDispatchDriver can be used directly or as a base class for a type-safe wrapper to an Automation server's methods and properties. To use COleDispatchDriver as a base class, derive a class from COleDispatchDriver and add methods to access the server's methods and properties.

Inside each of your wrapper methods, you would build an array of parameter types and call COleDispatchDriver::InvokeHelper, passing the values you want packed up on the IDispatch::Invoke call to the server. Here is the declaration for InvokeHelper:

```
InvokeHelper( DISPID dwDispID, WORD wFlags, VARTYPE vtRet,
➥void* pvRet, const BYTE FAR* pbParamInfo, ... );
```

- dwDispID—The displD you want to Invoke on the server.

- wFlags—Specifies whether you are accessing a property (get/set) or a method.

- vtRet—Returns the value's type.

- pvRet—The pointer to the variable to receive the return value.

- pbParamInfo—The pointer to a null-terminated array of bytes containing the types of the parameters to follow.

- ...—The variable list of parameters to pack up on the Invoke call to the server. Each variable in the list should have an entry in pbParamInfo, specifying its type.

As you can begin to appreciate, it could be a tedious, mundane process to build a COleDispatchDriver-derived wrapper for an Automation server by hand. To do any tedious, mundane task, there should be a wizard, and there is. The Visual C++ ClassWizard can generate a wrapper class for you.

Open the ClassWizard and click the button labeled Add_Class. Select the From a Type Library option from the drop-down menu. Browse to, or type, the path or filename of the .dll or .tlb for the server and click Open. The ClassWizard will load the file and show you a list of interfaces described in the type library. You choose the interfaces that you will be accessing and either accept or change the filenames for the wrapper class's header and implementation files. Click the OK button, and you're finished.

When you are in development of the server, at times you will need to add or remove a method or property to an interface or add or change the parameters on an existing method or property. These changes will throw your test program for a loop unless you modify or regenerate your driver classes. If you choose to modify the existing wrapper classes, do so with extreme care, paying close attention to the argument types and order described in BYTE parms, and the displD, arguments and the return type on the InvokeHelper call. If the changes to the server were rather extensive, it would be more efficient to use the ClassWizard to regenerate the driver classes for you. When you use the ClassWizard to regenerate the wrapper classes, delete the out-of-date header and implementation files. Alternatively, use new filenames and drop the out-of-date files from your project.

Automation Support in ATL

Whether building a controller or server in ATL, you have support from the native C++ compiler. If you are building a controller, and the server has a dual interface, the native compiler's smart pointers (classes built from the template class, _com_ptr_t) can be used to drive COM objects. If you are building the server, ATL has an IDispatch implementation that you can use.

The Client (Controller)

The #import directive will instruct the compiler's preprocessor to retrieve the type-lib/typeinfo from a .dll, .exe, or .tlb file and generate wrapper classes (_com_ptr_t smart-pointer classes) to access the server objects. The template class _com_ptr_t is a smart-pointer implementation that encapsulates interface pointers and eliminates the need to call AddRef, Release, and QueryInterface. It also hides the CoCreateInstance call when creating a COM object—for example,

```
#import "c:\win95\system\mshtml.dll" no_namespace
//TODO Under the hood - _com_dispatch_method w/DISPATCH_PROPERTYPUT
➥& DISPATCH_PROPERTYGET
HRESULT __stdcall com_dispatch_propget(IDispatch*, DISPID,
➥VARTYPE, void*) throw(_com_error);
HRESULT __cdecl com_dispatch_propput(IDispatch*, DISPID, VARTYPE, ...)
➥throw(_com_error);
HRESULT __cdecl com_dispatch_method(IDispatch*, DISPID, WORD,
➥VARTYPE, void*, const wchar_t*, ...)
 throw(_com_error);
```

CComDispatchDriver

CComDispatchDriver lets you retrieve or set an object's properties through an IDispatch pointer. Because this is limited in functionality to properties on an object only, this is rarely used. Most often, you'll use _com_dispatch_method, _com_dispatch_propget, and _com_dispatch_propput.

The Server

Adding an implementation for IDispatch to the server is even easier. ATL has a template class, IDispatchImpl, which is an implementation of IDispatch that uses the ITypeInfo interface on your type library. Remember that ITypeInfo has methods on it that can delegate IDispatch calls to an interface? All you have to do is add an IDispatchImpl declaration to your class's base list with a public access specifier and, voilà! Your server can now support simple controllers that want to talk to your object only through IDispatch.

There is one more thing—the IDL. Don't forget to add the **dual** keyword, derive your interface from IDispatch, and add the dispIDs—for example,

```
[
    object,
```

```
      uuid(62668191-51D3-11D2-AE5E-00E02916DB2F),
      dual,
      helpstring("IMyDriver Interface"),
      pointer_default(unique)
]
interface IDriver : IDispatch
{
      [propget, id(1), helpstring("property Width")] HRESULT
      ↪Width([out, retval] long *pVal);
      [propput, id(1), helpstring("property Width")] HRESULT
      ↪Width([in] long newVal);
      [propget, id(2), helpstring("property Height")] HRESULT
      ↪Height([out, retval] long *pVal);
      [propput, id(2), helpstring("property Height")] HRESULT
      ↪Height([in] long newVal);
};
```

Here's the definition of the template class, IDispatchImpl:

```
template< class T, const IID* piid, const GUID* plibid,
↪WORD wMajor = 1, WORD wMinor = 0, class tihclass =
↪CComTypeInfoHolder >
class IDispatchImpl : public T
```

This list should explain the parameters to the template class:

- T—A dual interface.

- piid—A pointer to the IID of T.

- plibid—A pointer to the identifier of T's type library section.

- wMajor—The major version of the type library. The default value is 1.

- wMinor—The minor version of the type library. The default value is 0.

- tihclass—The class used to manage the type information for T. The default value is CComTypeInfoHolder.

IDispatchImpl provides a default implementation for the IDispatch portion of any dual interface on your object. A dual interface derives from IDispatch and uses only Automation-compatible types. Like a dispinterface, a dual interface supports early and late binding; however, a dual interface differs in that it also supports vtable binding.

The following example shows a typical implementation of IDispatchImpl:

```
class CBeeper :
      public IDispatchImpl< IBeeper, &IID_IBeeper,
          &LIBID_BeeperLib >,
      public CComObjectRoot,
      public CComCoClass< CBeeper, &CLSID_Beeper >
{
   ...
};
```

`IDispatchImpl` contains a static member of type `CComTypeInfoHolder` that manages the type information for the dual interface. If you have multiple objects implementing the same dual interface, only a single instance of `CComTypeInfoHolder` will be used.

Special-Meaning DispIDs

All negative dispIDs are reserved, and a few have special meanings and are used by standard controllers. If you want your object to be friendly to the widest audience and the meaning of these special dispIDs to make sense for your object, advertise and implement these special dispIDs:

- `DISPID_UNKNOWN` (-1)—Used by `GetIDsOfNames` to indicate an unknown name.

- `DISPID_VALUE` (0)—Indicates the value property of an object.

- `DISPID_PROPERTYPUT` (-3)—Indicates the param that is the right side (or put value) of a `PropertyPut`.

- `DISPID_NEWENUM` (-4)—The standard `NewEnum` method. Returns a collection object that supports the `IEnumVARIANT` interface.

- `DISPID_EVALUATE` (-5)—The standard evaluate method.

Summary

You are now armed with the knowledge of how to build components that support Automation clients. This is especially important for you in this age of the Internet because many of the tools that use components can talk to components only through the Automation interfaces described here. The following are chapters that you might want to consider reading next:

- Chapter 6, "Using Aggregation to Simulate Inheritance." Learn about aggregation, the primary mechanism used by COM objects for code reuse.

- Chapter 7, "Breaking the Process Boundary Using Local Servers." Keep this chapter in the back of your mind as you read about moving your component from in-process to local servers. Automation support that you learned here will be easy to add to your local servers as well.

- Chapter 8, "Building COM Objects Using the ActiveX Template Library." You have had a taste of ATL in this chapter, so go for a full serving and build your knowledge of this lean, mean component framework.

CHAPTER 13

USING DISTRIBUTED OBJECTS

In this chapter, you will learn about the following:

- Understanding distributed objects with remote object instantiation

- Designing a distributed system

- How to build located objects

- Understanding the function and role of monikers

- How to create COM events and connectable objects

I n some ways, this chapter could be considered the book's climax. Although earlier chapters present useful and important information, this is the chapter that consolidates everything I've discussed so far and puts it to work building a true distributed object application. As you will see, working with distributed objects is not a simple matter of applying an object-oriented design to a problem and then snapping your fingers. Although the DCOM technologies can make the construction of distributed components easy (not quite as easy as snapping your fingers!), after a program design becomes distributed, you must tackle a host of new challenges.

Remote Object Instantiation

When you ask yourself what *distributed COM component* means, several things come to mind. Fundamentally, the DCOM technologies enable you to instantiate objects on remote machines or connect to objects already running remotely. I'll start this chapter by investigating the different ways that you can instantiate objects remotely. Later, in the section titled "Designing the Distributed Object Application," I'll discuss some techniques for connecting to remote objects that have already been instantiated.

What's involved in instantiating a remote object? Actually, quite a lot. Specifically, to create a remote object, the following events have to occur:

1. The client must request the creation of a new object.

2. The COM subsystem must determine that the server hosting the requested component resides on a remote machine.

3. The COM subsystem on the client machine must contact the COM subsystem on the remote server machine and request the launching of the remote server.

4. If the remote COM subsystem determines that the client program has sufficient security privileges and the server (and its stub DLL) is correctly registered on the remote machine, the server can be launched.

5. The remote server can create the new object and return an OBJREF to the client machine. (For a quick discussion of OBJREFs, see Chapter 9, "A Distributed Objects Overview.")

At the beginning of this sequence, you find the ubiquitous client. It is the client, of course, that indicates it wants a new object to be created. As you learned in previous chapters, DCOM-ignorant clients typically use the `CoCreateInstance()` function for this purpose. Although clients can continue to use `CoCreateInstance()`, DCOM introduces the new `CoCreateInstanceEx()` function. I'll explain this new function and discuss its similarities and differences to `CoCreateInstance()` later in the chapter.

I'm going to spend a little time on the second step because how COM determines which machine is hosting a remote server is largely a factor of whether the client in question is using `CoCreateInstanceEx()` or is of the older, DCOM-unaware variety.

Remoting Existing COM Components

The key to using DCOM is found in a concept that you've already heard a lot about: location transparency. COM's proxy-based, marshaled foundation provides a platform perfectly suited to the construction of distributed components. In fact, the COM programming model is so well suited to network distribution that your existing components can be DCOM-enabled without changing a single line of code and without recompiling or relinking.

This is a fascinating capability. Just think, every local server that you've built so far could be turned into a DCOM server in less than five minutes. COM accomplishes this feat easily because proxies know how to bundle up marshaled data and pass it to other processes or other machines. Make no mistake, the actual sequence of events involved in a remote method call is very different from the process of making a local method call, but both client and server code are insulated from these distinctions. By separating remoting functionality into the proxy/stub code and the operating system proper, component developers are spared from having to know where server code is running.

Beware the Temptation of Simple Distribution!

There's no dispute that distributing COM servers that were never designed to run on remote computers is a neat trick. Certainly, on some occasions it makes sense to move COM servers onto remote machines—to take advantage of more powerful processors and more memory, for example. However, the ability to remote older COM objects that were never explicitly designed for distribution is a red herring.

The main reason for this strong statement is that a computer network moves data much, much more slowly than a computer can move data around in memory (in-RAM operations are often measured in microseconds, whereas network messaging typically spans milliseconds). A COM component originally designed to run on a single machine might operate with perfectly acceptable performance when run locally, but might grind to a halt when executed remotely.

DCOM is an empowering technology, but it comes into its own only when you consciously design your systems and components with network distribution in mind. I'll be talking about some of these design considerations later in the chapter.

Transforming an existing COM component into a DCOM component is a matter of modifying the server's configuration information. As you know, component configuration data is stored in the system Registry, so remoting a legacy server involves adding and modifying Registry entries. These entries can be added to the Registry directly, using **REGEDIT** or **REGEDT32**, or you can use one of several other utilities that I'll discuss shortly.

Modifying the Registry

In Chapter 4, "Implementing a COM Client and Server," I discussed the **HKEY_LOCAL_MACHINE\SOFTWARE\Classes\AppID** Registry key. You'll recall that the AppID key is used to group configuration parameters for one or more distributed COM objects into a single centralized Registry location. To help manage the complexity of component configuration, several COM components can share the same AppID entry. Used intelligently, the AppID key simplifies the task of administrating large amounts of security and configuration data.

RemoteServerName is a key that can be found coming off a server's AppID CLSID key. This key tells COM that the specified server can be found on the remote machine named by **RemoteServerName**'s default value. Here's an example.

Suppose you have written a **HotDog** component, which has a CLSID value of **55555555-5555-5555-5555-555555555555**. A component's **HKEY_LOCAL_MACHINE\SOFTWARE\Classes\CLSID** section might look like this:

```
...\CLSID
     \{55555555-5555-5555-5555-555555555555} = "HotDog1 component"
        AppID = "{55555555-5555-5555-5555-555555555555}"
        \LocalServer32 = "C:\COM Servers\HotDog.EXE"
        \ProgID = "HotDog1"
```

As you can see, the fanciful **HotDog** component has an AppID entry with a GUID value that is the same as the component's CLSID. The local version of the **HotDog** component might have an AppID section that looks like so:

```
...\AppID
     \{55555555-5555-5555-5555-555555555555} = "HotDog1"
```

In the case of the COM (nondistributed) **HotDog** component, the AppID section will probably be empty. However, as a DCOM component, the AppID's Spartan digs are about to be livened up a bit. Suppose that you're running TCP/IP on your network and that you want to move the **HotDog** server onto a remote machine known by the logical host-name of oscar.junkfood.com. You can accomplish this in a couple of ways. In the first case, you can add a **RemoteServerName** entry with a value that corresponds to the remote machine name.

```
...\AppID
     \{55555555-5555-5555-5555-555555555555} = "HotDog1"
        \RemoteServerName = "oscar.junkfood.com"
```

Because the network is running TCP/IP, you have the option of either specifying your remote server name by using DNS syntax such as oscar.junkfood.com or using a standard TCP/IP address such as 162.70.122.31. Therefore, the preceding entry could also appear as

```
...\AppID
     \{55555555-5555-5555-5555-555555555555} = "HotDog1"
        \RemoteServerName = "162.70.122.31"
```

Assuming that **162.70.122.31** is the IP address of oscar.junkfood.com, the preceding two **RemoteServerName** entries are identical. Of course, using the DNS name protects you from having to change Registry entries if the remote machine changes its IP address.

DNS and IP are not the only name formats supported by DCOM. You can also specify a remote machine name by using the Universal Naming Convention (UNC). For example, if you're connected to a NetBEUI-based network and your remote machine name is OSCAR, you could use

```
...\AppID
     \{55555555-5555-5555-5555-555555555555} = "HotDog1"
        \RemoteServerName = "OSCAR"
```

or, alternatively,

```
...\AppID
     \{55555555-5555-5555-5555-555555555555} = "HotDog1"
        \RemoteServerName = \\OSCAR
```

Okay, now that you've modified your Registry, what is the end result? At the risk of sounding coy, nothing—at least, not yet. Although you've added a `RemoteServerName` key, all the old `HotDog1` configuration information is still in place. COM will always try to launch a server in the most favorable context (more about this policy later). Because launching a server remotely is the slowest way to start a server, COM will always try to launch the server locally first. In the case of the `HotDog1` server, the existence of the `LocalServer32` key indicates the presence of a server whose launch performance characteristics should be superior to those of a remote server. Therefore, despite the `RemoteServerName` entry, COM will still launch the server locally whenever a client requests a new `HotDog` object.

Luckily, *that's* a problem easily solved. By removing the `LocalServer32` key, you give COM no choice but to start up the server on the remote machine. With these changes complete, your component has become a bone fide DCOM class.

Note

Although the server is located on a remote machine (or more accurately, *because* the server is located on a remote machine), the proxy/stub DLL also must be correctly installed and registered on the client machine. Because a remote method call is out-of-process, the proxy/stub code is needed to marshal outgoing data from the client and to unmarshal incoming data from the server.

Simplifying Server Configuration Using `DCOMCNFG` and `OLEVIEW`

Now that I've made you excited about poking around in the Registry, let me tell you about an easier way to set the `RemoteServerName` Registry value. Every copy of Windows NT 4.x includes the DCOM configuration utility, `DCOMCNFG.EXE`. (Windows 95 DCOM includes a Windows 95–specific version of the utility, also named `DCOMCNFG.EXE`.) This utility is used to manage the whole range of DCOM-related configuration values stored in the system Registry, including remote server names and security information.

Figure 13.1 shows what `DCOMCNFG` looks like when it's first run on my main development machine. `DCOMCNFG` comprises a tabbed dialog box; the initial page displays a list of all the COM components that have an AppID entry.

You can click the Properties button to view a second set of property sheets that contain configuration data for the currently selected component. The first tab, shown in Figure 13.2, shows basic information about the server. The second tab, in Figure 13.3, is titled Location and contains information about where the component server should be launched.

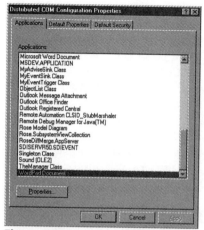

Figure 13.1   The initial display of the DCOMCNFG configuration utility.

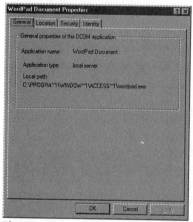

Figure 13.2   The DCOMCNFG server basic information dialog tab.

The Location dialog page has three different elements: a check box labeled Run Application on the Computer Where the Data Is Located, a check box labeled Run Application on This Computer, and a check box and edit field labeled Run Application on the Following Computer. For now, all you're concerned about is this last check box. When you select this check box and enter a remote computer name, DCOMCNFG will take care of creating all the appropriate Registry entries for you.

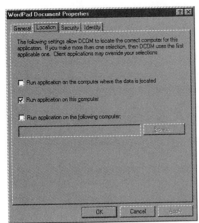

Figure 13.3   The DCOMCNFG server Location dialog tab.

Unfortunately, even if you use **DCOMCNFG**, you will still have to manually clear out any old configuration information. Another possibility is to use the OLE Viewer utility included with Visual C++ 5. You've probably become familiar with OLEView during your COM experimentation and have already recognized OLEView as an extremely valuable administrative tool. I find OLEView's user interface superior to that of **DCOMCNFG**, and OLEView provides access to much more information.

Remoting a local server by using OLEView is a matter of selecting the server in the Explorer-like interface and modifying the settings found on the Activation tab. Figure 13.4 depicts this dialog in action.

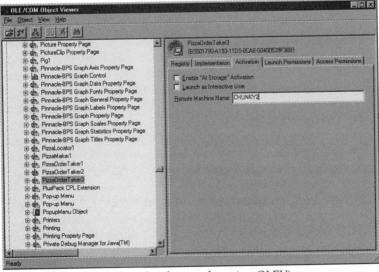

Figure 13.4   Remoting a local server by using OLEView.

Like **DCOMCNFG**, you'll have to clear out any old configuration information. However, unlike **DCOMCNFG**, OLEView provides a GUI for modifying every aspect of a server's configuration. Old configuration information can be removed from inside the utility, without having to resort to ugly **REGEDIT** gesticulations.

The biggest problem with relying on OLEView is that the utility is not a part of the operating system. Although it's certainly a more powerful and elegant utility than **DCOMCNFG**, you can be assured that **DCOMCNFG** will always be present on any Windows NT 4.0 (or later) machine. OLEView, on the other hand, has to be installed after the fact. A good rule of thumb is to rely on OLEView whenever you can (install it on every machine possible), but be prepared to use **DCOMCNFG** or **REGEDIT** in a pinch.

Tip

If you're working on a large network, you might want to place the OLEView binaries in a public share on your central development machine. This way, if you are working on a computer that does not have OLEView installed, you can simply download the utility from the development machine.

CoCreateInstanceEx

As I've already pointed out, the value of remoting COM servers never designed to be distributed is debatable. Although you will certainly find the occasional server that can be directly remoted and can provide immediate benefit, the truly useful and impressive COM applications are those explicitly designed with distribution in mind. This sounds good, but it's not immediately apparent what this means. Take a look at some of the technical implications of this goal.

Using the configuration options detailed in previous sections, I've shown how you can cause COM to short-circuit a call to **CoCreateInstance()** and enable new objects to be created on remote machines. This behavior is nice enough, but it is limiting. Because the name of the remote machine is etched in stone (in the Registry), clients will always be directed to the same place. If you rely solely on the **RemoteServerName** Registry key, multiple client programs running on the same machine will never be able to create objects on different remote computers. Instead, each client will be routed to exactly the same machine.

Don't worry, there's an easy way around these limitations. Applications that are DCOM-aware can be written so that they explicitly indicate to the DCOM subsystem which remote machine should host the new object. For example, this capability would enable a client program to raise a dialog box that asks the user for the name of the remote machine at run-time, rather than rely on a single hard-coded Registry value.

The key to this functionality is the new **CoCreateInstanceEx()** function. As the name implies, this new function performs the same duties as **CoCreateInstance()**, but with some additional capabilities. Listing 13.1 is a short snippet of code that shows **CoCreateInstanceEx()** in action.

Listing 13.1   CREATEEX.CPP—Making a Call to CoCreateInstanceEx()

```
// Create the remote PizzaMaker object
COSERVERINFO  ServerInfo;
MULTI_QI      MultiQI;

ServerInfo.dwReserved1 = 0;
ServerInfo.pwszName    = bstrHostname;
ServerInfo.pAuthInfo   = NULL;
ServerInfo.dwReserved2 = 0;

MultiQI.pIID           = &IID_IPizzaMaker;
MultiQI.pItf           = NULL;
MultiQI.hr             = NOERROR;

hResult = CoCreateInstanceEx(CLSID_PizzaMaker1,
                             NULL, CLSCTX_SERVER,
                             &ServerInfo,
                             1, &MultiQI);
```

I know what you're thinking, because I had the same reaction the first time I saw a call to CoCreateInstanceEx(). "I must do *all that* just to create an object!?!" CoCreateInstance() is nice and simple, whereas this monstrosity looks like the programming equivalent of a 747 cockpit. Although you'll ultimately find that CoCreateInstanceEx() is not overly complicated, it is ungainly. For this reason, most people will probably continue to use CoCreateInstance() and rely on CoCreateInstanceEx() only when the possibility exists that the object will have to be created on a remote machine.

The first three parameters to CoCreateInstanceEx() should look familiar to anyone who has had to use the CoCreateInstance() function. In fact, these three parameters are exactly the same for the two functions. The first argument is the CLSID of the new object instance, the second is an optional IUnknown pointer used during aggregation, and the third is the server launch context.

The next three arguments, however, are new. Argument four is the address of a COSERVERINFO structure that contains information about where the new object should be instantiated. The sixth argument is an array of MULTI_QI structures, and the fifth argument indicates how many elements are in the array. The MULTI_QI structure is used to simultaneously return multiple interface pointers from your new object.

COSERVERINFO

First things first. If you're planning on creating a new object instance, you must tell COM/DCOM where the object should be created. The COSERVERINFO structure that you fill in and pass in to CoCreateInstanceEx() contains information about which machine should host the new object. The structure contains the four fields shown in Table 13.1.

Table 13.1 COSERVERINFO Fields

Field Name	Description
pwszName	The name of the host on which to instantiate the object
pAuthInfo	Security subsystem authentication information
dwReserved1	Reserved for future use
dwReserved2	Reserved for future use

The first COSERVERINFO field is a Unicode string containing the name of the remote machine. The name can currently appear in any of the formats previously discussed, including DNS, IP, and UNC. As Microsoft extends the DCOM subsystem to support more network protocols, you will probably find that the addressing formats supported in this field will also be extended.

Note

If you pass COM a NULL string in COSERVERINFO's pwszName field, the subsystem will attempt to create the new object on the local client machine.

The **pAuthInfo** field is used to provide security information to the operating system. As long as you're using the default security provider, you can set the **pAuthInfo** field to NULL. If you are using a security provider other than NTLMSSP, you must pass in an appropriately filled-in **COAUTHINFO** structure. (Refer to Chapter 10, "Security," if you want to brush up on COM/DCOM security.)

The last two fields, **dwReserved1** and **dwReserved2**, are placeholder fields that Microsoft has reserved for future use. Your applications should set them to zero.

MULTI_QI

To understand the rationale behind the **MULTI_QI** array, you must review one of the biggest challenges surrounding the development of distributed systems. Namely, you have to remember that communication between machines over a network is extremely slow, at least by computer standards. Because using the network can be so expensive from a performance standpoint, one of the central tenants of distributed systems development is to never hit the wire unless you have to.

Keeping this in mind, we will trace the steps that a client program would go through to create a new Dog object and then retrieve the object's **IDog**, **IMammal**, and **IPet** interface pointers. Assuming that the client was using the **CoCreateInstance()** API, the initial call to the function would create the actual object instance. You can use this initial call to return an **IDog** interface pointer (remember, **CoCreateInstance()** can return an interface pointer other than **IUnknown**). That still leaves two calls to **QueryInterface()** to obtain the **IMammal** and **IPet** interface pointers.

Now, assume that each of these calls hit the wire, which is exactly what happens when you use a remote server. In this hypothetical example, you would have to make three separate round-trip network trips between the client and the server. This is exactly the sort of performance trap that you want to avoid. Fortunately, Microsoft addresses exactly this problem with `CoCreateInstanceEx()`.

For each interface pointer you want returned from the newly created object, you must pass in a `MULTI_QI` structure. If you want to retrieve more than one interface pointer, you must create an array of `MULTI_QI` structures and pass the array in to `CoCreateInstanceEx()` as the function's sixth argument.

Take a look at the `MULTI_QI` structure. The structure has three fields, described in Table 13.2.

Table 13.2   `MULTI_QI` Fields

Field Name	Description
pIID	The pointer to the identifier of the requested interface.
pItf	The returned interface pointer. Make sure that you initially set this field to NULL.
hr	The return value of the `QueryInterface()` call for this interface. Make sure that you initially set this field to NOERROR (zero).

Of course, if you're going to ask an object for an interface pointer, you must tell the new object which interface you want. That's the purpose of the `pIID` field. It corresponds to the fourth argument passed in to `CoCreateInstance()`.

The `pItf` field is an output parameter that will contain the returned interface pointer, if everything goes well. Because the DCOM subsystem is really just performing a server-side `QueryInterface()` on the new object, the possibility exists that the object won't support the requested interface (try asking for `IDuck` on a Dog object, and you'll see what I mean). The result of the `QueryInterface()` call is returned in the `hr` field and must be checked for every returned interface pointer that you intend to use.

The advantages of this approach should be clear to you. Now you can implement the hypothetical Dog example with a single API function call and a single round-trip network call. This represents a significant performance savings, albeit at the expense of some increased programming complexity.

The New `IMultiQI` Interface

With the introduction of DCOM, Microsoft has also introduced a new interface named `IMultiQI`. `IMultiQI` supports a single method, `QueryMultipleInterfaces()`, that allows for the querying of, well, multiple interface pointers (imagine that). `QueryMultipleInterfaces()` takes an array of `MULTI_QI` structures and an array size argument.

Unfortunately, to take advantage of this new interface, you must use classes that support it, and the current versions of ATL and MFC do not automatically support implementations of `IMultiQI`. You might, however, want to prepare yourself for the eventual adoption of `IMultiQI` by distributed classes that support a large number of interfaces. If you find that some of your DCOM clients do extensive interface querying and it's not possible or practical to consolidate these interface queries into an initial `CoCreateInstanceEx()` call, you might want to consider adding `IMultiQI` support.

Adding client-side support for `IMultiQI` is simply a matter of requesting an `IMultiQI` interface pointer in your client's `CoCreateInstanceEx()` call. Most of the time, at least for now, the interface pointer request will be rejected. This is certain to change, however, as Microsoft extends the ATL to allow for automatic `IMultiQI` support.

Determining When to Use In-Process, Local, or Remote Servers

As you can see, COM has to take many factors into account when it is determining where to start a server. Depending on the contents of the Registry, an optional **COSERVERINFO** structure, and a CLSCTX enumeration, COM has to decide to launch a server in-process, locally, or remotely. I want to take a little time walking through COM/DCOM's "thought process." You'll find this to be a valuable exercise because (trust me) at some point you *will* be faced with a situation in which servers are not being started where you think they should. Debugging this problem requires you to think like COM and to follow the same analysis that COM does when it's trying to determine where a server process should execute.

Before we jump right in, I want to make a notational point. The CLSCTX value passed in to `CoCreateInstance()` and `CoCreateInstanceEx()` plays an important role in what COM decides to do. As I walk through the server launch algorithm, I will make numerous references to the server context. Keep in mind that the server context is a value initially passed in to one of the aforementioned APIs, but that COM itself might end up changing this value internally as the algorithm progresses.

Without further ado, let's examine the process that COM follows when a client program requests the creation of a new object instance.

1. The COM subsystem checks whether the client has provided a **COSERVERINFO** structure. If the client program provides a **COSERVERINFO** structure indicating a non-**NULL** machine name, COM adds the **CLSCTX_REMOTE_SERVER** value to the server context.

2. If the specified class has a **RemoteServerName** Registry key associated with its AppID, COM adds the **CLSCTX_REMOTE_SERVER** value to the server context (if it's not already there).

3. If the client has provided a COSERVERINFO structure with a non-NULL machine name specified, but the machine name indicates the current machine, the CLSCTX_REMOTE_SERVER value is *removed* from the server context. Note that this is not a redundant step that conflicts with work done in step 1. The CLSCTX_REMOTE_SERVER value could have been passed by the client program in the original server context argument.

4. If the server context includes the CLSCTX_INPROC_SERVER value, COM will attempt to use an in-process server. COM will look for an InprocServer32 key in the class's Registry configuration, and if found, the specified DLL is loaded into the client's address space and used. The implication here is that COM views an in-process server as the most attractive option and will always use the in-process server code if it can.

5. Next, COM looks in the server context for the CLSCTX_LOCAL_SERVER value. If the value is found and there is a LocalServer32 key in the class configuration information, COM will start the server locally, in a new server process.

6. With no in-process or local server in sight, COM starts to consider the remote server option. COM first checks the server context to see whether the CLSCTX_REMOTE_SERVER value is present (remember that even though the client might not have passed this value in, COM itself might have added this value in steps 1 or 2). If CLSCTX_REMOTE_SERVER is present and the user provided a COSERVERINFO structure, COM modifies the server context value by removing the CLSCTX_REMOTE_SERVER value and adding the CLSCTX_LOCAL_SERVER value. COM then forwards the server activation request to the remote machine, where the COM subsystem on that machine will start the search for a local server implementation.

7. Finally, if the server context includes the CLSCTX_REMOTE_SERVER value, but no COSERVERINFO structure exists (the client is making a call to CoCreateInstance(), for example), COM goes looking for a RemoteServerName key in the class's configuration settings. If one is found, COM changes the server context from CLSCTX_REMOTE_SERVER to CLSCTX_LOCAL_SERVER and forwards the activation request on to the appropriate machine.

These steps have actually been simplified (believe it or not). For example, I've omitted any mention of COM's consideration of in-process handlers in these seven steps. An *in-process handler* is a specialized type of in-process server used during OLE object embedding.

COM also gives some additional consideration to objects that are being created out of a persistence stream, a topic that I won't be discussing in much detail. However, I will address the issue later in this chapter when I introduce the concept of object monikers.

Designing the Distributed Object Application

I now want to spend a little time discussing some of the application design issues related to building systems with distributed objects. My comments will be geared toward systems that are relatively large (many classes, many simultaneous users, and numerous machines). However, the lessons of this section can be applied to great benefit in smaller applications as well.

Scalability

One of the most desirable traits of a distributed object application is scalability. *Scalability* refers to the capability of a system to accommodate an ever increasing load (for example, more users or more data moving across the network) without a corresponding drop in performance.

Realistically speaking, you will always be able to exhaust the computing resources available to your clients and servers. At some point, as you continuously add more client machines, you will overwhelm the CPU and I/O capabilities of your server machines. A scalable system enables you to bring new server resources online without affecting overall performance.

Let's take a relatively naïve approach to application design. Suppose that your company wants to establish a Web site designed to accept customer orders for your product, Froggles. (You do know what a Froggle is, don't you?) Because you're anticipating a tremendous demand for your product (how many other companies that you know of are selling Froggles?), you will run many Web servers to keep up with the volume of traffic of incoming Froggle orders.

In your design, each Web server will become a DCOM client, forwarding the order request through a distributed object to a centralized Froggle-ordering server. You want to decouple the order objects from the Web server because you might need to initiate Froggle orders from a client platform other than a Web browser. Orders, for example, might come in from an automated telephone-based fulfillment center. Such a system would enable customers to call a toll-free number, punch in a credit card number, and place their order through a voicemail-like menu system. This telephone-based ordering system should be able to use exactly the same order objects as the Web-based system, even though the telephone-based system is not Web aware. Figure 13.5 shows one way that you could design this system.

In this diagram, all the clients (Web servers and phone clients) communicate with order objects on a single server. Is this a good design? It all depends.

Initial incarnations of this system might perform very nicely. As long as the volume of orders is kept low enough so that it doesn't max out the hardware hosting the order server process, this design should be quite serviceable. However, problems arise when the volume of incoming orders starts to overwhelm the single server machine. At this point, performance rapidly diminishes because incoming requests are queued up at the server and must wait before the order backlog is cleared.

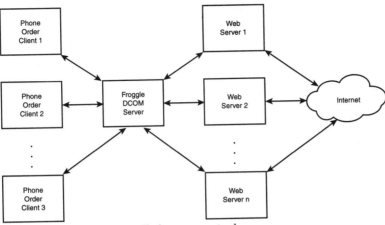

Figure 13.5   Assigning all clients to a single server.

You can solve this problem by adding a new server machine and redirecting half the clients to use the new machine. When the second machine becomes overloaded, you can add a third machine, and so on. Figure 13.6 depicts this approach.

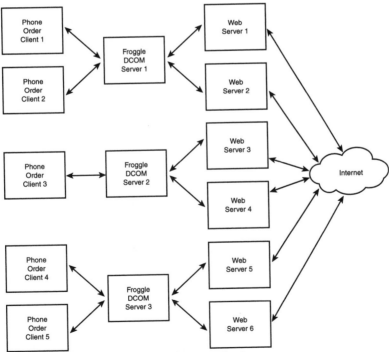

Figure 13.6   Splitting clients across multiple servers.

The biggest problem with this approach is that every time you add a new machine, you have to walk around to most of your machines and modify the client's configuration information so that it points to a different computer. This is a time-consuming and error-prone task, particularly when the number of client machines is large. Each machine represents an opportunity to update the wrong Registry key or to make a typo. On the other hand, if the order volume is growing at a slow rate that necessitates new servers infrequently (once a year, for example), this strategy could be perfectly acceptable.

Load Balancing

Assume that Froggle demand exceeds your wildest expectations and that you are hit with an absolute deluge of orders. New servers are swamped within days of being brought online, and the manpower effort required to administer and configure this system threatens to overwhelm your staff. What can you do?

One solution is to start buying larger and more powerful computers. However, this is seldom cost effective. You will almost always do better with a greater number of less powerful (and less expensive) machines networked together in a cooperative mesh. One cure for the administrative headaches associated with this approach is *load-balancing*.

In a load-balanced system, clients are not assigned to a particular server. Instead, clients consult with a third party, typically called a *broker*, to find out which distributed objects they should use. Because every client first consults the broker before connecting to server processes, the broker is free to assign clients to servers in a manner that will distribute the processing load evenly across machines. Figure 13.7 shows this strategy.

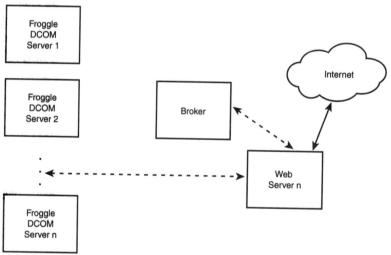

Figure 13.7   Load-balancing clients across multiple servers.

In distributing clients across servers, a broker can employ a host of different algorithms and heuristics, ranging from the simple and straightforward to the truly exotic. For example, in the round-robin algorithm, the broker maintains a list of all servers. Clients are routed to the next server in the list; when the list is exhausted, the broker starts again at the top.

A more sophisticated broker could be constantly monitoring the CPU usage of each server machine and route clients to a server process running on an underutilized machine.

Now, a question might be lingering on your lips. I've been preaching about the evils of hitting the wire, but using a brokering architecture implies two network trips (one to the broker and then one to the assigned server). Isn't this bad? In a word, yes. You don't want every single object method call to go through the broker. Instead, it's better for a client to get its server assignment as part of its initialization procedure, before it has started fielding order requests. This restricts all load-balancing overhead to client startup and completely neutralizes any performance penalty that you have to pay for using a broker.

This last point leads us to another important tenant of distributed systems development: Offload as much processing as possible to client or server startup. On my development teams, it's common to hear the mantra, "Let the server take half an hour to start up—just make sure the thing blazes after it gets going!" I've seen some client/server systems that literally take hours to get started, but are then capable of processing thousands of transactions per second.

Note

It's interesting to note that Microsoft has been making a lot of noise about its new Transaction Server product. Transaction Server provides a many wonderful features that are interesting to architects of large, transaction-based applications (for example, two-phased commits, resource pooling, and database connection sharing). However, the exclusion of load-balancing services seems a glaring omission.

Connecting to Service Objects

Most mid-size to large-size distributed object systems contain certain objects referred to as *services*. A *service object* is a single, global, distributed object instance used by multiple clients. The broker object described in the previous section is a good example of a service object. A broker that relies on a round-robin algorithm must be accessed by all clients to evenly distribute the load; because the broker maintains a list of servers and a "next server" pointer, every client that doesn't go to the same broker risks throwing off the load-balancing scheme.

A service object is typically created once when the system comes up and remains constant over the life of the system. This constancy saves the performance drain associated with a continuous churn of creating and destroying the same object over and over again.

There's really nothing too profound about the concept of service objects, but in the DCOM world, services raise a vexing question. If a service object is created early and remains alive forever, how do clients find these elusive services? After all, a client can't just call `CoCreateInstance()` or `CoCreateInstanceEx()` because these functions will create a whole new object. No easy answers exist to this question, built in to the DCOM subsystem, but there are several possibilities that we ourselves can purchase or implement.

Directory Services

In the world of distributed objects, we often talk about the concept of a *directory service* (you might also see this same capability referred to as a *naming service*, particularly in the CORBA literature). A directory service is a mechanism by which the administrators of a network or distributed software system can organize carefully structured information. We typically think of a directory service as managing more tangible network resources such as a printer or a user login account, but I think that's about to change.

Microsoft is touting its new Active Directory product as its strategic approach to directory services. It's certainly true that network administrators will use the Active Directory to maintain user and group accounts, manage printers, and control access to shared network resources. Because the Active Directory serves as the new management model for Windows NT 5.0, this will be particularly true when the next version of that operating system ships.

However, because the Active Directory is based entirely on COM/DCOM, you can create DCOM service objects that can be installed in the directory. A service object can be placed in the directory with a well-known name (for example, WinNT://MyDomain/Brokers/FroggleOrderBroker). Clients can then connect to the directory by using the known name and obtain an interface pointer to the service object.

The biggest problem with an Active Directory–based approach to matching DCOM clients with service objects is that the product is not yet available from Microsoft in its final form, at least not at the time of this writing. This obviously limits its usefulness, unless you have access to beta versions of the product (and you have no qualms about building applications, using beta code). This fact aside, you'll probably begin seeing the Active Directory assume a position of prominence as a DCOM matchmaking service, at least at those sites that have embraced Microsoft-only technology strategies.

Locator Objects

In the absence of a directory service, there is at least one other solution to the problem of connecting clients with service objects (when it comes to programming, isn't there *always* another way?). A *locator* is an object that is responsible for finding other objects. Locators are not brokers; they are short-lived objects whose single-minded purpose is to hop onto other machines and find services.

Note

The locator concept is best defined as a design pattern that describes a technique for finding other distributed objects. COM does not provide locator objects, nor are there standard interfaces or specifications that describe what a locator class should look like. Throughout this chapter, I will describe potential locator class implementations, but they are ultimately based on my decisions and priorities. You can, of course, design your own locator class to perform in a similar fashion but have a completely different interface.

Here's the scenario. You are a client that knows your service object is on a remote machine named SPAM. Your mission: to get an `IUnknown` interface pointer for your service object from SPAM to your client. Using a locator, the solution is conceptually simple. The client program creates a locator on SPAM. The locator finds the service object and returns an interface pointer. Q.E.D.

The only snag is the part I glossed over: "The locator finds the service object...." Creating the locator object gets you onto the right machine, but you still need a way for the locator to hook up with the service object. One solution uses something called the Running Object Table (ROT).

As you might have guessed, the ROT is a machinewide list of currently instantiated object instances and is maintained by the COM subsystem. COM does not automatically place new objects into the ROT; that task must be explicitly performed by your code. After your object has been placed in the ROT, another object (potentially running in a different process on the same machine) can consult the ROT and retrieve an `IUnknown` pointer to the ROT-hosted component.

Dealing with the ROT is complicated by the fact that you don't simply take an interface pointer and tell COM to put it in the ROT. Instead, you must create a special type of object called a *moniker*, hand the moniker a reference to your object, and then install the moniker in the table. Later in the chapter, in the section titled "Enter the Moniker," I'll walk you through a locator class implementation, and you'll see exactly how all the moniker works.

I'll give you one guess what the biggest problem is with the whole locator approach. Any ideas? It's SLOW. Really slow. Slow, slow, slow. Think about all the steps involved. Creating the locator object is only one network hit, but probably involves starting a locator server process on the remote machine (an expensive proposition). After the locator has been created, the client must call a distributed locator method to check the ROT for the service object. That's network hit number two. Of course, one of the nicer things about the locator approach is that it doesn't require a directory service and, even better, it works. If you're lucky, you can move all that sluggish locator overhead into the startup processing of your client, and users will barely notice.

Event Notifications and Connectable Objects

Connectable objects play an important role in most applications built with COM and OLE. The concepts of connectable objects and event notifications (sometimes called *COM events*) are not so much features of COM as they are design patterns that use COM to provide some extremely useful capabilities.

So far, I have been concerned exclusively with the mechanism that client programs use to contact COM objects residing inside server processes. Connectable objects, however, are concerned with communication in the opposite direction, from the server to the client. This feature becomes useful whenever you have a client that wants to be notified when important events happen inside an object.

Suppose that you are developing an application that controls the Froggle assembly line. Your application is composed of many classes: classes that control industrial robots, classes that control metal stampers, classes that manage fire control systems, and so on. An assembly line is a dynamic environment; at times, it can even be a dangerous place. No matter how much you and your computers are in control of the assembly line environment, accidents *will* happen. When something goes wrong, you most definitely want to know about it. With connectable objects, you can create a monitoring program that hooks into all your assembly-line control objects. If the metal stamper jams or the fire control system senses smoke, they can alert your monitoring program and sound the alarm.

Note

It's worth mentioning that, although they are certainly valuable in communicating exception "emergency" events, connectable objects are valuable in any situation in which you want to set up a notification relationship between two objects.

The concepts behind connectable objects are simple, although the actual implementation and COM interfaces are a bit baroque. COM events are passed between two objects; one object generates events and the other receives them. The generating object is called an *event source* and the receiving object is called an *event sink*. This is a crucial concept that bears repeating. COM events flow from sources to sinks, and I often use this terminology in the upcoming sections.

A connection between a source and a sink is formed when the sink provides the source with an interface pointer. The source holds on to this interface pointer, and when a particular event occurs, the source calls a method on the sink's interface. In the section titled "ATL Macros Supporting COM Events," I'll walk you through the creation of an ATL-based source and sink. You'll also learn about connection points and connection point containers, which are two of the core interfaces that COM uses to help in the management of sink interface pointers.

The Distributed Pizza-Ordering System

All this is obviously leading somewhere, and I would imagine that by this time you're ready to leap into some code. In the rest of this chapter, I'll introduce you to the third version of the PizzaOrderTaker application. You'll find that this PizzaOrderTaker example is a big jump from the examples you worked through in previous chapters. I've done this largely because distributing an application across the network not only complicates certain processes and procedures, but also opens up a world of opportunity and possibility.

As you work through the construction of the distributed pizza-ordering system, you might wonder from time to time why I choose to do something in a particular fashion. If I don't explicitly call your attention to a decision that I made or a potential design pitfall, I probably don't have a good reason for implementing a feature the way that I do. Building distributed systems can be tricky at times, and certainly there are things that you must look out for, but I am a firm believer that programming is a creative exercise, if not an artistic one. Most large systems are the result of many small decisions that generally can't be characterized as right or wrong and by several very large decisions that really must be right. In the rest of this chapter (and throughout this book, really), I'm more concerned with these big, important decisions.

In the PizzaOrderTaker1 and PizzaOrderTaker2 examples covered in past chapters, you've implemented the same local server in different ways. The Pizza Order-Taking Wizard is a client program that knows how to do only one thing—to interact with a COM object that supports the **IPizzaOrderTaker** interface. Figure 13.8 depicts the previous PizzaOrderTaker examples.

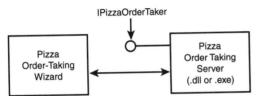

Figure 13.8   The PizzaOrderTaker examples so far.

You're now going to extend this example to incorporate several new elements. Figure 13.9 shows what the PizzaOrderTaker3 example looks like.

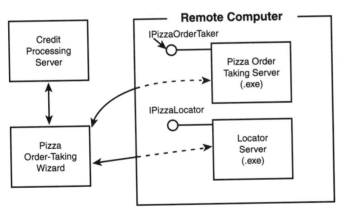

Figure 13.9   The PizzaOrderTaker3 example.

The Order-Taking Wizard will remain exactly the same. As in the PizzaOrderTaker1 and PizzaOrderTaker2 examples, the wizard will create an instance of an object that exposes **IPizzaOrderTaker** and then pass on the customer order information to the order-taking server.

The order-taking server is where you find some changes. Depending on how you want to configure your system, the pizza order-taking server can be set up to activate locally or remotely. You will proceed with the assumption that your server exists locally on the client machine. From the perspective of the order-taking object, the process of order-ing a pizza has two steps. In the first, the order-taking object calls out to a credit server responsible for debiting the customer's credit card and for ensuring that the pizza can be correctly billed. In step 2, the order-taking server uses a locator to find a pizza-making server running on a remote machine and then triggers the creation and delivery of the pizza. The thinking here is that the pizza-making server would be located at the restaurant, and clients (run-ning on your computer at home, for example) could communicate orders across the Internet.

Note

I mention the credit-processing server only for the sake of completeness. The example that I present in this chapter does not implement this server, mainly because the credit-processing server would be built in a virtually identical fashion as the pizza-making server (security concerns aside, of course).

You will also build a program called the PizzaMaker Server Spy. This small application is just a sink for event notifications sent out from a pizza-making server. When a pizza-making distributed object receives an order for a new pizza, the object sends out an event notification to the server spy, describing the requested pizza and detailing the delivery infor-mation. When the pizza is completed and "goes out the door," the pizza-making object sends another message to the server spy, indicating that the pizza is done and on the way.

The New PizzaOrderTaker Server

For the most part, the `PizzaOrderTaker3` class is very similar to the previous PizzaOrderTaker examples. The IDL, for example, remains exactly the same, although the new class has a different CLSID. The real changes have happened inside the various method implemen-tations, specifically inside the `OrderPizza()` method. Listing 13.2 shows `PizzaOrderTaker3`'s implementation of the `IPizzaOrderTaker` interface.

Listing 13.2   `PIZZAORDERIMP.CPP`—The Implementation of the Third
`ComPizzaOrderTaker` Class

```
// Get needed include files
#define INITGUID
#include "PizzaOrderImp.h"
#include "Utility.h"


//
// Useful constants
//
const ULONG        g_ulMaxBufferLen = 256;
const std::string g_strPizzaMakerHostKey =
      "Software\\Que\\PizzaOrderTaker Client\\1.0\\PizzaMaker Host";
```

```
// List of base pizza prices
ULONG g_aulPizzaPrices[] =
    {
        395,  // Individual
        595,  // Small
        795   // Large
    };

// List of base topping prices
ULONG g_aulToppingPrices[] =
    {
        50,   // Individual
        100,  // Small
        150   // Large
    };

// List of topping modifiers (topping prices are influenced
// by the size of the pizza, but some toppings
// (like artichokes—YECH!) are twice as expensive)
ULONG g_aulToppingMods[] =
    {
        0,    // Not a topping (here to catch errors)
        1,    // Pepperoni
        1,    // Sausage
        1,    // GroundBeef
        1,    // GreenOlives
        1,    // ProsciuttiniHam
        1,    // Pastrami
        1,    // GreenPeppers
        1,    // Mushrooms
        1,    // Onions
        1,    // Tomatoes
        1,    // Pesto
        1,    // JalapenoPeppers
        1,    // CheddarCheese
        1,    // FontinaCheese
        1,    // RicottaCheese
        1,    // FetaCheese
        1,    // Pineapple
        1,    // ExtraCheese
        1,    // Bacon
        1,    // Broccoli
        1,    // GenoaSalami
        1,    // Zucchini
        1,    // BlackOlives
        1,    // Anchovies
        2,    // ChickenBreast
        2,    // Shrimp
        2     // ArtichokeHearts
    };

//
```

continued on next page

continued from previous page

```
// Constructor and destructor
//

ComPizzaOrderTaker::ComPizzaOrderTaker()
   : m_eSize(Individual)
{
   VerboseMsg("In PizzaOrderTaker constructor.\n");
}

ComPizzaOrderTaker::~ComPizzaOrderTaker()
{
   VerboseMsg("In PizzaOrderTaker destructor.\n");
}



//
// IPizzaOrderTaker interface members
//

STDMETHODIMP
ComPizzaOrderTaker::ResetPizza()
{
   VerboseMsg("In ResetPizza.\n");

   // Clean out the topping list
   m_ToppingList.clear();

   // Reset the size to Individual
   m_eSize = Individual;

   return NOERROR;
}

STDMETHODIMP
ComPizzaOrderTaker::SetPizzaSize(PizzaSize eNewSize)
{
   VerboseMsg("In SetPizzaSize.\n");

   // Set the new size
   m_eSize = eNewSize;

   return NOERROR;
}

STDMETHODIMP
ComPizzaOrderTaker::GetPizzaSize(PizzaSize* peCurrSize)
{
   VerboseMsg("In GetPizzaSize.\n");

   // Get the current size
   if (peCurrSize)
      *peCurrSize = m_eSize;
```

```
      return NOERROR;
   }

   STDMETHODIMP
   ComPizzaOrderTaker::AddTopping(Topping eNewTopping,
                                  ToppingSize eNewToppingSize)

   {
      VerboseMsg("In AddTopping.\n");

      // Is this topping already in the list?
      if (FindTopping(eNewTopping) != m_ToppingList.end())
         return E_FAIL;

      // Create a new Topping tuple
      CToppingTuple* pTuple = new CToppingTuple;
      pTuple->eTopping = eNewTopping;
      pTuple->eToppingSize = eNewToppingSize;

      // Add the topping to the list
      m_ToppingList.push_back(pTuple);

      return NOERROR;
   }

   STDMETHODIMP
   ComPizzaOrderTaker::RemoveTopping(Topping eRemTopping)
   {
      VerboseMsg("In RemoveTopping.\n");

      // Find the topping tuple
      TupleListIter iter = FindTopping(eRemTopping);
      if (iter == m_ToppingList.end())
         return NOERROR;

      // Free the memory for the tuple and remove the list element
      m_ToppingList.erase(iter);

      return NOERROR;
   }

   STDMETHODIMP
   ComPizzaOrderTaker::GetNumToppings(ULONG* pulNumToppings)
   {
      VerboseMsg("In GetNumToppings.\n");

      // Get the current number of toppings
      if (pulNumToppings)
         *pulNumToppings = m_ToppingList.size();

      return NOERROR;
   }

   STDMETHODIMP
```

continued on next page

continued from previous page

```
ComPizzaOrderTaker::GetTopping(ULONG           ulListPos,
                               Topping*        peTopping,
                               ToppingSize*  peToppingSize)
{
    VerboseMsg("In GetTopping.\n");

    //
    // Retrieve the position's tuple
    //
    // GetTopping() provides position-oriented retrieval
    // because it's easy to manipulate and understand.
    // However, because the toppings are actually stored in a list,
    // positioned access is slow. Definitely room for improvement here.
    //
    // Note that list positions use first element-based access
    // and not zero-based access (i.e., the first element
    // is at position 1, not 0)
    //

    // Validate the list position
    if (!ulListPos || ulListPos > m_ToppingList.size())
        return E_FAIL;

    // Iterate through the list, counting
    TupleListIter iter = m_ToppingList.begin();
    ULONG ulCurrentElem = 1UL;

    do {

        // Is this a match?
        if (ulCurrentElem == ulListPos) {
            *peTopping = (*iter)->eTopping;
            *peToppingSize = (*iter)->eToppingSize;
            return NOERROR;
        }
        ulCurrentElem++;
        iter++;

    } while (iter != m_ToppingList.end());

    return E_FAIL;
}

STDMETHODIMP
ComPizzaOrderTaker::GetPizzaPrice(ULONG* pulPrice)
{
    VerboseMsg("In GetPizzaPrice.\n");

    // Start by setting the base price.
    ULONG ulPizzaPrice = g_aulPizzaPrices[m_eSize];

    // Now walk through the topping list, adding to the current price
    for (TupleListIter iter = m_ToppingList.begin();
         iter != m_ToppingList.end();
```

```
        iter++)
  {

     // Calculate the topping price
     ULONG ulToppingPrice = g_aulToppingPrices[m_eSize] *
                            g_aulToppingMods[(*iter)->eTopping];

     // Based on how much of the pizza is covered with this topping,
     // the topping price needs to be scaled
     switch ((*iter)->eToppingSize)
     {
        case FullPizza:                         break; // Do nothing
        case HalfPizza:    ulToppingPrice /= 2; break;
        case QuarterPizza: ulToppingPrice /= 4; break;
     }

     // Add the topping price to the total
     ulPizzaPrice += ulToppingPrice;
  }

  // And now return the result
  *pulPrice = ulPizzaPrice;

  return NOERROR;
}

STDMETHODIMP
ComPizzaOrderTaker::OrderPizza(DeliveryInfo* pDeliveryInfo,
                              CreditCard   , // eCreditCardType,
                              BSTR         , // bstrCreditCardNum,
                              ULONG*       pulPrice)
{
  HRESULT        hResult;
  IPizzaLocator* pIPizzaLocator = NULL;
  IPizzaMaker*   pIPizzaMaker = NULL;
  LPOLESTR       pszHostname = NULL;
  ULONG          ulPizzaID = 0;
  VerboseMsg("In OrderPizza.\n");

  USES_CONVERSION;

  // Set the price
  GetPizzaPrice(pulPrice);

  //
  // In a real system, at this point we'd probably go out to
  // another server and debit the customer's credit card first.
  // In other words, ordering a pizza involves at least two steps:
  // billing the customer and then making the pizza. Only
  // the latter part is implemented in this example.
  //

  // What host are we supposed to be looking for our PizzaMaker on?
```

continued on next page

continued from previous page

```
        pszHostname = LoadPizzaMakerHostnameFromRegistry();

        // Hook ourselves up to a locator object
        COSERVERINFO  ServerInfo = { 0, pszHostname, NULL, 0 };
        MULTI_QI      MultiQI    = { &IID_IPizzaLocator, NULL, NOERROR };

        hResult = CoCreateInstanceEx(CLSID_PizzaLocator1,
                                     NULL, CLSCTX_SERVER,
                                     &ServerInfo,
                                     1, &MultiQI);
    if (FAILED(hResult)) {
        // We'll let the client report the error
        // ReportError("Could not create a new PizzaLocator object.",
        ➥hResult);
        return hResult;
    }

        // Free up our hostname string
        CoTaskMemFree(pszHostname);

        // Just for convenience
        pIPizzaLocator = (IPizzaLocator*) MultiQI.pItf;

        // Look for any PizzaMaker objects that might be currently running
        // on the same machine as the locator
        hResult = pIPizzaLocator->Locate(A2OLE("PizzaMaker"),
                                IID_IPizzaMaker,
                                (PPVOID) &pIPizzaMaker);

        // Clean up some interface pointers...
        pIPizzaLocator->Release();
        pIPizzaLocator = NULL;

    if (FAILED(hResult)) {
        // We'll let the client report the error
        // ReportError("Could not find a running PizzaMaker object.",
        ➥hResult);
        return hResult;
    }

        // Create our array of ToppingInfo structures
        ULONG ulNumToppings = m_ToppingList.size();
        ToppingInfo* pToppingInfo = new ToppingInfo[ulNumToppings];

        // ...and fill it in
        ULONG ulToppingIndex = 0;
        for (TupleListIter iter = m_ToppingList.begin();
             iter != m_ToppingList.end();
           . iter++, ulToppingIndex++)
        {
            // Copy over the current topping
            pToppingInfo[ulToppingIndex].eTopping = (*iter)->eTopping;
            pToppingInfo[ulToppingIndex].eToppingSize =
            ➥(*iter)->eToppingSize;
```

```
    }

    // Tell our cooks to fire up the ovens!
    hResult = pIPizzaMaker->MakePizza(m_eSize,
                                      ulNumToppings,
                                      pToppingInfo,
                                      pDeliveryInfo,
                                      &ulPizzaID);

    if (FAILED(hResult)) {
        // We'll let the client report the error
        // ReportError("Error returned from MakePizza() method.",
        ➥hResult);
        pIPizzaMaker->Release();
        return hResult;
    }

    // Free up our topping array
    delete [] pToppingInfo;

    // Release our interface pointer
    pIPizzaMaker->Release();

    return NOERROR;
}

ComPizzaOrderTaker::TupleListIter
ComPizzaOrderTaker::FindTopping(Topping eSearchTopping)
{
    for (TupleListIter iter = m_ToppingList.begin();
         iter != m_ToppingList.end();
         iter++)
        if ((*iter)->eTopping == eSearchTopping)
            return iter;

    return iter;
}


LPOLESTR ComPizzaOrderTaker::LoadPizzaMakerHostnameFromRegistry()
{
    // Initialize data
    HRESULT hResult;
    HKEY    hKey = 0;

    // Open the base application registry key
    hResult = RegOpenKeyEx(HKEY_LOCAL_MACHINE,
                           g_strPizzaMakerHostKey.c_str(),
                           0,
                           KEY_QUERY_VALUE ,
                           &hKey);
    if (hResult)
        return NULL;
```

continued on next page

continued from previous page

```
                    // Now retrieve the hostname
                    BYTE  achHostname[g_ulMaxBufferLen];
                    ULONG ulHostnameLen = g_ulMaxBufferLen;
                    ULONG ulValueType;
                    hResult = RegQueryValueEx(hKey,
                                              "",        // The "Default" value
                                              NULL,
                                              &ulValueType,
                                              achHostname,
                                              &ulHostnameLen);

               if (hResult || ulValueType != REG_SZ) {
                  RegCloseKey(hKey);
                  return NULL;
               }

               // Close the subkey
               RegCloseKey(hKey);

               // Translate the hostname into a Unicode string
               // (caller must free the string by calling CoTaskMemFree()
               LPOLESTR  pszHostname;
               AnsiToUnicode((PCHAR) achHostname, &pszHostname);

               return pszHostname;
            }
```

The vast majority of this file should look familiar to you because it's very similar to your previous servers. Take a closer look, however, at the aforementioned `OrderPizza()` method because this little guy is quite different.

The first thing that `OrderPizza()` has to do is obtain an interface pointer to a pizza-making object. You know that the object is out there somewhere; you just have to find it. That's where your locator comes in.

Before you can create your locator, you must determine the name of the remote machine that's hosting your pizza-making object. In the PizzaOrderTaker3 application, this information is regarded as configuration information and is stored in the Registry. The `LoadPizzaMakerHostnameFromRegistry()` method goes out to the Registry and retrieves the name of the machine hosting the pizza maker. (The hostname is stored in the `HKEY_LOCAL_MACHINE\Software\Que\PizzaOrderTaker Client\1.0\PizzaMaker Host` key.)

With the remote machine name on hand, you can now create the locator object. In case you couldn't see this coming, you're going to be using the `CoCreateInstanceEx()` function here. Because this function enables you to create an object instance on a machine whose name is dynamically derived at runtime—which is what you're doing here—the function choice is natural.

Note that you could have used the good old `CoCreateInstance()` function. With a `RemoteServerName` Registry entry, you could use the older function to the same effect. Of course, this approach has some potential problems (apart from the fact that you want to learn how to use `CoCreateInstanceEx()` anyway). Although you wouldn't have to maintain your own Registry configuration information under the HKEY_LOCAL_MACHINE\Software\Que key, you'd still have to maintain the locator server's RemoteServerName entry. No win there. By using CoCreateInstance(), you also limit your system's flexibility. As you will see, your locator class is quite generic and can be used to find an instance of any class, on any remote machine. By using the RemoteServerName key, you limit yourself to creating locator objects on only a single remote machine.

```
// What host are we supposed to be looking for our PizzaMaker on?
pszHostname = LoadPizzaMakerHostnameFromRegistry();

// Hook ourselves up to a locator object
COSERVERINFO  ServerInfo = { 0, pszHostname, NULL, 0 };
MULTI_QI      MultiQI    = { &IID_IPizzaLocator, NULL, NOERROR };

hResult = CoCreateInstanceEx(CLSID_PizzaLocator1,
                            NULL, CLSCTX_SERVER,
                            &ServerInfo,
                            1, &MultiQI);
if (FAILED(hResult)) {
    // We'll let the client report the error
    // ReportError("Could not create a new PizzaLocator object.",
    ➡hResult);
    return hResult;
}
```

The preceding code snippet shows the setup and execution of the CoCreateInstanceEx() call. In this case, you're only asking that a single IPizzaLocator interface pointer be returned to you (no need to ask for an IMultiQI pointer in this simple example). IPizzaLocator is a custom interface with a single method, whose IDL definition is shown in Listing 13.3.

Listing 13.3   PIZZALOC.IDL—The IDL for the Locator Class

```
// Bring in needed system IDL files
import "wtypes.idl";
import "unknwn.idl";


//
//   Interface information for IPizzaLocator
//
[ object, uuid(DF113144-A33D-11D0-8CAC-00400539F36B) ]
interface IPizzaLocator : IUnknown
{
    HRESULT Locate([in] LPOLESTR                      pszItemName,
                   [in] REFIID                        riidResult,
                   [out, iid_is(riidResult)] void **ppvResult);
};


//
//   Class information for PizzaLocator1
//
```

continued on next page

continued from previous page

```
[ uuid(CA94F743-A33E-11D0-8CAC-00400539F36B) ]
coclass PizzaLocator1
{
    interface IPizzaLocator;
};
```

The `IPizzaLocator` interface's single method, `Locate()`, accepts three arguments. The first parameter is a string that identifies the sought-after object. This string will be used by the locator class to look up the target object in the remote computer's Running Object Table. The second parameter will receive an interface ID identifying the type of interface pointer you want returned. Finally, the third parameter is an output parameter that will contain the requested interface pointer to the found object (if the object is found).

The `iid_is(riidResult)` attribute used in the IDL declaration for `Locate()`'s third parameter is something new, but you can probably intuit what the syntax means. Because `Locate()`'s third parameter (the returned interface pointer) might or might not be an `IUnknown` pointer, you have to provide a means to indicate precisely what type of interface is being returned, so that the pointer can be correctly marshaled. (All interface pointers are not marshaled identically. They must be individually marshaled, like any other unique type.) The `iid_is()` attribute tells the MIDL compiler that it can use the interface ID passed in through the `riidResult` parameter for the purpose of marshaling the `ppvResult` interface pointer.

IDL and More IDL

IDL provides you with tremendously expressive power. In fact, I've found that working in IDL can be the easiest or the most difficult part of a software project. This is because simple and straightforward COM interfaces are described in IDL with a minimal amount of fuss and hassle. However, IDL can be used to describe, in minute detail, the intricate mesh of data that can be passed between COM clients and servers. Depending on your interfaces and the objects being used, this can become complicated.

To do IDL justice would require an entire chapter several times longer than this one. I haven't enough space here to document every little nuance of IDL programming. However, it's probably worth your time to explore the MIDL Books Online to develop a good feel for all the possibilities IDL opens up to you. You might also want to check out Don Box's excellent advanced COM/DCOM book *Essential COM* (Addison-Wesley, 1998). This book is full of detailed information about writing IDL.

As you can probably tell from the method arguments, the `Locate()` method follows `QueryInterface()` semantics. This innocuous-sounding feature is actually an important performance optimization. To understand why, imagine what would happen if `Locate()`

did not require the second parameter, the requested interface ID, and instead simply resorted to returning an `IUnknown` interface pointer. Because an `IUnknown` interface pointer is virtually useless by itself, the client would have to perform a `QueryInterface()` before anything useful could be done with the service object. In a distributed environment, that `QueryInterface()` call would hit the wire. By adding the `REFIID` argument, you can halve your on-the-wire time—a substantial performance boost.

In the case of the sample program, I've chosen the string `"PizzaMaker"` as the unique key that will be used to identify a pizza-making object in the ROT. You'll see this string again when I break down the `ComPizzaMaker` class and discuss the code that places the object in the ROT.

```
// Look for any PizzaMaker objects that might be currently running
// on the same machine as the locator
hResult = pIPizzaLocator->Locate(A2OLE("PizzaMaker"),
                                 IID_IPizzaMaker,
                                 (PPVOID) &pIPizzaMaker);
```

With the successful completion of the `Locate()` call, you now have access to a pizza-making distributed object. All that remains is to tell the object about the pizza that you want made (and where it should be delivered). This is a simple matter of querying the object for an `IPizzaMaker` interface pointer and then calling the `MakePizza()` method...I'm getting ahead of myself. Listing 13.4 shows the IDL definitions for the pizza-making interfaces and objects.

Listing 13.4   PIZZAMAKE.IDL—The IDL Definitions for the Pizza-Maker Object and the Pizza-Maker Sink Interface

```
// Bring in needed system IDL files
import "PizzaTypes.idl";


//
//   Interface information for IPizzaMaker
//
[ object, uuid(C07258C0-A196-11D0-8CA6-00400539F36B) ]
interface IPizzaMaker : IUnknown
{
    HRESULT MakePizza([in] PizzaSize                 ePizzaSize,
                      [in] ULONG                     ulNumToppings,
                      [in, size_is(ulNumToppings)]   ToppingInfo[],
                      [in] DeliveryInfo*             pDeliveryInfo,
                      [out] ULONG*                   pulPizzaID);
};


//
//   Interface information for connection point IPizzaNotifySink
//
[ object, uuid(BC42FDB5-A2E5-11d0-8CA8-00400539F36B) ]
interface IPizzaNotifySink : IUnknown
{
```

continued on next page

continued from previous page

```
        HRESULT OnNewPizzaRequest(
                    [in] ULONG                    ulPizzaID,
                    [in] PizzaSize                ePizzaSize,
                    [in] ULONG                    ulNumToppings,
                    [in, size_is(ulNumToppings)] ToppingInfo[],
                    [in] DeliveryInfo*            pDeliveryInfo);
        HRESULT OnPizzaComplete ([in] ULONG                    ulPizzaID);
};


//
//  Class information for PizzaMaker1
//
[ uuid(FC875E50-A1FD-11D0-8CA7-00400539F36B) ]
coclass PizzaMaker1
{
    interface IPizzaMaker;
    [source] interface IPizzaNotifySink;
};
```

This IDL file describes two interfaces. The first interface, **IPizzaMaker**, is exposed by the **PizzaMaker1** object and is the primary interface into the pizza-making server. The second interface shown here, **IPizzaNotifySink**, is not exposed by any objects inside the pizza-making server. Instead, the **IPizzaNotifySink** interface is exposed by sink objects that want to receive notification events from a **PizzaMaker1** distributed object.

Like **IPizzaLocator**, the **IPizzaMaker** interface has only a single method. **MakePizza()** takes several arguments that describe the attributes of the ordered pizza, the address where the pizza should be delivered (I'm assuming that the delivery will originate from the same location that makes the pizza), and an output parameter providing a unique order number that can be used to track the pizza. Take a closer look at these method arguments:

```
HRESULT MakePizza([in] PizzaSize                ePizzaSize,
                  [in] ULONG                    ulNumToppings,
                  [in, size_is(ulNumToppings)] ToppingInfo[],
                  [in] DeliveryInfo*            pDeliveryInfo,
                  [out] ULONG*                  pulPizzaID);
```

The **ePizzaSize** and **ulNumToppings** parameters are self-explanatory, but you might be wondering what's up with the next argument. The **ToppingInfo** parameter syntax should look vaguely familiar; it looks as if you're passing in an array of **ToppingInfo** structures (which would certainly make sense). However, what's that **size_is(ulNumToppings)** business all about?

When describing a method that accepts an array, the rules of C and C++ are ambiguous. For example, in C++ a pointer to a **ToppingInfo** structure can imply an array, or it can imply a single structure instance. This ambiguity is fine and good in an old-fashioned C++ program because everything resides in the same address space. If you're a function and I'm calling you, it doesn't matter if I hand you a simple structure pointer. Theoretically, we've already agreed on what I'm passing you (whether it's a single structure pointer or a structure array), and the C++ compiler only has to pass the 4-byte pointer value from the caller into the function. Because you and I are both in the same address space, you are free to interpret, in any way that you want, the chunk of memory to which the pointer refers.

Unfortunately, in the world of distributed objects, you don't have the luxury of a shared address space; after all, the remote object is on a completely different machine. The MIDL compiler, which is going to generate all your proxy/stub code for you, needs to know at compile time exactly what you're passing in to the method, so that it can package the method argument and pass it across the network to the server machine. If you're just passing in a single structure, that's fine. If you're going to pass an array in to the method, you also have to tell the compiler how big the array is. There is no way that the MIDL compiler can divine what your intentions are without a little extra help.

Luckily, the Microsoft IDL language provides a rich palette of IDL extensions that allow us great flexibility in describing how arrays and pointers should be marshaled. In fact, the `MakePizza()` method is a case in point. The `size_is(ulNumToppings)` modifier indicates to the MIDL compiler that you plan to pass in an array and that the array will contain `ulNumToppings` number of toppings. This flexibility illustrates one of the neat features of MIDL. Although it's probably accurate to say that working in IDL is more restrictive than writing normal C++ code, IDL can be very expressive and offers you flexibility.

Before you can call `MakePizza()`, you have to compose the `ToppingInfo` array. This means allocating a chunk of memory large enough to hold the requisite number of `ToppingInfo` structures and then iterating through the topping list, copying each structure from the list into the array.

```
// Create our array of ToppingInfo structures
ULONG ulNumToppings = m_ToppingList.size();
ToppingInfo*  pToppingInfo = new ToppingInfo[ulNumToppings];

// ... and fill it in
ULONG ulToppingIndex = 0;
for (TupleListIter iter = m_ToppingList.begin();
     iter != m_ToppingList.end();
     iter++, ulToppingIndex++)
{
    // Copy over the current topping
    pToppingInfo[ulToppingIndex].eTopping = (*iter)->eTopping;
    pToppingInfo[ulToppingIndex].eToppingSize =
    ➥(*iter)->eToppingSize;
}
```

With that out of the way, calling the method is a simple case of passing in the correct arguments and checking the return codes.

```
// Tell our cooks to fire up the ovens!
hResult = pIPizzaMaker->MakePizza(m_eSize,
                                  ulNumToppings,
                                  pToppingInfo,
                                  pDeliveryInfo,
                                  &ulPizzaID);
if (FAILED(hResult)) {
   // We'll let the client report the error
   // ReportError("Error returned from MakePizza() method.", hResult);
   pIPizzaMaker->Release();
   return hResult;
}
```

Even with all the new elements (that is, the locator object and the pizza-maker object), the `ComPizzaOrderTaker` class is still an easy class to understand. This is largely due to keeping the class interfaces simple but functional, which I suppose you could also call a design goal!

The Locator Class

Now that you've seen how the locator object is used, it's time to open the hood and see what makes the class tick. Although the class is simple, it provides a nice segue into a discussion of monikers and the ROT. Before that, though, take a look at Listing 13.5, which contains the declarations for the `ComPizzaLocator` class.

Listing 13.5   PIZZALOCIMP.H—The Declaration of the `ComPizzaLocator` Class

```
#ifndef PIZZALOCIMP_H
#define PIZZALOCIMP_H


// Get needed include files
#include "Resource.h"
#include "GUIDs.h"


class ATL_NO_VTABLE ComPizzaLocator :
    public CComObjectRoot,
    public CComCoClass<ComPizzaLocator, &CLSID_PizzaLocator1>,
    public IPizzaLocator
{
public:

    // Ctor and dtors
    ComPizzaLocator();
    virtual ~ComPizzaLocator();

    // IPizzaLocator
    STDMETHOD(Locate)(LPOLESTR        pszItemName,
                      REFIID          riidResult,
                      PPVOID          ppvResult);

    BEGIN_COM_MAP(ComPizzaLocator)
        COM_INTERFACE_ENTRY(IPizzaLocator)
    END_COM_MAP()

    DECLARE_REGISTRY_RESOURCEID(IDR_REGSCRIPT)
};

typedef ComPizzaLocator* PComPizzaLocator;


#endif
```

As you can see, `ComPizzaLocator` is a very normal-looking ATL class. As the IDL implies, a single method, `Locate()`, is used to implement the class's object-locating capabilities. Now move on to the implementation, found in Listing 13.6.

Listing 13.6   `PIZZALOCIMP.CPP`—The Implementation of the `ComPizzaLocator` Class

```
// Get needed include files
#define INITGUID
#include "PizzaLocImp.h"
#include "Utility.h"


//
// Constructor and destructor
//

ComPizzaLocator::ComPizzaLocator()
{
    VerboseMsg("In PizzaLocator constructor.\n");
}

ComPizzaLocator::~ComPizzaLocator()
{
    VerboseMsg("In PizzaLocator destructor.\n");
}


//
// IPizzaLocator interface members
//

STDMETHODIMP
ComPizzaLocator::Locate(LPOLESTR       pszItemName,
                        REFIID         riidResult,
                        PPVOID         ppvResult)
{
    HRESULT hResult;
    VerboseMsg("In Locate.\n");

    USES_CONVERSION;

    // Create a moniker for the PizzaMaker server
    IMoniker* pIMoniker = NULL;
    hResult = CreateFileMoniker(pszItemName,
                                &pIMoniker);
    if (FAILED(hResult)) {
        // We'll let the client report the error
        // ReportError("Could not create file moniker.", hResult);
        return hResult;
    }

    // Check whether there is a registered object
    hResult = BindMoniker(pIMoniker, 0, riidResult, ppvResult);
```

```
        if (FAILED(hResult)) {
           // We'll let the client report the error
           // ReportError("Could not bind to moniker.", hResult);
           return hResult;
        }

        // Clean up our various interface pointers
        pIMoniker->Release();
        pIMoniker = NULL;

        return NOERROR;
}
```

It shouldn't come as a shock to you that all the action here takes place inside `Locate()`. Despite its deceptively small size, many concepts are involved with this short piece of code. Understanding how `Locate()` works first requires some understanding of monikers.

Enter the Moniker

What is a moniker? Well, technically speaking, a *moniker* is any COM class that exposes the `IMoniker` interface. I am assuming, however, that you're less than satisfied with this technical description, so let's investigate some of the moniker concepts first.

Conceptually, a moniker is a small, lightweight object that acts as a reference to another object. Suppose, for example, that you're very hungry and I've just given you a moniker to a pastrami sandwich object (not to blur the lines between computer programming and reality *too* much). The moniker object itself is not a sandwich object (it doesn't support the `IEatMe` interface, as a sandwich object might). However, given a moniker, you can easily gain access to the object that the moniker is referring to. This is done by calling a method named `IMoniker::BindToObject()`.

I'm sure you must be wondering what the point is. After all, you're very hungry, and you just want that pastrami sandwich. Why fool around with this moniker business at all?

This question leads to two others: Why are we using monikers here, and what are the other uses for monikers? The answer to the first is simple. From a purely practical standpoint, you must understand monikers so that you can use the Running Object Table. Any object placed in the ROT must be wrapped with a moniker. Because you want to place your pizza-making distributed object into the ROT, you have to learn how to create and resolve monikers.

However, the lowly moniker has a more profound side. Monikers play an important part in many OLE and ActiveX subsystems (remember that OLE and ActiveX are really just a collection of programmatic subsystems built on top of COM/DCOM). Although the most common uses of monikers are far beyond the scope of this book, it's worth spending a moment discussing why monikers are so important to the rest of OLE and ActiveX. Then you won't go on your merry way, thinking that monikers are useful only for connecting to the ROT.

The most important reason for using a moniker is simply that you might not know where the object being referred to resides, particularly when you start talking about things such as object-embedding and hyperlinking across the Web. This is due, in large part, to a collection of OLE interfaces related to object persistence.

Monikers and OLE Object Persistence

Objects are not always created, used, and then destroyed in one sitting. Sometimes you want to create an object, use it for a while, and then save it someplace so that you can return to it later. In computer terms, the word *later* is ambiguous, but suffice it to say that there certainly are times when you would like to save your object, turn off your computer, and then return to that object the next time you start the machine.

With these criteria, it's clearly not acceptable to say that an object can exist only in a live state, loaded up in memory. The pursuit of object persistence is all about enabling objects to save their current state to some storage medium and then enabling programs to reconstitute objects from this state of suspended animation.

OLE supports a large number of interfaces exclusively concerned with object persistence. They're usually easy to pick out in a crowd: **IPersist**, **IPersistStorage**, **IPersistStream**, **IPersistMemory**... you get the idea. Most of these interfaces are geared toward saving and loading COM objects into and out of files. However, Microsoft has done a good job of ensuring that most persistence interfaces are sufficiently abstract to support other potential persistence stores, such as databases and Web pages.

Now you can return to the pastrami sandwich scenario, understanding what I mean about monikers referring to objects whose location is indeterminate. Suppose that the sandwich object was a persistent object stored in a local file. Keep in mind that the pastrami sandwich is a bona fide COM object; it just so happens that it hasn't been loaded into memory. Because the object is not in memory, you can't very well be handed a direct object interface pointer, can you?

You can, however, be handed a moniker object that knows enough about the object to load it from the file when you ask for it. Given the moniker, you can bind to the object without caring or knowing where the object is located. If the object happens to be in memory already, great! The binding operation should be very fast. On the other hand, if the moniker has to be loaded from a file or downloaded across the Web, that's fine, too. Your call to **BindToObject()** might take longer, but the result will be the same. In the end, you'll have an interface pointer that belongs to your pastrami sandwich, and when you're hungry, that's all that you care about.

The moniker concept can be extraordinarily powerful. If you write your programs so that they use only the **IMoniker** interface, you can be handed any type of moniker object and be completely divorced from having to know implementation details about the persistent object's location or storage mechanism. This means, for example, that you don't have to waste your time writing routines to manipulate files and then making sure that these same functions are linked into every one of the programs that needs them. Instead, you can rely on OLE (or ActiveX) to hide all that grossness from you, and you can concentrate on dealing with your objects through monikers.

OLE includes built-in support for nearly half a dozen types of monikers (you can also create your own moniker classes if you need to). However, in the PizzaOrderTaker3 example, you are concerned only with the file moniker. A *file moniker* is used to refer to a persistent object that resides in a file—no surprises there, I hope. The pizza-making objects that you are instantiating are clearly not persistent objects and do not support being streamed into a file. However, the file moniker is well suited to your needs because the moniker first looks in the ROT before deciding to load an object from its file. If the object is found in the ROT, the moniker doesn't even look for the file. Because of the assumption that a pizza-making object will always be registered in the ROT, this strategy will work just fine for you.

Food for Thought: A Locator Moniker

Now that you know about monikers and object brokers, you might be struck by the same idea as I was. It should be possible to create a new moniker class that completely encapsulates the search for remote service objects.

This "locator moniker" could respond to a `BindToObject()` request by querying a directory service for a broker object, asking the broker for a load-balanced service object, and then returning the service object to the original caller. In the absence of a directory service, the new moniker class could create its own locator, track down a broker (or the service object itself), and return the interface to the caller. The nice thing about this idea is that it enables you to migrate from a locator-based system to a directory service–based system without having to rewrite any application code.

Of course, I will leave the actual implementation of such a moniker class to you as an exercise (I can't have all the fun!).

Now that you have a feeling for what monikers are and how they are used, I can analyze the `Locate()` method in detail.

Back to the Code

The locator's purpose in life is simple. The `Locate()` method must look up an object in the ROT, and if it finds anything, it should return the pointer. Appropriately enough, the first thing that happens in `Locate()` is that the method creates a file moniker.

```
// Create a moniker for the PizzaMaker server
IMoniker* pIMoniker = NULL;
hResult = CreateFileMoniker(pszItemName,
                            &pIMoniker);
if (FAILED(hResult)) {
    // We'll let the client report the error
    // ReportError("Could not create file moniker.", hResult);
    return hResult;
}
```

The `CreateFileMoniker()` function used here is a standard API for constructing new file monikers. The function takes two arguments. The first is a string containing the filename and path of the target object, and the second is an output parameter that will contain an `IMoniker` interface pointer belonging to the new moniker. Because you are somewhat subverting the intended use of the file moniker, you will use the filename string simply as a unique identifier.

With a valid moniker in hand, it's time to resolve the object. You do this by calling the function `BindMoniker()`.

```
// Check whether there is a registered object
hResult = BindMoniker(pIMoniker, 0, riidResult, ppvResult);
if (FAILED(hResult)) {
    // We'll let the client report the error
    // ReportError("Could not bind to moniker.", hResult);
    return hResult;
}
```

`BindMoniker()` is an OLE-supplied convenience function that exposes a simplified interface to your moniker's `BindToObject()` method. `BindToObject()` requires that you provide it with an object called a *binding context*. A binding context is an object used to store additional information about the binding operation. In this case, you have no need of a binding context, and the implementation of `BindMoniker()` will provide a reasonable default.

`BindMoniker()` accepts four parameters, although the second argument is reserved and should always be passed as a zero. The first argument is your moniker pointer, and `BindMoniker()` ultimately ends up calling this interface's `BindToObject()` method. The third argument allows you to specify which interface pointer you want returned from the target object, after the moniker has been bound. The fourth and final argument will return the requested interface pointer if the call succeeds.

If the requested object has been properly registered in the ROT, the `BindMoniker()` call will return an interface pointer to the object, which the `Locate()` method will then return to the client. On the other hand, if the requested object is not found in the ROT, the moniker will try to find a file named PizzaMaker, from which it can supposedly load a persistent COM object. Because the moniker will not be able to find such a file, the call will return a `MK_E_CANTOPENFILE` (`0x800401EA`) error. It's not very elegant, but you can treat `MK_E_CANTOPENFILE` as your `"service object not registered"` error value. Alternatively, you may choose to modify the `Locate()` method to check for `MK_E_CANTOPENFILE` and map it onto one of your own custom error values.

The PizzaMaker Server

You're now going to break away from the pulse-quickening world of monikers and Running Object Tables to take a look at the pizza-making distributed object class. Like most other classes involved in this example, the `ComPizzaMaker` class is a bit contrived. It does not, unfortunately, make a pizza for you.

Digging into the `ComPizzaMaker` Declaration

I've already gone over the IDL for the `IPizzaMaker` interface. Listing 13.7 contains the declarations of the associated `ComPizzaMaker` class.

Listing 13.7   `PIZZAMAKEIMP.H`—The Declaration of the `ComPizzaMaker` Class

```
#ifndef PIZZAMAKEIMP_H
#define PIZZAMAKEIMP_H
```

continued on next page

continued from previous page

```
// Get needed include files
#include "Resource.h"
#include "GUIDs.h"


class ATL_NO_VTABLE ComPizzaMaker :
    public CComObjectRoot,
    public CComCoClass<ComPizzaMaker, &CLSID_PizzaMaker1>,
    public IConnectionPointContainerImpl<ComPizzaMaker>,
    public IConnectionPointImpl<ComPizzaMaker, &IID_IPizzaNotifySink>,
    public IPizzaMaker
{
public:

    // Ctor and dtors
    ComPizzaMaker();
    virtual ~ComPizzaMaker();

    // Overridden public methods
    HRESULT FinalConstruct();
    void    FinalRelease();

    // IPizzaMaker
    STDMETHOD(MakePizza)(PizzaSize      ePizzaSize,
                         ULONG          ulNumToppings,
                         ToppingInfo    aToppingInfo[],
                         DeliveryInfo*  pDeliveryInfo,
                         PULONG         pulPizzaID);

    BEGIN_COM_MAP(ComPizzaMaker)
       COM_INTERFACE_ENTRY(IPizzaMaker)
       COM_INTERFACE_ENTRY_IMPL(IConnectionPointContainer)
    END_COM_MAP()

    BEGIN_CONNECTION_POINT_MAP(ComPizzaMaker)
       CONNECTION_POINT_ENTRY(IID_IPizzaNotifySink)
    END_CONNECTION_POINT_MAP()

    DECLARE_REGISTRY_RESOURCEID(IDR_REGSCRIPT)
    DECLARE_PROTECT_FINAL_CONSTRUCT()

private:

    // Misc private methods
    void SendIncomingOrderEvents (PizzaSize      ePizzaSize,
                                  ULONG          ulNumToppings,
                                  ToppingInfo    aToppingInfo[],
                                  DeliveryInfo*  pDeliveryInfo,
                                  ULONG          ulNewPizzaID);
    void SendCompletedOrderEvents(ULONG          ulNewPizzaID);
```

```
    // Our static classwide pizza ID counter
    static ULONG m_ulPizzaIDCounter;

    // Private data members
    IMoniker* m_pIMoniker;
    DWORD     m_dwROTCookie;
};

typedef ComPizzaMaker* PComPizzaMaker;


#endif
```

Unlike the `ComPizzaLocator` class, this class declaration has a number of new elements. Most of these additions are related to connection points and COM events, which I'll explain in some detail. Before moving on to that topic, however, let me quickly point out the `FinalConstruct()` and `FinalRelease()` methods.

In Chapter 8, "Building COM Objects Using the ActiveX Template Library," I explain how ATL calls the `FinalConstruct()` method after the object is completely instantiated (that is, after all the class constructors have fired). In a similar vein, the `FinalRelease()` method is called right before the object is about to be deleted.

By convention, you should not place important construction/destruction logic in your ATL class constructors and destructors. Instead, this logic is commonly located in the `FinalConstruct()` and `FinalRelease()` methods. Following this rule of thumb will prevent your code from inadvertently conflicting with tasks performed by internal ATL classes during object creation or destruction.

The `DECLARE_PROTECT_FINAL_CONSTRUCT` macro is used to protect your object's reference count during the execution of your `FinalConstruct()` method. If you ever inexplicably encounter an error dialog like the one shown in Figure 13.10, your object has probably been deleted out from under you, and you should try incorporating the `DECLARE_PROTECT_FINAL_CONSTRUCT` macro into your class declarations.

Tip

Although you might encounter several such assertions throughout the ATL, any time you happen on an error dialog indicating that a variable containing the characters **Ref** equals zero, you should be suspicious. If you examine the ATL sources where the assertion was triggered, you'll typically find helpful comments left by the Microsoft programmers, suggesting that you use the `DECLARE_PROTECT_FINAL_CONSTRUCT` macro. (These comments are amusing, considering how little the Microsoft programmers comment their code. The ATL has even fewer comments than the MFC, which I didn't think was possible. I wonder if the comments are stripped out before the product is shipped....)

Figure 13.10 Missing the `DECLARE_PROTECT_FINAL_CONSTRUCT` macro?

Most of what's going on in `ComPizzaMaker` is directly related to the implementation of connectable objects, so let's dig in.

What Does It Mean to Be a Connectable Object?

As discussed previously, a COM event is a distributed method call made from a server to a client (as opposed to the more common client-to-server path). As always, the devil is in the details, and in the case of COM events, it's important to have a firm understanding of the interfaces that Microsoft has provided to support connectable objects.

The `ComPizzaMaker` class is a connectable object (that is, a source of events), and as such, it must expose several interfaces. When you talk about event sources in the abstract, you would like to see several criteria met. First, you would like a single source to be able to generate multiple types of events. By multiple types of events, I don't mean multiple methods; this requirement could clearly be met by using a single interface. No, what you want to see are event sources that can originate events from multiple methods and use many interfaces.

Second, you want your event source to be able to send events out to multiple subscribers. This means that you should be able to connect as many sinks as you want to a source and that when an event occurs, the notification should be sent out to each and every one of your registered sinks.

How did Microsoft go about satisfying these two criteria? Connectable objects are responsible for exposing something called a *connection point container*. A connection point container is used to hold on to a collection of—any guesses?—connection points. A *connection point* is an abstraction used to represent a single outgoing interface, that is, a single type of interface through which the source can originate events.

I think this topic would definitely benefit from an example. Think back to the Froggle assembly line example, in which a management program is responsible for monitoring the status of all the production facilities. (This program is often referred to as a management *console* by people who run in systems-management circles.) The management console is a DCOM client that interacts and drives many subsystem servers (a fire control server, a metal press server, and so on). Most of the time, the console tells the subsystem objects what to do. If you wanted to increase line production, for example, you would interact with the various line subsystems through normal COM interfaces.

However, when something goes wrong with a particular subsystem, the server will send an event notification to the management console, warning the application that a problem exists. In this case, the subsystem server is an event source and the management console is a sink. Now, take the case of the fire control subsystem. What sort of notifications could come from such an event source? How about...hmmm, I don't know...maybe...FIRE!! Listing 13.8 shows a hypothetical event notification interface used by a fire control subsystem.

Listing 13.8 FIRENOTIFY.IDL—The IDL for a Hypothetical Fire Control Subsystem Notification Interface

```
// Bring in needed system IDL files
import "wtypes.idl";
import "unknwn.idl";

//
//  Interface information for connection point IFireNotifySink
//
[ object, uuid(BFB13E10-D48B-11D0-8D08-00400539F36B) ]
interface IFireNotifySink : IUnknown
{
   // There's a fire here!
   HRESULT OnFire();

   // I'm not sure about a fire, but I see smoke
   HRESULT OnSmoke();

   // This is kinda fishy - the temperature's on the way up
   HRESULT OnUnusualTempRise();

   // The fire control system has been put into action
   HRESULT OnSysActivate();

   // The halogen fire suppression system has failed
   HRESULT OnHalogenSysFailure();

   // This is just a test
   HRESULT OnSysTest();
};
```

This interface looks just like any other COM interface declaration, an important point in its own right. There is nothing special or unusual about a notification interface; what makes the interface unique is the manner in which it's used.

Note

In Listing 13.8 (or Listing 13.7, for that matter), you might have noticed the I<name>NotifySink interface name or the consistent use of the On<name> method-naming convention. Many programmers use these conventions (I didn't make them up), but they certainly aren't requirements of a notification interface. I like this style because as you browse through source code, you can immediately tell whether the code is manipulating a notification interface or whether a method call is an event notification.

Your fire control subsystem is a connectable object that can generate events embodied by the `IFireNotifySink` interface. This interface represents the protocol used to connect the server to the client. The important thing to keep in mind, however, is that the object exposing the `IFireNotifySink` interface (the sink object) resides on the client and not the server. The server could end up holding on to an `IFireNotifySink` interface pointer, but the object itself is on the client.

Connectable objects expose an interface named `IConnectionPointContainer`, which enables you to look up a connection point object by interface ID. This step achieves your first design criteria; it allows for the support of multiple notification interfaces. If your fire control subsystem could also generate events through an interface named `IFroggleAlert`, this would imply that your connectable object holds on to two connection points: one for `IFireNotifySink` and one for `IFroggleAlertNotifySink`.

Now don't be fooled. The connection point object doesn't expose your notification interface. Instead, the connection point object holds on to a collection of notification interface pointers. These interface pointers are what the connectable object uses to send your client notification events on.

There's the theory, at least, from the connectable object's perspective. Later on, when I dissect the Server Spy, you'll see how notification sinks are registered with the connectable object (the connection points have to obtain their sink pointers somehow!). Now look at how connectable objects implement the support for COM events.

ATL Macros Supporting COM Events

We're still looking at the `ComPizzaMaker` header file because a good amount of programmatic infrastructure is required to provide connectable object support. This becomes readily apparent as soon as you look at the beginning of the class declaration, where two additional base classes have been thrown into the inheritance mix.

```
class ATL_NO_VTABLE ComPizzaMaker :
    public CComObjectRoot,
    public CComCoClass<ComPizzaMaker, &CLSID_PizzaMaker1>,
    public IConnectionPointContainerImpl<ComPizzaMaker>,
    public IConnectionPointImpl<ComPizzaMaker, &IID_IPizzaNotifySink>,
    public IPizzaMaker
```

The first new base class is a templated declaration of the `IConnectionPointContainerImpl` ATL class. This class provides an implementation of the `IConnectionPointContainer` interface, which is the interface used to access connection point objects.

In an ATL-based class, each connection point is incorporated into the inheritance chain, as illustrated by `ComPizzaMaker`'s derivation from the `IConnectionPointImpl` class. The `IConnectionPointImpl` template is parameterized on the name of your new COM class and the interface ID represented by this connection point. You must derive your COM class from one `IConnectionPointImpl` class for each notification interface that your class is going to support. For example, the fire control system component—which I conjectured might be an event source for events belonging to either the `IFireNotifySink` or `IFroggleAlertNotifySink` interfaces—would probably be declared something like this:

```
class ATL_NO_VTABLE ComFireControl :
    public CComObjectRoot,
```

```
   public CComCoClass<ComFireControl, &CLSID_FireControl>,
   public IConnectionPointContainerImpl<ComFireControl>,
   public IConnectionPointImpl<ComFireControl, &IID_IFireNotifySink>,
   public IConnectionPointImpl<ComFireControl,
➥&IID_IFroggleAlertNotifySink>,
   public IFireControl
```

Pretty straightforward stuff, but you're not done yet. Next, you make sure that the
`IConnectionPointContainer` interface implementation is added to your class's COM map.
(You don't have to add your connection point interface implementations to the COM map,
because connection point pointers are retrieved through the `IConnectionPointContainer`
interface protocol and not through a `QueryInterface()` call on your class.)

```
BEGIN_COM_MAP(ComPizzaMaker)
   COM_INTERFACE_ENTRY(IPizzaMaker)
   COM_INTERFACE_ENTRY_IMPL(IConnectionPointContainer)
END_COM_MAP()
```

Note the use of the `COM_INTERFACE_ENTRY_IMPL` macro inside the COM map. Like the
`COM_INTERFACE_ENTRY` macro, `COM_INTERFACE_ENTRY_IMPL` maps an interface onto an implementing class. However, whereas the `COM_INTERFACE_ENTRY` macro denotes that the
`IPizzaMaker` interface will be handled by the class owning the COM map (in this case,
`ComPizzaMaker`), the `COM_INTERFACE_ENTRY_IMPL` macro indicates that the
`IConnectionPointContainer` interface will be handled by the `<interface name>Impl` class
(in this case, `IConnectionPointContainerImpl`).

The last thing to worry about is the connection point map. The *connection point map* is
a list of interface IDs used to indicate to the ATL implementation of `IConnectionPointContainer`
which connection points are available.

```
BEGIN_CONNECTION_POINT_MAP(ComPizzaMaker)
   CONNECTION_POINT_ENTRY(IID_IPizzaNotifySink)
END_CONNECTION_POINT_MAP()
```

Creating the map is very similar to creating the COM map. You use the
`CONNECTION_POINT_ENTRY` macro to add support for a given connection point, passing in
the notification interface ID.

That finishes the declaration of the `ComPizzaMaker` class. Now it's time to look at the
code backing these declarations.

Implementing the `ComPizzaMaker` Class

Before you look at the code, I want to review exactly what you want the `ComPizzaMaker`
to do. Although the `MakePizza()` method won't perform any real task to speak of, we've
already identified several things that have to happen in order to correctly integrate with
the locator objects and notification sinks maintained within client programs.

When a `ComPizzaMaker` object is created, it must place itself in the machine's Running
Object Table. Doing this will enable a locator visiting the machine to connect to the pizza-
making distributed object and return an interface pointer to the owner of the locator. Conversely,
when the object is destroyed, it's important that the object remove itself from the ROT. If
you leave out this critical step, there's always the possibility that a visiting locator will think

that it has found a valid PizzaMaker and will try to return the object reference to the client. Try this with an invalid interface pointer, and something is bound to blow up.

The other thing that we've said we want to do is send out connection point notifications whenever an incoming pizza order is received and send out another notification when the pizza has been made. In both cases, this means going to your connection point container, retrieving a connection point, and then iterating across any interface pointers held on to by the connection point. This is not a difficult procedure, but several steps have to be followed closely.

Take a few minutes to look over the implementation of the `ComPizzaMaker` class, found in Listing 13.9.

Listing 13.9 `PIZZAMAKEIMP.CPP`—The Implementation of the `ComPizzaMaker` Class

```cpp
// Get needed include files
#define INITGUID
#include "PizzaMakeImp.h"
#include "Utility.h"


// Initialize our static pizza ID counter
ULONG ComPizzaMaker::m_ulPizzaIDCounter = 0x00;


//
// Constructor and destructor
//

ComPizzaMaker::ComPizzaMaker()
      : m_pIMoniker(NULL),
        m_dwROTCookie(0)
{
    VerboseMsg("In PizzaMaker constructor.\n");
}

ComPizzaMaker::~ComPizzaMaker()
{
    VerboseMsg("In PizzaMaker destructor.\n");
}


//
// Overridden public methods
//

HRESULT ComPizzaMaker::FinalConstruct()
{
    USES_CONVERSION;
    VerboseMsg("In PizzaMaker FinalConstruct method.\n");

    // Create the file moniker
    HRESULT hResult = CreateFileMoniker(A2OLE("PizzaMaker"),
```

```
                                        &m_pIMoniker);
   if (FAILED(hResult)) {
      // We'll let the client report the error
      // ReportError("Could not create file moniker.", hResult);
      return hResult;
   }

   // Get an interface pointer for the ROT
   IRunningObjectTable* pIROT = NULL;
   hResult = GetRunningObjectTable(0, &pIROT);
   if (FAILED(hResult)) {
      // We'll let the client report the error
      // ReportError("Could not obtain ROT interface pointer.",
      ➥hResult);
      m_pIMoniker->Release();
      m_pIMoniker = NULL;
      return hResult;
   }

   // Now place the moniker into the ROT
   hResult = pIROT->Register(0, GetUnknown(), m_pIMoniker,
   ➥&m_dwROTCookie);
   if (FAILED(hResult)) {
      // We'll let the client report the error
      // ReportError("Could not register Moniker in the ROT.", hResult);
      m_pIMoniker->Release();
      m_pIMoniker = NULL;
      pIROT->Release();
      return hResult;
   }

   // Release our IROT pointer
   pIROT->Release();

   return NOERROR;
}

void ComPizzaMaker::FinalRelease()
{
   // Remove our moniker from the ROT
   if (m_dwROTCookie) {

      // Get an interface pointer for the ROT
      IRunningObjectTable* pIROT = NULL;
      HRESULT hResult = GetRunningObjectTable(0, &pIROT);

      // Now remove the moniker
      if (SUCCEEDED(hResult)) {
         hResult = pIROT->Revoke(m_dwROTCookie);
         pIROT->Release();
      }
      m_dwROTCookie = 0;
   }
```

continued on next page

continued from previous page

```
        // And get rid of our Moniker
        if (m_pIMoniker) {
           m_pIMoniker->Release();
           m_pIMoniker = NULL;
        }
   }



   //
   // IPizzaMaker interface members
   //

   STDMETHODIMP
   ComPizzaMaker::MakePizza(PizzaSize      ePizzaSize,
                            ULONG          ulNumToppings,
                            ToppingInfo    aToppingInfo[],
                            DeliveryInfo*  pDeliveryInfo,
                            PULONG         pulPizzaID)
   {
      ULONG       ulNewPizzaID = ++m_ulPizzaIDCounter;
      VerboseMsg("In MakePizza.\n");

      // Start by notifying everyone who's interested that we
      // have a new pizza to make
      SendIncomingOrderEvents(ePizzaSize,
                              ulNumToppings,
                              aToppingInfo,
                              pDeliveryInfo,
                              ulNewPizzaID);

      // Now it's time to make the pizza.
      // In our fantasy world, it takes 10 seconds to make a pizza
      // (I wish! Wouldn't that be great!!)
      Sleep(10000);

      // Finally send out our notifications that the pizza is done
      SendCompletedOrderEvents(ulNewPizzaID);

      // Set the pizza id return parameter
      *pulPizzaID = ulNewPizzaID;

      return NOERROR;
   }



   //
   // Misc private methods
   //

   void ComPizzaMaker::SendIncomingOrderEvents(
                              PizzaSize      ePizzaSize,
                              ULONG          ulNumToppings,
                              ToppingInfo    aToppingInfo[],
```

```
                            DeliveryInfo*    pDeliveryInfo,
                            ULONG            ulNewPizzaID)
{
    CONNECTDATA cd;

    // Retrieve a connection point container interface pointer
    CComQIPtr<IConnectionPointContainer,
    ➥&IID_IConnectionPointContainer> pCPC(this);
    if (pCPC) {

        // Now look up our pizza notify sink connection point
        CComPtr<IConnectionPoint> pCP;
        pCPC->FindConnectionPoint(IID_IPizzaNotifySink, &pCP);
        if (pCP) {

            // Retrieve an enumerator for this connection point
            CComPtr<IEnumConnections> pEnum;
            if (SUCCEEDED(pCP->EnumConnections(&pEnum))) {

                // Iterate over our connections, one at a time
                while (pEnum->Next(1, &cd, NULL) == S_OK) {

                    // Do we have a valid object pointer
                    if (cd.pUnk) {

                        // Retrieve an IPizzaNotifySink interface pointer
                        CComQIPtr<IPizzaNotifySink,
                        ➥&IID_IPizzaNotifySink> pSink(cd.pUnk);

                        // Send out the event notification
                        if (pSink)
                            pSink->OnNewPizzaRequest(ulNewPizzaID,
                                                     ePizzaSize,
                                                     ulNumToppings,
                                                     aToppingInfo,
                                                     pDeliveryInfo);

                        // Release our reference count
                        cd.pUnk->Release();
                    }
                }
            }
        }
    }
}

void ComPizzaMaker::SendCompletedOrderEvents(ULONG  ulNewPizzaID)
{
    CONNECTDATA cd;

    // Retrieve a connection point container interface pointer
    CComQIPtr<IConnectionPointContainer,
    ➥&IID_IConnectionPointContainer> pCPC(this);
```

continued on next page

continued from previous page

```
            if (pCPC) {

                // Now look up our pizza notify sink connection point
                CComPtr<IConnectionPoint> pCP;
                pCPC->FindConnectionPoint(IID_IPizzaNotifySink, &pCP);
                if (pCP) {

                    // Retrieve an enumerator for this connection point
                    CComPtr<IEnumConnections> pEnum;
                    if (SUCCEEDED(pCP->EnumConnections(&pEnum))) {

                        // Iterate over our connections, one at a time
                        while (pEnum->Next(1, &cd, NULL) == NOERROR) {

                            // Do we have a valid object pointer
                            if (cd.pUnk) {

                                // Retrieve an IPizzaNotifySink interface pointer
                                CComQIPtr<IPizzaNotifySink,
                                ➥&IID_IPizzaNotifySink> pSink(cd.pUnk);

                                // Send out the event notification
                                if (pSink)
                                    pSink->OnPizzaComplete(ulNewPizzaID);

                                // Release our reference count
                                cd.pUnk->Release();
                            }
                        }
                    }
                }
            }
        }
```

Running Object Table Registration and Unregistration

Adding an object to the ROT takes place within the `FinalConstruct()` method, whereas removing the object from the ROT happens inside `FinalRelease()`.

You need two things before you can place the object in the ROT. First, because the Running Object Table will accept only objects associated with a moniker, you need a moniker object. Second, because your whole goal is to place your object in the ROT, you must have access to the table proper. You probably won't be surprised to find that you will gain this access through an `IRunningObjectTable` interface pointer.

Creating the moniker is a simple matter of calling the function `CreateFileMoniker()`.

```
// Create the file moniker
HRESULT hResult = CreateFileMoniker(A2OLE("PizzaMaker"),
                                    &m_pIMoniker);

if (FAILED(hResult)) {
    // We'll let the client report the error
```

```
   // ReportError("Could not create file moniker.", hResult);
   return hResult;
}
```

The `CreateFileMoniker()` function accepts a filename and returns a new moniker object (through an `IMoniker` interface pointer). It's as simple as that. Remember that in this particular case, you're not really passing in a filename to `CreateFileMoniker()`. You're just using the `"PizzaMaker"` string as a symbol to uniquely identify your pizza-making object.

With moniker in hand, you're off to see the ROT. Programs interact with the Running Object Table through an `IRunningObjectTable` interface; you can obtain one of these interface pointers by using the `GetRunningObjectTable()` function.

```
// Get an interface pointer for the ROT
IRunningObjectTable* pIROT = NULL;
hResult = GetRunningObjectTable(0, &pIROT);
if (FAILED(hResult)) {
   // We'll let the client report the error
   // ReportError("Could not obtain ROT interface pointer.", hResult);
   m_pIMoniker->Release();
   m_pIMoniker = NULL;
   return hResult;
}
```

The first parameter passed in to `GetRunningObjectTable()` is reserved and should be passed as zero, and the second parameter returns an `IRunningObjectTable` pointer. (I have high hopes that future versions of this function will enable you to pass a `COSERVERINFO` structure in the first argument and obtain `IRunningObjectTable` pointers for remote object tables.)

The last thing to do inside `FinalConstruct()` is place your object in the ROT. This is done using the `Register()` method belonging to `IRunningObjectTable`.

```
// Now place the moniker into the ROT
hResult = pIROT->Register(0, GetUnknown(), m_pIMoniker,
➥&m_dwROTCookie);
if (FAILED(hResult)) {
   // We'll let the client report the error
   // ReportError("Could not register Moniker in the ROT.", hResult);
   m_pIMoniker->Release();
   m_pIMoniker = NULL;
   pIROT->Release();
   return hResult;
}
```

`Register()` accepts four arguments. The first parameter specifies whether the reference counting is characterized as *strong* or *weak*. Here, you're passing in zero, which indicates weak reference counting. I'm not sure why Microsoft chose this terminology, but the concepts are easy to understand. If an object has strong reference counting, the ROT will call `AddRef()` on the object as part of the registration process and will call `Release()` on the object when the registration is revoked. (You can indicate strong reference counting by passing the value `ROTFLAGS_REGISTRATIONKEEPSALIVE` in to the `Register()` call.)

I can't think of a situation that would require strong registration, but the semantics of strong registration are interesting. If you place an object in the ROT with strong registration, you can release all your interface pointers without the object being destroyed. In fact, your object won't be destroyed until someone else comes along and unregisters the object.

The second of `Register()`'s parameters is an `IUnknown` pointer belonging to the object being installed in the table, and the third parameter is a pointer to the object's moniker.

`Register()` returns a special cookie value in the function's fourth parameter. The number—whose actual value has no intrinsic meaning as far as your application is concerned—is used to refer to this object in future dealings with the `IRunningObjectTable` interface. Interacting with the table through this cookie requires substantially less overhead than creating a new moniker every time you want to refer to the object.

With `FinalConstruct()` out of the way, you can turn your attention to `FinalRelease()`, which is where you're going to unregister the object. Because you've saved the registration cookie in a member variable, unregistering the object is a little easier than registering the object; no moniker is involved. Instead, you retrieve a pointer to the ROT and unregister your object, using the `IRunningObjectTable` interface's `Revoke()` method.

```
// Now remove the moniker
if (SUCCEEDED(hResult)) {
    hResult = pIROT->Revoke(m_dwROTCookie);
    pIROT->Release();
}
```

The `Revoke()` method accepts the registration cookie returned from the `Register()` call and removes the object from the ROT. With the object's registration revoked, future moniker-binding attempts using the `"PizzaMaker"` key will now fail.

Sending COM Event Notifications

We've already identified two times when you want your `ComPizzaMaker` object to generate events that will be broadcast to any connected sink objects. Take a look at how this is accomplished.

Sending out the `OnNewPizzaRequest()` event notification requires the completion of five steps (incidentally, the invocation of the `OnPizzaComplete()` method follows an identical path). Don't be intimidated. The whole process is very intuitive, and you'll be generating events before you know it.

The way to your notification interface pointers passes through your connection points, which in turn passes through your connection point container. That's where you'll start.

Because your class *is* the connection point container, you could start the ball rolling by performing a `QueryInterface()` on yourself, looking for the `IConnectionPointContainer` interface pointer. You *could* do that, but I'm going to show you how to produce the same result in a much more elegant manner.

```
// Retrieve a connection point container interface pointer
CComQIPtr<IConnectionPointContainer, &IID_IConnectionPointContainer>
➥pCPC(this);
```

This single line of code creates something called a *smart interface pointer*. Smart pointers are tremendously useful tools that should be an integral part of every COM programmer's repertoire.

A smart interface pointer is an object wrapper around a standard COM interface pointer. Unlike regular interface pointers, however, a smart pointer takes care of calling `AddRef()` and `Release()` for you. When a smart pointer is instantiated, the contained interface's reference count is incremented. In the smart pointer's destructor, the reference count is decremented. In addition to intelligent constructors and destructors, the smart pointer is equipped with an array of overloaded operators that provide appropriate behaviors. For example, `operator->()` returns the wrapped interface pointer, and `operator!()` returns `True` or `False`, depending on whether the contained pointer equals `NULL`.

The ATL ships with two smart pointer classes: `CComPtr` and `CComQIPtr`. The `CComPtr` class is a straightforward smart pointer implementation. It wraps an interface pointer of the type indicated in the template instantiation.

`CComQIPtr` is a little different. It also holds on to an interface pointer, but during instantiation or assignment, the class performs a `QueryInterface()`. The preceding line of code creates a smart pointer object and assigns the internally maintained interface pointer to the result of a `QueryInterface()` call. In this case, the `QueryInterface()` call requests an `IConnectionPointContainer` interface (the smart pointer will evaluate to `NULL` if the `QueryInterface()` operation fails). The end result is that the `pCPC` variable looks and acts like a normal run-of-the-mill interface pointer, but you're shielded from having to worry about when to call `AddRef()` and `Release()`.

Now that you have your connection point container interface pointer, you track down the connection point that belongs to `IPizzaNotifySink`. This step is accomplished by using the `FindConnectionPoint()` method supported by your connection point container.

```
// Now look up our pizza notify sink connection point
CComPtr<IConnectionPoint> pCP;
pCPC->FindConnectionPoint(IID_IPizzaNotifySink, &pCP);
```

Here you use a regular (non-`QI`) smart pointer. As you can see, the smart pointer can be used in virtually every situation in which you would use a regular interface pointer. The appropriate operators are overloaded such that the class retains the pointer semantics embodied in a standard C++ pointer.

You call `FindConnectionPoint()` by passing in the interface ID of the connection point that you're looking for. The requested connection point is returned in the second argument if the object supports the given interface. For those of you in the home viewing audience who are keeping track, that's two steps down, three to go.

```
// Retrieve an enumerator for this connection point
CComPtr<IEnumConnections> pEnum;
if (SUCCEEDED(pCP->EnumConnections(&pEnum))) {
```

Your next task is to retrieve the connection point's enumerator interface. Enumerators are semistandard interfaces used to manage and iterate over sequences of items. I use the term *semistandard* because there are many types of enumerator interfaces. For example, the `IEnumMediaTypes` enumerator is used in the ActiveMovie subsystem to iterate over the different media types supported by a multimedia data stream. The `IEnumMoniker` enumerator is used to iterate over a collection of monikers, and yes, the `IEnumConnections` interface enumerates over a connection point's collection of outgoing interface pointers.

The `EnumConnections()` method of the `IConnectionPoint` interface returns an enumerator designed to pass over a sequence of `CONNECTDATA` structures. `CONNECTDATA` has two elements: an `IUnknown` pointer and a cookie. As you'll see when you start to implement the sink objects, event connections between sources and sinks, like ROT entries, are manipulated by using cookies.

```
// Iterate over our connections, one at a time
while (pEnum->Next(1, &cd, NULL) == S_OK) {
```

The `Next()` enumerator method returns the next *n* elements of the iterated sequence, in which *n* is the value of the first parameter passed in to the method call. The next `CONNECTDATA` structure (or array of `CONNECTDATA` structures, if you asked for more than one) is returned in the second parameter. The third argument can be used to return how many elements were actually returned by the enumerator. This last argument exists because there's no guarantee that you'll get back as many elements as you asked for.

Given a valid `CONNECTDATA` structure, only one more thing remains for you to do. The `CONNECTDATA` structure contains an `IUnknown` pointer belonging to the sink object, and now you call `QueryInterface()` on the pointer and call the outgoing method. You use a `CComQIPtr` pointer for this purpose.

```
// Retrieve an IPizzaNotifySink interface pointer
CComQIPtr<IPizzaNotifySink, &IID_IPizzaNotifySink> pSink(cd.pUnk);

// Send out the event notification
if (pSink)
    pSink->OnNewPizzaRequest(ulNewPizzaID,
                             ePizzaSize,
                             ulNumToppings,
                             aToppingInfo,
                             pDeliveryInfo);
```

You'll recall that at the beginning of this odyssey, I remarked that the OLE connection point interfaces are rather baroque. Now you understand why. The "connection point container to connection point to enumerator to interface pointer" sequence of operations is difficult to wrap your mind around, but it provides tremendous flexibility with relatively low performance overhead. Luckily, the use of smart pointers helps keep the code size down to a few dozen lines.

Finishing the Server

All this is triggered from the `MakePizza()` method, which is called remotely by an order-taking object. `MakePizza()` is very simple. It sends out the incoming order event, waits for 10 seconds, and then sends out the pizza complete event. The method also maintains a static counter used to assign a unique ID to each pizza ordered.

The 10-second pause is intended to simulate the time required to make the pizza and send it out the door (how's *that* for service!). In a real system, of course, you would like the `MakePizza()` method to acknowledge the order and return from the method imme-diately, rather than block until the pizza is complete. You could, for example, spin off a worker thread, tasked with tracking the progress of the order, and have the `MakePizza()` method call return immediately. Chapter 11, "Using Different COM Threading Models," discusses threading in COM/DCOM servers.

Technically speaking, your pizza-making system is complete. But what's the use of cre-ating this entire infrastructure for event notifications unless you can actually see it put into action? On to the PizzaMaker Server Spy application!

The PizzaMaker Server Spy

Up to this point, all your connectable object code has been largely untested. One of the best things about the new PizzaMaker3 example is the Server Spy program that you will now address. This utility is the missing piece needed to fully demonstrate COM event func-tionality.

Here's how the Spy will operate. When the utility is first run, it will present the user with a dialog box asking for the name of a remote machine on which to look for a pizza-making object. The Spy will create a locator and try to connect to a remote object. If a PizzaMaker can't be found, the utility will create one.

After the Spy has found its remote PizzaMaker, the utility registers a notification sink capable of receiving events from your distributed `ComPizzaMaker` class. With connection points appropriately wired, the Spy presents its main window, which is shown in Figure 13.11.

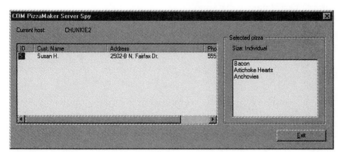

Figure 13.11   The Server Spy main window.

The main Spy window tracks incoming pizza orders in its central list box. You can select a particular order and see detail information displayed on the right side of the window. The Spy tracks the size and the toppings of ordered pizzas.

Listing 13.10 contains the source code for the Spy's main application object. Pay spe-cial attention to the `InitInstance()` method, which controls the entire flow of the application (like most of my quick-and-dirty programs, this utility is designed as a dialog-based MFC app).

Note

The Spy utility also shows how you can write programs that use both the ATL and MFC. Notice how the program declares both a global MFC application object and a global ATL module object.

Listing 13.10 `CLIENT.CPP`—The PizzaMaker Server Spy Application Class

```cpp
// Get needed include files
#define INITGUID
#include "GUIDs.h"
#include "Resource.h"
#include "Utility.h"
#include "SpyDlg.h"
#include "AttachDlg.h"


//
// Main application/client class
//

class CPizzaSpy : public CWinApp
{
public:

    // Public method inherited from CWinApp
    virtual BOOL InitInstance();
};


// Our one-and-only application object
CPizzaSpy TheApp;

// Our one-and-only ATL module object
QueATLModule _Module;


//
// The entire program is run out of this method
//

BOOL CPizzaSpy::InitInstance()
{
    // Standard initialization
    Enable3dControls();

    // Initialize OLE libraries
    if (!AfxOleInit()) {
        AfxMessageBox("Could not initialize OLE subsystem.");
        return FALSE;
```

```
    }

    // Initialize our ATL module
    _Module.Init(NULL, m_hInstance);

    // Ask the user for the name of the host
    CAttachDialog Attach;
    if (Attach.DoModal() != IDCANCEL) {

        // Bring up the main window
        CSpyDialog Spy(Attach.GetHostname());
        Spy.DoModal();
    }

    return FALSE;
}
```

The InitInstance() method begins by initializing the COM subsystem and initializing the ATL module object (note how the instance handle member variable from the MFC application object is passed in to the ATL module's Init() method). Next, you instantiate a CAttachDialog object and fire it off. The CAttachDialog class presents the user with the initial dialog requesting the name of the remote machine to connect to. After the remote hostname has been captured, you load up a CSpyDialog object, which will be the central focus of your attention.

The CAttachDialog class is simple because it's little more than a glorified entry form. Figure 13.12 shows what the dialog looks like, and Listing 13.11 shows the declaration of the class.

Figure 13.12   Connecting to a remote PizzaMaker server.

Listing 13.11   ATTACHDLG.H—The Declaration of the CAttachDialog Class

```
#ifndef ATTACHDLG_H
#define ATTACHDLG_H


// Get needed include files
#include "StdInc.h"
```

continued on next page

continued from previous page

```
#include "GUIDs.h"


class CAttachDialog : public CDialog
{
public:

    // Ctor & dtor
    CAttachDialog();

    // Overridden methods
    virtual BOOL OnInitDialog();

    // Public methods
    void        OnAttachHost();
    void        OnCancel();
    void        OnSelectLocal();
    void        OnSelectRemote();
    CString     GetHostname();

protected:

    DECLARE_MESSAGE_MAP()

private:

    // Member data
    CString        m_strHostname;
};


#endif
```

Not much goes on here, so I'm not going to dwell on the details. The various On<name> methods are event handlers called as the user selects the dialog's various buttons. The GetHostname() method is a public getter that can be used to retrieve the user's input after the dialog has been dismissed. Listing 13.12 shows the code backing the CAttachDialog class.

Listing 13.12   ATTACHDLG.CPP—The Declaration of the CAttachDialog Sink Class

```
// Get needed include files
#include "AttachDlg.h"
#include "Resource.h"
#include "Utility.h"


BEGIN_MESSAGE_MAP(CAttachDialog, CDialog)
    ON_BN_CLICKED(IDC_ATTACH,       OnAttachHost)
    ON_BN_CLICKED(IDCANCEL,         OnCancel)
    ON_BN_CLICKED(IDC_RAD_LOCAL,    OnSelectLocal)
    ON_BN_CLICKED(IDC_RAD_REMOTE,   OnSelectRemote)
END_MESSAGE_MAP()
```

```
// Constructor
CAttachDialog::CAttachDialog()
     : CDialog(IDD_ATTACH_DIALOG)
{ }


BOOL CAttachDialog::OnInitDialog()
{
   CDialog::OnInitDialog();

   // Select the local machine radio button
   CheckRadioButton(IDC_RAD_LOCAL, IDC_RAD_REMOTE, IDC_RAD_LOCAL);

   // Disable the hostname edit field and title label
   CEdit* pHostnameEditWnd = (CEdit*) GetDlgItem(IDC_HOSTNAME);
   pHostnameEditWnd->EnableWindow(FALSE);
   CStatic* pHostnameTitleWnd = (CStatic*) GetDlgItem(IDC_TXT_NAME);
   pHostnameTitleWnd->EnableWindow(FALSE);

   return TRUE;
}


void CAttachDialog::OnAttachHost()
{
   // Retrieve the hostname
   if (GetCheckedRadioButton(IDC_RAD_LOCAL,
   ➥IDC_RAD_REMOTE) == IDC_RAD_REMOTE) {
     CEdit* pHostnameEditWnd = (CEdit*) GetDlgItem(IDC_HOSTNAME);
     pHostnameEditWnd->GetWindowText(m_strHostname);
   }

   EndDialog(IDC_ATTACH);
}


void CAttachDialog::OnCancel()
{
   EndDialog(IDCANCEL);
}


void CAttachDialog::OnSelectLocal()
{
   CEdit* pHostnameEditWnd = (CEdit*) GetDlgItem(IDC_HOSTNAME);
   pHostnameEditWnd->EnableWindow(FALSE);
   CStatic* pHostnameTitleWnd = (CStatic*) GetDlgItem(IDC_TXT_NAME);
   pHostnameTitleWnd->EnableWindow(FALSE);
}


void CAttachDialog::OnSelectRemote()
{
```

continued on next page

continued from previous page

```
    CEdit* pHostnameEditWnd = (CEdit*) GetDlgItem(IDC_HOSTNAME);
    pHostnameEditWnd->EnableWindow();
    CStatic* pHostnameTitleWnd = (CStatic*) GetDlgItem(IDC_TXT_NAME);
    pHostnameTitleWnd->EnableWindow();
}


CString CAttachDialog::GetHostname()
{
    return m_strHostname;
}
```

The trickiest thing going on in this class (perhaps *tricky* isn't the right word) is the enabling and disabling of the edit field, based on what radio button is selected. Let's move on to the more interesting stuff.

The **CSpyDialog** class is the heart of the Spy utility. In Listing 13.13, you'll find the class declaration.

Listing 13.13 SPYDLG.H—The Declaration of the **CSpyDialog** Class

```
#ifndef SPYDLG_H
#define SPYDLG_H


// Get needed include files
#include "StdInc.h"
#include "GUIDs.h"


class CSpyDialog : public CDialog
{
public:

    // Ctor & dtor
    CSpyDialog(CString& strHostname);

    // Overridden methods
    virtual void DoDataExchange(CDataExchange* pDX);
    virtual BOOL OnInitDialog();

    // Public methods
    BOOL        AttachToHost();
    IPizzaMaker* ConnectToPizzaMaker(CString& strHostname);
    void        RemovePizzaEntry    (ULONG      ulItemIndex);
    void        OnExit();
    void        OnListClick();
    HRESULT     OnNewPizzaRequest    (ULONG          ulPizzaID,
                                      PizzaSize       ePizzaSize,
                                      ULONG           ulNumToppings,
                                      ToppingInfo     ToppingInfoArray[],
                                      DeliveryInfo*   pDeliveryInfo);
    HRESULT     OnPizzaComplete      (ULONG          ulPizzaID);
```

```
protected:

    DECLARE_MESSAGE_MAP()

private:

    // We have to have a hostname
    // Disallow default constructor
    CSpyDialog();

    // Member data
    CString        m_strHostname;
    IPizzaMaker*   m_pIPizzaMaker;
    CStatic        m_Hostname;
    CListCtrl      m_PizzaList;
    CListBox       m_ToppingList;
    DWORD          m_dwAdviseCookie;
};
```

```
#endif
```

Nothing too notable here, at least not without looking at the backing implementation code. You might have noticed that I made the default constructor of **CSpyDialog** private. This enforces the requirement that users of **CSpyDialog** always pass a remote hostname string in to the object's constructor. The hostname is obviously a critical piece of information, so it makes sense to put controls in place that make the hostname mandatory.

On to the class definition, found in Listing 13.14.

Listing 13.14   SPYDLG.CPP—The Declaration of the **CSpyDialog** Class

```
// Get needed include files
#include "Resource.h"
#include "Utility.h"
#include "TopUtil.h"
#include "SpyDlg.h"
#include "AttachDlg.h"
#include "PizzaNotify.h"


BEGIN_MESSAGE_MAP(CSpyDialog, CDialog)
    ON_BN_CLICKED(IDC_EXIT, OnExit)
    ON_NOTIFY     (NM_CLICK, IDC_PIZZA_LIST, OnListClick)
END_MESSAGE_MAP()


//
// Convenience structure
//
struct PizzaInfo
{
    PizzaSize   ePizzaSize;
```

continued on next page

continued from previous page

```
      ULONG        ulNumToppings;
};


//
// CSpyDialog methods
//

// Constructor
CSpyDialog::CSpyDialog(CString& strHostname)

    : CDialog(IDD_MGRCLIENT_DIALOG),
      m_strHostname(strHostname),
      m_pIPizzaMaker(NULL),
      m_dwAdviseCookie(0)
{ }


void CSpyDialog::DoDataExchange(CDataExchange* pDX)
{
   CDialog::DoDataExchange(pDX);
   DDX_Control(pDX, IDC_PIZZA_LIST,    m_PizzaList);
   DDX_Control(pDX, IDC_TOPPING_LIST,  m_ToppingList);
   DDX_Control(pDX, IDC_TXT_HOSTNAME,  m_Hostname);
}


BOOL CSpyDialog::OnInitDialog()
{
   CDialog::OnInitDialog();

   // Load the columns up into the Pizza list
   m_PizzaList.InsertColumn(1, "ID",         LVCFMT_LEFT, 35,  0);
   m_PizzaList.InsertColumn(2, "Cust. Name", LVCFMT_LEFT, 150, 1);
   m_PizzaList.InsertColumn(3, "Address",    LVCFMT_LEFT, 200, 2);
   m_PizzaList.InsertColumn(4, "Phone",      LVCFMT_LEFT, 100, 3);

   // Hook up with our server
   if (!AttachToHost())
      EndDialog(IDC_EXIT);

   return TRUE;
}


BOOL CSpyDialog::AttachToHost()
{
   HRESULT hResult;

   // Connect to the server
   m_pIPizzaMaker = ConnectToPizzaMaker(m_strHostname);
   if (!m_pIPizzaMaker)
      return FALSE;
```

```
// Create the sink object
TRACE("About to CreateInstance.\n");
CComObject<ComPizzaNotifySink>* pMgrSink;
 CComObject<ComPizzaNotifySink>::CreateInstance(&pMgrSink);
pMgrSink->SetSpyInstance(this);

// Register yourself with the server
TRACE("About to Advise.\n");
hResult = AtlAdvise(m_pIPizzaMaker,
                    pMgrSink->GetUnknown(),
                    IID_IPizzaNotifySink,
                    &m_dwAdviseCookie);
if (FAILED(hResult)) {
   ReportError("Could not connect sink.", hResult);
   m_pIPizzaMaker->Release();
   m_pIPizzaMaker = NULL;
   return FALSE;
}

// Set the hostname text
if (m_strHostname == "")
   m_Hostname.SetWindowText("< Local machine >");
else
   m_Hostname.SetWindowText(m_strHostname);

return TRUE;
}


IPizzaMaker* CSpyDialog::ConnectToPizzaMaker(CString& strHostname)
{
   HRESULT         hResult;
   IPizzaLocator*  pIPizzaLocator = NULL;
   IPizzaMaker*    pIPizzaMaker = NULL;
   BSTR            bstrHostname = NULL;
   ULONG           ulPizzaID = 0;
   VerboseMsg("In ConnectToPizzaMaker.\n");

   USES_CONVERSION;

   // Translate the hostname into Unicode
   if (strHostname != "")
      bstrHostname = strHostname.AllocSysString();

   // Hook ourselves up to a locator object
   COSERVERINFO  ServerInfo = { 0, bstrHostname, NULL, 0 };
   MULTI_QI      MultiQI    = { &IID_IPizzaLocator, NULL, NOERROR };

   hResult = CoCreateInstanceEx(CLSID_PizzaLocator1,
                                NULL, CLSCTX_SERVER,
                                &ServerInfo,
                                1, &MultiQI);
   if (FAILED(hResult)) {
```

continued on next page

continued from previous page

```
        ReportError("Could not create a new PizzaLocator object.",
        ➡hResult);
        SysFreeString(bstrHostname);
        return NULL;
    }

    // Just for convenience
    pIPizzaLocator = (IPizzaLocator*) MultiQI.pItf;

    // Look for any PizzaMaker objects that might be currently running
    // on the same machine as the locator
    hResult = pIPizzaLocator->Locate(A2OLE("PizzaMaker"),
                                     IID_IPizzaMaker,
                                     (PPVOID) &pIPizzaMaker);

    // Clean up some interface pointers...
    pIPizzaLocator->Release();
    pIPizzaLocator = NULL;

    // Were we able to find a running server,
    // or do we have to start our own?
    if (!pIPizzaMaker) {

        // Create the remote PizzaMaker object
        ServerInfo.dwReserved1 = 0;
        ServerInfo.pwszName    = bstrHostname;
        ServerInfo.pAuthInfo   = NULL;
        ServerInfo.dwReserved2 = 0;

        MultiQI.pIID           = &IID_IPizzaMaker;
        MultiQI.pItf           = NULL;
        MultiQI.hr             = NOERROR;

        hResult = CoCreateInstanceEx(CLSID_PizzaMaker1,
                                     NULL, CLSCTX_SERVER,
                                     &ServerInfo,
                                     1, &MultiQI);
        if (FAILED(hResult)) {
            ReportError("Could not create a new COM PizzaMaker object.",
            ➡hResult);
            SysFreeString(bstrHostname);
            return NULL;
        }

        // Set the interface pointer
        pIPizzaMaker = (IPizzaMaker*) MultiQI.pItf;
    }

    // Free up our hostname string
    SysFreeString(bstrHostname);

    return pIPizzaMaker;
}
```

```
HRESULT CSpyDialog::OnNewPizzaRequest(
                        ULONG       ulPizzaID,
                        PizzaSize   ePizzaSize,
                        ULONG       ulNumToppings,
                        ToppingInfo ToppingInfoArray[],
                        DeliveryInfo* pDeliveryInfo)
{
   // Copy out the delivery info
   CString strCustName((LPCWSTR) pDeliveryInfo->bstrCustName);
   CString strAddress((LPCWSTR) pDeliveryInfo->bstrAddress);
   CString strPhone((LPCWSTR) pDeliveryInfo->bstrPhone);

   // Copy over our topping array -- We'll reserve the first part
   // of the array for the pizza size and number of toppings attributes
   BYTE* pByteBuffer = new BYTE[sizeof(PizzaInfo) + (ulNumToppings *
   ➥sizeof(ToppingInfo))];

   // Blast in the pizza size and number of toppings
   ((PizzaInfo*) pByteBuffer)->ePizzaSize = ePizzaSize;
   ((PizzaInfo*) pByteBuffer)->ulNumToppings = ulNumToppings;

   // And now copy over the topping array
   memcpy(pByteBuffer + sizeof(PizzaInfo),
          ToppingInfoArray,
          (ulNumToppings * sizeof(ToppingInfo)));

   // Insert the new row into the table
   ULONG ulThisItem = m_PizzaList.InsertItem(
                        LVIF_TEXT | LVIF_PARAM,
                        0, ULongToStr(ulPizzaID),
                        0, 0, 0, (LONG) pByteBuffer);
   m_PizzaList.SetItem(ulThisItem,
                        1, LVIF_TEXT, strCustName,
                        0, 0, 0, 0);
   m_PizzaList.SetItem(ulThisItem,
                        2, LVIF_TEXT, strAddress,
                        0, 0, 0, 0);
   m_PizzaList.SetItem(ulThisItem, 3, LVIF_TEXT, strPhone, 0, 0, 0, 0);

   return NOERROR;
}


HRESULT CSpyDialog::OnPizzaComplete(ULONG  ulPizzaID)
{
   ULONG ulNumItems = m_PizzaList.GetItemCount();

   // Loop through all our items, looking for the right one
   for (ULONG ulLoop = 0; ulLoop < ulNumItems; ulLoop++) {

      // Is this the item to remove?
      if (m_PizzaList.GetItemText(ulLoop, 0) == ULongToStr(ulPizzaID))
      {
```

continued on next page

continued from previous page

```
            // Looks like it
            RemovePizzaEntry(ulLoop);
            return NOERROR;
        }
    }

    return S_FALSE;
}


void CSpyDialog::OnListClick()
{
    //
    // Thanks to Jeff Prosise for providing the hit testing
    // technique used by this method. This technique appears
    // in Jeff's book "Programming Windows 95 with MFC,"
    // (Microsoft Press, 1996).
    //
    DWORD dwPos = ::GetMessagePos();
    CPoint point((int) LOWORD(dwPos), (int) HIWORD(dwPos));
    m_PizzaList.ScreenToClient(&point);

    LONG lSelectionIndex = m_PizzaList.HitTest(point);
    if (lSelectionIndex != -1) {

        // Retrieve the selected item
        LV_ITEM ItemInfo;
        ItemInfo.iItem = lSelectionIndex;
        ItemInfo.iSubItem = 0;
        ItemInfo.mask = LVIF_PARAM;
        m_PizzaList.GetItem(&ItemInfo);

        // Set the pizza size text
        PizzaInfo* pPizzaInfo = (PizzaInfo*) ItemInfo.lParam;
        CString strSizeText("Size: ");
        switch(pPizzaInfo->ePizzaSize)
        {
            case Individual: strSizeText += "Individual"; break;
            case Small:      strSizeText += "Small";      break;
            case Large:      strSizeText += "Large";      break;
        }
        CStatic* pSizeTextWnd = (CStatic*) GetDlgItem(IDC_TXT_PIZZASIZE);
        pSizeTextWnd->SetWindowText(strSizeText);

        // Clear out the list box
        CListBox* pToppingListWnd = (CListBox*)
        ➥GetDlgItem(IDC_TOPPING_LIST);
        pToppingListWnd->ResetContent();

        // Display the selected item's pizza toppings
        CString strTopping;
        for (ULONG ulLoop = 0; ulLoop < pPizzaInfo->ulNumToppings;
            ➥ulLoop++) {
```

```
            ToppingInfo* pCurrTopping =
                      (ToppingInfo*) ((PCHAR) pPizzaInfo +
                                      sizeof(PizzaInfo) +
                                      (ulLoop * sizeof(ToppingInfo)));
            strTopping =
                ToppingUtil::ToppingEnumToStr(pCurrTopping->eTopping);
              switch(pCurrTopping->eToppingSize)
            {
              case HalfPizza:    strTopping += "  (On Half)";    break;
              case QuarterPizza: strTopping += "  (On Quarter)"; break;
            }
            pToppingListWnd->InsertString(0, strTopping);
        }
    }
}


void CSpyDialog::OnExit()
{
    // Clear out any outstanding pizza entries
    ULONG ulNumItems = m_PizzaList.GetItemCount();
    for (ULONG ulLoop = 0; ulLoop < ulNumItems; ulLoop++)
       RemovePizzaEntry(0);

    // Unhook our notify sink
    if (m_dwAdviseCookie) {

        TRACE("About to Unadvise.\n");
        AtlUnadvise(m_pIPizzaMaker,
                    IID_IPizzaNotifySink,
                    m_dwAdviseCookie);
    }

    // Release our server pointer
    if (m_pIPizzaMaker) {
       m_pIPizzaMaker->Release();
       m_pIPizzaMaker = NULL;
    }

    // ... and we're out of here!
    EndDialog(IDC_EXIT);
}


void CSpyDialog::RemovePizzaEntry(ULONG ulItemIndex)
{
    // We need to get at the user-param so that we can free up
    // our topping info
    LV_ITEM ItemInfo;
    ItemInfo.iItem = ulItemIndex;
    ItemInfo.iSubItem = 0;
    ItemInfo.mask = LVIF_STATE | LVIF_PARAM;
    m_PizzaList.GetItem(&ItemInfo);
```

continued on next page

continued from previous page

```
            delete [] (BYTE*) (ItemInfo.lParam);

            // And now remove the item
            m_PizzaList.DeleteItem(ulItemIndex);

            // If the completed pizza also happens to correspond to the
            // currently selected entry, clear out all the displayed
            // pizza info.
            if (ItemInfo.state & LVIS_SELECTED ¦¦ !m_PizzaList.GetItemCount()) {

                // First the size label
                CStatic* pSizeTextWnd = (CStatic*) GetDlgItem(IDC_TXT_PIZZASIZE);
                pSizeTextWnd->SetWindowText("Size: < None Selected >");

                // ... and then the listbox
                CListBox* pToppingListWnd = (CListBox*)
            ➡GetDlgItem(IDC_TOPPING_LIST);
                pToppingListWnd->ResetContent();
            }
        }
```

The action begins in the `OnInitDialog()` method. As part of the class's initialization (in addition to adding the columns to the list control), the Spy attempts to connect to the remote machine and obtain an interface pointer to a pizza-making object. This logic is contained in the `AttachToHost()` and `ConnectToPizzaMaker()` methods.

Attaching to the Remote Host

The `AttachToHost()` method is primarily responsible for creating the sink objects and then registering the sink with the remote server object. Before this can happen, however, you must find the object. This happens inside `ConnectToPizzaMaker()`.

By this time, you're an old hand at all this, so the `ConnectToPizzaMaker()` code should look very familiar. You begin by creating a locator object on the remote machine and then calling the object's `Locate()` method. Now you recognize that the call might fail (a server might not be running there, after all), so unlike the `PizzaOrderTaker3` class, which simply fails under such conditions, the `ConnectToPizzaMaker()` method will create a distributed object on the remote machine, if one can't be found. In either case, the `ConnectToPizzaMaker()` will get its hands on some object instance, and this interface pointer will be returned to the `AttachToHost()` method.

Making the Connection

After the Spy has obtained a remote interface pointer to the `PizzaMaker` object, it must establish the event connection. At this point, I want to take a break from the discussion of the `CSpyDialog` class and briefly examine how the event sink is implemented.

It's important to keep in mind that the `CSpyDialog` class is an MFC-based class that does not provide the implementation of a COM component. You are, therefore, missing an important class. After all, the source object generates events by making method calls on an interface pointer belonging to the client. So far, you don't have any COM object on the client.

The `ComPizzaNotifySink` class is just such a COM entity. This is a standard COM class that exposes the `IPizzaNotifySink` interface. To receive notification events, the `CSpyDialog` class must create a `ComPizzaNotifySink` object and then get an `IPizzaNotifySink` interface pointer to the source object. Listing 13.15 shows the declaration of the sink class.

Listing 13.15   `PIZZANOTIFY.H`—The Declaration of the `ComPizzaNotifySink` Sink Class

```
#ifndef PIZZANOTIFY_H
#define PIZZANOTIFY_H

// Get needed include files
#include "StdInc.h"
#include "GUIDs.h"


// Forward declaration
class CSpyDialog;


class ComPizzaNotifySink :
   public CComObjectRoot,
   public IPizzaNotifySink
{
public:

   // Ctor & dtor
   ComPizzaNotifySink();
   virtual ~ComPizzaNotifySink();

   // Public methods
   void SetSpyInstance(CSpyDialog* pSpy);

   // IPizzaNotifySink
   STDMETHOD(OnNewPizzaRequest)(ULONG         ulPizzaID,
                                PizzaSize     ePizzaSize,
                                ULONG         ulNumToppings,
                                ToppingInfo   ToppingInfoArray[],
                                DeliveryInfo* pDeliveryInfo);
   STDMETHOD(OnPizzaComplete)   (ULONG        ulPizzaID);

   BEGIN_COM_MAP(ComPizzaNotifySink)
     COM_INTERFACE_ENTRY(IPizzaNotifySink)
   END_COM_MAP()

private:

   // Member data
   CSpyDialog* m_pSpy;
};


#endif
```

In virtually every way, the `ComPizzaNotifySink` is like any standard COM class. You see here the declarations of the `OnNewPizzaRequest()` and `OnPizzaComplete()` methods required to implement `IPizzaNotifySink`, but you should also take note of the `SetSpyInstance()` method. If the `ComPizzaNotifySink` class is the object that will be receiving the event notifications, some mechanism must be in place for the sink object to communicate the notifications to the `CSpyDialog` class. By looking at the sink implementation in Listing 13.16, you can see how this interaction is accomplished.

Listing 13.16   `PIZZANOTIFY.CPP`—The Declaration of the `ComPizzaNotifySink` Sink Class

```
// Get needed include files
#include "PizzaNotify.h"
#include "SpyDlg.h"


//
// Ctor & dtor
//

ComPizzaNotifySink::ComPizzaNotifySink()
      : m_pSpy(NULL)
{
   TRACE("In sink construct.\n");
}

ComPizzaNotifySink::~ComPizzaNotifySink()
{
   TRACE("In sink destruct.\n");
}


//
// Misc. public method
//

void ComPizzaNotifySink::SetSpyInstance(CSpyDialog* pSpy)
{
   m_pSpy = pSpy;
}


//
// Notification methods
//

HRESULT ComPizzaNotifySink::OnNewPizzaRequest(
                        ULONG          ulPizzaID,
                        PizzaSize      ePizzaSize,
                        ULONG          ulNumToppings,
                        ToppingInfo    ToppingInfoArray[],
                        DeliveryInfo*  pDeliveryInfo)
{
```

```
        return (m_pSpy ? m_pSpy->OnNewPizzaRequest(ulPizzaID,
                                                   ePizzaSize,
                                                   ulNumToppings,
                                                   ToppingInfoArray,
                                                   pDeliveryInfo)
                       : NOERROR);
}

HRESULT ComPizzaNotifySink::OnPizzaComplete(ULONG  ulPizzaID)
{
    return (m_pSpy ? m_pSpy->OnPizzaComplete(ulPizzaID)
                   : NOERROR);
}
```

Assuming that someone (it boils down to the `CSpyDialog` object itself) has called the `SetSpyInstance()` method, the `ComPizzaNotifySink` class does nothing but channel incoming event notifications to identically named methods belonging to the `CSpyDialog` class. In this respect, the `ComPizzaNotifySink` object does nothing but act as an event funnel, shuffling events in through the front door and immediately redirecting them out the back door to the `CSpyDialog` class.

Now, the big outstanding question is how do you pass your `ComPizzaNotifySink` interface pointer on to the source? The answer can be found in `AttachToHost()`.

You begin by creating a new sink object and setting the internally maintained back pointer to the Spy dialog class.

```
// Create the sink object
TRACE("About to CreateInstance.\n");
CComObject<ComPizzaNotifySink>* pMgrSink;
CComObject<ComPizzaNotifySink>::CreateInstance(&pMgrSink);
pMgrSink->SetSpyInstance(this);
```

Here you declare a pointer to a COM object (parameterized by your sink class) and then call the static class-side `CreateInstance()` method that is a part of the `CComObject` class. On only a few occasions will you have to worry about calling the `CreateInstance()` method youself (which, predictably, creates a new instance of your COM class); creating sink objects is one such exception. Using the `CreateInstance()` method enables the Spy dialog to create a COM object, even though the program itself is not regarded as a server process.

Now that you have instantiated the sink object, you can attach it to the connection point residing on the server object. Technically speaking, this is accomplished by obtaining an `IConnectionPoint` interface pointer from the appropriate connection point and then calling that interface's `Advise()` method. However, an easy, more compact way of producing the same result is to call the `AtlAdvise()` helper function.

```
// Register yourself with the server
TRACE("About to Advise.\n");
hResult = AtlAdvise(m_pIPizzaMaker,
                    pMgrSink->GetUnknown(),
                    IID_IPizzaNotifySink,
                    &m_dwAdviseCookie);
if (FAILED(hResult)) {
```

continued on next page

continued from previous page

```
            ReportError("Could not connect sink.", hResult);
            m_pIPizzaMaker->Release();
            m_pIPizzaMaker = NULL;
            return FALSE;
        }
```

The `AtlAdvise()` function accepts four arguments, and I bet you could almost guess what they are. Argument one is an `IUnknown` pointer belonging to the source object, and argument two is an `IUnknown` pointer belonging to the sink object. The third parameter is the interface ID of the connection point to which the sink is being attached, and the final argument returns a cookie that you use when the time comes to sever the event connection.

When the dialog box is dismissed, the `OnExit()` handler is called. It's in this method that you unregister your notify sink, using the `AtlUnadvise()` function.

```
// Unhook our notify sink
if (m_dwAdviseCookie) {

    TRACE("About to Unadvise.\n");
    AtlUnadvise(m_pIPizzaMaker,
                IID_IPizzaNotifySink,
                m_dwAdviseCookie);
}
```

Finishing the Spy GUI

The only point left to discuss is how the Spy utility goes about using MFC to graphically display event information. I'm not going to spend much time going over this part of the code because it doesn't have much to do with COM/DCOM, but I will provide some comments.

The `CListCtrl` class provided by MFC enables you to associate a data pointer with every item in the list, and the Spy utility takes advantage of this capability. When a `NewPizza` event notification arrives, the `OnNewPizzaRequest()` method collapses all the pizza data into a single contiguous buffer and associates the buffer with the new line item.

When the user selects a line in the main list box, the `OnListClick()` handler is called. This method determines which item was selected, using a technique that I learned from Jeff Prosise's book *Programming Windows 95 with MFC* (Microsoft Press, 1996). The method extracts the relevant pizza information from the associated data buffer and fills in the detail section of the dialog box.

Note

By the way (I just want to vent for a second), sitting down to write the Server Spy program gave me the opportunity to revisit working with the MFC `CListCtrl` class for the first time in quite a while. Here's my question: Am I the only person on the planet who thinks that this control is far too difficult to use? I've never seen such a difficult control to program and with such a small rate of return. Okay, I'm stepping down from my soapbox now. Sorry. Please, don't sue me, Mr. Gates.

Running the Final Version

That about finishes the discussion of the Spy utility, and in doing so, it also concludes the discussion of the PizzaOrderTaker3 example. If you haven't done so already, I suggest that you fire up the entire system. I hope you have more than one computer available so that you can bring up the system in a distributed fashion. Although you can certainly run the whole thing on a single machine, that defeats the purpose, doesn't it?

Because the OLE connection point model fully supports multiple sinks attached to a single source, you may run as many instances of the Spy as you want, from as many machines as you want.

Summary

In this chapter, you learned how to effectively use distributed COM objects. Now you know how to instantiate a COM object on a remote machine.

I also explained how to find objects in the running object table, how to create moniker objects that point to your COM object, and how to load and unload the monikers from the running object table. The last part of the chapter describes how to use connection point interfaces to implement events in your COM server.

I'm going to let you catch your breath now. You've covered a lot of material here, and you've gained enough solid understanding of COM/DCOM basics to forge ahead on your own. As with any challenging programming endeavor, you'll never truly understand a new technology until you've used it for a while. No book is a substitute for experience. Good luck!

INDEX

M

X - Y - Z

WHAT'S ON THE DISC

The companion CD-ROM contains many useful third-party software, plus all the source code from the book.

Windows 95/98 Installation Instructions

1. Insert the CD-ROM disc into your CD-ROM drive.

2. From the Windows 95 desktop, double-click the My Computer icon.

3. Double-click the icon representing your CD-ROM drive.

4. Double-click the icon titled START.EXE to run the program.

NOTE

If Windows 95 is installed on your computer and you have the AutoPlay feature enabled, the START.EXE program starts automatically whenever you insert the disc into your CD-ROM drive.

Windows NT Installation Instructions

1. Insert the CD-ROM disc into your CD-ROM drive.

2. From File Manager or Program Manager, choose Run from the File menu.

3. Type *<drive>*\START.EXE and press Enter, where *<drive>* corresponds to the drive letter of your CD-ROM. For example, if your CD-ROM is drive D:, type D:\START.EXE and press Enter.